The Futures Game

Who Wins? Who Loses? Why?

Second Edition

Richard J. Teweles

Frank J. Jones

McGraw-Hill Book Company

New York   St. Louis   San Francisco   Auckland   Bogotá
Hamburg   London   Madrid   Mexico
Milan   Montreal   New Delhi   Panama
Paris   São Paulo   Singapore
Sydney   Tokyo   Toronto

Library of Congress Cataloging-in-Publication Data

Teweles, Richard Jack, date.
  The futures game.

  Rev. ed. of: The commodity futures game. 1974.
  Bibliography: p.
  Includes index.
  1. Commodity exchanges. 2. Financial futures.
3. Speculation. I. Jones, Frank Joseph. II. Teweles,
Richard Jack, date. Commodity futures game.
III. Title.
HG6046.T45 1987   332.64′4   86-10509
ISBN 0-07-063728-8

  234567890   DOC/DOC   9321

ISBN 0-07-063728-8

ISBN 0-07-063734-2 {PBK}

The editors for this book were William A. Sabin and Laura Givner,
the designer was Naomi Auerbach, and the production supervisor
was Thomas G. Kowalczyk. It was set in Baskerville
by Techna Type, Inc.

Printed and bound by R. R. Donnelley & Sons Company.

Contents

NINETEEN   The Meat Futures Contracts   423

TWENTY   Natural Resources: Metals and Petroleum   461

Bibliography   **609**

Preface

The deletion of the word "Commodity" from the title of the previous edition of this book indicates part of the reason why this new edition has become necessary. The broader word "futures" describes only one of the many changes in this area of the speculative market. Trading in financial instruments, currencies, and indexes of various kinds has been introduced, and the market share of these financially oriented contracts has increased significantly. In addition, the introduction of new contracts on more traditional hard and soft commodities has expanded the number of futures contracts traded from about 40 to more than 80. Exchange-traded options are also carving out an ever-increasing place in the industry. The CFTC and NFA have changed the rules of the game enough to justify a new chapter on compliance designed to help brokers and customers alike understand the rules and avoid problems. Sophisticated, relatively inexpensive computers have attracted increasing numbers of technically minded traders to the markets as they attempt to prove that the markets are not as efficient as some academicians maintain.

The sources of information material has been expanded into an entire chapter indicating material of general relevance to all the futures and related options markets. Material relevant to specific markets is indicated in the chapters on these markets. The bibliography has also been updated and expanded.

The authors of this edition give full credit to the contributions of the coauthors of the first edition: Charles V. Harlow and Herbert L. Stone. Some of their work is prominent in this edition and is timeless enough to justify a confident prediction that their thoughts will be present in any future editions of this work.

Finally, credit is due to James Alphier, who structured and composed most of the original version of the chapter "The Technical Approach." His tireless effort culminated in what we considered to be the definitive survey of technical analysis extant. In addition, his extensive comments and criticisms on other portions of the first edition were of considerable help.

A revision as substantial as the one represented by this new edition will inevitably contain errors and omissions. Readers are encouraged to correspond with the authors directly or through the publisher to indicate how they think this book can be improved in future editions.

Richard J. Teweles
Frank J. Jones

PART 1

Basics of
the Game

*A stock and a futures trader were good friends and compared notes
often on trading philosophies. When the stock trader fell on bad
times with a series of losses, he was forced to sell his membership.
Before leaving for another line of work, he reflected with his futures
trading friend. "Your trouble is that you weren't over here with me
trading futures," confided the friend. "But I don't know anything
about futures," the crestfallen stock trader replied.*

*In one way or another the advice "You've got to know the territory"
has been proffered for centuries. The four chapters in this part
are an effort to introduce the reader to "the territory" of futures
trading.*

*In Chapter 1—"Why Trade Futures?"—the idea of speculation, as
well as the specific evolution of trading in futures, is discussed.
Because many potential futures traders have had experience in
securities, specific similarities and differences in the two areas are
noted.*

*Chapter 2, "The Nature of the Futures Markets," places the trader in
the environment in which he is to operate. The nature of contracts,
the markets for those contracts, who plays the game, and the nature
of cash and futures prices are discussed in order that the trader*

may appreciate the relationships involved in the market and trader performance.

Chapter 3, "The Mechanics of Futures Trading," helps the trader to choose a broker and to understand clearly the procedures of opening and maintaining a futures account. Contract information, types of orders, regulatory requirements, and tax considerations are not heady stuff, but avoiding problems in these areas is imperative.

Chapter 4, "The Behavior of Futures Prices," lays the vital groundwork for a clear understanding of the behavior of prices, the relation between past and future price changes, and the question of trends.

Why Trade Futures?

When asked why he continued speculating,
James R. Keene, a famous speculator, replied,
"Why does a dog chase his thousandth rabbit?
All life is a speculation. The spirit of
speculation is born with men."
BERNARD BARUCH
Baruch: My Own Story

INTRODUCTION

This is a book about trading futures. Trading is an activity that cuts across many
disciplines—economics, mathematics, sociology, statistics, and psychology are among
the most obvious. Futures trading is carried on by individuals involved in related
cash markets as well as by floor traders and speculators. Speculators account for
more than half the dollar value of the open interest in futures, yet there are few
other fields in which there is more interest and less knowledge among the participants.

In this first chapter the economic role of the speculator and the history of trading
from its Phoenician beginnings are presented. Attacks on trading as an institution
are described, and speculation as an activity is analyzed, as are the specific differences between futures and securities. A final section—"Should You Speculate?"—leads the trader to considerations that, although personal, must include
general criteria.

ECONOMIC FUNCTION OF THE SPECULATOR

The usual justification made for speculation in futures is simple. Futures trading is beneficial to the public which ultimately consumes the goods traded in the futures markets. The benefit most often considered primary is the probability that hedging allows the risk of price changes to be shifted; hence the costs of production, marketing, and processing are reduced. If this is true, and if the cost savings achieved are passed on to consumers, futures trading will benefit the consumers on whose behalf the economy is supposed to function. Futures markets provide other important benefits, such as continuous, accurate, well-publicized price information and continuous liquid markets. Without the speculator futures markets could not function; therefore, if the futures markets operate for the social good, the speculator who makes the operation possible must also contribute to the social good. Speculators attempt to anticipate what prices are going to do and, by taking appropriate positions in the futures markets, make a profit if their judgment proves correct. They may or may not be correct and therefore may or may not make a profit, but in their very efforts to do so they do enough trading to provide the necessary base for liquid futures markets and thereby raise the efficiency of commodity marketing. Sometimes speculators are accused of making markets unstable by virtue of their speculation, but it is not necessary for them to prove that they earn their profits, if they do earn any, by stabilizing or destabilizing prices; they earn the opportunity to profit merely by being in the market, hence making the market possible. Furthermore, there is no proof that speculators not engaged in manipulation destabilize prices. Several studies have demonstrated that the speculator probably moderates rather than accentuates price volatility.[1] It is not unusual for cash markets to demonstrate greater price volatility when futures market volume and open interest are low than when they are high.

Not only is the volume of business done by trade hedgers at any given time frequently too small to provide the liquidity necessary for an efficient market, but a preponderance of hedgers frequently tends to want to buy at the same time or sell at the same time, and part-time speculators, along with professional traders and arbitrageurs, are needed to take the other side of some of these trades.

SPECULATING OR GAMBLING?

There are many who regard "speculation" and "gambling" as synonymous terms. One hears of "investing in securities" and "gambling in futures." Even some relatively sophisticated investors consider futures trading to be one step removed from a Nevada casino. Others regard speculation and gambling as distinctly different activities. The usual differentiation is based on the nature of risk and the social good. Gambling involves the creation of a risk for the sole purpose of someone taking it. The horse race, poker game, and roulette wheel themselves create risks that would not be present without them. Gamblers are willing to accept these risks

---

[1] One of the earlier of such studies was *Margins, Speculation, and Prices in Grains Futures Markets*, Economic Research Service (U.S. Department of Agriculture, 1967).

in return for the opportunity to win some money. No particular social good is accomplished unless one believes that gambling provides a needed outlet for the gamblers whose needs might be satisfied by something worse if they could not gamble.

Speculation is nothing more than an investment in which the realized rate of return may vary substantially from the expected rate of return. The terms "speculation" and "investment" cannot really be differentiated clearly from one another but rather represent the same activity, differing only in the degree of possible variation from expected returns. It is not accurate to differentiate between these terms solely on the basis of the length of time during which they will be held or the forms taken by returns. Both the intrinsic volatility of the asset and the amount of leverage utilized by the holder contribute to possible variation in expected returns.

Unlike gambling, speculation deals in risks that are necessarily present in the process of marketing goods and services in a free capitalistic system. As a soybean crop grows and is harvested, concentrated, and dispersed, the obvious risks of price changes must be taken by those who own the soybeans or have commitments to buy them, either in their original form or as oil or meal. These risks would be present whether futures markets existed or not. If the speculator were unwilling to take them, someone else would have to do so. Unlike the gambler who causes a game to be created merely to satisfy a desire to gamble, the speculator does not inject risk into the economy merely because of a desire to speculate.

The truth of the matter seems to lie somewhere between these two points of view. If hedgers operated in the futures markets solely to reduce their risks and passed their savings on to consumers, and if speculators made this all possible, there could be little quarrel with the argument that their services had social value. Actually, hedgers operate in the futures markets primarily to increase their profits and not just to reduce their risks. If they believe that to hedge against their inventories or to make forward sale commitments is the best course of action, they will do so. If they believe that a partial hedge is adequate, they might well hedge only part of their risk. In some cases, if they are quite certain that their judgment of the future course of prices is correct, they might carry their entire risk unhedged. Such selective hedging is far more common than is implied in many standard texts, which indicate that all risks are hedged and that most hedges work perfectly or nearly so.

Furthermore, many firms are not above attempting to take advantage of apparent opportunities in the futures markets by taking positions parallel with their cash positions—which, of course, amounts to speculations that increase risk rather than hedges that reduce it. If such speculation is successful, it works for the good of the company and its owners, and insofar as the economy is benefited by the health of companies and their owners, it is also benefited by the speculation. If speculation of this kind proves unsuccessful, however, and the company, its owners, and its customers are damaged, it is difficult to argue that the speculators who took the other side of the trade and made it possible benefited anybody.

The motivation of many individual speculators could well be identical with that of gamblers; that is, they are willing to take relatively large risks in return for the chance to gain large profits. In addition, they may derive some pleasure from the activity of trading, just as the gambler derives excitement from the game and not just from the monetary result of gambling. The major difference is that the activities of futures speculators are essential to hedging, which, on balance, is apparently beneficial to the social good.

THE EVOLUTION OF FUTURES TRADING

Trade carried on over great distances is an ancient activity of the human race. The great trade networks of the Phoenician, Greek, Roman, and Byzantine empires were primary sources of economic power for these old civilizations. Although much trading was done on barter or cash-and-carry bases, the Greek marketplaces and Roman trading centers utilized such characteristics of modern trading as fixed times and places to trade and even contracts for future delivery.[2]

The decline of the Roman Empire in Europe resulted in the rise of disorganized and hostile European feudal states. This system of self-sufficient feudal manors undermined the basic exchange of goods among peoples of widely separated lands. When the urban tradition of Rome disappeared in early medieval Europe, only a few cities in the south of France and in Italy retained their ties with distant Eastern trade depots. During the Middle Ages economic and political stability slowly returned. In the eleventh and twelfth centuries several feudal monarchs succeeded in expanding their land holdings and their authority and thereby sowed the seeds of the modern European state system.

By the twelfth century two great trading centers had begun to flourish on the European continent as a result of a general revival in trade. In northern Italy the cities of Venice, Florence, Genoa, Pisa, and Milan competed for trading rights with the Orient and also sought to expand their trade throughout Europe. At the same time northern European trade centered about the region of Flanders (now Holland and Belgium). This area, known since Roman times for its fine cloth, developed strong economic ties with England, which was then the most important wool-producing area in Europe. The Italian traders, specializing in such luxuries as fine silk, spices, rare metals, and exotic perfumes, crossed the paths of the Flemish traders of cloth, wine, salt fish, lumber, and metalware on land held by the Counts of Champagne. Evidence shows that as early as 1114 the Counts of Champagne had established trade fairs to encourage mercantile activity from which they extracted fees. It was at these markets in Champagne during the twelfth century that the first use of forward contracts in Europe probably occurred.[3]

Once established, the market fairs became the chief centers of international exchange in Europe. Traders came not only from Flanders and Italy but from Scandinavia, England, and even Russia. The Counts of Champagne provided the traders with protection, money changers, and even storage facilities. Trade fairs were eventually held on a year-round basis, rotating initially among several raw

---

[2] Lloyd Besant, ed., *Commodity Trading Manual* (Chicago Board of Trade, 1982), pp. 1–4.

[3] J. K. Sowards, *Western Civilization to 1660* (New York: St. Martin's Press, 1965), pp. 10, 384, and 391; Lee Dee Belveal, *Commodity Trading Manual* (Chicago Board of Trade, 1966), p. 3-a.

materials and manufactured goods but eventually specializing in only one or a few related commodities; for example, linen and wool at Troyes and leather and skins at Reims.[4]

Generally, the last few days of each fair were reserved for paying bills and settling the bargains struck during the fair. Because traders at the fairs often came from widely dissimilar geographic and ethnic backgrounds, disputes often arose over the settling of accounts, and because of these disputes a code of commercial law, called the "law merchant," was slowly developed. Violators of the code were taken before "courts of the fair," which were composed of the merchants themselves.

This emerging medieval code of mercantile law performed much the same function as the regulations established by today's commodity exchanges. It defined contract terms; determined methods of sampling, inspecting, and grading the commodity in question; and set down location and date for delivery of the goods. Although most transactions were of a spot nature, an innovation of the medieval fairs was the use of a document called a *lettre de faire* as a forward contract which specified the delivery of goods at a later date.[5] Although these *lettres de faire* were first issued only in the sale of cash commodities between a single buyer and seller, they later evolved into negotiable documents which might be transferred to several parties before arriving at the warehouse where the specified goods were stored. Because of the difficulties of travel, many merchants preferred to bring only samples of their merchandise to the fairs, and the *lettre de faire* helped to make trade by sample satisfactory to both buyer and seller. Its functions became similar to the bill of exchange widely used today.[6] In addition, it had some characteristics of the modern warehouse receipt. Signed by a reputable merchant in a distant city to indicate that a specified commodity was being held in his warehouse, the receipt (*lettre de faire*) could be sold to a third party, who would, in turn, either sell or take possession of the purchased goods. The forward contract trading by merchants in the late Middle Ages was in many respects like the modern commodity futures contract but differed in that the forward trades were not standardized and were consummated on a more personal basis.

Following the establishment of the Champagne market fairs, and later others like them at Bruges, Antwerp, and Amsterdam, and the proved viability of the representative sample as the basis for a commodity transaction, England created year-round meeting places at which traders could buy and sell commodities and manufactured goods. These meeting places were known as exchanges, an early example being the Royal Exchange opened in London in 1570. The Royal Exchange was later divided into specialized exchanges known as a group as the London Commodity Exchange.

Dealers soon began acting in the London commodity exchanges as intermediaries willing to absorb price risks that the merchants wished to avoid in return for the opportunity to profit in forward transactions. Although spot, or cash, trades

---

[4] Henry H. Bakken, *Theory of Markets and Marketing* (Madison, Wis.: Mimir Publishers, 1952), p. 317.

[5] W. C. Labys and C. W. J. Granger, *Speculation, Hedging, and Commodity Price Forecasts* (Lexington, Mass.: D. C. Heath and Co., 1970), p. 3.

[6] Belveal, loc. cit.

remained the essential part of the market, increasingly large numbers of traders took advantage of the forward contracts.

As the system evolved, sellers sold their goods to intermediaries, who would, in turn, seek out a prospective buyer. In this way sellers were almost certain to dispose of their goods at reasonable prices, and buyers could expect standardized levels of quality from dealers who offered goods for resale. At this point in the development of the marketing process grading systems and true futures contracts had not yet been devised, but they were on the horizon.

DEVELOPMENT OF THE FUTURES CONTRACT

The first recorded case of organized futures trading occurred in Japan during the 1600s.[7] Wealthy landowners and feudal lords of Imperial Japan found themselves squeezed between an expanding money economy in the cities and their primarily agrarian-based resources. The rents that they collected from their feudal tenants were paid in the form of a share of each year's rice harvest. This income was irregular and subject to uncontrollable factors such as weather and other seasonal characteristics. Because the money economy required that the nobility have ready cash on hand at all times, income instability stimulated the practice of shipping surplus rice to the principal cities of Osaka and Edo, where it could be stored and sold as needed. In an effort to raise cash quickly, landlords soon began selling tickets (warehouse receipts) against goods stored in rural or urban warehouses. Merchants generally bought these tickets in anticipation of their projected needs (they also suffered at times from the fluctuations of uncertain harvests).[8]

Eventually "rice tickets" became generally acceptable as a form of currency to facilitate the transaction of business. At times, however, stored rice reserves were inadequate to meet the needs of the nobility, and when this happened, many merchants extended credit at interest to the landlord before the actual sale of the rice tickets.

During the late seventeenth century the Japanese Dojima rice market was characterized by the fact that only trading in futures contracts was permitted. By 1730 the Tokugawa Shogunate, or Imperial government, designated and officially recognized the market as *cho-ai-mai,* or, literally, "rice trade on book." A number of rules of the *cho-ai-mai-kaisho* (the marketplace) were strikingly similar to the rules of modern American futures trading[9]:

1. Contract term duration was limited.
2. All contracts within any term were standardized.
3. A basic grade for any contract period was agreed on beforehand.
4. No contract could be carried over into a new contract period.
5. All trades had to be cleared through a clearinghouse.

---

[7] Henry H. Bakken, "Futures Trading—Origin, Development and Present Economic Status," *Futures Trading Seminar,* II (Madison, Wis.: Mimir Publishers, 1953), p. 9.

[8] Ibid., p. 10.

[9] Ibid., p. 11.

6. Every trader had to establish a line of credit with the clearinghouse of his choice.

The major difference between the *cho-ai-mai* market and today's futures market was that delivery of cash commodities was never actually permitted. This "futures trading only" concept caused the futures cash-price relationship to function improperly and resulted in erratic price fluctuations. In 1869 this discrepancy between prices in the spot (cash) market and those of the futures market prompted the Imperial government to order trading stopped. Testifying to the essential futures trading function of maintaining an orderly market, fluctuations in the cash price of rice reached chaotic proportions less than 2 years after the discontinuance of the *cho-ai-mai* futures market, and a disgruntled Imperial regime was forced to reopen it.[10] Significantly, physical delivery of goods was then allowed, and as a result the Japanese futures market was effectively wedded to the cash market, thus eliminating its initial instability.

It appears that the practice of tying the cash market to the futures market in Japan may have been influenced by Western trading practices on the Oriental rice-ticket market. As the economy in the United States expanded during the early part of the nineteenth century, commodity exchanges evolved from unorganized club-type associations into formalized exchanges, the first of which was the Chicago Board of Trade, established in 1848 with 82 members. Trading in Chicago was encouraged considerably by the trading standards, inspection system, and weighing system prescribed by the board.

It was on the Chicago Board of Trade on March 13, 1851, that the first time contract was recorded. This contract authorized the delivery of 3000 bushels of corn to be made in June at a price 1 cent per bushel below the March 13 price.[11]

The major commodity exchanges in the United States were established and are still situated in Chicago and New York. These sites were logically chosen because of their proximity to the major transport routes. New York, with its port located on the major ocean shipping routes, was ideally suited for international trade. Chicago, situated at the hub of rail and canal routes extending into the agricultural heartlands of the United States, inherited the bulk of internal trade.

Around the mid-nineteenth century forward contracts known as "to arrive" contracts, similar in nature to the medieval *lettre de faire*, gradually made their appearance. It was the accumulation of excess supplies at some times and their shortage at others in the expanding American money economy that caused the modification of the traditional cash-and-carry transaction. The first of these time contracts was not much more than a verbal agreement or a simple memorandum exchanged by both parties.

Because of the increase in the volume of trading at Chicago, the risk in forward contracts became too great to be transferred to intermediaries or specialized dealers, which was the common practice in the London markets at the time, but if another kind of intermediary—a third party—could be induced to assume the risk,

---

[10] Labys and Granger, op. cit., p. 6.

[11] H. S. Irwin, *Evolution of Futures Trading* (Madison, Wis.: Mimir Publishers, 1954).

the effect would be the same: namely, the assurance of a fair price for the seller and a reasonably uniform quality of product.

Although the first "to arrive" contracts were not transferable, the printed documents that were developed to specify the grade, quantity, and time of delivery of the goods soon were.[12] These alterations to the "to arrive" contracts resulted in the creation of a futures market in this country in which a contract was readily tradable before delivery. The intermediary drawn into the newly evolved marketing structure in the United States was the speculator, on whom the risk was placed.

Because of the volume of the futures contracts traded at Chicago and the replacement of the London-type dealer by the speculator, additional rules for orderly and fair futures trading had to be drawn[13]:

1. The commodity selected for trading had to be easily graded.
2. The grading of commodities had to be maintained by regular governmental inspection.
3. Payment had to be set at the time of delivery.
4. Prices had to be reported openly and be equally accessible to all traders.
5. Buyers and sellers were required to establish financial responsibility.
6. The number of buyers and sellers had to remain large enough to provide continuous opportunities for trade.

As already noted, the rules established in Chicago were much like those of the Japanese rice futures market of earlier date.

Futures trading on the Chicago Board of Trade quickly reached sizable proportions and was rapidly adopted by other exchanges. In New York futures trading had begun on the New York Produce Exchange and on the New York Cotton Exchange by 1870. That same year futures trading was initiated on the New Orleans Cotton Exchange, and by 1885 the New York Coffee Exchange was actively trading in futures. Since the second half of the nineteenth century a number of other commodity exchanges have been founded.

During America's history of futures trading some commodities, such as wheat, have retained their popularity with the trading public. Others, such as silk, butter, and pepper, have lost favor because of insufficient trading volume for a variety of reasons. Some, such as cotton and coffee, suffered a loss of public interest for a number of years but regained popularity later. Financial futures attained widespread acceptance quickly after their introduction and have maintained a high level of activity. The American futures market has developed into a vast and complex institution consisting of 11 exchanges and a large clearinghouse system. The exchanges range in size from the Chicago Board of Trade, which does about half of all trading based upon volume of all domestic exchanges combined, to the Chicago Rice and Cotton Exchange, which does about 1 percent of the total business. Trading takes place in about 80 futures contracts. There are constant additions to and deletions from the list of contracts traded as exchanges seek new

---

[12] Bakken, op. cit., p. 104.

[13] Labys and Granger, op cit., p. 6.

sources of business or eliminate new contracts which have failed to attract or which lose industry and public support.

With the exception of a short period during World War II, when the markets were closed, the growth of this institution has been continuous since about 1865 and in recent years has accelerated enormously. The history of futures trading in the United States, however, has not been problem-free.

ATTACKS AGAINST FUTURES TRADING

Futures trading has been subject to varying degrees of criticism as long as it has been in existence. Opposition grew particularly severe during the 1890s, when considerable legislation was proposed to restrict loose business practices of many kinds. In Germany all futures trading in grains was actually forbidden by a law passed in 1896, although the law was repealed 4 years later.

In the United States commodity exchanges were widely considered to be gambling dens full of parasitic speculators who drained off money that should have gone instead to producers or consumers of products. There were, and sometimes still are, attempts by the federal and certain state governments to abolish futures trading in whole or in part. In 1867 the Illinois Legislature passed an act that provided that the parties to futures contracts, referred to in the act as gambling contracts, should be fined $1000 and imprisoned up to 1 year in the Cook County Jail. Seven members of the Board of Trade in Chicago were actually arrested under this act. Although it was repealed the following year, many more than 100 other bills to abolish futures trading have been introduced in the United States Congress alone.

In 1890 one Congressman Butterworth of Ohio introduced a bill to place a prohibitive tax on dealers in futures, and, during the ensuing debate, Representative Funston of Kansas described the futures market as follows:

> Those who deal in "options" and "futures" contracts, which is mere gambling, no matter by what less offensive name such transactions be designated, neither add to the supply nor increase the demand for consumption, nor do they accomplish any useful purpose by their calling; but on the contrary, they speculate in fictitious products. The wheat they buy and sell is known as "wind wheat" and doubtless for the reason that it is invisible, intangible, and felt or realized only in the terrible force it exerts in destroying the farming industry of the country.

Although Congressman Butterworth's bill failed to pass, agitation continued, and in 1892 Senator Washburn, speaking in the United States Senate, asserted:

> As near as I can learn, and from the best information I have been able to obtain on the Chicago Board of Trade, at least 95% of the sales of that Board are of this fictitious character, where no property is actually owned, no property sold or delivered, or expected to be delivered but simply wagers or bets as to what that property may be worth at a designated time in the future. . . . Wheat and cotton have become as much gambling tools as chips on the farobank table. The property of the wheat grower and the cotton grower is treated as though it were a "stake" put on the gambling table at Monte Carlo. The producer of wheat is compelled to see the stocks in his barn dealt with like the

> peas of a thimblerigger, or the cards of a three-card-monte man. Between the grain-producer and loaf eater, there has stepped in a "parasite" between them robbing them both.[14]

Another bill that would have imposed a prohibitive tax on all futures trading in farm products failed to pass Congress in 1893 only because final action before Congress adjourned required a suspension of the rules of the House of Representatives and the necessary two-thirds majority vote failed by the narrow margin of 172 to 124. A similar bill considered by the next Congress actually passed the House but this time failed to gain approval of the Senate.[15]

Almost all the bills designed to abolish or restrict futures trading died before reaching a vote or were defeated. After World War II, however, the continuing demands for restrictive legislation were largely concentrated on two unrelated markets: onions and potatoes. In both cases the futures markets were blamed for causing wide fluctuations in prices that inflicted severe losses on the producers, processors, and marketers of these products. In previous attacks on futures trading those engaged in the production and marketing of the products traded were among the most vocal defenders of the futures markets. This time they were among the attackers. In particular, trading in onions was attacked by those who were supposed to benefit from the existence of the market as well as by the usual unsuccessful speculators. The market had few defenders other than the Chicago Mercantile Exchange, whose members did not relish losing the futures market in one of the products traded exclusively on that exchange.

After several years of argument Congress passed a bill in 1958 to prohibit futures trading in onions. The onion crop is a minor one, grown only in limited areas, but those engaged in the business of trading futures did not take the prohibition lightly. The Chicago Mercantile Exchange appealed to a United States District Court to get the prohibition set aside as unconstitutional, but the attempt failed. Some believe that those engaged in the onion trade who attacked futures trading were really concerned, as they maintained, about the wide fluctuations in price. Others believe that they were actually more interested in having accurate price information somewhat less publicized in order to capitalize on the ignorance of the farmers and consumers. The truth will probably never really be known, but there is some suspicion that the latter provided at least some basis for the trade's lack of enthusiasm for the futures market.

A similar law to prohibit trading in potatoes was considered several times during the years that followed. Although it was given serious consideration, it was not passed.

Although the equating of speculation in the futures markets with gambling is somewhat illogical, there were other reasons for the hue and cry. There has always been a widespread feeling that profits from speculation are somehow immoral,

---

[14] From a speech entitled "Regulation and Supervision of Futures Trading," by Bernard P. Carey, chairman, Chicago Board of Trade, delivered at a futures trading seminar April 28–30, 1965, at the Chicago Board of Trade.

[15] Holbrook Working, "Futures Markets under Renewed Attack." Reprinted from *Food Research Institute Studies*, 4, No. 1 (1963).

compared with profits from other seemingly more productive activities, although the concept of compensation received by other risk bearers, such as insurance companies, does not seem to cause similar resentment. This is the same sort of vague opposition that many people feel toward selling a future or security short. Somehow they believe that a price going up is good and a price going down is bad and, furthermore, that the short seller not only thinks that it will go down but makes it do so by selling short.

There are consistent and loud complaints by those who have lost money in futures and who are reluctant to believe that their losses are caused by their own failings. They prefer to blame factors beyond their control, which helps to restore their faith in themselves, if not their money.

For long periods the United States witnessed falling commodity prices even as the prices of finished goods rose. This divergence was caused by a number of factors which were difficult for many to understand and proved even more difficult to be corrected by those who did understand. It was easy for the farmers, who believed that they were paying too much for their food and clothing, to blame speculators, who appeared to be making considerable money without growing or producing anything tangible.

A common criticism of futures speculation is that it causes violent price moves, which work considerable hardship on those engaged in more productive pursuits. Wide publicity is given to the relatively rare but highly dramatic manipulations that cause many to conclude that speculation is not only gambling but a dishonest game besides. Almost any public speaker talking about futures trading can be sure that someone in the audience will ask about "that big soybean oil scandal of a few years ago" or some similar incident.[16]

Speculators can point to equally scandalous events in all types of business at all times and in all countries, but no responsible person wants to declare all types of business activity illegal. Manipulative devices, such as artificial corners, wash sales, spreading of false rumors, and the "bucketing" of orders, are illegal. All such activities are an abuse of speculative practice and certainly not an integral part of it. Nor does the fact that speculators are essential to the operation of futures markets mean that they dominate these markets. Major price movements are usually caused by basic changes in the supply or demand, or both, for a given product and only rarely by a group of speculators successfully creating self-fulfilling prophecies.

Considerable research has been done in an attempt to prove that speculation does or does not cause excessive price movement. No final conclusions can yet be drawn on this subject, but the weight of evidence indicates that speculation probably does more to smooth price fluctuation than to increase it. Even the demise of the much maligned onion market did something to prove this point. The fluctuations in the price of cash onions apparently were greater both before there was

---

[16] The Allied Crude Vegetable Oil Refining Corp., under the leadership of its president, Anthony De Angelis, went bankrupt in 1963 and caused substantial losses to a large number of prominent banks, brokers, and commodity dealers. This is considered to be one of the largest business frauds in recent history. The scandal was, however, based primarily on the issuance of fraudulent warehouse receipts rather than on any failure of the futures markets.

a futures market and after it was prohibited than while the market was functioning. There is no doubt that the presence of speculative traders results in more transactions than would take place without their activities, but to conclude that more transactions in themselves cause more price variation than there would otherwise be is unwarranted by the facts.

WHY DO SPECULATORS SPECULATE?

The specific motivation or combination of motivations of all the millions of speculators could not be discussed here in any detail even if reliable data were available. The broad incentives that attract most speculators are quite clear, however, and can be summarized briefly.

Certainly the greatest is the opportunity to make an important amount of money in relation to the capital base used. Not many speculators are naive enough to compare their activities with those of more conservative investors. Most of them are well aware of the risks that they take in return for the large and quick profits possible, although there are some who, like gamblers, are so convinced that they will win that they are unable to admit even to themselves that they might lose. Most of them learn all too quickly that it is a rare opportunity indeed that provides an important potential profit without an attendant large risk.

Other speculators are attracted almost as much by the stimulation of the speculation itself as they are by the opportunity for profit. For some it is the sheer excitement of the game; for others, it is the dynamics of the involvement with world politics, trade, currency fluctuation, wars, and other events that come to affect their own positions rather than just provide newspaper headlines. Aside from those who receive some masochistic pleasure from losing, it seems likely that even those motivated in large part by the desire to have something to get up for in the morning find the pleasure of speculating more satisfying when they win than when they lose.

SPECULATE IN WHAT?

The desire to speculate has always been so strong and widespread that hundreds of examples could be mentioned. Historically, there are some that are difficult even to comprehend today. One of the more fantastic is the trading that took place in tulip bulbs in Holland from 1634 to 1637. The high regard for the tulip held by society leaders spread throughout the country and reached the point at which everybody seemed willing to part with almost anything for rare tulip bulbs. Trading became frantic, and prices rose until entire fortunes were paid for bulbs. When the mania had run its course, the economy of Holland was shattered, and it was years before it recovered.

Similar effects were felt in the eighteenth century from the Mississippi land schemes of John Law in France and the South Sea Bubble that was perpetrated on the English public. The latter created a mood that fostered a rash of some of the most fantastic schemes in the history of finance and caused the ruin of thousands of people. There was the huge subscription for a company that was to manufacture a perpetual-motion wheel. A company was formed to repair and rebuild parsonage and vicarage houses, and among others were companies to supply London with sea coal, rebuild every house in England, settle the island of Blanco and Sal Tarthgus, repave the streets of London, insure horses, and transmute quicksilver into a malleable fine metal. The most preposterous of all was "A company for carrying on an undertaking of great advantage, but nobody to know what it is." Subscribers were to buy 5000 shares at 100 pounds each, with a 2-pound deposit. An annual return of 100 pounds for each share was promised, details to be announced in a month. The issue was oversubscribed in 5 hours, and the promoter left for the Continent that same night and was never heard from again.[17]

In the United States the Florida land boom of the 1920s was comparable to its predecessor bubbles. The results of the worldwide 1929 stock break are well known.

Some areas of speculation have been popular for many years. These include land; precious stones and metals; natural resources such as oil; rare items such as stamps, coins, and paintings; and securities, such as stocks, bonds, warrants, and options to buy or sell stocks.

The type and degree of skill needed for success may vary among these areas, as will the amount of capital required and the mechanics of buying and selling the items. In each case, however, the attraction is the potential profit, the stimulation received from the activity, or their combination. Certain of these items have characteristics that attract some speculators and repel others. The general characteristics of the futures markets are, in some respects, unique.

FUTURES VERSUS SECURITIES AND OTHER SPECULATIONS

One reason for the popularity of futures trading is undoubtedly the ease with which it may be done. Most brokerage houses deal in futures as well as in securities. Some have research departments of their own, and others subscribe to various services, but in either case the speculator looking for a suggested position will have little difficulty in finding one. Some individual registered representatives choose not to handle futures trades, preferring to specialize in securities or mutual funds, but in such cases other registered representatives in the same office are likely to be available. Few are really expert in futures trading, nor do they claim to be, but most are at least able to enter or close out positions efficiently and to pass pertinent information on to the trader if he or she wants it. In addition to full-line wire houses, there are firms that specialize in the handling of futures business. They usually have a considerable amount of factual information available

---

[17] Charles Mackay, *Extraordinary Popular Delusions and the Madness of Crowds* (London, 1841). Reprinted in 1932 by L. C. Page & Co., Boston, p. 55.

and are especially adept at the order and clerical end of the business, but there is no reason to believe that their market opinions are any better or worse than anyone else's.

Futures speculators who prefer to make their own decisions may be attracted by the relative ease of securing information. Important political and economic information is readily available in general and trade newspapers. Vital supply and demand information concerning specific futures is published in large quantities by various government departments and bureaus and is made available at frequent intervals. In addition to being mailed at low or no cost to anybody who requests it, such information is widely publicized in financial journals and on news wires. An adequate amount of accurate information about the handful of futures that are traded actively is considerably easier to obtain than about the tens of thousands of stocks, bonds, and mutual funds that are available. The problem faced by those who gather basic information about stocks is quite similar to the problem faced by those who gather basic information about futures. To date no model clearly superior to a random walk has been published to describe the behavior of stock and futures prices. Stock traders, however, may be able to take advantage of some slight trend tendencies and long-run cycles, and futures traders may be able to isolate some conditioned seasonals. Traders in stocks and futures are both faced with the results of information that becomes available while markets are closed, which means that markets are as "active" then as they are when they are open. In both securities and futures there are significant covariances among the prices of stocks representing related industries and among interrelated commodities such as feeds or edible oils.[18]

A basic difference between commodity and stock markets is that futures markets are primary and stock markets are secondary. The futures speculator in the long run must be concerned primarily with the real forces of supply and demand. Speculators in stocks must know about both the markets of the companies in whose stocks they are speculating and the market for the stocks themselves, in which case they must be concerned with the influence of floor specialists, whose influence on prices is somewhat controversial but exists to some significant degree with little doubt.

Like stock traders, futures traders have an advantage in liquidity over speculators in most other areas. There is seldom any difficulty in finding a buyer or seller at any time for even large positions, although, of course, the price may not be so favorable as desired. Positions can normally be acquired or disposed of within a minute or two when the exchanges are open, but if markets are active, an actual report of the transaction might not be received that promptly. There is no need to search out a buyer or seller or wait for an auction, as there would be in trading in paintings, and there are no loans to arrange or escrows to close, as in trading property.

Futures traders, unlike stock traders, must consider the limits that restrict the amount by which a futures price can rise or fall in one day and the range over which a future may be traded. These "limit moves" probably concern unsophis-

---

[18] Labys and Granger, op. cit., pp. 268–270.

ticated traders more than they should. For one thing, typical traders will seldom encounter them in a future in which they actually have positions. In addition, of course, they hardly find objectionable limit moves in a direction favorable to them. Their freedom of action is also not restricted by adverse limit moves that do not carry beyond the levels of risk they are prepared to assume. Furthermore, many futures markets do not provide for limit moves, and others do not restrict limits during delivery months.

Some traders are concerned that an adverse limit move will prevent a position from being liquidated with a reasonable loss. The loss, of course, was caused by the adverse price direction and not by the limit move. It should be made clear that a limit move does not cause a market to close; it merely precludes trades from being made beyond the limit. On reaching the maximum possible advance or decline a market may trade any number of times at that level or away from the limit. The purpose of limiting a move is to prevent unreasonable price moves based on overreaction to news. Securities markets deal with similar situations either by suspending trading until a fair and orderly market is again possible or by allowing prices to move over a large and (it may be noted) unlimited range. For a trader liquidity under the first condition is no better than in the futures markets when a market has advanced its permissible limit.[19] In a word, limit moves delay liquidation but neither preclude liquidation nor cause adversity.

Futures margins differ from stock margins in both concept and method of computation. Stock margins constitute a partial payment to the brokerage house. The remainder, or debit balance, in a margin account is a debt owed to the brokerage house on which interest is charged. The amount of the debt may be limited by the Federal Reserve, a stock exchange, or the brokerage house itself. Futures margins are actually good-faith deposits to protect a broker against risk in the event of adverse price moves in the interim between the establishment of a position and its liquidation either by delivery or by offset. Payment for the cash commodity needs to be made only in the highly unlikely event that delivery is actually made or taken.

Stock margins required typically fluctuate in a range of 50 to 90 percent, although both limits of this range have been exceeded for brief periods. Futures margins are based on fixed minimums per unit such as ounces, pounds, tons, or face values of financial instruments established by the exchanges, but individual brokers may require larger amounts if they believe the minimum involves undue risks for themselves or their clients. Requirements within a range of 5 to 10 percent of contract value are common, although the amount may be less than 5 percent in low-risk spread positions. The margin on 5000 bushels of corn, for example, might typically be about 15 to 22 cents a bushel with corn selling at $3 to $4. On a contract value in the area of $17,500 the deposit required might be only $750 to $1100. If 5000 bushels of May corn were bought against the sale of 5000 bushels of July corn, the total margin for the entire position might be as low as $250, and even this amount would probably be required by the broker rather than by the

---

[19] C. V. Harlow and R. J. Teweles, "Commodities and Securities Compared," *Financial Analysts Journal* (September–October 1972), 65–66.

exchange. When markets become unusually volatile, margins may be raised to protect the brokerage house from its clients and, perhaps, the clients from themselves. Even at such times margins exceeding 20 percent of contract value are unusual. Brokerage houses may offer varying margin levels to different clients provided that they equal or exceed levels established by the exchanges. The Commodity Exchange Act (CEA) provides for allowing the granting of special low margins to bona fide hedgers.[20]

The low margins not only provide the opportunity to establish large positions on a small capital base but also give the futures markets their somewhat undeserved reputation for extreme price volatility. Futures prices frequently remain in quite narrow ranges for long periods and are not more volatile than typical securities prices in similar price ranges. The price movements of futures, however, relative to the margin required can create large profits or losses relative to the available trading capital. Traders who find changes in values too great for their capital or nerve can reduce the leverage employed merely by utilizing more margin than is required and thereby trade on a more conservative basis. Too many traders take advantage of the possible rewards without accepting or recognizing the accompanying risks by fully utilizing the available leverage. This is why it is often maintained that bulls or bears can trade profitably, but not hogs.

The cost of trading futures is low in relation to trading in other areas. Commissions paid are usually less, considering the value of the merchandise traded, than those in land, precious goods, paintings, prints, or securities. Computation is simpler because commissions are based on the number of contracts bought or sold and are unrelated to the amount of money involved in a transaction, as they are in the security markets. For example, regardless of the price of 100 ounces of gold, which is equivalent to a stock round lot, the commission varies among brokers but is about $100, which covers both the purchase and the sale. The entire $100 is charged against the customer's account when a position is liquidated rather than $50 at the time of entry and $50 on liquidation.

The amount of record keeping required by a futures trader is minimal unless the position held is so large that it must be reported to the Commodity Futures Trading Commission. Reportable and maximum limits are so great that they are only of academic interest to most traders.

Tax rules covering profits and losses on futures positions are different from those covering securities despite the fact that both are capital items. Generally, gains in futures are deemed to be 60 percent long-term capital gains and 40 percent short-term capital gains regardless of how long positions have been held. They are also deemed to be taxable at year-end whether the positions are actually liquidated or not. Tax laws are subject to change, and there are various exceptions to these generalities, so traders are well advised to acquire the tax information applicable to them from their tax advisers or brokers.

The futures markets operate under rules and regulations of the exchanges and those of the Commodity Futures Exchange Commission. There are also various state laws affecting areas of trading not governed by federal law. There is also a

---

[20] General Regulations under the Commodity Exchange Act, Reg. 1.3(z)(1).

trade association, the National Futures Association (NFA), which operates in a manner comparable to that of the National Association of Securities Dealers (NASD) for securities.

There are those who are fond of pointing out that futures traders who are long on the contracts of most futures in the spot months risk getting unwanted deliveries. They usually refer to someone, invariably unnamed, who forgot about a wheat contract and came home to find wheat piled on the front lawn. In reality, futures traders have less to worry about concerning deliveries than securities traders. If they are short, they cannot get delivery at all. If they are long, they can avoid delivery merely by selling the position before the contract month arrives. If a position is carried into the delivery month, there is still no certainty that delivery will be received, but even if this occurs, the position can usually be disposed of before the close of the day's trading session. Even if this is not possible, the cost of carrying a delivered position for short periods is small, and the position can usually be sold when desired. Securities traders may well have far greater delivery problems if securities are misplaced. There is considerable time and trouble involved in disposing of securities if they are misplaced, as well as the expense of paying for a bond to protect the broker if they are found and sold by someone else. The cost may be particularly high in the case of bearer bonds.

Trading in futures is more like trading in securities than other types of speculation, but it should be noted that where there are differences between the two fields, futures trading is almost always the simpler. This, of course, does not imply that successful results in futures trading are more certain. The fact remains, however, that futures traders are not concerned with dividends, interest, rents, royalties, stock dividends or splits, rights offerings, handling certificates, proxies, ex-dividend dates, voting, call dates, conversions, or any other of the host of factors that might burden securities traders. Futures traders incur lower costs of trading relative to the amount of money traded because commissions are relatively lower than on most securities. Because the money they deposit as margin is a good-faith deposit and not a down payment, they owe their broker no money and hence pay no interest. Their costs of trading, of course, could become quite high if trading is frequent.

SHOULD YOU SPECULATE?

It is hardly proper for the authors of a book, brokers, or financial advisers to advise individuals to speculate or not to speculate. Some speculators make important amounts of money by speculating. They would not have been served well by someone who persuaded them not to risk losing any money and thus prevented their success. Similarly, it seems improper to suggest that everybody should speculate when it is known that most speculators are unsuccessful and therefore that the odds favor any particular new speculator losing. The decision to be conservative or aggressive with one's funds is best made by the one who is going to try to acquire more at the risk of losing whatever is already had. The logical basis for making the decision can be discussed productively, however.

The most common advice given to would-be speculators by many advisers is that they should speculate only when all of their financial responsibilities have been met, that is, when their insurance programs are adequate, when they have adequate equities in their homes, when their children's educations are complete or provided for, and when some money is available for emergencies. This approach is certainly cautious enough, but it might make some wonder what the purpose of speculating is. The reason most people want to increase their net worths is to raise their standards of living. If they have funds available to accomplish everything they regard as important, successful speculation can do little to improve their situations significantly, whereas unsuccessful speculation could leave them in positions that are far worse than those from which they began. In short, they have much to lose and little to gain.

In contrast, one with relatively little capital might appear to be irresponsible if a speculative venture is entered, but if a loss would not create despondency, an aggressive program might not be altogether unreasonable. Success might improve the financial condition of such a person to an impressive extent, whereas a loss could usually not cause great damage.

Regardless of the amount of capital available to traders for speculative purposes, their own natures are probably even more important than their available capital. There are those who are simply unable to take a loss or allow enough time for a profitable position to grow to its full potential. Some people are able to make a logical plan and follow it with a high degree of discipline. Others prefer to take things as they come rather than follow a rigid program. There are certainly activities to which the latter are well adapted, but speculation is not one of them.

There are those who find that the tension of carrying a position is so great that it interferes with their work or other activities to a degree that makes any profit they might gain not worth the anguish of realizing it. It is well and good to suggest "selling down to a sleeping point," but there are those who are so emotional that they cannot sleep if they have any position at all because they are so concerned about where the market will open in the morning. If it is necessary to trade on such a small scale that the chance for important gains is lost, it hardly seems reasonable to expend the energy needed to trade at all.

All potential speculators must consider their own capital positions along with their responsibilities and decide whether to risk some of what they have in an effort to gain more. They must also take adequate stock of themselves to determine whether the costs in time, energy, and stress involved in trading are worth expending for any profits that may be achieved. Speculating in futures may be an expensive mistake for some, but not speculating might prove equally or even more expensive for others in terms of opportunities lost. It is not the function of this book to convince readers that they should or should not speculate in futures. The purpose is rather to provide information about the nature and behavior of futures markets, information about the procedures used by successful traders and the pitfalls they face, fundamental and technical considerations, and information about specific markets to help readers make intelligent decisions for themselves.

2

The Nature of the Futures Markets

*"Futures markets are an anomaly to those
economists who study them least, an
anachronism to those who study them a little
more, and an annoyance to those who study
them most. . . ."* ROGER GRAY
*Fundamental Price Behavior
Characteristics in Commodity
Futures,* Futures Trading Seminar

INTRODUCTION

Trading futures is a skill, and no skill develops powerfully when one is wearing
blinders. For that reason prospective traders must understand, insofar as it is
possible, the nature of the environment in which they are to pit their skills against
those of others who play the same game.

This chapter, then, discusses the nature of the contract the participants hold
while playing the game, the nature of the organized markets for those contracts,
the nature of the open interest (i.e., the kinds of participants in the game), and
the nature of cash and futures price relationships. The last includes a detailed
analysis of the structure of the hedging process. Finally, a discussion of market
performance contains an analysis of the many connections between futures markets and price variability.

NATURE OF THE CONTRACT[1]

Regardless of whether the user of the traditional futures contract is a hedger or speculator, the common bond is the nature of the contract itself. That contract is a firm legal agreement between a buyer (or seller) and an established futures exchange or its clearinghouse in which the trader agrees to deliver or accept during a designated period a specified amount of a certain product that adheres to the particular quality and delivery conditions prescribed by the exchange on which that future is traded or make a cash settlement. The contract, if allowed to run to its termination, is fulfilled by a cash payment on the delivery date based on the settlement price for that day in some cases, and in the case of most tangibles, actual delivery of the commodity occurs.

During the time that the contract is open, the trader must agree to a series of conditions with a qualified broker (or the clearinghouse if the trader is a member) which calls for an initial margin deposit, a prescribed margin level that protects the broker from possible losses resulting from adverse price movements, and the right to close out (offset) an open contract at any time simply by properly instructing the broker to do so. The last condition is a bilateral one that permits the broker to close out the trader's position if the margin is seriously impaired.

This basic commitment has several ramifications. Although the contract defines the quantity, the quality, and the location at which the future may be delivered, there are, as a rule, alternatives available to the seller that allow for delivery of a commodity to be made with substantial deviations from the par specifications. The seller faces a scale of premiums or discounts in price because of such deviations, which might include different delivery locations or variations in the weight or grade of the commodity to be delivered. Deliveries must be made during the delivery month traded, but the actual day of the month is selected by the seller, who usually issues a notice of intention to deliver in the form of a warehouse receipt, a shipping certificate, or a bill of lading.

The trader holding a contract will usually be dealing through a futures commission merchant (broker) who is a member of an exchange and who will charge a commission for his or her services. It is the member broker who is responsible for the fulfillment of the contract if that broker is a clearing member of the exchange. If the broker is not a clearing member, the trades must in turn be cleared by a clearing member.

The contracts themselves are subject to legal provisions as well as the rules of the various exchanges, such as the setting of trading hours and trading regulations including minimum margins and the daily limits beyond which the prices of particular futures cannot move. These and other specifications of most futures contracts traded on all major exchanges are reviewed in Chapter 3.

There are, then, two major elements of the commitment assumed when a trader enters into a futures contract. The first is a promise of actual delivery of a future or a cash settlement at a designated date in a way that conforms to exchange

---

[1] The following discussion draws on Henry B. Arthur, "The Nature of Commodity Futures as an Economic and Business Instrument," *Food Research Institute Studies in Agricultural Economics, Trade, and Development,* 11, No. 3, 257–260.

specifications unless the contract has been previously offset. The second is a promise to respond promptly to adverse daily price changes by payment of cash to a member broker, who must in turn respond to a call for the cash from the exchanges' clearinghouses, the operation of which is discussed in the following section. The daily settlement process maintains the viability of the first promise to deliver or make a cash settlement. Traders who wish to cancel their commitments to make or accept delivery of actual commodities merely need to enter the market and offset their open positions. Over 98 percent of all futures contracts which provide for delivery are settled by offset rather than by deliveries.

Until actual delivery a transaction in a futures contract does not involve anything beyond the daily process of generating profits or losses against a good-faith margin deposit with a broker. There is no debit balance; hence no interest is charged. All net balances are on the credit side and are marked to the market after each day's trading. The actual buy and sell occur only after an intent to deliver is indicated by a short, at which point a specific buyer and seller are paired at the current settlement price.

NATURE OF EXCHANGE OPERATIONS

The need for holding futures contracts has grown at a rapid pace in recent years. To facilitate this growth about 80 futures contracts are traded actively on 11 exchanges in the United States and a much larger number in the rest of the world. Table 2-1 and Figure 2-1 illustrate the growth cycle since 1954 of futures contracts trading on American exchanges.

The dollar value of the contracts traded on the futures exchanges annually in the United States is measured in trillions of dollars. This dollar value varies widely because of the variation in the number of active futures contracts, volume, and price levels. It is certainly clear, however, that the volume of futures trading dominates that of physical cash trading in commodities which underlie the futures. The small number of actual deliveries against futures contracts further indicates the dominance of futures over physical trading. It is not unusual for futures trading to represent 20 times the size of the actual crop to be traded before the expiration of the crop year, and sometimes the figure is far higher. The size and value of each contract vary widely according to each commodity, as summarized in the contract facts discussion in Chapter 3.

Commodity exchanges may perform many functions, such as supplying accommodations for trading, handling, and grading cash commodities, but basically they exist to provide their members with facilities for trading items for future delivery. It is important to note that the exchanges themselves do not trade contracts, nor do they set the prices at which contracts are traded. They merely furnish a place where people in the commodity business, speculators, or their representatives can meet to buy and sell futures contracts and also establish rules and procedures designed to make such trading fair and orderly.

Most exchanges are voluntary associations of members whose primary business is producing, marketing, or dealing in the items underlying the contracts traded on the exchanges. The number of memberships ranges from about 200 on the

**TABLE 2-1 ANNUAL VOLUME OF CONTRACTS TRADED ON U.S.
FUTURES EXCHANGES, 1954–1983* (MILLIONS OF CONTRACTS)**

Year	Total	Year	Total
1954	4.3	1969	11.2
1955	4.1	1970	13.6
1956	4.5	1971	14.6
1957	4.1	1972	18.3
1958	3.9	1973	25.8
1959	3.8	1974	27.7
1960	3.9	1975	32.2
1961	6.1	1976	36.9
1962	5.2	1977	42.8
1963	7.1	1978	58.5
1964	6.4	1979	76.0
1965	8.4	1980	92.1
1966	10.5	1981	98.5
1967	9.5	1982	112.4
1968	9.3	1983	139.9†

* Volume figures provided by the Commodity Futures Trading Commission differ slightly from those provided by the Futures Industry Association. The commission's figures are reported on a fiscal year basis, i.e., October–September, whereas the association's figures are reported on a calendar year basis. Contracts are counted once, not twice, for each transaction.

† Not including exchange-traded option contracts, which accounted for an additional 2.6 million contracts in 1983.

SOURCE: Futures Industry Association, Inc., 1825 Eye Street, N.W., Suite 1040, Washington, D.C. 20006.

Kansas City Board of Trade to over 1400 on the Chicago Board of Trade and over 1800 on the New York Futures Exchange. Memberships are usually acquired from other members, subject to the approval of the exchange. In some cases an exchange may wish to expand membership, and so it sells memberships itself. In other cases an exchange may wish to reduce membership, and so it retires memberships as they become vacant.

A few exchanges permit "blackboard trading" to accommodate transactions in futures with only small interest. In this case, for inactive markets, orders are posted on a blackboard. When a broker gets an order, a transaction is made against the highest bid or lowest offer on the blackboard. This accounts for only a small amount of the total transactions. It is far more usual for trading to take place in a pit or around the outside of a ring. Each exchange differs in some respects from the others, but the similarities are many. All futures orders received by member firms are transmitted to the exchange floor by telephone or private wire for execution and are filled according to bids and offers in the respective trading areas by open outcry to all members present at the time. Typically, one commodity is traded in a pit or around a ring unless the volume is too small to justify so much space. Customarily, those trading the same delivery month of a future gather in the same area of the ring or pit so that brokers can fill their orders as rapidly and efficiently as possible.

Whenever volume is high and price changes are rapid, it is not uncommon for

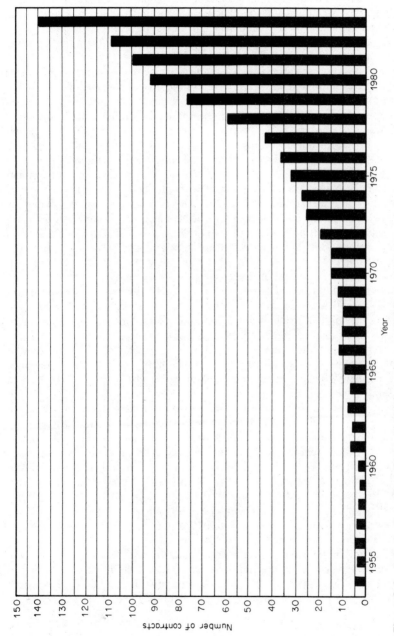

Figure 2-1 Annual volume of trading on U.S. futures exchanges, 1954–1983 (millions of contracts excluding options).

different prices to be bid and offered for the same delivery in different parts of the trading area at the same time. The trader must remember that these conditions might result in executions at prices that are never officially quoted, or, even more difficult to understand, these conditions might cause the return of an order marked "unable," even though the price on the order was well within the range of trading in that future.

Immediately after each transaction on an exchange a recorder, who is an employee of the exchange, writes out a record of the transaction, including its price and the time at which it was made, and then enters details into the exchange's reporting system by means of a computer terminal. The information is displayed on the trading floor and is also transmitted for display on tickers or quotation screens via electronic means to brokers and others who subscribe to the exchange's market data services. Futures exchanges typically report the future traded, the month, the price, and the time of sale but, unlike stock exchanges, omit the volume.

Some markets start each day's trading with an open auction in all contract months and continue to trade in that manner all day. Under this system all months in a particular future begin to be traded at the opening bell. Others open and close on a call basis, which means that each contract is called in turn until all orders currently on hand for that contract, except limit and stop orders away from the market, are filled.[2] After all contracts are opened, the market continues on an open auction or on the blackboard until halted by the closing call.

All this makes little difference to individual traders except that they must remember that spread orders in call markets (e.g., silver) cannot be filled on the opening or closing because only one future month at a time is being traded. The client may enter a spread order limited to a given difference in price which was noted on the tape or a broker's quote machine early or late in the day. When the broker tells the client that the order could not be filled, the customer sometimes assumes unfairly that the market was missed, not realizing that the order could not possibly have been filled.

At the end of each day the clearing organization which is related to the exchange assumes one side of all open contracts. If a broker is long, the clearing organization has the other, or short, position; if a broker is short, the clearing organization assumes the other, or long, side. The clearing organization guarantees its members the performance of both sides of all open contracts. Each broker, therefore, who is long or short on a futures contract deals only with the clearinghouse after a position has been initiated and not with the broker who actually took the other side of the trade when it was made. In effect, all obligations to receive or deliver commodities are with the clearing organization and not with other brokers or individual traders.

The clearing organization does not care about the prices at which each trade was entered because all profits and losses are settled daily in cash according to the latest settlement price. Because the clearing organization always has a zero net position, it can operate easily without any reference to entry or exit prices for

---

[2] These and other orders are discussed in detail in Chapter 3.

the individual trades on its books. Only the customer and broker are interested in these matters.

The total of the long or short positions held by all the clearing brokers which are outstanding at a given moment (and which are always equal) is called the "open interest." A broker who is long on a futures contract can meet this obligation either by accepting delivery during the delivery month or by selling the position to someone else who chooses to buy it. If the position is sold to someone who has chosen to be long, the open interest is unchanged. If the position is sold to a short who is buying in a position, the open interest is accordingly reduced. A broker who is short on a futures contract can meet this obligation by making delivery or by buying in the position either from someone else who wishes to be short or from someone on the long side who is selling out a position. The total size of the open interest and volume indicates the degree of current liquidity in a given market and is tabulated daily for each delivery month of every future by the clearing organizations of the exchanges. The Commodity Futures Trading Commission (CFTC) also publishes monthly and annual figures. The attempt by technicians to relate changes in open interest to simultaneous, preceding, or lagging changes in volume and price is discussed in Chapter 7.

Futures may be traded for delivery during any future month listed, but only a few months of the year ordinarily become active, usually in accordance with trade needs or customs, such as the normal harvest time of a crop. All months in which most futures are traded are listed with other pertinent contract facts in Chapter 3.

Some exchanges, such as the Chicago Board of Trade, the Chicago Mercantile Exchange, and the MidAmerica Commodity Exchange, each handle long lists of futures numbering about 20, whereas others, such as the Minneapolis Grain Exchange and the Chicago Rice and Cotton Exchange, might handle only one or two. Sometimes the same future is traded on more than one exchange. This is usually a matter of regional requirements, as in the case of wheat, in response to which Soft Red is traded in Chicago, Hard winter in Kansas City, and Northern spring in Minneapolis. Sometimes more than one type of a commodity can be delivered against an exchange contract; for example, Soft Red, Hard Red winter, Dark Northern spring, and Northern spring are all deliverable against the Soft Red contract on the Chicago Board of Trade.

NATURE OF THE OPEN INTEREST

Although exchanges differ in futures traded, location, size, and details of their operations, the people who trade on them are all similarly motivated. Basically, there are floor traders of various types, outside speculators, and hedgers. Speculators and hedgers, unlike floor traders, may or may not be members of the exchanges on which they trade, but whether they are or not primarily affects their commission and margin requirements and not the manner in which they trade or their reasons for trading. Because the remainder of the book centers on the activities and techniques of the market participants, they can be introduced briefly at this point.

Speculators

Speculators are interested in profiting from a price change in a futures contract. They are not interested in taking delivery or making delivery of the future in which they trade, although they may do so sometimes in connection with their speculating. Speculators may trade from the floor of an exchange if they are members or through a broker if they are not. They differ from one another in several ways. Some trade small positions and some quite large positions, even up to the limits imposed on speculative positions by the CFTC or by the exchanges, as illustrated in Chapter 3. Some prefer to trade from the long side, some from the short side, and some prefer to trade spreads rather than net positions. Spreading, like security arbitrage, is usually done by the more sophisticated traders.

One of the great differences among speculators is the length of time during which they are prepared to hold a position. A small number prefer to wait for a full move, which could take months, a year, or even more to develop, and will hold a position for as long as necessary. Position traders of this kind formerly had the additional incentive of being able to take advantage of the favorable long-term gains provisions of the Internal Revenue Code when trades were successful, but this incentive no longer exists. Most traders hold their positions for much shorter periods, and there are some who, whenever possible, get out the day they get in. These day traders are sometimes called "scalpers." Although they are seldom able to realize large gains in so short a time, neither do they sustain large losses on trades which are liquidated in one day. In addition, day traders receive more favorable margin requirements and, on many exchanges, benefit from a materially reduced commission rate. Unfortunately, many unsophisticated day traders develop a practice of liquidating only their day trades that go in the right direction and maintaining positions that go wrong; with the inevitable eventual record of an accumulation of many small profits which are more than countered by some large losses. Although commissions on individual trades may be small, the frequent trader, of course, is quite able to accumulate enough total commissions to overcome any gross profit which might somehow have been generated. The number of successful nonmember day traders in relation to the number who try day trading is quite small in the long run.

Floor Traders

Floor traders are members of the exchange who make their transactions in the pit or around the ring on the exchange floor itself, as contrasted with other members who choose to trade off the floor through member brokerage houses. Floor traders, like nonmember speculators, can trade for their own accounts. They can establish long-term positions or day-trade. Others act as scalpers, trading many times each day. Some try to buy at the current bid prices or sell at the current offer prices, knowing that they can reverse any positions thus established with little or no adversity. This practice is sometimes called "trading at the edge." Still others specialize in spreads by taking opposite positions between contracts when the price difference appears abnormal. Floor traders may work in one future or in several. They have such advantages as being able to trade with minimum commissions or margins. Trades liquidated in the couse of a day seldom require margin deposits, and trades liquidated at the same price at which they were established ("scratches") incur little or no commission expense. In addition, floor traders are able to take or liquidate positions quickly, but this in itself does not assure profits. A bad position taken quickly is bad nonetheless. A bad position liquidated quickly might have lost less if liquidated slowly. Floor traders trading for their own accounts are sometimes referred to as "locals." Some become quite prosperous; many others do not, despite the market information disseminated by some brokers indicating what the locals are doing, which sometimes leaves the impression that locals almost never lose.

Some members act as floor brokers, handling orders for others but seldom or never trading for themselves. These brokers specialize in orders emanating from futures commission merchants or from customers in the trade, such as processors, exporters, and warehousers. They receive only a small part of the commissions paid by customers to their commission houses, but brokers who handle the orders for large commission houses may gather in substantial volumes of business, and their total incomes can be quite impressive. The orders held by floor brokers at any given time are referred to as their "decks." They may trade for their own accounts if they wish, but they must not trade in such a way that anything they do is in conflict with their decks. As in any other fiduciary relationship, the customers' interests are to be placed first.

Hedgers

Futures trading grew out of the needs of the manufacturers, merchants, and dealers engaged in the business of producing, merchandising, and processing commodities. Some of the earliest markets featured the grains, and most of them are important today. Their salient point was that they existed primarily for delivery and therefore were characterized by rules governing merchandising transactions, standards ensuring grade and delivery terms, and clearing arrangements. Futures contracts soon came to be viewed as temporary substitutes for cash contracts, and traders found it rewarding to be able to establish prices for a future date.

The most important role played by early futures markets was in the hedging of inventories. During the peak marketing season tradespeople often bought more than enough to fill their current orders to be sure of being able to meet the demands of their customers until new supplies became available. The merchants and dealers of those grains incurred the risk of unfavorable price changes that could easily outweigh the other risks, such as fire, theft, or windstorm, they faced as a matter of course. Grain prices, then as now, were notoriously volatile because they were not only subject to the vagaries of supply and demand but also affected to an unusual degree by weather, unexpected political developments, and sometimes illogical changes in public psychology. Merchants and dealers with heavy inventories of an unsold crop could face disastrous losses in the event of a material drop in prices. Those same participants who made forward sales based on current cash prices and who relied on purchasing inventories later to meet their commitments rather than pay storage charges for the cash grain would have a similar problem if prices rose sharply.

The hedging function, then, naturally forcused on the role of transferring the risk of drastic inventory price changes to other holders in the futures markets. The other side of the transaction necessary to accomplish this might well have been taken by another hedger who was offsetting an opposite risk or was liquidating another hedge as a result of a change in his position in the cash market. More often than not it was taken by a speculator attempting to make a profit. It appears, on the surface, that this risk of price change would not be important in the long run because of the windfall profits that would compensate for disastrous losses. Most businesspeople learned in those early years, however, that they would gladly forgo large profits to avoid large losses because of the danger that they might not survive the large loss to enjoy the large profit if the loss came first. There was also the danger that a number of losses might precede a number of profits.

The traditional risk transferal concept of hedging has evolved into a dynamic concept of risk management which accents the maximization of expected return as well as the position of merely minimizing risk. In this regard hedging is now viewed by many sophisticated users as an important management tool which can facilitate buying and selling decisions and give greater freedom for business action not only in markets dominated by the necessity of carrying inventories from one period of time to another but also in nonstorage markets. The evolution of the hedging process and an analysis of the motivation and mechanics of hedging are covered in a subsequent section.

Distribution of the Open Interest

It is of considerable use to the trader to examine the distribution of the value of the total open interest among the participants over a wide range of markets for a significant period of time. Table 2-2 provides such data reported semimonthly over an 18-year period for commodities regulated by the Commodity Exchange Act (CEA).[3] The analysis does not include the unregulated markets at the time of the study, such as pork bellies, sugar, or cocoa, or markets that have since come into being and reflect important volume, such as cattle, plywood, lumber, orange juice, or silver. Even though many markets no longer viable, such as bran, middlings,

---

[3] Charles Rockwell, "Normal Backwardation, Forecasting, and the Returns to Commodity Futures Traders," *Proceedings of a Symposium on Price Effects of Speculation in Organized Commodity Markets, Food Research Institute Studies,* Supplement, 7 (1967), 107–130. Rockwell's approach was the first published study that utilized the commitments of reporting speculators, hedgers, spreaders, and nonreporting traders prepared by the CEA in a broad coverage of both markets and time. An earlier study by Hendrik Houthakker, "Can Speculators Forecast Prices?" *The Review of Economics and Statistics* (May 1957), reported evidence based on three markets over a shorter time period.

**TABLE 2-2   VALUE OF GROUP COMMITMENTS AS A PERCENTAGE
OF THE VALUE OF THE TOTAL OPEN INTEREST**

Trading groups*	Percentage of the value of total open interest for 25 CEA-regulated markets, 1947–1965
Nonreporting (small) traders:	
Small traders, long	53
Small traders, short	39
Reporting (large) traders:	
Large speculators, long	11
Large speculators, short	5
Speaders, long	18
Spreaders, short	18
Hedgers, long	18
Hedgers, short	38

* The CEA required that reports be filed for the day before, the day, and one day after a certain level of positions was held. These reportable positions, by commodity, are listed in Chapter 3.

SOURCE: Charles Rockwell, "Normal Backwardation, Forecasting, and the Returns to Commodity Futures Traders," *Proceedings of a Symposium on Price Effects of Speculation in Organized Commodity Markets, Food Research Institute Studies,* Supplement, 7 (1967), 117.

shorts, onions, and butter, are included in the study, it is reasonable to assume that the three broad conclusions[4] that follow continue to be applicable.

The first conclusion is that on the average both small (nonreporting) and large (reporting) speculators are net long and that reporting hedgers are net short. Large speculators, then, tend to be on the same side of the market as the small traders and opposite that of the hedger. The implications of this distribution in regard to the effectiveness of the futures market for hedging and to the rates of return to the participants are discussed later.

Second, the data indicate the degree of balance between the long and short positions of each group. The short-to-long position ratio is 74 percent for small traders, 45 percent for large speculators, and 47 percent for hedgers. As a group, then, it would seem that large speculators and hedgers have expectations that are more unbalanced than those of small traders. Whether the greater homogeneity in large trader expectations accompanies generally superior or inferior trading results is discussed in Chapter 13.

Third, the data in Table 2-2 confirm the long-suspected notion that large speculators form an elite population. The percentage of the total open interest attributed to the large speculator may vary considerably from market to market, but for all markets the holdings of the large speculator's total long and short positions are less than 20 percent of the total holdings of the small traders. If it can be conservatively assumed that the average large speculator holds a position at least 10 times as large as that of the average small trader, then large speculators probably constitute less than 2 percent of the total futures trading population.

[4] Ibid., 117, 118.

NATURE OF CASH AND FUTURES PRICE RELATIONS

Introduction

There is a basic truth about futures contracts. Most are temporary substitutes for cash items. The realization that delivery of real goods is often guaranteed if the contracts are held to maturity impresses upon speculators, both small and large, that speculation in futures is not just a numbers game which is conducted in Wonderland. Because of this, the trader should understand the relation between cash and futures prices. Perhaps this clarification can be made by indicating the complexities of the role of hedging in the futures markets.

There can be no serious exceptions to the statement that futures trading depends on hedging. Markets simply do not come into existence solely to furnish a speculative arena, nor do they persist if hedgers, the inhabitants of the land, do not find it rewarding to continue to use those markets. The higher the level of hedging, the higher the level of futures business. The relation between hedging and speculation is discussed in the final section of this chapter.

The trader should be apprised that the literature on hedging in futures markets is not the essence of clarity. It is often disjointed, and the thoughtful work is not generally available to the casual trader. In an attempt to define and develop the controversies as they have appeared, four classes of hedging theory are discussed,[5] each of which differs in the assumptions made about the attitudes of hedgers toward risk and motivation for using the futures markets.

Hedging Carried Out to Eliminate the Risks Associated with Price Fluctuations

The risk-elimination view of hedging usually begins with a naive illustration of the two kinds of hedges. A processor holds 100,000 bushels of cash wheat at $3.50 a bushel and is fearful of a decline in price. The processor immediately sells 100,000 bushels of futures contracts at $3.50 and is thereby short hedged. If the feared decline materializes and wheat drops to $3.35 a bushel, the profit on the short sale of futures exactly offsets the loss on the inventory. A long hedge is illustrated in much the same manner. A commercial business with a commitment to sell 100,000 bushels of wheat at a specific price and time in the future, which it has neither bought nor contracted to buy, can protect itself by buying a futures position equal in amount to its forward sale and therby fix its forward costs. Thus the hedging process is said to eliminate the risk of price fluctuation.

In real life hedging decisions are neither really so simple nor mechanical. The grade of the commodity owned or sold forward by the prospective hedger may not be the same as the contract grade traded on the futures exchange. There might also be variations in the discounts or premiums of "off" and "on" grades which

---

[5] This approach was employed by Roger W. Gray and David J. S. Rutledge, "The Economics of Commodity Futures Markets: A Survey," *Review of Marketing and Agricultural Economics,* **39,** No. 4, reported by the Food Research Institute, Stanford University, Stanford, Calif., 1972.

have been hedged in relation to the basic contract grade. Trade houses serving or buying from local areas might be confronted with conditions somewhat different from those affecting markets elsewhere. Sales and purchases of the cash commodities do not always correspond exactly with futures market contract units. Merchants and dealers might prefer to sell in amounts geared to contract units, but there is inevitably some variation. If elimination of risk is to be a reality, buyers in the field must report their purchases to be hedged before the market closes. Cash business can still be conducted after the futures close or before they open, which means that either some hedging must be delayed until the following day or, as noted later, some must be done in *anticipation* of further cash business.

Because of the "equal but opposite" connotation implied in the naive view of hedging, the concepts of hedging and insurance seem to be analogous. In fact, apart from the problems just discussed, the hedger is insured against price risk only if cash and futures prices move in parallel. The literature is replete with examples that indicate that cash and futures prices do *not* move in parallel.[6] The naive view of risk elimination must, then, give way to a risk-reduction concept.

Hedging Carried Out to Reduce the Risks Associated with Price Fluctuations

Even though it has often been found that cash and futures prices do not parallel one another, researchers have been able to muster considerable support for the proposition that a change in cash prices frequently results in a *similar* change in futures prices, particularly if some unexpected event causes a violent price change. Cash and futures prices, it has been ascertained, will not always move exactly together, but a material movement by them in opposite directions is quite unusual.

The arithmetical difference between the cash and futures prices at any time is known as "*the* basis." The usual difference reflects a premium or discount of the cash price versus the nearby future; for example, No. 1 soybeans in June might be quoted at 15 cents over the August future, in which case the basis would be expressed as "15 over." On the other hand, the individual hedger, concerned primarily with his or her own position, would be inclined to speak of "my basis." "*My* basis" refers to the difference between the price of "my" commitment in the actual product expressed as a premium or discount and the price of the specific future contract in which the individual hedger has affected a short hedge. "My basis" remains unchanged as long as the established price relationships remain in effect. The size of the premium or discount provides a benchmark against which the closeout prices of both positions may be measured. If the spread between "my" cash commitment and the nearby future contract remains unchanged or moves to a more favorable closeout basis, "my" transactions will have been successful.[7]

---

[6] Readily available source materials for the trader are the booklets on hedging published by many brokerage houses and exchanges.

[7] A complete discussion of "basis" is given by Henry B. Arthur, *Commodity Futures as a Business Management Tool* (Cambridge, Mass.: Division of Research, Graduate School of Business Administration, Harvard University, 1971), pp. 64–69.

Nothing, of course, precludes the basis from being quoted in distant options. Besides the current cash price being above or below that of futures options, nearby futures market prices may be above or below those more distant prices that reflect the same crop. In seasons in which supplies are normal or large the later contracts generally show a premium. Such a market is referred to as a "carrying-charge market." When supplies are tight, nearby contracts may reflect the scarcity of the cash market by selling at premiums over more distant contracts, in which case the market is said to be "inverted." Whether the current cash market is above or below prices in the futures market and whether the futures market is at carrying charges or inverted, and by how much, is vital to hedgers making price decisions. The same conditions can also influence speculators, who might attempt to make their decisions partly by considering what hedgers are likely to do.

If the risk-reduction premise is accepted as the major reason for indulging in the hedging process, the usefulness of any market must depend on how closely cash and futures prices move together. The methodology employed in such a search is predictable. First changes in cash prices and then changes in the basis must be measured. If the variation in cash prices is larger than the variation in the basis, the futures market can be considered an effective tool for reducing the risks associated with price fluctuations. Studies employing this kind of analysis have confirmed that there is considerably less variation in the difference between cash and futures prices than there is in cash or futures prices alone.[8] That there is a significant positive correlation between cash and futures prices is now regarded as the first axiom of the hedging process.

At this point the usual definition of the hedger as an aloof onlooker rather than a participant in the speculative market pricing process begins to blur. Indeed, the trader begins to understand that in most circumstances hedging is merely a form of speculation—speculation on the basis. The hedger differs from the speculator only because the variation in his outcome is generally less. What the hedger accomplishes is the specialization of risk, not the elimination of it. The short hedger, for example, passes to the speculator the risks of anticipating changes in absolute prices and retains the "basis risk," that is, predicting the demand for stocks. If he can forecast the volume and timing of demand for his product for a given level or risk, a short hedger might well be able to hold a much larger volume of hedged inventory than he could hold unhedged. Such a thought raises the possibility of hedging for profit as well as reduced risk.

Hedging Carried Out to Profit from Movements in the Basis

If merchants or processors feel that they have a comparative advantage in anticipating the yield on their inventories, the important question is no longer how *closely* cash and futures prices move together (the stability of the basis) but rather

---

[8] L. D. Howell authored two such studies for the USDA: *Analysis of Hedging and Other Operations in Grain Futures,* Technical Bulletin No. 971 (August 1948), and *Analysis of Hedging and Other Operations in Wool and Wool Top Futures,* Technical Bulletin No. 1260 (January 1962). He also coauthored, with L. J. Watson, *Relation of Spot Cotton Prices to Futures Contracts and Protection Afforded by Trading in Futures,* USDA Technical Bulletin No. 602 (January 1938).

whether such movement is *predictable*. Working[9] produced data on wheat prices that indicate that basis fluctuations are predictable. A more recent study has provided supporting evidence for corn and soybeans.[10] Working's conclusions invited a significant expansion in the possible motivations of hedging:

> 1. It facilitates buying and selling decisions. When hedging is practiced systematically, there is need only to consider whether the price at which a particular purchase or sale can be made is favorable in relation to other current prices; there is no need to consider also whether the absolute level of the price is favorable.
>
> 2. It gives *greater freedom for business action*. The freedom most commonly gained is that of buying; for example, when a particular lot of the commodity is available at a relatively low price, regardless of its absolute level (this freedom is related to but distinct from the facilitation of decision mentioned above); often, moreover, the freedom gained is to make a sale or purchase that would not otherwise be possible at what is judged a favorable price level, as when a cotton grower sells futures in advance of harvest, or a textile mill buys futures because cotton prices are judged to be favorable, but the desired qualities of cotton cannot be bought immediately in the spot market.
>
> 3. It gives a *reliable basis for conducting storage of commodity surpluses*. The warehousing of surplus commodity stocks is a very uncertain and hazardous business when based on trying to judge when the price is favorable for storage; hedging allows operation on the basis simply of judgment that the spot price is low in relation to a futures price.
>
> 4. Hedging *reduces business risks*. There is usually reduction of risk when hedging is done for any of the previous three reasons (though often not under the second reason), but any curtailment of risk may be only an incidental advantage gained, not a primary or even a very important incentive to hedging.[11]

The enlarged concept of hedging, which emphasizes the expected returns rather than simply reducing risk, came to be called "arbitrage hedging" and stemmed from the belief that hedgers develop a sophisticated understanding of factors that determine prices in the commodities in which they deal.

Working developed the concepts of "selective" and "anticipatory" hedging to deal with actions based on expectations. Selective hedging is partial hedging which occurs when hedgers have made subjective determinations on a price rise or fall in a coming period. Because of this determination, hedgers may leave some or all of their inventories unhedged. Thus a firm would employ short hedging only when a price decline is expected and would not carry short hedges at all when a price increase is expected. Anticipatory hedging would involve the purchase or sale of futures in anticipation of a formal merchandising commitment to be made later, and the operator would carry an open position in the futures market for a time without an offsetting cash commitment.

An excellent example of arbitrage hedging is reflected by soybean processors' use of the markets for soybeans, soybean meal, and soybean oil. The relation between the soybeans and their products enables processors to set hedging policies, for example, according to expectations of a large crop, a short crop, processing margins, and the relative demand for meal or oil.

---

[9] Holbrook Working, "Hedging Reconsidered," *Journal of Farm Economics,* 35, No. 4 (November 1953), 544–561.

[10] R. G. Heifner, "The Gains from Basing Grain Storage Decisions on Cash-Future Spreads," *Journal of Farm Economics,* 48, No. 5 (December 1966), 1490–1495.

[11] Working, op. cit., 560–561.

The major considerations of hedgers in making their decisions revolve around their particular bases and the premiums or discounts among forward future contracts. The literature developing these relationships has come to be known as the "supply of storage" theory.[12] The objective of the theory is to explain intertemporal (over time) differences between cash and forward prices or between cash and expected future cash prices in commodities with continuous inventories. Until recently futures trading was limited to commodities that could be stored for relatively long periods; hence a significant body of knowledge was built up. Price relationships for seasonally produced commodities with discontinuous inventories, such as Maine potatoes, or for continuously produced commodities in which no inventories are held at all, such as live cattle, must emphasize the forward pricing function.

The costs of holding inventory include carrying charges, such as interest and insurance, and the risk of price fluctuation. The benefits of holding inventory have been referred to broadly as the convenience yield, which arises from holding, per se, a certain level of inventory. If a processor, for example, inadvertently runs out of inventory, sales may drop precipitously, and the processor may not cover overhead expenses. Ensuring that inventory does not drop below a given level reduces the chance of incurring such out-of-stock costs. A processor may wish, too, to maintain a relatively stable retail price level for a product, even though raw material prices fluctuate considerably. The processor can accomplish this more efficiently by having a sizable inventory base that will allow a more stable average price. The convenience yield can offset some or all of the carrying costs associated with stocks. As soon as a short hedge, for example, is placed, the processor has fixed the rate of return to be earned if both the cash and the futures contract are held to maturity. For this reason the relation between the futures price and the cash price must be sufficient for the processor to recoup the net costs of storage from one time period to another.

If the first axiom of hedging is that cash and future prices tend to move in the same direction, the second general principle is that the price of the cash commodity and its futures price must become equal in the delivery month. If the futures price were higher than the cash price, the cash commodity would be bought, the futures sold, and delivery made. If the cash price were higher than the futures price, the processor would buy the futures and take delivery as the most desirable source of supply. Many traders notice, however, that cash prices are usually higher than

[12] M. J. Brennan, "The Supply of Storage," *American Economic Review,* 47 (March 1958), 50–72; Paul H. Cootner, "Speculation and Hedging," *Proceedings of a Symposium on Price Effects of Speculation in Organized Commodity Markets, Food Research Institute Studies,* Supplement, 7 (1967), 65–105; Nicholas Kaldor, "A Note on the Theory of the Forward Market," *Review of Economic Studies,* 7 (June 1940), 196–201; John Maynard Keynes, *The General Theory of Employment, Interest and Money* (New York: Harcourt, Brace, 1936); Lester G. Telser, "Futures Trading and the Storage of Cotton and Wheat," *Journal of Political Economy,* 66 (June 1958), 233–255; Holbrook Working, "Price Relations between July and September Wheat Futures at Chicago since 1885," *Wheat Studies,* 9 (March 1933), 187–238; Holbrook Working, "Price Relations between May and New Crop Wheat Futures at Chicago since 1885," *Wheat Studies,* 10 (February 1934), 183–228; Holbrook Working, "Theory of the Inverse Carrying Charge in Futures Markets," *Journal of Farm Economics,* 30 (February 1948), 1–28; Holbrook Working, "The Theory of the Price of Storage," *American Economic Review,* 31 (December 1949), 1254–1262.

the futures during the delivery month, and they wonder why they cannot buy the futures, take delivery, sell the commodity in the cash market, and pocket the difference. There are several reasons for the cash premium.[13] One is that cash and futures are not perfect substitutes until the last day of the month, which occurs after futures trading in that particular contract has ceased. Until that point, because delivery is made at the seller's option, the precise time of delivery is not known. This uncertainty can inject a premium into the cash commodity, which tends to decrease as the delivery month progresses. Factors among others that may be included are not knowing the precise quality of commodity that will be delivered and the possible inclusion of load-out or switching charges.

The trader should remember that there need be no particular incentive to deliver just because there is a gap between cash and expiring future prices. If lower demand is anticipated, the early-month deliverer may reason that the recipient (most likely a speculator) will have no use for the actual commodity and will have to redeliver (perhaps many times), while relieving the deliverer of storage charges. The merchant can deliver early in the month, fully expecting to stand for delivery again later in the month.

Tactics formulated by hedgers attempting to profit from movements in the basis revolve about four basic possibilities which may accompany either the short or the long hedge. A selling hedge or a buying hedge can be placed in a carrying-charge market or an inverted market, and price levels may increase or decrease after the placement of the hedge. Table 2-3 summarizes the possible outcomes from differences in cash and futures price movements. Generally, in a carrying-charge market, which is most common, merchants and dealers will buy the cash product freely because they are able to sell futures contracts favorably against their cash position, knowing that the premiums on the forward futures contracts will pay part or all of their carrying charges. The futures contract chosen will depend on the length of time that the merchant expects to hold the cash position and on which of the futures months traded is most favorably priced in relation to the others at the time the hedge is placed. A dealer or merchant who is long in the cash market and short hedged is, in effect, "long the basis"; that is, if the basis increases because the cash price gains on the futures month in which the hedge is placed, the hedger will make a profit by the amount of the improvement. Similarly, a merchant who has made a forward commitment to sell a cash commodity and places a long hedge by buying a futures position against the commitment is "short the basis." If cash prices drop in relation to the futures month in which the hedge is placed, the merchant will profit; if they gain, the merchant will lose.

When forward months are selling at discounts to nearby months, a buyer of the cash commodity has an especially difficult problem. If short hedges are placed in months selling at a discount, the buyer knows that cash and futures prices will tend to draw together as time passes and that there will not be a significant difference when the forward month becomes the cash month. This means that the basis will almost certainly become smaller, and because the buyer is long the

---

[13] As discussed by Thomas A. Hieronymus, *Economics of Futures Trading* (New York: Commodity Research Bureau, 1971), pp. 152–153.

TABLE 2-3   VARIATIONS IN GAINS OR LOSSES RESULTING FROM DIFFERENCES IN CASH AND FUTURES PRICE MOVEMENTS

Price movements		Results			
		To one who is "long" in the cash market		To one who is "short" in the cash market	
Cash price	Futures price	Unhedged	Hedged	Unhedged	Hedged
Falls	Falls by same amount as cash	Loss	Neither profit nor loss	Profit	Neither profit nor loss
Falls	Falls by greater amount than cash	Loss	Profit	Profit	Loss
Falls	Falls by smaller amount than cash	Loss	Loss, but smaller than unhedged loss	Profit	Profit, but smaller than unhedged profit
Falls	Rises	Loss	Loss, but greater than unhedged loss	Profit	Profit, but greater than unhedged profit
Rises	Rises by same amount as cash	Profit	Neither profit nor loss	Loss	Neither profit nor loss
Rises	Rises by greater amount than cash	Profit	Loss	Loss	Profit
Rises	Rises by smaller amount than cash	Profit	Profit, but smaller than unhedged profit	Loss	Loss, but smaller than unhedged loss
Rises	Falls	Profit	Profit, but greater than unhedged profit	Loss	Loss, but greater than unhedged loss

SOURCE: B. S. Yamey, "An Investigation of Hedging on an Organized Produce Exchange," *Manchester School,* **19** (1951), 308.

basis, he or she will lose accordingly. The difficulty of hedging in such markets is even more apparent when it is noted that the degree of inversion is virtually unlimited, whereas in a carrying-charge market, as already discussed, the degree of the carrying charge is limited by the possibilities of arbitrage.

Even under such conditions hedging may take place. Many hedges are placed for short periods, during which the unfavorable basis may not change or may become even more unfavorable, in which case a basis profit may even be realized. Alternatively, a cash dealer could buy "hand to mouth," perhaps buying only to fill orders in hand, or, if orders are held for future delivery, the dealer can cover the commitment by buying the relatively cheap forward futures contracts rather than the presently high-priced cash commodity. This places the dealer in the position of having a long hedge, which makes the dealer short the basis. Later the dealer can meet the commitment by buying in the cash market and selling the futures contract or taking delivery against the long futures position if the time, grade, and location of delivery all meet his or her requirements satisfactorily.

An oversimplified example illustrates the possible actions of a dealer in cash corn. Assume that in November the dealer has bought some cash corn from the country at $3.15 a bushel. Pending its sale to a processor or exporter, the dealer decides for any of myriad reasons to place a short hedge, assuming that she has no commitment for the sale of the corn. Perhaps corn for March delivery is then selling for $3.21 on the Chicago Board of Trade and the March contract is regarded as most satisfactory for hedging purposes. The dealer therefore may decide to sell an amount of March corn approximately equal to her cash position. Having placed a short hedge, she is now long the basis. When she sells her corn, the hedge will be removed, or lifted. If the price of corn in the futures market has moved up or down by the same amount as that of cash corn, the cost of hedging to the dealer is her commissions. In practice, of course, the dealer must consider related costs, such as the costs of moving the corn into storage, holding it, and moving it out again, all of which could have been avoided by selling the corn immediately after buying it. Typically, the cash and futures prices will move in the same general direction but not in exactly the same degree. If the cash price gains on the future, the basis will have widened and there will be a basis profit on the hedge itself. If the basis narrows, there will be a basis loss by the amount that it narrowed. With so little time between November and March, a material loss resulting from the cash price losing in relation to the futures is unlikely because in March they should differ by little or nothing. A large basis loss is therefore not a great risk.

The sale of the March futures contract could be made to another hedger who is short the cash market; to a hedger long the cash market who has sold his cash position and is now lifting, or buying in, his hedge; or to a speculator who is going long or covering a short position. The short position in the March contract can ultimately be eliminated in one of two ways. The dealer can wait until March and deliver her corn against the contract, or she can sell her cash corn on the cash market and lift her hedge either by offsetting it by purchase or by transferring the position to the new holder of the cash corn, who might also choose to be hedged in the March futures month. The latter procedure is so common that the transfer of the futures position itself frequently forms the basis for determining the selling price of the cash position. For example, a sale may be made at "3 cents under March," but exactly what is March? The price of March corn might vary several cents during the course of one trading day. A determination can be made simply by the dealer buying in her own March position for the purchaser of her cash corn and setting the price from that transaction. Such deals are given different names on different exchanges, such as "ex-pit transactions" or "sales against actuals." In these transactions the brokers agree to report identical prices to the clearinghouse without actually executing the trades.

If, in the example, March arrived and the cash corn which had been hedged was not yet sold, the hedger still might not deliver against her futures contract. She might conclude that the cash market was too low and, noting that the premium of the May futures contract over the March premium was favorable, might choose to buy in her March contract (offset) and remain hedged by selling May. This is called "rolling forward." If the dealer had known in November what she came to know in March, she could, of course, have saved a commission by selling the May corn as a hedge in the first place. It is obvious that if the basis had narrowed while the dealer was in a hedged position—that is, cash lost on the future—a loss on the basis would have been suffered.

Like speculators, hedgers must deposit margin against their positions, although normally their margin requirements are considerably less than those required for speculators. Sometimes margin may be handled by the hedger's bank. In such cases confirmations or statements involved in transactions will be provided for the bank as well as the hedger. Hedging involves certain costs, such as commissions and interest on margin requirements, but these may be regarded as costs of doing business. Most banks are willing lenders for hedging purposes and may be cautious about making loans to firms carrying large unhedged positions in the commodity markets. To some hedgers the ease of procuring cash loans may be the most important advantage of using the futures markets.

Because price relations are complex and the users of futures markets include producers, warehousers, merchants, and processors, hedging carried out to profit from movements in the basis requires detailed knowledge and skill in interpretation to be successful. An excellent summary of the specific needs, practices, and behavior of the individual trade user is offered by Hieronymus[14] and Arthur.[15]

Hedging Carried Out to Maximize Expected Returns for a Given Risk (Variability of Return) or Minimize Risk for a Given Expected Return

Recent studies have applied portfolio theory to hedging behavior.[16] The hedger is viewed as being able to hold several assets: for example, unhedged inventory, inventory hedged by a sale of futures, and inventory hedged by a forward cash sale are all possible decisions by the hedger, depending on the probability of the rate of return on each asset. The hedger herself is considered as acting in concert with her own utility for risk and reward and the inevitable play-off between the two at any given time in much the same way as the individual trader responded, as described in Chapter 5.

The theoretical studies are an attempt to formalize a discussion of hedging behavior and are based on the Markowitz theory of portfolio selection.[17] Further discussions of the models suggested in the literature are technical and are beyond the scope of this book. The implications of portfolio theory for understanding the nature of the futures markets are clear, however. The theory emphasizes that "risk is inherent in all marketing and processing strategies, not only those in which hedging does not take place, i.e., that futures markets facilitate 'risk management' rather than 'risk transferral.' "[18]

---

[14] Ibid., pp. 171–240.

[15] Arthur, op. cit., pp. 137–314.

[16] David J. S. Rutledge, "Hedgers' Demand for Futures Contract: A Theoretical Framework with Applications to the United States Soybean Complex," *Food Research Institute Studies,* 11 (1973), 237–256.

[17] H. Markowitz, *Portfolio Selection—Efficient Diversification of Investments* (New Haven: Yale University Press, 1959).

[18] Rutledge, op. cit., 254.

Any business contemplating the use of the futures markets as a management tool for choosing between various sets of marketing and processing strategies should answer initially several questions simply as a test of relevance.[19] These questions should include, What business are we in? What are the critical profit factors? How do price changes affect the critical factors? How do price change impacts compare with changes in the futures markets? Assuming that the answers to these questions indicate that risk management incorporating futures can contribute to the overall business objectives, varying points of view in developing hedging policies may be considered. Exhibit 2-1 attempts to structure these views.[20] Each of the column headings relates a business management function or interest. The first column assumes total independence of cash and hedging considerations. Hedging is employed merely to offset all or some of the net inventory price risks as they occur. The second column begins building the futures contract into the business operation, columns 3 and 4 include specific procurement and marketing functions which accent decision making by those responsible for the operations, and column 5 reflects the most sophisticated use of hedging. The vertical shading of the first panel is suggestive of the degree of risk incurred, which increases as the listings progress from top to bottom. The range includes an attempt at risk avoidance on the one hand and brash opportunism on the other. Real-world practices lie somewhere in between.

Critical Comment

The main purpose of including a discussion of the theory and practice of hedging is to educate the trader in the singular truth that futures trading depends on hedging. Two additional purposes must share top priority, however. The first is that the treatment of the vast majority of the literature with which the trader is most likely to come in contact is naive, if not outright incorrect. The most charitable judgment one can make of these approaches is that they are exactly what they claim to be—oversimplified examples. Many commission house offerings, as well as much of the early literature, tend to perpetuate pleasant myths in the interest of obviating the need for their own understanding and that of their readership.[21]

The second purpose of a discussion of hedging is to impress on the average trader the probable futility of attempting to relate a significant amount of this knowledge to the improvement of his or her own record. The differences of opinion and practices as well as the intricacies of the variables involved make it all but impossible to reduce the outcomes to general rules for the improvement of trading effectiveness. Better by far that the trader applaud the consistent use of well-

---

[19] Henry B. Arthur, "The Many Facets of Commodity Futures as a Tool of Management," *Workshop/72* (Coffee and Sugar Exchange, 1972), p. 36.

[20] Ibid., p. 42, op. cit., pp. 336–337.

[21] Since 1981 a considerable amount of scholarly work on hedging theory and practice has been published in *The Journal of Futures Markets,* published quarterly by John Wiley & Sons in affiliation with the Center for the Study of Futures Markets, Columbia Business School. The quality of studies in this journal is usually quite high.

EXHIBIT 2-1 Points of View in Developing Hedging Policies

Primary guide or → purpose Shading from protection to exposed position	Net position control (inventory risk)[1]	Gross position[2] (total commitment factors—"a larger market")	Procurement tool (time and cost)	Marketing tool (time and price)	Profit margins and incentives[3]
	1. Fully hedged (zero net position) Large volume "basis" operators 2. Partial hedge (constant, not zero, net position) Examples: Exclude Lifo base; hedge only seasonal accumulation 3. Variable hedge (planned or budgeted net position) Examples: Headquarters managed hedge; discretionary position within limits 4. Variable hedge (deliberate variances to profit from price swings) Examples: Cyclical position taking; leaning into the wind; special position taking situation	1. Maximize turnover without net exposure 2. Spreading and arbitrage[4] 3. Hedge excess over Lifo base 4. Hedge seasonal storage 5. Use of futures to economize cash tied up in inventories, or to shorten exposure without sacrificing current throughout 6. Disregard business needs; straight speculation	1. Take delivery on futures markets to get needed goods 2. Lock in margin through low-costing raw material (to cover a sale commitment) 3. Assure repurchase of temporarily liquidated Lifo base stocks 4. Anticipate storage accumulation by purchase of new crop futures 5. Use futures to attain target exposure when actuals not available 6. Pin down attractive cost for anticipated needs 7. Reach out, speculate regardless of commercial needs	1. Deliver actuals on futures market 2. Sell futures to lock in realization on goods in inventory 3. Sell futures to assure price for anticipated production 4. Cover risks on unpriced sales, requirements contracts, or "price date of delivery" 5. Liquidate unwanted risk by selling futures when cash won't move 6. Sell futures farther ahead than actuals can be booked in the market	1. Lock in margin where actuals are bought or sold on formula price to be based on later futures quotations 2. Deal in basis (this covers a wide assortment of specialized applications) 3. Use price or margin targets to determine how much business will be done, as in deciding how much to store or process 4. Pin down other half of a cash commodity trade in futures, awaiting opportunity to fulfill with actuals 5. Buy low, sell high, wherever the opportunity presents itself—all cash, all futures, or a mix including discretionary position taking

[1] This column assumes a commercial operation in which all decisions are based on cash market considerations. The net cash positions (or portions of them) are then hedged in futures.

[2] This column assumes that added cash positions will be undertaken simply because they *can* be hedged.

[3] The column for profit margins and incentives relates to operations in which the primary focus is not on protection from general price swings, but on earnings from residuals and differentials (basis), or even from deliberate position taking.

[4] Includes earning of storage by holding deliverable cash product against short futures. This is sometimes referred to as "cash and carry."

SOURCE: Henry B. Arthur, *Commodity Futures as a Business Management Tool*, Division of Research, Graduate School of Business Administration, Harvard University, Cambridge, Mass., 1971, pp. 336–337.

traveled markets by the trade, the expansion of those markets that may have fallen into comparative disuse, and the emergence of new markets (for example, for currencies, interest rates, stock indexes, petroleum, aluminum, and exchange-traded options on futures) which consolidate, renew, and expand oportunities for rewarding speculation.

The trader has been introduced to the nature of the futures contract and the considerable recent growth in its use. The nature of the exchanges that trade these contracts has been discussed, and portraits of the speculator and hedger which included the impact of each on the open interest have been drawn. Cash and futures price relationships were analyzed to give the trader an appreciation of the complexities of the hedging process.

At this point it might help to ask, "How well do the markets function?" The experienced trader may retort wryly. "Too well. They're *so* tough to beat." The trader, of course, is referring to the behavior of futures prices, which is of such importance that Chapter 4 is devoted entirely to a discussion of the characteristics of price changes. In a general sense, however, there has always been an implicit benchmark for judging whether futures markets should receive high or low performance marks. Because agricultural and raw materials commodities, which are featured in most futures markets, are subject to considerable price fluctuations (many are beyond the control of the producer or processor), markets that receive high performance marks are those in which there has been a noticeable reduction in price variability.

The question of price variability may be viewed generally from two positions—either that futures trading, in an institutional sense, tends to dampen or increase price fluctuations or that speculation itself significantly influences the variability of price changes. The various attacks on potato and onion futures trading as an institution[22] seemed to make more headway when price levels were depressed, just as similar investigations of the coffee, copper, and sugar markets were launched when prices were high. Some scholars have wondered about the pattern that exhibits concern for the *producer* of domestic commodities and the *consumer* of imported commodities.[23] Apart from such obvious bias, there is a continuing question whether the institution itself is worthy of the increasing trust that has been shown in its regard. A discussion of speculation and price variability follows later in the section.

One of the early dissatisfactions with market performance centered around the question of manipulation, which features corners and bear raids in the finest robber baron tradition.[24] Activity by such men as Hutchinson, Leiter, and Pattern in the years just before the turn of the century resulted in short-term price distortions, frequently because of inadequate supplies of a grain in the delivery position. The effectiveness of such corners gradually diminished as competitive balance appeared in the market, aided by legislation that now rewards the manipulator with 5 years of imprisonment, a $10,000 fine, or both.

---

[22] See Chapter 1.

[23] Gray and Rutledge, op. cit., 32.

[24] C. H. Taylor, *History of the Board of Trade of the City of Chicago* (Chicago: Robert O. Law Co., 1917).

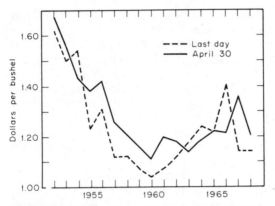

Figure 2-2   Closing prices of December corn contract on April 30 and expiration date, 1952–1968.

Historical evidence of the effects of futures trading on price fluctuations is not conclusive. Perhaps the most voluminous example of the divergent findings was provided by the U.S. Federal Trade Commission,[25] which in part concluded:

> Frequently attempts have been made to deal with the question of the stabilizing effect of future trading by comparing periods prior to the practice of trading in futures with periods since there has been such trading. Such a comparison, in order to prove anything, must first prove that the other things are equal—either that there have been no other changes between the two periods or that any other changes that may have occurred had no effect on the fluctuation of grain prices. Obviously, no such proof can be offered in the case under consideration . . . [vol. VI, p. 261].
>
> It seems to be conclusively proved by this bit of analysis that futures trading under existing conditions itself generates certain elements of risk and uncertainty. In other words, it causes some fluctuations. Its stabilizing influence must, therefore, depend upon its stilling or checking other causes of fluctuation that are more important than those it creates [vol. VI, p. 264].

More recent studies of onions tend to support the contention that a futures market diminishes the variation in cash prices[26] as well as the seasonal range in prices.[27] In the latter study an index of seasonal price variations was computed for a period before the advent of futures trading, during the actual trading period, and for a 4-year period following the ban on futures trading. The periods before and after futures trading registered similar harvest lows of about 75 and a subsequent spring high reading of about 145. During futures trading those figures were 87 and 118, respectively.

[25] *U.S. Industrial Commission Report* (1900–1901), House Doc. 94, 56th Cong. 2d Sess. House.

[26] H. Working, "Price Effects of Futures Trading," *Food Research Institute Studies,* 1, No. 1 (1960), 3–31.

[27] Roger W. Gray, "Onions Revisited," *Journal of Farm Economics,* 45, No. 2 (May 1963), 273–276.

Although financial instruments have been traded on futures exchanges for only a relatively brief period, a substantial amount of research has been done in this area because of concern that such markets might disrupt the underlying cash markets. Studies to date in Treasury bonds and GNMAs indicate no such disruption. Like older tests involving agricultural commodities, they seem to indicate that daily volatility in cash instrument prices is reduced because of the existence of the futures markets.[28]

As the trader may surmise by now, there can be no single meaning in the term "price variability." A look at continuous and discontinuous inventory futures markets will illustrate the variations.[29] In continuous inventory markets the price-of-storage theory ensures that the level of prices for *all* months responds to change in information as it develops. Of course, the interrelations between cash prices and futures prices (the basis) change, but these changes are generally much smaller than absolute price changes, as discussed earlier. When no inventories are carried, the function of a futures market is to conduct "forward pricing" (forecasting), and the relations among prices differ from the first case. Figures 2-2, 2-3, and 2-4 present price behavior in three crops for which production decisions take place in the spring before a fall harvest—corn, soybeans, and potatoes.

In each case the closing prices for December corn, November soybeans, and November potatoes on April 30 are compared with expiration prices for a number of years. Corn and soybean prices depict a tendency to move together (low variability), whereas the last-day (cash) price of potatoes is clearly much more variable than the futures price throughout the years analyzed. The implications from the standpoint of the *growers'* ability through hedging to reduce price variability from

---

[28] Gary R. Bortz, "Does the Treasury Bond Futures Market Destabilize the Treasury Bond Cash Market?" *The Journal of Futures Markets,* 4, No. 1 (Spring 1984).

[29] As developed by William G. Tomek and Roger W. Gray, "Temporal Relationships among Prices on Commodity Futures Markets: Their Allocative and Stabilizing Roles," *American Journal of Agricultural Economics,* 52, No. 3 (August 1970).

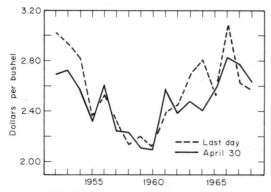

Figure 2-3 Closing prices of November soybean contract on April 30 and expiration date, 1952–1968.

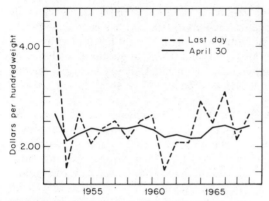

**Figure 2-4   Closing prices of November Maine potato
contract on April 30 and expiration date, 1952–1968.**

year to year are interesting. Because no potato stocks are carried from May to
November, the market in the spring cannot forecast any price other than the mean
November price until new crop information emerges. A forecast at the mean value
of past observations, when coupled with a near zero variance in springtime prices,
provides an excellent basis for hedging. On the other hand, as in the corn and
soybean markets, routine hedging may not be helpful in reducing annual price
variability because the variance in the springtime prices is about equal to the
variance in the cash prices at maturity. In summation, then, as Gray and Rutledge
note in their survey,

> ... the potato grower can greatly reduce *his* price variability through hedging, as the
> corn and soybean grower cannot. But it is implied on the *other* sides of these coins that
> corn and soybean price variabilities have been reduced (through generalized production
> and inventory response) as potato price variability has not.[30]

The question whether speculation itself significantly influences the variability
of prices is one of long standing. Many unresolved questions owe their longevity
primarily to problems of measurement, and the role of speculation is no exception.
Examples of the data on open interest, available monthly from the CFTC, are
presented in Tables 2-4 and 2-5; the indicated commitments are divided into
reportable (large) positions and nonreportable (small) positions. Reportable commitments are divided into noncommercial and commercial categories. The former
can be assumed to include speculators and the latter hedgers. Small traders are
residual, that is, the difference between the reporting traders and the total positions
indicated by the exchanges. Although most nonreportable positions undoubtedly
are held by small speculators, there is an unknown quantity of small hedging
positions included in this category.

The term "old" refers to old-crop futures and "other" to new-crop futures. Dates
assigned to new crops vary. For example, the first new-crop future of soybeans is

---

[30] Gray and Rutledge, op. cit., 35.

September, and for pork bellies it is February. Many futures such as financials, of course, have no crop years, so figures are indicated by calendar years. "Old" and "Other" noncommercial positions do not add to "All" because one leg of spread positions may be in the old crop and one in the new. The total of all long positions and the total of all short positions, of course, will be equal, and either total is synonymous with the term "open interest."

The monthly data indicate the changes in commitments from the previous month only in the "All" category. The percentage of the open interest represented by each trader is shown as well as the number of traders in each reportable category. Traders may appear in more than one category, and the numbers holding nonreportable positions are not shown.

An interesting category is "Concentration Ratios," which indicates the percentage of open interest held by the four largest reporting traders and by the eight largest reporting traders if there are that many.

A considerable amount of statistical information which summarizes or refines the open-interest data discussed briefly here is prepared by the economic analysis specialists of the CFTC and is available from the commission.

Because the terms "excessive speculation" and "undue price fluctuations" are subjective and the CFTC figures are the major source of reference, the trader can appreciate the problem of assessing the impact of the speculator. Because the positions or even numbers of nonreporting traders are not available, the total amounts of hedging and speculating in the market cannot be accurately known. The simplest solution is to assume that all nonreporting traders are speculators. Working, however, attempted to reclassify these nonreporting traders as hedgers or speculators and proceeded to construct a "Speculative Index."[31]

The Speculative Index may be understood more easily by first referring to Table 2-2. On the average, long hedging does not equal short hedging; therefore, for market balance long speculation is required to offset net short hedging. If H_L = long hedging commitments, H_S = short hedging commitments, and S_L = long speculating commitments, the degree to which short hedging is balanced by long hedging = H_L/H_S and the degree to which short hedging is balanced by long speculation = S_L/H_S. Together these ratios measure the hedging and speculative responses to short hedging.

The Speculative Index (T) isolates the amount of *net* short hedging ($H_S{}^\mu$), which must be carried by long speculation (S_L):

$$T = \frac{S_L}{H_S{}^\mu}$$

where S_L = long speculating commitments

$H_S{}^\mu$ = unbalanced short hedging commitments

In other words, long hedging (H_L) is subtracted from short hedging (H_S) to give the unbalanced short hedging commitment ($H_S{}^\mu$). If a commodity has more long

---

[31] Holbrook Working, "Speculation on Hedging Markets," *Food Research Institute Studies,* 1, No. 2 (May 1960), 199 ff.

TABLE 2-4   SOYBEANS—CHICAGO BOARD OF TRADE: COMMITMENTS OF TRADERS IN ALL FUTURES COMBINED AND INDICATED FUTURES, JUNE 29, 1984

Futures	Total Open interest	Noncommercial Long or short only Long	Noncommercial Long or short only Short	Long and short (spreading) Long	Long and short (spreading) Short	Commercial Long	Commercial Short	Total Long	Total Short	Nonreportable positions Long	Nonreportable positions Short
				Reportable Positions							
All	428,670*	20,870*	18,485*	56,890*	56,890*	156,230*	188,080*	233,990*	263,455*	194,680*	165,215*
Old	203,030	13,920	19,430	16,590	16,590	81,490	116,665	112,000	152,685	91,030	50,345
Other	225,640	28,005	20,110	19,245	19,245	74,740	71,415	121,990	110,770	103,650	114,870
Changes in Commitments from May 31, 1984											
All	−148,420	−44,345	2,305	−5,940	−5,940	−10,445	−81,940	−60,730	−85,575	−87,690	−62,845
Percentage of Open Interest Represented by Each Category of Traders											
All	100.0	4.9	4.3	13.3	13.3	36.4	43.9	54.6	61.5	45.4	38.5
Old	100.0	6.9	9.6	8.2	8.2	40.1	57.5	55.2	75.2	44.8	24.8
Other	100.0	12.4	8.9	8.5	8.5	33.1	31.6	54.1	49.1	45.9	50.9

Number of Traders in Each Category

All	162	28	20	41	41	64	66	121	121
Old	107	18	14	18	18	41	41	70	71
Other	116	24	22	17	17	36	46	72	78

Concentration Ratios

Percentage of Open Interest Held by the Indicated Number of Largest Traders

	By gross position				By net position			
	4 or fewer traders		8 or fewer traders		4 or fewer traders		8 or fewer traders	
	Long	Short	Long	Short	Long	Short	Long	Short
All	10.6	14.4	17.8	20.8	9.7	12.1	14.3	16.2
Old	15.7	22.7	24.0	33.7	15.2	18.9	20.9	28.0
Other	13.8	9.8	22.4	15.2	11.5	8.8	17.9	13.2

* Thousands of bushels.

SOURCE: Commitments of traders in commodity futures, CFTC, June 1984.

TABLE 2-5 PORK BELLIES—CHICAGO MERCANTILE EXCHANGE: COMMITMENTS OF TRADERS IN ALL FUTURES COMBINED AND INDICATED FUTURES, JUNE 29, 1984

Futures	Total Open interest	Reportable Positions									Nonreportable positions	
		Noncommercial				Commercial		Total				
		Long or short only		Long and short (spreading)								
		Long	Short	Long	Short	Long	Short	Long	Short		Long	Short
All	17,250*	2,799*	4,312*	2,513*	2,513*	1,338*	4,264*	6,650*	11,089*		10,600*	6,161*
Old	13,450	2,525	4,448	1,157	1,157	716	3,879	4,398	9,484		9,052	3,966
Other	3,800	1,280	870	350	350	622	385	2,252	1,605		1,548	2,195

Changes in Commitments from May 31, 1984

All	−129	399	162	402	402	−518	803	283	1,367		−412	−1,536

Percentage of Open Interest Represented by Each Category of Traders

All	100.0	16.2	25.0	14.6	14.6	7.8	24.7	38.6	64.3		61.4	35.7
Old	100.0	18.8	33.1	8.6	8.6	5.3	28.8	32.7	70.5		67.3	29.5
Other	100.0	33.7	22.9	9.2	9.2	16.4	10.1	59.3	42.2		40.7	57.8

Number of Traders in Each Category

	All	Old	Other
	162	147	40
	57	52	16
	65	60	16
	39	22	5
	39	22	5
	14	12	5
	18	18	3
	101	81	24
	107	93	22

Concentration Ratios

Percentage of Open Interest Held by the Indicated Number of Largest Traders

	By gross position				By net position			
	4 or fewer traders		8 or fewer traders		4 or fewer traders		8 or fewer traders	
	Long	Short	Long	Short	Long	Short	Long	Short
All	7.3	16.9	11.9	23.0	5.4	14.0	7.8	20.0
Old	6.8	21.0	10.5	28.8	6.7	20.1	9.2	27.9
Other	23.4	18.8	38.9	28.0	22.6	12.9	35.6	20.6

* Contracts of 38,000 pounds.

SOURCE: Commitments of traders in commodity futures, CFTC, June 1984.

speculation (S_L) than needed to carry net short hedging $(H_s{}^\mu)$ requirements, the Speculative Index will exceed 1.

The trader must bear in mind that the Speculative Index does not distinguish between markets in which long speculating commitments are greater than short speculating commitments or vice versa. The ratio indicates only that unneeded speculation is becoming more or less important when compared with unbalanced hedging. A more serious limitation of the Speculative Index is that it ignores spread or matching positions, which can be a significant percentage of the total open interest shown in Tables 2-4 and 2-5 for soybeans and pork bellies. Working simply defined the problem away when he limited speculation to the holding of a net long or net short position for gains,[32] and Larson developed a technique for estimating the classification of the total open interest.[33] However, precise measurement of the speculative commitment and its subsequent effects on price variability will have to wait for a more detailed publishing classification of open interest.

Because of these problems in measurement, the trader would expect difficulty in reaching a consensus regarding the impact of speculation on price behavior. In one study of the grains the following was concluded for soybeans:

> Clearly, this evidence does not support the hypothesis that "excessive speculation" causes or is even associated with market periods containing "unwarranted or undesirable price fluctuation." Of the 52 separate, semi-monthly dates on which classification of total open interest indicated that the unneeded speculative fraction was high relative to hedging requirements, 39 cases were identified as markets in which prices showed little movement. However, in 36 out of the 40 cases for which the calculated Speculative Index was low, price behavior was entirely different. Prices in these particular markets moved over wide ranges, sometimes rising and falling rapidly during a relatively short period of time, and often showing wide daily price ranges over an extended period of time.[34]

A study of 186 monthly observations from 1950 to 1965 computed the hedging ratios and the Speculative Indexes for potatoes, cottonseed oil, soybean meal, corn, soybean oil, soybeans, rye, wheat, and oats.[35] Most of the hedging ratios (H_L/H_S) were near 0.5, which reflects a situation in which long hedging is not sufficient to cover short hedging requirements. All Speculative Indexes were greater than 1, ranging from 1.12 for oats to 1.31 for soybeans, leading to the conclusion that the market had a tendency toward imbalance, with speculation as the dominant force.

Because the futures markets are growing at such a pace, it seems reasonable to conclude that the markets of the future will require greater, not lesser, levels of speculation in order not only to survive but to thrive. The failure of some futures

---

[32] Ibid., 187.

[33] Arnold Larson, "Estimation of Hedging and Speculative Positions in Futures Markets, *Food Research Institute Studies*, 2, No. 3 (November 1961).

[34] *Margins, Speculation, and Price in Grain Futures Markets* (Washington, D.C.: Economic Research Service, USDA, 1967), p. 35.

[35] W. C. Labys and C. W. J. Granger, *Speculation, Hedging, and Commodity Price Forecasts* (Lexington, Mass.: D.C. Heath and Co., 1970), p. 127.

contracts can be traced directly to the failure of sufficient speculative activity, which in turn led to the unbalanced or lopsided markets discussed in Chapter 4. The behavior of futures prices is significantly affected by the levels of hedging and speculation in the markets, and it is safe to say that if no speculation marked the trading landscape, the hedging interests would have to create a statistical equivalent to the speculator at great cost.

3

The Mechanics of Futures Trading

---

*"The man who says he knows all the answers
does not know all the questions."*

INTRODUCTION

Many people are reluctant to trade futures because they believe that the mechanics of trading are much more complicated than they really are. There are good reasons why some people should not trade futures, but the complexities of taking positions or understanding the bookkeeping are not among them. Some of the mystery is probably created by individual salespersons of brokerage firms who are loath to spend the time necessary to understand the technology themselves because of their greater interest in others of their firms' products.

Perhaps if a new futures trader preparing to make his or her first trade is followed, some confusion may be cleared away.

THE FIRM

Unless the new trader is actually a member of a commodity exchange, it will be necesssary to deal directly or indirectly with a member brokerage firm. Most firms that handle public business are futures commission merchants (FCMs) registered as such with the CFTC. Such firms are called brokers, commission houses, or wire houses. FCMs are of two general types, but their methods of operation are similar.

One type of broker is the mixed wire or commission house, which normally emphasizes listed securities but has other departments dealing with over-the-counter securities, bonds, stock options, mutual funds, futures, and, more recently, real estate and insurance. The other is the specialized broker, which deals exclusively in futures or even in a limited number of futures. Some of the latter were originally cash commodity firms that went into the futures business to add to their incomes. Many already had sufficient investment in memberships and wire facilities to make the addition of customer brokerage relatively inexpensive. A more recent addition is the introducing broker, which offers only limited service and trades in turn through a member firm.

Most clients who have traded in securities and become interested in futures find it convenient to begin their trading through the same broker through which they have traded securities if the broker is an integrated house. Many clients assume that large, well-known firms are strongly capitalized and that cash balances are therefore more secure. Others prefer the specialty firms because they believe that such firms provide more varied current information and better guidance. Still others trade through discount firms, which offer minimum service and minimum commissions. Such customers prefer to make their own decisions either because they believe they can outperform the professionals or because they believe that professional opinions are worthless anyhow.

After the firm has been chosen, the new trader must select the salesperson with whom to do business. This person may be a partner or a stockholder of the firm but more likely is an employee variously referred to as "associated person," "registered commodity representative" (RCR), "account executive," "investment executive," or some other euphemism for "salesperson." The salespeople frequently refer to themselves as "brokers," although the term "broker" really describes the firm which employs them. Most new customers spend little time or effort in their selection of this man or woman, which is probably an error. Trading may involve a significant portion of one's net worth, and the salespeople in many cases have a considerable impact on the results of trading in the accounts they handle.

In order to make a selection intelligently, the new customers should give some thought to the services expected from the RCR. If they wish to make their own decisions and do not wish to be solicited to make transactions, they may be primarily concerned with the service they expect. Such customers may be satisfied with relatively inexperienced but well-trained RCRs. Although such RCRs lack experience, they have considerable time and are grateful to have the few clients who deal with them. Therefore, the service rendered may be above average. A little time should be spent with the representative before trading begins to determine whether a good personal relationship is likely to develop. There is no need to trade with a salesperson simply because he or she happens to be the "broker of the day" or happens to be standing near the door when the customer happens to come in.

If the client is going to rely on the RCR to guide the trading in the account, the care given to the selection of the RCR is even more important. In addition to the ability to render good service, the RCR will need experience, good judgment, and integrity. These are not easy to evaluate, but neither are they impossible. One can choose one's broker as one would choose a lawyer, physician, dentist, or tax consultant—that is, by referral from others who have received satisfactory performance. A possible criterion is the RCR's personal trading. If results have been good, they may not necessarily be destined to continue to be good, but this is better than having to account for continuously poor results over a significant period. If RCRs do not trade their own accounts, one might wonder why. Presumably the RCR is economically motivated or would not be in the brokerage business. There may, of course, be mitigating circumstances, such as a rule of the firm precluding such trading or the judgment of the RCR that futures trading is not suitable for his or her financial situation or investment objective.

Some customers may wish to ask some questions about a firm's research department. It is not enough to know that there are some people in New York or Chicago who send out wires or prepare attractive-looking market letters and special reports. It is important to know that facts are separated from opinions and that the first are accurate and the latter useful.

OPENING THE ACCOUNT

Once the brokerage house and RCR have been selected, the opening of the individual brokerage account is a simple procedure. Various papers need to be signed, which will vary somewhat from broker to broker, but the following are typical.

The basic form is the customer's margin agreement, in which the client agrees to be responsible for any losses in trading, just as in a securities account. The form may be signed by an individual client or by more than one, in which case the clients must specify whether they wish to be joint tenants or tenants in common. If they choose to act as joint tenants with right of survivorship, the broker will accept instructions from all joint tenants. In the event of the death of any of them, the equity in the account belongs to the survivors. If the customers act as tenants in common, they own the account in specified shares. Typically, a husband and wife will be joint tenants, whereas unrelated customers, such as business partners, will open their accounts as tenants in common.

A risk disclosure statement is required by the CFTC of all futures commission merchants and introducing brokers that solicit futures or options business. These forms must be received, signed, and dated by new customers before trading begins. Their purpose is to attempt to make certain that new customers are aware of at least the basic risks present in futures or options trading. There are, of course, some risks not contained in the forms which should be clarified by the salespeople. Customers who choose not to read the forms or absorb their implications may still be bound by them, particularly if they sign an accompanying statement indicating that the forms were received and understood.

A form frequently requested is the authority to transfer funds. This form, formerly called the "CEA letter," was used for the transfer of funds between accounts used for regulated and unregulated futures. Since all futures are now regulated, the form is used primarily for routine transfers between futures and securities accounts owned by the same customer.

Futures may also be traded by partnerships or corporations. In a partnership all partners must agree to allow the account to be opened and must designate which partners can act for all. Corporate charters must allow futures trading, and the broker must be told which officers of the corporation are to be allowed to trade the account. Minors may be prohibited from trading by some brokers, but others permit accounts in the name of a minor if guaranteed by an adult.

Most brokers require that new accounts be financed with a minimum deposit such as $5000 or $10,000. Others require only the margin required by exchanges for a particular position, which may be only a few hundred dollars. Customers who deposit the bare minimums to cover only required initial margins should be aware of the regulations requiring prompt deposits of additional funds in the event of market adversity. Some brokerage firms allow more impairment than others, and there are varying opinions on what is meant by "prompt." Exchanges specify both minimum initial and maintenance margin levels, but many brokers have house rules that are more stringent than those of the exchanges. Although competition holds differences in bounds, many firms are concerned enough about client financial suitability to require deposits which are high enough to make certain that clients have at least enough money to absorb a minimum level of exposure to risk.

If orders in an account are to be placed by someone other than the client investing the capital, the broker will require a limited power of attorney, which is usually called a "trading authority." Such discretionary authority may be granted to the RCR, to a friend or relative of the customer, or to an account manager who will trade the account in return for compensation. A general power of attorney allows money to be withdrawn from the account in addition to granting authority to make trades. There is seldom any good reason to use this kind of document for trading purposes. Discretionary accounts are subject by some exchanges to minimum capital requirements that are somewhat greater than the minimum requirements for accounts not so managed. The client is usually responsible for all losses in the account, even in a discretionary account where the positions are ordered by someone else, so one should be cautious before signing a trading authority. This is especially true if the person who is to manage the account has any possible conflict of interest in the trading, such as generation of commissions. Those who wish to have their accounts managed or who wish to manage the accounts of others should take the time to note the latest exchange, state, and CFTC rules and regulations applicable to such accounts.

CONTRACT INFORMATION

The decision-making processes by which traders choose the futures in which to trade as well as the number of contracts and the particular contract month best for their purposes are discussed at length in subsequent chapters of this book, but a summary of basic information can be indicated at this point. The lists in Table 3-1 are not complete, but they do indicate the major futures exchanges in the United States, typical futures most actively traded on them, and pertinent contract data concerning them. From time to time changes occur in commissions

TABLE 3-1   CONTRACT INFORMATION

Futures	Exchange and local trading hours	Contract unit	Minimum fluctuation		Daily price limit‡	Order and report symbol	Contract months
			A price change of	Results in a profit or loss per contract of			
Currencies: British pounds*	International Monetary Market of CME 7:30 A.M.– 1:24 P.M.	25,000 B.P.	$0.0005	$12.50	$0.05 $1250/contract	BP	January, March, April, June, July, September, October, December, and the current month
British pounds	The London International Financial Futures Exchange 8:32 A.M.– 4:02 P.M.	25,000 B.P.	$0.0001	$2.50	$0.05 $1250/contract	LSP	March, June, September, December
Canadian dollars*	International Monetary Market of CME 7:30 A.M.– 1:26 P.M.	100,000 C.D.	$0.0001	$10.00	$0.0075 $750/contract	CD	January, March, April, June, July, September, October, December
Deutsche mark*	International Monetary Market of CME 7:30 A.M.– 1:20 P.M.	125,000 D.M.	$0.0001	$12.50	$0.01 $1250/contract	DM	January, March, April, June, July, September, October, December

Deutsche mark	The London International Financial Futures Exchange 8:40 A.M.–4:02 P.M.	125,000 D.M.	$0.0001	$12.50	$0.01 $1250/contract	LDM	March, June, September, December
Deutsche mark¶	Singapore International Monetary Exchange 7:35 A.M.–3:20 P.M.	125,000 D.M.	$0.0001	$12.50	$0.01 $1250/contract	SDM	January, March, April, June, July, September, October, December
Eurodollar*	International Monetary Market of CME 7:30 A.M.–2:00 P.M.	1,000,000 E.D.	$0.01	$25.00	100 basis points $2500/contract	ED	March, June, September, December, and spot month
Eurodollar¶	Singapore International Monetary Exchange 4:35 P.M.–3:20 A.M.	1,000,000 E.D.	$0.01	$25.00	100 basis points $2500/contract	SED	March, June, September, December, and spot month
French francs*	International Monetary Market of CME 7:30 A.M.–1:28 P.M.	250,000 F.F.	$0.00005	$12.50	$0.005 $1250/contract	FR	January, March, April, June, July, September, October, December

Note: See pages 79–80 for footnotes.

TABLE 3-1 (Continued)

Futures	Exchange and local trading hours	Contract unit	Minimum fluctuation		Daily price limit†	Order and report symbol	Contract months
			A price change of	Results in a profit or loss per contract of			
Japanese yen*	International Monetary Market of CME 7:30 A.M.– 1:22 P.M.	12,500,000 J.Y.	$0.000001	$12.50	$0.0001 $1250/contract	JY	January, March, April, June, July, September, October, December, and current month
Japanese yen	The London International Financial Futures Exchange 8:30 A.M.– 4:00 P.M.	12,500,000 J.Y.	$0.000001	$12.50	$0.0001 $1250/contract	LJY	March, June, September, December
Japanese yen¶	Singapore International Monetary Exchange 7:20 P.M.– 2:20 A.M.	12,500,000 J.Y.	$0.000001	$12.50	$0.0001 $1250/contract	SJY	January, March, April, June, July, September, October, December, and current month
Mexican peso*	International Monetary Market of CME 7:30 A.M.– 1:18 P.M.	1,000,000 M.P.	$0.00001	$10.00	$0.00150 $1500/contract	MP	January, March, April, June, July, September, October, December, and current month

Swiss francs*	International Monetary Market of CME 7:30 A.M.–1:16 P.M.	125,000 S.F.	$0.0001	$12.50	$0.0150 $1875/contract	SF	January, March, April, June, July, September, October, December, and current month
Swiss francs	The London International Financial Futures Exchange 8:36 A.M.–4:06 P.M.	125,000 S.F.	$0.0001	$12.50	$0.01 $1250/contract	LFR	March, June, September, December
Energy: Gas Oil	9:30 A.M.–12:20 P.M. International Petroleum Exchange London 2:45 P.M.–5:10 P.M.	100 tons	$0.25/ton	$25.00	$30.00 $3000/contract	LOG	Every month up to 9 months forward
Heating oil*	New York Mercantile Exchange 9:50 A.M.–3:05 P.M.	42,000 U.S. gallons (1000 barrels)	$0.0001/gal	$4.20	$0.02/gal $840/contract	HO	January, February, March, May, July, September, November, December
Light sweet crude oil	New York Mercantile Exchange 9:30 A.M.–3:10 P.M.	42,000 U.S. gallons (1000 barrels)	$0.01/barrel	$10.00	$1.00 $1000/contract	CL	Nearest six consecutive calendar months and January, April, July, and October (maximum 18 months)

TABLE 3-1 (Continued)

| Futures | Exchange and local trading hours | Contract unit | Minimum fluctuation | | Daily price limit‡ | Order and report symbol | Contract months |
			A price change of	Results in a profit or loss per contract of			
N.Y. Harbor regular leaded gasoline*	New York Mercantile Exchange 9:30 A.M.– 3:00 P.M.	42,000 U.S. gallons (1000 barrels)	$0.0001/gal	$4.20	$0.02/gal $840/contract	HR	15 consecutive calendar months
N.Y. Harbor unleaded regular gasoline	New York Mercantile Exchange 9:30 A.M.– 3:00 P.M.	42,000 U.S. gallons (1000 barrels)	$0.0001/gal	$4.20	$0.02/gal $840/contract	HU	15 consecutive calendar months
Propane	Petroleum Association of the New York Cotton Exchange Inc. 10:45 A.M.– 3:15 P.M.	42,000 U.S. gallons (1000 barrels)	$0.0001/gal	$4.20	$0.02/gal $840/contract	LP	The current month and the 11 succeeding months
Financial futures: Bank certificate of deposit*	International Monetary Market 7:30 A.M.– 2:00 P.M.	$1,000,000 face value	1 basis point $0.01	$25.00	80 basis points (0.80) $2000/contract	DC	March, June, September, December

						LFT	March, June, September, December
FT-SE 100 stock index	London International Financial Futures Exchange 9:35 A.M.–3:30 P.M.	£25.00 per full index point	£0.05	£12.50	£5.00 £1250/contract		
GNMA (CDR)*†	Chicago Board of Trade 8:00 A.M.–2:00 P.M.	$100,000 principal balance at 8%	1/32 point	$31.25	2 points (64/32) $2000/contract	GM	March, June, September, December (out 18 months)
Major Market Index*§	Chicago Board of Trade 8:45 A.M.–3:15 P.M.	100 × value of Major Market Index	1/8 point	$12.50	No limits	MX	3 nearby months including the present plus the last month in the next quarterly cycle
N.Y. Stock Exchange Composite Index*§	New York Futures Exchange 10:00 A.M.–4:15 P.M.	500 × value of N.Y. Stock Exchange Index	$0.05	$25.00	No limits	YX	March, June, September, December
Standard & Poor's 500*§	Index and Options Market/ Chicago Mercantile Exchange 9:00 A.M.–3:15 P.M.	500 × value of Standard and Poor's 500	$0.05	$25.00	No limits	SP	March, June, September, December

TABLE 3-1 (Continued)

Futures	Exchange and local trading hours	Contract unit	Minimum fluctuation		Daily price limit†	Order and report symbol	Contract months
			A price change of	Results in a profit or loss per contract of			
Standard & Poor's 100§	Index and Options Market/Chicago Mercantile Exchange 9:00 A.M.–3:15 P.M.	200 × value of Standard & Poor's 100	$0.05	$10.00	No limits	SX	March, June, September, December
Three-month Eurodollar interest rate	The London International Financial Futures Exchange 8:30 A.M.–4:00 P.M.	U.S. $1,000,000	1 basis point $0.01	$25.00	100 basis points $2500/contract	LED	March, June, September, December
Three-month sterling interest rate	The London International Financial Futures Exchange 8:20 A.M.–4:02 P.M.	£500,000	1 basis point £0.01	£12.50	100 basis points £1250.00	LIN	March, June, September, December

Instrument	Exchange and hours	Contract size	Minimum price movement	Tick value	Daily price limit	Symbol	Delivery months
Twenty-year gilt interest rate	The London International Financial Futures Exchange 9:30 A.M.–4:15 P.M.	Any gilt stock with a life of between 15 and 25 years as listed by LIFFE	1/32 per £100 nominal	£15.625	£2 per £100 nominal £1000/contract	LLG	March, June, September, December
U.S. Treasury bills*	International Monetary Market of CME 7:30 A.M.–2:00 P.M.	$1 million 90-day	1 basis point $0.01	$25.00	60 basis points $1500/contract	TB	March, April, June, July, September, October, December, January (out 21 months)
U.S. Treasury bonds*	Chicago Board of Trade 8:00 A.M.–3:30 P.M.	$100,000	1/32 point	$31.25	2 points $2000/contract	US	February, March, May, June, August, September, November, December
U.S. Treasury bonds	The London International Financial Futures Exchange 8:15 A.M.–4:10 P.M.	Any U.S. T-bond with a life of at least 15 years	1/32 point	$31.25	2 points $2000/contract	LTB	March, June, September, December
U.S. Treasury notes*	Chicago Board of Trade 8:00 A.M.–2:00 P.M.	$100,000 4–6 years	1/32 basis point	$31.25	2 basis points $2000/contract	TN	March, June, September, December
Value Line Composite Index§	Kansas City Board of Trade 9:00 A.M.–3:15 P.M.	500 × value of Value Line Index	0.05 index point	$25.00	No limits	KV	March, June, September, December

TABLE 3-1 (Continued)

Futures	Exchange and local trading hours	Contract unit	Minimum fluctuation		Daily price limit‡	Order and report symbol	Contract months
			A price change of	Results in a profit or loss per contract of			
Mini Value Line average stock index§	Kansas City Board of Trade 9:00 A.M.–3:15 P.M.	100 × VLA index	0.05 index point	$5.00	No limits	MV	March, June, September, December
Grains: Corn*	Chicago Board of Trade 9:30 A.M.–1:15 P.M.	5000 bu	$0.0025/bu	$12.50	$0.10/bu $500/contract	C	March, May, July, September, December
Flaxseed	Winnipeg Commodity Exchange 9:25 A.M.–1:15 P.M.	20 metric tons	C$0.10/ton	C$2.00	C$10.00/ton C$2000.00/contract	F	May, July, October, November, December
Oats*	Chicago Board of Trade 9:30 A.M.–1:15 P.M.	5000 bu	$0.0025/bu	$12.50	$0.06/bu $300/contract	O	March, May, July, September, December
Rapeseed	Winnipeg Commodity Exchange 9:25 A.M.–1:15 P.M.	20 metric tons	C$0.10/ton	C$2.00	C$10.00/ton C$2000.00/contract	RS	January, March, June, September, November

Commodity	Exchange / Hours	Contract size	Min. fluctuation		Daily limit	Symbol	Delivery months
Rye	Winnipeg Commodity Exchange 9:25 A.M.–1:15 P.M.	20 metric tons	C$0.10/ton	C$2.00	C$5.00/ton C$1000.00/contract	R	May, July, October, December
Soybeans*	Chicago Board of Trade 9:30 A.M.–1:15 P.M.	5000 bu	$0.0025/bu	$12.50	$0.30 $1500/contract	S	January, March, May, July, August, September, November
Soybean meal*	Chicago Board of Trade 9:30 A.M.–1:15 P.M.	100 tons	$0.10/ton	$10.00	$10.00 $1000/contract	SM	January, March, May, July, August, September, October, December
Soybean meal	10:30 A.M.–12:30 P.M. Grain and Feed Trade Assoc. London 2:45 P.M.–4:45 P.M.	20 tons	£0.10/ton	£2.00	£5.00 £100/contract	LMS	February, April, June, August, October, December
Soybean oil*	Chicago Board of Trade 9:30 A.M.–1:15 P.M.	60,000 lb	$0.0001/lb	$6.00	$0.01/lb $600/contract	BO	January, March, May, July, August, September, October, December
Soybean oil	10:15 A.M.–12:15 P.M. London Vegetable Oil Terminal Market Association 2:30 P.M.–5:00 P.M.	25 tons	$0.50/ton	$12.50	$20.00 from previous day's official closing price	LSO	February, April, June, August, October, December

TABLE 3-1 (Continued)

Futures	Exchange and local trading hours	Contract unit	Minimum fluctuation		Daily price limit‡	Order and report symbol	Contract months
			A price change of	Results in a profit or loss per contract of			
Wheat*	Chicago Board of Trade 9:30 A.M.– 1:15 P.M.	5000 bu	$0.0025/bu	$12.50	$0.20/bu $1000/contract	W	March, May, June, September, December
Wheat*	Kansas City Board of Trade 9:30 A.M.– 1:15 P.M.	5000 bu	$0.0025/bu	$12.50	$0.025/bu $1250/contract	KW	July, September, December, March, May
Wheat*	Minneapolis Grain Exchange 9:30 A.M.– 1:15 P.M.	5000 bu	$0.00125/bu	$6.25	$0.20/bu $1000/contract	MW	September, December, March, May, July
Wheat	Grain and Feed Assoc. London 11:00 A.M.– 4:00 P.M.	100 tons	5 pence/ton	500 pence	None	LWT	January, March, May, July, September, November
Meats: Broilers, iced*	Chicago Board of Trade 9:15 A.M.– 1:20 P.M.	30,000 lb	$0.00025/lb	$7.50	$0.02 $600/contract	IB	January, March, May, July, September, November
Cattle, feeder*	Chicago Mercantile Exchange 9:05 A.M.– 12:45 P.M.	44,000 lb	$0.00025/lb	$11.00	$0.015 $660/contract	FN	January, March, April, May, August, September, October, November

68

Commodity	Exchange / Hours	Contract Size	Min. Fluctuation		Daily Limit	Symbol	Delivery Months
Cattle, live*	Chicago Mercantile Exchange 9:05 A.M.–12:45 P.M.	40,000 lb	$0.00025/lb	$10.00	$0.015 $600/contract	LC	January, February, April, June, August, October, December
Hogs, live*	Chicago Mercantile Exchange 9:10 A.M.–1:00 P.M.	30,000 lb	$0.00025/lb	$7.50	$0.015/lb $450/contract	LH	February, April, June, July, August, October, December
Pork bellies*	Chicago Mercantile Exchange 9:10 A.M.–1:00 P.M.	38,000 lb	$0.00025/lb	$9.50	$0.02/lb $760/contract	PB	February, March, May, July, August
Metals: Aluminum	Commodity Exchange Inc. 9:30 A.M.–2:15 P.M.	40,000 lb	$0.0005/lb	$20.00	$0.05/lb $2000/contract	AL	January, March, May, July, September, December
Aluminum	London Metal Exchange 12:00 P.M.–5:00 P.M.	25 metric tons	£0.50/ton	£12.50	No limits	LAL	Date 3 months forward
Copper*	Commodity Exchange Inc. 9:50 A.M.–2:00 P.M.	25,000 lb	$0.0005/lb	$12.50	$0.05/lb $1250/contract	CP	January, March, May, July, September, December
Copper cathodes	London Metal Exchange 12:00 A.M.–5:00 P.M.	25 metric tons	£0.50/ton	£12.50	No limits	LKC	Date 3 months forward

TABLE 3-1 (Continued)

Futures	Exchange and local trading hours	Contract unit	Minimum fluctuation		Daily price limit‡	Order and report symbol	Contract months
			A price change of	Results in a profit or loss per contract of			
Copper wirebars	London Metal Exchange 12:00 A.M.– 5:00 P.M.	25 metric tons	£0.50/ton	£12.50	No limits	LKW	Date 3 months forward
Gold*	Commodity Exchange Inc. 9:00 A.M.– 2:30 P.M.	100 troy oz	$0.10/oz	$10.00	$25/oz $2500/contract	GO	February, April, June, August, October, December (out 23 months) plus current and 2 nearby months
Gold*	International Monetary Market of CME 8:00 A.M.– 1:30 P.M.	100 troy oz	$0.10/oz	$10.00	$50/oz $5000/contract	CG	January, March, April, June, July, September, October, December, and current month
Gold	9:30 A.M.– 12:10 P.M. London Gold Futures Market Ltd. 2:00 P.M.– 4:40 P.M.	100 troy oz	$0.10/oz	$10.00	No limits	LDG	Current (spot) month and the next succeeding 6 months
Gold, 1 kilo	Chicago Board of Trade 8:00 A.M.– 1:40 P.M.	1 kilogram (32.15 oz)	$0.10/oz	$3.22	$50/oz $1607.50/ contract	KI	3 nearby months including the current plus the next 7 even months

Commodity	Exchange	Contract size	Min. fluctuation			Symbol	Trading months
Gold†	Singapore International Monetary Exchange 7:30 P.M.– 3:15 A.M.	100 troy oz	$0.10/oz	$10.00	$50/troy oz $5000/contract	SGS	January, March, April, June, July, September, October, December, and current month
Lead	London Metal Exchange 12:00 P.M.– 5:00 P.M.	25 metric tons	$0.25/ton	$6.25	No limits	LLD	Date 3 months forward
Nickel	London Metal Exchange 12:00 P.M.– 5:00 P.M.	6 metric tons	£1/ton	£6	No limits	LNK	Date 3 months forward
Palladium*	N.Y. Mercantile Exchange 8:50 A.M.– 2:20 P.M.	100 troy oz	$0.05/oz	$5.00	$6.00/oz $600/contract	PA	March, June, September, December, plus spot month
Platinum*	N.Y. Mercantile Exchange 9:00 A.M.– 2:30 P.M.	50 troy oz	$0.10/oz	$5.00	$20/oz $1000/contract	PL	January, April, July, October, plus spot month
Silver*	Chicago Board of Trade 8:05 A.M.– 1:25 P.M.	1000 troy oz	$0.001/oz	$1.00	$0.50/oz $500/contract	AG	February, March, April, May, June, August, October, December
Silver*	Commodity Exchange Inc. 9:05 A.M.– 2:25 P.M.	5000 troy oz	$0.001/oz	$5.00	$0.50/oz $2500/contract	SV	January, March, May, July, September, December (out 23) plus current and 2 nearby months

TABLE 3-1 (Continued)

Futures	Exchange and local trading hours	Contract unit	Minimum fluctuation		Daily price limit†	Order and report symbol	Contract months
			A price change of	Results in a profit or loss per contract of			
Silver	London Metal Exchange 12:00 P.M.– 5:00 P.M.	10,000 troy oz	1/10 pence	£10.00	No limits	LSI	Dated 3 months forward
Tin	London Metal Exchange 8:30 A.M.– 5:00 P.M.	5 tons	£1.00/tonne	£5.00	No limits	LTS	Dated 3 months forward
Tin, high-grade	London Metal Exchange 8:30 A.M.– 5:00 P.M.	5 tons	£1.00/ton	£5.00	No limits	LTH	Dated 3 months forward
Zinc	London Metal Exchange 12:00 A.M.– 5:00 P.M.	25 metric tons	£0.25/ton	£6.25	No limits	LZN	Dated 3 months forward
Softs: Cocoa	10:00 A.M.– 1:00 P.M. London Cocoa Terminal Market 2:30 A.M.– 4:45 P.M.	10 metric tons	£1.00/ton	£10.00	Market closes for 15 minutes after £40 more and then resumes on limitless trading.	LCC	March, May, July, September, December

Commodity	Exchange and hours	Contract size	Minimum fluctuation		Maximum daily range	Symbol	Trading months
Cocoa	N.Y. Coffee Sugar Cocoa Exchange 9:30 A.M.–3:00 P.M.	10 metric tons	$1.00/ton	$10.00	$88.00 $880/contract	CM	March, May, July, September, December
Coffee, robusta	10:30 A.M.–12:20 P.M. Coffee Terminal Market Association of London 2:30 P.M.–5:00 P.M.	5 metric tons	£0.50/ton	£2.50	No limits	LCF	January, March, May, July, September, November
Coffee (contract C)	N.Y. Coffee Sugar Cocoa Exchange 9:45 A.M.–2:28 P.M.	37,500 lb	$0.0001/lb	$3.75	$0.04 $1500/contract	KC	March, May, July, September, December
Cotton, No. 2	N.Y. Cotton Exchange Inc. 10:30 A.M.–3:00 P.M.	50,000 lb	$0.0001/lb	$5.00	$0.02/lb $1000/contract	CT	October, December, March, May, July
Orange juice	Citrus Association of N.Y. Cotton Exchange 10:15 A.M.–2:45 P.M.	15,000 lb	$0.0005/lb	$7.50	$0.05/lb $750/contract	O	January, March, May, July, September, November
Potatoes, round white§	N.Y. Mercantile Exchange 9:45 A.M.–2:00 P.M.	50,000 lb	$0.01/50 lb	$10.00	$0.40/50 lb $400/contract	PC	November, December, January, February, March, April, May

TABLE 3-1 (Continued)

Futures	Exchange and local trading hours	Contract unit	Minimum fluctuation		Daily price limit‡	Order and report symbol	Contract months
			A price change of	Results in a profit or loss per contract of			
Rubber	9:45 A.M.–1:00 P.M. London Rubber Terminal Market Association 2:30 P.M.–5:00 P.M.	15 tons	£0.001/ton	£5.00/ton	£0.03	LRB	January, March, April, June, July, September, October, December
Sugar 11*	N.Y. Coffee Sugar Cocoa Exchange 10:00 A.M.–1:43 P.M.	112,000 lb	$0.0001/lb	$11.20	$0.005/lb $560/contract	SB	January, March, May, July, September, October (18 months including current month)
Sugar 12*	N.Y. Coffee Sugar Cocoa Exchange 10:00 A.M.–1:43 P.M.	112,000 lb	$0.0001/lb	$11.20	$0.005/lb $560/contract	SC	January, March, May, July, September, October (18 months including current month)
Sugar	10:45 A.M.–1:00 P.M. Paris 5:45 P.M.–N.Y. close	50 tons	1 French franc/ton	50 F.F.	Variable according to price	PSR	March, May, July, August, October, December

No. 6 raw sugar	10:30 A.M.– 12:30 P.M. The London Sugar Terminal Market 2:30 P.M.– 4:40 P.M.	50 tons	$0.020/ton	$10.00	$40.00/ton $2000/contract	LSS	March, May, August, October, December
Eggs, fresh shell	Chicago Mercantile Exchange 9:20 A.M.– 1:00 P.M.	22,500 dozen	$0.0005/dozen	$11.25	$0.02 $450/contract	E	All months
Woods: Lumber	Chicago Mercantile Exchange 9:00 A.M.– 1:05 P.M.	130,000 board feet	$0.10/thousand board feet	$13.00	$5.00/thousand board feet $650/contract	LB	January, March, May, July, September, November
Plywood (Western)	Chicago Board of Trade 9:00 A.M.– 1:00 P.M.	76,032 square feet	$0.10/thousand square feet	$7.60	$7.00/thousand square feet $532.22/contract	WP	January, March, May, September, November
Plywood	Chicago Mercantile Exchange 9:00 A.M.– 1:05 P.M.	150,000 square feet	$0.10/thousand square feet	$15.00	$7.50/thousand square feet $1125/contract	PY	8 months, using every other month starting with January and with the 2 nearby months repeated in the following year

TABLE 3-1 (Continued)

Futures	Exchange and local trading hours	Contract unit	Minimum fluctuation		Daily price limit‡	Order and report symbol	Contract months
			A price change of	Results in a profit or loss per contract of			
Options on futures:							
Option on British pound futures	International Monetary Market of CME 8:30 A.M.–1:24 P.M.	One IMM British pound futures contract	$0.0005	$12.50	No limits	XBP	March, June, September, December
Option on deutsche mark futures	International Monetary Market of CME 7:30 A.M.–1:20 P.M.	One IMM deutsche mark futures contract	$0.0001	$12.50	No limits	XDM	March, June, September, December
Option on Swiss franc futures	International Monetary Market of CME 8:30 A.M.–1:16 P.M.	One IMM Swiss franc futures contract	$0.0001	$12.50	No limits	XSF	March, June, September, December
Option on U.S. Treasury bond futures	Chicago Board of Trade 8:00 A.M.–2:00 P.M.	One U.S. Treasury bond futures contract	1/64 point	$15.625	128/64 $2000/contract	XUS	March, June, September, December

Options on three-month Eurodollar futures	Chicago Mercantile Exchange 7:30 A.M.–2:00 P.M.	One IMM 3-month Eurodollar futures contract	$0.01	$25.00	No limits	XED	March, June, September, December
Option on NYSE Composite Index futures	New York Futures Exchange 10:00 A.M.–4:15 P.M.	One NYSE Composite Index future contract	$0.05	$25.00	No limits	XYX	March, June, September, December
Option on Standard & Poor's 500 stock price index futures	Index and Options Market/Division of Chicago Mercantile Exchange 9:00 A.M.–3:15 P.M.	One Standard & Poor's 500 stock price index futures contract	$0.05	$25.00	$5.00 $2500/contract	XSP	March, June, September, December
Option on Value Line average stock index futures	Kansas City Board of Trade 9:00 A.M.–3:15 P.M.	One VLA stock index futures contract	$0.01	$5.00	No limits	XKV	March, June, September, December
Options on corn futures	Chicago Board of Trade 9:30 A.M.–1:15 P.M.	One CBOT corn futures contract	$0.00125/bu	$6.25	$0.10/bu $500/contract	XC	March, May, July, September, December
Option on Hard winter wheat futures	Kansas City Board of Trade 9:30 A.M.–1:15 P.M.	One KCBT Hard winter wheat futures contract	$0.00125/bu	$6.25	$0.25 $1250/contract	XKW	July, September, December, March, May

TABLE 3-1 (Continued)

Futures	Exchange and local trading hours	Contract unit	Minimum fluctuation		Daily price limit‡	Order and report symbol	Contract months
			A price change of	Results in a profit or loss per contract of			
Option on soybean futures	Chicago Board of Trade 9:30 A.M.– 1:15 P.M.	One CBOT soybean futures contract	$0.00125/bu	$6.25	$0.30 $1500/contract	XS	January, March, May, July, November
Option on live cattle futures	Chicago Mercantile Exchange 9:05 A.M.– 1:00 P.M.	One CME live cattle futures contract	$0.025/cwt	$10.00	No limits	XLC	February, April, June, August, October, December
Option on live hog futures	Chicago Mercantile Exchange 9:10 A.M.– 1:00 P.M.	One CME live hog futures contract	$0.025/cwt	$7.50	No limits	XLH	February, April, June, July, August, October, December
Option on gold futures	Commodity Exchange, Inc. 9:00 A.M.– 2:30 P.M.	One Comex gold futures contract	$0.10/oz	$10.00	No limits	XGO	February, April, August, December
Option on silver futures (5000 troy oz)	Commodity Exchange Inc. 9:05 A.M.– 2:25 P.M.	One CMX silver futures contract	$0.001/oz	$5.00	No limits	XSV	The nearest 4 of the following contract months: March, May, July, September, and December

Option on silver futures (1000 troy oz)	Chicago Board of Trade 8:05 A.M.–1:25 P.M.	One CBOT silver futures contract	$0.001/oz	$1.00	$0.50 $500/contract	XAG	Initially, June, August, October, and December of 1985, and June of 1986; however, may soon include all even months
Option on cotton futures	New York Cotton Exchange 10:30 A.M.–3:00 P.M.	One CTN cotton futures contract	$0.0001/lb	$5.00	No limits	XCT	March, July, December; active months are nearest delivery month plus 3 sequential
Option on sugar futures	N.Y. Coffee Sugar Cocoa Exchange 10:00 A.M.–1:43 P.M.	One sugar No. 11 futures contract	$0.0001/lb	$11.20	No limits	XSB	March, July, October, and first of these months in next year for which futures trading has begun

* The Commodity Futures Trading Commission regulates transactions in all futures traded on domestic markets. It has jurisdiction over dealings in futures and related spot transactions in the United States. Brokerage firms report to the CFTC the futures position of special accounts.

A special account is one whose contracts in any delivery month equal or exceed:

Wheat	500,000 bushels	Leaded gasoline	50 contracts
Corn	500,000 bushels	No. 2 heating oil	50 contracts
Soybeans	500,000 bushels	GNMA	100 contracts
Oats	300,000 bushels	Long-term U.S. Treasury bonds	300 contracts
Cotton	5000 bales	3-month (13-week) U.S. Treasury bills	100 contracts
Soybean oil	150 contracts	Long-term U.S. Treasury notes	100 contracts
Soybean meal	150 contracts	Domestic certificates of deposit	50 contracts
Live cattle	100 contracts	Foreign currencies	100 contracts
Hogs	50 contracts	3-month Eurodollar time deposit rates	100 contracts
Sugar, No. 11	150 contracts	S&P 500 index	300 contracts
Sugar, No. 12	100 contracts	NYSE Composite Index	100 contracts
Copper	150 contracts	AMEX Major Market Stock Index	100 contracts
Gold	200 contracts	All other commodities	25 contracts
Silver bullion	100 contracts	Effective December 5, 1984	
Silver coins	50 contracts		
Platinum	50 contracts		
Crude oil	50 contracts		

When a customer's position reaches the level specified, the brokerage firm identifies the customer to the CFTC and reports daily the customer's position while at or above the specified level. The customer must also submit reports to the CFTC. There is, however, a difference in the method of reporting. The customer reports whenever he or she trades in the reportable commodity. The customer reports trading and positions in all delivery months, while a brokerage firm merely reports the position in the delivery month with contracts in excess of the number specified by the CFTC.

† CDR—collateralized depository receipt.

‡ Normally prices can fluctuate only within these limits during a trading session. No trading can take place outside the limits set by the exchanges. The "daily limit" is the maximum price advance or decline from either the close or the settlement price of the previous day; the "daily range" is the maximum difference between the day's high and low prices. The limits apply to the price movement in all delivery months except (a) the spot month during maturity of some commodities and (b) when variable limits are activated.

All futures traded on the Chicago Board of Trade, New York Mercantile Exchange, International Monetary Market, New York Cotton Exchange, and Commodity Exchange Inc. and coffee and cocoa on the New York Coffee, Sugar & Cocoa Exchange, are subject to variable limits. Successive limit price moves for one or several delivery months will bring about automatic percentage increases in the limit. The increased limit will automatically revert to its original level after the designated periods of time or patterns of price behavior in the market. For details please contact your account executive.

§ No option for physical delivery—cash settlement only.

¶ Due to daylight saving time, trading on the Singapore International Monetary Exchange will begin 1 hour later from the last Sunday in April through the last Sunday in October.

SYMBOLS FOR DELIVERY MONTHS

Month	Year 1 Symbol	Year 2 Symbol
January	F	D
February	G	E
March	H	I
April	J	L
May	K	O
June	M	P
July	N	T
August	Q	R
September	U	B
October	V	C
November	X	W
December	Z	Y

SOURCE: A major futures commission merchant. Contract specifications in more or less elaborate form are available from most major brokerage firms. Because frequent changes occur, constant updating of this information is necessary. Brokers and customers should make certain that the data relied upon are accurate and current.

(which are negotiable to begin with), delivery months, opening times, closing times, and, of course, the list of futures itself. Most brokers will provide updated information, which they may designate as "contract specifications" or "contract information." There is no need for a customer, or even an RCR, to attempt to memorize much of this information. All that needs to be done is to obtain a current copy of such contract information and keep pertinent information for those futures in which one is currently interested.

Futures prices appear on brokers' quote equipment and on the financial pages of many newspapers, just as common stock prices appear in the same places. In stock trading the unit of trading is usually 100 shares. Futures, however, are traded in terms of contract units specified by the exchanges. For most grains and soybeans, for example, the full unit of trading is 5000 bushels. Traditionally, traders speak in terms of being long 10,000 bushels of corn rather than two contracts of corn. Brokers' boards, quote machines, and newspapers indicate the market value of grains and soybeans in terms of dollars, cents, and quarters of cents. Corn at $3.12½, for example, merely means that corn is valued at that price per bushel. It can be ascertained from "contract information" that a change of 1 cent per bushel on the standard contract of 5000 bushels represents a profit or loss to a corn trader of $50 on each contract. A change of ¼ cent is $12.50 on a 5000-bushel contract.

DAILY TRADING LIMITS

To prevent extreme price changes in one day, most exchanges limit the amount that many futures prices are allowed to move daily. This "daily limit" restricts the amount that a price may move above or below the settlement price of the previous trading day. For example, in cattle the daily limit is 1½ cents per pound. If cattle closed at 66.20 cents per pound on one day, then 67.70 cents would be "limit up" and 64.70 cents "limit down" on the next trading day. It might be noted that the range on the second day could be as much as 3 cents per pound because trading could be from limit up to limit down or limit down to limit up.

Despite widespread misconception on this point, a market does not close because a daily price limit is reached; it merely cannot trade past that point. Any amount of trading can take place at the limit if a trader is willing to take the opposite side, or, of course, a price can move down from limit up or up from limit down. Restrictions on limits can be modified by allowing wider moves after a move extended over a series of trading days. Sometimes limits are removed in the spot month or on the last day during which a given contract will be traded. Although daily limits are indicated in Table 3-1, the trader is well advised to maintain current data from a broker because limits change from time to time.

Many traders are overly concerned about the possibility of being locked into a position by an adverse limit move in those futures markets which provide for such limits. Although this is not a pleasant experience, it should be realized that the trader's real problem was caused by being wrong about the direction of price and not by the limit move. A limit move is designed to allow the market to have a cooling-off period and thereby encourage a smaller move than would otherwise have occurred. The alternative to a limit move is an *unlimited* move, which may provide far less comfort.

For those caught by an adverse limit move who cannot bear the thought of waiting for the next day's opening, it is often possible to acquire some degree of protection by spreading in the same market or in another market, such as a foreign one. It is even possible to liquidate the position altogether in some markets by acquiring a position in the spot market, which frequently has no price limits, opposite the unfortunate frozen position and then eliminating them both by a process frequently called a "switch." This process, of course, involves a cost.

TAKING A POSITION

When the account has been opened, the customer can take a position in one or more of the approximately 80 futures traded. The procedure, so far as the customer is concerned, is almost exactly like trading a security. An order is given to the RCR, who transmits it to the trading floor of the exchange upon which the selected future is traded. The transmission is usually done by private wire, but many firms use a telephone "hot line" to handle large orders or under conditions where time is short. It may be that an order is to be done on the opening or closing of a market, or an order may have a price limit close to the price at which the market is trading, and it is feared that the price of the market may move away if there is any delay.

When a trade is made, a report is sent back to the RCR, again either by private wire or by telephone. In the latter case, a report is also sent by wire to provide "hard copy" for the record. Orders are time-stamped when received, when transmitted, and when acted upon to assure the customer that instructions were followed promptly. Orders may be placed by customers personally, by letter, wire, or telephone. Most of them are placed by telephone.

The broker is required to mail the customer a confirmation of the trade as promptly as possible. This is usually done on the same day the trade is made. A confirmation of a new position indicates the exchange on which it was taken, the date, the price, and the size of the position. The confirmation of a position being liquidated contains the same information but in addition indicates the amount of profit or loss on the transaction and the total commission charged for entering and liquidating the position. This differs somewhat from a security confirmation of a closing transaction. Such confirmations do not indicate the profit or loss because the broker may not have access to this information. A stock can be bought at one brokerage house, held for years, and then sold at another. Futures positions are typically held for relatively brief periods and may not be readily transferred from one brokerage house to another. Futures transactions indicate the entire round-turn commission on the liquidating side, whereas security confirmations indicate one commission on the entry and another on the liquidation.

LIQUIDATING A POSITION

A speculator who has established a long position may liquidate it in one of two ways. It may be offset with a sale, or the contract can be held until expiration. In the latter case there would be an actual delivery in the case of most futures or a cash settlement in lieu of delivery in the case of the others. One who has a short position has basically the same possible routes to follow: the short position can be offset with a purchase, or, for most futures, delivery can be made if the trader has it in deliverable form and location or can acquire it. For those futures which provide for it, settlement at maturity must be made in cash. For virtually all speculators offset is the liquidation route chosen. Most do not want the cash commodity or do not have it available for delivery. Their purpose in being in the markets is to attempt to take advantage of price change, not to deal in cash products.

If delivery is to become a factor, it is usually of more concern to the speculator with a long position than to one with a short position because it is the latter who has the choice of whether to make delivery and when. Sometimes the holder of a long position holds the position into the delivery month, hoping that the amount of deliverable cash product is too small or too tightly held to make the risk of receipt of any great concern. In such a case the holder should become familiar with the rules of the exchange on which he or she is trading to appraise the odds of receiving early deliveries if any are made. Notices of delivery are posted on dates and at times specified by exchange rules. These notices are sometimes given to the long with the oldest position in terms of the date on which it was established and sometimes to the brokerage house with the oldest net long position. The latter might well mean that a trader with a long position held with a brokerage house which itself was net short could not get delivery at all. Considering the cost and trouble that an unwanted delivery can cause, a trader who is not highly sophisticated in futures market operations might do well to liquidate long positions routinely before the first date that notice of delivery is possible. These dates are available from any well-informed brokerage firm.

The trader who does choose to hold a position into a delivery month must also be aware of the last day of futures trading after which offset is impossible and delivery and cash settlement are the only routes open. Current rules covering notice days and the last days of trading for all futures are readily available from brokerage houses. Some exchanges and brokerage houses increase margins, often substantially, on the first notice day because of the risks of delivery and increasingly erratic markets as the open interest becomes thin.

TYPES OF ORDERS

A future may be bought or sold at the market, which means that the floor broker on the exchange must execute the order promptly at the most favorable price possible.

A limit may be imposed by the customer, which precludes the floor broker from paying more on a buy order or selling for less on a sell order. This limit assures the trader that he will get at least the price he wants if the order is executed but means that he will run the risk of not getting the order executed at all if the floor broker finds it impossible to fill it at the specified limit. Unlike the trader of listed security round lots, the futures trader who sees the correct price of a future "sell through his limit" on the tape, board, or quote machine cannot assume that his order has been filled. Because there are no floor specialists on the futures exchanges, it is possible and often reasonable for a transaction to take place too far away from a floor broker to allow him to complete it. This is not considered "missing the market" unless there is some evidence of carelessness.

Stop orders are often confused with limit orders but are actually quite different. A "buy stop" instructs a broker to execute an order when the price of a future rises to a specified level above the current market. The difference between a buy limit order and a buy stop order is exemplified as follows. A customer is inclined to buy December sugar, which is then selling at a price of 5.43 cents per pound. She tells her broker to buy her a contract at a price not to exceed 5.35 cents. This is a "buy limit." Another customer under the same circumstances tells her broker to buy a contract of December sugar but not until the price rises to at least 5.55 cents, at which point the order will be executed at the market. The buy limit order is usually placed below the current market and must be executed at the limit or better. The buy stop order is placed above the current market and may be executed at the price specified on the stop, above it, or below it, because it is executed at the market after the stop price is touched, at which point the stop is said to be "elected."

A "sell stop" instructs a broker to execute an order when the price falls to a given level, at which point it is to be executed at the market. Unlike a typical sell limit order, it is below the current market level and may be executed at a price at, above, or below the specified stop when it is elected.[1]

A sell limit order may be used to establish a new position or to liquidate an old one. A buy limit may be used to establish a new long position or to liquidate an old short.

A stop order may be used to limit a loss, protect a profit, or establish a new position. In the first case a client may have bought his sugar at 5.45 cents per pound and has instructed his broker to sell it if it falls to 5.37 cents in order to limit his loss to eight points. In the second case the sugar may already have risen from 5.45 to 5.65 cents and the customer places his sell stop at 5.53 cents because he wants to keep his position if the price continues to rise but does not want to lose back all his paper profit if the price declines. Some clients will raise their stops as the price advances in an effort to gain as much as possible from a major move, while making certain that they can probably lose back only a little of the gain. This device, frequently called a "trailing stop," has great appeal to new traders but works considerably better in theory than in practice for reasons discussed in Chapter 4. Many major price moves seem to have an uncanny tendency to elect all the trailing stops just before going into their accelerating phase. In the third case a client with no position believes that if the current price declines from 5.45 to 5.36 cents, it will continue to decline substantially, and the client would like to take a short position, although not until it declines to that point. She thereupon tells her broker to sell her contract of sugar at 5.36 cents stop. Buy stops are used for similar reasons; that is, to limit a loss, protect a profit on a short position, or establish a new long position but only after the price begins to rise.

---

[1] Some exchanges prohibit stop orders from time to time or allow only stop limit orders when they fear that stops might aggravate unusually volatile markets.

A somewhat more complex order is the stop limit. The client might instruct his broker not to buy sugar until it rises to 5.53 cents per pound and not to pay more than 5.55 cents. This is unlike the unlimited stop, which becomes a market order when the stop price has been touched. The limit price may be the same as or different from the specified stop.

A "market-if-touched (M.I.T.) order" is used somewhat like a limit order but with a minor difference. The limit order must be executed at the limit price or one more favorable to the client. The M.I.T. order is executed at the market when the market has traded at the price specified on the order, and so it may be filled at that price, above it, or below it. This order is often used by chartists who believe that a particular price is at the extreme of a trading range and who want to take a position immediately if that price level is reached with no risk of missing the market. M.I.T. orders are sometimes called "board orders." For example, a client long on pork bellies at 45.60 cents per pound who preferred to take his profit on a limit order might say, "Sell my July pork bellies at 48.50 cents." This instructs the brokerage firm to sell the contract at 48.50 cents or more. The order may be entered for one day or a specified period, or it may be open (good until canceled). Another client with a similar position who preferred M.I.T. orders would instruct her broker to sell her position at the market whenever a transaction took place at 48.50 cents or higher.

Sometimes a customer may wish to take a position within a short time but would like the broker on the floor of the exchange to use some of his personal judgment in the timing of the fill. The broker will do this if the order indicates that he is to fill it at the market but is to take his time and will not be responsible if by waiting too long or not waiting long enough the price is unsatisfactory to the customer. Such orders are marked "Take your time" (T.Y.T.), "Not held," or both. Customers may also specify the time at which they wish their orders filled; that is "on opening," "on close," or at a particular specified time.

"Alternative orders" provide for one of two possible executions: a customer may order 5000 bushels of corn at $2.45 a bushel and 5000 bushels of wheat at $3.56 a bushel but not want both. A far more common example of the alternative order is the placing of an objective and a stop, with instructions to cancel one if the other is filled. For example, having bought one contract of soybean oil at 24.50 cents a pound, a customer may order her broker to sell the oil at either 24.95 or 24.25 cents stop, whichever occurs first, and then immediately cancel the remainder of the order to avoid inadvertently reversing her position. This second kind of alternative order is popular with the trader who has carefully determined her objective and maximum loss point for a position and prefers to enter the order rather than watch the market and have to hurry to place one order or another as the market approaches one of the two points. Such an order also helps overcome the temptation to overstay positions.

"Scale orders" are used to establish or liquidate positions as the market moves up or down. The sugar trader may instruct his broker to buy a contract of sugar at 5.45 cents and another contract each time the price drops five points from that level until he has accumulated six contracts. When he sells out his position, he may order the broker to sell one contract at 5.70 cents and another contract each time the price rises five points until his six contracts have been sold.

"Contingent orders" are filled by the broker after the price of another contract or even another future reaches a specified level; for example, "Sell one July pork bellies at the market when August bellies have sold at 72.60." This order is used when the customer believes that August bellies will set the tone of the market but that profits will be maximized in the July contract.

"Spreads" may be established at a fixed difference rather than at specified prices because the spreader is concerned only with the difference rather than the level. She may therefore order her broker to "buy one July pork bellies and sell one February bellies at 180 points difference or more, premium February." Such an order could be used to establish a new spread position, which the trader believes will narrow, or to take the profit in a position at a narrower difference and be satisfied with the profit at 180 points difference.

DAILY OPERATING STATEMENT

It is essential that a trader be completely aware at all times of the status of his account. He must realize that it is the equity that is most important, not the closed profits and losses to date. Failure to accept this allows the trader to convince himself that he is ahead when he has taken some small profits but is keeping positions with large open losses in the hope that the markets will reverse and his losses will be recovered.

To avoid overextending an account the trader should distinguish his gross power from his net power. "Gross power" is the capital (credit balance or ledger credit) in a futures account increased or decreased by adjustments from all trades open at a particular time. The adjustments consist of margin requirements, commissions, and open profits or losses. Gross power can be used to margin new positions or can be withdrawn from the account. It is sometimes called "buying power" or "free credit."

"Net power" is gross power adjusted by the risk in open trades. This risk may be measured by the loss that would be suffered if all trades open were stopped out.

A trader, for example, has an account with $5000 and no open positions. For the moment, $5000 is her gross power. Let us assume that she has bought two contracts of cotton at 61.25 cents a pound, which require a margin of $900 per contract or $1800 for the entire position. The commission expense for the transaction is $90. Her gross power is therefore reduced to $3110. If cotton moves up 20 points a contract to 61.45 cents, the open profit of $200 can be added to gross power, which would then be $3310. As far as the broker is concerned, this amount can be used for new positions or withdrawn from the account. If a stop loss order has been entered at 60.80 cents, it is possible for each cotton contract to drop at least 65 points before it is sold. If the drop occurs, the value of the account will decline by $650. A cautious trader, therefore, would regard only $2660 as really available for use. This is her net power.

Traders use different devices to make certain that they are always aware of their equity. Some go to the length of withdrawing each day any excess created by improvement in their equity and depositing a check for the amount of the equity loss at the end of any day during which they suffer adversity. This makes them constantly aware that they are dealing in real money and not merely debits and credits.

A somewhat simpler method—one calculated to make the trader more popular with his broker—is to maintain a simple ledger sheet (see Exhibit 3-1). If the fluctuations in an account are alarmingly large, or if the trader is overextended, this statement will make the danger clear before, rather than after, a margin call or sell-out notice is received.

BUYING POWER

Sometimes a client may wish to know how much is available for new trades or how much cash can be withdrawn from his account. This amount is called "buying power," "excess," "excess margin," or "gross power," and in either case it would be the same at any given moment. To arrive at the figure it is necessary to subtract margin requirements on open positions from the equity in the account. This is just a way of saying that what is not being used is free to be utilized or withdrawn. The figure is computed by taking the credit balance, adjusting it by the open profit or loss, including commissions, on open positions to arrive at equity, and then subtracting margin requirements to arrive at the buying power or free balance. A well-run brokerage firm should be able to provide its clients with their buying power, equity, and open profit or loss almost immediately on request.

THE MONTHLY STATEMENT

The monthly statement sent by the broker to the customer lists the changes that took place in the account during the month. Such changes may result from the deposit or withdrawal of funds, the establishment or liquidation of positions, or the changes in the prices of futures positions held during the month and still held when the statement is mailed. The client must be familiar with the following terms to have a reasonably good understanding of the statement.

"Credit or cash balance" represents the funds deposited into the account, modified by the realized profits or losses from positions that have been closed out. The credit balance is not affected by open positions, even though they may represent paper profits or losses. The only way the original credit balance represented by the customer's deposit of margin may be affected is by an additional deposit, a withdrawal, or the closing out of a position at a profit or loss. The margin requirements established by the broker to support open positions do not appear on the statement but merely reduce the amount of the credit balance left free for taking other positions.

"Equity" is the amount of money the account would be worth if all open positions were liquidated. If there were no open positions in an account, credit balance and equity would be identical. If there were positions, equity would be determined by adding open profits less commissions to the credit balance and subtracting open losses plus commissions. Most firms indicate the net open profits and losses on

EXHIBIT 3-1   Daily Operating Statement

(Five weeks from ———— to ————)

	M	Tu	W	Th	F
Capital (includes unrealized gains and losses)	————	————	————	————	————
Margin on open trades	————	————	————	————	————
Gross power	————	————	————	————	————
Risk on open trades	————	————	————	————	————
Net power	————	————	————	————	————
Additions and withdrawals	————	————	————	————	————

	M	Tu	W	Th	F
Capital (includes unrealized gains and losses)	————	————	————	————	————
Margin on open trades	————	————	————	————	————
Gross power	————	————	————	————	————
Risk on open trades	————	————	————	————	————
Net power	————	————	————	————	————
Additions and withdrawals	————	————	————	————	————

	M	Tu	W	Th	F
Capital (includes unrealized gains and losses)	————	————	————	————	————
Margin on open trades	————	————	————	————	————
Gross power	————	————	————	————	————
Risk on open trades	————	————	————	————	————
Net power	————	————	————	————	————
Additions and withdrawals	————	————	————	————	————

	M	Tu	W	Th	F
Capital (includes unrealized gains and losses)	————	————	————	————	————
Margin on open trades	————	————	————	————	————
Gross power	————	————	————	————	————
Risk on open trades	————	————	————	————	————
Net power	————	————	————	————	————
Additions and withdrawals	————	————	————	————	————

all positions on the statement to show the customers exactly where they stand. This plays havoc with the common practice of ignoring open losses in the hope that they will go away but is a desirable way of making certain that clients know exactly where they stand. A statement that indicates net open profits and losses is frequently called an "equity statement." Many firms also indicate on the monthly statements considerable other information such as profits and losses for the year to date or the total of commissions paid. This not only helps the clients know where they are but also helps the firms' compliance departments when customers who lose maintain that they had no idea what was happening. Statements which are clear, sent promptly, and accepted without protest provide considerable cheer for a firm's attorney who is using ratification as a defense against a complaint from an unhappy loser.

Transfers of funds made among a customer's various accounts are also shown on the monthly statement. Transfers are indicated by a debit in one account and a corresponding credit in another. Such transfers may be made when the same customer is trading securities and options as well as futures. Some firms provide all the information on one statement. Most provide different statements for the various types of accounts, which are distinguished from one another by slight variations in the account numbers.

REGULATORY REQUIREMENTS

In addition to the rules of the various exchanges and the brokerage house which has been chosen, the trader may be concerned with some of the regulations imposed by the CFTC. This organization has many of the same functions relating to futures exchanges and trading that the SEC has relating to security exchanges and trading. Just as the SEC has delegated some of its functions to a trade association, the National Association of Securities Dealers (NASD), the CFTC has encouraged the creation of a counterpart organization, the National Futures Association (NFA). Most regulations of the CFTC and NFA, such as those which relate to licensing, capital requirements, and bookkeeping, are of concern primarily to brokerage houses and their employees, but some regulations apply to individual traders.

Individual traders, of course, are precluded from engaging in manipulative and other practices that may distort markets. Large traders are frequently required to report the sizes of their open positions or may be precluded from exceeding stated limits. To provide accurate information on the activities of large and small traders, the CFTC requires large traders to file reports that can be compared with the total number of open positions available from clearing organizations to arrive at the total of small positions. These reports are easily prepared and need be of no concern to the trader who complies. Most brokerage houses dealing with large clients are willing to prepare the forms on behalf of the clients if they are aware of any trading done elsewhere by the same clients. The current sizes of positions which must be reported may be easily learned by customers from their brokerage houses or from the CFTC.

Traders who carry unusually large positions may be concerned with maximum position limits in some, but not all, futures which are considerably above the reportable positions. These limits are set by the exchanges or the CFTC and are designed to preclude disorder in markets and help prevent manipulation. These limits not only apply to individual accounts but may be applied to multiple accounts directly or indirectly controlled by one person or to two or more traders acting in concert. They may be of concern to pool operators and others who manage large amounts of capital and related accounts.

Most individual traders do not trade on such a large scale that they should be concerned with these limits. Reportable positions typically range from about 25 to 200 contracts, and position limits may be 500 or more contracts. Exceptions are made for bona fide hedgers. For those who do trade on a grand scale, however, it should be noted that the CFTC takes its reportable position limit requirements quite seriously. Its attitude toward maximum position limits is downright humorless.

TAX CONSIDERATIONS

Commodity positions in the futures markets have long been considered to represent contracts to buy or sell rather than actual ownership of a commodity. The margin required by a broker is viewed as a performance deposit and not as a payment in the usual sense of the word. When a contract is liquidated, the profit or loss merely represents the price difference from the level at which the contract was made, adjusted by commissions and fees. There are those who quarrel with designations of futures positions as "property," but they have been generally accepted as such and are considered to be capital assets. Although they are not regarded as securities (chiefly because they are seen as primary rather than secondary investments and hence do not qualify as a transaction whereby money is invested in a common enterprise with the expectation of profits to be derived solely from the efforts of someone else), futures contracts are usually subject to capital gains treatment; however, it differs from that used for securities.

Futures trading does not create the deductible interest expense that stock trading on margin does because no interest is charged on commodity accounts unless they are in deficit or undermargined enough to require the broker to deposit its own funds with the clearing organization, pending the receipt of adequate funds from the client, in which case interest may be charged.

No state or federal taxes are charged directly on transactions. The cost of a trade for tax purposes includes the commission charged.

Before the passage of the Economic Recovery Tax Act of 1981, the rules affecting the tax treatment of futures positions were rather simple. Speculative positions held for 6 months or less were subject to short-term capital gains treatment. Those held for more than 6 months were treated as long-term capital gains. This was true even when securities and most other capital assets had to be held for more than 1 year to be accorded long-term treatment. Positions liquidated at varying times are required by the CFTC and by many exchanges to be liquidated on a first in, first out basis unless the customer specifically requests the broker to liquidate in a different order. Such instructions must be indicated on the trade confirmation. There is no problem with physical delivery of certificates because there are none. There is no provision in the futures markets for short sales against the box.

Capital Gains Treatment

The tax treatment of a futures position depends on whether it was speculative or a hedge. Hedging carried on in the day-to-day dealings of a business generally results in current operating expenses or credits—and therefore in fully taxable operating profits and losses rather than capital gains or losses.

Just where hedging ends and speculation begins and just who is a bona fide hedger have never been easy to determine. There appears to be little question that bona fide hedgers are benefited by lower margin requirements and that losses resulting from them are fully deductible and gains fully taxable as ordinary income. It is less clear, however, just what "bona fide" is and even what a "hedge" is. The definitions utilized by the CFTC, the IRS, and the futures exchanges have often differed materially. Brokerage houses have sometimes defined hedging somewhat liberally in order to allow large traders to utilize lower margin requirements.

The tax act of 1981 made some substantial changes in the tax treatment of futures, primarily to eliminate the use of tax straddles for tax purposes. Such straddles for many years had been widely used to defer the payment of taxes or convert short-term gains into long-term gains, or even both. Those who used such straddles effectively might reduce taxes, defer their payment for long periods, convert ordinary income into capital gains, or even achieve a combination of these benefits. Those who tried these same practices ineffectively provided a lucrative source of business for attorneys attempting to recover losses in trades which the customer had been told, or allegedly told, were without risk. Although many futures were used for so-called tax straddles, metals and financial instruments were especially popular.

The 1981 tax act effectively ended these tax games simply by modifying capital gains treatment. Regulated futures contracts (RFCs) and similar instruments such as forward contracts were henceforth to be treated at the same rates whether positions were long or short and no matter how long they were held. Gains on futures would be treated as 60 percent long-term and 40 percent short-term. With 40 percent of long-term gains taxable and the maximum tax rate 50 percent, a trader in the 50 percent bracket who was not affected by the alternative minimum tax would pay a total tax on gains of 32 percent (50 percent on the 40 percent short-term portion equaling 20 percent plus 50 percent on the taxable 40 percent of the 60 percent long-term portion equaling 12 percent).

It was further required that all open futures positions be marked "to the market" at the close of trading on December 31 and taxed accordingly whether the positions were open or closed. As a result, it was no longer possible to establish straddle positions with minimum risk or reward potentials, liquidate the losing sides, maintain the profitable sides, and deduct the losses. The never-ending battle between the IRS and those looking for ways to reduce, avoid, or eliminate taxes was thereby effectively moved to other arenas.

It should be noted that regulations evolving from this legislation and interpretations concerning them were not yet entirely clarified. The Tax Reform Act of 1984 answered some of the questions, particularly those involving options on RFCs, indexes, and foreign currencies. Most of these would be treated in the same manner as futures contracts. Nevertheless, those involved in hedging, cash-and-carry transactions, futures options, and other instruments that are like RFCs but are not RFCs are still well advised to consult a tax expert relative to any special problems that might concern them and not rely upon casual inexpert advice.

Other Issues

Tax problems have always varied widely among individual speculators and among businesses that deal primarily in commodities. There are many new products. Some seem to straddle the line between securities and futures. Some contracts, such as leverage contracts in metals, are similar to futures contracts purchased from a dealer on a principal basis just as securities are sometimes purchased from over-the-counter dealers rather than through brokers. Defining leverage contracts is difficult enough without using amateur sources to ascertain their correct tax treatment.

Further tax decisions involving futures will doubtless be made by the tax court as new laws are passed and old ones modified and as more regulations are issued and tested. Investors, traders, and dealers in futures would do well to consult with professional tax advisers before making any important assumptions about tax exposures departing from the ordinary. Employees of brokerage companies should be especially careful when giving advice involving tax or legal considerations.[2]

---

[2] Readers interested in studying tax developments can learn much from the material prepared by the Commerce Clearing House and by most large accounting firms. Some excellent specialized studies on tax subjects as applied to futures have been made available by the *Commodities Law Letter,* published monthly by Commodities Law Press Associates, 310 Madison Avenue (Suite 1926), New York, NY 10017. Various articles dealing wholly or partly with taxes have appeared in *The Journal of Futures Markets,* published quarterly by Wiley-Interscience Journals, 605 Third Avenue, New York, NY 10158.

4

The Behavior of
Futures Prices

*"Truth is allowed only a brief interval of
victory between the two long periods when it
is condemned as paradox or belittled as
trivial."* ARTHUR SCHOPENHAUER
From Copernicus to Einstein

INTRODUCTION

Scholars and traders alike are interested in gaining an understanding of the behavior of futures prices. Although the former might be interested chiefly in satisfying intellectual curiosity and the latter in making money through skilled forecasting, there is nothing to preclude a scholar from choosing to trade or a trader
from electing to take a scholarly approach to trading.

It should be realized at the outset that of all games played, the futures market
is certainly among the most difficult. Prices respond in often unpredictable ways
and to varying degrees to a huge number of unpredictable events. Given the
variation in both the inputs and the reactions to the inputs because of different
amounts of discounting by the markets, it is obvious that the inputs are basically
erratic and thus create a game not based purely upon skill or laws of probability,
resulting in extremely difficult analysis. Many strategies can be used in different
futures markets under varying conditions over different periods and may succeed
some of the times and fail at others. This is compounded by the fact that the

futures market game is a non-zero-sum game which is more difficult to analyze than a zero-sum game because of the influence on results of those who do not play the game but who absorb as fees, commissions, or interest income lost on cash margin some of the resources contributed by the players. Similar factors influence the stock market, which is considered by many to be the most intricate of all games, exceeding by a wide margin even such well-known statistical nightmares as chess and contract bridge. The stock market, however, provides dividend income, less leverage, and a well-established upward bias over the long run. This suggests that a person who has a carefully selected portfolio of stocks might gain profits over time merely by holding the portfolio with a minimum amount of culling as mistakes become recognized and better opportunities present themselves. Futures markets, however, do not yield dividend income. Furthermore, despite a historical long-term upward bias in some prices, large short- and intermediate-term price variations in positions held on a highly leveraged basis might easily preclude survival over the long term.

As if all this did not make matters difficult enough, the trader's search for truth is clouded by sometimes glib self-serving assertions of those with something to sell. The futures business is populated by a host of people who maintain that they have methods of predicting prices but whose methods are closely guarded "proprietary" secrets. Others hint at the great successes they have had with brokerage accounts, managed accounts, or their own trading, but somehow it is impossible to get enough statistical information to validate the assertions. Sometimes the samples used are too small to be meaningful, or the time over which results were achieved might be too short to be significant because unusual conditions might have unduly influenced results. The fact that the data utilized might be suspect is bad enough, but the danger that some of those who report the results might report them in a biased way makes intelligent analysis all the more difficult.

Those interested in analyzing short-run price changes in speculative markets must understand the concept of the efficient market and its accompanying statistical model, the random walk. It is up to the readers to decide whether to accept or reject this theory, but if they are to do so, they ought to make certain that their sources of data are unbiased. The efficient-market hypothesis suggests that futures prices are extremely difficult or even impossible to forecast. This concept is about as popular with many brokerage house research departments and publishers of advisory letters as the conclusions of the Surgeon General are to a cigarette manufacturer.

Even if the random-walk model best approximates reality in the short run, long speculators could still profit from long-run price changes if average upward price changes exceeded average downward price changes. If there is an upward bias, do speculators profit solely and simply because they bear the risks that hedgers transfer to them, or do they profit because they can forecast prices successfully? The "risk premium" concept is a common point of departure in the literature of futures price behavior, and the cases for and against the existence of such a premium are analyzed later in this chapter.

Whether or not there is a risk premium and, if so, whether it leads to a reasonable expectation of adequate profits, there may be enough observable biases in futures prices to give hope to a speculator attempting to forecast prices. Specific processes of decision making are discussed further in Chapters 6 and 7.

THE EFFICIENT-MARKET HYPOTHESIS

All serious students of futures or stock markets must understand the implications of the efficient-market hypothesis and determine for themselves whether to accept or reject its conclusions. There is almost as much debate about this hypothesis in the financial community as there is about religion among theologians. The debate may also go on as long without being settled. It should be noted, however, that this hypothesis is widely accepted in one form or another in the scholarly community and is apparently most often rejected not by those who have any evidence refuting the theory, if there is any such evidence, but rather by those who simply do not like its conclusions.

It is possible only to summarize the hypothesis here and indicate thje implications for the futures trader, but those who wish to read further will find no shortage of interesting and thought-provoking reference material.[1]

An efficient market is one in which there are large numbers of equally informed, actively competing people attempting to maximize profits. In such a market, at any moment, price reflects all available information, as well as all events expected to occur in the foreseeable future. Holbrook Working was the first in the futures field to offer a theory of expectations that rests on the premise that futures reflect anticipated changes in supply and demand rather than on their immediate values.[2]

It is generally agreed that the fundamental laws of supply and demand determine the long-run price behavior of futures. It is just as generally agreed that these laws have certainly failed in the short run to provide a similar insight. Most traders will agree that in the short run there is simply no significant correlation between "fundamentals" and prices, yet most traders establish and liquidate futures positions in the short run. It might be noted that even in the long run, supply and demand data are more useful in explaining why markets acted as they did rather than providing any help in forecasting what they are going to do.

Premises

Most students of the market have followed the lead of Harry Roberts in subdividing the concept of the efficient market into three levels.[3] Price changes in efficient markets are independent and follow a pattern popularly referred to as a "random walk."[4]

---

[1] Richard Brealey and Stewart Myers, *Principles of Corporate Finance*, 2d ed. (New York: McGraw-Hill, 1984), pp. 265–281; Richard A. Brealey, *An Introduction to Risk and Return from Common Stocks*, 2d ed. (Cambridge, Mass.: The M.I.T. Press, 1983); *The Random Character of Stock Market Prices*, ed. Paul H. Cootner (Cambridge, Mass.: The M.I.T. Press, 1964); Richard A. Epstein, *The Theory of Gambling and Statistical Logic*, 2d ed., (New York: Academic Press, 1977), pp. 295–303.

[2] Holbrook Working, "A Theory of Anticipatory Prices," *American Economic Review Proceedings*, **48** (May 1958), 191.

[3] H. V. Roberts, "Statistical versus Clinical Prediction of the Stock Market," unpublished paper presented to the Seminar on the Analysis of Security Prices, University of Chicago, May 1967.

[4] The common term "random walk" is used here, but it should be noted that statisticians distinguish between random walks and submartingales. A frequent error to be avoided is confusion of a random walk with a random variation.

The weak form of market efficiency indicates that prices reflect all information available from past prices. It would be reasonable to conclude that information about open interest and volume would also be reflected in prices if such information were of any predictive value in the first place. No evidence exists indicating that the market is not at least this efficient, despite the howls of anguish such a conclusion raises from those who use naive technical devices as a basis for trading decisions.

The second level of efficiency, usually called the "semistrong approach," maintains, with substantial statistical evidence, that all published information is already reflected in prices. This indicates that the successful trader had better plan on doing more than merely reading publications.

The third level of efficiency appears to leave some hope for the trader. In this strictest, or strong, form the efficient-market hypothesis maintains that prices reflect all information that can be acquired, even by hard-working imaginative researchers. This would indicate that prices reflect everything which is known or could reasonably become known, except, possibly, for inside information, which can lead to legal problems for the user of the information. Some might conclude that even if such information were to leak, it, too, would be reflected in prices. The result, if the strong form of efficiency describes reality, is that market prices reflect current values precisely and change only as new events dictate. Futures, like stocks, are therefore worth precisely what they are selling for, and the best estimate of tomorrow's opening price is today's closing price modified by any events which occur between them, including the reactions to the events. The availability of computers to digest and analyze data quickly and accurately has made markets even more efficient and therefore profits harder to gain than before. This would seem to contradict the implications of those who indicate that they have developed some complex (and usually secret) program to beat the market. It is the use of sophisticated analysis by alert traders that makes the market as efficient as it is.

Some have concluded that the markets are perfectly efficient or so close to it that there is no point in approaching them with any other attitude. Such a conclusion would indicate that the only approach to trading is the purchase of a logical portfolio which is expected to outperform risk-free investments by enough to make such investments reasonable. Others, however, point to the successes achieved by some traders, both individual and institutional, and conclude that the results are too good in terms of amount and consistency to be explained away by anything other than skilled performance. The die-hard efficient-market apologist is likely to answer that with millions of traders trading in a relative handful of markets, it would be remarkable indeed if nobody had a good record. If such an apologist were sufficiently cynical, he might point out that if enough monkeys were chained to enough pianos for long enough, one of them would eventually compose a sonata.

There are those who incorrectly conclude that the fact that prices change itself indicates market inefficiency. In an efficient market, however, actual prices only approximate anticipated or intrinsic value. In a world of uncertainty intrinsic value is elusive. Disagreements will cause discrepancies between intrinsic value and actual prices. If the market is highly efficient, actual prices will move randomly about the intrinsic value.

Of course, intrinsic values change. Soybeans *do* move from $6.85 to $7.50 a bushel, and there is nothing in the random-walk theory to suggest that superior intrinsic value analysis is useless in an efficient market. The trader will always do well if he can identify long-run supply-demand changes before such expectations are reflected in actual price changes. On the average, however, competition will cause most of the effects of new information regarding intrinsic values to be reflected quickly in futures prices. It is the random quality of new information and not changes in supply or demand that is responsible for the irregular behavior of futures prices. The duration and extent of such price adjustments will be random variables that will cause prices to overadjust, underadjust, sometimes precede the information, and sometimes follow it in a manner that causes successive price changes to be independent.

Behavior of Traders

If price changes are formed according to anticipations of supply and demand, it is important to analyze in more depth the behavior of traders in response to news. In a *totally* efficient (hypothetical) market, when no new information is available, no new market position would be taken and there would be no price changes. A general price equilibrium would be established in which no trader who had the will to buy or sell had the power and no trader who had the power (one who held an open position or the funds to establish one) had the will. As new information emerged, all traders would analyze it. If a change in positions were dictated, those changes would be effected rapidly and a new level of equilibrium would be established. In such a market only those traders would be successful who were better at analyzing and interpreting the information currently available to all traders because the history of equilibrium levels would tell them nothing about tomorrow's new input of information.

Moving from such an ideal market, an analysis can be made of the aftermath of the input of new information on a more realistic market consisting of "insiders" and "outsiders." The first group is made up of traders who by training or position learn about new developments quickly. The second group obtains new information only after the insiders have heard about it. Such a market would be less than strongly efficient.

As new information becomes available, a double response occurs: insiders react first and outsiders' reactions follow. The first response is clear. If the new information is bullish, insider response pushes prices higher. Conversely, if the new input is bearish, prices fall. The later outsider response cannot be disposed of so simply. If the new information is bullish, prices could rise again, remain unchanged, or drop. The first possibility could occur if the demand by the outsiders exceeded the supply offered by the insiders at the higher price established by the insiders. The second possibility could occur if outsider demand were exactly offset by insider desire to sell at the higher price. The third possibility is that outsider demand could not offset some increased insider selling at a higher price. The second case reflects the most efficient market, that is, when insiders correctly predict subsequent outsider behavior. Even if this response is not always forthcoming and the insiders do not perfectly anticipate the outsiders, the insiders are as likely to overestimate as to underestimate the outsiders' response to market news. Thus on each input of bullish news a trader could not establish a long position and expect prices to work higher, nor could he take a short position directly after the issuance of bearish news and have a high probability of profit.

The random-walk theorists agree that it is unlikely that their model describes the behavior of futures price changes exactly. Yet they assert that although successive price changes may not be strictly independent, the amount of dependence is unimportant. If there is no such strategy, then a simple policy of buy and hold will equal the results from any sophisticated procedure for timing. Therefore, unless a trader can improve on the buy-and-hold policy, the independence assumption of the random-walk model is an adequate description of reality.

All this does *not* mean that short-term traders will not or cannot make money trading futures; it *does* mean that on the average, those traders will not beat a buy-and-hold strategy with information they obtain from historical data.

Perhaps the clearest method of testing the random-walk theory is to assume for the moment that it is *true* and that it does present an excellent "jumping-off point" for the analysis of the behavior of futures prices. To many traders, this assertion may be heresy, yet if the theory is not backed by significant statistical evidence, it can be rejected.

EMPIRICAL STUDIES

Introduction

The first attempts to develop models to predict or even explain prices might well predate the Tulip Bubble, but credit for the first major attempt to apply modern mathematical and statistical techniques to a theory of speculative prices probably belongs to Louis Bachelier. His pioneering work in his doctoral dissertation, "Theorie de la Speculation,"[5] was utilized by Holbrook Working, who inspired much thought and research through his production of many highly respected studies of prices.

Those who have argued that futures price changes are random in nature have based their assertion on the following principles: (1) price changes are such that they could have been generated by independent trials from a simple chance model such as a roulette wheel; (2) no one has been able to show that price changes exhibit a systematic pattern, even though present statistical techniques are capable of detecting data that have come from a significantly nonrandom process.

The first point is merely suggestive because it is impossible to prove the existence of randomness. Holbrook Working, writing as early as 1934, observed:

> It has several times been noted that time series commonly possess in many respects the characteristics of cumulated random numbers. The separate items in such time series are by no means random in character, but the *changes* between successive items

---

[5] Gauthier-Villars, Paris, 1900.

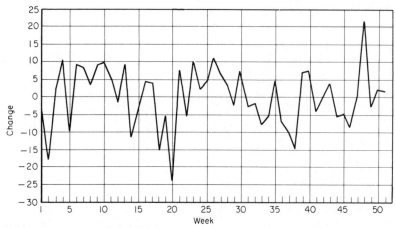

Figure 4-1   Changes from Friday to Friday (closing), January 6, 1956, to December 28, 1956, Dow Jones Industrial Average.

tend to be largely random. This characteristic has been noted conspicuously in sensitive commodity prices. . . .[6]

In support of this position it has been suggested that the output of a simple roulette wheel could duplicate many of the characteristic features of futures price movements. Results of this approach are illustrated in Figures 4-1 and 4-2. Although the illustration is based on price changes of a securities index, the principle is clear. Figure 4-1 represents the daily changes in closing prices of the Dow Jones Industrial Average for the year 1956. Figure 4-2 represents changes generated by the output of a random-number table. Even though the chance model demonstrated in Figure 4-2 cannot duplicate history except in the sense that one evening at a gambling casino duplicates another, the similarity of both series is striking enough to startle the would-be trader. Certainly the plotting of a series of price changes that could be generated from a random-number table is not calculated to inspire confidence in the recurring "patterns" supposedly embedded in price history.

In testing the random-walk assertion, statisticians have brought to bear several kinds of tests. In the pages that follow, results of runs analysis, serial correlation, filter rules, and spectral analysis are presented as evidence in the controversy.

Analysis of Runs

If a change in price (daily, weekly, monthly) is positive, it can be denoted by " +." A negative change can be labeled " −." A "run" is a consecutive sequence of the

---

[6] Holbrook Working, "A Random-Difference Series for Use in the Analysis of Time Series," *Journal of the American Statistical Association,* **29** (1934), 11.

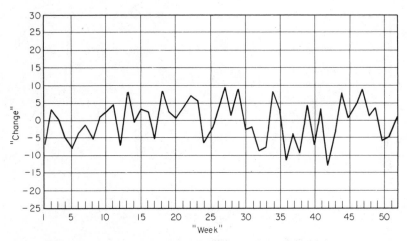

Figure 4-2 Simulated market changes for 52 weeks.

same symbol. Assume the following sequence of +'s and −'s on a close-to-close basis:

− − + + − + + + + − + − − + + − − − + − + −

The first four runs of this sequence are − −, + +, −, and + + + +. There are 13 runs in the entire sequence.

The purpose of a runs test is to determine whether the number of consecutive days of price movement in one direction is close to that expected by pure chance. Table 4-1 summarizes the observed versus the expected runs in a study of daily futures prices of July soybeans and July corn over an 11-year period. An exami-

TABLE 4-1 DISTRIBUTION OF LENGTHS OF RUNS OF DAILY JULY CORN AND SOYBEAN FUTURES PRICES, SUMMARY, 1957–1968

Length of run (days)	July soybeans			July corn		
	Observed run		Expected run	Observed run		Expected run
	Up	Down	Up or down*	Up	Down	Up or down*
1	359	364	345	359	365	361
2	202	169	172	201	185	180
3	82	88	86	78	75	90
4	26	48	43	40	40	45
5	8	12	22	12	12	23
6+	10	15	22	13	7	23
Total	687	696	690	703	684	722

* Expected on the assumption of .5 probability of rise or fall and 2755 close-to-close observations for July corn and 2888 observations for July soybeans.

SOURCE: Richard Stevenson and Robert Bear, "Commodity Futures: Trends or Random Walks?" *Journal of Finance*, No. 1 (March 1970), 74.

nation of these actual price changes shows that in this sample there were slightly more short (1- and 2-day) runs than expected and slightly fewer long runs (5 and 6 or more days) than would have occurred, on the average, by pure chance. The difference, however, is not significant and *could* have occurred by chance. The trader will note that these results, although slightly favoring a tendency toward reversals, in the main confirm the absence of identifiable nonrandomness in the length of runs through the 12 years observed. Also, as expected, the number of "up" runs of any given duration was about equal to the number of "down" runs of the same duration. The results of other statistical tests using runs have also been generally consistent with the hypothesis of independent price changes.[7]

Serial Correlation

Serial correlation measures the correlation among a series of numbers like futures prices with lagging numbers in the same series. Many different lags and many different time periods can be used to draw data for serial correlation tests. The presence of trends or reversal tendencies in futures prices can be detected with this approach. The object is to find patterns in short-term price changes that can be used to trade more profitably than with a naive buy-and-hold strategy. If an up move in price is followed more often than not by another up move, positive serial correlation is present. If the converse is true, the trader has isolated a tendency for negative serial correlation or a reversal characteristic.

Following Working's discovery that fluctuations of futures prices are economically warranted responses to new information, itself unpredictable, came a study that showed a slight nonrandom characteristic in price movements. Brinegar,[8] using a new statistic, found a weak but statistically significant tendency toward "continuity" of a trend (positive serial correlation) in the prices of wheat, corn, and rye, ranging from 4 to 16 weeks. The amount of continuity varied from commodity to commodity and from time period to time period and was especially associated with periods of large price movements. A second important conclusion from Brinegar's study is the evidence of a slight "reaction tendency" (negative serial correlation) for short intervals of apparently 1 to 2 weeks.

Larson[9] expanded these findings by studying the day-to-day changes in corn prices for two 10-year periods: 1922–1931 and 1949–1958. His contribution was to measure the pattern followed by prices after inputs of new information. Larson found that on the average about 81 percent of the price effect of new demand and supply information occurs on a single day, presumably the day of changes in news. There is then a reaction, averaging about 8 percent dispersed over 4 days, away

[7] See Holbrook Working, "Prices of Cash Wheat and Futures at Chicago since 1883," *Wheat Studies*, 2, No. 3 (November 1934), 75–124, and Sidney Alexander, "Price Movements in Speculative Markets: Trends or Random Walks," reprinted in Paul Cootner, ed., *The Random Character of Stock Market Prices* (Cambridge, Mass.: The M.I.T. Press, 1964), pp. 199–218.

[8] Claude Brinegar, "A Statistical Analysis of Speculative Price Behavior," *Food Research Institute Studies*, Supplement, 9 (1970).

[9] Arnold Larson, "Measurement of a Random Process in Futures Prices," *Food Research Institute Studies*, 1, No. 3 (November 1960).

from the initial price movement, even though the first movement is not sufficient to discount all the news. Finally, an additional 27 percent dispersed over 45 days results in a total price movement that is just appropriate. Many markets may operate as Larson's study suggests, differing from an ideal random-walk market principally in that traders react with varying skills to varying sources of information. For that reason some of the response to price making may be delayed, even though the delay is a small fraction of the total response and is dispersed over a considerable number of days in an unpredictable pattern.

Larson's evidence was important because, as Working later indicated,

> Economic reasoning suggests that the larger hedging orders should be expected to produce fairly large dips and bulges, of considerable duration. Experience of hedgers seems to bear out that reasoning. But Larson's evidence was the first to indicate clearly, from the behavior of prices, that these larger dips and bulges occurred frequently, in a large range of sizes and durations, their durations extending often to three or four days.[10]

Houthakker[11] has made a study that deals with the relative profitability of varying stop-loss order percentages as an indicator of serial correlation. Theoretically, if price changes were random, traders who tried to limit their losses by selling (buying) whenever the price of a future fell (rose) by a fixed percentage below (above) their initial prices would not find their average results better over a number of years than if they used no stops at all. If successive price changes were independent, a price decline (rise) of, say, 5 percent, which might be necessary to trigger a stop-loss, would not affect subsequent price changes. On the other hand, if a particular stop-loss percentage can be discovered, the use of which increases

---

[10] Holbrook Working, "Tests of a Theory Concerning Floor Trading on Commodity Exchanges," *Food Research Institute Studies,* Supplement, **7** (1967), 16.

[11] Hendrik Houthakker, "Systematic and Random Elements in Short-Term Price Movements," *American Economic Review,* **51** (1961), 164–172.

TABLE 4-2   TRADING RESULTS IN WHEAT FUTURES (1921–1939, 1947–1956) FOR VARIOUS STOP PERCENTAGES, IN CENTS PER BUSHEL

Stop percentage	Long positions				Short positions			
	May	Sept.	Dec.	Combined	May	Sept.	Dec.	Combined
100	+ 127	− 99	+ 59	+ 87	− 127	+ 99	− 59	− 87
20	+ 104	− 126	+ 55	+ 33	− 100	+ 112	− 16	− 4
15	+ 96	− 130	+ 69	+ 35	− 83	+ 73	− 24	− 34
10	+ 132	− 123	+ 90	+ 99	− 68	+ 90	+ 10	+ 32
7½	+ 135	− 74	+ 126	+ 187	− 55	+ 57	+ 27	+ 29
5	+ 122	− 47	+ 140	+ 215	− 34	+ 83	+ 79	+ 128
4	+ 133	− 15	+ 65	+ 183	− 19	+ 94	+ 53	+ 128
3	+ 116	− 5	+ 78	+ 189	− 19	+ 94	+ 70	+ 146
2	+ 42	− 4	+ 84	+ 122	− 24	+ 71	+ 30	+ 77
1	− 2	− 27	+ 73	+ 44	− 27	+ 60	− 11	+ 22
0	+ 18	0	+ 27	+ 45	0	0	0	0

SOURCE: Hendrik Houthakker, "Systematic and Random Elements in Short Term Price Movements," *American Economic Review,* 51 (1961), 166.

TABLE 4-3   TRADING RESULTS IN CORN FUTURES (1921–1939, 1947–1956) FOR VARIOUS STOP PERCENTAGES, IN CENTS PER BUSHEL

Stop percentage	Long positions				Short positions			
	May	Sept.	Dec.	Combined	May	Sept.	Dec.	Combined
100	+79	− 83	+112	+108	− 79	+ 83	−112	−108
20	+75	−114	+108	+ 69	−111	+ 94	− 36	− 64
15	+95	− 94	+119	+120	− 80	+ 91	− 48	− 37
10	+83	− 73	+141	+151	− 37	+107	− 47	+ 23
7½	+57	− 97	+151	+111	− 45	+103	− 27	+ 31
5	+21	− 47	+127	+101	− 23	+104	− 19	+ 62
4	+35	− 34	+125	+126	− 28	+117	− 56	+ 33
3	+36	− 11	+139	+164	− 12	+115	− 68	+ 35
2	+ 9	− 17	+156	+148	− 10	+105	− 53	+ 42
1	+29	− 24	+170	+175	− 9	+ 66	− 27	+ 32
0	+29	+ 2	+ 70	+100	0	0	0	0

SOURCE: Hendrik Houthakker, "Systematic and Random Elements in Short Term Price Movements," *American Economic Review*, 51 (1961), 166.

average net profit, then an instance of persistence in price trends will have been indicated. If the use of stop orders can lead to nonrandom outcomes for the trader, the problem becomes one of discovering what stop percentage is relevant. Stops placed too close to the entry price are activated by "noise," whereas if stops are placed too far away from the market, losses may be too great to be adequately offset by profits.

For his analysis, Houthakker chose wheat and corn futures during the periods October 1, 1921, to October 1, 1939, and February 1, 1947, to October 1, 1956. It was assumed that a trader bought or sold May wheat or corn on October 1, the September contract on February 1, and the December futures on June 1, liquidating each trade after 4 months unless stopped out beforehand. Commissions were not calculated.

Tables 4-2 and 4-3 summarize trading results for varying stop-loss percentages. A stop percentage of 5 means that the trader sells out at 95 percent of the purchase price, and a stop percentage of 0 means that any adversity below (above) a given entry point resulted in liquidation. A consistent long position in all three contracts of both wheat and corn was profitable, which implies a possible positive expected value over the periods covered.

In analyzing the stop percentages between 0 and 100, Houthakker cites some evidence of nonrandomness, even though the improvement is not always large.[12] The study notes that long positions in May corn give better results when stop percentages are relatively large but that the opposite is true for December corn. Results for being long on May and December wheat and short on September corn

---

[12] Roger Gray and S. T. Nielsen, "Rediscovery of Some Fundamental Price Behavior Characteristics" (paper presented at a meeting of the Econometric Society, Cleveland, Ohio, September 7, 1963). The authors supplied additional data, using the same "stop-loss" technique, which indicated that Houthakker's results were not necessarily typical of the markets analyzed. The tendency for trends was attributed by Gray and Nielsen to the influence of the government price support program and Houthakker's use of distant contracts.

also favor a moderate stop percentage. Stop-losses, of course, tend to reduce losses rather than increase profits. The trader could not expect a stop-loss policy, no matter how efficiently formulated, to furnish a profitable trading record.

Many efforts have been made to massage time series data in an effort to develop rules involving negative or positive serial correlation. Basically these involve buying after some indication of strength or weakness based upon a price move defined in terms of either time or amount. Most such rules work only in the periods selected, yield too little to justify the time, risk, and investment involved, or were successful only because of unusually large profits yielded by a small number of the input units. Rules might well work reasonably well if applied to the historical sample from which they were developed, but they might well fail if applied to the same market for other periods or to other markets.

Short-run rules which have worked historically might become known either through publications or by being promoted by the developer of the rules. Traders should be careful to note that consistent profits yielding either positive or negative serial correlation are, for many reasons, not easy to amass. First, few traders execute trades personally on the floors of exchanges. Orders based on time series typically must be placed market-on-close or market-on-opening, both of which typically result in high execution costs. These costs are typically underestimated (see Chapter 11). Working alludes to this problem by indicating that the professional scalper must buy or sell when a "dip" or "bulge" is actually forming, for it is only at such times that favorable prices can be obtained.[13] Such a consideration is paramount when it is realized that most trading rules are marginally profitable at best.

Second, because of the small margin of profit expected on the average, a trader may be tempted to increase the number of bushels traded, thereby substantially increasing the risks on any one trade. Unless the trader has considerable financial means, several losses on balance could do irreparable harm, both financially and psychologically. The question, then, not only of average profits but of average losses to be sustained deserves serious consideration in the setting of stop-losses.

Filter Rules

It remains to inquire into the possibility of applying filter techniques to futures prices. A major reason for examining filters develops from the concern that any dependence in the form of recognizable and usable price patterns will be so complicated that standard statistical analyses such as runs tests or short-run serial correlation tests will fail to uncover them. If prices exhibit patterns that persist over long periods of time, it can be concluded that the markets *have* a memory, that past price movements can help to forecast future price changes, and therefore that price changes are not independent. Such trend-following strategies, if successful, may eliminate or reduce the problems of commission costs, execution

---

[13] Holbrook Working, "Tests of a Theory Concerning Floor Trading on Commodity Exchanges," *Food Research Institute Studies,* Supplement, **7** (1967), 16, 17.

costs, and small average profits that have plagued the trader in results examined to date.

Most of the early work in trying to simulate technical trading rules centered on security prices. Alexander[14] developed a filter technique in order to apply a criterion similar to that used by some traders. The filter was defined as follows: As soon as the closing price moves up x percent from some initial point, the security is bought and held until its price moves down x percent from a high subsequent to the first purchase, at which time the long position is abandoned and a short position instituted; the short position is maintained until the closing price again rises x percent above a low subsequent to the previous sell, at which time the short position is covered and a long position is entered. Alexander used filters with varying values of x between 1 and 50 percent and applied the technique to American industrial stock price averages from 1897 to 1959. He concluded that his filter rule yields positive results for filters ranging from $x = 5$ to $x = 30$ percent. In other words, he finds a tendency for a price change in a stock price average to be followed by a subsequent price change in the same direction. The profitability of this filter technique may imply similar results for other trend-following techniques, but because the data consisted of changes in stock price *averages* and because changes in price *averages* have behavioral characteristics that differ from those of changes in the price of an individual stock, Alexander's results would not necessarily be meaningful in a pragmatic trading situation.

Cootner[15] examined the results of a rule that permitted a much more rapid response to changes of direction than Alexander's strategy. The decision rule was stated as follows: Buy the stock when the price exceeds a 40-week moving average by more than a given percentage (threshold amount), and sell the stock whenever the price dips below the moving average by *any* amount; sell the stock short whenever it falls below the moving average by more than the threshold amount, and cover the short sale whenever the price rises above the moving average by *any* amount. This rule was applied to the weekly closing prices of a sample of 45 stocks listed on the New York Stock Exchange over a period that generally included the years 1956 to 1960.

Rates of return using a 0 percent and a 5 percent threshold rate were provided, the latter rate lowering the excessive transactions that tend to occur when the stock price remains in a narrow range. Both strategies were superior to buy-and-hold *only* if gross profits were considered. After commissions neither strategy outperformed the simple investment rule.

In a careful analysis covering all the individual stocks of the Dow Jones Industrial Average, Fama and Blume[16] tested 24 filters ranging from ½ to 50 percent over

---

[14] Sidney Alexander, "Price Movements in Speculative Markets: Trends or Random Walks," No. 2, reprinted in Paul Cootner, ed., *The Random Character of Stock Market Prices* (Cambridge, Mass.: The M.I.T. Press, 1964), pp. 338–372.

[15] Paul Cootner, "Stock Prices: Random vs. Systematic Changes," reprinted in Paul Cootner, ed., *The Random Character of Stock Market Prices* (Cambridge, Mass.: The M.I.T. Press, 1964), pp. 231–252.

[16] Eugene Fama and Marshall Blume, "Filter Rules and Stock-Market Trading," *Journal of Business*, 39 (Supplement 1966), 226–241.

daily data for approximately 5 years, ending in 1962. When commissions are included, the largest profits under the filter technique are those of the broker. When commissions are omitted, the returns from the filter technique are improved but are *still* inferior to the returns from buy-and-hold for all except two securities of the 30—Alcoa and Union Carbide. In addition, empirical evidence is presented which indicates that Alexander's results tended to overstate the actual profitability of the filter technique versus buy-and-hold. Such bias, it is believed, appears because the use of indices overstates the profitability of short sales. Because short sellers must incur the cost of paying all dividends, the index is reduced by dividend payments, and therefore the time spent in being short will introduce a bias estimated at about 2 percentage points in favor of the filter technique.

A study by Stevenson and Bear[17] revealed some success in applying varying filters in July corn and July soybeans over the 12-year period 1957–1968. Three trading techniques are simulated. Trading technique 1 assumes that the trader buys the future at the opening on the first day of trading and enters a stop-loss order x percent below the purchase price. If the stop-loss is not executed, the future is sold on the last day of the contract. If the stop-loss is executed, no further position is taken until the following July contract begins to be traded. The reader will recognize this rule as similar to the one tested earlier by Houthakker.

Trading technique 2 is divided into plan A and plan B. Plan A waits for the closing price to move up or down x percent and then establishes a position in the *direction of the market move*. A stop-loss order is placed x percent below (above) the established position. If price moves in favor of the trader, the stop is moved each day so that the trader never risks more than x percent from the high closing price. If price moves against the trader, the stop-loss order is not moved. When a trade is closed out, the trader repeats the process. Plan A, then, to be successful requires a tendency toward a move of x percent to be followed more often than not by another move of *more* than x percent. Plan B uses the same procedure, except that it establishes a position *against* the market rather than *with* the market. This rule should help indicate whether the tendency in the markets tested is toward price reversals.

Trading technique 3 establishes a position *with* the market when price moves up (down) x percent and holds the position until a move occurs, either up or down, of x percent. Profits are not allowed to run.

For each of the trading techniques 1½, 3, and 5 percent filters were tested. Commissions were charged on all transactions, and the dollar returns in Tables 4-4 and 4-5 reflect a commitment of 10,000 bushels, or two contracts. A buy-and-hold policy over the 12-year period resulted in a profit in soybeans of $8545, or about an average of 3.5 cents annually. However, if it were not for the large profit of $10,654 realized in 1966 (about 53 cents a bushel), there would have been a sizable loss. Buy-and-hold results for corn over the same period produced a $5328 loss.

Trading technique 1 with a 5 percent filter worked well in soybeans but did not

---

[17] Richard Stevenson and Robert Bear, "Commodity Futures: Trends or Random Walks?" *Journal of Finance,* **21**, No. 1 (March 1970), 65–81.

TABLE 4-4 RETURNS FROM TRADING TECHNIQUES USING VARIOUS SIZES OF FILTERS, JULY CORN FUTURES, SUMMARY TABLE FOR 1957–1968

	1½% Filter				3% Filter				5% Filter			
	Profit	Loss	Net	Years profit	Profit	Loss	Net	Years profit	Profit	Loss	Net	Years profit
Buy and hold	$2955	$8283	$(5328)	5	$2955	$8283	$(5328)	5	$2955	$8283	$(5328)	5
Trading technique 1	1187	1940	(753)	2	1187	3440	(2253)	2	2849	4277	(1428)	4
Trading technique 2 (plan A)	460	9397	(8937)	1	2915	2381	584	7	3990	1577	2413	7
Trading technique 2 (plan B)	2978	5358	(2380)	5	5259	4332	927	6	2422	3241	(819)	4
Trading technique 3	203	8833	(8630)	1	2728	4235	(1507)	6	2527	3178	(651)	6

SOURCE: Richard Stevenson and Robert Bear, "Commodity Futures: Trends or Random Walks?" *Journal of Finance*, 21, No. 1 (March 1970), 77.

TABLE 4-5 RETURNS FROM TRADING TECHNIQUES USING VARIOUS SIZES OF FILTERS, JULY SOYBEAN FUTURES, SUMMARY TABLE FOR 1957–1968

	1½% Filter				3% Filter				5% Filter			
	Profit	Loss	Net	Years profit	Profit	Loss	Net	Years profit	Profit	Loss	Net	Years profit
Buy and hold	$21,210	$12,663	$ 8,547	4	$21,210	$12,663	$ 8,547	4	$21,210	$12,663	$ 8,547	4
Trading technique 1	10,556	3,132	7,424	3	10,556	5,832	4,724	3	21,210	6,784	14,426	4
Trading technique 2 (plan A)	4,502	11,159	(6,657)	3	15,744	3,428	12,316	7	19,241	2,140	17,101	8
Trading technique 2 (plan B)	9,098	8,942	156	5	4,676	13,550	(8,874)	3	5,635	16,107	(10,472)	2
Trading technique 3	3,589	15,858	(12,269)	3	2,380	11,518	(9,138)	3	16,462	4,130	12,332	8

SOURCE: Richard Stevenson and Robert Bear, "Commodity Futures: Trends or Random Walks?" *Journal of Finance*, 21, No. 1 (March 1970), 78.

result in a profitable corn trading rule, even though all filters reduced the loss accruing to the buy-and-hold strategy.

Trading technique 2 (plan A) provided the best results for both corn and soybeans. As the size of the filter increased, profitability increased when positions were established *with* the market, until results were optimized with a 5 percent filter. Eight of 12 years were profitable with the largest filter in soybeans, and 7 of 12 years yielded profits in corn. Plan B produced nearly inverse results when compared with plan A yet confirmed some tendency toward reversals in the shorter-run price movements.

Trading technique 3 did not perform so well as the other strategies. After commissions, only a 5 percent filter in soybeans did well.

Spectral Analysis

Spectral analysis is a modern statistical technique for decomposing a time series like futures prices.[18] This idea itself is not a new one because breaking down a time series into a "trend," plus a "cycle," plus a "seasonal" component, plus the unexplained remainder has been studied by standard economic procedures for many years. The trend is a very smooth, slow-moving component, corresponding to a very low frequency, and therefore seldom occurs. The cyclical component, which corresponds to the next lowest frequency, is followed by the seasonal (12-month) component and finally by all other shorter-term frequencies.

Spectral analysis can be compared with the swinging of the dial of a radio across a wave band. The signals received, however, are not words or music. At any particular frequency only the total *power* of the signal is measured. The static between "stations" would correspond to a purely random signal and would register as a small, constant amount. The "stations" themselves correspond to the frequencies of the transmission as well as the *strength* of each signal. Spectral analysis shows the size of the amplitude of each frequency found in a time series.

Monthly futures prices for a number of commodities for January 1950 through July 1965 were examined by Labys and Granger by spectral analysis.[19] In general, the series was flat and exhibited the behavior expected from a random-walk market. The only commodity that showed a slightly significant seasonal tendency which the authors would confirm was wheat. Cotton oil, potatoes, eggs, cocoa, corn, flax, lard, soybeans, soybean meal, soybean oil, cotton, rye, and oats generated the types of spectra that would generally confirm the random-walk model. Similar analysis was applied to weekly and daily futures prices. Fifteen years of weekly prices for corn, oats, rye, wheat, and soybeans were examined, and the shape of the spectra of these futures also confirmed the random-walk model. One year of daily prices for coffee, corn, oats, rye, rubber, soybeans, sugar, wheat, cocoa, and cotton was

---

[18] An excellent summary of spectral analysis is given in Walter C. Labys and C. W. J. Granger, *Speculation, Hedging and Commodity Price Forecasts* (Lexington, Mass.: D. C. Heath and Co., 1970), chap. 2.

[19] Ibid., pp. 66–70.

tested, and all but the last two indicated that the random-walk model provides a good explanation of price behavior. A small amount of negative serial correlation existed for cocoa and cotton.[20]

THE QUESTION OF TREND

Even if the random-walk model results in a crude approximation of the truth when it comes to explaining price changes in futures, traders can still profit. They can isolate, quantify, and trade those short-run, nonrandom changes that they can validate as offering, after commissions, a profit. This approach is discussed in detail in Chapter 7. A trader can still profit even if successive price changes are independent if their expected value is not zero. In other words, traders can make money in futures even if they cannot predict short-term price changes consistently. A trader can simply follow a trend.

Risk Premium Concept

The first explanation advanced to indicate how the idea of an efficient market and a trend might coexist centered around a risk premium concept. Keynes first advanced the hypothesis in an essay in the *Manchester Guardian Commercial* in 1923 in which he suggested that anyone could reap handsome profits by simply holding long positions in cotton futures throughout the crop year, year in and year out.[21] This affirmation came to be regarded as the "Keynesian theory of normal backwardation."[22]

Though for years severe problems in semantics were to persist in the literature, the theory in essence stated that although markets sometimes reflect carrying charges and sometimes are inverted, in either case a risk premium is a normal and continuing part of the difference between cash prices and futures prices. In other words, the theory required that the futures price be lower (biased downward) than the price expected to prevail at the later delivery period by an amount representing the speculator's reward for bearing the risk of price change in the interim.

---

[20] Statistically minded readers who would like to dig deeper into time series and spectral analysis, and similar techniques, might refer productively to Andrew D. Seidel and Philip M. Ginsberg, *Commodities Trading Foundations, Analysis, and Operations* (Englewood Cliffs, N.J.: Prentice-Hall, Inc., 1983). Studies are also available periodically on these and related subjects in various articles published by the Stanford Food Research Institute and in *The Journal of Futures Markets,* published by John Wiley & Sons, Inc., in affiliation with the Center for the Study of Futures Markets, Columbia Business School.

[21] Quoted in Roger W. Gray and David J. S. Rutledge, "The Economics of Commodity Futures Markets: A Survey," *Review of Marketing and Agricultural Economics,* 39, No. 4, 9.

[22] "Backwardation" is a British trade term which in American usage refers to the premium present in an inverted market or a situation in which cash prices exceed futures prices. "Contango," the opposite word, refers to a carrying-charge market in which futures prices exceed cash prices. Thus Keynes considered that risk cost (backwardation) was to be considered "normal" in both kinds of markets, inverse or carry.

The implication here is that short hedging will predominate, thereby leaving the speculator net long.

In its simplest form the theory predicted that under certain conditions it was necessary, *on the average,* for the price of futures contracts to rise. Early in the development of the theory there were three necessary conditions:

1. Speculators are net long.
2. Speculators are risk avoiders; that is, they require a history of profits if they are to continue to trade.
3. Speculators are unable to forecast prices.

It is clear that all these assumptions can be met if there is a rise, on the average, in futures prices during the life of each contract. It is equally clear that if speculators are net long, require a history of profits to continue the game, and have no ability to forecast the direction or extent of future price changes, then obviously all profits that accrue to them must unambiguously be considered as a reward for the bearing of risk, not unlike the flow of insurance premiums between an insurance company and the insured. The speculator is guaranteed an expectation of gain, on the average, by making it possible for the hedger to hedge. The size of the speculative gain, under these assumptions, hinges *only* on the size of the speculator's position and not on competence.

Statistical Evidence

Stone stated as early as 1901[23] in a report for the U.S. Congress that, among several commodities, an analysis of the cotton markets did not sustain the contention that the futures price is always less than the spot price:

> ... if, for example, we compare October futures in July with the spot price realized in October. Out of fifty-seven different futures ... compared with spot prices realized ... in the N.Y. cotton market from 1881–82 to 1899, in twenty-nine cases the futures proved to be higher than the spots realized 3 months hence, and in twenty-eight cases the futures prices were lower than the spots at maturity—that is, the speculative judgment anticipated the realized value of cotton a little too favorably in half of the cases and not quite favorably enough in the other half ... in the long run the speculative quotations for future delivery are neither uniformly above nor below the level of the proper cash value of cotton as determined at the future date, but ... they are tentative anticipations of such realizable value as the conditions of the supply and demand are most likely to determine at the time when the future contract matures.

In the same report results for 15 years (1883–1898) of Chicago wheat prices confirmed that if speculators were to rely on the Keynesian postulate of earning substantial profits by merely running risk and allowing one season's results to be averaged against the others, they would not fare well.[24]

---

[23] *U.S. Industrial Commission Report* (1900–1901), House Doc. 94, 56th Cong., 2d Sess., House, reviewed in Gray and Rutledge, op. cit., 14–15.

[24] Ibid.

A later report by the Federal Trade Commission[25] introduced evidence on which Working was later to comment:[26]

> One of the most critical and painstaking inquiries into the subject was that made by the Federal Trade Commission. It attacked the problem in several different ways. All the methods produced evidence, in price data subsequent to 1896, of some "downward bias" in futures prices of wheat and corn but not of oats; but for the 10-year period prior to 1896, the indicated bias was in the opposite direction for all grains. The method which the Federal Trade Commission appeared to regard as quantitatively most trustworthy . . . yielded for wheat, 1906–16, the estimate that it amounted to −2.39 cents (about 2.4 percent) for a twelve-month interval.

Early in the controversy considerable doubt was raised that a speculator could amass consistent and substantial profits by merely being net long. In spite of the evidence, it does not seem that the theoretical discussion ever turned to the statistics of the organized markets for confirmation. When other commodities were examined in due course, it became evident that hedgers could be net long for considerable periods of time. The implication that net short hedging would predominate was not always realized. Because the level of the net short positions of hedgers may vary considerably, so will the size of offsetting speculative long positions. Therefore, speculators may possibly have a history of profits *without* prices rising on the average: for example, prices rise 5 cents in the first period and fall 5 cents in the second period; speculators are long 20 contracts in the first period and only 10 contracts in the second period. Such action is still consistent with the assumed inability of speculators to forecast price changes. The opposite situation may be true also; that is, a rise in prices may not result in profits for traders who are long. Speculators may be long 10 contracts during a price rise of 5 cents and long 30 contracts during a decline of 3 cents.

The arena became packed with clamoring voices, and the ensuing controversy was instructive because it led the academic community to test what traders commonly refer to today as "seasonals." Indeed, if the presence of a trend in a commodity is to be related to the risks of carrying an inventory in that commodity, then any such trend *must* be related to the pattern of hedging.

Cootner has presented several examples[27] in support of the contention that risk premiums can exist in futures. From 1946 to 1974, bimonthly hedging and speculative positions were available for "large traders" as defined by the CEA. Beginning in 1974 exchanges themselves were required to publish volume and open interest information. The CFTC continued to provide a breakdown among hedgers, large speculators, and nonreporting traders, but the breakdown was provided on

---

[25] U.S. Federal Trade Commission, *Report on the Grain Trade*, 7 vols. (Washington, D.C., 1920–1926).

[26] Holbrook Working, "Theory of the Inverse Carrying Charge in Futures Markets," *Journal of Future Economics*, **30**, No. 1 (February 1948), 9.

[27] Paul Cootner, "Speculation and Hedging," *Food Research Institute Studies*, Supplement, **7** (1967), 84–103.

TABLE 4-6   WHEAT AVERAGE GAIN PER YEAR, 1947–1965, UNDER INDICATED STRATEGIES

Specifications	Strategy I	Strategy II	Strategy III
Cents per bushel:			
Short only	7.8*	8.5*	6.2
Long only	8.6*	9.4*	8.6
Long and short	15.9*	17.9†	14.8
Percentage of price:			
Long and short	7.7	8.7	7.3

Strategy I. Go short at bimonthly point when reported short hedging first drops below 3000 contracts. Cover short sales and go long at bimonthly point when reported short hedging first rises above 3000 contracts. Sell long positions when you go short. All positions are taken in the nearest future in which the position can be held for the entire period.

Strategy II. Same as Strategy I except that all positions are liquidated at the point prior to the change in the balance of hedging.

Strategy III. Same as Strategy I except that all short positions are initially taken in May and are switched to the July future (if necessary) on April 30. Long positions are initially taken in March and switched to May if necessary. Not tested for significance.

* Significant at the 5 percent level.

† Significant at the 1 percent level.

SOURCE: Paul Cootner, "Speculation and Hedging," *Proceedings of a Symposium on Price Effects of Speculation in Organized Commodity Markets, Food Research Institute Studies,* Supplement, 7 (1967), 89.

a monthly basis rather than on the former semimonthly basis.[28] Table 4-6 provides the results of three strategies of initiating long and short positions in wheat futures based on short hedging levels over a 19-year period. All three strategies were profitable for both long and short positions for the period. These results indicate that it was possible for speculators to profit merely by being long after the peak of net short hedging and short after the peak of net long hedging.

Table 4-7 presents some evidence for a seasonal in soybeans. The period covered is from the autumn of 1949 to the autumn of 1960. Details of the strategies are given in the notes for Table 4-7. The long and short strategy keeps the trader long for 6 months and short for almost the same period of time. This strategy offsets what otherwise might be considered an inflationary bias. The average gains for the years 1949 to 1960 are impressive, even though they *omit* the 1960–1961 crop year, which provided about 100 cents profit on the long side and 80 cents profit on the short. It is interesting to note that the peak in visible supplies is a good proxy for the peak in hedging.

Traders have long considered the possibilities of trading "intermarket" spreads, that is, being simultaneously long and short in different markets in which the impact of hedging comes at different periods of time. One spread is the relation between oats and corn reflected in Table 4-8. The domestic oats crop harvest is

---

[28] The reader who wishes to delve further into the area of the grouping of traders might refer to D. J. S. Rutledge, "Estimation of Hedging and Speculative Positions in Futures Markets: An Alternative Approach," *Food Research Institute Studies,* 14 (1977–1978), 205–211, and Ronald W. Ward and Robert M. Bear, "Allocating Nonreported Futures Commitments," *The Journal of Futures Markets,* 3 (1983), 393–401.

started in the spring and frequently lasts through the summer. The corn harvest, on the other hand, begins in September and is usually completed by the onset of winter. For corn, then, short hedging generally increases in the period just before the December contract goes off the board. Oats, during the same period, is a market in which the customary activity is one of hedge lifting. Again, details of the strategies are indicated in the notes for Table 4-8.

The trader should note that strategies 4 and 5 show a much smaller tendency for the price differential to rise because they are computed on a calendar basis rather than on a hedging basis. Thus, although buying two contracts of December oats and selling one contract of December corn on a hedging pattern resulted in an average rise of about 5 cents a bushel from 1947 to 1964, a similar strategy on a calendar basis yielded only about 2 cents a bushel. These results tend to support the existence of a risk premium.

Houthakker found, on the basis of monthly price observations, that his sample of speculators actually made money trading futures.[29] These findings required

---

[29] H. S. Houthakker, "Can Speculators Forecast Prices?" *Review of Economics and Statistics,* **39**, No. 2 (May 1959), 143–151.

TABLE 4-7   SOYBEANS: AVERAGE GAIN PER YEAR, 1949–1960,* IN CENTS PER BUSHEL

Positions	Autumn 1949 to autumn 1960†
Long positions:	
From peak in visible supply to April 30	18.2
From peak in hedging to April 30	21.3
Short positions:	
From April 30 to September 20	14.7
Long and short positions:	
Long from October 20 to April 30 and short	
from April 30 to September 20	38.7

* Since soybeans were in shorter supply than wheat during this period, long hedging tended to predominate earlier in the crop year than was the case for wheat, even though it is earlier in the soybean crop than in the wheat crop year.

Long positions were always taken in the May future.

Short positions were taken in the September future except in the periods 1949–1950 and 1950–1951, when the September future was not used. In those years the position was taken in the November future.

The September 20 terminal date was near the last day of trading in the September future. The last day was chosen because the long hedging positions in that month are usually taken to protect against late or poor harvests. The harvest usually begins late in September, and the hedging position is generally liquidated very late. It is the late September results which truly indicate the outcome. A smaller but still significant profit is obtained by terminating the short position on August 30.

† All results are significant at the 0.1 percent level.

SOURCE: Paul Cootner, "Speculation and Hedging," *Proceedings of a Symposium on Price Effects of Speculation in Organized Commodity Markets, Food Research Institute Studies,* Supplement, **7** (1967), 97.

TABLE 4-8   OATS—CORN: CHANGE IN PRICE DIFFERENTIALS OF DECEMBER CONTRACTS, 1947–1964

	Mean annual change (cents per bushel)	
Strategy*	To December 15	To November 30
1	4.79†	2.67
2	5.62†	3.45‡
3	3.84†	1.67
4§	2.37	−1.20
5§	−0.54	−1.72

* Hedging-oriented strategies: Buy 2 bushels of December oats and sell 1 bushel of December corn on bimonthly date when
(1) Reported oats net short hedging first exceeds reported corn net short hedging.
(2) Reported oats net short hedging exceeds 2000 contracts.
(3) Reported oats net short hedging minus reported corn net short hedging reaches peak. When oats short hedging always meets the conditions, trades are initiated on April 15.
Calendar strategies: Buy 2 bushels of December oats and sell 1 bushel of December corn on
(4) July 30.
(5) April 15.

† Significant at the 5 percent level.

‡ Significant at the 10 percent level. All other numbers are not statistically different from zero.

§ The figures are not significant at the 10 percent level.

SOURCE: Paul Cootner, "Speculation and Hedging," *Proceedings of a Symposium on Price Effects of Speculation in Organized Commodity Markets, Food Research Institute Studies,* Supplement, 7 (1967), 100.

additional changes in the risk premium theory. The trader will remember that the original risk premium concept required that speculators

(a) be net long,
(b) refuse to trade if they lost money in the long run,
(c) be unable to forecast price changes.

The only price behavior that apparently would tolerate all three conditions was one of rising prices on the average. The first breach in this concept occurred when it was discovered that short hedging did *not* predominate at all times for all futures and that speculators *could still* obtain a risk premium even if prices did not rise on the average. A speculator could simply be net long when hedgers were net short and net short when the hedgers were net long. Houthakker not only indicated that speculators earned profits but also devised a method of estimating the share of profits that should be attributed to actual forecasting skill versus the premium that would be received for merely bearing risk. The insurance premium analogy was no longer adequate in itself to explain speculators' profits. Of course, not everyone accepted these findings. Telser,[30] for one, rejected Houthakker's evidence

---

[30] L. G. Telser, "Futures Trading and the Storage of Cotton and Wheat," *Journal of Political Economy,* **66,** No. 3 (June 1958), 233–255.

of the ability to forecast on the basis that commissions were not charged against speculator income, the study was limited to only 9 years (1937–1939 and 1946–1952), and the method of estimating profits and losses was hampered by not including the changes in prices that were available to speculators in each month.

Rockwell enlarged on Houthakker's study in an important analysis covering 7900 semimonthly observations over 25 markets for the 18-year period 1947 to 1965.[31] Among other pertinent inquiries, Rockwell attempted to define the proportion of dollars flowing to speculators that could be attributed to the presence of a risk premium. In other words, how much money would accrue to a naive trader who is long when hedgers are net short and short when hedgers are net long? Two important conclusions emerged. First, prices rose consistently when speculators were net short, causing them considerable losses. Second, the profits that accrue to the naive speculator who is net long are so small that no significant tendency toward normal backwardation is observed. Rockwell pointed out, however, that these conclusions do not imply that there can never be strong upward or downward price tendencies in different markets or in different periods within a market. In other words, even though the overall generalization might be that the futures price is an unbiased estimate of the ultimate spot price, such a statement is critically dependent on the markets which are selected. Those who believe that the concept of normal backwardation is valid may gain some comfort from studies of the relatively highly volatile markets of the 1970s and 1980s. These studies indicated that the risk premium increased during those years. Whether the increase was caused by a change in the markets, a price bias in one direction which would make naive trading easier, or an increase in the wisdom of small traders is not so clear. Whether the increase was enough to overcome the risks and costs of trading is not so clear either.[32]

Rockwell's study is critically important for another reason, however. Although his study indicated rather conclusively that the risk premium theory is not viable for traders in a general way, his findings clearly promise a flow of profits to some traders solely on the basis of their forecasting skill. It is possible to define two levels of forecasting skill. First, a basic skill can measure the ability to be long in markets in which prices generally rise over the period examined and short when prices fall. Second, a special forecasting skill measures a trader's ability to forecast price movements that are shorter than the total period observed. The trader can see that these two definitions loosely parallel what might be called the fundamental and technical approaches to market forecasting. After these two approaches to decision making are developed in greater detail in Chapters 6 and 7, the trading results of the players in the game—hedgers, large speculators, and small speculators—are fully analyzed to arrive at an answer to the all-important question of who wins, who loses, and why. It is of interest to note at this point that traders might participate, without the prerequisite of any basic or forecasting skill, in

---

[31] Charles Rockwell, "Normal Backwardation, Forecasting and the Returns to Commodity Futures Traders," *Food Research Institute Studies,* Supplement, 7 (1967), 107–130.

[32] See Colin A. Carter, Gordon C. Rausser, and Andrew Schmitz, "Efficient Asset Portfolios and the Theory of Normal Backwardation," *Journal of Political Economy,* 91 (1983), 319–331.

biases that may be present without heavy reliance on whether or not there is a risk premium.

Other Causes of Bias

That there might be fruitful excursions into the question of whether price action could be lopsided for reasons other than the existence of a risk premium being paid to speculators has been stressed by such scholars as Gray. Gray has measured statistically the general tendency for futures prices to rise over extended periods of time for which the beginning and ending cash prices are generally unchanged.[33] If a trader holds a long position in a future, routinely rolls the position forward on maturity, and is able to generate consistent profits or losses when the cash price stays virtually unchanged, then that market may be said to be unbalanced, lopsided, or biased. Gray finds that corn, wheat, oats, beans (post-1955), and cocoa (post-1955) are examples of markets that do *not* offer the speculator a profitable bias. Soybeans (pre-1955), cocoa (pre-1955), wheat (Minneapolis), and coffee are examples of markets that *do* offer a significant bias over a considerable period of time. Markets that offer these biases are referred to as "thin" markets, or markets in which the amount of speculation does not keep pace with hedging requirements. Some markets outgrow their biases, such as soybeans and cocoa, and others do not. The latter, such as the markets for bran and shorts, fall into disuse and die. The futures market in coffee underlines the kind of pattern that characterizes a thin market. For many years after World War II coffee prices were high by historical standards, and prices for the near future were highest, followed by lower quotations for deferred contracts. This kind of pattern produces rather routine profits for the longs and losses for the shorts. It is interesting to note that in Rockwell's work, cited earlier, the markets with the smallest open interest displayed the largest bias, thus reinforcing Gray's analysis.

Another predictable bias can enter into the futures markets under the influence of a government loan program. Futures prices in wheat, for example, have regularly risen toward the guaranteed loan price, and even though that movement is predictable, it cannot take place until the movement into government hands has occurred. As Gray and Rutledge observe, "So long as the movement into loan is *anticipated,* it would be an irrational price which reflected it, for such a price, incorporating the anticipation, would prevent the event."[34] It is perhaps fitting that the chapter should close as it began, with a description by Working which illustrates the underlying premise of a futures market:

> The idea that a futures market *should* quote different prices for different future dates in accordance with developments anticipated between them cannot be valid when stocks must be carried from one date to another. It involves supposing that the market should act as a *forecasting* agency rather than as a *medium* for rational price formation when

---

[33] Roger Gray, "The Characteristic Bias in Some Thin Futures Markets," *Food Research Institute Studies,* 1, No. 3 (November 1960).

[34] Gray and Rutledge, op cit., 22.

it cannot do both. The business of a futures market, so far as it may differ from that of any other, is to anticipate future developments as best it may and to give them due expression in present prices, spot and near futures as well as distant futures.[35]

NOTES FROM A TRADER

The random-walk hypothesis is really a simple theory. It merely says that price changes are unpredictable when only previous price changes, not *all* available information, are used. Those holding that the random-walk model describes reality better than any other model do *not* say that the trader cannot make money—they merely promise the trader the fight of his or her life to beat the naive strategy of buy and hold after paying for the privilege of trying.

The tests that have been published so far lend a great deal of credence to the theory as an excellent "jumping-off point" to explain the short-run behavior of futures prices. This is not to say that all possible strategies have been tested and have failed to provide consistent profits. The ingenuity of traders in this regard has barely been scratched. Most of them feel they have 25 trading rules that will bring them riches beyond the dreams of avarice. But the present state of the statistical art warns, "Don't look around. Something's gaining on you. It's the random-walk theory, the new 'King of the Hill.' "

A stand such as this at the *beginning* of a section devoted to *successful* trading may be considered by many as unadulterated heresy. People make markets, and people do not release cherished falsehoods any more easily in the area of markets than they do in the area of science or philosophy. The fact that "patterns," usually described in an invincibly vague fashion, lead to profits about one-half the time they are traded does not dissuade the user. Instead, the capacity for definition is affirmed, and a new term, "false breakout," is coined. Indeed, the collection of empirical contradictions to any theory, albeit impressive, never succeeds solely by its presence in overturning the theory it contradicts. Rather, it is a better theory that must be advanced, or error simply becomes institutionalized by the collection of reams of "exceptions to the rule."

If short-run price behavior is described crudely by the random-walk hypothesis, then the theory itself becomes fair game. That it sets the tone for the game makes beating it a delicacy, never expected with certainty, yet always savored. The assumption of its tenets sharpens the trader for the battle. The trader *can* win, but only by discovering the truth of the biblical injunction "Broad is the path that leadeth to destruction." Financial salvation is a narrow gate through which pass only those traders who believe very little in luck as the cornerstone of their success. Sooner or later each trader affirms with Damon Runyon that "the race doesn't always go to the swift or the battle to the strong, but that's the way to bet." Indeed, one of the greatest contributions to traders' welfare made by advocates of the random-walk hypothesis is the presentation of objective evidence that shows how difficult it is to make money consistently in the markets.

---

[35] Holbrook Working, "Theory of the Inverse Carrying Charge in Future Markets," *Journal of Farm Economics,* **30,** No. 1 (February 1948), 14.

In moving from trading the markets in the short run to taking positions to profit from expected trends, the trader should realize that the work in this area affirms that, generally speaking, the market does not habitually shower loose dollars on the casual trader who plays the game. As someone remarked, a trader will have to leave his mouth open a long time before a roast pigeon falls in. That there are trends is undeniable. That these trends are easily forecast from factors known at any point in time is an assertion grounded in naïveté. To rely on a bias upward or downward for merely playing the game is to make a risk premium or a characteristic bias the raison d'être of trading. Unfortunately, there is no universal truth about such an assertion. Each trade made with such an assumption must be examined on its own merits and validated meticulously.

The foregoing points up what is perhaps the most important lesson to be learned from the behavior of futures prices. There *has* been serious work done in the field. A bibliography *does* exist, and familiarity with it will pay the trader definable dividends. One of the most rewarding is the ability to think critically about the methodology employed by any one person or institution selling positions in this or that commodity. The methodology at times has a great deal to do with affirming or disclaiming a particular conclusion. The trader should bring a healthy skepticism to the marketplace in the realization that well-trained scholars with a deep and abiding interest in the field do not find it incredibly difficult to disagree with one another. Somehow the vision on the one hand of pockets bulging with easy money and, on the other, the vision of the tip sheet which glibly asserts that sugar is most assuredly on its way up to a 500-point upswing will seem more and more mutually exclusive. To such affirmations the trader aware of the behavior of futures prices will remember to add that even a broken clock is right twice a day and that the capacity of the human mind to resist the intrusion of new knowledge seems close to infinite.

Playing the Game—
Trading

Armed with an understanding of the basics of the game, the trader is ready to become familiar with the decision-making processes. The seven chapters in this part attempt to isolate, describe, and analyze several elements of successful trading. Successful traders have discovered the importance of sound money management, which is often the least understood and most neglected aspect of trading. For that reason the part begins and ends with considerations that involve the management of funds committed to the futures game.

Chapter 5, "Risk, Reward, and You," supplies the trader with a personal profile of attitudes toward risk and profit at different levels of capital and leads the trader step-by-step in constructing a personal trading curve. Understanding the personal graph can help fit the trader's personality and value judgments about money with the type of trading the trader does.

Chapter 6, "Approaches to Trade Selection: Fundamentals," analyzes those factors that constitute what traders call the fundamental approach. Conceptual supply-demand considerations and applied price-quantity relationships are studied. The often blurred distinction between explaining price changes and forecasting them is presented, as are examples of successful explanatory and forecasting models.

*Chapter 7, "Approaches to Trade Selection: Technical Analysis,"
provides a panorama of technical tracking and forecasting methods
in a format that underlines the advantages and disadvantages of
each approach. Generous footnoting guides the trader to areas of
further market research which may be of interest. From the simple
arithmetic bar chart, the trader is led through various systems of
price tracking and forecasting, which include trend-following
methods, character-of-market approaches, and finally, strategies that
focus on market structure and more esoteric systems such as the
Elliott wave theory.*

*Chapter 8, "Spreads," may be considered by some to represent only a
choice of futures positions, but the subject is far broader than that
and deserves separate and more elaborate treatment. Opportunities
in these vehicles are flanked by different risks that must be carefully
evaluated.*

*Chapter 9, "Options," discusses the options markets that have been
introduced on several futures contracts. The differences and
similarities between options and futures with respect to their risk-
reward profiles are considered. The ability of options to limit the
risk of an investment due to either price increases or decreases is
also discussed.*

*Chapter 10, "The Game Plan," attacks the problem of the trading
plan directly by discussing its elements in some detail. The accent in
this chapter is on gathering specific information and organizing it
in a format that is useful, regardless of whether the plan accents a
fundamental or technical approach. The roles of stops and objectives,
as well as mistakes in plan formulation, are analyzed.*

*Chapter 11, "Money Management," concludes the section by
wrestling with the critical problem of money management, which
futures traders ignore to their enormous peril. Even if the essential
behavior of prices is understood and a rational strategy based on
fundamental or technical considerations is formulated and the
elements of a successful plan are followed, disaster will still strike if
basic skills are not developed in the area of capital management.*

5

Risk, Reward, and You

"Just as courage imperils life, fear protects it."   DA VINCI

INTRODUCTION

At this point the reader possesses more information about the basics of the futures game than the majority of the participants now playing. A 3-minute interview with a boardroom sample of traders (randomly selected, of course) will confirm that the information imparted in the first four chapters is not the subject of everyday brokerage office banter.

If such information is to be used intelligently, however, the reader must apply it to the decision-making process that leads to taking a position in the markets. Among the first decisions to be made are how to utilize one's capital and how much capital to risk. Treatment of these issues involves personal analysis and the concept of money management.

Money management is concerned essentially with four elements:

1. Objectives or preferences of the individual, including the person's present attitude toward money
2. Initial and subsequent dollar capital to be utilized or risked in trading
3. The expected value of the game
4. The probability of ruin

These elements are the fascinating subjects of this chapter and Chapter 11. Those playing the game are reminded that the issues of money management should share top billing with trade selection in the decision process. The first sections of this chapter discuss the concepts of probability as a numerical measure of optimism and utility as a numerical measure of preference or satisfaction. The *relationship* of probability to utility is used to construct the trader's personal trading curve and to make some useful analysis and interpretations of it.

OPTIMISM AND PROBABILITY

The futures trader operates in an atmosphere of uncertainty due to randomness. He cannot know with certainty what the outcome of any trade will be, but he can, and usually will, assign probabilities to the various outcomes based on his relative optimism or pessimism. A probability is merely a number assigned to an outcome to reflect the strength of the assigner's opinion (on a scale from 0 to 1) of the possibility that the outcome will occur; for example, he may feel that the probability of reaching his objective in a trade is .4, whereas the probability of losing is .6. A probability in such a situation can be considered an index of optimism or pessimism. If the probability of reaching his objective were changed to .5 instead of .4, it could be said that he became more optimistic. It does not matter whether his probability came from objective evidence, newsletters, hot tips, brokers' research, or personal intuition. Whatever the source, the numerical probability does measure *his assessment* of the likelihood of various outcomes, and it does help to determine his action and therefore the market price. Analysts and traders often attempt to estimate this probability, or optimism index, for large groups of traders. They may, for example, analyze the actions of large traders or insiders, or they may count the proportions of brokers and newsletters that recommend particular positions. These points are discussed in connection with contrary opinion in Chapter 7. If properly interpreted, such collective estimates can be useful. Even more useful and more easily measured, however, are the personal probabilities of the trader himself. Merely asking the right questions often provides useful insight.

PREFERENCES AND UTILITY

Suppose that a futures trader does assign probabilities to the various possible outcomes of a prospective trade. What principles does she use to make the decision whether or not to trade? How much is it worth to her to participate in a particular trade? Some will say that "worth" is the mathematical expectation of the gain or *expected value* or *average payoff* in money.[1] The rationale generally given for using

---

[1] The expected value, average payoff, or mathematical expectation is merely the sum of the possible *outcomes*, where each outcome is weighted by its probability; for example, in a trade in which there is a possible gain of $500 with probability .4 versus a possible loss of $200 with probability .6, the *expected value* or *average payoff* is $500(.4) − $200(.6) = $80. This indicates that if such a trade were made many times, it sometimes would result in a gain of $500 and sometimes in a loss of $200, but in the *long run* the average gain would be $80 *per trade*.

the expected value of money involves an argument about what will happen in the long run, that is, when the trade is repeated many times. It is easy to see the merit of such a decision criterion for a gambling house but not for an individual trader. In the first place, she trades relatively few times. Even more important, an approach that *would* give her maximum profit in the *long run* will do her no good if it leads to her economic ruin (treated in Chapter 11) in the short run. Some difficulties in choosing a simple criterion with which to make decisions are illustrated in the following examples.

The trader should put himself into each of the following four hypothetical situations and decide for each whether he would accept the bet.

1. He is offered a wager in which he will gain $200 if a (well-balanced) coin falls heads or lose $100 if it falls tails.

2. Her entire fortune (which took 50 years to amass) has a cash value of $5 million. She is now offered the opportunity to gain $10 million if a coin falls heads or lose her entire irreplaceable fortune of $5 million if it falls tails.

3. He has been planning a vacation this month in Florida and intends to spend all the cash he has available during that month. Assume that he now has $5000 available, which is more than ample for that purpose. He is offered a bet that will yield a profit of $5000 (which he would use for *additional* spending on his vacation) if the coin falls heads or a loss of $5000 (which would deprive him entirely of his long-planned vacation) if it falls tails.

4. She is desperate to see the Calgary Stampede. She has $5000 available in cash, but the total expenses for her and her family will amount to $8000. She is offered a chance for a profit of $5000 if the coin falls heads or a loss of $5000 if it falls tails.

The authors would accept the positions or bets in situations 1 and 4 but would say "no" in situations 2 and 3. What causes them to have different responses in situations 1 and 2? The two situations are similar in that favorable 2-to-1 money payoffs were offered when it seemed appropriate to offer even 1-to-1 money. What causes the difference in the authors' preferences? In situation 1, with equal probabilities, twice as much money can be gained as lost. In situation 2, with equal probabilities, it is also true that twice as much money can be gained as lost, but the gain of $10 million would not increase the satisfaction gained compared with the considerable dissatisfaction that would result from the loss of the entire $5 million fortune. Similarly, in situations 3 and 4, even though the money payoffs and probabilities are the same, the responses are different. These reflect the differences in the satisfaction to be gained from the money in the two different circumstances.

Apparently, in uncertain situations people do *not* act consistently with respect to their average monetary gain. They do, however, act consistently to maximize their own satisfaction. Much theoretical and experimental work has been done in this area, and useful models have been developed to measure the preferences or satisfaction that individuals exhibit for various bets and outcomes. Just as probability is merely a number (on a scale from 0 to 1) assigned to reflect the degree of optimism, so the *utility* of a bet or of an event is merely a number assigned (on *any* scale) to reflect the degree of preference or satisfaction.

The following material includes a brief discussion of these utilities along with some examples and a step-by-step procedure by which the reader can find his or her own utilities and construct a personal utility curve for futures trading (subsequently called the trading curve). The construction and interpretation of the personal trading curve will serve as a useful tool in money management and trading activities.

This chapter should be read with pencil in hand. The readers should make notes or calculations to make sure that the examples are clear to them.

UTILITY PROPERTIES

It can be shown that if a person is "rational" in the sense that he can express his preference between any two events and if he shows some measure of consistency in his preferences, then a numerical value, or utility, can be assigned to each event that will measure his satisfaction for that event; that is, of any two events, the one preferred will have a larger number (utility) assigned to it. In other words, if a person is guided entirely by his utility values, he will be acting in accord with his own true preferences. Therefore, once a person's utility values are found, they can be used to help him make rational decisions. In this chapter personal utilities are calculated and graphed in the personal trading curve. It is important to note here that each utility value reflects the preference for the particular event in the particular situation (e.g., see situations 3 and 4) at the particular time. Attitudes and preferences do change. It should also be pointed out that different people have different tastes and therefore different utility values.

It can also be shown[2] that the utility of any bet or venture to an individual will be equal to the average or expected value of his utilities for the different possible outcomes of that bet. The average or expected value is computed by adding the utilities of the various outcomes, with each utility weighted (multiplied) by the probability of the particular outcome. (As indicated earlier, these probabilities may be personal and reflect one's degree of optimism.) It is interesting to note that for a "rational" individual the utility of a bet is shown to be equal to the expected value of the utilities of the outcomes, without any assumptions or discussion of long-run effects or repeated trials. In other words, the relationship holds even if the prospect is to be faced *only once*. Utility, then, can always be computed by using ordinary probabilities and expected values.

COMPUTING PERSONAL UTILITIES

The computation of utilities, or measures of preference, is illustrated in the four examples that follow. Understanding these examples will make it possible for the reader to construct his or her own trading curve.

---

[2] John Von Neumann and Oskar Morgenstern, *The Theory of Games and Economic Behavior,* 2d ed. (Princeton, N.J.: Princeton University Press, 1947).

Example 5-1   Suppose that Mr. Merrill, a famous soybean speculator, has taken a position in the futures market and has set his objective so that if it is reached, he will gain $1500. He also has a stop set so that if the worst happens, he will lose $900. Suppose that for Mr. Merrill the utility of $1500 is 10 (the 10 is arbitrarily chosen) and the utility of $-$900 is (arbitrarily) -6; that is, $u(\$1500) = 10$ and $u(-\$900) = -6$. Assume further that Mr. Merrill believes his probability of success is ½. The utility of the trade, therefore, would merely be the average (expected value) of the utilities of the possible outcomes, that is, the sum of the utilities of the outcomes, with each utility multiplied by the probability of the particular outcome.

$$u(\text{trade}) = \tfrac{1}{2}(10) + \tfrac{1}{2}(-6) = 2$$

which would be halfway between -6 and 10, the utilities of the outcomes.

If Mr. Merrill's judgment of the probability of success were ⅔, his utility would become

$$u(\text{trade}) = \tfrac{2}{3}(10) + \tfrac{1}{3}(-6) = \tfrac{14}{3} = 4.7$$

which would be exactly ⅔ of the distance from -6 to 10.

Similarly, with a probability of success judged to be ⁹⁄₁₀, the utility of the trade would become

$$u(\text{trade}) = \tfrac{9}{10}(10) + \tfrac{1}{10}(16) = 8.4$$

which is ⁹⁄₁₀ of the distance from -6 to 10. Obviously, as the probability of success increases from 0 to 1, the utility increases from -6 (the utility of the worst outcome) to 10 (the utility of the best outcome).

In order to illustrate the difference between the expected *utility* (average of the utilities of the gains and losses) and the *expected gain* (average of the gains and losses themselves), the following example may be used.

Example 5-2   Consider a trade that, if successful, would yield a gain of $600 and, if unsuccessful, a loss of $500, where the probability of gain is .8. If the utility of a $600 gain is arbitrarily called 20 and the utility of a $500 loss, 10, the *expected utility* (or utility of the trade) is given by

$$u(\text{trade}) = .8(20) + .2(10) = 18$$

whereas the expected gain (in money) is given by

$$.8(\$600) + .2(-\$500) = \$380$$

Note that the amounts differ and, as illustrated in the four cases in the preference and utility section of this chapter, that expected gains do not necessarily reflect personal preferences as expected utilities do.

Example 5-3   In Example 5-2 the utilities of the best and worst outcomes were arbitrarily chosen to be 20 and 10, respectively. If, instead, other values had been chosen, the computed expected utilities would have been just as useful and would have reflected the same relative preferences for different bets;[3] for example, if the utilities of the best and worst outcomes had been chosen to be 1 and 0, respectively, the expected utility of the preceding example would have been

$$u(\text{trade}) = .8(1) + .2(0) = .8$$

---

[3] Two utility values (any two, e.g., for the best and worst outcomes) can be chosen arbitrarily. After they are chosen, however, all the other utility values are determined by the method of computation illustrated.

Note that when the highest and lowest utilities chosen are 1 and 0, respectively, the expected utility will always be equal to the probability of the best outcome. Such a choice of values is often made because it simplifies the computation of utility values.

Example 5-4 Utilities are similarly computed in situations in which there are *more* than two outcomes. For example, assume that a certain commodity trade could result in a payoff of $1000, $800, $500, or $200. Assume that the estimates of probabilities for the respective outcomes are .2, .1, .4, and .3. To calculate the utility of the trade, assuming that the utilities of the outcomes are

$$u(\$1000) = 22 \quad u(\$800) = 15 \quad u(\$500) = 7 \quad u(\$200) = 3$$

one merely calculates the average of the utilities; that is,

$$u(\text{trade}) = .2(22) + .1(15) + .4(7) + .3(3) = 9.6$$

In the following section the computational methods used in Examples 5-1 and 5-3 are applied to find the reader's personal trading curve.

THE PERSONAL TRADING CURVE

For the next 60 minutes prospective traders should pick a spot in which they are unlikely to be interrupted. During that time they are going to construct their own trading curves from questions they will answer during a self-administered trading profile interview (TPI). There are some ground rules that should be clear at the outset of the self-interview:

1. The TPI is *not* a test. One answer is no more correct than another. Rather, the TPI *measures* the reader's attitudes about gains and losses and about money at this point in time. The same TPI taken at a later date, especially after a large gain or loss or after a significant change in the trader's capital or income tax bracket, could well reveal a significant change in attitude. Trading curves derived from the TPI can easily measure such changes.

2. The dollar amounts risked, gained, or lost during the interview should be considered by the reader as *real* dollars with *real* purchasing power which, if lost, would represent some varying degree of pain. Lost dollars can be replaced by the reader only from savings or checking accounts, new earnings, or other sources. The pain of replacing $100 is obviously less than that of replacing $1000, and the reader's feelings should reflect that difference to *him or her*, in consideration of the total current situation.

3. The rewards to the reader should also be considered to be immediate and in cash, so that there will be virtually no lag between the time dollars are risked successfully and the ensuing payoff.

4. Many readers will be content to answer the questions in the TPI subjectively. Others will prefer to have paper and pencil handy. Either approach is satisfactory if the decisions reflect the reader's personal preferences and are not merely the result of some mechanistic computation. The reader should consider each trade and each level of risk capital separately and not relate them to preceding or sub-

sequent questions. Each question should be considered independently and answered carefully.

The personal trading curve is constructed by first choosing two possible outcomes of a trade. These outcomes are called the "best" and "worst" outcomes, and utility values of 1 and 0, respectively, are assigned to them. Then, using trades involving only those best and worst outcomes, other utilities are computed in Table 5-1 and the results plotted as a preliminary personal trading curve in Figure 5-1. For purposes of verification and improved accuracy, and to measure the consistency of the trader's decisions, additional utility values are computed in Tables 5-2 and 5-3. These values use trades with new best and worst outcomes. The results, along with those in Table 5-1, are plotted in Figure 5-2. Then, in the next section of this chapter, the trading curve is extended to include gains and losses that are larger than the initial best and worst outcomes.

Construction of a personal trading curve now proceeds in the form of a trading profile interview:

INTERVIEWER: What are the *largest* amounts you have had regular experience winning and losing on trades or investments?

TRADER: I've often had experience winning as much as $2000 on a single venture, and I've risked as much as $1000 on single trades.

The interviewer now fills out the first five of the six columns in Table 5-1. She enters $2000 and −$1000 as the best and worst outcomes on the top and bottom lines of Table 5-1 in column 6. She assigns a utility of 1 to the best outcome and enters it on every line of column 1. She also assigns 0 to the worst outcome and enters it on every line of column 2. She then fills out column 3 with a fairly

TABLE 5-1   COMPUTATION OF FIRST SET OF UTILITIES FOR TRADING CURVE

Utilities of		Probabilities of		Computed utility of trade (col. 5)	Reader's cash equivalent of trade, in dollars (col. 6)	
Best outcome (col. 1)	Worst outcome (col. 2)	Best outcome (col. 3)	Worst outcome (col. 4)			
1	0	1.0	0	1.00	2000	Best outcome
1	0	.95	.05	.95	1500	
1	0	.9	.1	.90	1250	
1	0	.8	.2	.80	1100	
1	0	.7	.3	.70	1000	
1	0	.6	.4	.60	800	Personal choices
1	0	.5	.5	.50	450	from TPI
1	0	.4	.6	.40	0	
1	0	.3	.7	.30	−400	
1	0	.2	.8	.20	−600	
1	0	.1	.9	.10	−800	
1	0	0	1.0	0	−1000	Worst outcome

uniformly spaced set of probabilities. These represent the respective probabilities of winning $2000 (the best outcome) for each of the different trades to be considered. Each line of Table 5-1 represents a separate and distinct trade. Column 4 is merely the complement of column 3. It shows the probability of *losing* $1000 (the worst outcome) for each of the trades. In column 5 the interviewer computes the utility of each trade by taking the average of the utilities (1 and 0 in each case); each utility is weighted (multiplied) by its own probability as in Example 5-3. The computation of the utility of .70 on the fifth line of Table 5-1, column 5, is made as follows:

$$1(.7) + 0(.3) = .70$$

The utility of .70 is the computed utility of the trade.

All that remains to be filled out is column 6, but filling it out properly is the essence of the trading profile interview. The trader must consider each line (trade) separately and carefully, always remaining cognizant of the four ground rules stated at the beginning of this section.

INTERVIEWER   (describing the trade indicated by line 2 of Table 5-1):   If you have a trading opportunity wherein you would either gain $2000 (best outcome) or lose $1000 (worst outcome) with probabilities .95 and .05, respectively, would you take that trade?
TRADER: Certainly! Who wouldn't?
INTERVIEWER: Obviously the trade has some worth to you. Would you pay me $800 cash for the opportunity to make that trade?
TRADER: What's going on here? You want me to hand you $800 in cash, right now, just for the opportunity to make that trade?
INTERVIEWER: If the trade ($2000 possible gain with probability .95 or $1000 possible loss with probability .05) is not worth $800 to you, forget it. If you think it is, then pay me the $800 now and enter the trade. Remember, whether you win or lose the trade, you don't get the $800 back. It's mine, once you give it to me.
TRADER: The trade is good. I'm *almost* (.95) certain to win the $2000. I'll pay the $800 and take the trade.
INTERVIEWER: In other words you feel that the cash value of the trade is *more* than $800?
TRADER: Right.
INTERVIEWER: I'm glad that's settled. Now, instead of $800 would you pay me $1200 to enter the same trade?
TRADER   (after some painful introspection and colorful rhetoric):   Yes.
INTERVIEWER: Then you feel that the trade is worth *more* than $1200 to you. Now, instead of $1200, would you pay $1400?
TRADER: That's a tough question; $1400 is a lot of cash to pay for that opportunity. On the other hand, that trade would yield $2000 with a very high probability (.95) and *almost* no chance (.05) of the $1000 loss. OK. I'll pay $1400, but not much more.
INTERVIEWER: You have just told me that the trade is worth *more* than $1400 to you. Would you pay $1600?
TRADER: Definitely not!
INTERVIEWER: Obviously the trade is worth *less* than $1600 to you, and in your preceding statement we decided it was worth *more* than $1400. How about $1500?
TRADER   (after much introspection):   That's difficult to decide. Maybe I would pay $1500 and maybe not. I'm sort of indifferent at that price.
INTERVIEWER: That's fine. Then the value of that trade to you is approximately the same

as the value of $1500 to you. Therefore, your utility for the $1500 cash is the same as your utility for that trade, already computed on line 2, column 5, as .95.

At this point the interviewer enters $1500 in column 6 of line 2 in Table 5-1. Note that the $1500 in column 6 is entered next to its utility, .95, in column 5.

By a similar careful and thoughtful process each line of column 6 is filled in. Each line represents a separate and distinct trade, with its own unique probability (column 3) of success. For each distinct trade in the table the best ($2000) and worst (−$1000) outcomes remain the same.

To illustrate the computation of utility for a negative amount of money, that portion of the trading profile interview (TPI) applicable to line 9 is also shown.

INTERVIEWER (now describing the trade indicated by line 9 of Table 5-1): Assume that you have a trading opportunity in which you would gain $2000 (best outcome) or lose $1000 (worst outcome) with probabilities .3 and .7, respectively. Would you take that trade?

TRADER: You mean the probability of winning $2000 is only .3? Why, I have more than twice the chance (.7) of losing $1000. That's not an opportunity. What do you take me for?

INTERVIEWER: Some people might welcome that opportunity. Obviously you have different preferences. For you that trade has a negative cash value. Would you take the trade if I handed you $100 right now? You keep the $100 win or lose, but if you accept the $100, then you must go through with the trade.

TRADER: Keep your $100.

INTERVIEWER: How about $300?

TRADER: That's better but still not enough to induce me to take that risky trade.

INTERVIEWER: Would you take the trade if I give you $400 to keep, whether you win or lose the trade?

TRADER: That's tempting. Maybe I would, but not a penny less than $400.

INTERVIEWER: That's fine. Then you would require a cash payment of at least $400 as an inducement to take the trade. That trade has a negative value for you, −$400 cash. Therefore, your utility for −$400 cash is the same as your utility for that trade, previously computed on line 9, column 5, as .30.

At this point the interviewer enters the −$400 on line 9 of column 6 in Table 5-1. Note that the −$400 in column 6 is entered next to its utility, .30, in column 5.

With the completion of Table 5-1, a preliminary trading curve is constructed by plotting the numbers in column 6 on the horizontal axis versus the numbers in column 5 on the vertical axis. Such a plot from Table 5-1 is shown in Figure 5-1. If a smooth curve were drawn through the points in that figure, it would show some interesting preliminary results. For values of $1000 to $2000 the curve is concave downward. The reader can examine Figure 5-1 in that region to see that

each added $100 increment of cash adds successively less utility value to the total.

For values of $0 to $1000, on the other hand, the trading curve is concave upward, and in that region, each additional $100 increment adds successively

more utility value to the total. The trader has quite different attitudes toward gains and losses in these two regions.

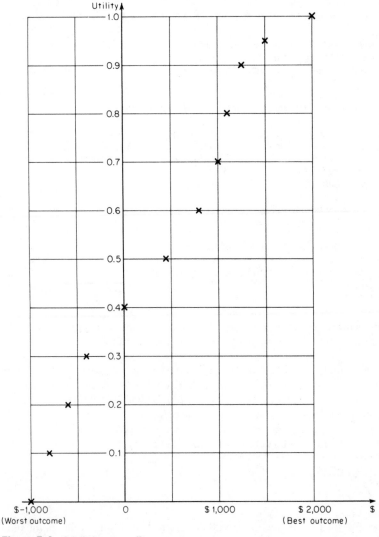

Figure 5-1   Preliminary trading curve.

For values of $-\$400$ to $-\$1000$ the trading curve seems to be linear. In that

region successively larger losses decrease the utility proportionately; for example, the decrease in utility going from $-\$400$ to $-\$600$ is the same as the decrease in utility going from $-\$600$ to $-\$800$ or from $-\$800$ to $-\$1000$. The trader's reactions to possible gains and losses in this region, where the trading curve is linear, will be quite different from the reactions in regions where the trading curve is concave upward or downward. Analyses of these differences are made in the following sections of this chapter.

For purposes of verification and improved accuracy, and to measure the consistency of the trader's decisions, additional utility values for some of the same dollar amounts are again computed. The results are shown in Tables 5-2 and 5-3. The computations are made from trades using new "best" and "worst" outcomes. The new results, along with the prior information from Table 5-1, are plotted in Figure 5-2.

To proceed with Table 5-2 the interviewer must first choose new "best" and "worst" outcomes for which the utilities are known. Any two values from column 6 of Table 5-1 will do. Assume that she chooses $800 as the new "best" outcome and $-\$800$ as the "worst." The utility of $800 is shown as .60 in column 5 of Table 5-1. The utility of $-\$800$ is shown as .10. These amounts are then entered in Table 5-2. The utility .60 of the new best outcome is entered in column 1 and the utility .10 of the new worst outcome in column 2. The outcomes themselves,

TABLE 5-2　COMPUTATION OF SECOND SET OF UTILITIES FOR TRADING CURVE

Utilities* of		Probabilities† of		Computed utility of trade (col. 5)	Reader's cash equivalent of trade, in dollars (col. 6)	
Best outcome (col. 1)	Worst outcome (col. 2)	Best outcome (col. 3)	Worst outcome (col. 4)			
.60	.10	1.0	0	.60	800	Best outcome
.60	.10	.95	.05	.575	650	
.60	.10	.9	.1	.55	550	
.60	.10	.8	.2	.50	400	
.60	.10	.7	.3	.45	250	
.60	.10	.6	.4	.40	150	Personal choices from TPI
.60	.10	.5	.5	.35	-100	
.60	.10	.4	.6	.30	-400	
.60	.10	.3	.7	.25	-450	
.60	.10	.2	.8	.20	-500	
.60	.10	.1	.9	.15	-600	
.60	.10	0	1.0	.10	-800	Worst outcome

* From Table 5-1.

† Same as in Table 5-1.

$800 and −$800, are entered on the first and last lines, respectively, of column 6 in Table 5-2. Then, as before, columns 3 and 4 are filled in with a set (it may be the same as before) of fairly uniformly spaced probabilities. Again, as before, in column 5 the interviewer computes the utility of each trade by taking the average of the utilities (this time .60 and .10 in each case), where each utility is weighted by its respective probability. The computation of the utility .55 in the third line of Table 5-2, column 5, is made as follows:

$$.60(.9) + .10(.1) = .55$$

The utility of .55 is the computed utility of the trade.

All that remains to be completed is column 6, and completing it is done by using the trader's profile interview, as before, in which the trader must again separately and carefully consider each line (trade) while remaining cognizant of the four ground rules stated at the beginning of this section. When Table 5-2 is completed in this manner, the results are plotted (column 6 on the horizontal axis versus column 5 on the vertical axis) as "2"s in the trading curve (Figure 5-2). (The results of Table 5-1, which were plotted in Figure 5-1, are plotted as "1"s in Figure 5-2.)

Further verification is achieved by completing Table 5-3 in a similar manner. New best and worst outcomes of $1500 and −$400 are chosen, again from Table 5-1, with their respective utilities, .95 and .30. [Note that this range of values ($1500 to −$400) is in the upper part of the original range ($2000 to −$1000), whereas the previous range of outcomes ($800 to −$800) was in the lower portion of the original range.] Table 5-3 is then completed, as were the preceding tables, and the results are entered as "3"s in the trading curve (Figure 5-2).

TABLE 5-3 COMPUTATION OF THIRD SET OF UTILITIES FOR TRADING CURVE

Utilities* of		Probabilities† of		Computed utility of trade (col. 5)	Reader's cash equivalent of trade, in dollars (col. 6)	
Best outcome (col. 1)	Worst outcome (col. 2)	Best outcome (col. 3)	Worst outcome (col. 4)			
						} Best outcome
.95	.30	1.0	0	.95	1500	
.95	.30	.95	.05	.9175	1200	
.95	.30	.9	.1	.885	1150	
.95	.30	.8	.2	.82	1100	
.95	.30	.7	.3	.755	800	
.95	.30	.6	.4	.69	600	Personal choices from TPI
.95	.30	.5	.5	.625	500	
.95	.30	.4	.6	.56	400	
.95	.30	.3	.7	.495	100	
.95	.30	.2	.8	.43	−100	
.95	.30	.1	.9	.365	−200	
.95	.30	0	1.0	.30	−400	} Worst outcome

* From Table 5-1.
† Same as in Table 5-1.

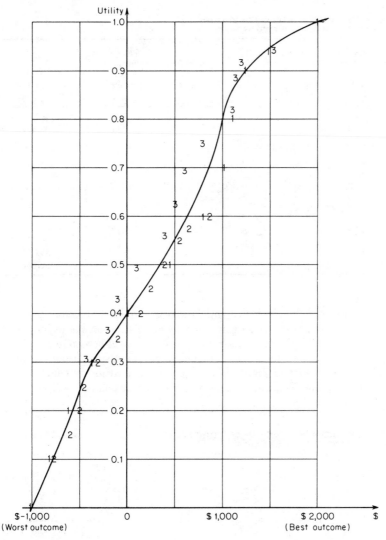

Figure 5-2 Trading curve.

Figure 5-2 represents the completed personal trading curve of the trader for gains and losses between $2000 and −$1000. The general shape can be more readily seen by drawing a freehand *smooth* curve, passing "near" most of the points. The next sections include comments on this curve and some analysis and interpretation of personal trading curves in general.

Tables 5-4, 5-5, and 5-6 are provided so that the reader can complete them during the self-administered trading profile interview (TPI). The reader should be sure to follow the ground rules discussed at the beginning of this section. The

**TABLE 5-4 COMPUTATION OF FIRST SET OF UTILITIES
FOR TRADING CURVE TO BE COMPLETED BY READER**

Utilities of		Probabilities of		Computed utility of trade (col. 5)	Reader's cash equivalent of trade, in dollars (col. 6)	
Best outcome (col. 1)	Worst outcome (col. 2)	Best outcome (col. 3)	Worst outcome (col. 4)			
1	0	1.0	0	1.00	2000	} Best outcome
1	0	.95	.05	.95		
1	0	.9	.1	.90		
1	0	.8	.2	.80		
1	0	.7	.3	.70		
1	0	.6	.4	.60		} Personal choices from TPI
1	0	.5	.5	.50		
1	0	.4	.6	.40		
1	0	.3	.7	.30		
1	0	.2	.8	.20		
1	0	.1	.9	.10		
1	0	0	1.0	0	−1000	} Worst outcome

reader should feel free, however, to change the best and worst outcomes to those that represent the relatively large gains and losses that *he or she* experiences regularly. Whatever the best and worst outcomes are should be entered in Table 5-4 and Figure 5-3. After the tables are completed, the results (from all three tables) should be plotted in Figure 5-3, which is provided for that purpose. A smooth curve can then be drawn to pass near most of the points.

**TABLE 5-5 COMPUTATION OF SECOND SET OF UTILITIES FOR
TRADING CURVE TO BE COMPLETED BY READER**

Utilities of		Probabilities of		Computed utility of trade (col. 5)	Reader's cash equivalent of trade, in dollars (col. 6)	
Best outcome (col. 1)	Worst outcome (col. 2)	Best outcome (col. 3)	Worst outcome (col. 4)			
		1.0	0			} Best outcome
		.95	.05			
		.9	.1			
		.8	.2			
		.7	.3			
		.6	.4			} Personal choices from TPI
		.5	.5			
		.4	.6			
		.3	.7			
		.2	.8			
		.1	.9			
		0	1.0			} Worst outcome

**TABLE 5-6 COMPUTATION OF THIRD SET OF UTILITIES FOR
TRADING CURVE TO BE COMPLETED BY READER**

Utilities of		Probabilities of		Computed	Reader's cash equivalent
Best outcome (col. 1)	Worst outcome (col. 2)	Best outcome (col. 3)	Worst outcome (col. 4)	utility of trade (col. 5)	of trade, in dollars (col. 6)
		1.0	0		} Best outcome
		.95	.05		
		.9	.1		
		.8	.2		
		.7	.3		
		.6	.4		} Personal choices from TPI
		.5	.5		
		.4	.6		
		.3	.7		
		.2	.8		
		.1	.9		
		0	1.0		} Worst outcome

In the next section the boundaries of the trading curve are extended beyond the original best and worst outcomes so that the reader can also get a graphic interpretation of personal attitudes toward the gains and losses that are larger than those with which he or she has had regular experience.

EXTENDING THE TRADING CURVE FOR LARGER GAINS AND LOSSES

In this section the trading curve is completed. It not only includes that portion of the curve illustrated in Figure 5-2 but is extended to include gains larger than $2000 and losses larger than $1000. The interpretation of the shape and scatter of points for these larger values will yield significant information concerning the sizes and kinds of trades that should be accepted or avoided. Such information can be invaluable to the trader as well as to the trader's broker or adviser.

As a first step in extending the curve, Figure 5-4 is prepared with gains and losses ranging from − $3000 to $5000 and with the utility scale ranging from − 3 to 2. The next step is to plot all the points from Figure 5-2 (or from Tables 5-1, 5-2, and 5-3 if it is easier) on this new scale of Figure 5-4. Then computations are made in Tables 5-7 and 5-8 to determine utilities for larger gains and losses, also to be plotted in Figure 5-4.

Utilities for Larger Gains

In Table 5-7 utilities are computed for large *gains* of $2500, $3500, and $5000. Each of these utilities is computed three times in order to give some information about the trader's consistency in making decisions. As in the preceding trading

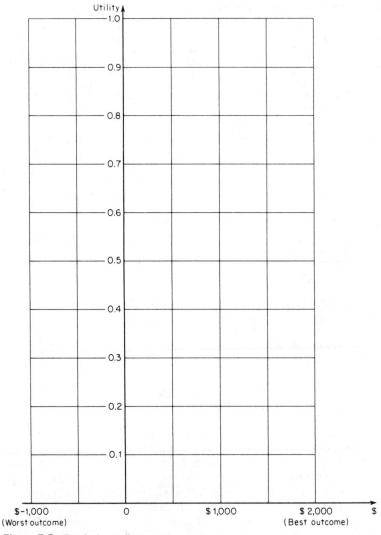

Figure 5-3   Reader's trading curve.

profile interview (TPI), each of the nine trades in Table 5-7 is to be separately considered by the trader. He must consider the possible gain G, the possible loss L, and the probability p of a winning trade. After sufficient examination of this information, the trader, as before, decides on an amount of cash C which for him, at this moment, is the equivalent of the trade. For example, in considering the second trade (gain $3500, loss $0 probability .50) in Table 5-7 the TPI could proceed as follows:

INTERVIEWER: Would you accept a trade in which you would gain $3500 with probability .50 or lose $0 with probability .50?

TRADER: Certainly I would. There's no risk in that one.

INTERVIEWER: Would you pay me $500 for that trading opportunity?

TRADER: Yes.

INTERVIEWER: Would you pay me $1000 for that opportunity?

TRADER: Probably not, but maybe a little less.

INTERVIEWER: How about $900?

TRADER: I think I would be indifferent about paying $900 for that trading opportunity. I would not pay $1000, and I would be willing to pay $800, but I don't know about $900.

The amount of $900 is then recorded in the Cash C column of Table 5-7 for that trade. The utility .74 of $900 is then taken (approximated) from Figure 5-2 and written in the $u(C)$ column next to the $900. Similarly, the utility .40 of the $0 loss is taken from Figure 5-2. The desired utility 1.08 of the $3500 gain is then computed by using the formula in Table 5-7 and its footnote.

The interview and computation should proceed in this manner through each of the other trades in Table 5-7. For example, in the sixth trade the interviewer would begin as always by first asking the trader if he would accept the trade ($5000 possible gain with probability .40 versus $400 possible loss with probability .60). If the trader accepts, the interviewer proceeds as before to find the largest amount

TABLE 5-7   COMPUTATION OF UTILITIES FOR LARGER GAINS

Trade					Reader's cash equivalent of trade	
Gain, in dollars G	Computed* utility $u(G)$	Loss, in dollars L	Utility from Fig. 5-2 $u(L)$	Probability of winning p	Cash, in dollars C	Utility from Fig. 5-2 $u(C)$
	$\dfrac{u(C) - .4(1 - p)^*}{p}$					.80
						.74
2500	.97	0	.40	.70	1000	.70
3500	1.08	0	.40	.50	900	
5000	1.15	0	.40	.40	800†	
	$\dfrac{u(C) - .3(1 - p)^*}{p}$					
2500	1.10	−400	.30	.50	800	.70
3500	1.30	−400	.30	.50	1000	.80
5000	1.75	−400	.30	.40	1200†	.88
	$\dfrac{u(C)^*}{p}$					
2500	1.00	−1000	0	.40	0	.40
3500	1.40	−1000	0	.40	500	.56
5000	1.33	−1000	0	.30	0	.40

* Utility of gain $= u(G) = \dfrac{u(C) - u(L) \cdot (1 - p)}{p}$, where G, L, p, and C are as indicated in the table headings.

† Example of obviously inconsistent decisions (most inconsistencies are much less obvious).

he would be willing to *pay* for that trading opportunity. That amount is then entered in the Cash column, and the utilities of the Cash C column and the Loss L column are estimated from Figure 5-2. The desired utility 1.75 is computed from the formula in Table 5-7.

After all nine utility values $u(G)$ of the large gains are computed in Table 5-7, they are plotted in Figure 5-4 as X's. The trading curve can now be extended to the right to $5000, and a *smooth* curve can be drawn through the points in Figure 5-4.

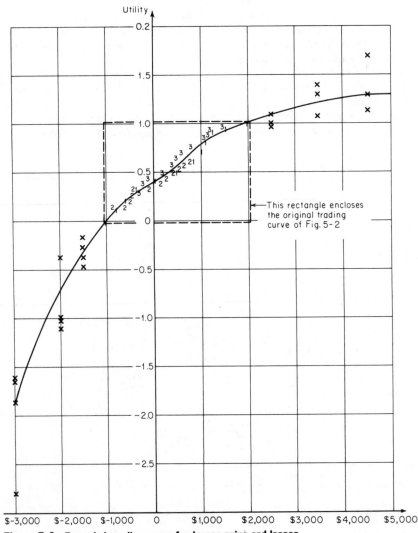

Figure 5-4   Extended trading curve for larger gains and losses.

TABLE 5-8 COMPUTATION OF UTILITIES FOR LARGER LOSSES

		Trade			Reader's cash equivalent of trade	
Gain, in dollars G	Utility from Figs. 5-2 and 5-4 u(G)	Loss, in dollars L	Computed* utility u(L)	Probability of winning p	Cash, in dollars C	Utility from Fig. 5-2 u(C)
			$-\dfrac{1.25p - u(C)^*}{1 - p}$			
3500	1.25	− 1500	− .13	.50	500	.56
3500	1.25	− 2000	− .37	.50	100	.44
3500	1.25	− 3000	− 1.87	.60	− 1000	0
			$-\dfrac{p - u(C)^*}{1 - p}$			
2000	1	− 1500	− .47	.70	500	.56
2000	1	− 2000	− 1.00	.70	0	.40
2000	1	− 3000	− 1.65	.80	200	.47
			$-\dfrac{.75p - u(C)^*}{1 - p}$			
1000	.80	− 1500	− .53	.70	0	.40
1000	.80	− 2000	− 1.20	.80	0	.40
1000	.80	− 3000	− 1.60	.80	− 200	.32
			$-\dfrac{.56p - u(C)^*}{1 - p}$			
500	.56	− 1500	− .37	.70	− 400	.28
500	.56	− 2000	− 1.09	.80	− 500	.23
500	.56	− 3000	− 2.74	.90	− 500	.23

* Utility of loss = $u(L) = -\dfrac{u(G) \cdot p - u(C)}{1 - p}$, where G, L, p, and C are as indicated in the table headings.

Note how these points are spread out at $3500 and even more at $5000, especially compared with the small spread at any particular dollar value between the original boundaries ($2000 and − $1000). This spread indicates inconsistencies in the trader's decisions. Most of them are not readily apparent, but two in Table 5-7 are. Pointing these out will give the reasons for large differences in some of the computed utility values. The first inconsistency occurs between the third and sixth trades in Table 5-7. Both offer the same gain of $5000 with the same probability .4 of winning. The third trade is better than the sixth, however, because the loss is $0 rather than $400, yet the trader has indicated that he is willing to pay more ($1200) for the sixth trade than ($800) for the third. A similar inconsistency exists between the decisions on the second and fifth trades. Because of his tendency toward inconsistent decisions in trades involving potential gains greater than $2500, this trader should plan such trades with great care.

Utilities for Larger Losses

In Table 5-8 utilities are computed for large *losses* of $1500, $2000, and $3000. Each of these utilities is computed four times, and then all the utilities are plotted in Figure 5-4. As before, each of the 12 trades is treated separately by considering its gain G, its loss L, and its probability p of success. Using that information, the trader (perhaps with the help of an interviewer) decides on an amount of cash C which, for him, is equivalent to the trade.

Consideration of the ninth trade (gain \$1000, loss \$3000, probability .80) in Table 5-8 begins with the interviewer asking the trader if he will accept the trade. If the trader answers "no," then the interviewer may ask if he will accept the trade if given an inducement of, say, \$500. An affirmative answer will bring forth a lesser offer. The interviewer will proceed in this manner until she finds the smallest amount the trader will accept as an inducement for him to proceed with the trade. In Table 5-8 for the *ninth* trade that amount is − \$200. It is then recorded in the Cash C column of Table 5-8 for that trade. The utility .32 of − \$200 is taken from Figure 5-2 and written in the $u(C)$ column next to the − \$200. Similarly, the utility .80 of the \$1000 gain is taken from Figure 5-2. (For the first three trades in Table 5-8 the utility of the \$3500 gain is approximated from Figure 5-4.) The desired utility − 1.60 of the \$3000 loss is then computed by using the formula in Table 5-8 and its footnote.

After all 12 utility values $u(L)$ of the large losses are computed in Table 5-8, they are plotted in Figure 5-4 as X's. This extends the trading curve to the left to − \$3000, and the smooth curve of Figure 5-4 can also be extended to the left and downward.

Note that the points in Figure 5-4 are slightly spread out at − \$1500, much more spread out at − \$2000, and considerably more at − \$3000. This shows the growing inconsistencies in the trader's decisions as his losses grow large. He would do well to plan carefully when considering trades in which he will risk more than \$1500.

Comments on the Extended Trading Curve

An analysis and interpretation of trading curves follows in the next section of this chapter and in the notes from a trader. It would be useful, however, to comment on the completed trading curve shown in Figure 5-4.

From the aforementioned discussion of inconsistencies and the spread of points on the curve, it can be seen from Figure 5-4 that the trader makes uniformly consistent decisions on trades involving gains as high as \$2500 and losses as large as \$1500. Beyond those values extra care in planning is necessary. As experience is acquired, these boundaries could be expanded considerably. Periodic construction of trading curves will note such expansion.

The general shape of the curve is also of great interest. From small losses of \$200 to gains as high as \$1000 the curve is slightly concave upward. This indicates

that the trader's utility for gains of those amounts increases at an increasing rate. The trader therefore has a slight tendency to accept even an unfavorable (negative expected value) trade in those amounts. Those with such tendencies are sometimes called "risk lovers." Many traders act as risk lovers for small gains and losses.

As our trader's *gains* increase beyond $1000, the shape of the trading curve becomes concave downward, which indicates a decreasing utility for incremental

gains. The trader's decisions in regard to larger trades will be more conservative, and he will have a tendency to take only favorable (positive expected value) trades. Such are the actions of a "risk averter." Many traders act that way for large gains and losses.

For *losses* greater than $200 our trader's curve is also concave downward, in-

dicating that as losses grow, the trader's pain (dissatisfaction) increases at an increasing rate. He abhors large losses and has a tendency to avoid risking much capital on any one trade. If he is convinced that a trade is going badly, he will quickly close the position and take his loss to avoid a larger loss.

Tables 5-9 and 5-10 and Figure 5-5 are provided so that the reader can complete

**TABLE 5-9   COMPUTATION OF UTILITIES FOR LARGER GAINS
TO BE COMPLETED BY READER**

		Trade			Reader's cash equivalent of trade	
Gain, in dollars G	Computed* utility $u(G)$	Loss, in dollars L	Utility from Fig. 5-3 $u(L)$	Probability of winning p	Cash, in dollars C	Utility from Fig. 5-3 $u(C)$
2500		0		.70		
3500		0		.50		
5000		0		.40		
2500		−400		.50		
3500		−400		.50		
5000		−400		.40		
2500		−1000		.40		
3500		−1000		.40		
5000		−1000		.30		

* Utility of gain = $u(G) = \dfrac{u(C) \; - \; u(L) \cdot (1 \; - \; p)}{p}$, where G, L, p, and C are as indicated in the table headings.

**TABLE 5-10 COMPUTATION OF UTILITIES FOR LARGER LOSSES
TO BE COMPLETED BY READER**

		Trade			Reader's cash equivalent of trade	
Gain, in dollars G	Utility from Figs. 5-3 and 5-5 $u(G)$	Loss, in dollars L	Computed* utility $u(L)$	Probability of winning p	Cash, in dollars C	Utility from Fig. 5-3 $u(C)$
3500		−1500		.50		
3500		−2000		.50		
3500		−3000		.60		
2000		−1500		.70		
2000		−2000		.70		
2000		−3000		.80		
1000		−1500		.70		
1000		−2000		.80		
1000		−3000		.80		
500		−1500		.70		
500		−2000		.80		
500		−3000		.90		

* Utility of loss $= u(L) = -\dfrac{u(G) \cdot p - u(C)}{1 - p}$, where G, L, p, and C are as indicated in the table headings.

the personal trading curve and, by using the information in this and the next section, analyze the results.

ANALYSIS AND INTERPRETATION OF THE TRADING CURVE

Scatter of Points and Choice of Best and Worst Outcomes

Widely scattered points within the original boundaries of his trading curve reflect inconsistencies in the trader's decisions. These inconsistencies result typically from one of two causes. The first is usually easy to rectify. It comes about because of the superficial evaluation of some of the trading opportunities presented in the table. Correction involves careful reevaluation of some of the trades.

If, after reevaluation, a wide scatter remains, it may be indicative of the second cause of inconsistencies, which is related to the boundaries (best and worst outcomes) chosen. The boundaries should be close to the maximum gain or loss *regularly* achieved. If both best gain and worst loss are too small, the trading curve often approximates a straight line and the scatter of points is usually small. In this case the boundaries should be moved farther apart and the tables reevaluated. If the curve is still linear, especially if the points are reasonably spread, it is good evidence that it is the true shape of the curve, not merely the result of improper boundaries.

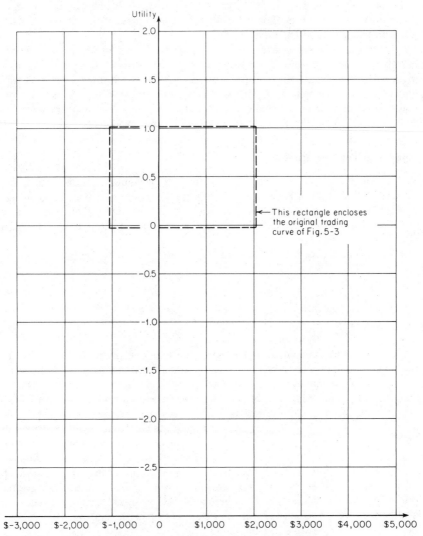

Figure 5-5   Reader's extended trading curve for larger gains and losses.

If either the best gain or the worst loss is too large, the points on the trading curve may be widely scattered and not fit any smooth curve. This often results if the subject has had no real experience with gains or losses of the magnitude that he is graphing, in which case bringing the offending boundary in toward the other will enable him to construct a set of points that will fit a smooth curve reasonably well.

When the trading curve is extended to include larger gains and losses, widely scattered points still indicate inconsistent decisions. For these large amounts, however, the scatter pattern yields valuable information. It helps to define upper limits to the trader's risks and objectives if he wants to act rationally and consistently in planning and executing trades.

Curves with excessive scatter may be of value to a broker attempting to evaluate her client's ability to think critically about expected gains and losses. An assessment of the client's attitudes toward gains and losses would supplement the usual questions about his capital, savings, and insurance and yield more detailed information. An analysis of the shape and scatter of points would help the broker to advise the client on the sizes and types of trades and positions to take.

Shape of Trading Curve

When a smooth (trading) curve is drawn through the computed utilities, different regions of that trading curve can be identified as concave downward, concave upward, or approximately linear. Sometimes the entire trading curve may have one shape, and sometimes different regions within the same curve have different shapes.

A curve that is concave downward indicates that successive constant amounts

of gain add smaller and smaller increments to the trader's utility (satisfaction). In the region in which his trading curve has that configuration (a) the trader would prefer to keep his money rather than take fair (or unfavorable) bets,[4] and (b) if he were forced to take a fair bet, he would prefer smaller fair bets to larger ones. A person with this attitude toward gains and losses is a risk averter. Most persons are risk averters for large enough sums of money. As indicated above, a risk averter will avoid unfavorable or fair bets. Depending on the degree of risk aversion (concavity of the curve), he may even avoid slightly favorable trades. He will take moderately favorable trades but not large positions, preferring instead to keep some cash or to diversify. Only for extremely favorable bets will the risk averter prefer large positions. The latter temptation should be resisted, however, because of the increased probability of ruin that can accompany increasingly larger positions. This topic is treated in Chapter 11.

A curve that is concave upward indicates that successive constant amounts of

---

[4] A fair bet is one whose average or expected value is zero. An unfavorable bet has a negative expected value. A favorable bet has a positive expected value.

gain add larger and larger increments to the trader's utility (satisfaction). For the amounts of money for which his trading curve has that configuration (*a*) the trader will prefer fair (or favorable) bets to keeping his money, and (*b*) he will prefer larger fair bets to smaller ones. A person with this attitude toward gains and losses is a risk lover. Many traders are risk lovers, especially for small amounts of money. The risk lover will take fair or favorable trades and, in fact, will prefer large positions. He may even take them in slightly unfavorable trades. Of course, if a trade is sufficiently unfavorable, the risk lover will keep his cash and not trade. Those two situations express his preferences—all or nothing. He prefers not to diversify and would prefer large positions. A risk lover who trades often and follows his preferences has a high probability of ruin because he will often take large and sometimes unfavorable positions. He should be careful to enter only favorable trades, and the size of his positions should be consistent with a low probability of ultimate ruin. The principles of money management, as discussed in Chapter 11, are most important to the risk lover.

A trading curve that is linear indicates that successive constant amounts of gain

add proportional increments to the trader's utility (satisfaction). For the region in which his curve has that configuration the trader will accept favorable trades, decline unfavorable trades, and be indifferent to the size of fair bets. In summary, the person with this trading curve will always prefer to maximize the mathematical expectation of *gain* (because doing so will also maximize his utility). Maximizing the average gain is good in the long run, but even this trader must be aware of the probability of ruin to give himself a better chance of reaching the "long run."

Figure 5-6 represents five different risk attitudes in the continuum from one extreme to the other. From left to right the curves are characterized by an increasing preference for risk.

It is important to note that the risk attitudes, and therefore the trading curve, of an individual can change for a number of reasons, including additional experience, gains or losses, changes in capital, changes in the personal income tax rate bracket, and loss of income source. This can be shown dramatically by comparing trading curves prepared both before and after a large gain or loss or a series of gains and losses. The trader would do well to prepare new trading curves at

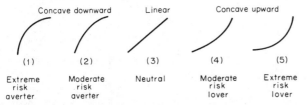

Figure 5-6   Trading curves representing different risk attitudes.

regular intervals so that they can be compared with previous ones and interpreted. The preparation and interpretation of a trading curve, after the first one, takes little time and can be an important step toward successful money management in the futures game.

NOTES FROM A TRADER

The concept of utility may appear academic to some, but it actually explains much of what makes one person act differently from others under similar circumstances. Two people may react completely differently, yet each is acting in a manner that is right for him. One may risk an important amount of money trying for an even greater amount, whereas another would not even consider risking what he has. The first is not necessarily bold or irresponsible (depending on whether he wins or loses his big bet), nor is the other wisely cautious or cowardly; they merely have different utilities for gaining or losing money. There are other utilities, not discussed in detail here, that also account for trading decisions. There is utility for time, for example. One person may wish to devote many of her waking hours to making more money, whereas another may feel that her time should better be spent for other activities more important to her. There are different utilities for avoiding pressure, so there are those who would forgo making more money because they do not wish to pay the price in sleepless nights and spoiled weekends waiting breathlessly for markets to open.

It is the wise individuals who make an honest effort to understand themselves well enough to give proper credit for their accomplishments where due and proper blame for their failures as well. Students in school almost invariably say "I got an A" and "He gave me an F." Such students, later in life, might say "I called that corn market perfectly" and "My broker sure touted me a miserable hog position" or "I wanted to get out and my broker wouldn't let me." Such foolishness may be a little soothing for traders' morale in the short run, but, unfortunately, it does not help them understand themselves, which is the first step to improved trading.

The trader's personal trading curve can give insights to possible biases which, if not overcome, can lead to poor decision making. The trader with biases is not unique. However, the trader who recognizes personal biases and controls them with a well-conceived plan to avoid impairing trading results is a member of a select group.

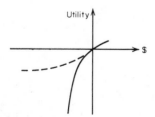

Figure 5-7

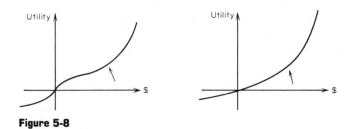

Figure 5-8

The authors have noted some predispositions following some experience with administering the TPI:

1. An exceptionally large scatter of points at any dollar level for gains or losses may indicate enough inconsistency to suggest that complete trading plans should be made during periods when the markets are closed to avoid accepting levels of risk and reward that are incompatible with the trader's feelings (assuming that the trader understands the game).

2. The trading curve may bend sharply and flatten at an extremely low dollar level. This indicates that increased dollar gains beyond that point do not occupy a high priority in the trader's value system. A person with such a curve might first question whether she should be a trader at all. If she concludes that the curve is shaped as it is because of her own inexperience and she still wants to try her hand at trading, she could begin by trading spread positions or commodities with less than average volatility until her confidence grows enough to change her attitude and her curve so that it does not turn downward so sharply.

3. The shape of the trading curve in the "loss" region is extremely important. In Figure 5-7 the *solid* line showing the curve in the loss area reveals that the person described suffers acute pain even from relatively small losses. He would find it easy to decide on a stop-loss point, enter an order at that point, and feel little or no temptation to change it. On the other hand, the person with the curve indicated by the *dashed* line would feel little pain from even relatively large losses. This might sound good, but pain in trading is like most pain in that it is nature's way of warning that all is not well. Such a person is likely to let losses run, either ignoring them or rationalizing them; he will suffer disaster sooner or later. A broker who notes these tendencies in a client should encourage use of a stop-loss procedure or recommend that the client not make his own trading decisions.

4. The trading curves in Figure 5-8 denote a quality that can best be described as greed. The owners of such curves may be rational risk averters or mild risk lovers in the lower dollar values, but they reach a point (of sharp upward curvature) at which they are seized by a consuming desire to "shoot the works." Their types are frequently seen at the casino, where up to a point, say $250, they play by risking small increments of their total capital. Above that point they are suddenly possessed by a fever that demands higher and higher risks, regardless of the

probabilities of success. Their counterparts are the traders who chortle happily as they talk about pyramiding their profits into amounts beyond the dreams of avarice. A sensible alternative for a trader so predisposed is to have a managed account (preferably an account managed by someone who has studied this book thoroughly) or to trade so lightly that the fun involved in the activity is greater than the cost of playing the game.

6

Approaches to Trade Selection: Fundamentals

> *"Decide, v.i. To succumb to the preponderance*
> *of one set of influences over another set."*
> AMBROSE BIERCE
> *The Devil's Dictionary*

DECISION MAKING

Introduction

It is popular among traders to conclude that if they provide capital and nerve, it is only necessary to acquire a reliable source of good trades to achieve great success in the futures markets. It is additionally popular to accept as truth several conclusions that are at best questionable but which, in truth, may be useless, fanciful, or downright false. Neither this book nor any other is able to provide all the answers leading to profitable trade selection, but the reader may be well served by the suggestion of some of the more important questions.

Readers who make an effort to supplement what is presented here may be well advised to beware of articulate but biased sources. This is particularly true when such sources justify their conclusions without evidence, with inadequate samples, or with claims of proprietary (undisclosed) methods or results.

Some brokers are customer-oriented, disclose the truth as they know it, make no material omissions of facts, and render honest and efficient service. Others exaggerate, imply market knowledge which may actually be of little or no value, or may indicate trading results for their clienteles or their own accounts which differ markedly from the true results.

Some services, advisers, and account, fund, or pool managers have developed approaches to trading based upon successful experience in enough kinds of markets over long enough periods to justify their efforts to attract trading capital. Others have had limited or narrow experience, which does not justify risking other people's money. Still others conceal or actually misrepresent their experience and trading results.

Some writers for financial magazines and newspapers write scholarly articles about futures which can provide traders with valuable insights and information. Other such writers demonstrate a capacity for writing which vastly exceeds their capacity for thinking. It is not asking too much of writers to support opinions with evidence or to disclose the existence of contrary opinions with equal or greater believability.

There are many reputable people who are engaged in the futures industry in one way or another. Some of them provide information and services of considerable value. Others provide information or services with little, no, or even negative value. Readers are not being advised here to be distrustful or cynical; rather, they are being advised to be alert to the wide range of the quality of advice and service available in the futures industry, investigate before they invest, and try to make certain that their interests are being adequately considered.

The Efficient Market—A Reprise

Whether the markets are efficient and, if so, to what degree has been argued for years. The argument will probably rage forever. The fact that the answer is unknown, however, does not mean that the question should not be faced.

Those who believe that the market is completely efficient are best advised to buy and hold carefully selected portfolios or trade in indexes which act as portfolios. Those who believe that there is efficiency but that it is incomplete should make certain that the information upon which they are basing their trades is valuable, not generally known, and legally acted upon. Those who believe that the market is not efficient at all should be certain that their conclusion is based upon something beyond hope, idle conjecture, or the advice of others which might be based upon self-serving motivations.

The amount of truly scholarly research pointing to strong and possibly complete efficiency is almost overwhelming. Detractors of this conclusion are all too often uttering opinions with insufficient evidence to support their positions or to counter the evidence offered by those with opposing points of view. It is popular to dismiss those who believe in strongly efficient markets either as people who live in ivory towers or as people who tried to profit in the markets, failed, and are trying to explain away their failure.

All those who believe in the efficiency of markets do not live in ivory towers. Some who believe in a market's efficiency have acquired considerable wealth in that same market. Some who most loudly disparage this approach to the nature of markets include those with little or unfavorable experience themselves.

Specific Approaches

It is popular to indicate that there are two general approaches to trade selection: fundamental and technical. This is often followed by an implication that traders tend to select one or the other of these and use it exclusively or predominantly.

Actually, there are more than merely these two approaches. Some traders react primarily to subjective feelings about markets based upon their judgment. Of course, such traders may well be considering factors which others would label as fundamental or technical but which are not specifically identified or quantified. Others rely entirely or partially upon a host of inputs which some may regard as strange, unusual, unreliable, or downright absurd. These can include inputs ranging from the astrological to voices heard in the night. If any esoteric methods work consistently for traders, they are well advised to use them. It should be noted that even the common separation of the fundamental and technical approaches can be called into question. Many fundamentalists are aware of the technical condition of the markets, and many technicians speak of trading only in the direction of the fundamentals.

Despite the blurring of the distinctions between these two approaches to trading and the possibility that one or both are worthless, some discussion of them is warranted.

The Fundamental Approach

The popular distinction between the fundamental and technical approaches to the market has to do with the factors considered or at least emphasized. Fundamentalists are concerned with changes in supply and demand factors which influence the price of the future being traded. Most are concerned with relatively long periods. The technician is concerned primarily with information about the market rather than about the item itself which is being traded. Most, but not all, technicians are more short-term-oriented than are fundamentalists.

In the long run conventional economic wisdom would conclude that the price of a commodity must ultimately reflect the equilibrium point of the combined forces of supply and demand. Isolating, quantifying, and evaluating in some reasonable way the respective weight of each supply-and-demand factor is the primary task of the fundamentalist.

To grasp the magnitude of such a task traders must grapple with economic theory. At this point the inevitable question arises: "Why is theory important? Give me the facts!" There are at least three problems with facts. First, it is not always easy to say exactly what a fact is. A court of law provides an excellent illustration of the effort that must be expended to isolate "facts," especially when different witnesses who appear quite credible and who have believable demeanors contradict one another.

The second trouble with the facts is that the number of them is overwhelming and almost unbelievable. For example, the wheat trader is dealing in a product grown in a huge number of countries. Some of these countries consume most of what they produce; others export varying amounts of their crops depending upon supply and demand conditions. Furthermore, although some countries attempt to distribute information quickly and accurately, others sometimes conceal, withhold, or misrepresent facts. The fundamentalist must attempt to consider human consumption, animal consumption, the amount of wheat to be retained as seed, and the minimum amounts to be carried over as reserves. The supply is based on quantities planted and harvested as well as the yields realized from the harvests. The yields may vary greatly from one region to another and from one crop year to the next. Government programs may affect supply, demand, or both. Import and export restrictions and political considerations may have great effects on prices. The amount of wheat used as feed will depend upon the numbers of creatures which consume the wheat, and so the wheat trader may be concerned with the numbers of cattle and poultry in the world and where they are located. In addition, wheat may compete as feed with corn, rye, oats, soybean meal, and a number of other products, and so the relative prices of all such competitive feeds may well affect the price of wheat. This list is far from complete, and few traders like to specialize in only one market. The number of known facts affecting the supply and demand for wheat available to traders is far beyond their ability to absorb them, regardless of their energy levels or organizing skills. When the number of unknown facts about wheat which can affect price is added, the total becomes completely unmanageable. To consider additionally other markets equally or even more complex, such as currencies, silver, or stock indexes, makes the problem mind-boggling. Simplification of reality by the development of models becomes a necessity but creates the risk of omitting or weighting too lightly a seemingly minor factor which may well prove to be the dominant factor during the very period being considered.

The third trouble with facts is that the individual trader seldom can know in advance the degree to which a particular set of emerging facts has been expected (discounted). Many disappointed traders have puzzled over markets that opened lower following news that they believed would have to be considered to be bullish or markets that opened higher following news that they would have believed to be bearish.[1]

The fundamentalist is confronted not only with a long list of factual relationships but also with the compound relationships described by that demanding gossamer prefix "expected." Hence the multiplicity of relationships increases dramatically. The soybean analyst must double the broad inputs of carry-over, new-crop production, and imports to *expected* carry-over, *expected* new-crop production, and *expected* imports. Whereas the fundamentalist might appear to be required to reason as well as possible concerning the combinational change that could occur among three dominant variables, it is actually necessary to consider six variables, with the ensuing proliferation of possible outcomes. Demand for soybeans explodes from an analysis that includes the demand for oil and meal, the amount of beans crushed, and exports into the *expected* demand for oil and meal, the *expected* demand for meal, the *expected* crush of beans, and the *expected* export figure.

---

[1] The reader interested in pursuing fundamental model building will find an excellent exposition of this subject in Andrew D. Seidel and Philip M. Ginsberg, *Commodities Trading Foundations, Analysis, and Operations* (Englewood Cliffs, N.J.: Prentice-Hall, Inc., 1983), pp. 320–393.

The soybean trader who is trying to compress price prediction by considering only a simple relationship of the anticipated size of the new crop to the size of the old crop is faced by the following bewildering set of possibilities added to the problems of acquiring accurate data, which may or may not have predictive value:

A large crop follows a large crop when either, both, or neither was expected.
A large crop follows a small crop when either, both, or neither was expected.
A small crop follows a large crop when either, both, or neither was expected.
A small crop follows a small crop when either, both, or neither was expected.
A small carry-over or large carry-over precedes any of the foregoing combinations.

Successful traders must understand and give meaning to the relevant facts about a future and determine which of these facts are likely to dominate prices during the period being observed. In doing so the traders must theorize. There are those who attempt improperly to draw a contrast between theory and facts. The proper contrast is not between theory and facts. The proper contrast is between good (useful) theory and bad (irrelevant) theory. Good theory should lead to good practice. If theory does not do this, it is simply not good theory.

Traders who wish to understand why prices are what they are or what factors might cause prices to change materially must become familiar with the forces that affect supply and demand and the possible significance of the effects. Traders working toward developing a model that explains prices should also be aware, however, that a model that explains prices is not necessarily a model that predicts which factors will change, and in what proportions, or what the market effects of the changes will be. In brief, a highly skilled fundamentalist may have a thorough understanding of a market's structure but still have no information that will lead to the profitable establishment of market positions.

The advent of inexpensive computer capacity, more sophisticated software, and increasing skills among users has resulted in increased efforts being made to analyze market fundamentals. Unfortunately, however , the ability to analyze and digest information quickly might serve only to make markets even more efficient and profits, therefore, even more difficult to realize. Regardless of all these and other intricacies involved, the fundamentalist trader's estimate of future price action must rest on an explicit or implicit theoretical base. Such a base must include the dynamics of price equilibrium, which in turn considers the nature of the various supply and demand curves, including the elasticity of each, and the response of all material factors to changes in the others.

Although equilibrium is a meaningful concept for referring to the direction of the long-term forces working on price and quantity changes, it should be noted that disequilibrium is the normal condition of a trading market. In that the demand for many commodities can change much more quickly than the supply, adjustments may require long periods. For example, much of the cocoa crop is still grown by small farmers in Ghana and Nigeria. The price of cocoa for a period of 2 or 3 years affects the quantity of beans supplied in the following periods. If cocoa prices are high during one period, the farmers will be financially able to expand planting or, equally important, able to afford insecticides and fertilizers to ensure a greater yield from the trees they have. As greater yields are realized, prices drop, expenses are cut, and the cycle is slowly reversed. Similar conditions exist in other markets such as sugar and livestock.

Model Building

It is possible to construct a flowchart of an industry which illustrates the magnitude of the forces that affect the price of a particular commodity at any particular time. These relationships include hundreds of variables, some of which are quantifiable to some degree. Theoretically, if the flowchart is correct and all the factors that affect the price of the commodity have been included and weighted according to their importance, a mathematical formula might be produced to explain the average price of the commodity for each period being considered.

Because such an exercise would require many years of preparation if it could be done at all, simplification of these relationships is necessary. This simplification, known as model building, attempts to reduce the number of variables from that approaching the infinite to a few dominant factors that retain the power to explain.

As a simplification of reality, a model has limitations recognized by good theory. A serious one is that many factors affecting the price structure must, by definition, be eliminated from consideration. The trader must develop sufficient insight into the supply-demand factors of a given commodity to be able to identify the *dominant* price-making influences at any point in the crop year. For example, the planting of new cocoa trees will certainly have the effect of increasing the production of cocoa in the long run. The lag in such incremental supply, however, is approximately 5 years. The most sanguine fundamentalist would admit that the price of cocoa futures will reflect many shorter-term influences in the meantime, such as figures that may indicate that cocoa users face a second year of reduced carryover inventory levels. Therefore, caution must be used in the selection of individual elements when models are constructed.

In eliminating so many factors from consideration in the interest of simplification, care should be exercised to ensure that such simplification will not give way to contradiction of reality. For example, a case for sharply higher prices might be made for wheat futures if new-crop production fell below total estimated usage and if a simple two-variable model were constructed. However, assume that wheat futures have fallen. If a less casual study indicated that old-crop carry-over had been at a 20-year high, the model for supply would have to be expanded to include carry-over as well as new crop production to avoid future contradiction.

Explaining versus Forecasting

The trader should be clearly aware of the significant differences in meaning and value between explanatory and forecasting models. Building a model merely to explain the elements that enter into price can be enormously difficult. Building a model that predicts with significant accuracy where prices are going to go is at a minimum far more complex and might well be impossible. One of the most insistent myths surrounding fundamental analysis in futures is that *explaining* price changes is equivalent to *forecasting* price changes. On the contrary, an explanation is seldom equivalent to a prediction. In fact, explanation frequently requires only that the trader be equipped with 20/20 hindsight.

In an explanatory model the variables used to explain a price at a particular time are also measured at the same time and thus must be currently available with the price they seek to explain. For example, assume that the trader has found that the price of hogs is a function of the quantity of hogs available, the prices of substitutes (beef and veal, lamb and mutton, fish and poultry), the income position of buyers, and consumer preference and that no further variables are needed to explain past prices. Assume further that the proper quantities for all past years are absolutely known for all four of these variables and that they have been weighted properly. As magnificent as such a model of price behavior would be, it would enable the trader only to *understand* past hog prices, not to *predict* future hog prices. The problem of turning explanatory variables into forecasting variables would still remain. For example, one determinant of the price for hogs—the quantity of hogs available—is reported quarterly in December, March, June, and September. Unfortunately, no one has yet been able to forecast consistently the quantity of hogs before these reports are issued. If, as already discussed, the behavior of futures prices is based partly on *expectations* and *changes* in expectations, it becomes a formidable task to predict price changes even if the trader were given a perfect preview of the figures to be reported. Unless the trader were also privy to accurate estimates of what figures were *expected,* he or she might still be unable to forecast the price changes that might follow the input of new information.

On the other hand, there are really only two general ways in which a *forecasting* model can be built. The first approach, using the preceding example, is to forecast the *next* hog quantity from a knowledge of past hog quantities. This simple extrapolative technique would have proven worth only if the explanatory variable, lagged for one 3-month period, were found to have predictive value when estimating the quantity of hogs in the next report. For example, assume for a moment that the trader has access to 10 years of figures reflecting the quantity of hogs available as evidenced by the annual December report. It is now March, and the trader wishes to forecast accurately the March quantity-of-hogs figure soon to be released. If the only source of information is the December hog quantity figure, the trader has an *explanatory* variable lagged by 3 months. If the pattern of December figures offers a significant clue over the years to the up-coming March figure, the trader can use this lagged explanatory variable to *predict* future variables. The published material to date, however, does not give the trader much encouragement in this regard.

The second method of forecasting isolates a variable that is predictive of hog quantities apart from past hog quantity figures. For example, the trader may find that quarterly changes in hog quantities are related to changes in the price of beef. However, for this information to be of forecasting, rather than explanatory, value, the price of beef in the *present* period would have to correlate highly with the quantity of hogs available in a *future* period. Again, research indicates that this approach to forecasting does not easily yield significant results.

Building a Forecasting Model

The bridge from explaining past price changes to forecasting future price changes is not easily crossed. Many traders are sure that someone, somewhere, knows everything, in that this person is knowledgeable enough to list all the sets of supply and demand conditions that would cause *all* bull or bear markets. In reality, traders do extremely well to isolate, quantify, and evaluate any set of conditions *sufficient* to cause a particular bull or bear market, even if viewed retrospectively. The development of a forecasting model requires even more rigor.

There is no requirement that traders be omniscient in order to make money. It is enough that they isolate and quantify any set of sufficient conditions for bull and bear markets in the futures they are trading. Traders following this strategy will simply not trade a future (regardless of its price fluctuations, all of which are caused by sufficient conditions of which they are unaware) until they see the sufficient conditions they have previously validated materialize. Then, and only then, will the traders take a position in the market.

Such a strategy is similar to that which might be followed by someone paid to predict fires. He might miss a great many fires caused by, say, chemical combinations of which he was completely unaware, but the specific knowledge that rags soaked with flammable fluids usually combust might be enough to earn him a generous living.

The fundamentalist attempting to build a forecasting model by searching for the factors that will dominate a current market might find insurmountable the problems to be solved. Some traders begin to feel comfortable with traditional supply-demand analysis just in time to lose most of their capital in one trade because a price which can go no lower or no higher finds a way to do so and perhaps by a considerable amount. Such traders find out too late that the supply coming into a market does not always decrease when the price falls. In fact, the fear of a further fall in price may be an inducement to offer an even greater supply on the market, thus causing price to weaken beyond the point that was indicated by traditional equilibrium analysis. The same possibility exists on the demand side, where the fear of a further price rise may induce a tremendous demand in the short run which can outstrip all economic projections and account for many a tragic tale of getting short "too soon." The inapplicability to the trader of "equilibrium" prices in the short run is reflected by rather substantial totals in the loss column each year. There are traders who remember when the price of soybeans was considered unbelievably high when it exceeded $4 per bushel. Others believed that world sugar could not possibly sell much below 15 cents per pound for long because that was "its cost of production." And who would have believed that the price of a contract of onions would ultimately fall to the price of the burlap bags in which the onions were shipped?

The significance of information is difficult to evaluate. As time passes, new information appears which must be considered. Some information must be selected from the mass available in order to develop a manageable model. The model must incorporate expectations as well as statistical data. New information and its impact are unpredictable. The random quality of new information rather than actual changes in supply and demand is responsible for the disequilibrium which is usually the norm in futures prices.

Prices might be related to quantities other than carry-over, production, imports, exports, usage, government monetary and fiscal policies, and the myriad of other factors which influence futures prices "fundamentally." The relationships of price to volume, open interest, and forces of speculation and hedging may also be considered in the search for explanatory and predictive variables. It is little wonder that some battered and discouraged fundamentalists may try other approaches to trade selection. Some believe that from experience they have developed such a finely honed sense of judgment that they can simply observe a market and "know" that the level of prices is too high or too low. Most such traders find that the market is a more formidable opponent than they had thought, and eventually they are leveled along with the prices. Others, however, actually do seem to sense when a market is "tired" and ready to fall or is poised for an upturn. Traders with this ability may have developed or been born with specialized sensitivity or judgment beyond that of other less fortunate mortals. Perhaps trading, like chess or operatic singing, can usually be learned only to a point beyond which most people cannot go because of the lack of some natural endowment.

Still other fundamentalists crushed by the sheer weight of elusive and mercurial data may find it satisfying to conclude that all fundamental data are reflected quickly and accurately in trading statistics anyhow, and they thereby feel justified in turning toward the less bewildering world of technical analysis.

NOTES FROM A TRADER

It is not the purpose here to indicate that fundamental analysis is a waste of time. Knowing what factors influence supply or demand for a future and to what degree might well alert a knowledgeable and observant trader to changes taking place in a market which might yield handsome profits. Rather it is the purpose to make clear that there is much more to such analysis than reading or hearing about a government report or political development and then expecting a market to wait for a leisurely entrance at a favorable price level. Most roads to high economic returns are marked by several rocky detours along the way.

Basic Data

Errors in basic data will obviously lead to errors in forecasts. The trader must realize that every statistic, whether generated by government or private sources, has a band of error about it. There are many problems in specifying what factors influence prices and how and when to measure them. Masses of data are meaningless unless they are grouped in some manner; however, there is the problem of the most representative totals or averages for various markets, seasons, or time periods.

No matter how accurate the estimate of a crop size, for example, may be, that estimate is based on a sample. Samples are less than perfect reflections of reality for many reasons, the most important of which is cost. At some point the return in the form of increased accuracy is not so great as the increased cost. The trader should remember that accuracy is also impaired because of revisions to data that are constantly being made. The words "preliminary" and "estimate" liberally dot most factual summaries.

The Analytical Framework

Even though there are no substitutes for competent statistical tools in the process of appraising the outlook for prices, the trader must bear in mind that such tools are not reliable substitutes for judgment. Because judgment is present continually, it can be extremely difficult to reproduce, on a quantifiable basis, fundamental studies performed at a particular point in time. As one study concluded, when referring to the estimation of certain variables in the pork bellies market, the procedure used "was not systematic, was not documented, and could not be duplicated."[2]

An important source of error is in the construction of the model itself. Explanatory models attempt to specify historical price responses to supply-demand forces which involve a complicated set of varying leads and lags. Forecasting models bear the additional burden of having to lead actual price response. Because models are but a simplification of reality, no model can include all the relevant factors. A second source of error may be the choice of equation form. Some relationships are linear, whereas others are curvilinear and may be more difficult to identify. Some relationships may best be studied in terms of changes rather than levels. Finally, estimates of elasticity are subject to a range of error which may arise from inaccurate basic data or a poorly constructed model.

Opportunity Cost of Capital

Traders employing the fundamental approach are not concerned so much with the question of *when* prices will move significantly up or down as they are with the probability of *whether* prices will move in a given direction and the possible extent of such a move. If prices move immediately through the objective indicated by a trader's study, the trade presents no hazard. However, if prices move opposite to the trader's expectation, the trader is confronted with the vexing problem of losses or, at least, forgone alternative opportunities. If such action persists for months and other trades are rejected because capital has been unavailable for commitment, the cost of capital becomes a real consideration.

Increased Market Efficiency

Implicit in the fundamental approach is the search for the discrepancy between the actual price of a future and its intrinsic value, as indicated by the price model formulated. As information systems become more complex and computer capability becomes more accessible, it seems logical to predict a damping effect on the quantity and degree of discrepancy that a given market will allow to remain unexploited.

It will be remembered that the concept of an efficient market is implicit in the random-walk model developed in Chapter 4. The implications of this model for

---

[2] Vance L. Nimrod and Richard S. Bower, "Commodities and Computers," *Journal of Financial and Quantitative Analysis*, 2, No. 1 (March 1967), 64.

the fundamentalist are clear. The closing price of a future for any one day or month is generally as good a clue as any fundamental factor to the closing price on the following day, week, or month. If the full import of such a truth dawns on a trader with something less than instant clarity, the trader may be comforted to learn that a sage observer of futures markets for many years has wryly observed:

> It is remarkable how long a known fact can in effect remain unknown, for lack of sufficient thoughtful attention to it; the near randomness of speculative price movements has long been widely recognized, in the limited form of recognition that no simple method was known for reliable prediction of speculative price movements.[3]

At least one study has documented the fact that futures prices are almost as active when markets are closed as they are during formal market hours[4]; that is, prices vary almost as much overnight and over any weekend as they do during the actual trading period. Such continuation of activity underscores the never-ending search by traders for new information. It seems that expectations never sleep. (Given the trend toward 24-hour markets by linkups among American, European, and Far Eastern cities, perhaps analysts and traders will also have to forgo sleep.) Prices are pulled inexorably toward events that are unknown but about to transpire. Indeed, on those plains of expectations bleach the bones of countless traders who insist that in the short run there must be a significant correlation between basic market factors and prices.

---

[3] Holbrook Working, "Tests of a Theory Concerning Floor Trading on Commodity Exchanges," *Proceedings of a Symposium on Price Effects of Speculation in Organized Commodity Markets, Food Research Institute Studies,* Supplement, 7 (1967), 14.

[4] Walter Labys and C. W. J. Granger, *Speculation, Hedging, and Commodity Price Forecasts* (Lexington, Mass.: D.C. Heath and Co., 1970), pp. 81–82.

Approaches to Trade Selection: Technical Analysis

*"Nothing is more difficult, and therefore more
precious, than to be able to decide."*
NAPOLEON I
Maxims

INTRODUCTION

Technical analysis refers to a study of the market itself rather than of the external factors that affect the supply of and demand for the various commodities, currencies, financial instruments, and other items which are traded in the futures markets. Technicians utilize the statistics generated by the markets. By tracking and smoothing these data, the technicians attempt to describe and explain short-term price movements. Those who rely on their judgment to make trading decisions may use technical devices to enhance their judgment.

Other technicians go further. They believe that past actions of the market alone may be utilized to reach meaningful conclusions about future prices; that is, the way the market behaved yesterday may indicate how prices will behave today. Such technicians, of course, reject even the weak-form explanation of market efficiency and dismiss the random walk. Research into this area is attributed, as usual, to naive academicians or traders who simply do not really understand markets. Technicians typically do not believe that price fluctuations are random and unpredictable. They believe that the study of transactions taking place can help traders anticipate impending price movements with sufficient accuracy so that they realize an adequate rate of return to cover any effort expended or risk accepted.

The fundamentalist reasons inductively, seeking to isolate and quantify dominant factors. By taking into consideration the expected supply and expected usage of products underlying futures, including such factors as carry-in, carry-out, production, exports, free supplies, substitutability, money supply, trade balances, and a host of others, fundamentalists try to deduce intrinsic value. If current prices indicate that the market is sufficiently above or below presumed equilibrium levels, appropriate action is taken in the futures market.

Some technicians consider their version of fundamentals but prefer to emphasize technical devices. Others go further and contend that fundamental analysis is a completely futile procedure. They point to many of the problems faced by fundamentalists. The factors the fundamentalist is examining are in many cases estimates subject to important revision. Furthermore, the technician asserts that there are so many fundamental elements in play at any time that an important one can often be overlooked or those being analyzed may be weighted improperly. Even if all relevant supply-demand factors can be estimated with total accuracy, the technical analyst still believes that the result would be of only limited value in appraising prices. As two advocates of the technical school declare:[1]

> Of course, the statistics which the fundamentalists study play a part in the supply-demand equation—that is freely admitted. But there are many other factors affecting it. The marketplace reflects not only the differing value opinions of many orthodox (commodity) appraisers, but also all of the hopes and fears and guesses and moods, rational and irrational, of hundreds of potential buyers and sellers, as well as their needs and resources—in total, factors which defy analysis and for which no statistics are obtainable—In brief, the going price as established by the market itself comprehends all the fundamental information which the statistical analysts can hope to learn (plus some which is perhaps secret from him, known only to a few insiders) and much else besides of equal or even greater importance.

Even a cursory look explains why the technical approach to futures trading has had little trouble gathering followers. Only three series of data are required: price, volume, and open interest. These data are easy to get and to store and are available with almost no time lag. The models that the technician constructs with this statistical information are relatively simple and straightforward, applicable to anything that can be traded on a free market, anywhere, at any time. One noted technical analyst has stated, "The technician of 1900 would be completely at home in the markets today."[2] The same certainly could not be said of the turn-of-the-century fundamentalist.

These considerations have appeared to be especially attractive to many traders searching for a better and easier way to make decisions. In the last several decades a vast amount of work has been done to erect a maze of technical tools—all with the aim of anticipating future prices from trading statistics.

---

[1] Robert D. Edwards and John Magee, *Technical Analysis of Stock Trends* (Springfield, Mass.: John Magee, Inc., 1957).

[2] John Magee, *The Stock Advisory Service* (Springfield, Mass.: John Magee, Inc., 1964).

Every technical approach, from the simplest to the most complex and esoteric, falls into one of four broad areas of technical analysis: patterns on price charts, trend-following methods, character-of-market analysis, and structural theories. Volumes could be—and have been—written about many of the methods contained in these four basic areas. To go into great detail on any one method would be beyond the scope of this book, but a comprehensive survey is presented, with ample references for further study of the key methods within each area.

PATTERNS ON PRICE CHARTS

The use of patterns of movement on price charts is one of the oldest methods of market analysis known. The approach is said to have gained great popularity in 1901 when William Peter Hamilton, then editor of *The Wall Street Journal*, stunned his readers by recounting in detail precisely what James R. Keene was doing when he successfully promoted the first public offering of stock in U.S. Steel. Hamilton was said to have had an informant in Keene's inner circle, and Keene himself believed this. *The Wall Street Journal* readers were amazed to learn that all of Hamilton's deductions were made by simply tabulating—and shrewdly analyzing—the price and volume action of U.S. Steel stock on the market.[3]

Although Hamilton used only common sense in analyzing the price movement of U.S. Steel, it was not long before many other researchers attempted to catalog and codify any number of price patterns with supposed forecasting value. At first it was said that the "pools" (secret groups of wealthy speculators who manipulated stock prices) revealed their actions to the trader who charted prices and volume. In later years, when the pools were banished by legislative fiat, the charts were supposed to show "changes in psychology." Whatever one believes is being measured, this entire approach rests on the assumption that certain repetitive patterns of price and volume action will often occur before significant price movement.

Bar Charts

The most popular tool for storing price and volume history in searching for these repetitive patterns is the bar chart. In standard procedure each day (week, month, or year) is represented by one vertical bar on a graph. The bar is drawn to cover the range between the extreme high and low prices of the day, and a "tick mark" indicates the close. This is illustrated in Figure 7-1, which shows three consecutive days of price action for wheat. Each day is plotted to the right of all preceding days until a record of prices is compiled. Below each price plot on the graph another bar could be drawn to indicate volume of trading for that day.

A number of variations are possible on this standard procedure. Some techni-

---

[3] William Peter Hamilton, *The Stock Market Barometer* (New York: Harper & Brothers, 1922). Hamilton explained in some detail the kind of reasoning he used in his deductions. Hamilton's exposition of the basic premises employed in technical analysis remains one of the best available, even after more than half a century.

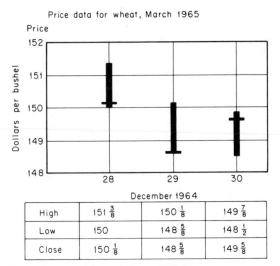

Figure 7-1 **Constructing a bar chart.**

cians will graph the close only. A "midrange" price can be entered on the graph, which consists of the high plus the low divided by 2. The opening price can be shown as well. All of these procedures have advantages and disadvantages, and each technician must decide which one he or she considers most useful.

As traders record daily (or weekly) price action, they will begin to observe those patterns that the chartists assume are of a recurring variety.[4,5] Figure 7-2 illustrates a number of patterns that have been well publicized. The price action of May soybeans in Figure 7-3 reveals how these and other popular patterns may be noted and used by a trader. *A, B,* and *C* may be said to form a "head-and-shoulders" top, which is completed during the first week of December. Following classical lore, measuring from the head *B* to *D* on the "neckline" indicates a minimum objective of 10 cents below the "breakout" at *E,* or $2.14. *F* illustrates an "exhaustion gap," and *H* shows the "resistance" met by the 10-cent rally from *G* as prices "pull back" into the "left shoulder" (*A*) area. *I* represents a "double bottom" which takes 11 weeks to form before supporting a 7-cent rally to *J.* Throughout this entire time "trendline" *T*1/*T*2 is drawn across three important tops and is used as a benchmark

---

[4] Edwards and Magee, loc. cit. This work is the definitive source of information on chart patterns and their analysis. Other works are William Jiler, *How Charts Can Help You in the Stock Market* (New York: Commodity Research Publications Corp., 1961), and Martin J. Pring, *Technical Analysis Explained* (New York: McGraw-Hill, 1980).

[5] Two out-of-print works which detail methods of technical analysis using price charts are Richard W. Schabacker, *Technical Analysis and Stock Market Profits* (New York: B. C. Forbes Publishing Co., 1934), and Robert Rhea, *The Dow Theory* (Binghamton, N.Y.: Vail-Ballou Press, 1932). Both books can be found in many big-city libraries. More modern publications will overlap all or most of their content, but these books are based on original research.

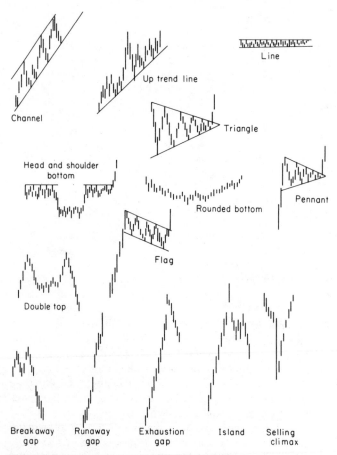

Figure 7-2   Typical chart patterns. The mirror image of most of these patterns has an opposite implication.

to indicate the development of the downtrend, as well as possibly helping to time its ending.[6]

It should be clear from this brief discussion that the field of bar charting could be discussed in great detail. Because of a multitude of alleged patterns, quite an extensive vocabulary has been developed to describe all manner of price-action phenomena.[7]

---

[6] A strong exponent of using charts to trade commodities, and one who believes in paying special attention to "measuring implications" of price patterns, is Houston Cox, *A Common Sense Approach to Commodity Trading* (New York: Reynolds & Co., 1968). A slightly revised edition of this book, *Concepts on Profits in Commodities,* was published in 1972.

[7] An excellent source for the technician, especially one who is mathematically inclined, is Andrew D. Seidel and Philip M. Ginsberg, *Commodities Trading* (Englewood Cliffs, N.J.: Prentice-Hall, Inc., 1983).

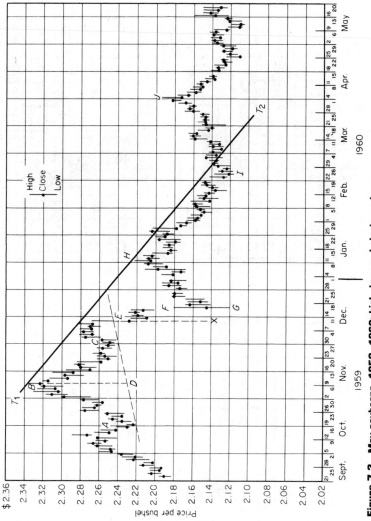

Figure 7-3   May soybeans, 1959–1960: high, low, and closing prices.

Point-and-Figure Charts

Point-and-figure chartists make two assumptions that bar chartists do not. First, they view the volume of trading as unimportant, a mere side effect of price action with no significance. Second, they dismiss the importance of how much time has

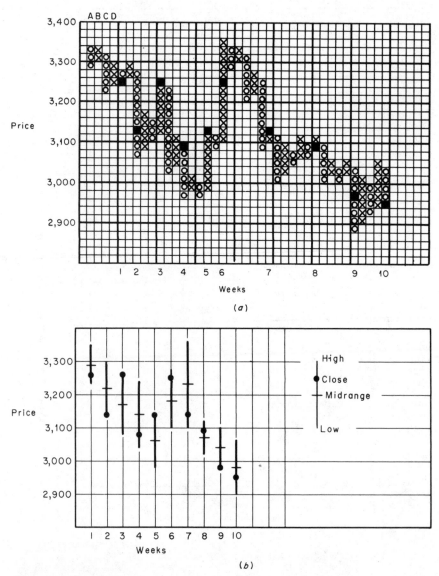

Figure 7-4   Point-and-figure chart versus bar chart. (a) Point-and-figure chart for a 10-week period in cocoa: each X or O represents a change of $20; (b) bar chart for cocoa covering the same 10 weeks as (a).

elapsed as price moves from one level to another. Only one thing matters, and that is the direction of price change. Point-and-figure charts are constructed to show the direction of price change and nothing else.

Figure 7-4 illustrates a typical point-and-figure chart for cocoa. The chartist had decided in advance to smooth price action broadly by indicating every fluctuation of $20 or more and has scaled the chart accordingly. Each box on the chart equals $20.

If the price of cocoa rises by $20, an "X" is used to indicate the price change. As long as the price of cocoa continues to rise, new X's will be entered on top of those preceding, one for each $20 of rise. If the price of cocoa rises by $300 with no interruption of as much as $20, 15 X's will be placed on top of one another in the same column. This will continue until the price drops by the minimum amount decided upon previously, in this case $20. Once this happens, an "O"[8] is placed in the column to the right. Each additional $20 drop causes an "O" to be placed below the preceding "O" as long as the price continues down with no $20 interruption. When a $20 rise finally occurs, an "X" is placed in the next column to the right, and the sequence continues as prices dictate.

The P & F chart is a record of price reversals with no reference to time. For comparison purposes a weekly chart of cocoa for the same period is shown in the lower half of Figure 7-4. The closing price for each week is blacked in on the chart to make the comparison easier. Clearly, the more often the price of cocoa reverses direction by $20, the greater the number of vertical columns used up.[9]

Any amount of price fluctuation can be shown on a point-and-figure chart. A chartist with an extremely short-term orientation and access to all successive prices during the day could construct a chart to show reversals of as little as one minimum fluctuation. A single day's action could use up scores of columns. On the other hand, a trader with an unusually long-run view could construct a chart to show reversals of no less than 30 or 40 points. With such a large unit of reversal a considerable history of price fluctuation could be compacted into a small chart, but some traders would consider the amount of information too sparse to be sufficiently informative.

Despite their unique construction, point-and-figure charts are used much like bar charts.[10,11] Figure 7-5 illustrates many of the popular bar-chart patterns in a point-and-figure format. The most important difference in claims made for these two tools for charting, and perhaps the only substantive difference, is that many chartists believe that the *extent* of future price moves can be predicted by using

---

[8] Some technicians will use an "X" in both up and down columns of price movement.

[9] The two standard works on the interpretation of point-and-figure charts are Alexander Wheelan, *Study Helps in Point and Figure Technique* (New York: Morgan, Rogers and Roberts, 1962), and A. W. Cohen, *The Chartcraft Method of Point & Figure Trading* (Larchmont, N.Y.: Chartcraft, 1960).

[10] The first published work on point-and-figure charts is Victor De Villers, *The Point & Figure Method of Anticipating Stock Price Movements* (New York: Traders Press, 1972). This book shows how importantly De Villers was influenced by the Dow theory and other classical technical concepts.

[11] An exceptionally intricate theoretical rationale of the use of point-and-figure charting is presented in John W. Schulz, *The Intelligent Chartist* (New York: WRSM Financial Service Corp., 1962).

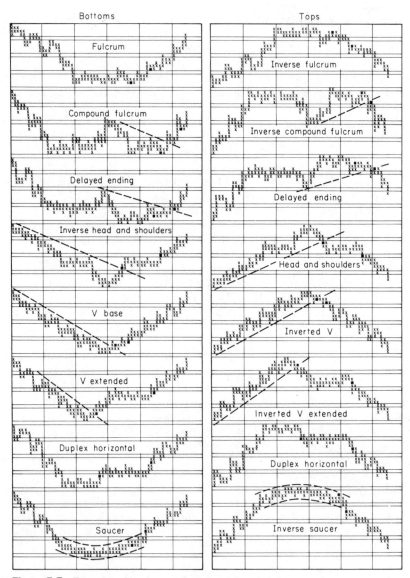

Figure 7-5 Examples of patterns of point-and-figure charts.

point-and-figure charts. This is accomplished by a consideration of what is known as "the count."

In its simplest form the count is the number of squares across an area of lateral movement on a point-and-figure chart. Chartists who use the count believe that a direct relation exists between the number of squares used up during a lateral movement and the size of a subsequent rise or fall out of this congestion area.

There are several variations on precisely how to use the count to project the extent of the future move.[12]

Old-Time Price Patterns

In many old books and courses considerable space is devoted to the observations of "veteran traders" who have detailed simple price patterns that allegedly have predictive significance. Although these principles of chart reading fell into obscurity for many years, a recent flood of reprints of these old works has led to renewed interest.[13] Possibly the reason these patterns are largely ignored in modern publications is that invariably they are presented with no accompanying rationale and are described as being short-term in nature.

An example will illustrate one bit of market folklore: the "stair-step" principle. To put this principle into operation the following elements must be present:

1. There is a rise in price of at least three upward waves and two downward waves, working steadily higher.

2. The bottom of each downward wave is below the top of the preceding upward wave.

3. When the bottom of the last downward wave is penetrated, the principle says, "when the last step is broken, all will be broken."

Many of these old-time patterns are described in far more objective and explicit terms than their more modern counterparts. The objectivity and explicitness did not impair the relegation of the methods to apparently well-deserved obscurity.

Striking the Balance—Advantages and Disadvantages of Using Price Patterns in Trading

The Advantages. (*a*) The trader does not even have to prepare charts. Many services sell up-to-date charts for modest prices, and some brokerage houses will even supply them gratis. (*b*) It cannot be denied that successful analysts, past and present, have used price-pattern concepts successfully. Although studies[14] on

---

[12] Wheelan, loc. cit.; Cohen, loc. cit.; and Schulz, loc. cit., all present several variations of "the count" in point-and-figure charts. An ardent point-and-figure chartist who believes that the projection of price targets is a worthless pastime is James Dines, *How the Average Investor Can Use Technical Analysis for Stock Profits* (New York: Dines Chart Corp., 1972). Dines's book contains several variations on basic point-and-figure techniques.

[13] Some extensive and detailed old works with interesting technical methods are the several courses written by Mark and Jared Pickell, Ralph Ainsworth, Burton Pugh, and W. D. Gann. These courses have long been out of print and can be picked up only occasionally through such specialty dealers as Allan C. Davis, 1617 Linner Road, Wayzata, Minn. 55391, and James Fraser, 283 S. Union Street, Burlington, Vt., who maintain sizable inventories of books and courses on speculation.

[14] Alfred W. Cowles, "Can Stock Market Forecasters Forecast?" *Econometrica*, 1 (1933), 309–324, and Daniel Seligman, "The Mystique of Point & Figure," *Fortune* (March 1962). These studies do not increase the prestige of chartists or price forecasters in general.

the accuracy of chartists' forecasting have yielded disappointing results, they have also unearthed the occasional practitioner who has achieved substantially successful results over a long period of time. Individuals making successful forecasts from this kind of analysis are not unknown, though they are, admittedly, few. (c) Even if the use of any specific price patterns for forecasting purposes is considered unacceptable, it is nevertheless true that a study of price charts can reveal information about market action that may assist the trader in making a decision. For instance, a trader contemplating the purchase of two different commodities might well use a different operating plan in a commodity whose chart showed a steady descent to ever lower levels, as opposed to another whose chart showed prices soaring to record highs.

The Disadvantages.   (a) The use of most chart patterns has been widely publicized in the last several years. Many traders are quite familiar with these patterns and often act on them in concert. This creates a "self-fulfilling prophecy," as waves of buying or selling are created in response to "bullish" or "bearish" patterns. After this chartist buying or selling is exhausted, prices will very often reverse direction to create vicious "chart traps." Just as positive or negative fundamental information can be discounted in the prices, so can positive or negative technical information be discounted. (b) Chart patterns are almost completely subjective. No study has yet succeeded in mathematically quantifying any of them. They are literally in the mind of the beholder. This subjective element makes it impossible to put any of them to an objective test to see how they have worked in the past. (c) The few analyses done to date of the records of the chartists themselves have not been encouraging. Chart-oriented advisers have, in almost all cases, given advice that was no better than random. Even with the few who have distinguished themselves, there is no evidence that their success rests solely in chart reading. It is safe to assume that whatever predictive value there may be in price patterns is not easily comprehended.[15]

TREND-FOLLOWING METHODS

Isaac Newton can be given credit for probably the best-known assumption on which most technicians operate: "A price trend once established is more likely to continue than to reverse." This is simply a restatement of Newton's first law of motion, applied to price action. If this concept is accepted as true, then a successful trading strategy can be built on the simple principle of buying strength and selling weakness. The only problem remaining is the optimum way in which to carry it out.

---

[15] Ibid. Seligman's study unearthed one point-and-figure chartist whose results over a long period were exceptionally good and much better than chance alone would indicate. Nonetheless, it was obvious that this chartist used many other factors besides charts in achieving this result. For a cynical view of any successful trader see Fred Schwed, Jr., *Where Are the Customers' Yachts* (Springfield, Mass.: John Magee, Inc., 1955), Space Age Edition, in the chapter entitled "A Brief Excursion into Probabilities."

Moving Averages

An average is defined as "the quotient of any sum divided by the number of its terms." Thus a 10-day average of soybean closing prices is the sum of the last 10 days' closings divided by 10. A moving average of prices is a progressive average in which the divisor number of items remains the same, but at periodic intervals (usually daily or weekly) a new item is added to the end of the series as, simultaneously, an item is dropped from the beginning.

If one is constructing a 10-day moving average of soybean closes, the average on the tenth day is the sum of days 1 through 10 divided by 10. On the eleventh day the eleventh day's close is added to the total and the close of day 1 is subtracted. This new sum is then divided by 10. On day 12 the close of that day is added to the total and the close of day 2 is subtracted. This total is divided by 10, and so on. Table 7-1 illustrates the computation of a 10-day moving average based on the closing prices of May 1961 soybeans.

Figure 7-6 shows a 10-week moving average of soybean closes. An examination of this chart will reveal the important properties of moving averages. The 10-week moving average smooths out the erratic week-to-week changes in actual prices and thereby indicates the underlying trend. Further, the moving average lags behind prices and crosses the current price only when a new direction is established. These same properties are characteristic of moving averages calculated for any time span.

Shown on the chart are "buy" and "sell" signals, given when price penetrates the 10-week moving average. Technicians acting on such signals are following the strategy of buying strength and selling weakness. They hope that the prevailing

TABLE 7-1 COMPUTATION OF A 10-DAY MOVING AVERAGE FOR A TYPICAL MAY SOYBEANS CONTRACT

Date	Close, in cents	10-day net change*	10-day total†	10-day average‡
3/15	290.000			
16	291.500			
17	294.000			
3/20	290.500			
21	291.500			
22	300.500			
23	304.000			
24	204.500			
3/27	301.250			
28	305.250	. . . .	2973.000	297.30
29	297.750	+ 7.750	2980.750	298.08
30	300.250	+ 8.750	2989.500	298.95
4/3	300.500	+ 6.500	2996.000	299.60
4	299.750	+ 9.250	3005.250	300.53
5	302.250	+ 10.750	3016.000	301.60

* Difference (plus or minus) between latest close and the tenth close, counting back.

† Sum of 10 latest closes.

‡ The 10-day-total column divided by 10. These figures in sequence make up the moving average.

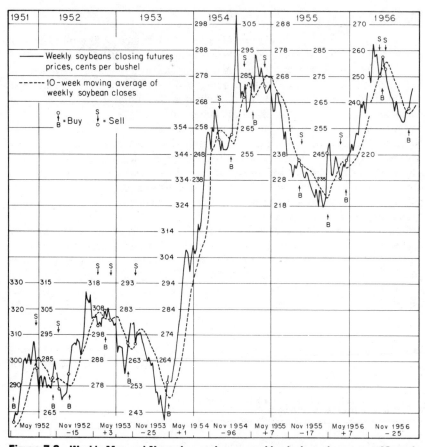

Figure 7-6   Weekly May and November soybeans: weekly closing price versus 10-week moving average. Prices of contracts adjusted to each other for continuity.

trend, like the buy signals of late 1953, will continue long enough to compensate adequately for the kinds of whipsaw losses that resulted from the first two signals of 1952.

There are countless systems that use moving averages, but all are based on variations of just two factors:

1. The length of time used in computing the moving average. It is here that an important trade-off is involved. The shorter the length of time, the more sensitive the moving average will be to any change in trend. New trends will be acted on earlier and do not need much time to establish themselves. The trader pays for this sensitivity because the shorter the moving average's length, the greater the number of trades that will be made. This means greater commissions and a larger number of whipsaw losses. A longer period of time used to calculate the moving

average will reduce the number of trades and the number of whipsaw losses but will signal new trends much later—often so late that the trend will be closer to completion than initiation.

2. The kind and amount of penetration required. In an effort to reduce false signals, many technicians demand more than just a simple penetration of the moving average; for instance, requiring that the price in Figure 7-6 penetrate the moving average by 5 cents as a prerequisite for acting on any signal would eliminate several whipsaws. Other technicians try to eliminate "meaningless penetrations" by requiring "a material length of time" to elapse before a "signal" is followed. Still others try to measure the angle of penetration and require that the angle be "significantly great" before a trade is made.

These strategies, however, are subject to the same limitations described above. Too small an amount of penetration, however measured, does little to reduce whipsaws. Too large a penetration eliminates trades that would have yielded adequate profits and reduces the profits on those which are accepted. Although considerable effort over many years has been expended in attempts to establish the sizes of successful filters, nothing printed to date appears to help traders attempting to make sufficient profits after execution costs to justify their risks.

Striking the Balance—Advantages and Disadvantages of Using Trend-Following Methods

The Advantages. (*a*) A trend-following technique is, by definition, objective. All the elements must be clearly defined before it can be put into practice. This means that traders can, if they have the facilities, determine how well any technique has worked in the past and define its important characteristics. Any number of variations can be back-checked in an attempt to optimize results. (*b*) Any trend-following method provides traders with a sizable part of their operating plans, with all the attendant benefits in terms of results and peace of mind. Because their action points are so clearly defined, the traders are not so likely to be beset by uncertainties. (*c*) Trend followers believe, along with many famous traders, that "the big swing makes the big money." By employing any trend-following method it is impossible for a big move to occur without their participating in it.

The Disadvantages. (*a*) Traders who use trend-following methods begin with at least two counts against them. First, whipsaws are inevitable and frequent. Second, all signals acted upon are late by definition. To compensate for both of these liabilities, the trader must realize frequent enough or large enough profits on the successful signals. (*b*) A future moving within a trading range will provide the trend follower with seemingly endless losses until a major trend is initiated. Large numbers of long positions will be taken on strength near the top of the range and short positions on weakness near the bottom. In that even cursory observation indicates that most markets fluctuate in trading ranges most of the time, it seems clear that trend followers will probably suffer losses on most of their trades. "Rules" developed in some markets will not work in others or even in the same markets during other periods. Attempts may be made to adapt the rules to volatility, but predicting volatility is no easier than any other kind of market prediction.

CHARACTER-OF-MARKET ANALYSIS

The trader using character-of-market methods operates on premises completely different from those of the chartist or trend follower, both of whom have constructed a number of techniques based on the interpretation of price action. Those technicians who employ a character-of-market approach believe that a deceptive veneer has been painted over the true picture of supply and demand.

The character-of-market analyst seeks statistical measurements of supply and demand that are independent of price or at least uses price information much more subtly than the chartist or trend follower. The important question asked by those traders who use this approach to technical analysis is, "What is the *quality* of a given move in price?" The trader then tries to commit his or her capital in line with price movements of good quality and to avoid, or even take an opposite position to, movements of poor quality.

As noted before, the technician has only three series of trading data to work with: price, volume, and open interest. Nevertheless, so many combinations and permutations of these data have been employed in character-of-market methods that it is possible here to touch only on the most illustrative and basic.

Oscillators

In a broad sense all time series oscillate. Trends, seasonals, and cycles can all be regarded as oscillating time series. Like so many other definitions in the area of technical analysis, the definition of "oscillator" is different for different people. As used here, the term "oscillator" refers to a family of technical indicators based on measurement of price changes rather than price levels. The simplest type of oscillator is based upon the distance the price of a future has traveled over a given period. For example, a 10-day oscillator is constructed by taking the price on the latest day and subtracting the price of the tenth day previous. The number obtained is either positive or negative, depending on whether the price has risen or fallen in the last 10 days. The same procedure is followed during subsequent trading days.

The calculation of oscillators can be carried to surprising complexity, usually as rules are developed to filter out the latest series of unsuccessful trades. Some oscillators are specially smoothed, some are weighted, and some are modified in conjunction with one or more additional factors (such as volume). Sometimes all of these options are used. Time periods employed for constructing oscillators can range from 2 to 3 days (or even less if the trader has access to intraday data) to several weeks or longer. The use of *any* oscillator, however, rests on one or both of these contentions:

1. A price rise or price decline can become overextended if it gathers too much velocity. If the price of any future enjoys an unusual gain that is compacted into a short time span, the presumption is that buying is temporarily exhausted and part or all of the gain will be retraced. Such a market is said to be "overbought." The opposite kind of price action would lead to an "oversold" market. By constructing an oscillator the technician seeks to monitor excessive rates of price change that could lead to exhaustion and subsequent price reversals.

2. A price trend can simply peter out as it steadily loses momentum. In this case a price trend continues but generates less and less energy until it dies. A top is signaled when, for instance, the price continues to make new highs for the move but the oscillator moves from large positive numbers to small positive numbers. The reverse is true for a bottom. Used in this way, an oscillator is a tool for measuring the exhaustion of a price trend.

These two concepts are not mutually exclusive. Figure 7-7 shows the daily action of November 1970 eggs against a 20-day price change oscillator. For this period levels in the oscillator above + 300 (meaning that price had advanced more than 300 points in the preceding 20 days) spotlighted markets that were overextended on the upside. Similarly, levels in the oscillator below − 300 indicated that price had become oversold.

During this period the penetration of "trendlines," drawn across key tops or bottoms in the oscillator, indicated exhaustion in the current price trend. In line with this concept of exhaustion, it will also be noted that the oscillator can peak or bottom ahead of price in many instances, thus signaling possible reversal.

Striking the Balance—Advantages and Disadvantages of Using the Oscillator

The Advantages. (*a*) Overbought or oversold signals generated from oscillators will usually work well in trading markets, which occur more frequently than trending markets. If there is no dominant trend, points of upside and downside exhaustion can, in theory at least, be identified with a fair degree of accuracy. (*b*) Signals of an overbought or oversold market can act as a valuable check on a trader's emotions. No matter how bullish a situation may appear, a high positive reading on the oscillator at the same time could be a sobering influence. The reverse is also true. (*c*) History is replete with examples of price trends that peaked or troughed, whereas accompanying rate-of-change oscillators showed a clear loss of momentum well in advance.

The Disadvantages. (*a*) Acting on overbought or oversold oscillator signals will lead to financial disaster in any market with a dominant price trend. During a powerful bull or bear swing an oscillator will repeatedly move into "overextended" territory and will often stay there for a long time. This danger cannot be avoided because a trader who could consistently anticipate dominant price trends in advance would not be using an oscillator as a trading device. (*b*) Zones that represent overbought or oversold markets must be decided on the basis of history. If the

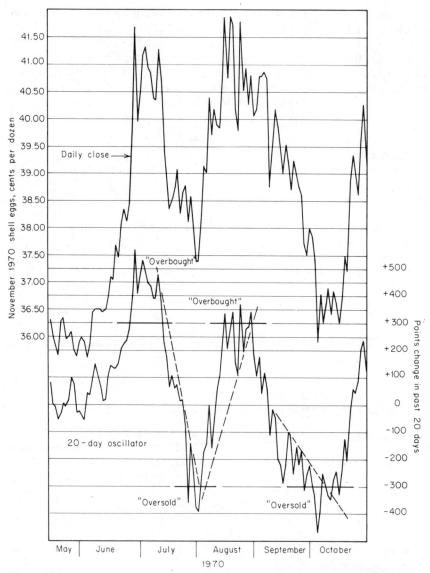

Figure 7-7   November 1970 shell eggs: daily close versus 20-day net change oscillator for May—October 1970.

future being followed suddenly becomes either more or less volatile, whether still in a trading range or not, previously determined zones will be worthless. All futures do change their volatility over time. (*c*) Loss of momentum before key tops and bottoms are reached is well documented, but this phenomenon is much easier to see in retrospect. In Figure 7-7 trendlines are drawn on the oscillator itself to determine loss of momentum. These trendlines could have been drawn in many other ways, and several of them would not have yielded satisfactory results. In practice, declining momentum will indicate a pause in the price trend or a reversal, and there is no way to tell which. Using this technique, analysts can often explain past price action, but they cannot easily predict future price changes.

Traditional Volume and Open-Interest Methods

"Volume" refers simply to the aggregate number of contracts or bushels of futures traded in a given period; it is a measure of the combined futures market supply and demand for that period. "Open interest" is the total purchase or sale commitments outstanding. At any time, the purchase commitments or number of contracts "long" is equal to the sale commitments or number of contracts "short." The different types of trades and their effects on the open interest are listed below. "Old" buyers are those who have outstanding long positions, whereas "old" sellers have outstanding short positions in the market. "New" buyers or sellers are those who are just entering the market to take a long or short position.

Transaction	Effect on open interest
Purchases by old sellers from old buyers	Reduced
Purchases by old sellers from new sellers	Unchanged
Purchases by new buyers from old buyers	Unchanged
Purchases by new buyers from new sellers	Increased
Sales by old buyers to new buyers	Unchanged
Sales by old buyers to old sellers	Reduced
Sales by new sellers to old sellers	Unchanged
Sales by new sellers to new buyers	Increased

The open interest increases only when new purchases are offset by new sales. Decreases in open interest occur only when previous purchases are sold and are offset by the buying in of previously sold contracts. Since it is the effect on open interest that is reported and not the type of transaction, the technician interested in this aspect of market behavior must infer the latter from the former.

Volume and open-interest data are reported daily in newspapers and by wire services. They are also printed and distributed at different intervals by the CFTC and by various advisory services. Most technicians use the totals for both the volume and open interest of a given future rather than the figures for individual contract months.

Significant changes in volume and open interest may last for a few days or for extended periods. Changes must be related to their respective seasonal patterns before a meaningful analysis may be undertaken. The seasonal changes are usually more substantial and more significant for open interest than for volume. Those who fail to consider seasonal influences are in danger of making serious misinterpretations of apparent large increases or decreases of the raw data.

Because there is no measurable seasonal pattern for volume, technicians generally compare it with that of the immediate past. For example, if the total platinum volume has hovered around 500 contracts a day and suddenly increases over a period of a few days to 750 contracts a day, a significant change in market psychology may be occurring according to those who believe that volume is significant.

General rules have been formulated to indicate how significant net changes in open-interest and volume figures may be analyzed in conjunction with price analysis.

The tendencies for volume alone may be summarized as follows:

1. When a major price advance is under way, volume tends to increase on rallies and to decrease on reactions.

2. Conversely, during a major price decline, volume tends to increase on down moves and decrease on rallies.

3. Volume expands sharply as bottoms and tops are approached.

Open interest, when compared with price action, tends to act in the following ways:

1. If prices advance and open interest advances more sharply than a seasonal analysis would suggest, aggressive new buying would seem to have taken place.

2. If prices advance and seasonally adjusted open interest declines, the advance has been fueled by short covering and might be regarded as technically weak.

3. If prices decline and aggressive new selling is taking place, the market may be considered to be technically weak.

4. If prices decline and open interest decreases beyond seasonal expectations, the decline has been fed by discouraged longs who have liquidated their unprofitable positions, leaving the market relatively strong technically.

A perhaps oversimplified form of some of the relations among volume, open interest, and price is sometimes given as follows:

If prices are up and   (a) volume and open interest are up—the market is strong;
                       (b) volume and open interest are down—the market is weak.
If prices are down and (a) volume and open interest are up—the market is weak;
                       (b) volume and open interest are down—the market is strong.

Like so much of the explanatory and predictive data in the futures markets, all of this sounds quite logical. The value of these observations has little or, at best, only cursory statistical support.

Striking the Balance—Advantages and Disadvantages of Using Traditional Volume and Open-Interest Methods

The Advantages.   (a) The basic principles of interpreting volume and open interest appear quite logical. It seems reasonable that the expansion and contraction of volume and open interest compared with price action should yield worthwhile clues to the balance of supply and demand in the market. (b) The trader following volume and open-interest principles uses a three-dimensional model rather than one of single dimension found in other technical approaches. There are many other ways in which price action can be viewed, and many more shadings can be used to describe bullish or bearish behavior. (c) If the forecasting ability of volume and open interest is denied, there is still a significant amount of information to be obtained by simply monitoring such data. The trader knows which contracts are most active, the size of the market in which he or she is dealing, and any important properties of trading activity.

The Disadvantages. (a) This type of analysis is replete with a number of ill-defined terms: "low volume," "increase in open interest," "decline of greater than seasonal expectation," and several others. To make use of this approach, technicians must quantify their terms to avoid meaningless generalities. (b) General rules for volume and open-interest interpretation are well publicized. Application of these classical principles leads to the problem of the "self-fulfilling prophecy" discussed among the disadvantages of using price patterns. Volume and open-interest behavior which is clearly bullish or bearish can be discounted in the present price level as easily as other more familiar supply-demand factors. (c) The validity of these standard principles rests on unproved assertion. No publicly available studies that use volume and open-interest decision rules confirm their value in actual trading.

On-Balance Volume

The bulk of character-of-market analysis originates from the belief that "big-money-eyed" traders consistently take positions prior to substantial price moves in any future. The "big money" is seen, for instance, as surreptitiously acquiring sizable long positions before price advances, well ahead of the "ignorant masses." This quiet buying is known as "accumulation." When these same interests are selling their longs and going short at the top of a rise, before a large decline, their activity is called "distribution." Tracking the supposed clandestine flow of accumulation and distribution has led to the growth of countless technical methods over the years.

An old approach to measuring accumulation and distribution by the action of price and volume—one which has enjoyed a popular renaissance since the early 1960s[16]—is currently known as "on-balance volume," or OBV. Easily calculated and graphed, OBV attempts to provide information on the quality of price movements by yielding a volume curve that can be compared directly with the price curve.

Table 7-2 illustrates a hypothetical OBV calculation. Each day's closing price is compared with the closing price of the preceding day. If the latest day has a higher closing price, *all* the volume of trading that day is assigned a plus sign. If the latest day's close is lower than that of the preceding day, all the volume is assigned a minus sign. These daily plus and minus volume figures are added to a cumulative running total. This cumulative total is the OBV. The absolute level of the OBV curve is of no significance; the technician is interested only in the contour of this

---

[16] Joseph Granville, *Granville's New Key to Stock Market Profits* (Englewood Cliffs, N.J.: Prentice-Hall, 1963), has popularized this approach in recent years.

TABLE 7-2 COMPUTATION OF ON-BALANCE VOLUME

Date	May soybean oil daily closing price	Volume (number of contracts)	OBV (cumulative volume)
March 1	27.09	—	—
2	27.15	+3000	+3000
3	27.22	+2500	+5500
4	27.07	− 800	+4700
5	26.85	−1200	+3500
8	27.01	+2500	+6000

curve when it is compared with the contour of price, either graphically or in tabulated form.

The dominant theory behind OBV, as previously noted, assumes that large-scale accumulation or distribution can take place in the market. Because this activity would have to be done quietly, it is further assumed that worthwhile accumulation or distribution is carried out under the cover of small net or deceptive price changes. The OBV curve is believed to illustrate the true state of affairs by showing whether the volume of trading is highest during periods of rising or falling prices. When the bias in volume deviates significantly from the price curve, unusual activity is presumed to be taking place.

Under normal circumstances the OBV curve will move parallel to the price of the future under surveillance. As long as this relationship remains, the trader using OBV will have no particular interest. However, when the OBV curve begins to diverge from price, notice is taken because many analysts believe that such divergence indicates accumulation or distribution. In Table 7-2, for instance, the price of soybean oil dropped a nominal eight points between March 1 and March 8. Yet the OBV record shows that 6000 more contracts changed hands on days of rising price than on days of falling price. If this kind of behavior continued for a significant period of time, the technician would conclude that soybean oil was being intensively accumulated. Moneyed interests would be presumed to be buying heavily, putting prices up for a day or so before quietly allowing them to drop on low activity until they moved again into a satisfactory buying area. In theory, this process would continue until accumulation was completed. Prices would then move much higher as the "big money's" analysis was proved correct and the "crowd" began to act on the now favorable news developments affecting soybean oil.

There are more complicated ways to calculate and use OBV, such as using weighting devices or other modifications, but the basic principles of interpretation followed by subscribers to this device remain the same.

Striking the Balance—Advantages and Disadvantages of Using OBV

The Advantages. (a) If there is, in fact, important money from intelligent sources that quietly assumes positions in advance of large price moves or if such substantial buying or selling takes place for any reason, it cannot help but leave a record in daily transactions. OBV pinpoints periods in which a substantial excess of volume takes place at higher or lower prices, thus giving the technician a "lead" for further study. (*b*) Whatever interpretation is used, OBV gives the analyst information with which to quantify the volume of any price move. Even if the trader is not looking for "signals" per se, the knowledge that the largest volume occurs on rising or falling prices, and how it compares with price, can be helpful in appraising market action.

The Disadvantages. (*a*) Research to date indicates that the profit-making ability of the large trader is impressive.[17] These studies have shown that large traders succeed mainly by trading *short-run* price fluctuations. Such conclusions do not support the relatively longer-term accumulation-distribution thesis on which much of OBV analysis rests. (*b*) No objective rules of interpretation have ever been presented by advocates of OBV,[18] thus ensuring the impossibility of performing any tests that would determine whether the use of OBV would lead to nonrandom trading results. (*c*) On theoretical grounds the calculation of the most commonly used form of OBV is open to serious question. Each day's price change is determined by transactions on both the buying and selling side, and it does not seem reasonable to assign *all* the volume to the plus or minus side simply because the close one day is higher or lower than the close of the preceding day. If pork bellies, for example, were up 130 points during the day but closed down 5 points, it would not seem proper to assign all the volume that day to the minus side. Calculation of basic OBV may be too simplistic.

Analysis of Open Interest to Determine Activities of Large and Small Traders

Another way to measure accumulation and distribution is the proposal made by many technical analysts to differentiate between "smart money" and "stupid money." Those making this differentiation believe that there are, essentially, two categories of traders: winners and losers. For example, in the stock market, exchange specialists have often been identified as a winning group and odd-lotters as a losing group. Techniques long in use with these and other groupings can be applied to futures as well. An attempt is made to identify the winning group and the losing group and then discover in a timely manner what one or both of these groups are doing. Positions are then initiated either with the winning group or opposed to the losing group when either shows a strong preference for one side of a market.

Technicians might conclude, for example, that large traders were the most frequent winners and small traders the most frequent losers. Such technicians would then be required to obtain from the government, from exchanges, or from the market itself, through some technical devices, information in the form of reasonably current indications of what these groups were doing.

---

[17] C. S. Rockwell, "Normal Backwardation, Forecasting, and the Returns to Speculators," *Food Research Institute Studies*, Supplement, 7 (1967), 107–130.

[18] Granville, loc. cit., presented many objective collateral OBV calculations but failed to present a completely quantifiable set of decision-making rules.

Striking the Balance—Advantages and Disadvantages of Using Open Interest to Reveal the Activities of Large and Small Traders

The Advantages.   (*a*) Similar techniques have been used with some purported success in the stock market for many years. The breakdown of open interest available on futures yields series of data that are analogous to those used in stock market analysis. (*b*) Whether or not traders successfully construct valid technical indicators from open-interest breakdown, knowledge of the current interplay among hedgers, large traders, and small traders might be helpful in explaining market action in any future. (*c*) This kind of analysis can be intriguing to those who think it has value because so little research has been published in this area.

The Disadvantages.   (*a*) The work that has been done on the behavior of large and small traders argues against the value of open-interest breakdowns. Small traders, rather than acting consistently on the wrong side of the market, are better described as trading haphazardly. Large traders are consistent winners but are short-term-oriented as a group.[19] It might be concluded that there is no available information on "stupid money" and that "smart money" data are available but come too late and too infrequently to have value. (*b*) Open interest is available to the public only with a time lag of days or weeks, thereby making the information virtually useless. (*c*) The fact that there is so little published work in this area may not reflect the failure of futures traders to take advantage of its latent value. It may rather indicate that detailed timely data are unavailable or that traders have tested the approach and found it of no value.

Contrary Opinion

. . . the supposedly stolid Dutch were overcome by the Tulip Craze, the volatile French had their Mississippi Bubble, while the sturdy English had their South Sea Bubble.

As I read the account of these madnesses, I was tempted to shout, "This cannot have happened". Yet within my own lifetime I have seen similar deliriums in the Florida land boom of the 1920's and the stock market speculation that led to the 1929 crash. Something of the same crowd madness may have been at least partially responsible for Hitler's rise to power in Germany.

These crowd madnesses recur so frequently in human history that they must reflect some deeply rooted trait of human nature . . . if his book showed how baseless are man's moods of wild hope, it also showed that man's moods of black despair are equally unfounded. Always in the past, no matter how black the outlook, things got better. . . . Whatever men attempt, they seem driven to try to overdo.[20]

---

[19] Rockwell, loc. cit.

[20] Bernard Baruch, *Baruch: My Own Story* (New York: Henry Holt & Co., 1957), p. 219.

With these words, Bernard Baruch explained how he related an account of the "madness of crowds"[21] written in 1841 to the extremes of psychology that he had observed in his own experience. His astute decision to sell his holdings in 1929 has been credited to his reading this book at an opportune time. Baruch apparently never attempted to utilize the lessons of history contained in Mackay's book in any systematic way, but a stock market analyst named Humphrey Neill did ponder on the implications of swings in mass psychology. The result was a new way of thinking called "contrary opinion."[22]

Neill's contention was that crowd madness did not have to go to the point of making history before it could be detected and used to advantage. His belief was that any crowd, such as stock or futures traders, could frequently be carried to extremes of action and opinion. Astute observers could recognize these extremes and act opposite to the prevailing psychology to their own advantage. In other words, they would adopt a "contrary opinion." Neill attempted in his book to demonstrate that this phenomenon extends beyond trading stocks or futures. He noted that popular expectations before many major world events were directly opposite to what actually happened. Only its use in futures trading, however, is considered here.

In market letters and boardroom talk the term "contrary opinion" appears frequently. Apparently most traders have come to believe that the contrarian takes positions opposite the prevailing opinion almost as a reflex action. This popular notion is far too simple; the true contrarian does more than merely lean against the current state of thinking.[23]

Before money is committed to a trade, the contrarian insists that certain basic elements be present. First there must be a strong consensus about the future price or behavior of a future. This opinion must be almost unanimous—virtually taken for granted—before there is any chance that mass psychology has been carried to extremes. Examples of widely held opinions that would interest a contrarian would be "Beans are going much higher," "September bonds will go off the board weak," "February bellies will gain on the May," and "Cocoa will take its lead from next month's purchase figures and not do much until then." Any of these opinions unfulfilled could represent a trading opportunity. Note that the opinion need not be only one of price direction. A normally popular future that has been unusually neglected is one example of a consensus that could provide a contrarian with much food for thought.

A second and equally important prerequisite is that the strong bias of opinion

---

[21] Charles Mackay, *Extraordinary Popular Delusions and the Madness of Crowds* (London: L. C. Page & Co., 1932), reprinted from the 1841 edition. Several reprints of this book have since been published; it documents scores of historical occurrences in which people lost all semblance of reason and were dominated by mass psychology.

[22] Humphrey Neill, *The Art of Contrary Thinking* (Caldwell, Ohio: The Caxton Printers, 1960), is the definitive source of information on contrary opinion.

[23] R. Earl Hadady has acquired a wide reputation in the area of contrary opinion. In addition to several periodicals, including *The Professional Chart Service, The Commodity Spread Trader,* and *Market Vane,* Mr. Hadady has published a book, *Contrary Opinion; How to Use It for Profit in Trading Commodity Futures* (Pasadena, Calif.: Hadady Publications, Inc., 1983).

be supported by "weak" reasons. In determining how strong or weak these supporting reasons are, the contrarian differs sharply from the fundamentalist. The trader using contrary opinion is not interested in how important the facts are or even whether they are true. The reasons behind an opinion are judged strong or weak only according to the manner in which they have been disseminated and the reaction they have produced.

To the contrarian, supporting reasons are weak if they have one or both of these characteristics:

1. The facts have been widely publicized and well known for some time.

The presumption here is that any such facts are already discounted in the current price. For example, suppose that the great majority of traders are bearish on wheat. If such a position is popular because a coming bumper crop has been apparent for several weeks and prices have already dropped substantially, the question of how much risk remains on the downside may well be raised. If news of the impending record crop has generated most of the selling it warrants, any favorable developments will be a surprise to most traders.

This kind of well-publicized fact is especially weak if its realization is far in the future. If, for example, the expected bumper crop is many months away from being harvested, a great many things could happen in the meantime (including the discovery that the crop is not nearly so large as the earlier estimates) to change the present bearish psychology sharply.

2. The facts of the situation are not known but only supposed.

This sort of situation can occur anywhere but is more common in international commodities, such as sugar, cocoa, copper, silver, coffee, and currencies. Opinion is formed on the basis of preliminary indications that have all been in agreement but for which no hard evidence is yet available. Cocoa may be regarded as an exceptionally bullish situation on the basis of preliminary crop estimates long before any solid facts are in on the crop size. Even if the crop is small, such expectations may already have been discounted in the current price. Other than extravagantly bullish news could find the market vulnerable to decline following the first factual reports.

If the trader who uses contrary opinion can find a situation in which there is a near-unanimous opinion supported by weak reasons, he or she has, at least in theory, found a trade with high potential and low risk. The low risk comes from the probability that the factors that caused the consensus have been discounted. The high potential comes from the element of surprise that can be a dominating influence when mass psychology carries to extremes and only one-sided news is expected. If the reason behind the crowd's opinion turns out to be entirely invalid, which has happened frequently in the past, the contrarian gains a bonus.

Striking the Balance—Advantages and Disadvantages of Using Contrary Opinion

The Advantages. (a) More than the premises of almost any other technical approach, the premises behind contrary opinion are solidly logical. When strong feelings prevail toward a particular future, it is indisputable that conditions in that market are abnormal. Most known facts are likely to have been discounted completely or partly, offering little potential to the trader who is following the lead of the majority. Of equal importance, such a market is extremely vulnerable to unexpected developments not in line with current thinking. (*b*) Even if a contrary opinion approach is not used to signal trades, it can be valuable to the trader who wants to keep emotions in check. Watching for weak reasons behind strongly held opinions will keep the trader from being carried away by the arguments of the moment and losing perspective. (*c*) A contrary approach can often turn up important facts for both the technician and the fundamentalist. Contrary opinion is more than a means of generating signals. It is a way of thinking that can be conceptually and practically useful. In the final analysis the success of contrary opinion depends completely on neglected facts coming to the fore. By directing attention away from popular thought patterns contrary opinion is one method whose primary purpose is to enable traders to think for themselves and possibly to unearth key factors on which trades may be based.

The Disadvantages. (*a*) Collecting an accurate sample of opinions can be most difficult. Myriad sources must be consulted to determine whether there is a strong consensus toward any future. Newspapers, brokerage house letters, private advisory letters, brokers themselves, their clients, and the "signals" currently being given by popular trading methods are only a few of the inputs needed to monitor a consensus situation that may be shaping up. It can be an arduous—sometimes almost impossible—task to uncover the prevailing psychology, even given a strong consensus. (*b*) Even if the state of prevailing opinion is known, the depth of that opinion may be hard to evaluate. One group of traders expecting lumber to "consolidate and retrace recent large gains during the next few weeks" is certainly not so bearish as others who expect a major collapse. Weighting these and other shades of opinion can be a perplexing problem. (*c*) Although contrary opinion can provide the trader with numerous psychological advantages, it can spawn at least one large psychological disadvantage. Used heavily, it can breed arrogance. (*d*) Points of extreme mass psychology in any future are quite infrequent. Even the most adept contrarian may have to wait a long time between trades. (*e*) The approach is not as precisely quantitative as is generally believed. Because of this, contrary opinion has not yet been put to an objective historical test to determine its validity and characteristics, as some other technical methods have. (*f*) It is much easier to initiate trades by following a contrary opinion method than to know when or where to close them. In closing a trade, the contrarian must rely heavily on other methods or personal judgment.

STRUCTURAL THEORIES

The final quadrant of technical analysis is as controversial as it is varied. Structural theories include the seasonal approach, which is widely respected and used among technicians. It is similar to the cyclical approach, although the latter reflects longer time cycles and different inputs. Some who utilize structural theories base their decisions upon inputs which many would consider bizarre. Such exotic theories are not discussed here, but if a trader is able to make money in the markets consistently by analyzing comic strips or following voices heard in the night, that person would be wise to do so.

Technicians who use structural theories do not construct indices for predictive purposes as is the case in character-of-market analysis, nor do they rely on trend following as an aid in making decisions. Structural theorists believe, rather, that an intensive study of historical performance will reveal understandable and repeating price patterns in the market itself.

This approach is quite different from that discussed earlier of looking for non-random price patterns on charts. Such price patterns as are deemed to be predictable are expected to occur at irregular intervals, consume a relatively brief period, and predict prices only for brief periods. Their form is quite general and may assume many variations. Those who use seasonals, along with those who use such other components of time series as trends or cycles, consider them to be far more comprehensively based. Prices are seen as "following a blueprint" that can provide valuable guidance at all times. The trader who understands this blueprint will know where prices stand within the structure and can determine where they are going next.

Seasonal Price Movements

The most respected structural blueprint attempts to define times of the year when futures prices have a high probability of moving in one direction or the other. These seasonal price trends are usually due to the particular way a future is produced and/or distributed. In grains, for instance, the sudden increase in supply at harvest time should lead to lower prices. Later in the season, as supplies are used, prices could be expected to rise. Indeed, the desire to stabilize seasonal price fluctuations was one of the most important reasons leading to the birth of the Chicago Board of Trade.[24] It was believed, and subsequently confirmed, that a futures market could at least moderate the violent seasonal price tendencies in grains.[25]

Traders using seasonals believe that although futures trading has moderated formerly more marked price tendencies, these price tendencies have not been eliminated. They contend that there are specific times in some futures markets that remain significant each year. Some of these traders believe that the seasonals provide profitable trading opportunities. Others believe that, as a minimum, seasonals influence prices enough to be considered as an element in broader trade selection methods.

Because, ultimately, any seasonal price pattern is produced by an interplay of production and consumption factors, some would consider such patterns to belong in a fundamental rather than a technical approach to trading. Others might argue that seasonals are repeating patterns of price action that can be discovered and measured from observations alone without regard to factors underlying production and consumption. There is, of course, considerable overlap in these "two types"

---

[24] See Chapters 1 and 2.
[25] See Chapter 4.

of seasonals. This is not unusual in discussions of fundamental and technical analysis, which often blend together rather than remain distinctly separate.

Traders who believe in using seasonals almost exclusively for trade selection go so far as to develop a "calendar portfolio" of seasonals which purports to indicate action to be taken in various futures at specific periods. Sometimes these seasonal "blueprints" suggest particular periods during the year during which rising or falling prices are likely. Others attempt to indicate particular months during which the high or low for the entire year is most likely to occur.

Another form of seasonal analysis particularly favored by some full-service brokerage houses that specialize in futures is called a "conditioned seasonal." This is a concept which maintains that a price move will follow the occurrence of some specific precondition. Examples of such allegations are "Potatoes will advance into January if they make a new high in November" and "January soybeans will gain on deferreds if Chicago stocks are low in November."

Striking the Balance—Advantages and Disadvantages of Using Seasonals

The Advantages. (a) If any clear, repeating seasonal tendency has been isolated, the trader can usually then determine the dominant reason for its existence. As long as that reason exists in succeeding years, the presumption is that prices will probably repeat their performance. (b) Seasonal information can be used to argue for or against trades accepted in any other form of analysis. The trader who wishes, for example, to short orange juice during the last half of October is made aware of a strong tendency for prices to rise at that time of year. When any commitment is made, seasonal information may help in appraising the risks. (c) If nothing else, careful analysis of seasonals can help the trader to achieve a better understanding of the basic forces affecting the balance of supply and demand in any single future.

The Disadvantages. (a) The means by which futures are produced and consumed are always in a state of flux. For this reason the life span of the best validated seasonal tendency can prove to be quite limited. (b) Any seasonal tendency that becomes well known is almost certain to be totally smoothed out as more and more traders act on it. Seasonal forces can be discounted in the price like any other fundamental or technical inputs. (c) Although seasonal trading is almost unique in its ability to indicate entrance and exit dates to positions in advance, little is said about interim risk. In holding positions for long periods, traders are subject to the chance of considerable risk while waiting for the presumed gain. Such traders might be forced out of positions by variation margin calls before they realize their ultimate profits. Even those who could afford to hold their positions would have to consider the possibility that the losses might continue to grow because the seasonal is overwhelmed by other factors. How is the trader to control losses in seasonal trades? The answer is not clear. Those who choose to utilize the seasonal approach to decision making must realize that seasonal analysis usually provides little information on interim risk. Judgment must be utilized to determine if a seasonal trade is on course, and the trading plan must be broad enough to deal with interim adversity.

Time Cycles

Seasonals, no matter how derived, deal with repeating annual phenomena. For at least the last century, however, a great many investigators have concluded that there is a longer-term structure in futures prices.[26] Even longer-term cycles have been isolated and documented. In 1875 Samuel Benner wrote a short book wherein, among other things, the prices of pig iron and corn were predicted for the next several decades. Had a hypothetical trader, with the required money, warehouses, and other resources, bought and sold pig iron during the years indicated, dollar gains would have exceeded losses by a ratio of 31 to 1.[27] Benner's predictions on corn were less spectacular, but gains still shaded losses by a margin of 3¼ to 1, and the average annual gain from trading in cash corn would have exceeded 7 percent compounded. Results like these, achieved over a span of more than 80 years, strongly suggest that Benner's success might have been correlated with underlying cyclical phenomena.

Technicians who use time cycles to forecast prices employ a unique modus operandi. They believe that back records of prices contain evidence within themselves of at least one and usually several time cycles during which prices are carried up or down. Whether a computer or paper and pencil is used, the trader attempts to isolate and quantify the important cycles in any future. These cycles are then combined to yield a prediction of the dates of future high and low prices. The trader then takes action accordingly.

Most of those who use time cycles simply maintain that important price highs and lows are spaced by distinct repeating intervals over periods typically ranging from 2 to 6 years. Among the oldest such cycles observed is the 67⅓-month cycle, which some believe is followed by the corn market.

Others use complex and sometimes highly sophisticated mathematical models designed to define precisely the timing, shape, amplitude, and other characteristics of the time cycles being investigated.

Although any trader can use a record of futures prices to discover price cycles after the fact, this approach has never been overly popular. The literature on the subject is sparse, and only a few services emphasize this approach. Traders must decide for themselves whether the relative lack of interest in the method presents an opportunity or whether it means that traders lack the patience to trade with cycles or have concluded that the method is of no value.

Striking the Balance—Advantages and Disadvantages of Using Time Cycles

The Advantages. (a) Some evidence may indicate that time cycles are real phenomena and not statistical fantasies. Sophisticated mathematical tests can

---

[26] Perhaps the first person to investigate time cycles in a scholarly way was Hyde Clark, who alleged an 11-year cycle in specualtion and famine in 1838. Influenced by Clark, William Stanley Jevons published *The Periodicity of Commercial Crises and Its Physical Explanation* and *The Solar Period and the Price of Corn* at the University of Manchester in 1875. Jevons's thesis was that repetitive cycles in sunspots affected crop yields, and therefore prices, on a predictable basis.

[27] Samuel Benner, *Benner's Prophecies of Ups and Downs in Prices,* privately printed, Cincinnati, Ohio, 1875 (reprinted by The Foundation for the Study of Cycles, 124 South Highland Avenue, Pittsburgh, Pa. 15206).

indicate the probabilities that observed cycles are due to chance. Trading futures on the basis of time cycles is at least theoretically possible. (b) Even if time cycles are not used to signal commitments, such research might at least be helpful in appraising the risk underlying trades.

The Disadvantages. (a) Not all the evidence indicates that cycles are real phenomena. Mathematical techniques to date have not supported the contention that repeating time cycles of any length are present in futures prices. (b) Even if cycles are accepted as real phenomena, there is still much about them that is not known. It is impossible to know for any particular future what causes observed cycles, how many cycles are currently influencing prices significantly, or even the curvatures of the cycles. That there is nothing approaching a complete cycle model is a major obstacle to the technician attempting to use cyclical data. Any time cycle isolated by a trader might prove to be useless as hidden properties of the cycle become apparent, other undetected cycles nullify or override it, or all cycles are overwhelmed by powerful shorter-term influences. (c) Most of the published research in commodity price cycles has been conducted with cash rather than with futures prices. Cash and futures markets often do not move in tandem. Futures have a limited life, and some represent different crops, which makes it difficult to analyze prices in a meaningful way. (d) Even with complete and accurate knowledge of a cycle, the trader can never have a complete picture. Important current developments can ruin the clearest cyclical indications, with prices getting back "on track" too late to help the trader or, perhaps, not getting back at all.

The Elliott Wave Theory

As must be common to all who publish investment services, I received frequent letters from individuals who had developed "infallible" methods or systems for forecasting the stock market. My usual reply was that the individual go on record with me over a market cycle after which I would determine whether I cared to investigate the matter in detail. In most instances, at some point in the cycle the system went haywire and correspondence died on the vine.

Elliott was one of three notable exceptions. He wrote me from California in late 1934 that a bull market had begun and would carry for some distance. . . . In March 1935 the Dow Rail average crashed under its 1934 low, accompanied by an eleven percent break in the industrial average. Having recent memories of 1929–32, this development scared the lights out of the investing public. On the bottom day for the industrial average, the Rails having leveled off four days previously, I received a late evening telegram from Elliott in which, as was always his way, he *dogmatically* affirmed that the break was over and that another leg of the bull market was beginning. This break, looking back, was Primary Wave No. 2 of the Cycle movement then under way under Elliott's Wave Principle although, at the time, I had no idea as to his method.[28]

It was in this way that the Elliott wave theory first became known to Charles Collins and then to an ever-wider audience. The theory was discussed by R. N.

---

[28] Hamilton Bolton and Charles Collins, "The Elliott Wave Principle—1966 Supplement," *The Bank Credit Analyst,* 1245 Sherbrooke Street West, Montreal 109, Quebec, Canada.

Elliott in various articles published between 1938 and 1946 and by others in various publications since that time.[29] Elliott himself died in 1947, at which time many of his papers disappeared.

Elliott's basic precept involved a modified cyclical approach to forecasting based upon counting charted waves of advances and declines in stock prices. These waves, Elliott believed, fell into patterns so complete and so comprehensive that one could know at any time where prices stood in their development, how much potential they had on the upside or downside, and roughly how much longer a trend would persist.

Elliott's basic theory was that prices move in a five-wave sequence in line with the direction of the main trend and in a three-wave sequence during "corrective" movements against the main trend. Each wave is broken up into subwaves of its own (either three or five waves), and these waves, in turn, break down into smaller subwaves, and so on. In principle, Elliott waves can be carried down to the level of each individual trade. The theory can also be extended to a larger scale, in which each wave is seen as a subwave of a larger wave, which in turn is part of a still larger wave. In this case, according to Elliott, the result might be waves in prices centuries long. Given this all-inclusive system of categorization, it is theoretically possible for the trader to know where prices stand at all times.

Elliott's wave counts are based on the Fibonacci Summation Series. This series, starting with 1,2,3,5,8,13,21,34,55,89, was developed about 700 years ago by one Filius Fibonacci, an Italian mathematician. Each of the numbers in the series equals the sum of the preceding two numbers. Although Fibonacci designed the series primarily for his students, a virtual cult has developed around it. It has been affirmed that both living and inanimate objects obey a number of laws that revolve around the mathematical properties of this series. Some believe that the series enabled scientists to predict how populations of animals will multiply, how plants will grow, and how crystalline structures will form naturally.

The ratio of any number in the series to its next highest is 61.82. This ratio is sometimes designated as the "golden mean," and it has found some interesting uses in architecture. Many of the numbers in the series and the mean itself are yielded by various combinations of measurements applied to the great pyramid of Cheops.

---

[29] The most comprehensive single work on the wave principle is Hamilton Bolton, *The Elliott Wave Principle—A Critical Appraisal* (Montreal: Bolton, Tremblay & Co., 1960). Bolton, Tremblay & Co.'s *Bank Credit Analyst* has also published a number of supplements for irregular years, starting with 1961, that seek to update Bolton's original work and provide current interpretations. Cox, loc. cit., is a strong advocate of using Elliott's principles for commodity trading. William O'Connor, *Stocks, Wheat & Pharaohs* (New York: Weiner Books Co., 1961), is an offbeat source of information on Elliott applied to futures prices. The book is out of print but available in many big-city libraries. O'Connor not only uses unique principles of interpretation but is the only source that places great stress on daily charts for identifying Elliott waves in the very short run. Elliott's two monographs are long out of print and almost impossible to obtain, as are past issues of his advisory letters. R. N. Elliott, "The Wave Principle," *Financial World* (1939), reprinted by BCA Distributors, Ltd., Montreal, 1963, consisting of a series of articles that appeared in *Financial World Magazine*, is his only work still readily available. Additional discussions of the theory may be found in *Techniques of Professional Chart Analyst* (New York: Commodity Research Bureau, Inc.) and *Elliott Wave Principles* (New York: Frost and Prechter, 1978).

Elliott's efforts to adapt his wave theory to prices, the Fibonacci Series, and the golden mean have all been utilized by technicians in attempts to predict prices. There are those who believe this to be one of the most interesting and accurate technical methods extant. Others believe that phenomena which exhibit the proper numerical relationships are held up as proofs of the theory, whereas those which provide the wrong numbers are ignored or conveniently explained away. Such cynics point out that there are enough numbers available in nature and the results of various human endeavors to prove almost anything.

Striking the Balance—Advantages and Disadvantages of Using the Elliott Wave Theory

The Advantages. (*a*) During the time that Elliott was using his method he compiled a spectacular record of forecasting stock prices. Following in his footsteps, both Collins and Bolton continued to make surprisingly accurate predictions of the stock market averages. (*b*) The fact that Elliott's work relies so heavily on the Fibonacci Series carries great weight with those who believe that the series explains much of nature. It has been hypothesized that these relationships are so all-inclusive that they extend into the psychological arena, with price fluctuations of securities and futures reflecting their subtle but all-pervasive influence.

The Disadvantages. (*a*) Elliott never hinted that his "law" might apply to futures prices. His forecasting work centered almost exclusively on the Dow Jones Averages. Even in individual stocks, research performed indicates that application of Elliott's principle is quite intricate and possible only in selected instances. (*b*) The entire concept of the Elliott wave theory rests on counting "waves." Yet it is impossible to answer objectively the question "What *is* a wave?" Elliott himself gave no answer to this question. This means that the technician is forced to use highly subjective judgment to label a wave on the chart and also to identify the time scale which the wave fits. Waves, sometimes involved in major moves, frequently break up into many more than five subwaves. Either the theory is wrong or some of the waves should not be counted for some unknown reason. This problem occurs quite frequently in Elliott's analyses. (*c*) The theory is so flexible that it is possible to get several radically different wave counts by using the same price data, and leading Elliott interpreters are in almost constant disagreement. A particularly disturbing corollary to all of this is that the more back data the trader has accumulated, the greater the number of possible counts. In most endeavors additional information usually clarifies; with Elliott, additional information can just as easily add to the confusion. (*d*) One flexible aspect of the theory is the fluid concept of "extensions"; for example, a five-wave move can, under Elliott's rules, extend itself without warning into nine waves. These and other features of the theory make it difficult to come to any decisions at any given moment and easy to see the correct count (and decision) after the fact. (*e*) Elliott, beyond question, intended that his wave principle mold current prices into a comprehensive structure that would provide guidance at all times, but virtually any future chart will show long "blank" spots in which it is impossible to get any sort of wave count. Because one of the fundamental tenets of the theory is that *all* waves can be categorized, the existence of these blank spots means either that the premise is invalid or that the count at these times is subtle enough to escape all observers. (*f*) It is not generally realized that Elliott was a mystic who also believed in numerology. In his monograph,[30] published in 1946, he discussed how mathematical relationships in the Great Pyramid of Gizeh not only predicted future world events but tied in with his own wave theory as well! Although the trader should keep an open mind in regard to the claims of technical analysis, a trading method that is in agreement with pyramid numerology should, indeed, be cautiously evaluated.

NOTES FROM A TRADER

Isolating, quantifying, and successfully trading nonrandom elements in futures trading data requires unusual determination and discipline. Technicians must deal with the efficient-market concept and not just ignore it in the hope that it will go away. The probability that the market is strongly or completely efficient is high, although this will probably never be proved or, at least, will never be believed by everyone. If true, the efficient market is a powerful adversary, and in attempting to forecast, technicians must beware of trying to get more out of an experience than the wisdom that is in it lest they become like Mark Twain's cat that "sits down on a hot stove lid. She will never sit down on a hot stove lid again—and that is well; but she will never sit down on a cold one any more."

There seems to be an overwhelming urge among many technicians to develop a simple, totally mechanical system that works with a high degree of accuracy. The professional trader becomes aware that the search for a foolproof trading system in which all observations promptly find their preordained place has the same large challenge and the same small promise as the search for any all-encompassing system in any other discipline, be it medicine, philosophy, or law. The mature trader recognizes that although judgment can be reduced, it can never be eliminated, and many losing trades will mar even the best trading results.

Technical analysis does offer the advantage of smoothing market data and thus makes tracking data somewhat easier. This in turn may help traders exercise sound judgments in making market decisions. Just as fundamental analysis may only explain relationships between supply and demand and not be predictive, technical analysis may serve only to describe what markets have done and not be predictive either. Although neither approach may be predictive, both may provide inputs to help sound judgments to be made if forecasting is possible at all.

Technicians must accept certain facts. Sophisticated mechanical devices may serve only to make markets even more efficient and, hence, forecasting more, not less, difficult. If any faith is to be placed in "trading rules," there is no place for

---

[30] R. N. Elliott, *Nature's Law—The Secret of the Universe*, privately published, New York, 1946. Long out of print. The title perhaps indicates Elliott's view of the importance of his methodology.

a loose definition of terms. Despite these and other problems there are at least two important lessons to be retrieved from technical analysis. First, almost all methods generate useful *information*, which if used for nothing more than uncovering and organizing facts about market behavior will increase the trader's understanding of the markets. Second, the trader is made painfully aware that technical competence does not ensure competent trading. Speculators who lose money do so not always because of bad analysis but because of the inability to transform their analysis into sound practice. Bridging the vital gap between analysis and action requires overcoming the threat of greed, hope, and fear. It means controlling impatience and the desire to stray away from a sound method to "something new" during times of temporary adversity. It means having the discipline to "believe what you see" and to follow the indications from sound methods, even though they contradict what everyone else is saying or what "seems" to be the correct course of action.

The rewards are great and they are attainable. As one astute observer of the markets remarked,

> . . . commodity price developments are watched by relatively few traders, most of them quite set in their ways; even in the most active futures markets, the volume of serious research by participants seems to be quite small. It is therefore possible that systematic patterns will remain largely unknown for a very long time.[31]

---

[31] Hendrick Houthakker, "Systematic and Random Elements in Short Term Price Movements," *American Economic Review*, 51 (1961).

8

Spreads

"Why worry about realized losses?
They are more than overcome by potential
profits."

INTRODUCTION

Spreads may be considered by some to represent only a choice in a type of commodity position, but the subject is far broader than that and deserves separate and more elaborate treatment.

Most unsophisticated commodity traders are converted security traders who bring their habits with them. They are much more likely to be long the market than short and know little or nothing about spreads. The professional trader is at least as conversant with the short as with the long side of the market and knows considerably more about spreads.

SPREADS

Spreads may represent a high percentage of the open interest of a commodity, especially among large speculators and commercial traders. They may be entered for either technical or fundamental reasons. The word "spread" has several meanings to commodity traders, but all imply a price difference. Spread in its most general sense applies to the difference between the cash and future prices of the same commodity. In its more restricted senses it may refer to the differences in the prices of various contract months on the same future exchange or the differences in prices between the same or different months in the same or related futures on exchanges located in different cities.

A spread also describes the actual position taken by a trader who is simultaneously long one commodity contract and short another. The trader may hold equal but opposite positions (legs) in two or more different contracts of the same commodity on the same exchange, such as long 10,000 bushels of Chicago March wheat and short 10,000 bushels of Chicago May wheat. This is usually called an intracommodity or interdelivery spread. An interdelivery spread between, say, May wheat and December wheat would be characterized as an intercrop spread. The trader might also consider an interexchange spread such as long 10,000 bushels of Kansas City wheat and short 10,000 bushels of Chicago wheat in the same or different delivery months. The trader might also establish an intercommodity spread consisting of equal but opposite positions in two different but related commodities on the same or different exchanges; for example, he or she could be long 10,000 bushels of corn and short 10,000 bushels of wheat or long 25,000 bushels of oats and short 25,000 bushels of corn. Opposite positions in unrelated commodities are not considered spreads. A trader may be long copper and short sugar, but these would be considered merely separate positions because there is usually little or no price covariance between copper and sugar.

Historically, the terms "spread" and "straddle" had some shades of difference, but they have since become interchangeable among commodity traders, and in practice the word "spread" is now more commonly used in the futures markets. There was once some tendency for traders to speak of spreads in connection with grain positions and straddles in connection with other commodities, such as cotton. The terms "spread positions" and "hedge" are used interchangeably but incorrectly by some traders. A hedge refers to the concurrent holding of two opposite commodity positions, one in the cash, or spot, market and the other in the futures market. A spread position also refers to two concurrent and opposite positions, but both are in the futures markets. In its more general sense spread describes the price difference between the cash and futures markets in a hedged position. "Arbitrage" is a word related broadly to the others described herein, but it generally suggests two positions entered simultaneously, or virtually so, one long and the other short, "locking in" a price difference so great that a profit is virtually assured. In the commodity markets this condition would exist if the price of a distant contract exceeded the price of a nearby contract by an amount of more than the carrying charge. Another example might be a distorted difference between London and New York or Chicago futures prices caused by changes in transportation costs or currency values. Opportunities may arise from time to time in several futures traded on both foreign and domestic exchanges, but differences in contract sizes might well make taking advantage of such differences difficult. Silver has been one of the more popular vehicles for this kind of trading.

Arbitrages may also be executed in the securities markets by trading the same security on two different markets at different prices or the same security in different forms, such as common stock against convertible bonds, convertible preferred stock, rights, or options. A riskier form of arbitrage might be based upon an assumed merger of two companies whose stock does not adequately reflect the merger. Generally distortions in both securities and futures markets are small and exist only for brief periods, so such opportunities exist primarily for the professionals who have the ready capital to trade on a large scale, good communications, and low execution costs. Individual traders who lack these advantages will rarely if ever discover a realistic arbitrage opportunity and are probably well advised to devote their efforts to achieve profits to some other area.

Significance of Price Differences

Most of the following discussion centers on the taking of a spread position, but it is worth noting how important the spread differences among the prices of various contract months are to the intelligent establishment of a position. Suppose that it is August and that a trader believes that the price of wheat is likely to go up. He decides to establish a position of 10,000 bushels to take advantage of the expected price rise. He is aware that wheat is then trading for delivery in September, December, March, May, and July. How does he decide which to buy?

There are several factors to consider. One is the crop year which he believes presents the greater opportunity. The crop year for wheat begins on July 1. If he wants to take his position in the forthcoming new crop, he has little choice because the only new-crop contract trading in August is the July of the following year. If he believes that the greater opportunity is offered in the current, or old, crop, he must choose among the September, December, March, and May contracts. One factor affecting this decision is the amount of time believed needed for the expected upward price move to develop and when it is expected to begin. If he expects something to happen within a few days because of some near-term development, such as important export business, he could buy any of the old-crop contracts. He would probably lean toward the September delivery because there is less time available for the tightness in wheat to be alleviated, and it would best reflect a tight cash market.

If he expects to retain his position for some months, there is no point in considering September and no great attraction in the December contract. He can gain considerably more time by acquiring the March or May contract, thereby saving the commission that would be incurred if he bought an earlier contract and later "rolled forward" into a later leg.

The choice between the March and May contracts must still be made. Too many traders make this decision with little or no thought at all or, worse, for the wrong reasons. They may choose the March merely because they have been following that contract or buy the May because that happens to be the contract that their salesperson happens to keep on his quote machine or on a quote board in his office. The decision would better be made logically on the current price difference, or spread, between the March and May futures prices.

To clarify this point, assume that the carrying charge on a bushel of wheat is 12 cents a month. That would be the approximate cost of handling, storing, insuring, and financing 1 bushel for 1 month. The cost of carrying a bushel of wheat from the beginning of trading in the March contract to the beginning of trading in the May contract would therefore be 24 cents for the 2-month period. It would be virtually impossible for May wheat to sell for significantly more than 24 cents over the March delivery for long. If it were to do so, it would become profitable for an arbitrager to buy the March and sell the May at the unusually wide price difference. She would be prepared, if necessary, to take delivery of her March wheat on or after March 1, hold her short May position as a hedge, and then deliver her cash wheat against the May contract at her discretion anytime after May 1. More likely, the abnormal spread difference would dissolve quickly, and the arbitrager could simply liquidate both legs of her spread position and realize her profit. In either case, she would be certain of a gain approximating at least the difference between the approximate 24-cent theoretical carrying charge and the wider spread difference at which she had taken her position. Of course, she might gain or lose from a change in the carrying charge while she was holding her position. In addition, her own carrying charge might differ from the theoretical carrying charge.

Because opportunities like this are so obvious to professional traders and profits in the real world are not so easily attained because of market efficiency, the spread difference between March and May would almost certainly stop widening short of the 24-cent full theoretical carrying-charge difference. Yet if the spread difference were perceived as being near the practical limit, it would be of considerable help to a net position trader trying to make an intelligent decision. At near the full carrying charge he would probably place his long position in the March rather than the May contract. The prices of both contracts might rise equally, and he would realize the same gain in either one. Both might lose equally, and he would suffer the same loss in either one. If the spread difference changed, however, it would almost certainly do so either because March went up more than May or down less, and in both cases the trader would find the March contract the better alternative. March could not lose materially on May, and there is no limit to the amount that it could gain on May in a strong market. Not only could it sell for May, but there is no 12-cent barrier to its premium. Because clocks run only one way, nobody has yet found a way to buy the May contract of a commodity, take delivery, and then redeliver it against the previous March contract. When nearby contracts sell for more than distant contracts, the market is described as "inverted." Premiums of nearby contracts over premiums of distant ones can become quite large in strong markets—in some but not all futures markets.

If, with wheat at or near a full carrying charge, the trader believed that wheat was going to go down rather than up and he wanted to go short on either March or May, his decision would be just as obvious. He would certainly go short on the May contract rather than on the March. Here again, the spread difference could change materially only if May lost on March, because March could not lose on May unless carrying charges themselves increased. If the trader's judgment proved wrong and the market turned higher, the probability would be that March would gain on May. This would result in a loss greater than what would have been incurred on May during the same period. With May offering the added attraction of providing two additional months for the trade to work out profitably or for temporary adversity to be overcome, the choice of March would be a poor one indeed.

The traders who must be most alert to price differences if they are to profit from them are the position spreaders.

Spread Positions

Position spreaders are less interested in the direction of price than in the difference between two prices. Instead of deciding that a given contract price is too high or too low, they are interested in taking advantage of price differences that they consider abnormal. The possible positions open to these traders are intracommodity, intercommodity, or intermarket spreads, or a combination of them. The logic of those taking such positions is best made clear by example.

Intracommodity Spreads

Intracommodity spreaders try to take advantage of price differences that they believe are too wide or too narrow in the same market at the same time. They might note that May corn is selling for 18 cents over March and expect a strong market in corn to develop soon. If this should happen, they believe that not only would the general price level of corn go up but the March contract would gain on the May. If they are right, there is no limit to the amount that March could gain because it could not only close the prevailing discount but also sell for more than May by a substantial amount. If they are wrong, there is little to lose because here, again, March cannot sell below the May for long by much more than a reasonably full carrying charge. A spread trader would take advantage of this opportunity by buying the March contract and selling an equal amount of the May against it. This position could be characterized as a "bull spread," and the trader could be said to be "long the spread." The position could be established either by putting on both sides at the same time or by entering one side at a time in order to try to effect a more favorable difference. The latter, called "legging in," takes unusual skill and sometimes results in losing the opportunity observed in the first place.

When the spread has been established, the spreader merely has to wait for March to gain on May as much as she thinks it is going to and then take off (lift) her position. She does this by selling out her March contract and buying in her May. The removal of a spread position is often called "unwinding" or "backspreading." Here, again, she can take off both sides simultaneously by instructing her broker to remove the spread at the current market difference or at a difference of a fixed number of cents. She could also take off (lift) one side (leg) at a time and hope to improve her total profit by doing so. Like entering a spread one side at a time, removing it by lifting one leg at a time is not a good practice. Most trades seem to develop a peculiar knack for taking off the wrong side of their spreads first and then watching a profit achieved over a period of weeks dissolve in a few days or hours.

One of the questions most frequently asked by inexperienced traders is, "Why spread in the first place?" If a trader like the one described above thinks corn is going to go up, why not just buy the March? If the spreader is correct in her analysis, she will make a profit on her March contract, lose on her May, and show a net profit on the difference because the March profit will exceed the May loss. It is obvious that she would have had a greater profit per contract if she had just bought the March. Her action in taking the spread, however, is not quite so foolish as it may appear. By taking the spread position she has reduced her margin requirement. The margin on one contract, 5000 bushels, of March corn long against a short contract of 5000 May might be only $250 for the entire position, compared with a margin of $750 or more required for the March corn alone. If the price of March corn were to rise by 12 cents per bushel and that of May by 4 cents, the return on the margin utilized would be greater on the spreads than it would have been on the net position. The profit on the net March would have been $600 on a $750 margin requirement, or 80 percent. The spread position would provide a profit of $600 on the March and a loss of $200 on the May, but this would represent a net gain of $400, or 160 percent of the $250 margin requirement. If she chooses to be more aggressive, the trader could carry 15,000 bushels in a spread position for the same margin required for a net position of 5000 bushels. This would increase the percentage of net profit on the margin required but, of course, would expand the possible net loss risked as well.

It should be noted that the analysis of the corn situation may have been wrong in the first place and that corn might go down and not up. In that case a net position in March corn could be painful or even ruinous, whereas the spread position could hardly prove too painful because of the limited amount that the March contract could lose on the May. The cost of this "insurance" is not great because the commission on the spread position is only slightly more than the commission on a new position, and the funds needed to margin the position are considerably less. The spread trader may well have increased her potential profit and at the same time reduced investment and not materially increased her relative risk. It is even possible that the spreader could be completely wrong in her analysis and still make money just because she spread. The price of corn could fall drastically, and the price level of May could lose on that of March simply because more net traders choose to sell it or have to sell it because of pressure to liquidate as their margins erode. March, of course, still could not lose too much on the May because of the ever-present watchfulness of the arbitrager. This latter situation merely indicates that not all spreads work and that it is possible to make money for the wrong reason. A cynic might observe that luck beats brains every time.

It should be noted that in the preceding discussion it was assumed that the price of the nearby contract would gain on the price of the more distant contract in a rising market and lose in a falling market. This is true often enough, and so the position is often called a bull spread because it tends to work in rising markets. Careless traders may forget that it is not always true, and, in fact, one who is bullish in some commodities might well choose the opposite positions and be correct most of the time. Bull spreads involving long the nearby position and short the distant typically work best in the case of storable commodities and in the same crop year—for example, long March corn and short May corn or long January pork bellies and short July pork bellies. Storable commodities in which the classic bull spread tends to work include the grains, soybean and soybean products, sugar, orange juice, plywood and lumber, pork bellies, and usually, copper. In the case of some nonstorables, such as cattle, hogs, and Treasury bills, there may be little or no correlation between different commodity delivery months, and spread traders may find themselves simply with two almost unrelated positions, one long and one short. There are even some perverse futures such as potatoes and the precious metals which typically react in a manner opposite that of most storable commodities, and so in bull markets, the nearby contract actually tends to lose ground on the distant. Changes in carrying charges in the case of the previous metals are caused most frequently by changes in financing charges. As the price level rises, therefore, the distant contracts will not only rise along with the nearby but also tend to rise more because financing charges will be incurred on a higher base price. A spreader in these markets is really trading financing costs which will change with price level. Typically, therefore, the silver or gold traders who want to be long for an anticipated long-term rise are foolish to buy the nearby contract. They not only make less money if the market rises but also may find themselves paying commissions to roll positions forward while obtaining no benefit for the expense incurred.

In this area, as is the case with most rules, one must beware of the exceptions. There is little point in establishing a bear spread by selling the nearby contract short and buying the distant when the nearby is already relatively so low that it cannot lose any more ground. If the nearby contract involves the spot month, its price might be warped by certain technical problems such as delivery points and not reflect its usual reaction to movement in the more distant contracts. Nearby contracts are often expected to reflect strength in the tightness of cash commodities. Some markets, however, respond to other fundamental, technical, or speculative forces, and the result is that price differences might not act as may have been expected.

There is hardly any limit to the number of combinations open to the intracommodity spreader, but certain positions tend to be relatively popular, such as intercrop spreads of July soybeans against November, July cocoa against December, July world sugar against October, and May wheat against July.

Intercommodity Spreads

Some commodities are used for the same general purposes as others and therefore are interchangeable to a degree. The easier it is to substitute one for the other, the closer the relationship of their prices. Oats and corn are a case in point, as are hogs and cattle. Some traders may have observed historical ratios between the prices of related commodities such as silver and gold and may believe that undue widening or narrowing of the price difference may offer an opportunity. If a spreader believes that the price relation between two commodities is unrealistic, he can sell the higher-priced commodity, buy the lower-priced one, wait for the relative price levels to approach normality, and then take his profit. The advantages of trading in this manner are similar to those of intracommodity spreads. The margin on cattle against hogs is usually about the same as it would be for either hogs or cattle taken alone. This is greater than in the case of the intracommodity spread, in which the margin on the spread is considerably less than it would be on one side alone. Unlike the intracommodity spread, however, the intercommodity spread seldom involves a commission reduction when there is more than one commodity. Because drastic changes in the price levels of both commodities are likely to be similar, the risk of ruinous losses is considerably reduced at the cost of the opportunity to achieve windfall profits.

Among the more popular spreads of this kind are those involving soybeans and the products produced from the soybeans, namely, soybean oil and soybean meal. A spreader usually assumes that a crusher will find either oil or meal more profitable at a given time and that one of the product prices will be the stronger. If the current prices do not reflect the strength of one of the products adequately, the spreader can buy the product that she feels should be the stronger and sell the other against it. If she believes that the value of the two products combined is too low relative to the value of the beans, she can sell one contract of beans and buy one contract each of soybean oil and soybean meal. This position is usually called a "reverse crush" because it is opposite to the position taken by the soybean crusher, who is typically long on beans, which he crushes in order to be able to sell the products. A contract of oil plus one of meal does not exactly equal the amount of oil and meal that could actually be produced from the contract of 5000 bushels of beans, but it is usually close enough to yield a profit if the beans prove to be selling too high on the products. If the trader thinks that beans will gain on the combined products, she can buy the beans and sell the products, just as a crusher does. The establishment of such a position is sometimes called "putting on running time."

Other popular intercommodity spreads include wheat versus corn, hogs versus bellies or cattle, gold versus silver, long-term versus short-term financial instruments, and oats versus corn. Traders should make certain to note material differences in contract sizes or values to be sure that the sides are comparable. In the case of oats versus corn, for example, trades frequently spread one contract of corn against two contracts of oats because they consider a contract of oats to be worth only about 56 percent of a contract of corn.

Intermarket Spreads

Many commodities are traded on more than one market. Wheat is traded on the Chicago Board of Trade, the Kansas City Board of Trade, and the Minneapolis Grain Exchange. Chicago trades basically Soft Red winter wheat; Kansas City, Hard Red winter wheat; and Minneapolis, spring wheat. There is, however, a close relation among all these types, which are interchangeable for many purposes. In some cases the type trading on one exchange is deliverable against the type trading on another. All three basic types of wheat are deliverable on the Chicago Board of Trade. In this case the important limiting factors include the cost of transportation between cities, as well as differences in the characteristics of the different types of wheat. If speculators believe that price differences are out of line between commodities being traded in two cities, they sell the higher-priced contract and buy the lower-priced one. In spreads of this kind there is no commission advantage and seldom much, if any, margin advantage.

Popular positions include Winnipeg oats versus Chicago oats, New York cocoa and sugar against the London equivalents, Chicago against Kansas City or Minneapolis wheat, and New York gold or silver against Chicago or London.

Combinations

The fact that traders decide that Winnipeg oats are too low relative to Chicago oats does not mean that they should be long on *December* Winnipeg oats and short on *December* Chicago oats. If they think that oats are too high relative to corn, it does not follow that they should be long on *March* corn and short on *March* oats. The fact that they chose both contracts in the same delivery month may indicate that they have not thought enough about their spread positions. In most futures markets the nearby contract will gain on the distant in strong markets because of the influence of strong cash markets on the nearby contracts, and carrying charges will decrease or inversion will increase. During weak periods in such markets nearby contracts tend to lose on the distant, and carrying charges will increase or inversion will decrease. The long side of a spread trade should probably be the contract that is lowest-priced in terms of the prevailing spread differences in the commodity, and the short side should probably be the contract that appears highest-priced at that time. Traders should be careful to consider, however, that going to different delivery months will involve possible elements of change caused by variations in finance costs. They should also remember that bull spreads in some futures markets involve buying the spread and in others selling the spread. Nevertheless, for the best logical choice of both sides to be in the same delivery month would be sheer coincidence more often than not; yet this choice is all too often made by spreaders giving their positions only superficial thought.

Low-Risk Spreads

Many traders contemplating speculation in futures markets are in great fear of the risk involved. In order to reduce fear, many writers and speakers interested in attracting new commodity speculators are fond of discussing the "no-risk spread." The usual example given is an intracommodity spread being traded at the full carrying charge so that a trader can buy the nearby contract and sell the distant with virtually no risk at all except for a material change in the carrying charge. Actually, attractive opportunities of this kind are quite rare. Other traders will take spread positions before the contracts reach the full carrying-charge difference, with the result that the spreads may never get there. The closer the actual prices approach the apparent ideal, the more likely it is that there is such extreme weakness in the nearby lower-priced contract that there is no reason for it to gain on the distant contract. The low-risk trade, therefore, may involve little risk but will have little potential. Traders who wait for full carrying-charge situations involving real potential may spend a long time waiting for a trade that will never be made successfully.

Other more obscure examples of low-risk spreads involve combinations of positions now used primarily by professional traders and not too often by them. The butterfly spread involves three positions of unequal size in the same commodity. It is actually a spread of spreads with a common leg in the center. For example, one could be short one contract each of February and August pork bellies and long two May contracts. It will be noted that the inside leg is twice the size of and opposite in direction to the outside legs, or "wings." In the example given, the trader is said to be short the spread. If he were long the wings and short in the larger center position, he would be said to be long the spread. The latter position is sometimes referred to as a sandwich spread.

A similar spread may be established with no common contract in the middle. An example would be short January bellies, long March, long May, and short July. This is sometimes referred to as a condor spread.

If a combination of bull and bear spreads is applied to two closely related commodities rather than one, it is sometimes designated as a tandem spread. One might find such a spread utilized between cattle and hogs, hogs and bellies, Treasury bills and bonds, GNMAs and T-bonds, or other closely related financial instruments. For example, a trader may establish one spread position long on September Treasury bills and short on December bills and at the same time go short on September Treasury bonds and long on December bonds.

The low profit potential of such spreads and the difficulty of finding and recognizing realistically attractive opportunities have caused these spreads to be obscure, and they shall probably remain so except among highly sophisticated professional traders.

Tax Spreads

There were formerly large numbers of traders who entered spread positions primarily to achieve some tax advantage, such as postponement of gains to later years, conversion of short-term capital gains to long-term capital gains, conversion of ordinary gains to capital gains, or a combination of both favorable conversion and postponement. Combination spreads such as butterflies were especially popular for this purpose because of their extremely low risk. The profit potential in such trades was a secondary consideration, although traders were not averse to achieving a monetary gain in addition to their tax advantage if possible.

Low risk and the lack of a predominant profit motive eventually attracted considerable displeasure from the Internal Revenue Service, which began disallowing deductions from such trades, especially those from silver spreads. Current tax laws have caused the "tax spreaders" to try their luck elsewhere, but many cases resulting from disallowed trades were still wending their way through the courts long after the laws were changed.

Taxes were discussed briefly in Chapter 3, but detailed coverage of this subject is beyond the scope of this book and probably beyond that of some brokers and others who are sometimes too generous with advice in this complex and hazardous area. Because bad advice can lead to audits, disallowances, expense, and other forms of anguish, it might be wise to get advice from those best qualified to give it rather than from those with something to sell.

Problems

Although many of the traders who turn to spread trading do so with the expectation of finding it a simpler and safer approach to futures trading than is the trading of net positions, they may find themselves wrong on both counts. Not all the special problems encountered by spread traders can be discussed here, but some examples may help.

Many technicians rely heavily upon charts in selecting trades or in timing entrances to and exits from market positions. The chartist's first problem is determining what to put on the chart. For net positions, it is usual to indicate the opening, high, low, and closing prices of the commodity being monitored.

A trader interested in the price difference between two contract months of a commodity has a far more complex problem. The trader, may, of course, simply chart the two positions separately and attempt to learn by observation which of the two is acting stronger or weaker relative to the other. If it is considered more desirable to chart the spread difference itself by subtracting the price of one contract from the price of the other, it may be difficult or impossible to represent the differences realistically. Spread transactions are not indicated separately from net trades on any generally available quote system or in the columns of financial publications, so a considerable amount of guesswork becomes necessary. The differences between the closing prices or midranges of both contracts are often charted, but midranges may occur at quite different times and may represent materially different ranges, or both. The closing price of one or both of the contracts may reflect an aberration such as an unusually large order to buy or sell on the close of the market. This might result in a substantial change in the spread difference if closing prices are utilized for charting, but it would almost certainly be insignificant and correct itself at the opening of the market on the following day. There is really no way to judge,from the day's ranges of the individual contracts where the spread was really being traded during the day and certainly no way of knowing whether volume in the spread was light or heavy. The lack of readily accessible data may make it impossible even to determine the ranges of spreads during the trading day. Spread quotes may or may not exist on trading floors.

The observer of intermarket spreads may have an additional concern if the commodities followed have different contract sizes. For example, he may be interested in trading hogs versus cattle. The trader's spread chart may indicate the difference in price between hogs which have a 30,000-pound contract and live cattle which have a 40,000-pound contract. Noting a "chart signal" indicating to him that the price of hogs should gain on the price of cattle, the trader might act upon this by buying one contract of hogs and selling one contract of cattle. If the price of hogs rises and the price of cattle falls, the trade will prove to be profitable. If both prices should fall, the trader will still achieve a satisfactory result provided that the price of cattle falls as far as or farther than the price of hogs. If prices rise, however, a problem may well occur. The price of hogs could rise, by, say, 120 points and the price of cattle by only 100 points, which would be quite consistent with the chart signal but not too satisfactory to the trader, who would suffer a loss of $400 on the cattle while enjoying a gain of only $360 on the hogs.

The solution to this problem may appear quite simple but actually only lead to further complications. The trader could establish a position of four contracts of hogs and three contracts of cattle, thereby providing equal long and short positions of 120,000 pounds each. This would make a profit certain if the signal worked but involve too large a monetary risk for a trader with minimum capital. Other combinations of related commodities might require even larger positions to achieve equality, or equality might even be impossible from a practical point of view.

An alternative solution is to attempt to build the price difference into the chart itself by multiplying the actual price of cattle by 4/3 or the actual price of hogs by 3/4 and then charting the somewhat artificial difference. The assumption might be that market action would now be sufficient to offset the price difference, but there might be some question as to whether the chart signals themselves would remain accurate enough to support trading decisions. That is, of course, assuming that chart signals based upon unadjusted prices were valid in the first place.

It is quite common, and probably wise, for technicians to progress from "paper trading" into "real-world trading." In the case of spreads, even paper trading can prove quite difficult to evaluate among those not inclined to lie to themselves. How can they ever really know where a trade would have been entered? Unless a spread clearly widens or narrows well beyond their price objectives, can they ever be really sure that the positions could have been liquidated at a profit? If stops are to be utilized and the trade fails, how can the trader know with any reasonable accuracy what the liquidation price would have been?

If trading in the real world is begun, additional problems might arise that were not even considered during the planning stage. Futures markets may open or close at different times, so news may affect the commodity that is being traded, whereas the other side of the spread is in a future which is closed and therefore unable to respond to the same news. This may be serious during a closing period when news adverse to the spread may cause a severely aberrant close, which may result in a substantial margin call. If one side of the spread is in a foreign market, currency variations may add an additional element of risk.

Futures may have different trading limits, which means that traders may lose more on one side of a spread than they make on the other, with the result that they find themselves not nearly so well protected by being spread as they may have thought. Traders who are short on wheat and long on corn find small comfort in their spreads in a sharply rising market when they discover that they are making 10 cents per bushel per day on the corn while losing 20 cents per bushel per day on the short wheat.

Execution costs of spreads tend to be high and only partly because of the greater commissions incurred. More serious is the fact that spreaders entering a position have to enter the long side at the offer and the short side at the bid, although the existence of spread quotes on the exchange floor might reduce or eliminate this problem. When they liquidate, they may again face the same problem. This may not seem to involve particularly large numbers, but it may actually cause the profit from the spread to be materially less than had been expected. This must be added to the initial problem of predicting a realistic number of winning trades. The problem is further compounded if one leg of the spread is to be placed in a thin distant contract. This may be tolerable if the trade proves to be successful, but if it is stopped out, the resulting loss may be substantially greater than had been anticipated.

It is not unusual for traders to deal in both spreads and net positions. If such traders have an open position long on March wheat and short on May wheat and now get an indication that they should be long on May wheat, they face a whole new range of decision making.

None of this should be taken to indicate that spread trading cannot be done successfully, for that is not the case. Too often, however, spread trading is offered as a rather simple low-risk way of trading commodities which is especially good for the beginner. That is not the case either. Spread trading may be more difficult than net trading and may involve greater rather than less risk.

Mistakes

The most frequent mistake made by those who trade spread positions is establishing them for all the wrong reasons. A common example is the net position trader who has an open loss that continues to get worse until he receives a margin call. He could, of course, solve his immediate problem by reducing or eliminating his position, but for some reason he regards a realized loss as something so much worse than an open loss that he will do anything to avoid it. This error is so widespread and usually so disastrous that it is worth examining in some detail.

Presume that a cocoa trader is convinced that the price of May cocoa at $2528 per ton is such a bargain that it is worth the full use of his available trading capital of $6000. The margin requirement for one contract of 10 metric tons of cocoa at the brokerage house of his choice is $2000. He therefore buys three contracts of May cocoa at $2528 and waits for great wealth to come his way. Unfortunately, the news items concerning cocoa become unfavorable. Ghana announces that its crop looks better than had been expected. Holland and Germany speak of decreased consumption, and suddenly May cocoa is at $2414 and "not acting well." The trader is convinced that this adversity is temporary and that the forthcoming rise will be bigger than ever, and he wishes only that he could buy the cocoa now instead of when he did. Nevertheless, his broker's shortsighted margin clerk, concerned only with numbers, points out that the open loss is $3420 and that there is insufficient margin remaining to support three cocoa contracts.

The trader now has several choices. First, he could deposit additional funds, but he has none available for this purpose. Second, he could sell one cocoa contract and keep the other two, but he does not like the prospect of having to make $171 per ton on each of his two remaining contracts to compensate for the $114 open loss on each of the three contracts he has bought. Third, he could admit that he was wrong about the cocoa market and liquidate all three of his contracts. This he finds impossible to do because he would have a realized loss of more than $3400 in addition to the necessity of admitting to himself, his wife, his broker, and his accountant that he is not as good a trader as he would like to have them think. So he seeks a way to postpone the inevitable by buying time. Accordingly, he orders his broker to sell three contracts of July cocoa at its present price of $2375 a ton. The margin requirement on a cocoa spread is only $500 compared with the $2000 on a net long or short position, so his total margin requirement is reduced from $6000 to $1500. The equity in the account was reduced from $6000 to $2580 by the decline in May cocoa, so the margin call is easily satisfied by spreading the May cocoa against the new July position.

On close examination it should be apparent that the trader has not really improved his position and may have made it worse. He has reduced his margin requirement from $6000 to $1500, but he would have had no requirement at all if he had simply sold his May cocoa. His new plan, if he has one, is probably to cover his short July position after cocoa stops going down and take his "profit." It should be clear, however, that his position will be no better than if he had just taken off his May cocoa and reinstated it. It is probable that the May will drop just as much as July if July goes down, and therefore his July closed profit will be equaled by an additional May open loss. The commission expense of trading the three July contracts is just the same as that incurred in taking off the three May. The moment the July short position is lifted, the margin requirement reverts to $6000 and the trader has the same problem he had before because there has been no equity improvement. A common procedure for such people would be to take off July early one day and hope that May rises enough by the close to overcome the margin call—which, of course, might happen. Because the trend of cocoa has been down, however, it is at least as likely that cocoa will go down during the day and make matters worse. In the end he might trade his July cocoa several times, paying a commission of about $300 every time he does until he has a margin call even on the spread position and his situation has become hopeless. At this point he will probably blame the cocoa exchange, his broker, or his bad luck, when actually he was guilty of overtrading, failing to take a loss quickly, and spreading for the wrong reasons. Aside from a rally in the May futures on the day he covers his July position, the only other way out of his predicament is an improvement in the spread itself resulting from the May contract gaining materially on the July, but in a bear market the reverse is more likely. The chances of spreading a bad position and then recovering either by successfully day-trading one side of the spread or by seeing a material improvement in the spread position itself are extremely thin ones.

A second serious error common among spreaders is choosing a spread in preference to a net position primarily to reduce margin and then putting on such a large spread position, just because the margin is low, that they ultimately take more risk and pay more in commissions than they would have paid with a net position. Such traders fail to realize that a spread provides some but not complete protection. A spreader might consider a price difference warped and thereby offering an opportunity, but it might well become even more warped and result in a loss before it returns to normal, that is, assuming it was warped in the first place and did not merely reflect some condition overlooked by the spreader.

A corn trader, for example, may consider May corn cheap at $2.82 and consider the purchase of 5000 bushels for an anticipated 18-cent gain, for which she would risk a 6-cent loss. The required margin might be $750 and the round-turn commission $80. The gain would yield her a gross profit of $900 and a net profit of $820. The gross risk would be $300, and the total anticipated risk would be $380. The $820 profit would be about 109 percent of the margin required, but the trader concludes that she would do even better by spreading because her broker will carry 5000 bushels of May corn long against 5000 bushels of December corn short for only $250. She believes that the expected 18-cent gain in May corn will result in its gaining 9 cents on December corn during the same time, which would represent a potential net profit of $350, or about 140 percent on the $250 margin. The commission on the spread position of about $100 would be only slightly higher than the commission on the net trade and so would not materially overcome the benefits of a higher return, a lower margin, and risk, at least perceived, at a lower level.

This seems so attractive to the trader that she is reluctant to leave idle the remainder of the $750 margin that the net corn position would have required. She thereupon decides to utilize the same capital for the spread and puts on three of the spreads, or 15,000 long May corn against 15,000 short December. If her trade succeeds, she will realize a gross profit of $2700 less a total commission of about $180, or $2520 on her $750 margin. What she fails to consider is the effect of possible adversity. It is unrealistic to assume that one could be prepared for a possible loss of less than 5 cents on a spread of this kind, but some unexpected event like an adverse government report on the corn crop could easily cause a loss of 5 cents or even more. A 5-cent loss on the spread would be $750 plus the $180 commission, which would more than wipe out the trader's capital. This is a far greater loss than could reasonably have been suffered on a net position. As a result the apparently safer position with a smaller investment has become a far greater risk with an equal investment and a larger commission.

Even when a spread can be established on the basis of an available quote, some traders are tempted to establish a spread one leg at a time or to remove it one leg at a time. This has at least one clear disadvantage and usually two. The spread commission is lost. Instead of paying the spread commission of about $100 for a corn spread, for example, the customer must pay the full $80 for each side, or a total of $160 for both. Second, most traders have an uncanny ability to put on the wrong leg first or take off the wrong one first. This is so probably because most of them try to choose the exact moment that a market will turn, which is almost impossible to do. For example, suppose that the corn spread previously discussed has worked favorably and that May corn has gained the planned 9 cents on December. The trader could take off the spread at the prevailing difference and realize her profit. She could also cover her December short and allow the May to continue to rise. Instead, she will probably yield to the temptation to take off the May because it is the profitable side and stay short on December, hoping that it will go down, overcome its paper loss, and allow her to show a profit on both legs of the spread. Actually, what seems to happen all too often is that the May side is taken off on a day when corn is strong, and it is that very strength which caused the spread to succeed. It is also taken off early in the day because the trader wants as much time as possible for December to react. So corn continues strong, and the 9-cent profit that was realized over a period of months is lost in hours.

A mistake that is not quite so serious, but quite common, is the haphazard choosing of contract months. The trader could have timed the transaction by watching a chart indicating the difference between May and December corn, but at the moment of entry July might be a better choice than May or March better than December. The choice should be based on all pertinent factors, not on the casual choice of contracts on a spread chart or a broker's quotation screen.

An error that may prove to be downright disastrous is the failure to realize the risk-reward consequences of being short on the nearby leg of an intramarket spread and long on the distant. This means that the potential reward of the trade is limited to the full carrying charge between the contracts utilized for the spread, whereas the risk of loss is virtually limitless. Selling the nearby leg in an inverted market may have merit if near-term weakening of the market is anticipated, but selling the nearby at a deep discount to the deferred contract may be extremely hazardous in some markets. Such positions are sometimes established by somewhat unsophisticated traders who believe all spread trades to be conservative. They were formerly sometimes used by traders spreading for tax purposes who did not always fully realize the risks of their positions.

NOTES FROM A TRADER

Spread trading is not so simple as taking net long or net short positions in a commodity. The advantages are sometimes so great, however, that it is well worth the time and energy needed to master them. Most spread positions involve less risk than net positions and frequently less investment. The extra commissions incurred are usually a small consideration compared with the advantages. The avoidance of catastrophic losses is one of the greatest advantages of spread trading. Futures markets sometimes have sudden violent price movements. When one of these movements is in favor of a trader, he realizes a welcome windfall profit, but when one is against him, he is no longer a futures trader. Many speculators with experience in trading are happy to forgo the opportunity for such windfall profits if the equal chance for a disastrous loss can be avoided. Spreads accomplish this reduction of risk because what is lost on one side in an unusually large adverse move is frequently matched by an approximately equal gain on the other side. The cost of this insurance against disaster is quite low. For a new trader spreads may provide an opportunity to enter the commodity markets with minimum capital and risk.

Options

---

*"We must learn to explore all the options and
possibilities that confront in a complex and
rapidly changing world."*   JAMES FULBRIGHT

REGULATORY BACKGROUND

Exchange-traded stock options began at the Chicago Board Options Exchange (CBOE), an "offshoot" of the Chicago Board of Trade, during 1973. Exchange-traded stock options expanded in both the number of stocks covered and the trading volume, not only at the CBOE but also at the American Stock Exchange and some regional stock exchanges. Prior to the listing of exchange-traded stock options, there were over-the-counter options on stocks, but they never entered the mainstream of Main Street investments.

U.S. commodity options—that is, options on some agricultural products—were traded on U.S. futures exchanges but were prohibited in 1936. In the early and mid-1970s, options on futures contracts traded in foreign cities, mostly London, were traded in increasing volume in the United States. However, questionable sales practices and many allegations of fraud in these options received considerable press, and these options were banned as of June 1, 1979. The only commodity options then remaining were the so-called dealer options, which were options on physical commodities sold by those having a commercial interest in the underlying commodity. To continue in this business, dealers had to have been in the commodity option business as of May 1, 1978, and meet other requirements. Dealer options continue but are small in coverage and volume.

The regulatory process for approving the trading of options on U.S. futures exchanges began on January 29, 1981, when the CFTC published proposed rules for a pilot program for exchange-traded options on nonagricultural futures contracts. These rules were adopted by the CFTC on November 3, 1981, and became effective on December 3, 1981.

Exhibit 9-1 shows the futures options contracts listed according to this program. The Treasury bond futures option, the gold futures option, and deutsche mark futures option, and, to a lesser extent, some other options contracts have proved successful.

During December 1982, the CFTC approved a pilot program for options on select nonagricultural "physicals" whereby each exchange could list one such option. Then during November 1983, the CFTC amended its programs for options on futures and options on physicals so that each exchange could list two options in either category rather than only one option in each category. As Exhibit 9-1 indicates, the CME (with an option on its deutsche mark futures contract) and Comex (with an option on its silver futures contract), which have been quite successful, and the CBT (with an option on its silver futures contract), which has not been successful, participated in this second-round program.

The next major step in the U.S. commodity options program occurred during late October 1984, when U.S. futures exchanges were allowed to trade options on two of their agricultural futures contracts. The agricultural futures contracts listed by the exchanges according to this program are shown in Exhibit 9-2.

EXHIBIT 9-1   Commodity Option Pilot Program

Exchange*	Futures contract	Date listed for trading
Initial pilot:		
CBT	Treasury bond	October 1, 1982
Comex	Gold	October 4, 1982
CSC	Sugar	October 1, 1982
CME	S&P 500 Index	January 28, 1983
NYFE	NYSE Composite Index	January 28, 1983
KCBT	Value Line Index†	March 4, 1983
Second round:		
CME	Deutsche mark	January 24, 1984
Comex	Silver	October 4, 1984
CBT	Silver	March 29, 1985

*CBT—Chicago Board of Trade
CME—Chicago Mercantile Exchange
CSC—Coffee, Sugar & Cocoa Exchange
Comex—Commodity Exchange
KCBT—Kansas City Board of Trade

MCE—MidAmerica Commodity Exchange
MGE—Minneapolis Grain Exchange
NYCE—New York Cotton Exchange
NYFE—New York Futures Exchange

†Traded on the floor of the CBT.

EXHIBIT 9-2   Agricultural Commodity Option Pilot Program

Exchange	Futures contract	Date listed for trading
CBT	Soybeans	October 30, 1984
CME	Live cattle	October 30, 1984
KCBT	Wheat (Hard Red winter)	October 30, 1984
MGE	Wheat (Hard Red spring)	October 30, 1984
MCE	Wheat	October 30, 1984
NYCE	Cotton	October 30, 1984
CME	Live hogs	February 1, 1985
CBT	Corn	February 27, 1985
MCE	Soybeans	February 8, 1985
MCE	Gold	August 17, 1984

The CFTC and Congress expanded the pilot program on nonagricultural futures and nonagricultural physical commodities (such as silver and gold) from two to five contracts on August 24, 1984. The contracts listed according to this expanded program are shown in Exhibit 9-3. This 3-year pilot program was scheduled to expire on October 1, 1985, but it was extended prior to that date. Subsequently, on April 29, 1986, the CFTC voted to replace the pilot program on nonagricultural futures contracts and physical commodities with a permanent program. With respect to the separate 3-year pilot program on agricultural futures, which expires on January 25, 1987, the CFTC also voted to expand it from two contracts to five on April 8, 1986.

Another addition to the options program came on April 26, 1985, when the American Stock Exchange, through a CFTC subsidiary, listed an option on physical gold with a cash settlement. The Philadelphia Stock Exchange, through a CFTC subsidiary, listed an option on a "physical" 90-day Eurodollar on May 10, 1985. This Eurodollar option is based on cash settlement and is the first European-type option listed by an exchange, which means that the options cannot be exercised by the long prior to expiration.

FUTURES VS. OPTIONS

Futures

Futures are symmetrical; that is, the seller (short) and the buyer (long) are subject to symmetrical gains and losses. Figure 9-1 shows the potential profit and loss of long and short futures positions which were initially transacted at a price of $100. If the price increases from $100, the long profits by the amount of the price increase and the short loses this amount, and vice versa for a price decrease. Thus, the profits and losses for buyers are symmetrical.

EXHIBIT 9-3   Expanded Commodity Option Pilot Program

Exchange	Futures contract	Date listed
CME	British pound	February 25, 1985
CME	Swiss franc	February 25, 1985
CME	Eurodollar	March 20, 1985
CBT	Silver	March 29, 1985
CBT	Treasury note	May 1, 1985

For futures contracts, symmetry applies in other ways also. Both longs and shorts put up margin, but on neither side does the margin represent a payment; it is simply earnest money or a good-faith bond. If the underlying price remains constant, say at $100, both receive their full margins back. Commissions must also be paid, of course.

In addition, prior to the notice and delivery days, both longs and shorts can liquidate their futures positions by offset at the exchange, longs liquidating their position by selling and shorts liquidating by buying. Deliveries cannot occur prior to the notice-delivery period. During the delivery period, however, both the long and the short may be obligated to participate in delivery, with the short making delivery and receiving payment and the long taking delivery and making payment.[1]

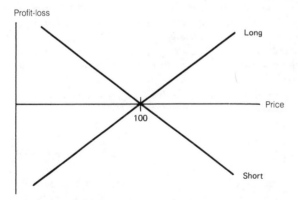

Figure 9-1   Profit-loss profile of long and short futures.

---

[1] For futures contracts with multiple delivery days, the shorts have somewhat more flexibility than the longs in that the shorts can choose the delivery day on which they will deliver. Presumably, however, the longs will not maintain their long positions during the delivery periods unless they wish to take delivery. In addition, for futures contracts with multiple delivery grades, the shorts may choose which of the various deliverable grades they will actually deliver. Market participants, however, usually know which grade will actually be delivered, and the futures contracts are priced on the basis of this "cheapest deliverable" grade. Both of these privileges of the short represent the "seller's option" of the futures contract. Both of these aspects of the seller's option affect the symmetry of the long and the short in futures contracts only in a minor way.

Options

Buyers and sellers of futures contracts have for the most part similar rights and obligations. Prior to the delivery period, neither has the right to demand that the delivery process occur. During the delivery process, both have the obligation to participate in the delivery process. Options are by design asymmetrical—buyers and sellers of options have unequal rights and obligations. The options buyer has the right to initiate the delivery process at any time, while the seller has the obligation to respond to the long's choice at this time.[2] Thus, the long is in a superior position because the long has the right and the short has the obligation.

This asymmetry leads to a true story of a conversation between a potential options customer and a broker. The potential customer asks the broker, "What's the difference between futures and options?" The broker, after a long pause, responds, "That's a complicated question, but I guess the main difference is that futures are symmetrical and options are asymmetrical." The customer quickly asks, "You mean that to trade options I have to learn the metric system?" Although options are more complicated than futures, learning the metric system is not necessary, and options do provide more speculative flexibility than futures, which makes it worthwhile to deal with this complexity.

There is a quid pro quo for this asymmetry. The long, to compensate the short for accepting this obligation, must pay the short a fixed amount of money at the time the transaction is made. The amount of this payment is called the option *premium* and is a market-determined price.

In the futures markets, neither the short nor the long pays the other; margin is only earnest money. If the underlying price remains the same, both the long and the short receive their margin back. In options, however, the buyer pays the seller for accepting the obligation mirroring the long's right. And if the underlying price remains constant, the short retains this amount, the option premium, and the long loses this "payment."

At this point it is necessary to introduce a third difference between futures and options.

PUTS AND CALLS

In futures, with symmetrical rights and obligations regarding delivery and payment, an investor can go long or short. In options, with asymmetrical rights and obligations, the long has the rights and the short has the obligations with respect to delivery. Given the asymmetry of rights and obligations with respect to options and consistent with the two sides of delivery—taking delivery and making delivery—there are two types of options: *calls* and *puts*. Calls permit buyers to call for or demand delivery at any time they choose. Puts permit buyers to put or make delivery at any time they choose.

---

[2] This is the case for "American" options. In "European" options the options buyer can initiate delivery only at the expiration or maturity of the options contract.

Because options apply to the right of the long to take (call) or make (put) delivery, one other aspect of delivery must be specified. This aspect is called the "strike price." The strike price, which is independent of the current market price, is the price at which delivery is made from the short to the long, in the case of a call, or from the long to the short, in the case of a put. Options (both calls and puts), like futures, also have maturities, or dates on which trading in them ceases.

In futures, one may trade, for example, a March contract, on which one could go long or short. With options there are both March calls and March puts, each of which has various strike prices. For example:

March calls @ $100   March puts @ $100

March calls @ $102   March puts @ $102

March calls @ $104   March puts @ $104

Figure 9-1 shows a profit-loss profile for long and short futures positions. The profit-loss profile for each is symmetrical. For example, from any given initial price, if the price increases by $1, a long future profits by $1; if the price decreases by $1, the long future loses by $1. Next consider the profit-loss profile of calls and puts.

Calls

Consider calls first. Assume that we are dealing with a March call on a gold futures contract at a strike price of $400. Assume that the gold futures price is also $400 at this time. Assume that the price of this call, paid by the buyer to the seller, is $20. This price is called the call "premium."[3] The premium is determined in the same way that futures prices are determined: by bidding and offering on the exchange. The premium is the option price which is the counterpart to the futures price.

This premium exemplifies a fundamental difference between futures and options. In futures, there is no passing of money between the long and the short—both put up a margin, which is earnest money, not a payment. In options, however, the premium is paid by the buyer to the seller—the premium is truly a payment which the buyer transfers to the seller. If the underlying price remains constant, in the above example, the seller keeps this amount and the buyer loses it.

Note the profit-loss profiles of the long and the short in the above example. To do so it must be recognized that the long has the right to "call for" delivery of a (long) futures contract at any time prior to the option's expiration for $400, and the short, then, has the obligation to deliver the long futures at $400. The notification of the exchange by the long with regard to the desired delivery date is called an "exercise." The identification of the corresponding short by the exchange

---

[3] The premium is quoted in terms of the price of what underlies the futures contract. For example, if the price of gold is $400 per ounce, the premium will be quoted as $20 per ounce. But with 100 ounces of gold per futures contract, the total premium on one option will be $2000 ($20 per ounce × 100 ounces).

is called an "assignment." The expiration of the option occurs at the termination of trading. Although the long has the right to call for delivery at any time prior to expiration and the short, then, has the obligation to make delivery, at expiration all outstanding long calls must be exercised or they expire and are worthless.

The exchange accomplishes the exercise and assignment in the above example by assigning the long call that is exercised a long futures contract at $400 and the short call to which it is assigned a short futures position at $400.[4] If, for example, the gold futures contract has a price of $420 at the time, the long futures position has an immediate profit of $20 and the short futures position an immediate loss of $20.

One important aspect of option prices or premiums should be recognized. Consider the premium of a gold futures call with a strike price of $400. Assume that the underlying futures price is $400. If the call is exercised, the exerciser will be assigned a futures contract at the strike price of $400. Because the underlying futures price is also $400, there will be no profit or loss as a result of exercise. This does not mean that the option price or premium will be zero. The call will have value during the time prior to the call's expiration because the futures price may increase above $400 and there would be a profit on exercise. This component of the option premium is called "time value."

An option's premium can thus be divided into two components: *time value* and *intrinsic value*. The intrinsic value is the immediate profit that would result from the exercise of an option. For a call, there is an immediate profit from exercise only if the underlying futures price is above the strike price of the call. For example, if the underlying futures price is $420, the exercise of a $400 call results in the assignment to the exerciser of a long futures position of $400. With the futures price at $420, there is an immediate profit of $20 due to exercise. Thus, the call has an intrinsic value of $20, but the option price will be greater than $20. There is an additional value to the call because the underlying futures price may increase above $420, giving the long call a profit even greater than $20. The value of the option premium in excess of $20 is called time value. Thus, in this example, if the option premium is $30, the time value is $10 because the intrinsic value is $20.

An option which has intrinsic value, that is, whose underlying futures price is greater than the strike price, is said to be "in the money." If the underlying futures price were equal to the strike price, as in the above example when both were $400, there would be no intrinsic value to the option and the option premium would be entirely time value. An option whose underlying futures price is equal to the strike price is said to be "at the money."

Consider the third possibility—the case with the underlying futures price being less than the call's strike price. For example, assume that the underlying futures price is $380 for the call whose strike price is $400. If the buyer of the call exercised

---

[4] The common methods of assignment are random assignment and assignment by the age of the short option, with the newest options being assigned first.

the call, he would be assigned a long futures contract at the strike price of $400. But because the underlying futures price is $380, he would have an immediate loss of $20.

The buyer of the call would, of course, not exercise the call in this case. The buyer of the call has the right to decide when and whether to exercise, and she would not exercise if the exercise would result in a loss. Instead, she would let the call *expire worthless*. A call whose underlying futures price is less than the strike price is said to be "out of the money." The buyer of a call which remains out of the money until expiration will allow it to expire worthless. The buyer's loss, then, will be what was paid to buy the call—the option premium. Obviously, the entire value of an out-of-the-money call, prior to expiration, is time value—it has no intrinsic value.

All options, prior to expiration, have time value. In-the-money options also have intrinsic value. At-the-money and out-of-the-money options have zero intrinsic value. The time value of an option is greatest when the option is at the money (futures price equals the strike price), and the time value decreases as the option goes more in the money (the futures price increases for a call, or the opposite for a put) or out of the money (the futures price decreases for a call, or the opposite for a put).[5]

Not surprisingly, the time value declines for in-the-money, at-the-money, or out-of-the-money options as the options approach maturity. Thus, as an option matures, its time value declines. The reason is that the less time there is remaining, the less the probability that the futures price will increase to give the option some value at expiration, or greater value at expiration. And all options with no time left until expiration have zero time value. The combination of time value and intrinsic value for in-the-money, at-the-money, and out-of-the-money options is summarized in Exhibit 9-4.

In general an option premium depends on five factors:

1. *Strike price.* The higher the strike price, the less intrinsic value a call option has (opposite for put option).

---

[5] While few options traders understand the technical reasons for these facts, most do know them and act accordingly.

EXHIBIT 9-4 Intrinsic Value and Time Value of Options

	Calls		Puts	
	Time value	Intrinsic value	Time value	Intrinsic value
In the money	+	+	+	+
At the money	+	0	+	0
Out of the money	+	0	+	0

2. *Underlying futures price.* The higher the underlying futures price, the greater the intrinsic value a call option has (opposite for put option).

3. *Volatility of underlying futures price.* The higher the volatility, the more likely it is that an out-of-the-money option (put or call) will go into the money and, thus, have intrinsic value.

4. *Level of short-term interest rate.* Both call and put premiums decrease slightly as the short-term interest rate increases.

5. *Time to expiration.* The greater the time to expiration, the greater the possibility that the underlying futures price will change such that the option (put or call) becomes in the money and, thus, the greater the premium (put or call).

The call premium decreases as factors (1) and (4) increase but increases as factors (2), (3), and (5) increase. The put premium increases as factors (1), (3), and (5) increase and decreases as factors (2) and (4) increase.

Now consider the profit-loss profile of a long call at various futures prices at the time of expiration of the option's contract, as summarized in Exhibit 9-5.

Consider, again, a call option on gold futures with a June expiration and a $400 strike price. Assume that the June futures contract is priced at $400 at the time

EXHIBIT 9-5 Profit-Loss Profile of Call

A. Long Call			
Futures price at option's expiration	Premium paid by long	Long's profit or loss at expiration	Net profit or loss by long
360	−20	0	−20
370	−20	0	−20
380	−20	0	−20
390	−20	0	−20
400	−20	0	−20
420	−20	20	0
440	−20	40	+20
460	−20	60	+40
480	−20	80	+60

B. Short Call			
Futures price at option's expiration	Premium received by short	Short's profit or loss at expiration	Net profit or loss by short
360	+20	0	+20
370	+20	0	+20
380	+20	0	+20
390	+20	0	+20
400	+20	0	+20
420	+20	−20	0
440	+20	−40	−20
460	+20	−60	−40
480	+20	−80	−60

the call is purchased (that is, the call is at the money) and that the premium paid by the long to the short for the call option is $20.[6]

Initially the long pays the short $20 for the call. Thus, the long loses $20 and the short benefits by $20 due to this initial purchase by the long and sale by the short. There may also be additional profits or losses realized by the long and the short at the expiration of the option's contract for various prices of the underlying futures contract.

Assume, first, that the price of the futures contract remains at $400 at expiration. Thus, the long call is assigned a long futures contract if he or she exercises, at the strike price of $400, and the short call is assigned a short futures contract at $400. Neither experiences a profit or loss due to only the exercise or assignment. Thus, there is a net profit of $20 to the short due only to the $20 premium paid by the long to the short and a net loss of $20 to the long, as seen in Exhibit 9-5.

Now assume that the futures price is $420 at expiration. The long call, if it is exercised, will be assigned a long futures contract at the strike price of $400 and the short call a short futures contract at $400. Thus, the long would experience an immediate profit, because of exercise, of $20 and the short a loss of $20. This profit and loss, however, are offset by the payment of the $20 premium from the long to the short, and, thus, on a net basis both the long call and the short call break even, as indicated in Exhibit 9-5.

Similarly, if the futures price is $440 at expiration, the long will profit by $40 at expiration due to exercise and the short will lose $40 due to assignment. After the $20 premium initially paid by the long call to the short call is netted out, the long call will have a net profit of $20 and the short call a net loss of $20.

The result can be extrapolated for any higher futures price at expiration. In general, longs will always exercise at expiration when the option is in the money. The profit to the long or the loss to the short is always equal to the ultimate futures price minus the strike price, with the profit to the long and the loss to the short due to exercise and assignment, minus the initial premium paid by the long to the short.

Consider next the futures price at expiration being less than the initial futures price. Assume that the futures price is $390 at expiration. If the long call is exercised, it will be assigned a long future at the strike price of $400. But because the futures price is $390, this will lead to an immediate loss of $10 to the long call and a profit of $10 to the short call. But this is where the asymmetry of options comes to the fore. The long, due to the quid pro quo for paying the option premium ($20 in this example), has the "option" of whether to exercise the call or not. And the long would not exercise an option if it led to an immediate loss of $10. The long, who has the choice or the option, would let the call expire worthless. Thus, the long would lose only the initial premium of $20. And the short would profit

---

[6] There are, of course, commissions on both futures and options on futures. These commissions are ignored in this chapter but, in practice, will not be ignored by your broker, and as a result, you cannot ignore them either.

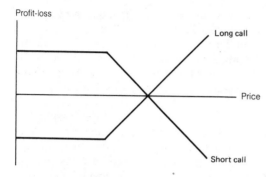

Profit-loss

Long call

Price

Short call

Figure 9-2 Profit-loss profile for long and short calls.

by only the initial premium of $20. In this case, the short would not actually realize the extra $10 in profit because the call would not be exercised.

In general, the long would never exercise an out-of-the-money call—a call whose strike price was greater than the underlying futures price—and would let it expire worthless. Thus, for out-of-the-money calls, the long would lose the premium initially paid to the short and no more. And the short would profit by the premium initially paid by the long and no more. The profit-loss profile for long and short calls is shown in Figure 9-2. There are asymmetries in these profiles. The long can lose no more than the initial premium but can profit by an unlimited amount, and the short can profit by no more than the initial premium but can lose an unlimited amount. These asymmetries result from the fact that the long can choose whether to exercise the option or not.

It is interesting to note, however, that the long call is a bull strategy (that is, it profits if the underlying futures price increases and loses if the futures price decreases) and that the short call is a bear strategy. But neither is like a long futures (which is a bull strategy) or a short futures (which is a bear strategy) because futures, whether long or short, have unlimited profits *and* losses, whereas the profits and losses of long and short calls are limited in one direction and unlimited in the other direction. These differences are illustrated in Figure 9-3 and summarized in Exhibit 9-6.

Long futures and long calls are both bull strategies, but long futures have both unlimited profits and unlimited losses, whereas long calls have unlimited profits and limited losses. There is a strategy that has the opposite, that is, limited profits and unlimited losses on the upside. Short futures and short calls are both bear strategies, but short futures have both unlimited profits and unlimited losses, whereas short calls have limited profits and unlimited losses. There is also a strategy that has the opposite, that is, unlimited profits and limited losses on the downside.

Both of these additional strategies relate to the other type of option: puts.

Puts

Calls enable the longs to *take delivery* from the shorts at the strike price. Puts enable the longs to *make delivery* to the shorts at the strike price. So for a put, the longs have the "option" of whether to exercise the put or not, and exercising means making delivery and collecting from the shorts an amount equal to the strike price. And for the put, the shorts take delivery at the strike price and pay an amount equal to the strike price if the longs exercise their options.

Consider the profit and loss possibilities for long and short put holders in the example above. A put on gold futures with a $400 strike price has a premium of $20 when the underlying gold futures price is also $400. The profit-loss profile for long and short puts as the gold futures price increases and decreases is shown in Exhibit 9-7.

As with the call, the long pays the short $20 for the put, that is, for the option of making delivery at the strike price of $400, which is independent of the underlying futures price. If the put option is exercised by the long, the long put is assigned a short gold futures contract at the strike price of $400 and the short put is assigned a long futures position at $400.

Consider the profit and loss possibilities for the long and short puts if the gold futures price remains at $400 at the put's expiration. In this case, if the long puts were exercised, they would be assigned a short futures contract at $400 when the underlying futures price was $400, for no profit or loss. Thus, the longs would be indifferent to exercising the puts or letting them expire worthless. This, in general, is the case for *at-the-money* puts or calls. If the exercise had been made, the shorts, who would have been assigned a long futures contract at $400 when the futures price was $400, would also break even.

Thus, overall, if a put is at the money at expiration, there will be no profit or loss to the longs or shorts due to exercise and assignment, but the longs will, in this example, have a $20 loss and the shorts a $20 profit due to the $20 premium paid by the longs to the shorts at the time the transaction was made.

If the futures price were $420 at expiration, the long puts, if they were exercised, would be assigned short futures positions at $400 when the futures price was

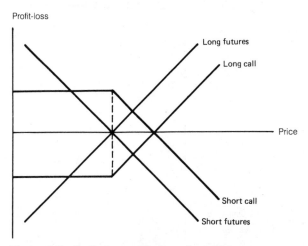

Figure 9-3   Profit-loss profile for calls and futures.

EXHIBIT 9-6 Profit-Loss Profiles for Various Strategies

	Type of strategy	Profit or loss			Payment (−) or receipt (+)
		Price increase	Price constant	Price decrease	
A. Basic Strategies:					
Future—long	Bull	Profit—unlimited	Break even	Loss—unlimited	0
Future—short	Bear	Loss—unlimited	Break even	Profit—unlimited	0
Call—long	Bull	Profit—unlimited	Loss—limited	Loss—limited	−
Call—short	Bear	Loss—unlimited	Profit—limited	Profit—limited	+
Put—long	Bear	Loss—limited	Loss—limited	Profit—unlimited	−
Put—short	Bull	Profit—limited	Profit—limited	Loss—unlimited	+
B. Combination Strategies:					
Straddle—buy	Volatility	Profit—unlimited	Loss—limited	Profit—unlimited	−
Straddle—sell	Stability	Loss—unlimited	Profit—limited	Loss—unlimited	+
Spread, vertical—bull	Bull	Profit—limited	Profit or loss—limited	Loss—limited	+ or −
Spread, vertical—bear	Bear	Loss—limited	Profit or loss—limited	Profit—limited	+ or −

EXHIBIT 9-7   Profit-Loss Profile of Put

A. Long Put

Futures price at option's expiration	Premium paid by long	Long's profit or loss at expiration	Net profit or loss by long
350	−20	50	+30
360	−20	40	+20
370	−20	30	+10
380	−20	20	0
390	−20	10	−10
400	−20	0	−20
420	−20	0	−20
440	−20	0	−20
460	−20	0	−20
480	−20	0	−20

B. Short Put

Futures price at option's expiration	Premium received by short	Short's profit or loss at expiration	Net profit or loss by short
350	+20	−50	−30
360	+20	−40	−20
370	+20	−30	−10
380	+20	−20	0
390	+20	−10	+10
400	+20	0	+20
420	+20	0	+20
440	+20	0	+20
460	+20	0	+20
480	+20	0	+20

$420. There would be an immediate $20 loss. In this case the longs would not choose to exercise. They would let the puts expire worthless and not lose due to exercise. They would, however, still have losses of $20 due to the premiums paid. On the other side of the transaction, the shorts would also have no profit or loss due to exercise and assignment, but they would have $20 profits due to the premiums received. Thus, the longs would have a $20 loss and the shorts a $20 profit, both due to the exchange of the $20 premium.

In general for a put, when the underlying futures price is above the put strike price, the put is said to be out of the money and the long will let it expire worthless rather than exercise it. In this case, the long will experience a loss equal to the initial amount of the premium and the short a profit of the same amount. The profit and loss of the short and the long, respectively, for any out-of-the-money puts are $20, as shown in Exhibit 9-7.

Assume that the futures price is less than the strike price—say $390—at the option's expiration. If the long puts are exercised, they will be assigned a short futures contract at $400. They will thus have immediate profits of $10. In this case the longs choose to exercise. On the other side of the transaction, the short puts will be assigned a long futures position at $400 when the futures price is $390, and there will be an immediate loss of $10. The short has no choice in the matter of whether the put is exercised.

On a net basis, the long put has a $10 profit due to exercise, but because of the $20 premium paid for the option there is a net loss of $10. The short put loses $10 due to the assignment but receives $20 and so has a net profit of $10, as shown in Exhibit 9-7.

In general, if the futures price is below the put strike price at expiration, the puts are said to be *in the money,* and the longs will choose to exercise because they will profit due to the exercise. The amount of the long puts' profit will be equal to the difference between the strike price and the futures price. This will also be the amount of the short puts' loss. Of course, to get their net profit or loss, the $20 premium, which represents a loss to the long put and a profit to the short put, must be included. These results are shown in Exhibit 9-7 where the put is in the money, that is, where the futures price is below the strike price of $400. Figure 9-4 shows a graph of the profit-loss profiles of the long and short puts in this example.

Two observations can now be made which relate to the questions at the end of the last section. A long put is a bear strategy with unlimited profit potential if the market does move down and limited loss potential, the premium paid, if the market moves up. A short put is a bull strategy with limited profit potential if the market moves up and unlimited loss potential if the market moves down.

Note also that a call is in the money if the strike price of the call is less than the underlying price and out of the money if the strike price is greater than the underlying price. Contrariwise, a put is in the money if the strike price is greater than the underlying price and out of the money if the strike price is less than the underlying price. In-the-money puts and calls will both be exercised by the long because it will be to the profit of the long to do so. Out-of-the-money puts and calls will both be allowed to expire worthless by the long because exercising them would cause a loss.

STRATEGIES

Calls, puts, and futures contracts provide various types of bull and bear strategies—that is, bull and bear strategies with various combinations of limited and unlimited profit and loss potential. These combinations are summarized in Exhibit 9-6.

Investors have considerable flexibility in choosing a strategy on the basis of their bullish or bearish sentiments, the strength of their sentiments, and their tastes for or aversion to risk. We will consider separately various bull and bear strategies.

Bull Strategies

A long futures position is a bull strategy with unlimited profit and loss potential. If the market is flat, a long futures strategy breaks even. A long call is a bull

Profit-loss

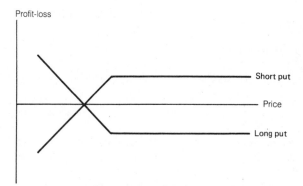

Figure 9-4   Profit-loss profiles of long and short puts.

strategy with limited loss potential but unlimited profit potential. But if the market is flat, this strategy experiences a loss equal to the premium paid in order to have the option to limit the loss due to adverse price moves. A short put is also a bull strategy, and it has a limited profit potential and an unlimited loss potential. But if the market is flat, there is a profit equal to the premium collected for giving someone else the option to limit the loss, which at the same time limits the profit potential of the short put.

Which of these three bull strategies is best? The answer to this question is an unequivocal "It depends." It depends on three factors.

First, it depends on the size of the option premium. If the call premium were zero, one would choose the long call with its unlimited profit potential and limited loss potential. As the premium increased, one's preferences would move toward the long futures and being subject to the unlimited loss, because for the long call there is a certain loss of the premium. And if the put premium were great, one might even sell a put to experience the profit equal to the put premium, even if the market stayed flat.

The choice also depends on risk tolerance. One who was completely averse to risk would not accept unlimited loss under any circumstances and thus would always buy a call and never buy a futures contract or sell a put to implement a bull strategy. This is the major reason why buying calls is so popular with many retail investors.

The third factor that determines the choice of one of the three bull strategies is the certainty of one's sentiments, in this case bull sentiments. If one thought that Voltaire's Dr. Pangloss ("All is for the best in this best of all possible worlds"), was unduly pessimistic, one would be long on futures in order to experience every dollar of profit from the upward move, unreduced even by the call premium of a long call. Those who "sorta thought" the market would move up but were constantly looking over their shoulders to see if it would "tank" would probably use long calls so that they would not have to exercise their necks so much. And those who thought that the market would move up but would not be surprised if it remained flat might sell puts because it is the only bull strategy that shows a profit in a flat market.

Thus, even though there are three bull strategies, each has different profit and loss possibilities, and the choice among them depends on:

- The level of the call or put premium
- Risk tolerance
- The degree of one's bullish expectations

Bear Strategies

Similarly, there are three bear strategies: short futures, long puts, and short calls. With short futures there are unlimited profits in the downward direction and unlimited losses in the upward direction. If the market is flat, one breaks even. Long puts lead to unlimited profits but limited losses. But if the market is flat, there is a loss equal to the call premium paid to limit the loss. And for a short call, profits are limited but losses are unlimited. But if the market is flat, there is a profit equal to the put premium received.

The choice of the best bear strategy among the three depends on the same three factors on which the choice of the bull strategy depends.

COMBINATIONS OF FUTURES AND OPTIONS—THE TINKERTOY APPROACH

Basically, futures are rather simple instruments. You can "buy 'em or sell 'em." In either case you have unlimited profit and loss potential. Their relative simplicity results from this symmetry.

Options are more complicated. Long calls offer unlimited profits for price increases and limited losses for price decreases. Short calls have limited profits for price decreases and unlimited losses for price increases. Long and short puts are different from either of these. It is this lack of symmetry that leads to the relative complexity of options.

But as one usually "gets what one pays for," the complexity of options also leads to a richness or a greater variety of strategies. As we have already seen, long and short calls and long and short puts provide for a greater variety of bull and bear strategies, in terms of limited and unlimited profit and loss potentials, than long and short futures. This is one of the elements of richness that options provide.

The other aspect of richness that options provide results from the types of strategies which can be "built" with options. More strategies can be built with options than wooden structures can be built with Tinkertoy parts. Consider some of the things we can build with these "Tinkertoy" options.

Futures

The first things that can be built with options contracts are futures contracts. We can build either long or short futures contracts with combinations of calls and puts. Specifically, a long call and a short put is equivalent to a long futures position, and a short call and a long put is equivalent to a short futures position. For an illustration of these results, consider the options examples given in Exhibits 9-5 and 9-7.

Exhibit 9-8 shows the results of a combination of a long call, from Exhibit 9-5, and a short put, from Exhibit 9-7. Both long calls and short puts are bull strategies. Because the long call has unlimited upside profit and limited downside loss, and because the short put has limited upside profit and unlimited downside loss, the combination of these two has the same profit-loss profile as a long future.

That the combination of a long call and a short put is equivalent to a long future is shown in part A of Exhibit 9-8. Column 4 in part A shows the sum of column 2 (for a long call) and column 3 (for a short put). The outcome in column 4 is the same as for a long future—that is, a dollar-for-dollar profit for increases above the initial price of $400 and a dollar-for-dollar loss for price decreases below $400. Thus, by connecting a long call to a short put one can build a long future.

EXHIBIT 9-8   Combinations of Options

	A. Combination of Long Call and Short Put		
(1) Futures price at option's expiration	(2) Net profit or loss for long call	(3) Net profit or loss for short put	(4) Net profit or loss for long call and short put
350	−20	−30	−50
360	−20	−20	−40
370	−20	−10	−30
380	−20	0	−20
390	−20	+10	−10
400	−20	+20	0
420	0	+20	+20
440	+20	+20	+40
460	+40	+20	+60
480	+60	+20	+80
	B. Combination of Short Call and Long Put		
(1) Futures price at option's expiration	(2) Net profit or loss for short call	(3) Net profit or loss for long put	(4) Net profit or loss for short call and long put
350	+20	+30	+50
360	+20	+20	+40
370	+20	+10	+30
380	+20	0	+20
390	+20	−10	+10
400	+20	−20	0
420	0	−20	−20
440	−20	−20	−40
460	−40	−20	−60
480	−60	−20	−80

Note that in this example the call and the put both had the same strike price, and both were initially at the money. If the initial futures price was not such that the call and put would be at the money, one could build something very close to, but not exactly the same as, a long future out of the near-the-money call and put. The effective delivery month of the future built is the same as the expiration months of the call and put used.

One could also build a short futures position—a bear strategy—out of a short call and a long put—both bear strategies. Column 4 in part B of Exhibit 9-8, which shows the sum of column 2 (for a short call) and column 3 (for a long put), has the same profit-loss profile as a short futures contract.

Thus, futures contracts can be built from combinations of options contracts. So puts and calls can be used not only in their own right but also to build futures contracts. One may still choose to use futures contracts. But issues such as margins and pricing may affect this choice.

Puts from Calls and Futures

Because futures can be built from puts and calls, it should not be surprising that one can build puts from calls and futures and calls from puts and futures.

For example, one can build a long put by combining a long call and a short future. This is shown in Exhibit 9-9, wherein column 4 shows the sum of column 2 (the profit-loss profile for a long call) and column 3 (the profit-loss profile for a short future) and is the same as the profit-loss profile for the long put as shown in Exhibit 9-7.

Positions can be combined not only numerically, as shown in Exhibit 9-9, but also graphically, as in Figure 9-5, which shows how a long call and a short future can be combined to form a long put. In fact, calls were listed on stock options prior to puts, but traders were able to "convert" a combination of a long call on the stock with a short position in the stock into a long put on the stock—this was called a conversion.[7]

EXHIBIT 9-9 Building a Long Put—Numerical Representation

(1) Futures price at expiration	(2) Net profit or loss for long call	(3) Net profit or loss for short future	(4) Net profit or loss for long call and short future
350	−20	+50	+30
360	−20	+40	+20
370	−20	+30	+10
380	−20	+20	0
390	−20	+10	−10
400	−20	0	−20
420	0	+20	−20
440	+20	−10	−20
460	+40	+60	−20
480	+60	−80	−20

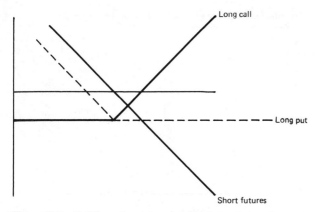

Figure 9-5   Building a long put—graphical representation.

Similarly in futures options, the four types of options can be built by the combinations indicated below:

Long put = long call + short futures
Short put = short call + long futures
Long call = long put + long futures
Short call = short put + short futures

Other Strategies

We have shown that long and short futures can be built from combinations of puts and calls and long and short puts and calls from calls, puts, and futures. But that is not so exciting. It brings nothing new to the party.[8] Now we can show, however, that we can use our "Tinkertoy" options to build entirely new types of strategies, that is, strategies with entirely new types of profit-loss profiles. Many such strategies can be built. The most common are discussed in this section.

Straddles.   A "straddle" is a combination of either (1) buying a call and buying a put (called a "buy straddle") or (2) selling a call and a put (a "sell straddle") of the same strike price and month. Consider the buy straddle first. In terms of the above examples, assume that both the call and the put were bought with $400 strike prices when the price of the underlying futures was $400. The premium for both the call and the put was $20, so the buyer of these two options had to pay $40 for the combination.

---

[7] Conversions and the opposite—reverse conversions—are also used as arbitrage strategies by professionals.

[8] But at times you accomplish one of these at a cheaper price than that of the alternative.

EXHIBIT 9-10   Profit-Loss Profile for Buy Straddle—Numerical Representation

Futures price at option's expiration	Profit or loss for long call	Profit or loss for long put	Net profit or loss for long call and long put
350	−20	+30	+10
360	−20	+20	0
370	−20	+10	−10
380	−20	0	−20
390	−20	−10	−30
400	−20	−20	−40
420	0	−20	−20
440	+20	−20	0
460	+40	−20	+20
480	+60	−20	+40

The profit-loss profile for this buy straddle is shown numerically in Exhibit 9-10 and graphically in Figure 9-6. The buy straddle shows a loss if the price is flat or relatively flat. Specifically, there is a loss for futures prices between 360 and 440, with the maximum loss of 40 if the market is flat at 400. If the market increases above 440 or decreases below 360, there is a profit, which is unlimited. Thus, this strategy loses if the market is stable and profits if the market moves sharply, either upward or downward. For this reason, the buy straddle is sometimes called a "volatility spread."

A sell straddle consists of selling both the call and the put considered above. The profit-loss profile for the sell straddle is shown in Exhibit 9-11 and Figure 9-7, numerically and graphically, respectively. The sell straddle, not surprisingly, has the opposite profile of the buy straddle. It shows a profit if the price stays flat or relatively flat. Specifically, it shows a profit for prices between 360 and 440, with the maximum profit of 40 (the amount of the premium initially received) at

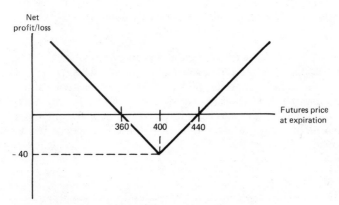

Figure 9-6   Profit-loss profile for buy straddle—graphical representation.

EXHIBIT 9-11   Profit-Loss Profile for Sell Straddle—Numerical Representation

Futures price at option's expiration	Profit or loss for short call	Profit or loss for short put	Net profit or loss for short call and short put
350	+20	−30	−10
360	+20	−20	0
370	+20	−10	+10
380	+20	0	+20
390	+20	+10	+30
400	+20	+20	+40
420	0	+20	+20
440	−20	+20	0
460	−40	+20	−20
480	−60	+20	−40

the initial price of 400. If the price increases above 440 or decreases below 360, there is a loss, which is unlimited. This strategy shows a profit in stable markets and a loss when markets are changing in either direction. It could be called a "stability spread."

Straddles add both stability and volatility strategies to our previous list of bull and bear strategies.

Spreads.   In futures, while there are many types of spreads, the most common type of spread involves buying one delivery month and selling another delivery month of the same contract.

In options, these same general types of spreads exist, but since there are two types of options, calls and puts, there can be both call spreads and put spreads of these types. To give examples of these, assume that for the gold futures options above, there are both options on the June futures contract (June options) and options on the September futures contract (September options). Assume also that

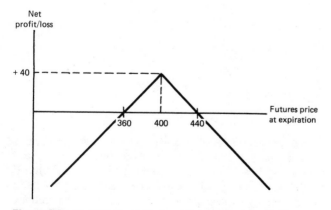

Figure 9-7   Profit-loss profile for sell straddle—graphical representation.

there are puts and calls with $400 strike prices for these months, as summarized below:

June 400 call   June 400 put
September 400 call   September 400 put

There are two types of spreads between months involving both calls and puts, as summarized below:

Call spreads (horizontal)

Sell June 400 call/buy September 400 call
Buy June 400 call/sell September 400 call

Put spreads (horizontal)

Sell June 400 put/buy September 400 put
Buy June 400 put/sell September 400 put

These call and put spreads are referred to also as "calendar spreads" or "horizontal spreads." They are not clearly bull, bear, neutral, or nonneutral strategies but strategies that, more subtly, hope to profit from the more or less rapid decay of the time value of the nearby option rather than the deferred option. The profit-loss profiles of these horizontal spreads are not shown here.

There can also be options spreads with the same delivery month but across strike prices. Assume that with the puts and calls considered above there are also puts and calls available with $420 strike prices. With the initial $400 futures price, the $420 strike price call would be out of the money and the $420 strike price put would be in the money. The various June contract combinations available are summarized below:

June 420 call   June 420 put
June 400 call   June 400 put

The types of spreads across strike prices that are possible with these options are:

Call spreads (vertical)

Buy 420 call/sell 400 call
Sell 420 call/buy 400 call

Put spreads (vertical)

Buy 420 put/sell 400 put
Sell 420 put/buy 400 put

These spreads across strike prices are called "vertical spreads." Each of them is either a bull strategy or a bear strategy. But what is new about these vertical spread strategies is that whether bull or bear, they all have both limited profit and limited loss potential, something none of the strategies considered heretofore have had.

To consider the profit-loss profiles of these spread strategies, assume that initially the underlying futures price is $400 and that the premiums of the options are as

EXHIBIT 9-12 Calculation of Profit-Loss Profiles of Vertical Spreads

	Premium	350	400	420	450
A.					
Buy 420 call	−5	0	0	0	+30
Sell 400 call	+20	0	0	−20	−50
Net premium	+15	—	—	—	—
Net on exercise	0	0	−20	−20	−20
Net profit or loss	+15	+15	−5	−5	−5
B.					
Sell 420 call	+5	0	0	0	−30
Buy 400 call	−20	0	0	+20	+50
Net premium	−15	—	—	—	—
Net on exercise	0	+20	+20	+20	+20
Net profit or loss	−15	−15	+5	+5	+5
C.					
Buy 420 put	−25	+70	+20	0	0
Sell 400 put	+20	−50	0	0	0
Net premium	−5	—	—	—	—
Net on exercise	+20	+20	0	0	0
Net profit or loss	+15	+15	−5	−5	−5
D.					
Sell 420 put	+25	−70	−20	0	0
Buy 400 put	−20	+50	0	0	0
Net premium	+5	—	—	—	—
Net on exercise	−20	−20	0	0	0
Net profit or loss	−15	−15	+5	+5	+5

follows:

Option	Premium
420 call	$5
400 call	$20
400 put	$20
420 put	$25

On the basis of these premiums, the profit-loss profiles of the four vertical spreads indicated above are calculated in Exhibit 9-12 and shown graphically in Figure 9-8.

As shown, the sell 420 call/buy 400 call (Exhibit 9-12, part B) and sell 420 put/buy 400 put (part D) are bull strategies with maximum profits of 5 and maximum losses of 1.5.[9] The buy 420 call/sell 400 call (Exhibit 9-12, part A) and buy 420

---

[9] Note that even though the sell 420 call/buy 400 call spread (strategy B) and the sell 420 put/buy 400 put spread (strategy D) are both bull spreads with maximum profits of 5 and maximum losses of 15, they are not fully equivalent. In strategy B, the spreader collects 5 for selling the 420 call and pays 20 for buying the 400 call, thus paying a net 15. Since there is a net payment, this spread is called a "debit spread." On the other hand, in strategy D, the spreader collects 25 for selling the 420 put and then pays 20 for buying the 400 put, thus collecting a net 5. Since there is a net collection, this spread is called a "credit spread." So the initial amount that must be put up to do these two spreads differs. Debit and credit spreads are also margined differently, but that topic is not considered herein.

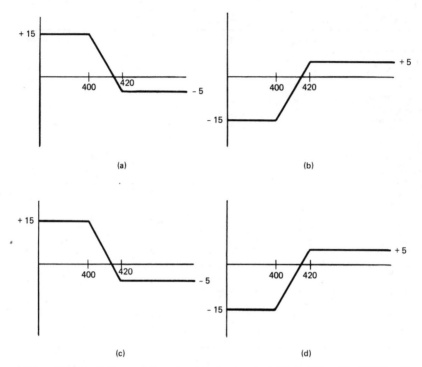

Figure 9-8 Profit-loss profiles of vertical spreads. (a) Buy 420 call/sell 400 call; (b) sell 420 call/buy 400 call; (c) buy 420 put/sell 400 put; (d) sell 420 put/buy 400 put.

put/sell 400 put (part C) are bear strategies with maximum profits of 15 and maximum losses of 5. These vertical spread strategies have both limited profit and limited loss potential.

This section on other strategies has considered buy and sell straddles and bull and bear vertical spreads (with puts and calls). The profit-loss profiles of the strategies considered are also summarized in Exhibit 9-6. There are other more complicated strategies involving combinations of puts and calls that are not considered here.

OVERVIEW AND CONCLUSIONS

Because of their symmetry, futures are relatively easy to comprehend. Primarily because of their asymmetry, options are more difficult to comprehend and apply. The reward for wading through and conquering this difficulty, however, is a much richer menu of strategies involving not only neutral and nonneutral as well as bull and bear strategies but also combinations of unlimited and limited profit and loss possibilities.

This richer menu, however, puts an added responsibility on investors. They must more explicitly specify their taste for profits versus their tolerance for risk. That is, they must more specifically know "what they're about" in an investment sense.

NOTES FROM A TRADER

One of the most consistent phenomena in finance is the trade-off. Efficient markets demand a price for any real benefit. This concept also applies to the options markets. The opportunity for a profit requires payment in the form of risk. Reduction of risk will almost certainly reduce the chance for a profit.

A major advantage frequently claimed for options by brokers of these instruments is the protection to the buyers of options against margin calls caused by sharply adverse market moves. The terror of margin calls due to a series of unfavorable limit moves is eliminated.

This advantage is bought only at a price, however. The option buyer starts with a loss, i.e., the premium paid for the option. Holders of futures contracts who liquidate their contracts at the same prices at which they were entered lose only commissions. Given the same circumstances, however, option buyers lose their premiums (at least the time value of the premium) as well as commissions. In effect, they have entered a race starting behind the starting line. The price of a loss limitation is the higher probability of losing.

On the other hand, sellers of options contracts collect rather than pay a premium, but the price for starting ahead of the starting line is being subject to margin calls in the event of adverse market moves. Nevertheless, more sophisticated speculators typically exhibit a preference for selling options and collecting premiums, even though they are subject to margin calls, rather than buying options and paying premiums.

Options have many uses. But the fundamental aspect of options is that the long option, whether a long put or a long call, has a limited loss—no more than the initial premium paid can be lost. On the other hand, short options have unlimited loss—in this sense short options are like futures contracts. Thus, the premium paid by the trader who is long an option is the price of being able to sleep at night. For this reason, many traders will never be short an option. On the other hand, the pros have a bias toward the short option side—they will accept the unlimited downside to collect the premium.

Options can be used as a substitute for stop orders. For example, if traders have an acceptable profit in a long futures position, they can put a stop order in at a somewhat lower price. Alternatively, they can buy a put to protect their profits. A major difference between these two approaches is that if prices reverse and decline to the lower level and then again increase, the trader is out of the market during the final period of price increase if a stop order is used but still in the market if a long put is used. On the other hand, the trader must pay the premium on the put. For example, a trader who holds a long gold futures position at a price of $400 could buy a $400 put for protection against losses. But the put premium must be paid. This combination of a long futures and a long $400 put is equivalent to a long call at $400. Similarly, to protect a profit on a short futures position, the trader could buy a call. The use of long puts and calls to protect the profits in futures positions may make the rule "never hold a position going into a report" obsolete.

Options can also be used when futures contracts are at their price limits because options contracts have no price limits. For example, if a trader has a long futures position and the market is limit down, the trader can buy a put and exercise the put, which gives the trader the right to a short futures position, which then makes the trader flat. However, the cost of this transaction may be high. First, the put premium includes time value, and the early exercise deprives the holder of the long put of this time value. To avert this loss, the trader could simply hold the long put until the next day on which futures trading commences and liquidate both the put and the futures contract. Even then, the price of the put at the time it is bought will be based not on the limit price of the futures contract but on the market's assessment of what the equilibrium futures price is. For example, if Treasury bonds were locked at a limit of 77-00 but the market assessment of the equilibrium price were 76-16, the price of the 78 put would include 1-16 of intrinsic value consistent with the assessed 76-16 price, not 1 point of intrinsic value consistent with the 77-00 limit price, plus the corresponding time value. For example, on February 28, 1983, the April gold futures contract closed limit down at $423.70, the April $480 put hit $80, and the April $500 hit $110. Thus, if traders had bought and exercised the $480 put, the effective liquidation price of the long futures position would have been $400, and the effective liquidation price of the futures contract with the $500 put would have been $390. Both are significantly less than the $423.70 limit-down price. These differences represent the amount by which the market's perception of the equilibrium price was less than the $400 price limit and also the initial time value of the options. In this regard, the options premiums give an indication of the market's assessment of the equilibrium futures price—however, an adjustment must be made for the time value of the option.

It should also be expected that when futures are at their limit, the liquidity of the options contracts may be less because the futures contracts will not be available against which to arbitrage. Finally, many futures contracts have spot month contracts which are traded without price limits and can be used even when the other contract months are at their limits.

Options may also be used to reduce margin requirements. While the premium must be paid for long options, short positions are margined, and some mixed strategies such as vertical spreads may require no margins.

10

The Game Plan

*"Would you tell me, please, which way I ought
to go from here?"*
*"That depends a good deal on where you want
to get to."*   LEWIS CARROLL
Alice in Wonderland

INTRODUCTION

This chapter is not for everyone. There are those who do not like to follow plans.
It's their money. Others are not able to follow plans. All such people are not wrong.
Some trade intuitively and make little or no money but enjoy what they are doing.
Others make enough money often enough to indicate that their intuition has value.
It seems logical to some that such intuitive trades are based on input and that the
input could be quantified. Those who trade in this manner, however, are often
unable to indicate just what factors cause them to enter or exit trades exactly
when they do and credit some extraordinary sensitivity which they cannot articulate. Most people do not claim to have this inherent timing ability, however, and
so have a choice of following a plan or trading haphazardly. Those among this
less fortunate group should read on.

Many traders find themselves in a position like that of the German High Command when it faced its adversary across the Channel during World War II. The
invasion of Britain was planned but never executed, whereas the Battle of Britain
was executed but never planned. Similarly, many futures traders seem to go

through life planning trades they never execute and executing trades they never plan. The preceding chapters in this part have dealt with various elements of the decision-making process of futures trading. The objectives of the individual trader and the size of his or her initial capital commitment were analyzed in Chapter 5, which deals with risk and rewards, and the trade selection process was thoroughly discussed from the fundamental and technical approaches. The tasks that remain are to synthesize specific information into a game plan that will provide for any eventuality in a trade and to complete the consideration of the elements of money management begun in Chapter 5.

Bernard Baruch, who was no mean trader in his own right, knew the danger of arguing with numbers. He was fond of pointing out that two and two equals four. Once he said that "two and two make four and no one has ever invented a way of getting something for nothing."

Many speculators less intelligent than Baruch, and much less prosperous, seem to go through life unaware of this simple truth. They take positions based on impulse instead of reason and then wait to get lucky. They have not learned that even the best speculators consider themselves fortunate to be right on most trades or even to make significant profits during most years. Some traders find that their trading has resulted in more losses than profits, that the size of their average loss exceeds the size of their average profit, and that execution costs and commissions must be added to their losses and subtracted from their profits. Such traders eventually learn that two and two equals four.

The speculator has no more hope of winning on every trade than the gambler has of winning on every roll of the dice or every turn of the cards. The gambler learns to use words like "maybe," "usually," and "perhaps," and the speculator should learn the same. The speculator can no more know all the contingencies of determining price change than a card player can know the makeup of every hand before the cards are dealt.

If speculators plan their trades properly, it is at least possible for them to have the odds on their side in the long run, which is something few gamblers who do not own casinos can hope to achieve. Over a long period the skilled speculator who follows a well-thought-out plan in a disciplined manner may well have favorable results. Any gambler can win in the short run, but in the long run probabilities prevail and most will lose. No reasonable person would expect good luck to prevail and skill to fail for long periods—at least not so long as two and two still makes four.

Although not universally considered even by skilled traders, the disciplined use of good plans is widely credited by many as one of the most important reasons for their success. In the following pages the manner of developing a plan and the elements it should contain will receive careful consideration. Mistakes in formulating as well as implementing such a plan will be noted so that losing tactics may be avoided. It should be evident, however, that no chapter in this book or any other, no tract, nor any lecture can make successful futures traders out of everyone. There is a considerable amount of art, and perhaps luck, that affects results, and so no simple set of rules can ever guarantee profits. Furthermore, if every trader became successful, there would be no losers to provide the profits acquired by the winners.

THE BROAD PLAN

Reduced to its most basic elements, the trading plan provides the reasons for logically entering and getting out of any position, whether or not it proves ultimately profitable. Once a position is taken in the markets, a price level can do nothing but rise, fall, or remain unchanged, and a trading plan must provide a blueprint for entering a trade and establishing the action to be taken by the trader in *any* of the *three* eventualities.

Although there are several key elements of a game plan to be considered, the core of a plan must indicate, unequivocally, how the trader is to exit from trades that have been entered. Such an approach consists of not one exit plan but three. There must be a plan for accepting losses if a position shows adversity, a plan for accepting profits, and a plan for getting out of a trade if the price change over a significant period is negligible.

The most efficient procedure for exiting from a trade that shows a loss is by means of a stop-loss order if the trader knows how much adversity he is willing to absorb. If he has decided before entering the trade how much loss is acceptable, all he has to do is place a stop-loss order at that point. If the logical exit point is known, failure to place a stop-loss order is almost certainly foolish and may well lead to disaster.

If a trade shows a profit, the guidelines to the trader who is composing a game plan are not nearly so clear-cut. Several possibilities exist, and a case can be made for each of them. If the trader has decided upon her objective before entering the trade, the obvious procedure is to enter a limit order immediately to exit at that objective. Trading by price objectives may not, however, suit a trader who uses other methods of trade selection. A trader need not be a trend follower to believe in letting profits run until some gauge, technical or fundamental, gives a "signal" for opposite action. In this case the exit plan might read, "sell at the stop-loss point or when Indicator X gives a sell signal, whichever comes first."

One method of trading calls for holding a position until a certain amount of time has passed and then accepting whatever profit or loss exists. This may work well if a trade is profitable, but given enough time, the loss on a trade may approach the national debt. It would appear that this approach works best, if at all, only for positions which are to be held for short periods.

Whatever plan for accepting profits is used, a vital consideration is that the trader recognize that accepting profits is ultimately the name of the game. Unless he decides to replace judgment with luck, he should have in mind one or more clear conditions that tell him to close out his trade and take whatever profits there are. Many successful traders have learned that it is easier to make money than it is to keep it, and the trader who ignores the necessity for a plan on where to realize profits ultimately learns the painful truth to the saying that "trees do not grow to the sky."

The problem caused by trades that do virtually nothing after they are entered is not too serious. If it happens often, the trader may find that she is trading the wrong futures or responding to the wrong events. For the occasional trade that "goes dead" there are two possible solutions. Either an arbitrary time limit can be placed on the trade (so that it can be closed out if little net change has occurred at the end of this allotted time), or it can be held until the delivery month approaches. The method of trade selection will determine which concept is followed.

The trader with well-conceived exit plans not only has completed a large part of her total trading plan but will find that in the heat of actual trading she now has important peace of mind. Knowing exactly where to exit a trade and why is the best medicine for maintaining calm nerves in the futures trading game. The alternative to such planning probably causes traders to make their greatest mistake, namely "watching the market" and making decisions on the basis of impulsive reactions to random price moves or margin calls. Watching the market does not alter the basic price directions that are possible once a position has been entered, that is, up, down, and sideways. The dangers of watching a market include the often overwhelming temptation to cut profits quickly, ride losses, or overstay positions going nowhere. All tend to tie up capital, waste energy, and confuse and demoralize the trader.

KEY ELEMENTS OF THE PLAN

Capital

Basically, any plan worthy of the name contains certain key elements. One of the first decisions to be made by any speculator who has decided to trade futures is the amount of capital that he is willing to devote to this trading. The extremes that limit this decision are clearly definable. The minimum is the margin on the books of the broker offering the most liberal terms. The maximum is the net worth of the trader plus all he can borrow. In practical terms, neither of these extremes would be considered by a reasonable person, although there is little doubt that both routes have been followed more than once.

The actual amount of the trader's net worth to be utilized for trading depends on many considerations. These were discussed at length in Chapter 5, but some should be noted here because they influence construction of the trading plan. One is the motivation of the trader. If trading is to be only a stimulating avocation, it might serve its purpose just as well if done on a small scale. Another consideration is the personal aggressiveness of the trader expressed by his desire to make money in relation to his willingness to risk losing what he already has. Some traders might be willing to risk a substantial proportion of their net worth in an effort to increase the total by an important amount. Others might be willing to risk only a comparatively small amount of capital because of fear of loss, the difficulty of replacing what might be lost, or personal responsibilities. These considerations in turn may be based on the age of the trader, the effort that was expended to accumulate the capital that must be risked, the size of his family, his health, the type of job he holds, the attitude of his family toward his trading, and his nerve. Basically, a trader should not take a risk disproportionate to the importance to himself of the potential profit. Traders vary in their reactions to different types of trades, which helps explain why one trader will enter a trade rejected by others and reject others that somebody else may find appealing. Sooner or later each trader should become familiar with his own trading curve and select trades partly in accordance with it.

In formulating a plan, a trader is faced with the major question of the types of technical and/or fundamental data on which to base her trade selections. Before she embarks on the all-important trade-selection process, however, she should probably consider the related problems of learning where the data are to be found and how to obtain them regularly with the expenditure of reasonable time, effort, and cost. For example, one might use a point-and-figure chart based on a ¼-cent reversal in an active soybean market only to learn that scanning miles of ticker tape to search for the ¼-cent reversals is impracticable and that buying such data might cost too much or be too slow to be of any use.

If a trader must study data to make intelligent decisions, she must have a place to do her studying and the time in which to do it. Part-time trading is difficult, and haphazard preparation under adverse conditions makes satisfactory results highly unlikely. The trader must know what types of orders she prefers, preferably for carefully considered reasons, and how to communicate her instructions to her broker without missing markets. These last items may seem mechanical and routine, but they may prove more difficult to resolve satisfactorily than they first appear, and they *must* be resolved satisfactorily.

Trade Selection and Evaluation

No rational person would undertake trading in futures unless he felt that he possessed some method of selecting profitable trades. Recommending any single trade-selection method is not the province of this book. In-depth surveys have been presented of technical and fundamental trading methods so that the reader will be aware of many lines of inquiry. These possibilities may be expanded for all active futures. The purpose of this discussion is to illuminate some of the vital factors that must be considered when a trader chooses a particular method of trade selection and to present some general guidelines on how the method chosen may be evaluated.

Choosing a Trade-Selection Method.   Would-be traders are bombarded constantly with advertisements and claims. They are informed of methods by private advisory services, brokerage houses, and acquaintances. Few of these methods are worth serious study, and some can produce dangerous errors in thinking. Because most methods are alleged to be wildly profitable, choosing a method by the sole criterion of its having produced the largest past profits is probably an exercise in futility. Instead, careful consideration should be given to other important characteristics that should mark any method of trade selection.

At some point the trader must make a general determination of the factors that will cause him to enter into a market position. He may follow the guidance of some other person or a service, or he may gather sufficient fundamental and technical data of his own to justify a position. Some traders engage primarily in technical research. Others rely on basic fundamental research and seek out situations they believe to be undervalued or overvalued. Still others rely on their own feelings, which may be designated as a "judgment," "the touch," "a hunch," or "intuition" depending on how much dignity one wishes to lend to this often fatal approach. The trader's attitudes preceding the trade entry will help determine the strategy; that is, whether he will lean toward short-term trades or positions held for extended periods, prefer the long or short side of the market, or search out net positions, spreads, or options. If he considers being against the speculative crowd as of great importance, he might often have to prefer the short side. If small margins and the elimination of drastic adverse moves are sought, some spread positions may be preferred.

A popular opinion holds that "fundamentals will give the main direction of prices, and technical factors will provide the timing." Although it is true that most fundamental methods are concerned with long-term factors, one has only to consult a futures calendar to realize that daily fundamental factors affect a number of futures, and there is no logical base for assuming that short-term methods of trade selection based on such information could not be devised. Moreover, a valid technical method can easily be long-term-oriented as well as short-term-oriented. The authors cannot conceive of a technical method that indicates when to take action but gives no clue to the anticipated direction of price. The trader should realize that fundamental and technical methods are often independent means of analyzing markets and as such are not necessarily complementary or contradictory.

Apart from the basic approach, other factors may be considered. Does the trader wish to follow a well-publicized method or a more obscure method which has been purchased or is based on the trader's own research? Advantages and disadvantages may be noted for both approaches. In the first instance the trader may feel that one or more popular methods of trade selection embody valuable truths and that discipline is the one missing element needed to trade them profitably. An analogy has been made that there are hundreds of thousands of pianos in the United States but only a handful of virtuosos. A disadvantage in trading many popular methods, however, is that large numbers of traders may act on such signals. This may result in poor executions because signals from these methods may be efficiently discounted. Even worse, such methods have often caught the public fancy because they rely on axioms of market behavior that appear to be logical but have no basis in fact. They are testimony to a saying often attributed to Jesse Livermore: "With ease, human beings believe what it pleases them to believe."

Perhaps scores of obscure trading methods, some mechanically complicated, are privately printed and sold to limited numbers of people for prices ranging from $10 to several thousand. An advantage to procuring one of these methods may be that the approach to markets may be viable, but the seller may not have the discipline or the desire to trade himself. If this is the case, the quality of the seller's research is not necessarily low. Another reason for buying a method may be that the method of trade selection is sound but the trading plan incomplete, with no allowance made, for example, for money management considerations. In this case both the inventor and the clients may have experienced losses because of poor planning and not because trade selection was inherently poor. Since the importance of a complete plan is usually overlooked, the chances are that any valid private method of trade selection that the trader locates will become available to him because of this reason. The disadvantages of securing private methods are clear and are probably applicable most of the time. That these methods are available calls into question their efficacy. Assuming that their originators are economically motivated, if the trading methods were successful, there would be little need to broadcast their availability to others.

It is possible that the trader may conclude that most, if not all, methods of trade selection available to her are of little use and may wish to do research of her own. If this is the case, she must overcome the almost insuperable obstacle of fooling herself. To avoid self-deceit the trader should vow to be as conservative as possible in validating her method and even then to add an extra margin for error. Results in the real world are seldom as good as they look on paper, using hindsight. Worse than this, frequently some overlooked problem in the method of trade selection is apparent only after the trader's capital has been lost. The number of handwritten worksheets and computer printouts detailing methods of trade selection, all with "excellent" results, must approach infinity.

The frequency of trades should be considered. Some traders may feel comfortable trading every day, whereas others may prefer only a handful of trades every year. Two factors will have an influence on how many trades are made over any time span. The first is the number of markets followed. If a trader follows many futures, he will trade more actively over a significant period of time. The second factor is whether the method used is designed to select trades for long-term or short-term price changes. As a general rule a long-term method will select fewer trades than a short-term method.

Whatever method of trade selection is chosen, the trader must have enough confidence in it and be comfortable enough with it to build it into her trading plan. Once a method of trade selection has been integrated into the total plan, it should not be changed or substituted while trades are being contemplated or made. If, after unhurried consideration, a better method of trade selection appears or an improvement on the existing method seems feasible, the entire trading plan should be redrawn, with the new method of trade selection inserted.

Because of the time factor, the trader may feel that he prefers to use the trade-selection method of a broker, an advisory service, or some other organization. If so, he has saved himself considerable work in this area, but a crucial problem remains. Whether a trade-selection procedure is based on his own or someone else's work, it *must* be validated by the trader himself.

Evaluating a Trade-Selection Method. Trading futures with a trade-selection method that has not been validated makes a mockery of the rest of the trading plan. There are few methods of trade selection available to the trader that will not bear the claim that they have been exhaustively validated. The trader is best advised to ignore such claims and validate the method himself. If he does so, two important advantages will accrue. First, he will have certain knowledge of how the method has performed to date without having to rely on the claims of others who are more likely to have a vested interest in displaying impressive results. Second, validating a method of trade selection makes the trader more aware of its properties in a way that cannot be duplicated. This information can lead to valuable peace of mind during the periods of adversity inevitably encountered by even the most successful traders.

A number of considerations must distinguish all worthwhile trade-selection methods or the generation of "buy" and "sell" signals. These are as follows:

1. The method must rest on a solid, logical theory. If the basic concept doesn't make a modicum of sense, the trader would do well to leave the pioneering stages to others.

2. The method must have a back record with the following properties: (*a*) The back record must be in real time, not hypothetical time. If a trader is employing a signaling method and "tests" the signals over some period *in the past,* such a test is in hypothetical time. If a trader compiles a record of signals *before the fact,* the test is in real time. Although considerable back testing must be done, a significant portion of the back record must be in real time. Almost any perseverant person can invent a system that will produce vast hypothetical profits over any past period. Few methods will work under real-time conditions when interpretative principles cannot be modified by hindsight. (*b*) The real-time record of signals must include many different types of markets. Some methods work quite well when prices are in a relatively narrow trading range; others succeed in dynamic trending markets. Still other methods are most profitable when price action is somewhere between these two extremes. It may require a considerable amount of time to produce a back record that is extensive enough for purposes of evaluation. If the trader is too impatient to obtain a back record or is falsely persuaded by others that his requirements are not reasonable, he runs a serious risk of evaluating the method by using what is known as "biased sample." This approach would be equivalent to a poll taker determining national attitudes toward taxation by polling only those people who work on Wall Street.

3. The signals themselves must have the following properties: (*a*) The entry and exit prices at which the method suggests action should be realistic. Wheat, for example, might give a buy signal at $3.40, calculated on Tuesday night. If it opens on Wednesday at $3.45 and then rises from there, the entry price must be considered as $3.45 or the trade must be abandoned. It is surprising how many back signal records use the closing price of the signal day rather than a realistic price on the day the trader would act. The same point can be made about exit prices. If the method suggested a stop-loss price of 68.50 cents a pound on a short pork bellies trade and the price rallied 100 points in the last minute of trading to close at 69.00, the exit price should be figured at 69.00. Not only must the most conservative entry and exit prices be used in compiling the record of any method, but it is sound practice to make an extra allowance for "execution costs" in compiling a back record. Adding an extra commission on each trade is one possible procedure. Almost all professional traders will insist that they have never seen a method that made adequate allowance for execution costs. (*b*) Results should be consistent; a number of methods will fail badly when tested in this way. The question the trader should ask is, "To what extent does *each* profitable trade support the overall result?" A method that "would have" transformed $10,000 into $20,000 over a span of 100 trades is not deserving of confidence if the entire gain was achieved by five spectacular winning trades plus 48 nominal losses. A method that made less cumulative profit but had its gains evenly distributed among the

successful signals might be much more deserving of confidence. (*c*) The signals must be validated by using sound statistical principles. It can then be determined how worthwhile any signaling method is likely to be and what the probability is that observed results could have been duplicated by chance alone. Chapter 11, "Money Management," covers this important point in more detail.

A hypothetical method with a logical theory behind it embracing a 3-year back record that includes 20 active futures with 600 real-time signals, of which 450 were profitable, would not require much thought to suggest that it might be worth testing for some months. Careful, realistic research on the trader's part might greatly simplify this evaluative step. Nevertheless, it should be done. Jumping to a false conclusion about the validity of a method from a sample of observed trades that is too small or misinterpreted is probably one of the most common errors of the investing public.

4. The method must provide for a realistic way to exit every trade other than exhausting one's capital and being sold out by one's broker. If the trading method utilized permits predetermination of the exit point, stop-loss orders should almost certainly be used. Such stops should not be placed at obvious points suggested by books that explain how to get rich in the futures markets. But stops should be used by most traders. Without them, the question all too often is not *whether* the trader will lose all of his trading capital but only *when*.

Number of Markets to Follow

An important element of the game plan mentioned briefly to date has to do with the number of futures to be followed and, of that number, how many to trade actively at a given time. The trader who speculates only as an avocation and who relies on detailed analysis of fundamental information or elaborate technical analysis may find it difficult to follow all active futures without making significant errors. The margin of difference between success and failure in futures speculation is narrow enough without having to deal with opportunities that were inadvertently overlooked or losses that were taken on trades that should not have been entered in the first place. Concentrating on only a few markets permits the accumulation of a larger amount of valuable fundamental knowledge and gives a better feel for the technical action of a particular market. The limitation of such concentration is that many markets may present opportunities for a time but then trade within narrow limits for extended periods while new or previously inactive markets become active. A willingness to trade in any market that becomes active provides an adequate number of opportunities, but it is possible to be tempted into too many positions or to know too little about a situation to justify taking the necessary risks. Because concentration in selected areas provides fewer opportunities, there may be a tendency to compensate by plunging heavily into riskier positions that will result in large profits if right and large losses if wrong.

Time Horizon

The expected life span of a trade deserves some thought. The overall objective is to realize the greatest possible return on the capital commensurate with risk which has been made available for trading. As in any other risk venture, "return" is a function of the time required, not just the number of dollars returned. A small profit attained in 2 or 3 days may justify the time expended and the capital risked, whereas a small profit that takes months to realize may be worth little even if the chance of attaining it is quite high because of the unavailability of the capital tied up in margin while the trade is open. The trader who makes a quick paper interim profit on the way to what may be a significantly greater objective must give considerable thought to her wisest course of action. Exhibit 10-1 may help to clarify this problem.

If a trader has bought pork bellies for a 4-cent (400-point) gain over a 1-month period, she may be willing to accept a 100-point profit the first day or a 200-point profit during the remainder of the first week. Any point significantly over the line connecting the entry price with the price objective may be considered attractive at any time. Some traders may even wish to enter orders each day to liquidate their positions at a point significantly over the line but within a reasonable day's range. Any order taken alone is unlikely to be filled, but over a lifetime of trading a large number will be.

Considering such alternative price objectives allows the trader to avoid the problem of casting aside a well-conceived plan to take a small profit impulsively, which may be as sure a road to ultimate ruin as any. Most traders willing to seize the opportunity to realize a quick small profit are much less willing to liquidate a position when faced with a quick small loss. Replacing possible large profits with small ones but leaving large losses because stop-loss points are considered inflexible produces a series of small profits and large losses, and this requires a ratio of gains to losses far too favorable for most traders to achieve.

Adding to Positions

The simplest type of plan might provide only for entering a position and liquidating it, but some traders prefer something more elaborate. A trader might intend, for example, to add to an initial position after the price has moved in a direction favorable to him. He is averaging *with the market*. Having bought a contract of sugar at 9.25 cents a pound, he could average by buying an additional contract at 9.65 cents, or, having sold short a contract of copper at 71.50 cents a pound,

EXHIBIT 10-1   Alternative Price Objectives.

he could average by selling another at 68.50 cents. The logic of this procedure is that the new price level offers the opportunity to increase the potential profit while the open profit already achieved allows the possible loss on the expanded position to be little or no greater than it was on the original position. It might even be less if the paper profit was large enough when the new units were added. The sugar trader was willing to risk 40 points from the current price, and so when he bought his first contract of sugar at 9.25 cents, his 40-point risk would have come out of his working capital if the market had gone against him. When he added his second unit at 9.65, the market continued to rise, but if it had reacted 40 points and he got out, he would have lost 40 points on the second unit but nothing on the first except his paper profit. If he had added a third unit, or line, at 10.05 cents, he would no longer have lost any of his capital on a 40-point reaction because he already had a 120-point open profit to act as a buffer. The disadvantage of trading in this manner is that each new unit offers less potential and more risk than those previously added because the market is closer to its ultimate objective by the amount of the price change that has already taken place. The result of poorly timed additions might well be the loss of profits already achieved in order to try to gain even larger profits. The trader who regards equity as the ultimate measure of her financial strength does not consider the loss of paper profit different from the loss of any other kind of capital, and this might well be the most logical attitude.

Averaging *against the market,* the alternative to averaging with it, provides for the addition of new lines after the initial position shows a loss. Use of this averaging technique against the market assures the trader of making more money than the trader who averages with the market when he proves to be right in his selection of a position and his timing. It also means that his worst positions will be his largest because so much adversity has provided him with the "opportunity" to add so much. He best positions will be his smallest because they provide no opportunity to add to the original line. Eventually the averager against the market is likely to find himself in a position that deteriorates so far that he can no longer support it, much less add to it. It has been said that sooner or later all that an averager will have left is averages. One cynic has called it the "anchor method."

Both types of averagers face the problem of how many units to add to their initial positions and when to add them. Adding a number of units at the new levels greater than the number originally established is a technique too aggressive for most traders to accept. The trader, for example, who buys one contract of cotton, adds two more on strength and then three more on still more strength, and continues to add in this way eventually risks buying such a large number of units near the top of a price move that even a relatively slight reversal quickly eliminates all the paper profit that was gained on the smaller number of units acquired at lower price levels.

Stops

The trader should estimate the amount of loss that might have to be suffered in the event that a trade proves unsuccessful. This amount may be determined from a price level indicated by chart analysis or a percentage of some dollar figure deemed to provide a valid guide, such as a percentage of the margin or of the current price level of the future. It may also be nothing more elaborate than the monetary loss the trader is willing to take before abandoning the trade. The potential profit may then be compared with the potential loss. Many traders erroneously believe that the potential profit must be at least twice the potential loss before a position is justified, whereas others correctly are willing to vary the ratio according to what they regard as the *probability* of achieving the profit. They may feel, for example, that a potential profit of a given amount is worth seeking even at the risk of a loss of an equal or even greater amount if the chance of achieving the gain is materially greater than that of suffering the loss. The opportunity for even a small profit can be quite attractive if the risk of losing a small amount is minimal. This concept is discussed in detail in Chapter 11. Regardless of the favorableness of the ratio of expected profit to expected loss, some trades must be passed just because the dollar amount of loss that must be risked is too great for the trader's capital to bear. Erosion of his capital by the attrition of one bad (or unlucky) trade after another is a hazard that no trader can eliminate, but to risk consistently so much of his capital in trades that "can't miss" that recovery is not reasonably likely is a certain road to ruin. For some perverse reason the trades that cannot miss are always the ones that seem to.

There is some difference of opinion concerning the relative wisdom of actually placing orders to liquidate a position at predetermined points and liquidating when the market touches one of them. Generally it is difficult to justify failure to enter an order when the objectives and stop points have been determined. Actually entering the orders assures that a carefully prepared plan will not be replaced by impulse during the heat of a trading session. A satisfactory profit that was expected, achieved, and then lost in the effort to try for more can be completely demoralizing. A reasonably small planned loss that is replaced by an unreasonably large unplanned loss can be more than demoralizing; it can be ruinous. To spend an important amount of time watching short-term ripples in a market in order to avoid entering orders in advance is usually a useless expenditure of time and energy.

Some traders are reluctant to enter stop-loss orders because of some vague feeling that somebody will force the price toward their stop price until their position is lost, after which the market will promptly go the other way. As often as not, this is an excuse to avoid putting in the stop.

A trader who decides not to use stops should at least consider their use carefully before rejecting them. If the market does not move to the stop point, no harm has been done. If the stop is elected and the price moves well beyond that point, the trader may have been saved from complete disaster. If the price moves just a little beyond the stop point, the trader often has time to reconsider without the bias of having to defend a position she is presently holding. If she wants to reinstate, she may do so, and the only cost to her is the added commission, which the market may have saved for her anyhow by going far enough past her stop.[1] The only really painful course that the market could take would be to elect the stop and reverse

---

[1] Some exchanges grant reduced commissions for day trades, which make the total cost of liquidating and then reinstating a position quite minor.

almost immediately. If this happens to a trader often, he is probably placing stops at rather obvious points, such as just below recent lows or above recent highs. Moving markets have a tendency to reverse temporarily and clean out stops before continuing their moves, and traders should take this into consideration before using stops. Difficulties in this area result not from the use of stops but from their improper use.

Few traders are sufficiently well disciplined to be able to dispose of a position showing a loss quickly. Those who are might not be able to reach their brokers quickly enough to act before a small loss becomes large. Even those who have both the necessary discipline and good communications with their brokers seldom gain by not having the orders entered in advance.

THE PLAN IN ACTION

Form of the Plan

Plans may be mental or written, but written plans are preferable for most traders because they are more likely to be complete and to be followed conscientiously. Each trader may develop a plan form of his own to complement his own style of trading. Exhibit 10-2, although not exhaustive, probably contains most of the elements that most traders will wish to consider for each position entered, but it is best for the trader to devise the form that he finds most useful. Some may wish to add or delete items or leave more or less room than is provided in the illustration for specific items. Errors are more likely to result from a plan that is too sparse than from one that is too elaborate. The time and energy spent in thinking through a plan are doubtless worth the money saved through trading haphazardly. A brief explanation of the purpose and use of most of the items in the plan exhibited follows.

The first item, "futures position," can be completed by indicating the future chosen and the contract month after either "long" or "short." If a spread position is to be entered, both blanks could be filled in or a third blank marked "spread" could be added. If a trader keeps her plan forms filed together, she will be kept aware of her overall position. Considering each trade on its own merits may result in the trader's having a number of positions all long or all short. Certain events, such as war or currency devaluation, may cause many seemingly unrelated futures to move sharply in the same direction and leave the trader with a greater loss than she was prepared to take. This should be considered when adding new positions.

The margin for any new position, whether long, short, or spread, should be considered before a trade is entered, not after. Margins can be changed by exchanges or individual brokers and sometimes by considerable amounts. If the trader had expected to be called for an amount materially smaller than is actually required, she may find herself faced with an unexpected shortage of margin immediately after a trade is entered.

The commission per contract must be considered in order to make certain that the possible profit compared with the possible loss is adequate to justify the trade. The trader who decides to scalp 25 points in cattle only to realize that this would

EXHIBIT 10-2   Trading Plan Summary.

1. Futures position: Long _____ Short _____ Per contract or per spread: Margin ____ Commission ____ Trade # _____

2. Type of plan: ☐Scalp ☐Full move ☐Averaging with position ☐Averaging against position ☐Other

3. Entry plan:

Line number	Conditions necessary for entry of lines			Quantity	Cumulative quantity	Average price
	Date	Price	Other			

4. Actual entries:

Line number	Date	Quantity	Price	Cumulative quantity	Average price

5. Liquidation plan:

Line number	Conditions for liquidation of line			Quantity	Remaining quantity	Final objective	Interim objective	Initial stop	Adjusted stop	Final date
	Date	Price	Conditions							

(A) Net dollar gain to final objective _____ X Probability of achieving objective _____ = $ _____

(B) Maximum dollar risk _____ X Probability of reaching stop point = $ _____

(C) Expected dollar value,(A) minus (B) = $ _____

6. Actual liquidation:

Line number	Reason for liquidation (check one)				Other	Date	Quantity	Price	Gross dollar gain or loss	Commission	Net gain	Net loss
	Planned date	Final date	Objective reached	Stop elected								

Summary·Actual dollars gained _____ Actual dollars lost _____

7. Other factors (where applicable)

Technical comments _____
_____
_____

Seasonal _____

Historical price level _____ High _____ Neutral _____ Low _____ Consensus _____ Government loan equivalent _____

Price nearest option month _____ Carrying charge _____ Cash price _____

Crop year supply-demand comments _____
_____

Near term supply-demand comments _____
_____

Landmarks necessary to indicate trade on course (include dates where applicable) _____
_____

Perils (include dates where applicable) _____
_____

Comparable years

Year	Results	Comments
19__		
19__		
19__		

_____
_____
_____
_____
_____
_____
_____
_____

8. Trade evaluation:

Entry plan versus actual entry   Liquidation plan versus actual liquidation
☐ Good ☐ Fair ☐ Poor   ☐ Good ☐ Fair ☐ Poor

Mistakes committed:
Entry _____
Liquidation _____

represent a $100 gross profit, which must be reduced by a commission of perhaps $60, finds that he is trading for the benefit of a cattle broker rather than for himself.

The "type of plan" may depend on the nature of the opportunity or the personality of the trader. Some people prefer to trade in one consistent manner, whereas others believe themselves flexible enough to trade in different ways at different times or at the same time in different trades. If additional lines are not to be added to the initial position, a quick profit, or scalp, may be expected, or perhaps a major change in price level over a relatively long period would be possible, in which case the trader may hold his position for a full move. If additional lines are to be added, they may be made when the market has moved favorably for or against the trader. In either case he must determine what factors, if any, will cause him to add a second line, a third line, or more lines. Additions may be made at fixed intervals, as predetermined price levels are reached, or on the basis of some other factor that seems important to the trader, such as a reaction after a rise in price. Adding new lines by utilizing paper profits is called "pyramiding."

The "actual entries" may differ from the "entry plans" because of the manner in which orders are filled; for example, a trader may have planned to enter a position in platinum on the opening of the market at a price of about $439 an ounce only to be surprised by an opening at $445 because of some unexpected news. If differences between the planned entries and actual entries are so great and so material that they affect trading results to any great degree, a change in the method used to enter trades is indicated.

The "liquidation plan" is the heart of any plan form. In providing for an exit from a trade that covers any eventuality, the trader avoids the demoralizing experience of riding losses or taking profits impulsively. It is also important that such a plan forces a trader to think through the expected dollar value of a trade before he enters, not afterward. The "expected value" concept is covered in detail in Chapters 5 and 11, but the computational aspects are not difficult and may be introduced at this time.

Assume that a trader believes that she has isolated, quantified, and validated a nonrandom technical device that results in profits in 65 percent of the indicated trades over a reasonable period of time. Further assume that the technical device has signaled a particular trade that, if successful, should result in a net profit of $780, whereas the execution of a stop would mean a $600 loss. Multiplying the profit ($780) by the probability (.65) of achieving the profit gives $507. Similarly, if the dollar risk on the trade ($600) is multiplied by the probability (.35) of losing, the result is $210. The expected dollar value of the trade, $297, is computed by subtracting $210 from $507. Obviously the expected value of a trade should be positive or the trade should be rejected.

The summary following the section "actual liquidation" refers to the *actual* dollars gained or lost on the trade. The trader should check his record of closed profits and losses frequently to ensure that results generally parallel expectations, both in the number of profits and losses and in the average dollar amount of profits and losses.

The section on "other factors" can be adapted by each trader to summarize the factors he considers important. "Technical comments" may include chart formations, volume, open interest, or response to news.

The "seasonal" item is noted because some traders think that many futures have seasonal trends. There is nothing wrong with sometimes attempting to take advantage of a contraseasonal move, but the trader should at least be aware that he is doing it.[2]

Noting the "historical price level" makes it certain that the trader knows whether he is trading at prices that have been proved unusually high or low in the past. This might not dissuade him from buying at historically high prices or selling at historically low prices, but it guarantees that he is doing it knowingly rather than inadvertently.

The "consensus," particularly of brokers and services that influence a number of traders, helps to determine whether a contemplated position is with or against the crowd. This factor, again, may not be considered critical, but it does help one to avoid being the last to buy or sell.

The "government loan equivalent" or other government price influences (where they apply) should be considered with the historical price level to help determine whether the current price of a future is too high or too low. If the price seems historically high, for example, but the loan level has been increased drastically, the market price may appear to be not nearly high enough rather than too high.

The relation of the cash price to the near-term contract often is a clear indicator of near-term strength or weakness. A change in the relationship may provide an early indication of a change in price direction of the futures market.

"Landmarks" point out events that can reasonably be expected to happen if the trade is to be considered on course; for example, the results of a government report which is scheduled to be released on a given date should generally be in line with expectations of what the report will indicate.

"Perils" are closely related to landmarks because a report that contains statistics unfavorable to the trader's position may prove to be a peril instead of a landmark. Some perils, of course, such as a freeze in Florida when a trader is short on orange juice or a large unexpected release from the government stockpile of copper when the trader is long on copper futures, cannot be definitely dated.

The "comparable years" section simply indicates past years in which conditions were similar to those in the current year. If the direction of price or timing in those years is not consistent with the trader's intended position, she should have some reason to believe that there are conditions existing in the present year that are different enough from conditions in the past to justify her position. Because the list of "other factors" may be wide and deep, additional space should be provided for their notation.

The "trade evaluation" section of the plan is a control of the trader's discipline. Sooner or later price movement must have elected a stop or an objective or time must have run out. In any case, the result of most trades should be in accordance with the objectives and risks covered in the plan. The trader should eventually have a plan form that is detailed enough and a discipline that is strong enough

---

[2] Seasonal movements, like most of the other apparent consistencies in the futures markets, have a natural tendency to disappear or become distorted when they become well known. If a trader believes that she has discovered a consistency, she would do well to keep it to herself.

so that there is seldom a significant variation within his control between the possible results, good or bad, and the actual results.

A Specific Plan

A plan is so basic to successful trading that it is worth pausing to explore in depth some of the thought that goes into its construction. Assume that a speculator has decided to enter the futures markets and will risk $10,000 for this purpose. He has selected a brokerage house and a registered representative, opened an account, and deposited his money. He has also decided to limit his trading to wheat until he becomes knowledgeable enough to enter other markets.

It is October, the recently harvested wheat crop was a large one, and current prices are low. The trader has decided that the current price level adequately reflects the size of the crop and that there is no logical reason for it to go much lower. He also concludes that potential foreign and domestic demand, as well as anticipated commercial hedge lifting, should result in a price rise. The chart he keeps also indicates that the decline in price has stopped, and he interprets this as a signal that bullish forces are about to become dominant and that a rise is probable. He therefore decides to enter a long wheat position.

Having decided to buy wheat, the trader must make a rational choice among the various markets where wheat is traded. This decision will be based on the estimated location and time of the greatest demand for wheat and on the type of wheat that will be in the shortest supply. If the trader decides that the anticipated demand will be reflected in Soft Red more than in Hard Red and in winter more than in spring wheat, he will probably take his position on the Chicago Board of Trade rather than on the Kansas City or Minneapolis exchange. He will then have to determine which contract will best reflect the expected tightness. He can do this either by making a fundamental judgment or by looking at wheat charts from other years with similar fundamentals and noting what happened then. He may also consult charts of other commodities in an effort to find similar patterns. It appears to the trader that the December contract does not provide him with enough time before having to risk taking delivery, but believing that a rising market will cause inversion he prefers nearby contracts to those more distant. He therefore compromises by selecting the March contract. He notes that in recent years during which wheat prices have risen, March gains on May, and May gains on July. Therefore, a spread position in which March is bought against a short position in July might be profitable. Because the trader has adequate capital available for margin and because he believes that the risk of a net long position is reasonable, he decides merely to buy the March wheat, which is selling at $3.54½ a bushel.

Analysis of the recent market, as well as analysis of those in years with similar characteristics, indicates that a gross profit of 30 cents a bushel has a .55 probability of being achieved by December 15, whereas a decline to $3.39½ a bushel would indicate that the market is not "acting right" and that the trade should be abandoned. The probability of the latter is judged to be .45. If the price were to rise by 30 cents, the gross profit on a contract of 5000 bushels would be $1500, which would leave a net profit of $1440 after deduction of the $60 round-turn commission currently charged by the trader's broker. If the trade had to be closed out unfavorably at $3.39½, the decline of 15 cents a bushel would represent a loss of $750 plus the $60 commission, or a total of $810. Considering that the expected value of a profit is $792 ($1440 × .55) and that the possible loss is estimated at only $364.50 ($810 × .45), the trader regards the expected value of the trade of $427.50 ($792 − $364.50) as adequate and decides to enter the trade. He is aware that the chance of having to liquidate a little below his stop point exceeds the chance of having an order filled above his profit objective, but he considers even the worst-case expected value positive enough to justify a position.

Because he thinks that the ratio of profit to loss is small and because so much time may be needed for the position to reach its potential, he decides not to tie up much available capital in this trade. The modest objective and close stop-loss level preclude any additions to the original position on either strength or weakness. The speculator decides that the most he is willing to lose on this trade if it proves to be unsuccessful is 10 percent of his trading capital, or $1000. Note that he is concerned more with the amount of his trading capital that he might lose than with the percentage of his margin or the change in the price of the wheat itself. Accordingly, he buys 5000 bushels of wheat at $3.54½ and immediately enters an open order to sell the 5000 bushels at $3.84½ or at $3.39½ stop O.C.O. (one cancels the other, or order cancels order). A reminder is written on the trading plan to liquidate the position at the close of the market on December 15 if neither the objective nor the stop-loss point has been reached by that time. The amount of thinking and planning represented by a plan even as simple as this probably exceeds that done by many traders, which may be one reason why so many people lose money trading.

A refinement of the plan outlined here is a provision for accepting something less than a 30-cent profit before December 15 in order to consider the time needed to make a profit as well as its amount. As an extreme example, a rise of 20 cents on the same day that the position was taken would leave the trader in the position of possibly waiting for 2 months or more to make 10 more cents at the risk of losing back the 20 cents plus at least the other 15 cents to the stop point. It may appear to be logical to accept the 20 cents because the additional gain is too small to justify the possible loss from the new price level. By the same token, it is never possible to make 30 cents in a position if a profit is always taken at 20 cents. One possible solution is simply to wait for the other 10 cents in accordance with the plan. Another is to have the plan provide for such possibilities by allowing profits to be taken if they are achieved quickly. For example, it may provide for a profit of 16 cents to be taken during the first week, for 19 cents during the next 2 weeks, for 24 cents during the next 2 weeks, and for waiting for the objective of 30 cents thereafter. It is important, however, to work these possibilities into the plan rather than modify the plan haphazardly in accordance with impulses.

COMMODITY POOLS AND MANAGED FUNDS

Most of this book considers investments in futures contracts based upon decisions made by investors themselves or advice given to them by their brokers. Others, however, prefer to turn their funds over to external professional managers. There are three primary ways of using professional management services. There are both public and private pools or funds and individually managed accounts. In addition, advisory services provide futures advice, usually in written form, without actually controlling customer funds. Most of this section deals with public commodity pools, but many of the comments and conclusions apply to the other types of managed accounts as well.

Professional fund managers typically charge a fee, usually front-end, and retain a portion of any profits for managing investors' funds. It would appear uneconomical for investors to turn their funds over to professional managers, but many do for one or more of several reasons.

The primary reason is probably the perceived expertise of the professional manager. Investors may think that professional managers have access to better information about futures markets or know better how to interpret it. Or the perceived expertise may relate to quantitative ability or computer skill.

There may be other reasons more subtle than perceived expertise. One involves diversification. Investors may believe that the widely accepted benefits of diversifying in securities markets apply as well to futures markets. A pool has sufficient capital to diversify its investments into many futures markets, and this is assumed by many scholars and investors to reduce risk.

Lower transaction costs might attract some investors to pools. The more an investor pays in transaction costs, the less he has to invest in the markets and the sooner he will lose all of his funds if his positions go against him. Even if he is successful, he must overcome the cost of trading before he gains enough to justify his time and risk. Because of their size, some pools may be able to negotiate lower commissions than individual traders. Although this may be true in some cases, even small investors can often negotiate favorable commissions or patronize discount brokers. Furthermore, many pools charge commissions that are even higher than standard retail rates. Funds sponsored by brokerage houses have, of course, an interest in survival, but they also have an interest in generating commission income.

The leveraged nature of futures trading may offer another advantage of pooled trading. Futures contracts are highly leveraged vehicles usually requiring margins of between 0.5 percent and 10 percent of the value of the positions held. This can result in substantial profits if the prices of the positions held move in the investor's favor. As usual, however, the cost of this opportunity is the acquisition of risk that is at least equally as substantial. This means that small market moves against an individual investor can lead to margin calls, exhaust the investor's capital, or even require the deposit of funds beyond the capital the investor had planned to utilize for futures trading.

Many commodity investors have been correct in their assessments of the direction in which markets would move only to find that a small adverse move exhausted their funds and that as a result they were out of the market, although they eventually proved to be correct. There are all too many futures investors who were correct about market direction but not right soon enough and as a result lost their trading capital. They can sympathize with the football coach who never lost a game but admitted that a few games ended too soon.

Professional investors rarely use their maximum leverage. Instead, they usually keep half or more of the total funds they manage in a low-risk investment such as Treasury bills. By being less than fully invested, they can withstand greater adversity and survive to trade another day.

Individual investors could also refrain from investing up to the extent of leverage permitted. They could deposit more than the required margin or put half or more of their funds in money market funds or savings accounts. This might appear to make considerable sense, particularly if a fund is charging fees based upon funds deposited but not utilized. Actually, however, most individual investors do not exhibit such conservative behavior but prefer to work their funds to the maximum. According to fund advocates, professional investment managers have sufficient discipline to limit their market exposure, whereas individual investors do not and therefore are "blown out" of the market on any adverse move.

Most funds do not require individual investors to deposit funds beyond their initial investments and thus offer some of the same appeals as options. Total exposure is known in advance, and investors are able to weather temporary adversity without losing their investments.

Thus, professionally managed funds are thought to be preferable to individually managed funds because of greater expertise, greater and less expensive opportunities for diversification, lower transaction costs, and the opportunity to utilize leverage at a reasonable cost and with a quantifiable total exposure. These advantages must be weighed, however, against the costs of utilizing professional managers.

Some charge so much in fees and profit sharing that long-run profitability is virtually impossible. Some account managers exhibit no more trading skill than anyone else. Their sources of information may have no great value, and their technical devices are defeated just as rapidly by efficient markets as are the chart signals used by the most naive individual investors. Managed funds that outperform individuals over time probably do so more because of disciplined trading than because of superior expertise or understanding of markets. It might be more economical for individuals merely to understand discipline and use it rather than pay for it in the form of fees covering distribution costs and the holding of idle funds as well as possibly higher commission rates.

Structure of a Commodity Pool

A commodity pool or fund is a partnership, usually consisting of one general partner and several limited partners. The general partner is typically the commodity pool operator (CPO)—the person who organizes the pool and bears an unlimited risk of loss. The limited partners invest their funds in the pool. Their risk is usually limited to the amount of funds invested.

Trading decisions are made by a commodity trading adviser (CTA), who is chosen by the CPO. The adviser is usually compensated by fees and a percentage of any profits achieved. Remaining shares of profits may be distributed to the partners or utilized to increase the scale of trading.

There are usually two other major participants in a commodity pool. One is the clearing agent, or the clearing member of the exchange or exchanges, who clears the trades on the exchanges. Often the CPO serves also as the clearing agent.

The other is the selling agent or distributor (there may be more than one agent or distributor), who actually sells or distributes the shares of the pool to the investors, or limited partners. Selling agents or distributors are typically brokerage house salespeople. A pool may not begin to invest the funds raised from investors (open) unless a specified minimum level of total capital is achieved. The selling agents may share in the initial costs of setting up a pool, even if it does not ultimately succeed in opening. The structure of a commodity pool is summarized in Figure 10-1.

Organizing a commodity pool results in sometimes substantial costs. Registration with such appropriate government agencies as the SEC, the CFTC, and perhaps, state agencies, along with various legal, accounting, and printing activities, including the preparation of a prospectus, may involve costs of hundreds of thousands of dollars. If the fund opens, these costs are usually charged against the deposits of the investors. In addition, the CPO and the CTA usually receive a front-end fee. What remains after these charges is available for investment in the markets. In addition to his fee, the CTA frequently may take some percentage of any profits generated.

The selling agent also receives a commission for each share of the pool he sells to the limited partners. The clearing agent receives a clearing fee for each commodity trade done through him by the CTA. The selling brokers also often receive a "trailing commission," that is, a portion of the clearing commission for each trade done by the CTA.

There are many possible variations among the detailed structures of pools and in the distribution of their costs and fees. Such details are available from the prospectuses, or offering circulars, which should be available to prospective investors.

Performance of Commodity Funds

The rapid proliferation of commodity funds began in 1978. They grew rapidly as measured by the amount of money managed through 1982. This resulted from aggressive selling efforts aided by the good performance which many funds enjoyed during that period. Within the group, there were, of course, some big winners

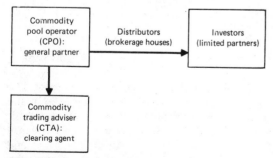

Figure 10-1   Structure of a commodity pool.

EXHIBIT 10-3   Commodity Fund Performance*
Number of Advisers with Gains (+) or Losses (−) in Equity

	1979		1980		1981		1982		6/12/83 (12 months ending)	
	+	−	+	−	+	−	+	−	+	−
Public funds	9	1	14	3	13	7	27	13	3	44
Private funds	NA	NA	6	0	10	3	14	3	8	16

*From managed account reports.

and big losers, but the overall performance of the funds in the years 1979 through 1983 is clearly indicated in Exhibit 10-3.

A convenient source for following the performance of the major public commodity funds has been the "Funds Review" section of the monthly periodical *Futures Magazine*. Monthly tables list between 50 and 100 of the funds and identify their general partners, underwriters, and trading advisers. These tables also indicate changes in the unit values and distributions of the funds since their opening dates.

The performance of most funds worsened during the early 1980s. The most likely reason for this deterioration was the price behavior of the markets. Most fund trading advisers prefer trend-following systems, especially if computerized. Basically most believe that "the trend is your friend" and that their profits are greatest when they identify major trends and ride them, being long through prolonged uptrends and short through downtrends. In choppy markets—that is, markets where there are frequent changes in the direction of prices after small moves—they often get "whipsawed" and prefer to stay out of nontrending markets altogether.

For trading advisers to realize good profits, it was not necessary for all futures markets to be trending—only a few strong trends are necessary to achieve good profits over a period. But during 1982 and 1983, most markets were choppy and nontrending. The performance of trading advisers became sharply worse. Some funds lost so much equity through adverse market action or withdrawals by disenchanted investors that they were forced to close.

Public Funds, Private Funds, and Investment Advisory Services

It has been indicated that there are three similar but different ways that investment advisers may be utilized to manage individuals' commodity investments.

The first and most common involves the public commodity fund or pool. The public fund, similar to the stock or mutual fund, is offered to the public by the brokerage houses or other distributors. Since the fund is offered to the public, it can be advertised, and solicitations can be made by brokers for the fund. Because the fund is offered to the public, it must be registered with the Securities and Exchange Commission (SEC), and as part of the registration process, a prospectus must be made available. The fund must also be registered with the states under the blue-sky laws. However, neither the SEC nor the states have any ongoing regulatory authority over a fund.

The public fund must also be registered with the CFTC. In addition, its CPO and CTA must be registered with the CFTC. In this context, the track records of the CTA must be made available. The CFTC also has an ongoing regulatory authority over a fund—this is mainly used to assure disclosure of the performance of the fund. In a public fund, the investment increments are typically small—for example, $5000.

Private funds or pools are again pools of several investors' funds, which are combined and managed together. A private fund, however, cannot be offered to the public; that is, it cannot be advertised, and solicitations to the public cannot be made by brokers. Because of this, it does not have to be registered with the SEC. States also exempt private funds with certain characteristics. The private fund is, however, regulated by the CFTC, which also enforces the same type of disclosure that public funds make.

Whereas public funds are generally marketed to investors, private funds are typically composed of a small group of investors who contribute a larger amount of funds—typical minimum contributions are $20,000 to $25,000. To avoid SEC registration, only "accredited investors" can participate, that is, investors who can "fend for themselves." These accredited investors may be institutional or business investors or individuals with substantial net worth or income. And most states exempt state registration for pools with at most 35 accredited investors.

The third way in which investors can have their funds managed in futures markets by a professional adviser is via an individually managed account. In this way the investors' funds are not mingled with other investors' funds and invested together; instead, their funds are individually managed. In this case, although the manager has to be registered with the CFTC as a CTA, the investment itself does not have to be approved or regulated. A typical minimum amount accepted by professional managers is $50,000. Many CTAs manage several such individual accounts.

Individual investors may also manage their own funds, that is, make their own investment decisions, but rely to varying degrees on investment advisory services. These investment advisory services are usually used on a subscription basis and make explicit investment recommendations, usually in periodic publications.

Selecting a Fund

Several factors should be considered before an investment is made in a managed fund. The track record of the adviser is considered by some to be quite important. A record of the past performance of an adviser may be supplied by the adviser herself or by the broker representing the fund.

Heavy reliance upon track records can create problems. It makes it difficult for new, potentially successful advisers to become established. It takes a track record to get funds, and it takes funds to develop a track record. A good track record may result from certain types of markets which may establish misleading short-term results. There may have been changes in personnel who helped create the good record. A good track record may result in the attraction of so much capital that it can no longer be successfully managed.

Some investors rely upon the techniques used by the adviser. Some prefer fundamental analysis and others technical analysis. Many of the latter are impressed by computerized approaches to trading. Other investors consider primarily the reputation of the pool organizer, who is the general partner of the fund.

Initial and continuing fees should be carefully considered. Heavy up-front claims on the initial investment consisting of organization costs and selling expenses combined with trading costs and profit sharing may require trading results that cannot reasonably be maintained over time. The investor should determine not only what can be lost if trading is unsuccessful but also what return can be expected if trading is successful. Although the total loss is limited, this provides little satisfaction if such a loss is probable sooner or later or if excellent gross results would provide the investor only with what could be netted in investments with far less risk.

As a minimum, investors should be aware of the reputation of those with whom they are dealing. It is difficult enough for sophisticated traders of high integrity to be successful in futures trading. Investors who choose to invest with fly-by-night boiler-room operators must take some of the blame for the ultimate loss of their capital.

MISTAKES

As in most other activities requiring skill, success or failure in trading futures is largely a matter of how many mistakes are made. Most of them occur in the area of planning, but one of the greatest is not having a plan at all because no plan, no matter how poorly constructed, will allow for the loss of a trader's entire trading capital. A plan should give the trader a chance to try again. The alternative to planning is "watching the market," which usually results in trades being made in response to haphazard impulses triggered by random news items or hunches. It also results in considerable time being wasted watching a tape or a quotation board, time that could be used more productively by doing almost anything else. Boardroom traders too often take a small profit as quickly as possible and then rationalize by saying "You never go broke taking a profit," or they ride a loss and say "I'm locked in."

It should be remembered that the primary advantages of planned trading include the limitation of losses in relation to available capital and a formula for getting out of a trade, regardless of the direction taken by price. If a trader devises a plan that permits him to risk all of his trading capital or does not allow him to get out of a trade unless it goes in only one direction, he had better spend some time thinking about plans before he does much trading. Jay Gould is credited with having said "The perfect speculator, the perfect gambler, if you will, must know *when* to come in; more important, he must know when to stay out; and most important, he must know when to get out once he is in."

Aside from not having a plan at all, the greatest possible mistake probably is to have a plan and not follow it. The temptations to make errors when a plan is not followed may be overwhelming. When the profit objective has been reached, the market has obviously been "acting well," and the trader must beware of "waiting for a while" to see what happens next. If still more profit is made, he can put in a new stop at the level of his original objective and make more money. The danger, however, is a reaction just after the initial objective is reached and before a stop can be inserted at a favorable point. If reasonable profits are attained and then lost back, the chance of success in the long run becomes remote. Even worse is making excuses not to take a loss when the stop point is reached. Every trader is able to rationalize riding losses by convincing himself that recovery is virtually certain from the new level, that if he were not already in the trade he would certainly enter it now, that further adversity is simply impossible, or that it is the wrong day or wrong time of the day to take the loss. The fact remains that the risk level influenced the size of the position being carried, and this in turn influenced the amount of capital being risked, which was the maximum considered reasonable. Any further loss therefore becomes unreasonable by definition. One solution to this problem is to remove temptation by putting in the stop order to liquidate the position immediately after the position is taken and leaving it in regardless of current news, time of the day, or anything else. Unfortunately the alternative to a planned loss is an unplanned loss, and the trader who habitually receipts for unplanned losses is firmly embarked on the road to ruin.

Perhaps the most stultifying mistake that can befall a trader is the assumption that success is virtually certain if he adopts a rational trade-selection strategy and intelligently follows the elements of a successful plan as developed in this chapter. Unfortunately there is a final obstacle to success—money management—which is the proper concern of the closing chapter of this part for those who play the game.

NOTES FROM A TRADER

A most important aspect of planning is to *have* a plan. Another is to follow it. A plan not followed is like an automobile seat belt not buckled. A plan should be kept to oneself. When other people are looking over the trader's shoulder, things start to go wrong, because she begins to attach some importance to their reactions to what she does, when they really should not affect what she does at all.

There is always some apparent reason for trying for still more profit or not taking a loss. If the trader lacks the discipline to set objectives and risk limits and to act when either is reached, he should not trade futures.

The trailing stop seems to be an infallible device for taking advantage of big moves with modest risk. For reasons developed thoroughly in Chapter 4, this device rarely works.

Plans may be difficult to devise and adapt to one's own trading preferences, and even a carefully conceived plan may not work. Markets may act in a way in which they have never acted before, and all the work that went into a plan's preparation may appear to have been wasted. Discouragement from time to time is part of the game, and famines have a way of following feasts. Despite any apparent disadvantages, there can be no doubt that trading with a game plan is far better than trading without one.

11

Money Management

*"It is remarkable that a science which began
with the consideration of games of chance
should become the most important object of
human knowledge. . . . The most important
questions of life are, for the most part, really
only problems of probability."*
PIERRE SIMON DE LAPLACE
*Théorie Analytique des Probabilités,
1812*

INTRODUCTION

Games of speculation are different from gambling games in both the economic
and legal senses, but to the typical speculators the similarities of the two activities
greatly exceed the differences. Their reasons for engaging in either one are the
same: profit, excitement, diversion, compulsion, or some of their combinations.
Most important, many of the rules are quite similar, and therefore the extensive
thought applied to gambling games is quite applicable to the futures trading game
as well.

Traders, like gamblers, will find it far more difficult to handle their money in a
logical and disciplined manner than to learn the rules of the game. Anyone, for
example, can learn to play draw poker—the ranking of possible hands and local
interpretations of the rules and procedures—in an hour or so. Many people, how-

ever, have played the game for years and have lost consistently because of poor money management. Most of these losers bemoan their bad luck, just as losing futures traders tend to blame their brokers, unexpected events, or bad luck for their own errors in money management.

It is impossible to develop a set of rules in this chapter to serve as a guide for all traders under all conditions. Trading is an individual decision-making process, and each trader brings his or her own unique intellectual and behavioral background to bear on the problem of approaching futures trading most profitably. Traders have different goals in the markets, different attitudes toward their profits and losses, and different preferences in their styles of trading, to say nothing of a host of other differences such as time available, tax considerations, and financial and psychological strength. Traders who hope to succeed in the long run must be able to recognize and develop their behavioral skills in order to determine a set of objectives most logical for their concept of maximum advantage. To employ a money management system effectively a trader must consider its four basic elements:

1. Initial capital
2. Objectives
3. The expectation of the game being played
4. The probability of ruin

The first two were discussed in preceding chapters. The remaining two are considered in the pages that follow. The discussion here does not consider subjective motivations in great detail because it would require an extensive foray into psychology involving a wide range of personal drives such as a guilt-ridden risk lover's desire to lose his money.

EXPECTATION OF THE GAME PLAYED

Probability

A game, as discussed here, may consist of one or more trials which a gambler would call bets and a speculator would call trades. The expectation, or average payoff, of the game being played indicates whether it consisted primarily of fair bets (those with zero expectation), good bets (those with a positive expectation), or bad bets (those with a negative expectation). If the game consisted of only one trial, the expectation of the game and the trial would be the same. A basic element of expectation is the long-run relative frequency of an event occurring. This element is probability, expressed as a number ranging from a low of 0 to a high of 1.

An example is provided by a game centering on the flipping of a coin. The probability of "heads" is .5 and the probability of "tails" is .5. Another example is provided by the draw poker player who is holding four spades and draws one card to his hand hoping to find a fifth spade to make a flush and, it is hoped, win the pot. The probability of drawing that fifth spade from a deck of cards without a joker is .191; the probability of not drawing it is .809.

It should be noted that the gambler or player of a social card game has a decided advantage over the speculator in the futures or stock market in that the gambler is able to determine the precise probabilities inherent in the game and to act accordingly. (This is not to say, of course, that the player will actually use that advantage or that knowing the probabilities will enable the player to profit from playing the game.) A roulette player may be interested in betting on red versus black or odd versus even. She can readily determine that the wheel has 36 numbers, half odd, half even, half on a red background, and half on black. In addition, most American roulette wheels have a "0" and "00" on a green background, on both of which the casino wins all red, black, odd, and even bets. The player knows, therefore, that there are 18 chances to win and 20 chances to lose, regardless of how she bets. The probability of winning is .4737 ($^{18}/_{38}$) and the probability of losing is .5268 ($^{20}/_{38}$).

Unlike the coin flipper, who knows that after many flips approximately half will have resulted in heads, the futures trader who concludes that sugar is going to increase in price is far less certain of measuring the probability of this event occurring before an unreasonably large adverse move. He may believe that the chance of an adequate rise in price before a substantial drop is .7, but this probability is subjective. Regardless of the thoroughness of his fundamental or technical research, the futures trader is applying his knowledge of the past to make his evaluation of the future. But in an area as dynamic as the futures markets conditions as well as probabilities change frequently. Even a huge number of samples to serve as a guide cannot lead to certain determination of the probabilities of success or failure because of the complex and fluid nature of the game and the rules under which it must be played.

Payoff

Those who play a game or trade a market normally hope to get more out of it than they put into it. The emphasis here is placed on money payoff rather than psychic costs and income (most people seem to get more satisfaction out of winning than losing, anyway). The money payoff of a game (gambling or trading) can be used to measure what may be won versus what may be lost, modified sometimes by an admission charge to a casino or a commission charged by a broker. A player may be in a position, for example, to win $1000 if she wins or to lose $500 if she loses. In this case her "money odds" may be said to be 2 to 1 of winning.

It should be clear that the mathematical *expectation* of a game depends on the probabilities and payoffs. Specifically, it is the sum of the possible payoffs with each payoff weighted (multiplied) by its respective probability. The player who stands to win $1000 or lose $500 with a probability of winning of .5 has a mathematical expectation, or average payoff, of $1000 × .5 − $500 × .5 = $250 and obviously might consider playing the game because in the long run she will average a $250 gain per play of the game. Suppose, however, that a player stands to win only $500 if he wins or lose $1000 if he loses. He might be tempted to reject the game out of hand, but what if the probability of winning were .9 and the probability of losing only .1? The expectation of the game would be $500 × .9 − $1000 × .1 = $350, still a positive value. On the basis of monetary expectation, the second game is more favorable than the first, for which reason the often-given advice to take a position in the stock or futures markets only if the trader will make two or three times or more what he may lose is ordinarily so foolish. Those giving such advice rarely speak of the *probability* of winning or losing, and without it the expected monetary value of taking the position cannot be determined. A game in which the player may win twice as many dollars as he stands to lose is no different in expectation from a game in which he may lose twice as many dollars as he may win if his probability of winning the first game is .33 and the probability of winning the second game is .67. Expectation, in short, is nothing more than the average payoff, which is derived by modifying the payoff of an event by its probability of occurring.

Depending on the combination of probability and payoff, a game may be said to be favorable if its expectation is more than zero or unfavorable if less. Returning to the roulette player discussed above, it will be recalled that the probability of her winning was .4737 and of losing, .5263. In the usual casino the player will be offered a money return equal to the money that she risks; that is, a player who bets a dollar on red, black, odd, or even will lose the dollar if she loses and win a dollar if she wins. Usually there is no charge for admission to a casino, so the payoff to the player is even (or the odds may be said to be 50-50). The mathematical expectation of the game to the player betting on one of the four items listed would therefore be 47.37 cents of each dollar bet, and the expectation of the casino would be the other 52.63 cents. The house "take" or "advantage" is the difference of 5.26 cents on a one-dollar bet, or 5.26 percent of all bets. The player may be said to be making a bad bet, and because the house has the other side of all players' bets, it may be said to be making all good bets, each by the same margin.

The futures trader who tries to discover whether he is in a better or worse position than the roulette player finds his analysis difficult. He is aware precisely of only one aspect of his expectation of winning, and that is some part of his payoff. He can probably determine the commission that he will have to pay and estimate the opportunity cost on the capital that he utilizes for margin. The remaining element of the payoff, that is, how much he will win or lose because of market action, is far more difficult to determine accurately. A disciplined trader can, of course, determine the points at which he intends to liquidate his position, win or lose. He may even be sufficiently disciplined to enter orders at the two points he has determined—one intended to take his profit at the objective and the other to stop his loss when he has all the adversity he cares to suffer on a trade. If he sets his objective at a definite limit and leaves an open order in at that point, the chance of his getting exactly his price on a *successful* trade is quite high. He obviously cannot get less, and only infrequently will a market act so favorably for him that he will be filled at a price that is better than the one he has asked. On a losing trade, however, the outcome is far less certain. If he enters a stop-loss order which is elected, that order can be filled at his stop price, but also at better or worse. A fill at a better price than the stop specified is even rarer than a fill at a price that is better than a limit on the order at a trader's objective, but a fill at a price that is worse than that specified on a stop-loss order is quite common, and sometimes the fill is *much* worse. On balance, therefore, if the trader wins, his objective will usually be exactly as planned, but if he loses, the loss will frequently be greater than expected. (This is one of the major reasons why trading in the real world seldom turns out to be so profitable as one's paper trading has indicated that it should be.) The sophisticated trader must learn eventually to take this into consideration and plan in advance for the "execution costs" of his trades to include not only commissions but also some extra adversity on his losing trades. He may well have learned that the cost of extra adversity over a long period of trading may approach the far more obvious cost of commissions.

Despite his problems of probability and payoff, the trader must reach a conclusion concerning his chance of being ahead after making one or a series of trades, determine how much he expects to gain if he wins and how much he expects to lose if he loses, and use this knowledge in planning how to play the game. He may, of course, also decide not to play at all after completing an evaluation of his expectation.

Fair Bets

It is obvious that if a game consisted of one or more fair bets, it would involve a zero expectation and be an even game. It might be concluded that participants in such a game must be playing basically for fun and that no one has the right to expect to win in the long run. This, however, is not the case. Although the amount of money a person has does not affect the expectation on a single play of the game (whether the flip of a coin or a trade in plywood), the capital available to the players can be of tremendous importance in determining their eventual financial outcome.

If two players are betting on coin flips and one has significantly more capital than the other, that player's chance of eventually winning all the other's money, hence ruining him, is considerable. The greater the difference in relative capital and the more of his capital the poorer of the two players bets, the greater the probability that the richer will ruin the poorer and the faster it will happen. Even though the coins will work toward 50 percent heads and 50 percent tails, the probability of "runs" of heads or tails also increases as the game progresses. The probability, for example, of a series of 10 heads being flipped consecutively in 10 trials is not great, but if one continues to flip a coin for days at a time, the probability of 10 heads appearing in a row *sooner or later* actually will become rather high. If this event should be favorable to the poorer player, he will increase his capital and the richer player will be somewhat impaired, but if the series favors the richer player, the poorer can well be ruined. The richer player can expect to have his run sooner or later. That is why a gambling casino competing against small players does not even need its favorable probability to win on balance from a high proportion of its small opponents. This also helps the large futures trader to win even more from smaller traders as time goes on. In futures trading, as in so many other areas of financial endeavor, the nature of the game favors the rich getting richer.

Good Bets

The player making a good bet, which may be referred to as favorable or positive, has in her favor a mathematical expectation of winning money each time she makes it. A game consisting of one such bet or a preponderance of them is a favorable game. (Some consider each bet a game, and a series of bets would then be a series of favorable games, but the difference in semantics is of more interest to game theorists than to futures traders.) Positive expectation merely requires some combination of probability and payoff (including the cost of playing the game) that makes the bet or game financially favorable to the player. The coin flipper, for example, may be betting even money that he can flip one head before his opponent flips two, or he may be betting that he will flip a head before his opponent flips a tail, but he will win a dollar if he wins and lose 50 cents if he loses. He may need to flip one head to win a dollar at the risk of losing one dollar if his opponent flips a tail, but he gets paid a dime for playing the game. Better still for the fortunate player such as a racetrack which has a positive expectation of winning a high proportion of wagers placed but still charges its patrons for the opportunity of entering the premises, to say nothing of collecting fees for allowing them to park their cars outside, is some combination of these favorable terms.

Bad Bets

One might ask why individuals would make bad bets, that is, those in which they have a negative expectation when probability and payoffs are considered. One reason, of course, is that some players do not realize that their bets are bad or how bad they are. Others choose to play in negative games, knowing that they are unfavorable, because they have motivations explained by psychological drives rather than logically based financial factors. Presumably some people find a masochistic pleasure in losing or pride themselves on their courage in playing David to the bookmaker's Goliath. Some maintain that they enjoy playing the game enough to warrant the inevitable cost of playing, but here again the subjective world of individual psychological makeup (or mix-up) would have to be examined. This chapter assumes that the reader is interested in making good bets and playing favorable games.

In passing, it might be noted that there can be a high probability of eventually winning a game by ruining the opponent, even in a game in which each bet is bad, provided that it is not *too* bad and that the player making the bad bets has capital materially exceeding that of his opponent and that bets are large. This happy circumstance, however, can never accrue to a futures trader who is trading badly because he is always small in relation to the combined size of his opponents. Large traders who tried to overcome an unfavorable approach to futures trading would almost certainly find themselves among the small traders within a reasonably short time.

Strategy for a Favorable Game

Futures traders typically have, or think they have, a positive expected payoff, and it is that kind of game that is examined in more detail for a logical approach to ultimate victory. Readers should not treat this subject lightly. The *manner* in which they play the futures trading game is far more likely to cause their ultimate success or failure than is any other aspect of their trading, including their method of selecting trades.

It would be of considerable value if a money management strategy applicable to all traders could be offered here. This is impossible, however. The number of possible variables in the solution of all possible trading strategy problems would extend this book into at least a 5-foot shelf. Factors that would have to be considered include not only differences in personal attitudes toward profits and losses but also the specific probabilities that traders believe are inherent in the trades they select. The varying differences in probabilities of success and various ratios of profit to loss, differences in commissions, and different possible combinations of "good trades," "better trades," and "best trades" make for a huge number of possible variations. A single trader with an elaborate system of selecting trades may enter positions with wide variations in probabilities, payoffs, temporary adversity possibilities, commissions, required capital commitments, and time requirements. Too, there may be times when certain completely unexpected events create biases that were not taken into consideration and unexpectedly cause many simultaneous positions to have good or bad results at the same time. A trader, for example, may have long positions in four futures presumed to be reacting to different forces, with all four trade entries based on apparently independent technical signals. An event may occur that will prove to be bearish on *all* futures, and the trader will suffer four losses. Had he been short, he would have had four profits.

An individual trader facing this problem must consider the data he has available that apply to his own methods of trade selection and, even recognizing some of the subjectivity in money management and determination of probabilities, at least do his best to solve his problem logically. This is considerably better than making decisions haphazardly and hoping that everything will turn out well. The numbers that might apply to a mythical trader and what they mean to her should be a useful subject for detailed examination.

Assume that a trader has initial trading capital of $10,000. She has developed a technical trading method that she believes will indicate trade opportunities that will offer a profit opportunity equal in dollars to the risk of loss when commissions and other execution costs are considered. On the basis of her research or experience, the trader believes that her chance for a profit on any given trade is .55 and that her chance for a loss, therefore, is .45. Her mathematical advantage on each trade is .10. (She may feel that some trades will give her more advantage than that, but she has learned to temporize optimism and always take the conservative approach to any of her trading decisions.) Assume also that the trader plans to trade indefinitely rather than aim for some specific objective, that no change is expected in her presumed probabilities on the basis of her continuing research, and that her attitudes toward her gains and losses will remain unchanged as her fortunes ebb and flow. If she is successful, her gains could range between reasonably satisfactory and huge, depending on the frequency of her trades. As she proceeds from her research into real-time trading, the trader should be alert to benchmarks to make sure that she is on course.

Real-Time Validation

As has been indicated, life in the real world has a way of being more difficult than paper trading has shown it should be. Traders implementing their untested plans should make some effort to be sure that they are "on course." The statistics will vary with the plan being used, results expected, and degrees of variation from the expected acceptable to the trader, but at some point a method counted on to yield a given number of profits should begin yielding them.

The trader who anticipates a 10 percent advantage could make use of the figures in Table 11-1. This table can help to show him how many losses he should have suffered in a given number of trades. Suppose, for example, that he has taken three losses in his first five trades and is concerned because he believes he should have had only two. The first line of Table 11-1 indicates that he has a probability of .9497 of having more than zero losses, .7438 of having more than one, .4069 of having more than two, .1312 of having more than three, and .0185 of losing on all five. Three losses in five trades represent more than 40 percent, and in the column headed by "40" he will note that the chance of three or more losses was .4069. Three losses in five trades, therefore, should come as no great shock. By the same token, if he had lost on all five of his first five trades, he should also note carefully that there was a chance of only .0185 of this happening if in fact his probability of winning had been .55. Some traders might go back to their paper trading for a while, even at this early juncture, but others might go on trading despite the uncomfortable odds of more than 50 to 1 that the real world is not doing what their paper worlds said it should. If after 30 trades such a trader has had more than 18 losses (more than .60, hence $P = 60$), he will know that he is still in an unpleasant area with only a .0334 chance of being right, and if he has had more than 21 losses, the chance of his being on a satisfactory course is an almost ridiculous .0016. As he approaches his hundredth trade, his percentage of

TABLE 11-1   PROBABILITY OF MORE THAN p PERCENT UNSUCCESSFUL TRADES WITH A PROBABILITY .55 OF WINNING (10 PERCENT ADVANTAGE)[a]

No. of trades \ P→	0	10	20	30	40	50	60	70	80	90	100
5	.9497		.7438		.4069		.1312		.0185		.0000
10	.9975	.9767	.9004	.7340	.4956	.2616	.1020	.0274	.0045	.0003	.0000
20	1.0000	.9991	.9811	.8701	.5857	.2493	.0580	.0064	.0003	.0000	.0000
30	1.0000	.9960	.9960	.9306	.6408	.2309	.0334	.0016	.0000	.0000	.0000
40	1.0000	1.0000	.9993	.9717	.7376	.2624	.0283	.0007	.0000	.0000	.0000
50	1.0000	1.0000	.9998	.9835	.7615	.2385	.0165	.0002	.0000	.0000	.0000
60	1.0000	1.0000	.9999	.9903	.7820	.2180	.0097	.0001	.0000	.0000	.0000
70	1.0000	1.0000	1.0000	.9942	.7998	.2002	.0058	.0000	.0000	.0000	.0000
80	1.0000	1.0000	1.0000	.9965	.8156	.1844	.0035	.0000	.0000	.0000	.0000
90	1.0000	1.0000	1.0000	.9979	.8294	.1706	.0021	.0000	.0000	.0000	.0000
100	1.0000	1.0000	1.0000	.9987	.8426	.1574	.0013	.0000	.0000	.0000	.0000
150	1.0000	1.0000	1.0000	.9999	.8909	.1091	.0001	.0000	.0000	.0000	.0000
200	1.0000	1.0000	1.0000	1.0000	.9209	.0791	.0000	.0000	.0000	.0000	.0000
250	1.0000	1.0000	1.0000	1.0000	.9440	.0560	.0000	.0000	.0000	.0000	.0000
300	1.0000	1.0000	1.0000	1.0000	.9592	.0408	.0000	.0000	.0000	.0000	.0000
400	1.0000	1.0000	1.0000	1.0000	.9778	.0222	.0000	.0000	.0000	.0000	.0000
500	1.0000	1.0000	1.0000	1.0000	.9877	.0123	.0000	.0000	.0000	.0000	.0000

[a]In this table and in Tables 11-2 and 11-3 probabilities shown for trades 5 through 30 were derived from binomial distributions; for 40 through 500 they were derived from normal distributions that approximate binomial distributions.

losses should be clearly closing in on the expected .45. The chance of anything over .50 losses at this level is only .1574; over .60, only .0013. And over .70, the chance statistically approaches the impossible.

Tables 11-2 and 11-3 provide the same information for traders who believe that they have a probability advantage of .20 (.60 − .40) or .30 (.65 − .35). Traders with greater advantages have an inkling much sooner than those with smaller advantages of whether they are on course, and at each level the chance of their judging correctly whether they are on course is higher than the chance for those with smaller advantages at the same level. A trader with a .30 advantage, for example, who has traded 100 times and who has had more than 50 losses knows that there are only eight chances in 1000 that his real-world trading is in line with his researched expectations.

A trader following her program has two tasks in the area of validation. One is determining statistically or by excellent judgment whether her results are approaching her expectations at various levels of real-time trading. The other is deciding on the level that will cause her to abandon this method if results are less than favorable. One trader with losses indicating only a .20 chance of his being right may continue trading, whereas a second may go back and do more research, and a third may throw up his hands in disgust and buy U.S. Treasury bills.

PROBABILITY OF RUIN

Conceptual Foundation

Success presents few problems to most traders; it is the loss of trading capital, or ruin, that must be considered primary. Consideration of ruin demands an early

TABLE 11-2   PROBABILITY OF MORE THAN p PERCENT UNSUCCESSFUL TRADES WITH A PROBABILITY .60 OF WINNING (20 PERCENT ADVANTAGE)

No. of trades \ P→	0	10	20	30	40	50	60	70	80	90	100
5	.9222		.6630		.3174		.0870		.0102		.0000
10	.9940	.9537	.8328	.6178	.3670	.1663	.0548	.0123	.0017	.0001	.0000
20	1.0000	.9964	.9491	.7501	.4045	.1277	.0222	.0017	.0001	.0000	.0000
30	1.0000	.9997	.9829	.8238	.4216	.0972	.0083	.0002	.0000	.0000	.0000
40	1.0000	.9999	.9951	.9017	.5000	.0983	.0049	.0001	.0000	.0000	.0000
50	1.0000	1.0000	.9981	.9256	.5000	.0744	.0019	.0000	.0000	.0000	.0000
60	1.0000	1.0000	.9992	.9430	.5000	.0570	.0008	.0000	.0000	.0000	.0000
70	1.0000	1.0000	.9997	.9561	.5000	.0439	.0003	.0000	.0000	.0000	.0000
80	1.0000	1.0000	.9999	.9661	.5000	.0339	.0001	.0000	.0000	.0000	.0000
90	1.0000	1.0000	.9999	.9736	.5000	.0264	.0001	.0000	.0000	.0000	.0000
100	1.0000	1.0000	1.0000	.9794	.5000	.0206	.0000	.0000	.0000	.0000	.0000
150	1.0000	1.0000	1.0000	.9938	.5000	.0062	.0000	.0000	.0000	.0000	.0000
200	1.0000	1.0000	1.0000	.9981	.5000	.0019	.0000	.0000	.0000	.0000	.0000
250	1.0000	1.0000	1.0000	.9994	.5000	.0006	.0000	.0000	.0000	.0000	.0000
300	1.0000	1.0000	1.0000	.9998	.5000	.0002	.0000	.0000	.0000	.0000	.0000
400	1.0000	1.0000	1.0000	1.0000	.5000	.0000	.0000	.0000	.0000	.0000	.0000
500	1.0000	1.0000	1.0000	1.0000	.5000	.0000	.0000	.0000	.0000	.0000	.0000

**TABLE 11-3   PROBABILITY OF MORE THAN p PERCENT UNSUCCESSFUL TRADES WITH A
PROBABILITY .65 OF WINNING (30 PERCENT ADVANTAGE)**

No. of trades \ $P \longrightarrow$ 0	10	20	30	40	50	60	70	80	90	100
5	.8840		.5716		.2352		.0540		.0053		.0000
10	.9865	.9140	.7384	.4862	.2485	.0949	.0262	.0048	.0005	.0000	.0000
20	.9998	.9879	.8818	.5834	.2376	.0532	.0060	.0031	.0000	.0000	.0000
30	1.0000	.9981	.9414	.6425	.2198	.0301	.0014	.0000	.0000	.0000	.0000
40	1.0000	.9995	.9766	.7463	.2537	.0234	.0005	.0000	.0000	.0000	.0000
50	1.0000	.9999	.9869	.7707	.2293	.0131	.0001	.0000	.0000	.0000	.0000
60	1.0000	1.0000	.9926	.7938	.2062	.0074	.0000	.0000	.0000	.0000	.0000
70	1.0000	1.0000	.9957	.8098	.1902	.0043	.0000	.0000	.0000	.0000	.0000
80	1.0000	1.0000	.9975	.8258	.1742	.0025	.0000	.0000	.0000	.0000	.0000
90	1.0000	1.0000	.9986	.8401	.1599	.0014	.0000	.0000	.0000	.0000	.0000
100	1.0000	1.0000	.9992	.8527	.1473	.0008	.0000	.0000	.0000	.0000	.0000
150	1.0000	1.0000	.9999	.9003	.0997	.0001	.0000	.0000	.0000	.0000	.0000
200	1.0000	1.0000	1.0000	.9309	.0691	.0000	.0000	.0000	.0000	.0000	.0000
250	1.0000	1.0000	1.0000	.9512	.0488	.0000	.0000	.0000	.0000	.0000	.0000
300	1.0000	1.0000	1.0000	.9653	.0347	.0000	.0000	.0000	.0000	.0000	.0000
400	1.0000	1.0000	1.0000	.9819	.0181	.0000	.0000	.0000	.0000	.0000	.0000
500	1.0000	1.0000	1.0000	.9905	.0095	.0000	.0000	.0000	.0000	.0000	.0000

decision—and one of the most critical decisions in the area of money management. The risk of ruin in favorable games increases directly as more of the available trading capital is utilized for each trade. Increasingly conservative approaches also result in less profit potential, either because less will be gained on each winning trade or because there will be fewer trades. An intelligent median must be chosen.

Assume that the trader decides to use $2500, or one-fourth of his $10,000 capital, for each trade and plans to continue making $2500 commitments indefinitely. His risk of ruin is heavily concentrated in the early stages of his trading program. If he loses on his first two or three trades, he is in serious trouble, and if he loses on his first four trades, he is out of the trading business. The chance of his losing on his first trade is .45. His chance of losing on all four of his first four trades is only $(.45)^4$, or .04. If he is ahead after the first four trades and finds himself with trading capital five or six times the size of his $2500 commitments, four losses (consecutive or net) can no longer ruin him, but then he also faces an increasingly high probability of having more than four net losses as he continues his trading over time. The probability R of his eventual ruin is given by the formula

$$R = \left(\frac{1 - A}{1 + A}\right)^c$$

where A is the trader's advantage in his trades expressed in decimal form and C is the number of trading units with which he begins.[1] If a trader is willing to risk one-third of his capital in a trade, he has three initial trading units. If he risks

---

[1] William Feller, *An Introduction to Probability Theory and its Applications*, 3d ed. (New York: John Wiley & Sons, 1967). A good source of basic probability theory is Samuel Goldberg, *Probability: An Introduction* (Englewood Cliffs, N.J.: Prentice-Hall, 1960).

one-twentieth, he has 20 trading units. The trader being considered here will risk $2500 of his $10,000 on each trade and so has four trading units when his trading begins. His chance of eventual ruin is $[(1 - .1)/(1 + .1)]^4$, or .45. He may find this number uncomfortably high and may examine his chance of succeeding if he risked only one-tenth of his capital on each trade rather than one-fourth. The trader may consider survival more important than maximizing expected profits as fast as possible but having to accept more risk to do so. Some traders, of course, may choose maximization and accept the added risk that goes with it. The risk of only $1000 of the trader's $10,000 capital on each trade provides a dramatic example of the virtue of taking small risks if survival is the major motivation. The chance of losing all of the $10,000 capital in the first 10 trades drops to $(.45)^{10}$, or less than one chance in 3000. Even if he continued to trade indefinitely, risking $1000 on every trade in order to gain $1000, his chance of ruin would be only .1341. The probability of success on any given trade has remained unchanged, but the trader's chance of survival has increased from .55 to .87 merely by his trading on a more conservative scale.

One of the most difficult and important decisions to be made by the trader is what to do if his account grows on schedule, thereby further indicating that his favorable research projections were correct. If his original capital of $10,000 has grown to $20,000, his chance of being ruined if he continues trading on a scale of $1000 has become much smaller than the original .1341 because it would now take 20 net losses rather than 10 to ruin him. The probability of this happening is only .018. The chance of his continuing to add to his capital over time becomes more and more certain as it builds in size if he does not greatly increase his scale of trading. Having reached $20,000, he has an even greater chance of reaching $30,000, and having reached $70,000, say, he has a chance of then reaching $80,000 that is even greater still. On the other hand, when the trader reached $20,000, he could have become more aggressive. He could have begun trying for $40,000 with the same degree of probability as he originally had of reaching $20,000 from $10,000. The chance R of being ruined before reaching a higher specified level from any given starting point is provided by the formula

$$R = \frac{[(1 + A)/(1 - A)]^W - 1}{[(1 + A)/(1 - A)]^{C+W} - 1}$$

where A is the trader's advantage, C is the original trading capital expressed in trading units, and W is the number of those same-sized units he hopes to accumulate.[2] In the case of the trader being considered in detail here, his original capital is $10,000, which represents 10 trading units. With his .10 advantage his chance of getting to $20,000 successfully is .8815. If he arrives at the $20,000 level and chooses to try for $40,000 by using $2000 units of trading, his chance of arriving at $40,000 is again .8815. Each time he doubles his money, he will have the same chance of doubling it again by doubling his trading units. This assumes that he will not eventually find himself trading on a scale that will raise

[2] Ibid.

market liquidity problems, thereby decreasing his assumed .10 advantage, and that he will not pass his "stress point" and damage his judgment. Such a program may seem quite exciting because a trader has to double his original $10,000 only seven times to accumulate $1,280,000. Before he is too quick to give up his virtual certainty of continuing to accumulate money (if he never raises his scale of trading), he should realize that if he doubles his scale of trading, his overall risk of ruin will increase considerably. The chance of success in seven successive series with a chance of .8815 of winning each series is $(.8815)^7$, and the chance of ruin is $1 - (.8815)^7$, or an uncomfortable .5866. Even this may be exaggerating the real chance of success because (a) the presumed .10 advantage may have some high hopes mixed in with the research; (b) independence of results often does not exist, which makes runs of "bad luck" more likely than the computed probabilities would indicate; and (c) the growth of execution costs and market liquidity problems, as capital grows, becomes increasingly likely.

Traders must work out their own probabilities, given their own facts, judgments, and attitudes, but it may be of interest to note in Table 11-4 the probabilities faced

TABLE 11-4   TRADER'S CHANCE OF RUIN WITH A .10, .20, OR .30 ADVANTAGE IN ATTEMPTING TO EITHER DOUBLE THE INITIAL CAPITAL OR TRADE INDEFINITELY

		.10 Advantage Probability of		.20 Advantage Probability of		.30 Advantage Probability of	
C	W	Success	Ruin	Success	Ruin	Success	Ruin
1	1	55	45	60	40	65	35
1	∞	18.2	81.8	33.3	66.7	46.2	53.8
2	2	59.9	40.1	69.2	30.8	77.5	22.5
2	∞	33.1	66.9	55.6	44.4	71.0	29.0
3	3	64.6	35.4	77.1	22.9	86.5	13.5
3	∞	45.2	54.8	70.4	29.6	84.4	15.6
4	4	69.1	30.9	83.5	16.5	92.2	7.8
4	∞	55.2	44.8	80.2	19.8	91.6	8.4
5	5	73.2	26.8	88.4	11.6	95.7	4.3
5	∞	63.3	36.7	86.8	13.2	95.5	4.5
6	6	76.9	23.1	91.9	8.1	97.6	2.4
6	∞	70.0	30.0	91.2	8.8	97.6	2.4
7	7	80.3	19.7	94.5	5.5	98.7	1.3
7	∞	75.5	24.5	94.2	5.8	98.7	1.3
8	8	83.3	16.7	96.2	3.8	99.3	.7
8	∞	79.9	20.1	96.1	3.9	99.3	.7
9	9	85.9	14.1	97.5	2.5	99.6	.4
9	∞	83.6	16.4	97.4	2.6	99.6	.4
10	10	88.1	11.9	98.3	1.7	99.8	.2
10	∞	86.6	13.4	98.3	1.7	99.8	.2
11	11	90.1	9.9	98.9	1.1	99.9	.1
11	∞	89.0	11.0	98.9	1.1	99.9	.1
12	12	91.7	8.3	99.2	.8	99.9	.1
12	∞	91.0	9.0	99.2	.8	99.9	.1

KEY: C is the trader's initial capital in units; W is the number of additional units the trader is attempting to gain; the symbol "∞" indicates that the trader expects to trade indefinitely. The format of this table was derived from Edward O. Thorp, *Beat the Dealer* (New York: Random House, 1962), p. 63.

by traders with advantages of 10, 20, and 30 percent in their favor on each trade, including all costs, with payoffs equaling losses. The effects of different sizes of commitments and the length of time during which trading is planned to continue become quite clear. For example, if a trader has an assumed 10 percent advantage, capital of $10,000, and a plan to risk $2000 (one-fifth of her capital; hence her capital represents five original trading units), with the payoff and dollar risk also $2000, and if the trader expects to trade indefinitely, her chance of success will be .633 and her chance of ruin .367. If she reduced her exposure and objective on each trade to $1000, her chance of long-term success would increase to .866 and her chance of ruin would drop to .134. If a trader thought that her advantage was .30 (.65 − .35), her chance of ruin (if she risked only one-tenth of this capital and traded indefinitely without increasing her scale of trading, if successful) would be a minuscule .002. It should be obvious that a greater advantage vastly increases the chance of success in trading, just as it does in gambling, but it should now also be obvious that a trader with less probability of success who trades conservatively can actually have a better chance of long-term success (winning the game) than a trader with a higher probability of success who chooses to trade more aggressively. The trader with a .30 advantage, using one-fourth of her initial capital on each trade, faces a chance of ruin of a little more than .08. The trader with only a .10 advantage, however, can achieve about the same low risk merely by trading in units of one-twelfth of her capital. The outlook for the time that it would take for each to make important profits, assuming success, would vary considerably.

Multiple Positions

The problem of how much of a trader's available capital should be committed to one trade is compounded when the trader decides to add lines to an original position. This may occur when he follows a program of averaging or when he believes that he has a new reason for taking a position beyond that already existing. This might happen, for example, when a chartist is following various signals and notes a second signal which indicates that he should enter a position when he already has a similar one based on a previous chart signal. He might conclude that these signals should be treated separately and distinctly or even that the second signal will reinforce the first and make its favorable outcome more certain. This situation deserves some thoughtful consideration before it is carried too far. No reason for adding units to an open trade makes a favorable outcome certain. A large number of signals all followed will eventually cause a trader to hold a position so large that an unfavorable outcome will ruin him.

To deal with this situation, which results in great opportunity accompanied as usual by great risk, the trader should consider a protective policy. One such policy might be a limitation on the number of multiple lines to be accepted. This, in turn, will depend on how large his trading capital is and how great a risk he thinks each unit entails. A trader who risks only 2 percent of his capital on each line will still be risking only about 8 percent on four lines of the same future. An 8 percent loss is painful but not disastrous. A trader who risks 15 percent on a line, however, would find himself with a loss of about 60 percent if all four lines failed.

Stop-Loss Points

When the trader has determined how much risk he is willing to face in a trade, he has a starting point from which he will determine his stop-loss level and, it is hoped, place an actual stop-loss order. If he believes that a logical stop-loss can be placed at a point involving less than his acceptable maximum risk, the closer stop is, of course, to be preferred. Placing stops may involve many criteria, some of which are regarded as important by some traders but not by others. It would appear that there are two considerations that cannot be ignored by any trader. First is the amount of money that would be lost if the stop were violated. Second is the current price volatility of the future being traded. In regard to the first of these points, whether the stop points themselves are based on the current market price of a future, the margin required, a chart point, or the day of the month multiplied by the phase of the moon, the number of dollars of loss, including execution costs, can easily be expressed as a percentage of the trader's capital. The trader should also have an informed idea of the maximum number of net losses he may reasonably have to suffer, based on his experience or research. If he risks so much that reasonable adversity will ruin him, his route is suicidal. It should be reiterated that ruin does not consist of a series of losses; it consists of a series in which the number of losses exceeds the number of profits by enough to cause ruin, regardless of their order. For example, if a trader with $4000 risks a total of $1000 on each trade, she will be ruined if she loses four times in a row. She will be just as ruined, however, by a bad period during which she has four patterns of one profit followed by two losses. She will have four profits, eight losses, and no money, even though she never had more than two losses in a row. Because an adverse series becomes increasingly likely as trading is carried on over time, it is obvious why trading too large a position is so deadly.

The second point that must be considered by any trader determining stop points is the degree of volatility in the markets he or she is trading. Traders who base their stops on current prices or chart patterns must take into consideration how logical stop-loss points may change drastically as futures are traded at higher or lower levels or as current volatility becomes greater or less. Stop-loss levels should be adjusted to recent volatility, but even this must be defined by the trader on a logical and validated basis. Is "current" defined as the range of prices for the last week, month, 6 months, or something else? Of course, next week may prove to be greatly different from last week, but this is an unavoidable risk that always accompanies speculation. Volatility, like most of the other vital data in futures trading, is fluid and nonstationary, unlike the more stable mass of data to be considered by coin flippers, poker players, and dice shooters. The importance of stop-loss strategy cannot be overestimated. This element of strategy will affect the trader's mathematical expectation in the following manner. If the stop-loss is placed far from the current price, the probability of losing will be small but the amount of the loss may be large. If the stop-loss is placed close to the current price, the probability of losing will be greater but the amount of the loss will be small. Consistently placing stops too close and getting stopped out in "noise" areas or placing stops so far away that the inevitable losses will be unreasonably large will lead to almost certain ruin.

Strategy Following Significant Success

When an account has grown impressively, a trader has a difficult decision to make, but it cannot be avoided. If a $10,000 account has grown, on schedule, to $20,000, which was the objective hoped for when trading in futures was started, the action to be taken is obvious. A check is requested and deposited in a convenient savings and loan institution, and the futures account is closed. If, however, the trader is thinking in terms of acquiring a chateau in France, a chauffeured limousine, and a cellar of Rothschild wines, he must prepare for the next phase of his trading. Again, no definitive course of action acceptable to all traders can be marked out here, but the alternatives are clear. The trader can leave well enough alone and continue trading in the same way and on the same scale as before. Now that he has $20,000, however, he may be concerned that if he trades on the same scale as he did when he had only $10,000, half of his new level of capital will appear to be idle. If he chooses instead to double his scale of trading, he can achieve his ultimate goals faster, if he reaches them at all, but with the usual added risk and stress. If he doubles his commitment to each trade in his effort to reach $40,000 from $20,000 as rapidly as he reached $20,000 from $10,000, he risks finding himself back at $10,000 in only half that time. After all, it took 10 net successful trades, each yielding a $1000 gain, to reach $20,000, but it would take only five net trades, each resulting in a $2000 loss, to bring his trading capital back down to $10,000. A delicate balance of probabilities and personal feelings must be considered by each trader at critical points such as these and decisions made according to his own mix of knowledge and emotions.

Strategy Following Significant Adversity

Even presuming that a trader's basic method is viable, if adversity precedes success, she will find her position difficult. The fact that failure came first does not ensure that success is inevitable after that point. All that is completely certain is that the trader's capital is impaired. If she continues to take risks similar to those she has already taken, the chance of ruin becomes ever greater. Most traders would choose to employ a defensive strategy, but here again there is a price to pay.

A defensive strategy can consist basically of one of two courses of action. One is the elimination of trades, for the time being, that have the least chance of success. The other is the elimination of any trades that require the risk of too many dollars in relation to the lower level of the account. Of the two the second would appear to be the better. Regardless of the quality of a trade, the probability of success is never 1, and therefore there is always some chance of loss. Furthermore, trades that are known to have poor ratios of success to failure would never be utilized, regardless of the condition of the account. The range between the most acceptable and least acceptable trades for the typical trader is not wide, considering all the uncertainties of trading. It is unlikely that any trade can ever have much more than a .8 probability of success, and it is also unlikely that a trader would be willing to accept knowingly a trade below about .65 (assuming in both cases an even money payoff). This practical range of only about .15 does not provide much room to maneuver.

If there is a limit on dollar risk in relation to the total number of dollars in the account in a given trade, then trades exceeding this risk can, of course, be eliminated, but this will reduce the number of trades available to recover the dollars lost, and recovering money lost may take longer than losing it in the first place. If the trades with smaller risks also have smaller profit potentials, as is likely, the trader must again face an ugly statistic. He might have lost half his money by having a series of trades that yielded 10 net losses and followed with a new series yielding 10 net profits only to find that he was only halfway back to his original level of capital because his profits were smaller than his losses. A loss of 60 percent from a given level requires a profit of 150 percent merely to get even. Profits of 150 percent are not easy to achieve, getting even is not the most exciting goal, and, of course, the trades entered to attempt recovery would themselves entail the risk of further loss.

Systems

The trader, like the gambler, should learn early the fruitlessness of wasting time and money trying to profit from a game with a negative expectation by the use of some clever strategy. It is to be hoped that a trader's research has resulted in some method of selecting trades that will yield better results than random selections. The mathematical expectation of a game is not affected by the strategy of varying the size of individual bets. If a trader has a valid method that yields on the average 65 wins for 35 losses in a series of independent trials, he will have the same ratio of wins to losses, regardless of his betting strategy, and no system of risking more or less, depending on the result of his recent trades, will change the ratio. If a game is fair, it will remain fair; if it has a positive expectation, it will remain positive, and if negative, it will remain negative, and the latter two will maintain their biases with no change in degree.[3] No mechanical system can change probabilities one iota.

Money management "systems" designed to overcome a negative expectation in any game, whether trading or gambling, are usually based on some common misconceptions about the statistical law of large numbers, itself frequently incorrectly called the "law of averages." The designers of systems almost invariably depend on some theory that numbers will average out in time to yield profits. A coin having fallen tails a number of times owes some heads, and so one should bet on heads to take advantage of the certainty that the average number of heads flipped will approach 50 percent of all flips sooner or later. A coin, however, has neither a memory nor a conscience, and one may overlook the significance of the difference between percentages and absolute numbers. Certainly, as the coin is flipped longer and longer, the percentage of heads or tails flipped will inevitably approach 50, but not because a short-term series of tails will be immediately followed by a series of heads. Rather, in the long run, the law of large numbers

---

[3] Richard A. Epstein, *The Theory of Gambling and Statistical Logic,* rev. ed. (New York: Academic Press, 1977), p. XIV. Some of the conclusions that follow were drawn in part from this same scholarly reference, especially its section entitled "The Basic Theorems," pp. 52–73.

declares that a large number of subsequent trials will overwhelm any apparent aberrations in any part of the series. In a word, as a game is played longer and longer, the *percentage* of wins and losses will inevitably approach the statistical expectation, but seemingly unusual differences will occur just as inevitably. A pattern of 100 flips of a coin alternating precisely from heads to tails would be almost as miraculous as a consecutive series of 100 heads or 100 tails. This means that streaks of luck (both good and bad) are expectations, not aberrations.

Although variation in the sizes of bets will not change the statistical chance of ultimately winning or losing the game (if the size of bets is varied), the ultimate amount of money won or lost and the time it will take to win or lose could be affected. This results entirely from the different average level of capital involved in the game, not a change in the probability of winning or losing on each game or trade. A betting system intended to overcome the disadvantage of a basically bad bet is sometimes called the "gambler's fallacy," and it could be called the "futures trader's fallacy" just as well. The number of futures traders who have spent good money for systems and who have lost money following them is legion, as is the number of gamblers who have followed the same ruinous path.

Betting and trading systems are sought with more zeal than are perpetual motion machines and sources of everlasting youth. The chance of finding a reasonably simple system that will consistently "beat the odds" is no greater than the chance of satisfying a craving for any other delusion, but the idea refuses to be laid peacefully to rest. There will probably always be people who believe that the coin being flipped, having yielded a series of heads, is due for tails, the clear fallacy of the "maturity of the chances" notwithstanding.[4] A series of bad trades having been suffered just as clearly will indicate to many that a series of good trades is due. Bad luck indicates that good luck is coming and vice versa as surely as a pendulum will retrace its path. This idea of retribution or symmetry permeates philosophical thinking throughout history, back to the ancient Chinese, and will probably influence the actions of gamblers and traders as long as dice roll and people trade in securities and futures.

All systems, regardless of their complexity, are based on wagering or trading that depends on the outcome of previous trials. Some of these systems, which involve multiplicative, additive, or linear betting, can become extremely complex, but the basic premise remains the same. Linear systems have a fixed additive constant. Additive systems increase stakes at an arithmetic rate. Multiplicative systems increase bets geometrically, depending on the immediately preceding result. One of the best-known geometric systems is the "Martingale." The Martingale system has many proponents because many people who have used the system have won games and credit the system with the win, whereas actually all it has done is offer a high probability of small gains and a small probability of a

---

[4] The "maturity of the chances" is a doctrine that, in effect, attempts to assign dependence to basically independent events by attributing to them a memory that they lack by definition. A roulette player may, for example, bet on black after four consecutive reds have come up because a black "is due." The poker player, having failed to complete the last few straights and flushes that he tried for, believes that the next one will be achieved almost with certainty. The horse player may play the favorite each time three favorites in a row have lost because, after all, most of them should win each afternoon.

large loss. If the system is used for a long period of time, however, the chance of suffering a large loss becomes greater. If the game is continued indefinitely, the large loss becomes certain. The basic idea behind Martingale (or any other progression system) is that the bet size will be increased each time a bet is lost until a win covers the most recent string of losses and leaves the player even or ahead. For example, a player who loses one unit can follow by betting two. Therefore, if he wins, he will be ahead one unit, and if he loses, he will be behind three. If he wins, he will bet one unit and start a new series. If he loses, he will bet four units. If he wins, he will be ahead a total of one unit and start a new series. If he loses, he will be behind seven units and will bet eight. Sooner or later he will win, and when he does, he will be ahead one unit for his series. He therefore figures to win one unit for each series, although some series will be longer than others.

The Martingale player soon finds out, however, that he is caught between two bet (or trade) limitations: the lower and the upper. If the least he can bet or use as margin is reasonably close to the upper limit, it will not take many progressive increases of his bets following losses to equal or exceed the upper limit. In gambling the lower and upper limits are determined by the casino. In trading the lower limit is determined by the margin requirement and the upper by the capital or stress point of the trader or liquidity problems in markets; hence good results as bets become larger become increasingly unlikely. The time required for a progression to become unreasonable in trading is undoubtedly shorter than in gambling, and the time available even in gambling is too short in itself for long-term success to be expected. The gambler forced to double his $1 bet in a series of 20 losses would have to risk more than a million dollars to have the opportunity of winning his series on the twenty-first bet. This is ludicrous enough even without considering that minimum bets must often exceed $1 and that a house limit often restricts the maximum to about $500. The ninth loss of a geometrically increased $2 bet would carry the player past a $500 house limit. The player might argue that nine losses in a row are highly unlikely. This is true for any particular series of nine bets, but the player who continues playing for a long period will almost certainly have nine losses in a row sooner or later, as will the futures trader.

The system player would do well to test her system against a random-number table. If ostensibly it can, say, double her capital before she loses it with a high degree of probability in a game involving many independent events, then merely by "betting smart" she should be able to beat the random-number table in a paper game by doubling her capital three or four times in long games before she is ruined. (A person who did this and published her results would have the first such publication in history.[5])

Size of Commitments

Despite the fact that varying the size of commitments will not change probabilities, it could well change an outcome by ending the game sooner or later than might

---

[5] An elaborate discussion of systems may be found in Allen N. Wilson, *The Casino Gambler's Guide* (New York: Harper and Row, 1970), pp. 234–258. The mathematics of system fallacies is covered in Epstein, loc. cit.

otherwise be the case. The trader, as well as the gambler, must be vitally concerned with loss of the money he has available for trading because its loss eliminates any chance of winning or even trading unless he can later replace his capital. In a word, ruin precludes success and must be avoided if at all possible. Sizing of commitments according to the nature of the game has a vital effect on the possibility of ruin. The correct guiding principles may surprise many traders and gamblers. For fair or unfavorable games, the strategy of betting should be aggressive, and for favorable games, the approach should be conservative.

If a futures trader who regarded futures trading as a basically losing game intended to take only one position and had a specific money objective in mind, his best strategy would be precisely the same as that of a gambler facing the same problem. If the expectation of a profit is negative or zero, but the game is still to be played for some reason, the best chance available to reach the objective is obtained by making a large commitment and playing the game only once. Of course, the capital might be lost and the objective not reached, but the probability of reaching the objective is less for any other strategy. As one decreases the size of one's commitments in an unfavorable game, the chance of eventually reaching one's objective becomes ever smaller and the chance of ruin greater.

The informed futures trader, unlike the gambler who competes against a casino's odds, is presumed to be playing a favorable game against a far better capitalized adversary (the market) and should wager accordingly. Her wisest policy is simple. *She should trade on a small scale.* The specific amounts risked, of course, depend on the size of her capital, her objectives, and how long she expects to continue her trading. If she intends to trade indefinitely, her positions should be modest in relation to her capital, and errors should be made on the conservative side. Because the probabilities favor her winning in the long run, her primary objective in the management of her capital is to make every effort to *reach* the long run. The best way to defeat herself is to risk so much that she cannot realistically recover from adversity on one trade or a series of bad trades. Regardless of how good the odds are, there is some chance of losing, and there is a certainty of periods of severe adversity even when the system used is valid and the expectation favorable. The longer a game is played, the more inevitable such periods of adversity become. Adverse runs should not be surprising. They are to be expected and should be planned for. The best way is to expose so little capital that ruin will not be the result when nothing seems to go right.

The trader who maintains that his research is valid and that he has a positive expectation on every trade may argue that he can afford to risk one-fourth of his capital on every trade because the chance of his losing four times in a row is quite small. He would be correct in making this assertion, but he should think further before engaging in such an aggressive course. The chance of losing four times in a row, even with favorable probabilities, becomes quite high after several series and after a long series is virtually certain. Even worse is the fact that the trader does not need four losses in a row to be ruined; he needs only one point in his series of trades at which he has lost on four trades *on balance.* Even with a high expectation of success on any given trade, his chance of surviving a long game without being a net loser by four trades at any given time would be poor. If the capital risked were reduced from one-fourth to one-tenth, the chance of being ruined on any series of 10 trades would be infinitesimal and his chance of surviving a long series of trades would become high. In any case, the trader must determine the size of his commitments by his probability estimates, the payoffs, and his own degree of optimism with regard to what his trading talent is worth.

In summary, frequent small commitments in a favorable game will almost certainly yield an ultimate profit, whereas continued large-percentage commitments will almost certainly cause ruin. In an unfavorable game large commitments made over a short duration provide the only chance of winning and the best expectation (or rather the least bad expectation) results from playing once. One who is ahead in a game with a negative expectation may be said to be losing at a negative rate. If one with a dollar to risk insists on playing a slot machine, his best strategy is to bet his entire dollar in a one-dollar machine and then quit, win or lose, rather than put 20 nickels in a nickel machine.

The inviting, but usually fatal, temptation to bet too heavily in favorable games is probably what leads so often to the most usual type of overtrading; that is, risking too much of one's capital on any one trade. The other types of overtrading, which include trading too many positions at the same time and trading too often, may also cause severe damage, but trading on too large a scale is probably worst of all.

NOTES FROM A TRADER

If money management now appears to be an area that requires considerable thought, that is full of dilemmas and contradiction, and that is generally quite frustrating to the reader, he or she has made real progress. The first step in solving this problem, as in solving most others, is to recognize its existence and face up to it. Ignoring it merely because its solution is difficult and indefinite and relying instead on blind luck is hardly an intelligent alternative.

Money management principles contain so many decisions that must be made by traders on an individual basis that no specific program which is adequate for all traders can ever be devised. This does not mean, however, that some basic principles that are useful for all cannot be suggested. Some poker players like to bluff frequently, while others seldom or never bluff. There are winners to be found among those belonging to either school, most of whom think that those who do not agree do not know how to play poker. Those holding either conviction, however, cannot possibly make money by consistently drawing to bad hands and paying more for the privilege than the hand is worth. There are rules that must be followed by all traders and gamblers if they are to live long enough in the world of games to reach the long run while still solvent. Most of these rules for basic survival are to be found in the area of money management, in which few traders are especially interested, rather than in the area of trade selection, which is the basic interest of most of them.

A wise principle of money management is to make mistakes on the side of the too conservative. It is better to accumulate money too slowly than to lose one's trading capital quickly. If debating whether to buy one unit or two, buy none. If debating whether to take a position, pass it by. As an account grows, consider withdrawing some or all of the profits. If aggressiveness is desired, the number of dollars risked can increase as the account grows, but the risk percentage can be held unchanged or even reduced at the same time. The unexpected always seems to be costly rather than profitable. A trader who assumes that he will be right 65 times out of every 100 trades he makes each year assumes that he can look forward to about 30 winning trades net in the next year (65—35). Somehow a considerable number of things will go wrong. If he has a hundred trades and the number of net wins is not 30, it will almost certainly be smaller. He might find himself with only 20 net profitable trades instead of 30. Execution costs will be higher than expected, especially because bad trades will go further through his stops than he thought reasonable, but the less frequent windfall profits that should logically compensate seem rarely to arrive on time, and then they are smaller or more infrequent than had been anticipated. Errors will almost always impair results and rarely improve them. Oversleeping and missing the opening of the market will not cause one to miss a position that opens unfavorably, but a market that opens within a satisfactory range and then moves toward the trader's objective without any retracement is likely to result in an opportunity lost forever. If the market opens sharply in the anticipated direction, even the trader who wakes up on time may be inclined to wait and try to enter it at a more favorable level. If the market provides the hoped-for adversity, the trader will enter some trades that will work and some that will not. If adversity never comes, however, only the good trades can be missed, not the bad ones. With all this the trader might consider himself lucky to find himself with only about 10 net good trades remaining to make his year profitable. Even the most favorable "trading system" will depend for its ultimate favorable results on a surprisingly few net good trades. It does not take many errors (bad luck) to miss them. Furthermore, 65 correct decisions in a hundred was probably an overly optimistic estimate in the first place.

It is interesting to observe the way most futures traders play the futures game in relation to the possible ways that money games can be played:

1. The most effective approach to the objective of maximizing results is to play a favorable game on a small scale.

2. Less desirable, but still providing a reasonable chance of success, is playing a favorable game on a large scale with enough profits coming early in the game to avoid ruin.

3. A basically unfavorable game may yield profitable results (presuming that one insists on playing unfavorable games) if one plays seldom and bets heavily.

4. The only road that leads inevitably to disaster is playing an unfavorable game continuously.

The trader who trades on impulse or uses some other invalid method of making trading decisions is following the fourth route—which is crowded with bumper-to-bumper traffic.

Some of Finagle's laws as applied to speculators and market researchers are especially valuable to traders concerned with money management[6]:

---

[6] Compiled in the original form by John W. Campbell, Jr., late editor of *Analog Science Fiction Magazine*.

1. If anything can go wrong with a research project, it will.

2. No matter what the result, there is always someone willing to fake a better one.

3. No matter what the result, there is always someone eager to misinterpret it.

4. No matter what occurs, there is always someone who believes it happened according to his pet theory.

5. In any collection of data the figure that is most obviously correct—beyond all need of checking—is the mistake.

6. Even if it is impossible to derive a wrong number, still a way will be found to do it.

In the area of money management, as in no other, traders should beware of self-deceit. Successful traders do not lie to themselves. They do not substitute hope for facts. Fagin's cynical comment in the musical production of *Oliver* is quite appropriate for consideration by an economically motivated trader attempting to evaluate the money management program that he or she has been using. "In this life, one thing counts, in the bank, large amounts!"

Losers and Winners

In every game there are winners and losers. The scorecard in the futures game, which is brutally simple, consists merely of a credit or debit in a trading account over a period of time long enough to exclude luck, either good or bad, from playing a prominent role. Because more speculators lose than win, the part title makes allowance for that sobering fact by reversing the consideration of the outcomes.

Chapter 12, "The Futures School for Losers," creates satirical composites of the classic losers. Habits that reinforce unsuccessful trading results are examined with tongue in cheek in the hope that familiarity will breed a determination to avoid the losers' lineup.

Chapter 13, "Maxims: Good and Bad," subjects the conventional wisdom of market lore to critical analysis. That there are platitudes to reinforce any position the trader desires to take should not surprise the reader. This study of market maxims underlines the innate desire of many traders to avoid coming to grips with the actual behavior of futures prices and the implications of that behavior for their own.

Chapter 14—"Who Wins? Who Loses? Why?"—concludes the part by focusing for careful study on the returns to the players of the futures game. Hedgers, large speculators, and small traders reflect varying trading results in the long run. Studies are examined to shed light on the question of the distribution of profits and losses and the skills employed by the winners. These skills involve behavioral as well as analytical competence, and one systematic approach to understanding the role of feelings and thoughts is presented.

12

The Futures School for Losers

"The capacity of the human mind to resist the intrusion of new knowledge is infinite."

INTRODUCTION[1]

Some futures traders learn their lessons at the School of Experience early and well. They go on to realize profits and enjoy the exciting dynamics to be found in the world of futures. Others never learn much of anything and spend their lives at the Futures School for Losers repeating the same mistakes or happily discovering minor variations. This school has campuses in most areas of the world and traces its beginnings to the seekers of lodestones and to Dutch traders of tulip bulbs. It might help future traders who wish to avoid attending the school to interview members of the present student body who have been attempting to graduate, unsuccessfully, for many years.

THE STUDENT BODY

Herbert Hoyle has had more friends, relatives, and counterparts at the school than anyone else. Herbert himself enrolled as a student more than 50 years ago just

---

[1] Some of the material in this chapter was originally published in articles in *Commodities* (March and August 1973 and February 1986).

after averaging up his security holdings on a 20 percent margin, starting in August 1929. He has spent all the years since trying to develop a simple set of mechanical rules (secret, of course) that will help him to achieve a substantial profit each year at a constant rate while using a small amount of capital and entailing virtually no risk. Herbert became seriously interested in his project some years ago when he noticed that his rules worked spectacularly, particularly when applied carefully to the body of historical data from which they had been developed.

"I noticed," says Herbert, his eyes narrowed, "that December wheat sold at a significantly higher price on September 8 than it had on July 20 throughout the entire period covered by my records at the time (four years). On the July 20 following the completion of my research, I quietly bought all the December wheat that I could afford (5000 bushels), but unfortunately a recent reduction in the government loan price had not been fully discounted, and I lost 14 cents a bushel. I decided that henceforth wheat should be bought only in years when there was no adjustment in the loan price, and I changed my rules accordingly.

"The following year I bought wheat again on July 20 but lost 19 cents a bushel by September 8. I noticed too late that the difference in price between wheat and corn was wider than it had been for the last five years, and I had failed to consider the importance of this in my earlier conclusions. There was no point in abandoning my work, since of the six observations I now had, four had worked successfully, and the other two could be easily filtered out. The following year I was a little unlucky. There was no change in the loan price, but the spread between wheat and corn prices was even wider than it had been the year before, so I naturally did not buy the wheat. In fact, utilizing the information I had gained, I sold it short instead. When it rose 47 cents a bushel by September 8 with no reaction greater than ¼ cent a bushel, I was a little disappointed, of course, but then I suddenly realized the significance of the late Lenten season, which obviously cancels out the effect of the wheat-corn spread. Of my seven observations, actually five had worked, although I did not benefit by the latest one, and two were filtered out. The eighth year was really quite upsetting. I again bought the wheat on July 20, and it was 4 cents higher on September 8, just as I had expected in light of the narrow wheat-corn spread and early Lent. Because of some rumor of heavy French exports in August, wheat prices dropped more than 50 cents, and before they could rally back, my margin was gone and my broker sold me out ⅜ cent off the bottom. My record, however, really is six wins in eight years, with the other two years filtered out. Now I am sure that I have all the important factors, and if I can get $500 together before July 20, I expect to make some really important money in the wheat market from now on, unless my creditors attach my account again before the realizing move takes place."

Herbert's rules, including the filters and exceptions, eventually filled 37 type-written pages (single-spaced), which Herbert kept in a padlocked drawer for se-curity reasons along with instructions to pass the notes along to his children in the event of his passing or being committed to an institution.

Despite his discouraging start, Herbert Hoyle proved to be among the most successful of the school's students. He spent many years carefully reviewing his 37 pages of rules, filters, and exceptions so that he would be able to select dates to enter and exit most markets. His original research, based upon 8 years of trades, was eventually expanded to 28 commodities and resulted in an extraordinarily successful proprietary system of trading carefully measured by consistently undocumented hypothetical results. Herbert calls his method the Hoyle Theory of Relativity. He is currently offering his system on a local television station, under the sponsorship of the Buckette Shoppe Brokerage and Boiler Room Company. It can be obtained at periodic seminars held at local motels (ample parking and light refreshments are offered—reservations suggested).

Herbert would have liked to test his trading system in his personal account, but his wife's threats of what she would do if he compounded his earlier losses dissuaded him. So Herbert took the next best step. He took a job with Buckette Shoppe, which not only sponsors his television show but also hired him as a registered commodity representative. This has enabled him to experiment with his trading system in the accounts of his customers, particularly those which are discretionary, but the customers always seem to withdraw their capital after a series of losses without being reasonable enough to allow the system to demonstrate its Account Recovery Subsystem.

Glenda Gullible finds Herbert Hoyle's scholarly fundamental approach far too complicated and believes that the soundest approach to trading is a basically simple one. Glenda initially tried to achieve wealth at the horse races after buying a book suggesting that the proper approach was to bet on the favorites to show on the last race each day early in the season. The theory held that the winning bettors would all have gone home by the last race and that the handicappers had not yet had time to evaluate sufficient data to weight the horses properly. Glenda became discouraged when she realized that her profits did not equal the cost of her racetrack admissions, her parking, her hotdogs, and the cleaning bills for her checked sportcoat. Neither did they exceed her losses.

Glenda next tried to make some money playing blackjack at Nevada gaming palaces after reading a book suggesting that it was necessary only to keep track of picture cards and fives and always double down on two nines. Unfortunately, when Gloria finally screwed up enough courage to take a bus to Las Vegas, her results were not nearly so good as they had been when she dealt herself several thousand hands on her dining room table. She encountered a flinty-eyed dealer who worked with five decks of cards and dealt them from a card shoe so rapidly that Glenda could not keep count. It was then that Glenda turned to futures trading.

"There is no point examining the fundamentals," Glenda tells us, "because everything is reflected in prices anyhow. The most important thing is to trade only consistently with the basic trend. Never trade against the trend! When it is up, only be long. When it is down, only be short. The basic trend may be easily determined in many ways, but one of the best is with a line chart. Just draw a line along recent bottoms in a rising market or recent tops in a falling market, and you have a clear picture of a market's direction and its rate of movement.

"The best way of all, though, involves the proper use of moving averages, which requires some intelligence (I.Q. exceeding 55) and some knowledge of mathematics (addition and subtraction). I have discovered something really remarkable," continues Glenda in a confidential tone of voice. "When you use moving averages of different time spans, like 3 days and 10 days, in markets that are moving around at all and plot these averages as lines on a chart, the 3-day line will cross the 10-

day line from time to time, although I am not certain what causes this." Glenda leans back in her chair to give the listener time to absorb the implications of her revelations. "In order to make the lines clear during periods of narrow price fluctuations I find it best to use colored pencils. It is wise to use chartreuse for the *3-day* average and turquoise for the *10-day* average. When the chartreuse line is below the turquoise line, I sell short, and when it goes above, I cover and go long. Of course, I get whipsawed once in a while, but at least when there is a major trend, I am in the market the right way and I stay with the move until it has run its course." Unfortunately, while Glenda was trading there proved to be more narrow trading markets than trending markets (which was also true before Glenda began trading as well as after), so Glenda has been whipped and sawed rather thoroughly. She is currently working to improve her system either by requiring sharper crossing of the lines (as measured by a plastic protractor) or by waiting for some period of time to elapse after a crossing before considering a position to be worth taking. So far the ideal period to wait has proved historically to vary from 1 to 254 days, but Glenda believes that the key is on the chart somewhere and needs merely to be discovered. Currently she is unable to trade anyhow because she has lost two-thirds of her capital trading unsuccessfully and spent the other third on chart paper, colored pencils, and the protractor.

Seymour Software believes that his computer programs will help cover the losses that he previously incurred following astrological signs. His faith is inherited from his ancient ancestor, Lodestone Software, who spent his entire life attempting to convert lead into gold but did not consider until just before he became senile what gold would be worth if it became as plentiful as lead.

Seymour has programmed into his computer all the data which never yielded profits before because he believes that the computer ought to be more intelligent than its programmer. He has successfully blended together moving averages of 19 durations with three types of oscillators, four cycles, and the average temperature in seven typical corn belt counties. All of this has been modified by Finnegan's Finagling Factor; that is, the number by which all other numbers must be multiplied to make the computer output work retroactively.

Seymour's car has weathered rather badly lately because his garage contains 3 tons of computer runs, but he hopes one day to make enough money trading to have his car painted and reduce the balance due on his home computer.

Legin Legout is a part-time student because his sole interest is spreads. He has a deep conviction, based upon pure conjecture, that spreads are the best and probably the only way to beat the futures markets. Legin's philosophy is that a loss on one side of a spread will always be countered by a profit on the other side and that therefore the risk in trading is reduced to a point where a profit is assured in the long run. He engages in endless debates on this subject with the Professor of Spreads, Straddles, and Options, Dr. Scartissue Chips, but it seems unlikely that the two will ever agree. The professor seems to have a blind conviction that there is some sort of correlation between risk and reward; that is, if spreads reduce the risk in a transaction, the reward will be reduced by as much or more, and if the reward is not reduced, the risk has not been reduced either. Legin just shakes his head and mutters something about those who can do, do, and those who cannot do, teach.

Legin is especially incensed by the professor's failure to understand the ease of trading spreads. The professor seems to have a naive notion that the primary factor causing a spread trade to succeed or fail is the direction of the market, which is the most difficult single factor for an analyst to determine. Because a spread trade may still fail to yield a profit even if market direction is correctly determined, the professor believes that spreads are even more difficult to deal with than net trades because more must be judged correctly about spreads, and determining market direction is difficult enough.

Legin is currently considering withdrawing from the class because of the professor's ignorance about charting. The professor has been talking recently about the difficulty of charting spreads because one is really charting two individual markets which may be quite different from spread differences prevailing on the exchange floors, especially if closes are used. He is also talking about aberrations caused by different contract sizes and such ivory tower drivel as covariance. Legin feels that the evidence gathered in his two experimental trading programs to date is overwhelming. Although he ultimately lost all of his trading capital in both cases, he lasted longer than most of the people who began net trading at the same time. The professor maintains that lower risk per transaction has been countered by enough lowered expectation per transaction to make the expectation of the program one of lasting longer but leading ultimately and inevitably to ruin. He pontificates about the fruitlessness of playing a 10-cent slot machine rather than a dollar machine with the same capital. Legin was going to respond to this foolish analogy but was too busy developing a new GNMA-sugar program to waste time on naive debate.

Frieda Fantasy turned to futures trading many years ago after suffering grievous losses trading Czarist bonds. She has become a recognized expert in the art of spreading positions to avoid realizing losses. Frieda is especially pleased with her results so far this year, during which she has not had a single closed loss. She believes that she is finally about to overcome the misfortunes she has borne during the last 26 years, having lost money in 25 of them. (She broke even one year when she was too busy dealing with her divorce and bankruptcy proceedings to trade.) Frieda has told everyone who will listen of her market successes this year, during which she has had six consecutive profits. She has taken particular pains to keep three boardroom acquaintances informed because she is currently trying to induce them to allow her to trade their accounts in return for 3 percent a month of their invested capital plus one-half of all closed profits unadjusted by open losses.

"In January I bought December silver," relates Frieda, "because of the continuing imbalance of supply and demand, the outlook for more use of film because of the recent invention of a new type of camera, and substantial sales of a series of medals portraying famous Indian chiefs by a private mint. I was a little early, and December silver dropped 600 points, and I thought I had better buy time, so I sold March against my long December. The market dropped another 300 points, just as I thought it would, so I took my profit in the March. To take advantage of the short-term irrational weakness in the market and to protect my December position I sold a May contract. Sure enough, the market continued down and I was able to take a $200 profit in the May and managed to sell July after a further drop of only 50 points. This market has been like a money machine. I have now taken six straight profits on the short side, and now I have a no-risk position short September and still long that original December which will probably yield the greatest profit of all."

Frieda proudly displays her six confirmations showing the $1470 profits on the short-side transactions. She carries them with her at all times, believing that they will help her sell her managed-account program, which she has recently had copyrighted as The Frieda Fantasy Infallo Program. Unfortunately, the market rallied a little after Frieda's seventh short sale, and she now has a $150 open loss on the short September silver as well as the open loss of $2375 on the original purchase of the December silver, but this does not dishearten Frieda. She has a plan. "When the market takes its next dip, I'll cover September and stay with the December. This will give me seven profits in a row, so even if December doesn't recover, I'll still have seven profits out of eight, and the random-walk boys can't laugh that off." A visitor has some questions to ask Frieda about some aspects of her logic as well as how she will provide the margin required to support her December position after she liquidates the September, but Frieda has been led away for her daily tranquilizer injection.

William Wilde really wanted to be a gladiator but was born in the wrong place at the wrong time. Unable to realize his primary ambition, he turned to futures trading. "This whole business is kill or be killed," says William, holding up his clenched fist and facing the emperor. "The way to beat this thing is to probe for the big one and then milk it dry." William accomplishes this by waiting until he sees what he believes to be a great opportunity and then moving in with all his resources. "The way to determine the size of an initial position is to divide your credit balance by the margin deposit required and buy all you can. When the market goes your way even a little, your base is big enough so even the small move will create enough additional capital to allow you to pyramid quickly; then you keep on pyramiding until you have all the money that you can carry home."

William is quite confident at the moment that he is about to achieve a great victory because he has just succeeded in replacing the $2000 he lost by holding seven pork bellies 2 days too long with money he borrowed from the credit union, and he is hoping that the 25,000 bushels of wheat he intends to buy in the morning will rise quickly enough for him to repay the loan before his wife learns of it and orders him out of the house again. William's ultraconservative friend, Long T. Bonds, asks what he is going to do if wheat goes down and he finds himself in debt to the credit union without the means to pay back the obligation. "When the going gets tough," replies William, "the tough get going." "But," Long persists, "isn't it true that in any game in which probabilities are involved the longer you play, the more certain it becomes that a series of losses will occur? And isn't it also true that you are never even prepared for the first loss, much less a series of them?" Utilizing all of his keen reasoning power, William replies, "If you can't stand the heat, stay out of the kitchen."

Martha Mule once read in a booklet that cash and futures prices have a tendency to meet during the delivery month sooner or later. This made a tremendous impression on Martha, who ranks the importance of this bit of information somewhat above the Bill of Rights. She is currently long one contract of October live cattle, which is selling 4 cents a pound below the cash price of cattle as quoted on the newswire in the brokerage office. "Someone is going to make that 4-cent difference," brays Martha, "and it might as well be me." When Martha placed the order with her broker, her registered representative volunteered to check with the research department in Chicago for an opinion on the potential in Martha's trade. Although the research department was about to leave for a hamburger and a milk shake for lunch she did take the time to reply, and the broker, Tradum Offen, called Martha back with the bad news. "In order to be sure of making the 4-cent difference," Tradum said, "you must have considered such things as location of the cattle, differences in grade, and possible problems with certification for delivery by the exchange. Also, presuming that the 4-cent difference is made up before futures trading stops in October and not after, it could be met just as well by the cash price dropping to meet the futures price as by the futures price rising to meet the cash, in which case, you would make no money. As a matter of fact, the cash price could drop 8 cents and the futures 4 cents and you could lose." Her sharp mind functioning in its usual manner, Martha replied, "Have you a late quote on November soybeans?" "The futures business is one thing and the cash is another," continued Tradum after telling Martha that November soybeans are limit up (Martha is short). "It is not wise to play another person's game." "I have to move my car," replied Martha shrewdly. "It's in a loading zone."

By the time she returned from moving her car, she had received delivery of the contract of cattle. Only then did she learn that it was the last day of trading and the cattle cannot be redelivered. Shortly thereafter one of Martha's cattle died, and two others are not looking well. Martha still has the remainder of her contract of cattle and has spent a busy morning writing letters to the CFTC, the Chicago Mercantile Exchange, Dow Jones, and the State Consumer Frauds Division bitterly complaining of the false and misleading cash prices reported on the newswires by an incompetent wire operator and questioning how any honest trader could possibly beat a game with such unfair rules. Nothing worse has happened to Martha since she took delivery of a carload of onions only to learn that trading had ended in that commodity forever and her onions were sprouting through the bags in which they were delivered. She did succeed in selling some of the bags to a dealer in secondhand burlap for almost as much as it cost her to have the bags deodorized. Martha would like to tell of some other of her experiences, but she has to leave for court to fight the ticket unjustifiably placed on her car for parking in the loading zone.

Ivan Bentaken has had trouble all his life with unreasonable people. In school, whenever he was prepared for show-and-tell, he never got called on, but when he was unprepared, his name was invariably called. In the Little League he was called out on every play. Police officers herd him out of traffic to give him tickets, although everyone else is clearly going faster. Now he trades futures. He recently opened his third futures account to replace the one he has just closed with another broker, whom he is suing for recommending the purchase of corn, which went down 9 cents a bushel following a surprisingly bearish crop report issued 2 weeks after the purchase. "My broker obviously knew of the report and got me to buy the corn so that he or his firm's partners could bail out," declares Ivan, his eyes blazing. "Even if he did not know of it, he is derelict in his fiduciary relationship · to me because he should have known of it. After all, his firm claims to have a research department in Chicago right in the Board of Trade Building."

Having calmed down enough to discuss his trading philosophy, Ivan talks of objectives. "A $1000 account really ought to provide an average return of several hundred dollars each month and sometimes $1000 or more. After all, it would yield over 5 percent in a savings and loan with no risk at all (to say nothing of the use of a notary public at no charge). If you don't get a chance for greater reward, it's foolish to take the extra risk.

"You have to be especially careful of brokers," he continues. "They are always foisting advice on you—urging you, for example, to use stops and objectives to make sure that you are always getting out of your position one way or the other. I had a big profit a few months ago, took the profit, and went into another position, which also resulted in a profit, but I would have made more just by staying with the first position. My broker did not make a single move to stop me from switching the position. I am still waiting for the CFTC to do something about it, but they won't answer my letters anymore. Three or four years ago I doubled my money in the first six months of the year, and my broker thought that was a big deal, but I had a friend across the street who tripled his money during the same period. My friend's broker is quite conservative and told me that he really only expected an annual yield of 80 percent. I figured that if he only did half that well, I was certain of 40 percent, so I opened an account. In spite of his virtual guarantee, I lost my money on my first two trades in only a week, so I am having my lawyer file a suit based on material misrepresentation, lack of suitability, and churning."

Following the loss of his suit and the payment of damages because the judge maintained that the case was frivolous and without merit, Ivan had no change in his luck. He sold his home just before prices rose sharply and invested the proceeds in a recreational vehicle dealership just in time to face the gasoline crunch. He filed suits against his real estate broker for inducing him to sell his house and against the former owner of the recreational vehicle dealership for fraud, but he lost both suits. Ivan's anger was not relieved when he discovered that the buyer of his home was the former recreational vehicle dealer.

With what remained after he paid his legal expenses, Ivan opened a commodity account with a broker who had direct contact with the exchange trading floors over a hot line. The broker suggested that bad trades made quickly were no better than bad trades made slowly, but Ivan interpreted this as mere modesty.

When the prime rate went to 8¼ percent, Ivan was sitting at his broker's elbow ready to act. "Selling at the all-time high can't be too bad," Ivan said, and he went into T-bill futures with all of his funds ready for the turn downward. When interest rates passed 15 percent, Ivan spent his last change for a stamp so that he could mail his complaint and his demand for a reparations procedure to the CFTC. "If the hot line can reach the exchanges, it can reach the Federal Reserve just as quickly," he says grimly. "Worst of all, I had intended to use the money to buy platinum futures, and I am claiming my lost profit on that too." Ivan's broker has retired at the age of 83, and Ivan's case is behind 911 others with the CFTC. To date he has received no reply to his request for accelerated action, so he is contemplating filing suit against the CFTC if the ACLU will provide an attorney willing to work on a contingency basis and bear all expenses of discovery and trial.

Erika Von Director believes that acting is everything, so she bases all her trading decisions on the manner in which markets are acting during the infrequent periods when she knows what is happening. When her broker calls her with a trading suggestion, Erika checks her charts and then follows the suggestions that have acted well recently (gone in the direction of the broker's suggestion for a least one day). When she is advised to take a loss, Erika usually replies that "the market is acting as if a reversal is about to occur." When advised to take a profit, Erika studies her charts and proclaims that "it is premature to liquidate the position because the market is acting well." Because any position that shows a profit has had to act well, Erika has great difficulty in liquidating positions at a profit. Erika once read in a book that prices tend to act best just before they collapse and worst just before they rally, so Erika sold the book.

A friend once suggested that Erika determine objectives and stops in advance and place orders at those points in the market, but Erika prefers to use her judgment and make decisions at points at which market action indicates that she should take action. She is not disturbed by the fact that the moment when she usually takes action is always one during which she happens to be in the brokerage office or on the telephone with her registered representative. "You should never place stops," intones Erika, "because they will invariably drive the market just to your stop, knock you out of your position, and then run the market just to where you thought it would go in the first place!" When asked whether her problem might not be the placement of her stops, and just who buys or sells the hundreds of contracts needed to touch off her stops on her one or two contracts, Erika says, "You just don't understand the futures markets." She says this with the same haughty air that her ancient ancestor, a Carthaginian general, assumed when explaining the strategy he planned to use against the approaching Romans.

Deposit N. Witharawal believes in following a strategy of observing statistical runs. Knowing his own trading limitations, which are legion, Deposit follows the advice of his broker, who is always sincere and occasionally lucky. Whenever Deposit has a series of successes with small positions, he adds money to his account and takes large positions just in time for the inevitable series of losses. Following this, he withdraws most of his capital in order to trade a minimum amount until his broker recovers his touch. "I couldn't believe it," sobs Deposit, "I no sooner withdrew part of my remaining funds than he was right nine times in a row. I had to pass up four of his suggestions and take positions in the other five only about half as big as I had taken on the way down. On one of those five, I couldn't take the adversity necessary to achieve the profit, so I had a loss. The broker claims to be ahead for the year, but it certainly doesn't show in my account. He claims it has something to do with money management, but I think he is misrepresenting his results." Following the advice of Ivan Bentaken, Deposit is about to make a claim against the broker for the difference between the results in his account and those he believes he should have had according to the broker's record.

Oscar Ostrich believes that all adversity is temporary. When all is going his way, Oscar can be found telling of his successes to the small group of gray men in gray suits with gravy on their ties who spend all day in the boardroom because their wives drive them from their homes. When markets go against him, however, Oscar is not there. Sometimes he can be seen walking slowly around the block, moving his lips in silent prayer, hoping to find a miraculous recovery in his positions by the time he completes the circuit. More frequently he cannot be found at all.

"If I didn't have bad luck, I would have no luck at all," he tells all who will listen. "I was doing all right until I got into those 12 contracts of May sugar. I am usually in the boardroom or keep in constant touch with my broker so I know at all times where I am. However, I got busy and I had no time to call or even read a paper for nine days. By the time I was informed, news that the crop was 72 percent greater than expected had become known to everyone but me, and the market sold down so far that I got sold out." Someone suggests that if Oscar had placed a stop in the market, he would have suffered little, but he is busily digging a hole in the school's sandbox in order to plunge his head into it.

Wheeler Bandini is known to every registered representative in the brokerage business except the youngest and least experienced, and they will undoubtedly meet him soon. He can always be recognized by the nature of his proposals, which involve unorthodox transactions, huge amounts, and considerable time, effort, and cost to the broker (all wasted). "I have access to 8 million pounds of Mexican coffee, which I can place anywhere you want within 24 hours," he confides, "if there is some way we can place a hedge against it and cinch the big difference between the present futures market and my cash coffee. Of course, I would expect no margin on the short futures position because this is a bona fide hedge." Or, "I am in touch with a shipload of nonquota sugar being brought in by some Cuban refugees, and if we can dispose of it through your cash department, I would be glad to split the profit with you." Or, "I handle the financial affairs of a group of 220 brain surgeons who won't make a move without my say-so. If I open a futures account with $3 million, how might we both benefit a little from it?"

Wheeler is not a major menace except to himself when attempting to cross the street unaided and to unsophisticated brokers so anxious to build a profitable clientele that they accept his hallucinations at face value. This has happened twice. In each case an account was opened and an order actually placed against Wheeler's cash positions, but he disappeared into the night, leaving behind a disconnected telephone and an "address unknown." One of the students attempts to ask Wheeler why he does what he does, but Wheeler is furtively slinking down the corridor, eating strange-looking mushrooms and muttering something about getting the exclusive right to market the entire Russian output of platinum through a holding company he is about to form.

Wheeler benefits especially from the addition of new markets. He was absent from brokerage offices for almost 3 years because of two deals he tried to promote, both unsuccessfully. One involved an approach to several large oil companies in order to arouse interest in a supertanker carrying high-grade light petroleum en route from Saudi Arabia to Rotterdam, but no one expressed any interest. He filed suit against one of the companies for allegedly having him thrown down a flight of stairs, but he dropped the case when the company threatened to file charges of trespassing, loitering, and littering against him.

His next exploit involved trying to interest the Israeli government in a shipment of plutonium in exchange for a large number of submachine guns to be exchanged with an unnamed government in the Caribbean area for a large quantity of high-grade cigars. This deal fell through when the Israeli official suggested a commitment to the psychiatric ward of the Hadassah Hospital in Jerusalem.

Wheeler has now become quite interested in the financial instruments futures markets. At the moment he is urging Seymour Software to form an advisory company, in which he would furnish advice on the direction of interest rates to major banks, savings and loan companies, the U.S. government, the Rothschilds, and others who have a real need for the ultimate in sophisticated hedging techniques. Seymour has expressed some interest in the idea and has suggested a date with Ivan Bentaken's lawyer to form the advisory company. So far, however, neither Seymour nor Wheeler has determined how to acquire enough cash to pay the lawyer, who is unwilling to work in return for 40 percent of the company.

Barbara Brass is known to every broker in the country, although she invariably does business elsewhere. She is always the first to mail in the coupon that appears with a firm's advertisement. When the registered representative begins calling prospective clients, he always reaches Barbara first. "Put me on your market letter list for a few months," demands Barbara, "and send me daily charts on price, open interest, and volume covering orange juice, cotton, and rapeseed for the last few years. Also, would you have your research department take a look at the spread relationship between April heating oil and February live cattle during the third quarter of leap years and let me know what they have to say? I can be reached evenings after 10:30."

Once this initial contact has been made, the broker need have no concern about Barbara remaining in touch, especially when reports are due. "When is the cold storage report on bellies coming out, and what does the floor expect it to say?" asks Barbara on line one while the broker's best client is on hold on line two, waiting to place an order for 4000 shares of stock at the market. Within one minute after the report is issued, Barbara will be certain to call back to learn the figures and ask for the reaction on the floor and some estimate of where the market will open in the morning. She would call her own broker, of course, but does not wish to disturb him, especially because Barbara has no position in bellies anyhow.

Barbara is most in evidence at workshops and seminars presented as business-building devices by brokerage firms. She can be easily recognized by the dog-eared notebook and charts she is carrying and by the holes in her shoes. Just as the broker pauses for breath before making his major point about the enormous opportunity in the cocoa market because Ghana and Nigeria have invaded one another, Barbara raises her hand and asks, "How much wheat is transported into Kansas City by barge in relation to the amount transported by rail, and how much does each barge hold? Also, when does it get too cold for barge traffic, and what historical implications has this had for the Chicago–Kansas City wheat spread?" While the speaker tries to answer Barbara's questions without admitting that he has no knowledge whatever of the Kansas City freight structure, the well-dressed man sitting near the door who was about to ask how to open a $10,000 account looks at his watch, puts his checkbook back into his pocket, and leaves.

During the refreshment period following the speech, Barbara backs the speaker into a corner to ask him why the tomato paste market did not succeed, considering all the pizzas that are sold in the United States. By the time the broker escapes from the corner and cleans the coffee off his suitcoat that Barbara has spilled on it, the entire audience has left. Barbara picks up four copies each of all the literature, takes all the remaining cookies and doughnuts, gets her parking ticket validated, and leaves muttering something about the unproductiveness of the evening.

Benjamin Franklin Bartlett believes that there is a wisdom in maxims that covers any contingency likely to be faced by a trader. Benjamin has had two articles published, one attempting to reconcile "Absence makes the heart grow fonder" with "Out of sight, out of mind" and the other explaining why "Birds of a feather flock together" is completely compatible with "Eagles don't flock." His "Thoughts on Maxims as Applied to Trading" is the definitive work on the subject and has formed the basis for the chapter that follows.

13

Maxims:
Good and Bad

If, could, should, might:
Weasel words are always right.
                    CANDY TREAT

INTRODUCTION

The bulk of the work done by Benjamin Franklin Bartlett is presented in this chapter. The reader should be aware that many of Bartlett's conclusions have been attacked and ridiculed by an unfriendly reviewer whose work is noteworthy, partly because it is stimulating and partly because he has made a fortune trading futures, unlike Bartlett, who is currently in charge of preparing french-fried potatoes at a small hamburger stand. The reviewer, Rich Kreesus, believes that success in trading futures requires more than the judicious choice and observation of old saws. He believes that some may present a real danger to novices or undisciplined traders, in some cases because they accept them and in others because they do not. There is some old saying that will justify almost any action or lack of action. Many people are not disturbed by the fact that equally plausible maxims might appear to justify diametrically opposed actions. They just blithely choose the one that encourages their doing what they want to do anyhow. Sociologists have named this phenomenon "selective perception." The most favored alibis comfort traders when they have taken a loss or a smaller profit than they should have. There is real danger in confusing alibis with wisdom, and it might help to provide a small part of Rich Kreesus's master list of alibis at this point:

1. I should have entered a stop and been out long ago.
2. I should not have used a stop—they shoot for them.
3. I should have let my profit run.
4. I should have got out when I hit my original objective.
5. I should have had a bigger position.
6. I should have had a smaller position.
7. I should not trade in the soft commodities.
8. I should not trade in the hard commodities.
9. I should not trade in financials.
10. I should have left my money in the bank.
11. I should have averaged with the market.
12. I should not have averaged with the market.
13. I should have averaged against the market.
14. I should not have averaged against the market.
15. I should have bought time by spreading temporarily.
16. I should have just got out—the first loss is the best loss.
17. I should have listened to my broker.
18. I should know better than to listen to my broker.
19. I should never trade on the market opening.
20. I should never trade on the market closing.
21. I should have got out before the report.
22. I should have held my position through the report.
23. I should have been in the nearby contract.
24. I should have been in the distant contract.
25. I should have considered the seasonal.
26. I should know that seasonals are too simplistic to consider.
27. I should never have met the margin call.
28. I should have met the margin call and gone a few more days.
29. I should never have told my wife about my account.

Rich concludes that no list of maxims can replace the time and effort that must go into the careful preparation of a trading plan. In fact, he derides maxims as conventional expressions of wisdom that are overly general, have no predictive value, and belong more in an explanation of the efficient-market theory than in a trading plan. It is best left to the readers to study some of Bartlett's work on maxims and judge for themselves whether maxims are consistent and adequate tools for skilled, experienced traders. The following summary of Bartlett's work on maxims has been rather thoroughly edited by Rich Kreesus, who could not resist editorializing from time to time. In fact, he has even taken the time to insert maxims of his own choosing which lead to conclusions that are in sharp contrast with those of Bartlett. The first group of maxims deals with risk and reward.

RISK AND REWARD

One of the first decisions to be made by any trader has to do with his objectives. How much of his capital is he willing to risk to acquire more? In a word, is he willing to accept the degree of risk that goes along with the opportunity to achieve important monetary gains?

Many traders consider the willingness to accept risk as the same kind of courage that is usually associated with Medal of Honor winners. There is no shortage of maxims to encourage them, and these are led, of course, by "When the going gets tough, the tough get going." This can be supplemented by "Danger and delight grow on one stalk" and "Everything is sweetened by risk." If these fail, there is always "Worry, like a rocking chair, keeps you busy but gets you nowhere." Fagin lends encouragement with his "In this life, one thing counts, in the bank, large amounts!" If even more encouragement is needed, one can always rely upon "The man, the woman, who risks nothing, does nothing, has nothing, is nothing." One would be foolish indeed to pay any attention to such fools as Da Vinci, who said, "Just as courage imperils life, fear protects it," or Pushkin's reluctant gambler, who said, "I cannot sacrifice the necessary to win the superfluous." The ancient writer who wrote "Who will pity a snake charmer bitten by a serpent, or any who go near wild beasts" may have given advice that was good for the Alexandrians 2000 years ago but would hardly apply to a modern cocoa trader.

SELECTION

One of the first decisions to be made by any trader is whether the wiser policy is concentration or diversification of positions. Traders who choose diversification have widely quoted the maxim "Don't put all your eggs in one basket" to justify their choice. The more aggressive speculators who choose to concentrate in order to achieve more potential in a given position can retort with "It is much easier to watch a few than many" or "Put all your eggs in one basket and watch the basket."

In reality, either of these two broad policies may be correct for people with different objectives or different styles of trading, or for the degree of aggressiveness they might choose to select in their pursuit of profit. The relatively conservative traders can always say, "Patience is a virtue," whereas others who are willing to accept greater risks might answer, "There are two ways to get to the top of an oak tree: climb it, or sit on an acorn."

The choice of specific trades may be made more difficult by trying to reconcile such conflicting popular advice as "Never sell after a big decline" with the equally popular "Never buy after a long decline." Under given conditions either of these may prove correct; but if both are correct, a future cannot logically be either bought or sold after a long decline. If traders are discouraged by the necessity of dealing with difficult decisions, they might find some comfort from George Bernard Shaw's observation that "for every complex problem, there is a simple solution, and it is wrong!"

A trader may not be too badly injured by heeding the advice to "Buy what will not go down in a bear market." The implication is that such a choice will probably lead the next rise, which is possible, but it also may be out of favor with many traders because it is not considered to have much potential, and although it might not go down, it might not go up either. Similarly, one might heed the advice "never buy something that won't go up in a bull market," only to discover that he or she has been persuaded not to buy something that merely has not gone up yet and is just about to do so.

Potential buyers who want a rule that will allow them to do anything that they really want to can turn to "When a bear market turns to bull, buy what has gone down the most and also what has gone down the least." This sounds plausible, but security buyers who buy a high-grade preferred stock because it has gone down the least might also find that it will also go up the least. If they hedge by buying what has gone down the most, they may find that they have bought stock in a company whose stock is discounting its impending bankruptcy, at which point it will continue down to zero. They learn the truth of the warning "Many a healthy reaction has proved fatal."

The choice of a purchase should be made on the basis of the opportunity inherent in the trade and not because the buyer wants to acquire a given amount of money for an automobile, a trip, or a new suit. There is considerable validity in the warning "Never speculate for a specific need," as any poker player can attest if he has played for his supper and subsequently gone hungry. The potential in a trade is proved by the trade itself and not by the desires of the buyer or seller.

Potential sellers of a position find their choices no easier than those of the buyers. They are told to "Sell what has gone up the most because it will react the most" and, at the same time, to "Sell what has gone up the least because what could not go up must come down." If they observe the former, they could find themselves short in a market rising most rapidly; if they choose the second alternative, they might find themselves short in a market so completely demoralized that the only real possibility is an ultimate move higher or little move at all for a long period. One of the near certainties in speculation is that when everyone is bearish, a market must go up because there are no sellers left, just as when everyone is bullish, a market must go down because there are no buyers left. The reasons to justify these seemingly unlikely moves will appear after the moves have taken place.

There are those who argue, with considerable logic, that it is best to sell something before it goes down rather than after. Those who warn "Never sell something because it seems high-priced" leave the trader in a position of selling positions only if they seem to be low-priced. This is difficult to reconcile with the successful trader's ability to buy low and sell high, which appears to be an infallible route to success.

Both a trader who prefers selling on rallies and another who would rather sell something that could not go up might prove to be correct at one time or another. The first can maintain that "The warrior who is first to weaken in battle is often seen as the leader of a retreat," whereas the other can insist that it is wise to "Sell short what will not go up in a bull market."

OPINIONS

Traders who find it difficult to select positions for themselves might choose the seemingly easy course of accepting the advice of others whom they consider to have superior judgment or better sources of information. To do so, of source, they must ignore the admonition "Don't rely on the advice of insiders." They must also disregard the comment of a highly regarded successful trader: "Given time, I believe that inside information can break the Bank of England or the United States Treasury."[1] For some reason that trader has discounted the elaborate survey that indicated that people who work in the grain trade have managed to lose their own money about as fast as anyone else and that farmers frequently manage to lose even faster than most.[2]

Some traders may believe that information which is generally available is as good as any other information because the difference between winning and losing is the interpretation of information rather than the information itself. After all, even the sophisticated social commentator Will Rogers asserted that "All I know is what I read in the papers." Those who accept this are not deterred by the cynic who warned that "If you buy headlines today, you'll end up by selling newspapers tomorrow."

It would appear that brokers would be interested in giving traders good advice in the interest of keeping this business, building their capital, and receiving referral business, but the results obtained by those who slavishly follow the suggestions of registered representatives of brokerage houses have been something less than outstanding. Many customers eventually come to accept the remark of a cynical trader to the effect that "The only sure tip from your broker is a margin call." Another said, "Few people ever make money on tips. Beware of inside information. If there was any easy money lying around, no one would be forcing it into your pocket." One would probably be well advised to "Beware of one who has nothing to lose," because "Markets are never wrong; opinions often are" and "Opinions are worthless; facts are priceless."

If a trader does have enough faith in someone else to accept his judgment, she would probably be well advised to follow it through to the conclusion of the trade. There are many speculators who have suffered a large loss in a position suggested by someone else only to find that their adviser had seen the error of their selection quickly and liquidated with a much smaller loss or even a profit. This is why one successful speculator advised a friend, "If you get in on Smith's tip, get out on Smith's tip."

Contrary-opinion advocates suggest that one ascertain the prevalent opinion of the trading public in some way and then take the opposite position on the basis that "The public is always wrong." At least, it tends to be wrong at critical junctures.

---

[1] Bernard Baruch, *Baruch: My Own Story* (New York: Holt, Rinehart and Winston, 1957), p. 123.

[2] Blair Stewart, *An Analysis of Speculative Trading in Grain Futures*, Technical Bulletin No. 1001 (U.S. Department of Agriculture, Commodity Exchange Authority, October 1949), pp. 67 and 68.

This assumes, of course, that the trader can take note of the same facts available to the remainder of the trading public and be able to accept an opposite position. It is well and good to advise sagely, "Buy when others sell and sell when others buy," but how could everybody follow the advice without making it meaningless?

TIMING

Most successful traders are convinced that timing represents the ultimate difference between profit and loss in trading. "When to buy and sell is more important than what to buy and sell" would be accepted as sound advice by virtually all experienced traders. Most would also agree that "A bull can make money, and a bear can make money, but a hog never can," including Baron Rothschild, who gave as a major reason for his success his rule, "I never buy at the bottom and I always sell too soon."

When to take profits can cause endless problems if one chooses not to develop and follow a plan. Hardly anyone would quarrel with the basic admonition to "Cut losses and let profits run." Just when to cut the losses or how far to let the profits run is difficult to determine. One might agree with such thoughts as "The real money made in speculation has been in commitments showing a profit right from the start." Those who follow this advice probably provide the fuel for the relatively common phenomenon of the false breakout.

"Sell when the good news is out" probably has a better reputation for validity than it deserves. Some markets discount news to a far greater degree than others. Accordingly, the first response to news might reflect all the change in price that there is going to be, but in other cases it might be only the beginning of a major change in the price level. In the latter case buying when the good news is out rather than selling might prove to be by far the better alternative. "Never sell on strike news" is in the same category. Some strikes are anticipated and some are not. Some end quickly and present a welcome opportunity to work off surplus inventory, whereas others last for extended periods and result in temporary or even permanent loss of markets, in which case selling on strike news might prove wise.

"Sell on the first margin call" appears to be valid because it really suggests that a position be abandoned before all of the trader's capital has been lost. Much would depend, of course, on the amount of loss that took place before the margin call was received. In most cases considerable attrition must already have taken place, which might imply that a well-constructed plan would not have allowed the position to have been held long enough for the margin call to have been received at all. Margin calls usually indicate that a speculator has been overtrading or has not cut losses soon enough.

It is debatable whether an attractive trading opportunity always exists. Accordingly, some traders maintain that "There is no need to be always in the market" because they are convinced that money cannot consistently be made by trading every day or even every week. Most speculators agree that overtrading is one of the worst possible errors that can be made, and accordingly they advise, "Trade too often and be the broker's good friend; trade less often to be your own true friend."

Others, however, may be going too far when they say, "When in doubt, do nothing." This might lead to considerable trouble. If a trader is out of the market and in doubt, he might do nothing and miss a profitable opportunity. Even worse, he might be in a market with a losing position and be in doubt. Accordingly, he might do nothing but watch his small loss become a large one. A trader could take the opposite course and listen to those who suggest, "When in doubt, do something" and "If you would not buy, sell." Most experienced traders find themselves consistently beset by doubts, and they could hardly react by consistently doing nothing or always doing something. If their doubts become too disturbing when they have an important position, they might well observe the old adage "Sell down to a sleeping point."

The best way to resolve such problems is to have a carefully prepared trading plan and do one's best to suppress doubts while the plan has time to work. This probably would provide more profitable results than a program based on impulse. Impulse usually results in entering positions at high prices and selling them at low prices because futures and stocks "Look best at the top of a bull market and worst at the bottom of a bear market." It is only human to want to buy when the market looks good and to sell when it looks bad, which is why it has been said that "The human side of every person is the greatest enemy of the average investor or speculator." The trader might be well advised when he is told, "Trust your own opinion and back your judgments only when the action of the market itself confirms your opinion."

Even when a plan has been devised, it is not always easy to follow it logically if any credence is given to popular maxims. For example, it is often said, "Don't try to get the last eighth." On the same point it has been written that "One of the most helpful things that anybody can learn is to give up trying to catch the last eighth—or the first. These two are the most expensive eighths in the world. They have cost stock traders, in the aggregate, enough millions of dollars to build a concrete highway across the continent."[3] These sound quite logical, but if a trader never tries to reach the exact entry point or objective specified in her trading plan, how does she ever reach either? A trader might bid $1.71½ for 10,000 bushels of oats when the market is at $1.72¾. If the market hesitates at $1.72, she might be tempted to raise her bid to be sure not to miss the market. If her objective were $1.78 and the price appeared to be meeting resistance at $1.76½, she might sell at the market in order to be sure to get out. If her order is filled at $1.76, she has covered her costs by too little to justify the risk incurred. Those last eighths she failed to gain represented too much of the potential profit in the trade to be given up. When the market turns just short of an entry or liquidation point, it can be highly annoying, but if more flexibility is needed, the plan should provide for it. There are times when placing a market order is the best way to take or liquidate a position, but there are other times when placing a limit order is wiser. In the

---

[3] Edwin Lefevre, *Reminiscences of a Stock Operator* (New York: George H. Doran Co., 1923), p. 65.

latter case the trader has little choice but to wait for the last eighth. If this fails too often, he can blame the perversity of the market rather than his own ineptness in devising plans. Although such logic will make him no money, it might make him feel better. As Shalom Aleichem said, "The girl who can't dance says the band can't keep time."

CHARACTER OF THE MARKET

Some maxims provide some general advice for traders concerning the nature of the market itself. As in the other areas, however, some of them sound logical, but there is frequently a maxim that sounds just as logical but suggests an opposing course of action. One might hear one sage maintain that "The market has no past," only to hear another say that "Nothing new ever occurs in the business of speculation or investing in securities or futures," which implies that much can be learned from the past. Most traders and all technicians would agree with the latter, although in trading, as in most other ventures, there are any number of people who will not or cannot learn from history, as well as some who cannot learn from anything.

There are those who believe, often with good reason, that one should "Never quarrel with the tape." They believe that the current price of something is all that really counts, and if it is not in line with what was expected, the wise course is to "Quit while the quitting is good." They feel that it is not productive to be too curious about all the reasons behind all the price movements because so much time might be spent learning about the factors which could influence a trade that no trade would ever be made; also, so much effort might be used to justify retaining a position when the tape says it should not be retained that severe losses would result. That is why "Wishful thinking must be banished."

Those who believe that inactive markets should be avoided are fond of asserting, "If money cannot be made out of leaders, it will not be made out of the market as a whole." They must contend with the equally popular and probably more accurate assertion that "the leaders of today may not be the leaders of tomorrow." Trading in today's leaders may result only in trading where there is no longer any opportunity and not trading where there is. Those who are unable to agree with either view can take the middle road by accepting the proposition "All stocks and futures move more or less with the general market, but value will tell in the long run." Just how much move indicates a genuine move toward economic value is not so easy to determine. One must remember that "value has little to do with temporary fluctuations in prices" and that this problem will always be with us because "The market will continue to fluctuate."

Some traders even personify a market. They believe this: "Plot the pattern of a bull market and you will have also plotted the pattern followed by nature for most living things: a slow start and gradual acceleration in growth that terminates at maturity." Most bull markets actually do appear to follow this sort of pattern.

NOTES FROM A TRADER

There is hardly a maxim that someone could not find fault with. There are one or two, however, that most traders believe sooner or later. Many of those who believe them later would have done better to believe them sooner. One of these is "Put half your profits in a safety-deposit box." Although it should be possible to find an investment wiser than cash in a safety-deposit box, it hardly seems necessary to utilize any profits gained to take larger and larger positions with the ever-increasing risks that accompany them. Although it may not seem logical, it is probably true that money is easier to make than it is to keep.

Adversity is part and parcel of trading. The only benefits that come from adversity are the knowledge and strength gained. It detracts nothing from the truth to acknowledge it with such seemingly inane statements as "Winners never quit and quitters never win" or one more profound like "God grant me the serenity to accept the things I cannot change, the courage to change the things I can, and the wisdom to know the difference." The point of one is just as valid as the point of the other. The simple truth is that most successful speculators have been bloodied at least once before achieving success, but all have tried again. Perhaps one need not accept the cynical proposition that "A speculator who dies rich has died before his time."

14

Who Wins?
Who Loses?
Why?

Who Wins?

"The race is not always to the swift nor the battle to the strong—but that's the way to bet."   DAMON RUNYON

Who Loses?

"The greatest tragedy in all history is the murder of a beautiful theory by a gang of brutal facts."   ANONYMOUS

Why?

"I contradict myself. I am large, I contain multitudes."   WALT WHITMAN

INTRODUCTION

The purpose of this concluding chapter of the trading section is to focus on the results of those who play the futures trading game and to suggest reasons for the outcomes. Traders of a cynical bent might take the position that such an inquiry should precede the trading section, not succeed it, for if futures trading is a zero-sum game, or worse, in which total profits and losses are equal at best, it is possible, theoretically at least, for the participants to engage in a kind of suicidal rotation in which no one wins in the long run. In such a dismal activity the only possible continual advantage could be only to the brokers if the commissions charged as entry fees for the game exceeded all the brokers' costs. Under these conditions potential traders might well conclude that the game is suited only to those hardy thrill seekers who might be characterized as gladiators who look on each trade as a game of "kill or be killed." Unless the shape of their trading curves indicates exceptionally active greed factors, many people might well find such a game totally unsuitable. Fortunately, there are some facts about the outcomes of futures trading that square well with hypotheses that are not quite so bleak.

DISTRIBUTION OF PROFITS AND LOSSES

The Blair Stewart Study

Probably the best-known analysis of the trading record of speculators is that by Blair Stewart, as a consulting economist for the Commodity Exchange Authority.[1] The complete trading records of 8922 customers of a Chicago commission firm which went bankrupt in the 1930s were turned over to the CEA for analysis. The study is restricted to results in grain futures (wheat, corn, oats, and rye) for a 9-year period, 1924 to 1932.

Futures market participants were divided into two broad classifications—hedgers and speculators. Three broad groups were distinguished among the speculators: scalpers, who were defined as buying and selling on small fluctuations in prices and closing the day with near even positions; spreaders, who were long and short on positions of equal amounts; other speculators, who represented all remaining traders. The Stewart study focused on the results of the last group:

	Profit traders			Loss traders		
Commodity	Number	Total net profits	Average profit per trader	Number	Total net losses	Average loss per trader
Wheat	2045	$1,508,407	$738	5496	$ 9,411,620	$1712
Corn	1525	$1,183,993	$776	2403	$ 2,222,602	$ 925
Oats	589	$ 124,038	$211	997	$ 772,132	$ 774
Rye	497	$ 293,042	$590	816	$ 825,838	$1012
All grains*	2184	$2,064,800	$945	6598	$11,958,200	$1812

* The "all grains" figures are not equal to the totals of the figures for the individual grains because some traders made profits in one or more grains but lost on their futures transactions in one or more of the other grains.

The overwhelming conclusion from the general summary is that the vast majority (75 percent) of the speculators (other than scalpers and spreaders) lost money. There were 6598 speculators in the sample with net losses compared with 2184 with net profits, or three times as many loss traders as profit traders. Net dollar speculator losses of approximately $12 million overwhelmed net dollar profits

---

[1] Blair Stewart, *An Analysis of Speculative Trading in Grain Futures.* USDA Technical Bulletin 1001 (October 1949), p. 57.

of nearly $2 million by six times. Speculators were not discriminating—they lost in every commodity, consistently and impressively.

The distribution of profits and losses indicated that for most traders the game was not played for high stakes. Eighty-four percent of the winners during the 9-year period won less than $1000. Stewart's sample of traders who held reportable positions did not indicate that large speculators were any more successful than small traders, although the sample was too small to warrant any such generalization.

Other significant points included the following:

1. Speculators showed a clear tendency to cut their profits short while letting their losses run.

2. The speculator is more likely to be long than short.

3. The entire period was one in which prices declined, and speculators suffered a disproportionate share of the total losses during the last 3 years, when the price decline accelerated.

4. No occupational group was able to claim results that differed from the general conclusion in regard to aggregate profits and losses. Managers in the grain business were somewhat more successful than other groups, yet they could produce aggregate profits in dollars that were only 28 percent of aggregate losses.

5. There was a clear tendency for long speculators to buy on days of price declines and for shorts to sell on price rises. This action indicates that traders were predominantly price-level rather than price-movement traders.

6. It cannot be known to what degree the trades for the sample were influenced by the brokerage firm at which all were made. The bankruptcy of that firm could, of course, have resulted from one factor or from a combination of many factors, but if one of these was the loss of its customers' capital resulting from its advice, the conclusions resulting from a study of the sample could be quite misleading.

The study also presented two case studies which isolated in detail the trades of the largest winner and loser. The loser traded virtually throughout the 9-year period, and his losses were more than $400,000 in wheat futures. In the spring of 1928 he had amassed a moderate profit, which he was to give back and follow with heavy losses resulting from a seasonal strategy, beginning in 1928, of buying wheat heavily at harvest time and selling it in the subsequent spring. The most successful trader struck quickly in 1924 by being long on corn, wheat, and rye, staying with his position until October of that year, and then fading away with profits of almost $300,000. He did not trade again during the 9-year period.

The Hieronymus Study[2]

Hieronymus was able to secure the summary records of closed trades for a commission house for the calendar year 1969. Even though conclusions derived from

[2] Thomas A. Hieronymus, *Economics of Futures Trading* (New York: Commodity Research Bureau, 1977), pp. 259–263.

a 1-year inquiry must of necessity be tentative, it is instructive to compare recent results, however selective, with Stewart's observations 35 years earlier. The aggregate results for three major metropolitan offices of the firm are as follows:

Number of accounts	462
Number of accounts with profits	164
Total profits (dollars)	$462,413
Profit per account (dollars)	$2,819
Number of accounts with losses	298
Total losses (dollars)	$1,127,355
Loss per account (dollars)	$3,783
Average result (loss) (dollars)	$1,439
Net loss, all accounts (dollars)	$664,942
Commissions paid (dollars)	$406,344
Put to clearinghouse (dollars)	$258,598

Thirty-five percent of the firm's customers (versus 25 percent in the Stewart study) closed 1969 with a profit. A total of $1,589,768 changing hands between winners and losers and involving 462 people is an *average* of $3441, and so the game cannot qualify as one representing staggering sums. This is confirmed by a frequency distribution, which indicates that half the winners and losers won or lost less than $1000 and that 84 percent won or lost less than $5000. Except for a few big losers (16 over $15,000) and fewer big winners (6 over $15,000), the clients of the commission house tended to pass money back and forth, paying commissions in the shuffle. It is interesting to note that a large number (170) of accounts were traded only once or a few times at most. This group, although constituting 37 percent of the total number of accounts, contributed 64 percent of the total losses. Regular traders (those who won or lost at least $500 and contributed $250 in commissions during the year) did better as a group, and their net profits were nearly enough to offset their net losses. Regular traders (42 percent) paid $364,647 of the total $406,344 in commissions, or almost 90 percent, which strongly suggests that the regular traders relieved the one-time traders of their money and then deposited it with the firm in the form of commissions.

The Houthakker Study[3]

The conclusions of Houthakker's early studies were consistent with the conclusions of later work by others done in greater detail and with more statistical evidence. Small traders tended to prefer the long side of the market to a considerable degree. They also apparently had less forecasting ability than did large speculators.

These studies were limited to only wheat, corn, and cotton and covered only three periods. Wheat and corn were observed from 1937 to 1940 and from 1946 to 1952, whereas cotton observations covered the period 1937–1952. Elimination of the data for the war years (1941 to 1945) for the two grains might make a comparison of conclusions from these markets with conclusions from the cotton market questionable.

---

[3] Hendrik Houthakker, "Can Speculators Forecast Prices?" *The Review of Economics and Statistics* (May 1957).

A major contribution of this work was the inspiration it provided for others to broaden and deepen the research into the questions it sought to answer.

The Rockwell Study[4]

The Rockwell study, based on Houthakker's earlier method of analysis, makes use of more than 7900 semimonthly observations covering 25 CEA-regulated markets for 18 years, beginning in 1947, as described in Table 14-1. The study does not include the markets such as pork bellies, cocoa, and sugar which at that time were unregulated and which constitute a significant percentage of futures trading in more recent periods. Three different market aggregations were used: "All Markets," covering 25 markets; "Large Markets," including only Chicago wheat, New York cotton, and soybeans; and "Small Markets," which included the remaining 22 markets. A reasonably stable general price level occurred from the beginning of the period to the end, as shown in Table 14-1.

For the 18-year period in all markets there is a positive total return of about $750 million on the long open interest, as illustrated in Table 14-2. About 40 percent of the return to the long open interest goes to the small speculator, and the remainder is divided fairly equally among the large speculator, the hedger, and the spreader.

If, in all markets, those holding long positions account for about $750 million in profits, there must be an offsetting $750 million loss to those holding short positions. Again the small speculator bears approximately 40 percent of this loss.

The large speculator again makes a profit, albeit a small one ($25 million) when compared with gains on the long side. It is important to note that the large speculators are the *only* group that has an aggregate profit on the short side for All Markets. The short hedger bears 40 percent of the short-side losses in All Markets, about equal to those of the small speculator. The hedger, however, does not offset short losses with long profits because long-side gains account for only 20 percent of the long profits.

In the Small Markets small speculators lose money on their long positions. Their long losses are offset by large speculators and long hedgers, and so the total dollar return to those holding long positions in the Small Markets is virtually zero. On the short side only the large speculators make money and they achieve these profits mainly at the expense of the short hedgers.

In the Large Markets the small speculator makes almost 50 percent of the long-side profits. On the short side the large speculators make a little money, but the short hedgers lose more than twice the amount of their gains on the long side. The total return on the long open interest in the Large Markets ($751.4 million) contrasts markedly with the insignificant return on the long open interest in the Small Markets.

---

[4] Charles Rockwell, "Normal Backwardation, Forecasting, and the Returns to Commodity Futures Traders," *Proceedings of a Symposium on Price Effects of Speculation in Organized Commodity Markets, Food Research Institute Studies,* Supplement, 7 (1967), 115. Portions of this study have been referred to in Chapters 2 and 4. Before proceeding, the trader should review the breakdown, in percentages, of the value of the open interest by participant in Table 2-2.

TABLE 14-1   DESCRIPTION OF DATA AND PRICE LEVELS

Commodity and markets*	Period of observation From	Period of observation To	Number of semi-monthly observations	Change in price level of nearby contract,† dollars Start	Change in price level of nearby contract,† dollars End	Annual percentage price change From start to end	Annual percentage price change Between maturity years
Wheat, Chicago Board of Trade	7/47	6/65	432	2.39375	1.42250	−2.3	−2.2
Wheat, Kansas City Board of Trade	7/50	6/65	360	2.30375	1.43500	−2.3	−1.6
Wheat, Minneapolis Grain Exchange	7/50	6/65	360	2.36125	1.59750	−2.2	−2.5
Corn, Chicago Board of Trade	7/47	6/65	432	2.30375	1.32250	−2.2	+1.4
Oats, Chicago Board of Trade	7/47	6/65	432	1.02000	0.67750	−1.9	−5.1
Rye, Chicago Board of Trade	7/47	6/65	432	2.52000	1.15750	−3.0	−1.6
Soybeans, Chicago Board of Trade	7/47	6/65	432	2.78000	2.96000	+0.36	−0.7
Soybean meal,‡ Chicago Board of Trade	7/47	6/65	432	87.50	71.10	−1.0	−12.0
Soybean oil,§ Chicago Board of Trade	7/50	6/65	360	0.1245	0.1008	−1.3	−3.1
Cotton, New York Exchange	7/47	6/64	408	0.3898	0.3328	−0.9	−2.8
Cotton, New Orleans Cotton Exchange	7/50	6/60	240	0.3569	0.3278	−0.8	−4.3
Cottonseed meal, Memphis Merchants Exchange Clearing Association	7/47	6/60	312	79.90	54.00	−2.5	−9.4
Cottonseed oil, New York Produce Exchange	7/47	6/65	432	0.2350	0.1232	−2.6	−0.6
Lard, Chicago Board of Trade	7/47	6/62	360	0.1960	0.0870	−3.7	−1.6
Flaxseed, Minneapolis Grain Exchange	7/50	6/62	288	3.7150	3.1900	−1.2	+2.0
Shell eggs, Chicago Mercantile Exchange	7/47	6/65	432	0.5262	0.3490	−1.9	−0.1
Frozen eggs, Chicago Mercantile Exchange	7/61	6/65	96	0.2635	0.2687	+0.5	−4.6
Potatoes, New York Mercantile Exchange	7/47	6/65	432	2.96	2.58	−0.7	+5.0
Wool tops, Wool Association of the New York Cotton Exchange	7/47	6/62	360	1.570	1.666	+0.4	−4.7
Grease wool, Wool Association of the New York Cotton Exchange	5/54	6/63	257	1.413	1.190	−1.7	−0.2
Bran, Kansas City Board of Trade	7/47	6/56	216	58.50	33.20	−4.8	−7.8
Shorts, Kansas City Board of Trade	7/47	6/56	216	60.00	38.90	−3.9	−9.8
Middlings, Kansas City Board of Trade	7/55	6/56	24	37.00	35.15	−5.0	−3.4
Onions, Chicago Mercantile Exchange	9/55	6/59	91	2.10	1.30	−9.5	−1.0
Butter, Chicago Mercantile Exchange	7/47	6/53	144	0.6775	0.6120	−1.6	−2.4

* "Large markets" are wheat at Chicago, cotton at New York, and soybeans.
† The nearby contract is the first contract that expires after the first observation; generally it is July.
‡ Soybean meal is for the Memphis Merchants Exchange Association until July 1953.
§ Soybean oil is for the New York Produce Exchange until July 1950.

SOURCE: Rockwell, op. cit., 115.

TABLE 14-2 AGGREGATE PROFITS BY TRADING GROUPS: LONG, SHORT, AND NET
(in millions of dollars)

Trading group	Large markets		Small markets		All markets*	
	Long	Short	Long	Short	Long	Short
Small traders	369.7	−303.6	−68.1	−1.4	301.6	−305.0
Reporting speculators	114.8	3.1	38.8	22.2	153.5	25.3
Reporting spreaders†	159.0	−159.0	5.5	−3.4	164.5	−163.1
Reporting hedgers	108.1	−291.2	25.4	−18.8	133.5	−310.1
Total long open interest*	751.4		1.5		752.9	
Small traders, net	66.1		−69.5		−3.4	
Reporting speculators, net	117.8		61.0		178.8	
Reporting hedgers, net	−183.2		6.5		−176.6	

* Because of rounding, totals are not necessarily exact sums of the components shown.
† This category is included only for balance purposes. The sum of the net positions is not zero because of its omission.
SOURCE: Rockwell, op. cit., 119.

A summary follows of the significance of the net returns to each group for the 18-year period, as presented in the last three rows of Table 14-2. It should be noted that the profit flow in the three Large Markets determines to a great extent the behavior of the All Markets aggregate.

1. When the short-side losses of small traders are compared with their long-side profits, the group shows a small net loss for All Markets.

2. Large speculators win consistently (though unevenly) in Small and Large Markets, and their total winnings ($178.8 million) come almost entirely at the expense of hedgers in the Large Markets.

3. In the Small Markets hedgers do much better ($6.5 million) than they do in the Large Markets, and the profits of the large speculator ($61 million) are made at the expense of the small speculator.

4. The losses of hedgers in the three Large Markets provide the profits for large speculators and almost enough profits for small speculators to offset their losses in the 23 Small Markets.

Even more instructive is the presentation in Table 14-3 of the annual profits in All Markets for all participants. The small speculators lose in 11 of the 18 years. Their average loss is $15.1 million and their average profit, $23.7 million. If the largest profit years are removed (1950–1951 and 1960–1961), the average profit drops to $10.5 million, well below the average loss. There is little consolation to the small speculators in the realization that 68 percent of their profits for the 18-year period may be attributed to only two years.

The large speculators, on the other hand, show a profit in 15 of the 18 years. Their average yearly profit is almost $13 million, even though they account for perhaps less than 2 percent of the total value of the open interest, whereas their average annual loss is only $3.4 million. If the two largest profit years are removed, the average profit is $9.6 million, still virtually three times the average loss of $3.4 million. The consistency of the profit-making capacity of the large speculators is impressive.

The hedgers, during the 18-year period, show a $6.5 million profit in the 22 Small Markets, yet their loss in the Large Markets is so large ($183.1 million) that they suffer an All Markets loss of $176.6 million. Recent research by Working[5] is consistent with these findings. Working indicated that the major proportion of hedging losses may spring from market execution costs, which can be considerably greater than the reduced member commissions paid by most large hedgers. Because hedgers' orders tend to be large, any buys and sells would tend to make price bulges and dips which scalpers would trade. Such action, if true, renders understandable why the amount of speculation in a given market is closely tied to the amount of hedging. Hedgers may be the major source of income of the large speculators. Because most hedging is short hedging, most large speculator profits should come from the long side of the Large Markets. This may be verified by referring to Table 14-2.

If the annual rates of return to the participants are defined as gross profits as a percentage of contract value, Table 14-4 can present the trader with an idea of the individual rates of return by trading groups. Even though commissions, taxes, and capital reserves are omitted, the fact that margin requirements are only 5 or 10 percent of the contract value means that the actual returns on margin money may be as much as 10 to 20 times the returns indicated here. Regardless of the

TABLE 14-3　ANNUAL PROFITS FOR ALL MARKETS
(in millions of dollars)

Year	Small traders, net	Large speculators, net	Hedgers, net	Total
1947/48	16.2	19.5	−34.2	115.9
1948/49	−13.5	−0.5	13.8	−48.2
1949/50	7.9	17.0	−24.9	153.3
1950/51	47.5	28.9	−76.11	229.5
1951/52	−10.5	7.8	2.7	126.2
1952/53	−44.3	−4.3	46.4	−171.9
1953/54	12.8	16.3	−29.7	113.4
1954/55	−17.0	5.1	12.0	−27.7
1955/56	2.5	12.7	−15.5	73.9
1956/57	−6.4	6.5	−0.1	5.8
1957/58	−9.4	0.9	8.4	−27.4
1958/59	−3.6	1.4	2.5	−3.7
1959/60	−14.6	4.5	10.2	−38.3
1960/61	63.3	35.2	−98.6	217.8
1961/62	−19.4	−5.4	24.8	−95.9
1962/63	−3.6	2.1	1.6	50.5
1963/64	−24.1	10.0	14.1	−75.0
1964/65	13.0	21.2	−34.1	155.0
Total	−3.4	178.8	−176.6	752.9

SOURCE: Rockwell, op. cit., 120.

[5] Holbrook Working, "Tests of a Theory Concerning Floor Trading on Commodity Exchanges," *Proceedings of a Symposium on Price Effects of Speculation in Organized Commodity Markets, Food Research Institute Studies,* Supplement, 7 (1967), 5–48.

level of absolute profits, the relative profits of the different trading groups may be compared.

For All Markets the rate of return on the long open interest is 4 percent annually. The hedgers make about this amount on net long positions, and so the large speculators pick up what the small traders lose on the long side in Small Markets as well as what the hedgers lose in the Large Markets. On the short side the large speculators win from the small traders and the hedgers in both Small and Large Markets. Again the large speculators are the standouts in the Large and Small Markets. Their overall return of 6.1 percent is earned because they do well in both their long and short positions and because the ratio of their long to their short positions is large during the periods when short hedgers are losing. The small traders lose so much on their short positions that the resulting profits on their long positions do not overcome the deficit. If the hedgers are offsetting existing or expected positions in the cash market, the overall loss (-1.7 percent) may provide an insight into the gross cost of placing a year-long hedge.

Until recently the risk premium concept, as developed in Chapter 4, was the consistent, if overworked, springboard into any discussion of the distribution of profits and losses in futures trading. The naive strategy (being net long when hedgers are net short and being net short when hedgers are net long) does not result in an acceptable explanation of the profit flow. The failure to isolate and measure persistent evidence that speculators are paid for merely playing the game implies that speculative profits must be explained by reference to the trader's forecasting ability. Forecasting ability, however, may be defined as two broadly differing skills. The first is the basic ability to be long in markets when prices are going up on the average and net short in markets when prices are going down on the average. This measure of forecasting skill indicates the long-run ability of a given trading group to stay on the "right" side of a given market and is referred to as "basic skill." On the other hand, a second level of forecasting ability is the "special skill" that a trading group exhibits when it makes profits from price movements that are shorter in duration than the total period under observation.

Table 14-5 presents a division of the rates of return according to basic and

TABLE 14-4   AGGREGATE RATES OF RETURN BY TRADING GROUPS (percent)

Groups and positions	Large markets	Small markets	All markets
Total positions:			
All groups	6.1	0.0	4.0
Small traders, long	5.6	-2.0	3.0
Small traders, short	-5.8	-0.0	-4.1
Large speculators, long	10.1	4.3	7.6
Large speculators, short	0.5	5.0	2.7
Hedgers, long	5.3	1.7	3.8
Hedgers, short	-7.1	-0.6	-4.3
Net positions:			
Small traders, net	0.6	-1.2	-0.0
Large speculators, net	7.2	4.6	6.1
Hedgers, net	-3.0	0.1	-1.7

SOURCE: Rockwell, op. cit., 122.

**TABLE 14-5   DIVISION OF RATES OF RETURN ACCORDING TO BASIC
AND SPECIAL FORECASTING SKILLS BY NET TRADING
GROUPS°** (percent)

Trading and skill groups	Large markets	Small markets	All markets
Small traders, net:			
Rate of return from special forecasting skill (R^F)	−0.1	−1.2	−0.4
Rate of return from basic forecasting skill (R^B)	0.7	0.0	0.4
Total rate of return (R^A)	0.6	−1.2	−0.0
Large speculators, net:			
Rate of return from special forecasting skill (R^F)	5.0	3.9	4.8
Rate of return from basic forecasting skill (R^B)	2.2	0.7	1.3
Total rate of return (R^A)	7.2	4.6	6.1
Hedgers, net:			
Rate of return from special forecasting skill (R^F)	−0.9	0.8	−0.6
Rate of return from basic forecasting skill (R^B)	−2.1	−0.7	−1.0
Total rate of return (R^A)	−3.0	0.1	−1.7

° The decomposition in a given market of the total actual rate of return (R^A)
into basic forecasting skill (R^B) and special forecasting skill (R^F) is discussed
in Rockwell, op. cit., 127.
SOURCE: Rockwell, op. cit., 127.

special skills. Small traders make important money only in the Large Markets,
where rising prices result in a positive figure for basic skill (R^B). Small traders
exhibit a consistent negative value for special skill (R^F). Large speculators, as is
obvious by now, make money on the evidence of both skills. There are no "minus"
values for the large traders in the Large Markets, Small Markets, or All Markets
summary. Almost 80 percent of the total profit of the large traders comes from
their special skill and only 20 percent from their basic skill. The large traders,
then, are not rewarded chiefly by executing the strategy of buy and hold in an
extended up move or sell and hold in an extended down move; instead, they are
rewarded chiefly by trading price changes in the relative short run.

Working's study[6] of the detailed record of one professional trader in cotton
futures for a brief period is important for several reasons. In his attempt to test
the theory that most floor trading is scalping and that the execution costs of
hedging are perhaps the chief source of income to speculators in futures markets,
the definition of "scalping" was considerably enlarged to cover not only the smallest
dips and bulges that occur but those that last up to a few days. In the large, well-
traveled markets professional scalping tends to specialize, sometimes into three
distinguishable classes—unit-change scalpers, day-trading scalpers, and day-to-
day scalpers. Unit-change scalpers, who stand ready to buy one tick below the

---

[6] Ibid.

last sale or sell one tick above it, almost invariably end the trading session in a zero net speculative position. Day traders tend to concentrate on dips and bulges of greater than unit size and may decide to hold some small percentage of their positions overnight. Day-to-day scalpers more often than not are prepared to carry most or all of their positions into the next trading session or for 2 or 3 successive days.

As indicated by the Stewart study, nearly all speculators, on or off the floor of the exchange, make some attempts at scalping. Price-level traders may wait for price dips before getting long or for price bulges before initiating a short position. These traders, of course, run the risk of missing the market completely in those trades that, by definition, are the most successful. An alternative is to place orders "at the market," which ensures some execution costs at the hands of floor traders who are, themselves, scalping. The small trader is not on the exchange floor and cannot easily, for example, buy "on a dip" while the dip is forming.

Because the professional scalper derives profits from trading dips and bulges of varying time lengths, it seems difficult to understand why the ability to recognize price trends is asserted by floor traders to be the most important requirement for successful scalping.[7] The adage "Cut your losses and let your profits run," heard by every trader alive, including those who came down with the last rain, has always been regarded as a basic rule of successful trading. Yet the effort to comply with the directive is successful only for the trader who can consistently anticipate the continuation of price trends. Such success is highly doubtful for reasons considered at length in Chapters 4 and 7. How, then, can the concepts of scalping and trend following coexist?

Working's thoughts, following a study of a 2-month record of floor trading by a professional trader, explain why the adage "Cut your losses and let your profits run" combines in one statement two entirely different approaches that are important for different reasons:

> (a) because a "trend" is the converse of a dip or bulge, trend recognition is a means of recognizing dips and bulges; (b) a scalper recognizes, in order to partially offset the losses that he incurs from trends whose beginnings he mistakenly regards as initial moves in a dip or bulge; and (c) the adage, "cut your losses and let your profits run," which is highly respected by floor traders, deserves such respect even if its application cannot be made a source of net gains. By letting profits run, to the best of his ability, a scalper derives such profits as he can from the emergence of unpredictable trends that happen to be in his favor, partially offsetting inevitable losses from the emergence of trends that run against him. By setting a limit on the amount of loss that he allows himself to incur, per unit of the commodity, a scalper accepts unnecessary loss to a greater extent than he avoids further loss (a consequence of the supposition that brief price trends are a source of net loss); but the practice, while slightly reducing his overall rate of profit per unit of the commodity, allows him to trade safely on a scale several times as large as would be prudent if he did not thus limit his losses per unit . . . effort to deal as successfully as possible with brief price trends is necessarily an integral part of professional scalping; and therefore, evidence that a floor trader makes such efforts does not, by itself, warrant classing him as a trend trader.[8]

---

[7] Ibid., 44.
[8] Ibid., 45.

The Ross Study[9]

In a study of 2637 customers chosen at random from among the customers of a large brokerage firm during 1970 and 1971, Ross provided no more comfort than his predecessor researchers for speculators looking for an easy way to acquire great riches. The total losses after commissions of the sample group exceeded the total profits of the winners by more than double. The losing group actually showed net profits of $2.6 million before commissions but was overwhelmed by total commissions approximating $8 million.

What results might have been obtained in today's markets where discounts are available is a matter of conjecture. The general level of commissions is higher, so the discounted commissions might not differ much from the undiscounted levels of 1970. Another factor which, as usual, is difficult to evaluate is the effect of the advice given to the traders by the brokerage firm at which they were trading.

Additional Evidence

The authors have been able to confirm that the average expectation of a trader making net profits in any given year will be one in four. The records of one respected brokerage firm indicated that for 10 years, beginning in 1962, the percentage of traders concluding the year with net profits ranged from a low of 14 percent to a high of 42 percent, with an average of 26 percent. In 1969, 23 percent of the accounts made money, compared with 35 percent in the Hieronymus sample of 462, which was approximately 10 percent of the size of the firm the authors examined. At any rate, the three estimates do not seem to be mutually exclusive in their implications for any given year. As the rates of return for the CFTC trader classifications are examined, however, it will be seen that there is a significant difference between making profits in any *one* year and making *consistent* profits over a period of many years.

SKILLS OF THE TRADER

Forecasting Skills

The bald, unyielding fact is that small traders, as a group, seemingly possess no basic forecasting or special forecasting skill. They hold 46 percent of the value of all contracts and their gross profits are zero. Substantial losses occur when commissions are included. On the average, then, a small trader has the expectation of losing money—the losses over a reasonable period to equal commissions. It is evident that small traders do not require a history of profits to continue trading. The explanation of such a phenomenon may take several directions. First, the needs of some small traders may be met by merely playing the game. Having something that is dynamic and fast-paced to get up for in the morning is so exciting

---

[9] Ray L. Ross, "Financial Consequences of Trading Commodity Futures Contracts," *Illinois Agricultural Economics*, **15**, No. 2 (July 1975).

that the trader may be more than willing to risk losing money for the privilege of speculating. Second, traders may continue to trade because they believe they can forecast prices. The fact that they cannot consistently do so does not deter them because they tend to remember profits and forget losses. Third, the small trader may continue to trade because his or her group is amorphous and consists not of a crowd but of a parade. The successful small trader becomes large as a result of competence, whereas the unsuccessful small trader is eventually forced to withdraw from the market and is replaced by new blood. Fourth, small traders may be convinced that their latest mistake is also their last mistake and that, having learned, there is nothing ahead but smooth sea and blue sky.

On the other hand, small traders have years in which they post impressive profits. Referring to Table 14-3, it may be seen that in the years 1950–1951 and 1960–1961, for example, small traders show returns four and six times larger, respectively, than the average profit of the five other profitable years. This performance may well be explained by the tendency of small traders to rely on the existence of positive serial correlation as the basis for their trading strategy; that is, small traders tend to rely on long-run trend-following methods for profits, in which they assume that the tendency of a rising market is to continue to rise and the tendency of a falling market is to continue to fall. Such trading theories result in trading strategies of buying strength and selling weakness, which may enable the small trader to reap extremely high profits in years when such trends are of long duration. Unfortunately, in the long run, more markets are trading markets than long-trending markets; that is, there seems to be more of a tendency for price reversal than for price continuation.

Large traders generally tend to view markets as trading markets rather than trending markets. They may rely more heavily on the presence of negative serial correlation; therefore, they may tend to sell certain rallies and buy certain declines. Such a result is consistent with an examination of the returns of large traders in such big profit years as 1950–1951 and 1960–1961. In those years large traders show a return, respectively, of 3 and 3.7 times the average profit of the other 13 profitable years, considerably lower than those for the small trader.

It should be emphasized that there is a considerable difference between a winner in any given year and a consistent winner over a significant period of time. Although the studies to date have indicated that a trader in any given year has an approximate probability of one in four of achieving a net profit, the probability of extending his or her supremacy consecutively drops precipitously. Of the 25 percent who win in any given year, only 2 percent manage their skills in a consistent manner than ensures their reappearance in a ratio approaching 15 of 18. For the remaining 23 percent *sic transit gloria*.

It is important to note that the dismal profitability of the small traders results in no small part from their inability to manage money intelligently. Of the four elements of money management, the two discussed in detail in Chapter 11 are probably the chief culprits—the expectation of the game being played and the probability of ruin. The small traders seldom approach the expectation of the game in the spirit of fair, good, and bad bets as determined by the profitability of the event occurring, the ratio of gain to loss, and the cost of playing the game. In their desire to play a speculative game to the hilt, in which results, either good or bad, occur quickly, they do not give the probability of ruin the cool reflection it deserves, and the small speculators remain generally unconvinced that they cannot change the mathematical expectation of the game by the way they play the game.

There are quantitative and qualitative reasons for the supremacy of one trader over another. Many of the quantitative skills, which certainly may be acquired through patience and intellectual diligence, have been the subject of much of this book. Many of the skills that must be developed, however, deal with behavior and the reaction of the trader to ongoing events and conditions.

Behavioral Skills

It is difficult to discuss the development of skills that cannot be internalized adequately except by experience. The fact that such behavioral skills exist is clearly illustrated by a neophyte who, having been sensitized to a particular behavioral skill, may say, "Why didn't you tell me that before?"—to which the professional trader replies, "I did." People make markets. The nature and behavior of people, although not reducible to a formula, is at least agreeable to analysis. The behavior of the trader should move toward the kind of behavior necessary for survival.

Few studies since World War II have dealt specifically with the behavior of traders. One, by Blair Stewart, has been examined. Another, by Ira Glick, deals with the professional trader. Others have made limited attempts to analyze the characteristics of the amateur speculator.

Glick's study[10] analyzed three styles of trading that professional traders on the Chicago Mercantile Exchange believed could lead to success:

> One successful pattern is exemplified by the scalper, and, from the trader's point of view, is probably the most difficult to realize. The typical scalper is thought of as young, relatively new in the occupation; flexible, aggressive and exhibitionistic in his behavior, and *always* minimizing losses.
>
> A second career pattern for success is the older, more mature trader, actively and in a large way engaged in some phase of the egg business. He has excellent sources of information and is regarded as intelligent, able to view and grasp the total market situation in terms of a span of time and a diversity of factors. He is thought of as being wealthy and as having many wealthy friends, probably some of whom are also in the cash egg business.
>
> A third successful career line is quite similar to the above type, but this type of successful trader does not often appear on the exchange floor. Instead, he is thought of as purposely staying away from the (physical) marketplace, developing his trading strategy and tactics on the basis of good sources of objective information and executing his purchases and sales through representatives on the trading floor. . . .[11]

Narrow studies made by the authors and others do not provide much information that is not readily observable to practitioners in the futures industry. Speculators tend to classify themselves either as fundamentalists or as technicians, with most

---

[10] Ira O. Glick, "A Social Psychological Study of Futures Trading," an unpublished Ph.D. dissertation (Department of Sociology, University of Chicago, 1957).

[11] Ibid., pp. 245–246.

preferring the latter. Technicians, most of whom rely wholly or primarily on charts, generally conclude that market patterns are the same in all or most markets and, hence, tend to trade in more different markets than fundamentalists.

Most such traders rely for information primarily upon their brokers, general financial publications, services, and newsletters. Few engage in any individual research of any depth. Most lose but feel that they are learning how to avoid losing in the future, and so they continue to trade. Many seem to continue trading and losing in the same manner as before, apparently blaming unusual conditions or bad luck for their lack of success.

Although much information is contained in these studies, they do not really contain a systematic insight into the behavior of the futures trader. A systematic approach would serve not only to explain the trader's present behavior but also to outline useful paths for change in the future. Perhaps one day a psychologist with an understanding of speculators' behavior will explain why traders continue to rationalize methods that have not worked, follow advisers who have rarely been right, fail to follow their own plans, and otherwise refuse to confront reality.

It appears that the ability of traders to confront reality may well have much to do with their eventual success. Such traders are able to adapt to various market and trading conditions. If their plans include the use of stop-loss orders, they place such orders, and having placed them, they do not find excuses to cancel them. Such traders do not get so carried away with greed or so cowed by fear that they are unable to act rationally.

Unsuccessful traders cope with unpleasant reality in quite a different way. They depend not upon changing themselves or their methods but rather on fantasizing or changing the ways they view reality. They tend to be selectively perceptive and retentive; that is, they tend to see and remember what fits their needs and expectations. They prefer simple, easily constructed mechanical systems which tend to have dollar results approaching 50 percent profits and 50 percent losses. When commissions and execution costs are subtracted, the normal expected path of such traders' capital is a gentle downward slope that terminates considerably short of their capacities for self-deception.

Such traders tend to devise new filters after each series of trades that might have eliminated losses and converted them into profits. They also explain away a loss or two by blaming them upon unusual news items or especially disruptive untimely reports. They conclude, therefore, that their 50-50 results really sprang from a system destined to yield 70-30 or 80-20 in the long run. The long run, however, never seems to arrive. The capacity of such people to misinterpret reality appears to be limitless.

No matter how successful traders become, they still find it difficult to live in the real world. Where members of the animal kingdom must adjust to the external environment on its terms, human beings can manipulate reality over a broad range by the use of symbolism. Traders must realize that desirable qualities can be bestowed by words alone and that such words can be affixed more readily to the occasion than the occasion can be modified to fit the actual meaning of the words. Traders do not enjoy being wrong. Besides ruining their credit balance, being wrong does not build a good image of the self. Yet mistakes must be constantly perceived and remembered for no other reason than that under no other conditions can they be controlled.

Successful trading is reached, if at all, by following a series of successive approximations. Early in the process ignorance is the rule, and traders know that they know nothing. Following a sometimes long apprenticeship in which the vocabulary symbols are acquired, a false sense of competence spreads like a thin veneer and serves to entertain friends with the glibness of skills not yet acquired, though seeming to be. Given enough time, patience, and perseverance, successful traders enter into that third state in which they believe that they know something and no more. In this state they are "inner-directed" and not "other-directed."[12] The "other-directed" individuals react to what others believe about them. Their roles and values tend to be derived from what their peers expect of them. The "inner-directed" individuals hold to the thoughtful courses they set for themselves. Instead of being solely radar-equipped, as in "other direction," the "inner-directed" individuals rely on a gyroscope that is not at the mercy of whim or caprice. The successful traders' gyroscopes are finely tuned. They realize that without a thoughtful approach to trading they face the same problem that the German High Command faced in World War II, in which the invasion of Britain was planned but never executed, whereas the Battle of Britain was executed but never planned. Many traders never move beyond the point of development where they tend to execute trades that are never planned or plan trades that are never executed.

Traders must understand that decisions with favorable consequences evolve into a viable approach to trading only if they are consciously reduced to principles and followed with *great effort*. Traders who buy or sell on impulse find sooner or later that mere feelings about trading are 50-50; that is, there is no significant statistical correlation between good feelings and profitable trades. Therefore, to avoid the results of emotional activity, successful traders must be prepared to give up in trading what they find most rewarding in interpersonal relationships—good feelings. The propensity for traders to resist such depersonalization is high, and there is a constant temptation to spill out over the boundaries of the well-defined role of trading. Good feelings will come as a result of the successful plans that have been conceived and executed by a meticulous, thoughtful trader. Traders who share their thoughts about their trading philosophy with their brokers can do much to relieve stress between the two. This, in turn, might also influence trading results by achieving the benefits yielded by team play.

NOTES FROM A TRADER

The problems to which traders have set their faces have developed because their aspirations are infinitely expansible; the solutions lie in the hope that their knowledge and behavior are infinitely perfectible. In between the recognition of the problems and the acquisition of the quantitative and qualitative skills needed for

---

[12] David Riesman, *The Lonely Crowd* (New Haven, Conn: Yale University Press, 1950).

their solutions lies a series of searches that must, many times, include the experience of failure. Indeed, no successful traders the authors have known can follow their paths backward very far without running into failure. It is not the act of failure, however, that differentiates the ultimately successful or unsuccessful traders. Rather, it is that the successful traders get up, spend a few days healing, reaffirm what they know, and go about the business of adding to their store of wisdom. In such a growth process the quality of persistence looms large and is virtually irreplaceable.

In the high-risk areas of the world of finance, the cold facts of probabilities cannot be changed by wishful thinking or by bemoaning the cruel realities of life. Some people win frequently and accumulate large sums. Others are destined to lose frequently and, at least as a group, lose the large sums that are won by the smaller group of winners. The chance of success may be helped by thinking straight, negotiating low execution costs, dealing with a broker who observes high standards of performance, and setting reasonable goals. Regardless of their intellectual capacity and the strength of their personal discipline, however, most players in the futures game are destined to lose to the few. Those who cannot accept this truism are well advised to turn their attention elsewhere.

The person involved responsibly, both intellectually and behaviorally, with the experience of trading may, to paraphrase Theodore Roosevelt, know at his best the triumph of high achievement, but if he fails, he will have failed while daring greatly, and so his place will never be with those timid souls who know neither victory nor defeat. Perhaps, then, in the final analysis, it may be as rewarding to travel as it is to arrive.

The Broker
in the Game

There are at least two reasons for the inclusion of Chapter 15,
"Building, Maintaining, and Servicing a Futures Clientele." The first
is the obvious one of providing the futures broker with a guide to
ongoing activities which show no clear beginning or ending. In that
sense the chapter will have served its purpose if it proves useful as a
yardstick for measuring the broker's individual performance. The
second reason, however, is as important as the first. The chapter
should be studied by traders so that as clients they may be aware of
the principles on which the performance of a knowledgeable broker is
based. The setting of standards does two things: first, both broker
and client will more readily recognize substandard performance
because good performance is defined; second, avenues to better
performance are explored by which improvement in the quality of
services rendered may be effected as much by client awareness as by
the broker's presentation. Chapter 16, "Compliance: I'll See You in
Court," describes how brokers can avoid legal problems that will be
costly, take up valuable time, affect their reputation, and perhaps
result in something even worse.

15

Building, Maintaining, and Servicing a Futures Clientele

"To profit from good advice requires more wisdom than to give it."

INTRODUCTION

Registered commodity representatives who specialize in futures are, like their counterparts in the securities area, basically sales representatives. They must build clienteles by using effective prospecting methods, maintain them by replacing lost clients, and serve their active clients efficiently. It is a truly rare person who has enough skill and knowledge to perform capably as a sales representative and as a researcher at the same time. Both research and sales are full-time jobs for most people if done competently. The function of futures sales representatives is to locate potential clients who, because they are served honestly and well, will remain clients over time.

BUILDING A FUTURES CLIENTELE

Sales Personality

The impression made by registered commodity representatives on their clients is based on attitude, appearance, and ability to communicate. The attitude that all sales representatives should have is obviously beyond dispute. They should believe that their products are good for all concerned: their clients, their firms, and themselves. The clients' interests must come first, but the firm and its salespeople should also gain from satisfactory service. Long-term success is virtually impossible if all do not benefit adequately and fairly. The brokerage company must make a profit from its business, the sales representatives must be able to earn adequate livings handling their accounts, and customers must be financially or psychically rewarded to justify their trading. Some salespeople believe that no client ever profits in the long run. Others are so disturbed by the high percentage of traders who lost money that they are unable to function effectively. Such salespeople would help all concerned, including themselves, by selling some other product or by making a living in some other way. If the sales representative can accept the fact that trading futures is right for some people and wrong for others and tell all of them the truth about the business, assuming that they are interested in such knowledge, then enough sincerity can be shown to permit effective selling. If people are induced to trade who clearly should not trade, or if others are persuaded not to trade who might enjoy trading, profit from it, or both, or if a salesperson pretends to know what is not known, no one is helped. The proper attitude for most good sales representatives is derived in large part from the enthusiasm that comes from a real understanding of what they are selling and what motivates the people who are buying.

Sales representatives' appearances are dictated by the same standards that apply to anyone else in the investment field. They should look successful enough to avoid having their customers wonder why they are offering financial advice when they look like failures themselves. They should not, however, dress so extravagantly that they give the impression that they have acquired all the money that their clients have lost. Extremes of dress are almost certain to prove offensive to some people, who may respond by patronizing someone else.

Sales representatives communicate with their customers personally or by telephone or by mail. They must know how to speak, write, and spell. If their speech, vocabularies, or writing abilities are inadequate, they should recognize the deficiencies and do something about them beyond hoping that an office stenographer will note and correct errors. Effective formal courses in speech are available, and most communities have clubs dedicated to the improvement of public speaking. Group prospecting, such as addressing a luncheon meeting of a civic club, is too effective a sales device not to be utilized merely because a sales representative is too inexperienced or shy to learn to speak well. Vocabulary and spelling may also be improved by taking positive steps that can be fun as well as economically rewarding. Formal courses in letter writing are part of the program of virtually all business schools.

Product Knowledge

It has been said that futures traders pass through three stages. First, they know not and know that they know not. Then they know not and know not that they know not. Then they know and know that they know. The first and third stages are relatively safe, but most traders seem to enter the dangerous second stage rather quickly and stay there. Worse, many registered commodity representatives are there as well and are even more dangerous than individual traders because of their influence on others. Many inexperienced traders are led to believe that registered commodity representatives know more than they really do because of their fluency in the language of the business and their knowledge of its mechanics.

Some registered commodity representatives study securities and futures constantly in a truly professional manner and are really well informed. Others who become quite humble when they realize how little they do know approach trading with the caution it deserves. Too many, however, cover their lack with glib pretense and superficiality. It behooves the trader to ascertain the category into which a registered commodity representative fits.

To become established as a professional in the area of product knowledge a registered commodity representative need not build a reputation for enriching all clients or selecting winning positions infallibly. A client who expects to find a person with such a reputation to service an account is hopelessly naive, unreasonable, or both. There are, however, some constructive steps that may be taken by sales representatives. They can become thoroughly informed of the services offered by their firms and by the exchanges. They can master the rules, regulations, customs, and mechanical procedures that apply to their jobs and learn enough about the legal, accounting, and tax aspects of trading to provide their clients with general guidance, but they should never try to replace qualified lawyers or accountants. Some of this basic knowledge is necessarily possessed by most sales representatives because of the requirement that an examination be passed (see the appendix at the end of this chapter). Like all other professionals, sales representatives in the futures field should keep pace with all developments and changes and be aware of the implications they may have for clients. Different futures become popular or unpopular. Sometimes new ones appear on the futures exchanges and the old become dormant or disappear completely. Relatively new areas of activity such as trading currencies on futures exchanges or the resurgence of trading in options on futures on exchanges may offer new opportunities.

An important step toward professionalism is becoming familiar with the old and new literature in the industry. In addition to the obvious sources of current information (financial magazines, newspapers, and services), there is the scholarly work done in futures and the closely related areas of probability, money management, and utility theory, all of which professional salespeople should become acquainted with in order to better understand their products and the customers who buy them. It is not a matter of unreasonable expense or effort for registered commodity representatives to build themselves libraries of appropriate books and government and private research publications. The rapid rate of growth of the futures trading industry makes it mandatory for salespeople and clients alike to keep abreast of changes.

One of the most important words to learn in the area of product knowledge is "validation." Half-truths and unsupported opinions such as "Gaps on the chart must be closed" or "When a 3-day moving average line crosses a 10-day moving average line, a trading opportunity is evident" should not be inflicted on unsophisticated clients, who will as a result almost certainly lose their trading capital. Suggestions concerning areas of "support" and "resistance" that are based upon casual observation of dog-eared charts may be quite useless, even if they are made by sincere representatives of brokerage firms appearing on television or at "seminars."

Registered commodity representatives who induce their clients to make decisions on the basis of such fragile foundations will sooner or later lose both the clients and their reputations and well deserve to lose both. The same applies to those who give thoughtless advice in the area of money management. One of the most popular of these high-sounding but questionable concepts is "Always keep a cash reserve." Obviously a cash reserve is useless if it is never to be put to work. Even more common is the frequently offered advice to set profit objectives at some dollar multiple of the risk; for example, if a trader is to risk 4 cents in a corn trade, his objective should be no less than 8 cents. Hence he is ostensibly taking a favorable 2 to 1 bet. Actually this is meaningless if no weight is given to the probability of achieving the profit or suffering the loss. Trading corn with a stop of ¼ cent and a goal of a profit of $1.25 a bushel hardly offers a trader odds of 500 to 1, whereas a position with a risk of 4 cents and a goal of 4 cents is well worth taking if the probability of achieving the 4-cent profit is four times the probability of suffering the 4-cent loss.

Knowledge of the Firm

Sales representatives should realize that there is no ideal firm in terms of size or specialization. Each has its advantages and limitations, but sales representatives should make an effort to understand the strengths and weaknesses of their own companies and capitalize on their strengths and compensate for their weaknesses. If the weaknesses prevail on balance, they might do well to make a change.

Basically, there are two types of firms in the futures field. One is the full-line wire house, which, in addition to futures, offers stocks, bonds, mutual funds, and sometimes various other types of financial merchandise such as insurance, real estate, and tax shelters. The other is the specialty house, which limits its offerings to futures and options. The full-line house is usually considerably larger than the specialty house in terms of capital, number of branches, and number of personnel. The sales personnel for the first can offer clients the advantage of trading in various types of financial merchandise with one firm, thus simplifying record keeping and transferring funds among their various financial ventures. Sales representatives with specialty firms can sometimes offer more sophisticated services in terms of speed, interpretation of news, and operational knowledge because neither they nor their back-office personnel have to diversify in so many complex areas. Some specialty firms prefer to act primarily as order takers and compete with wire houses by discounting commissions.

Sales representatives must thoroughly understand the structures of the firms with which they are associated. Clients have the right to know whether firms holding a significant amount of their capital are financially stable. Sales representatives should either be fully aware of their firms' financial conditions or have good reason to explain why they are not. They should know which exchange memberships are held by their firms and which of them are clearing memberships. If the number of clearing memberships is relatively limited, sales personnel should be prepared to deal with the questions of clients rightfully concerned about the possibility of having recommendations concentrated among the futures traded on the exchanges to which the firms belong rather than among those presenting the best opportunities.

Registered commodity representatives should be familiar with their firms' market letters and other published materials as well as with those issued by competitors. They should be able to explain other services such as charts, floor information, futures calendars, and offers of specific trading recommendations, and they should know how to interpret their clients' confirmations and monthly statements.

The one area in which nearly all sales representatives expect more than their firms can deliver is that of providing consistently successful specific recommendations of market positions. The life of registered commodity representatives would be easy indeed if all they had to do was pass on the recommendations of their firms' research departments to clients, who would then make significant amounts of money within a short time. Telling clients the glad news of their latest gains is among the pleasantest experiences sales representatives can have, whereas breaking the news of yet another catastrophic loss is among the worst. Regardless of the size or degree of specialization of their firms, sales personnel must realize that their good intentions are probably beyond question. They would like their clients to make money in the markets because they profit from commissions paid and know that it is easier to retain satisfied clients than it is to replace clients with new ones, particularly as their reputation for losing clients becomes known. Furthermore, clients who are successful in the market have ever-growing accounts, and the commissions they pay grow accordingly if they do not withdraw all their profits. In addition, they are far more likely to refer new accounts to the firm than if they were losers.

The magnitude of the problems faced by a futures firm, regardless of the purity of its intentions, should not be underestimated by its employees or its customers. Making profits in the futures markets is possible for the skilled, disciplined trader who is carefully managing an adequate but not unreasonably large pool of capital. If the firm recommends positions and its recommendations are followed by many of its clients, it acts much as if it were loosely managing many accounts, each influenced to some degree by its owner. If the firm is consistently successful, the amount of money it influences will grow almost geometrically as the accounts of its customers grow and new customers are attracted by tales of success. Ultimately, the firm's own clients will drive prices so high when they buy and so low when they sell that the firm's recommendations will become self-defeating. Although the futures markets are generally sufficiently liquid to handle the business of individual traders, they cannot absorb concentrated orders of unusual size without distortion. Despite this problem, customers almost invariably demand and receive trade recommendations from the firms with which they deal in addition to the more reasonable basic data and current market information. The fact that long-term success is virtually impossible does not seem to deter many customers or sales forces from demanding specific trading advice. It is interesting to note in passing that customers who ask for valid and specific records covering significant periods of time are far more likely to receive a reason why the records are not available than to receive the records themselves. The sales representatives should be aware that customers who follow a firm's recommendations precisely over a period of time are quite likely to lose money and virtually certain to blame them for their losses. If they make money, customers are likely to credit their own ability to select trades wisely.

Prospect Knowledge

Identification of potential futures clients is difficult except in a most general way. Many surveys have been conducted by financial publications and futures exchanges. The Chicago Board of Trade surveyed 60 of its member firms and published a summary of the responses in *A Profile of the U.S. Futures Market* in October 1983. It concluded that there were about 200,000 active speculative accounts. Over half of the traders were over 50 years old, and over two-thirds were college graduates, of whom about half held advanced degrees. Most had incomes well beyond the national average. The largest groups classed by occupation were farmers and engineers. Over half the traders were self-employed. Most traders (96 percent) were male, and 80 percent were married.

Although efforts to describe the potential clientele for a business are laudable, the wide band of characteristics attributed to the trader to date is too general to be really useful to sales representatives. Pure conjecture would lead one to such conclusions as "Potential clients should have adequate resources," which would eliminate most young people, who have not yet had time to acquire speculative capital, as well as people in the oldest segment of the population, who are often more concerned, and properly so, with capital preservation than with growth. Farmers are familiar with futures. Engineers like trying their hands at developing trading systems. The excess of male traders harks back to the former practice of many brokerage firms of rejecting female accounts or, at least, discouraging business from women.

The job of all salespeople is to identify the buying motives of their clients and to present selling points that will appeal to those buying motives as much as possible. In a broad sense futures clients are motivated by some combination of the desire to make significant money and the desire to play an exciting game for the sake of playing it. The two most common conflicting motives with which registered commodity representatives must deal are greed and fear. Most investors would be glad to realize substantial gains from futures trading but are afraid to pay the price, namely, the risk of loss.

Registered commodity representatives should be prepared to give honest answers, whether the questions asked are actually asked or only implied. Most potential clients can be expected to ask what gains can be expected from successful trading. Sales representatives' answers should be based on something more than pure conjecture, hope, or selective perception but must in no way offer any assurances of profits. The sales representatives should realize that the fears expressed by prospective clients may not be their basic ones. Many people are concerned with possible substantial deficits, endless limit moves, or physical delivery of the future in which they are trading, but their real doubt is most likely based on simple ignorance or the apprehension attendant on losing money. They must be made to realize that the risk of loss must be accepted in any venture in which the profit potential exceeds the interest paid on a bank savings account. The sales representative should neither fan the greed nor quell the fear beyond reason but should try to contain both within reasonable bounds. Clients who expect to double their money monthly and others who are afraid that opening a small futures account could easily result in a foreclosure on their homes are equally guilty of faulty thinking and should be corrected.

One frequent problem centers on the question, expressed or implied, of the sales representative's own success in the futures markets. In effect, if the opportunities are as vast as often implied, why is he not rich himself? Handling this question is neither so difficult nor so embarrassing as one might think. Basically, the good sales representative deals with this question as with all others; that is, merely by telling the truth. One possibility, of course, is that he *is* rich and has accumulated his wealth by following his own advice. There are many others, however. The sales representative may be too young to have accumulated enough capital to justify speculating. He may be conservative in nature and more concerned with not losing than with the chance of winning. The sales representative, like any other customer of a financial firm, should adapt his financial merchandise to his own nature. It is also possible that he has a talent for guiding others, although he cannot play the game well himself. This situation is analogous to that of the athletic world, in which many excellent coaches have never been good players and many good players could never succeed as coaches. Other sales representatives feel that trading their own accounts would create a bias in their handling of clients' accounts and that they would have to make a choice between one direction or the other. They may conclude that in their own trading they would make important money 4 or 5 years out of 6, which is true of most successful professional traders, but that by handling accounts of others they will make reasonably good money 6 years out of 6.

The motivations and fears of their clients should be clear to the sales representatives. Both are described at considerable length in other chapters.

Skill in Selling

In addition to natural talent, some training is necessary to develop an effective sales representative. Procedures of the firm as well as the principles of selling must be learned. Some of this training is the responsibility of the firm employing the sales representative, although this responsibility is frequently abdicated by having inadequate classes conducted by people who have little more expertise in the subjects taught than the trainees themselves or by those with expertise but without the ability to teach. Regardless of the quality of their firms' training, sales representatives should be willing to improve themselves by learning what they can about the futures area and how to present themselves and their ideas effectively.

The principles of describing the product, meeting a client's objections, and closing sales in futures positions are similar to those in selling any intangible product and are not presented here in detail. Most of them can be handled merely by knowing enough about the field to answer questions and making suggestions reasonably and honestly. Prospecting for new clients is so important and, for some, so difficult that it warrants some discussion.

When thoroughly trained sales representatives have passed the necessary tests and obtained the required registrations, they are ready to begin prospecting. This is not a popular activity with most sales representatives, but in the investment business it is never ending. Not only would most sales representatives like to have the largest clientele possible, but they would also prefer to improve its quality.

Some sales managers reduce the subject of prospecting to its essentials: simply walk, talk, and meet the people. Finding customers thus becomes a simple numbers game. Approach enough people enough times and the result will be a number of interviews. Conduct enough interviews and the result will be the conversion of prospects into clients. Continue the process long enough and the result will be a large clientele of high quality. Basically, this philosophy of prospecting is quite correct, but new sales representatives may well question the source of all the people to whom they are supposed to walk and talk. If 10 contacts ultimately result in one interview and three interviews produce one new account, a hard-working sales representative can use up a great number of names within a short time. Replenishment of a real prospect list at a reasonable cost is not so simple as it may appear.

Some firms rely heavily on newspaper advertising, particularly of the kind that requires some sort of reply. Favorites include the coupon that is returned for literature, an invitation to call a sales representative who will provide desired information, and an invitation to a lecture. All of these usually provide names that result in new business and so are popular with sales representatives. For their employers who pay for the advertisements, however, this method is somewhat less popular. Although most people interested in trading futures read newspapers and magazines or watch television, most people, hence most readers or viewers, do not trade futures, and advertising rates must be high enough for the media to cover the costs of reaching their entire unspecialized audiences. A small number of publications and television stations are devoted entirely to securities and futures, but most of them appeal to those already engaged in investing rather than to potential investors. When the costs of preparing advertisements or television "shows" are considered in addition to the costs of following up leads developed from such media, the expenditures for each new name placed on a firm's prospect list may approach or even exceed the revenues reasonably expected to be gained from new accounts. Some of this may be justified by the firm's desire to engage in institutional advertising simply to keep its name before the public. When this motive is combined with the effort to gain new business, the total cost may be judged reasonable.

Lectures, often dignified by the title "seminar," are sometimes effective but are also sometimes delivered by the wrong speaker to the wrong audience. Not infrequently they are given by people new to the business who have not yet developed a clientele to an audience that has not formulated an approach to trading. Alternatively, they may be presented by more experienced sales representatives. Some may have changed locations or firms, and others may be trying to replace a clientele that has been lost or which must be constantly renewed because of attrition. There may or may not be a correlation between knowledge of trading and skill in making a presentation, but sometimes glibness is confused with wisdom, and some members of "seminar" audiences have been damaged by what they thought was sound advice. Even well-promoted, effectively delivered, and efficiently followed up lectures often result in the opening of only rather small, low-profit accounts, for sophisticated traders with large accounts seldom feel the need to attend. Workshops held regularly once or twice a week at the same location to examine current markets in a professional manner (not merely by indicating trend lines on a chart with a pointer) have proved quite successful for some brokers at a reasonable cost. The same prospective clients may return several times, thus allowing time for confidence to build, and they may bring friends. In addition, workshops tend to appeal more than general lectures to serious students of the market.

Conducting a seminar is a skill in itself and deserves some thought. Certainly the lecture should be carefully planned in every detail. A trader who will learn sooner or later that a well-prepared plan is the key to successful trading can hardly be impressed by a meeting at which the microphone does not work, the reading material is in short supply, the slides are shown upside down, or the number of chairs provided differs substantially from the size of the audience. Some problems can be avoided by asking for reservations by coupon or telephone. Although some who make reservations will not appear and others will come without reservations, a good approximation is at least possible. Some way of obtaining names and addresses inoffensively must be arranged if the productivity of the lecture is not to be defeated. Those who attend can sign in at the door, or a door prize can be offered. Names and addresses can be written on the ticket stubs to be drawn.

If the audience contains people of varying degrees of sophistication, the level of the talk should be determined by the least knowledgeable, but the talk must move fast enough to hold the attention of those who are more familiar with the markets. If analogies are used, the speaker should be careful to go from the familiar to the unfamiliar and not from one unfamiliar activity to another. Slide projections should be large enough to be seen clearly by those at the back and along the sides of the room. Questions should be answered at the end of the presentation to avoid breaking its continuity by permitting diversion into areas of interest to only small segments of the audience. When questions are allowed, answers should be concise. Long-windedness tends to stifle questions from other prospects who might open accounts if they could get just one more answer but are afraid that a question will result in another 20-minute speech and that they will never get home. Sixty seconds for each answer is usually long enough.

It is wise for speakers to consider in advance the most frequent objections to their products. If objections can be turned into selling points by treating the objectionable aspects to better advantage, then sales representatives have nothing to fear if they know their material and their answers are ready and well phrased. If questions that are difficult to treat favorably are expected, speakers can do much to lessen or forestall their adverse effect by raising them themselves before the audience does and by phrasing them as favorably as possible. Typical questions might involve the delivery of the cash commodity, the tremendous adversity that might be caused by a series of adverse limit moves, the unusual metal and interest rate markets of a few years ago, or the advantages and disadvantages of trading options rather than futures contracts.

Mass mailing undoubtedly brings in leads but has most of the disadvantages of advertising in mass media, especially the high cost per lead. Because traders have so few common characteristics other than speculative capital and a willingness to accept a risk, it is most difficult to define a mailing list that could prove especially useful, even presuming its availability. Lists of doctors, dentists, airline pilots, and those who have written to exchanges for information are especially overworked. Even sales representatives who "work a list" often do so ineffectively. It is important to keep good records when contacts are made, eliminating names only when accounts are opened or when it becomes evident that they never will be. Too often a sales representative is unwilling to approach prospects who would become accounts only after four, five, or even more contacts. It is usually unwise to attempt to sell accounts or positions to people by mail or telephone. It is more productive to rely on interviews, during which the sale of an account is easier. It is also easier to determine whether a prospect would make a suitable account at a face-to-face meeting.

Unannounced personal calls are unquestionably sometimes effectively made but are generally unpopular both with prospects and with sales representatives. Prospects, especially busy ones, often resent being disturbed at a time conventient only to the sales representative, and many sales representatives believe that the time consumed in seeking out a qualified prospect is beyond reason, especially in large cities. In addition, it places the sales representatives in a difficult psychological position. They are selling a trading activity that is supposed to present a handsome profit potential while they themselves are walking door-to-door looking for customers. Any attempt to explain this away because one is new in the business is futile, for customers will soon realize that they can pay their commissions to a sales representative who is too well established to take the time to ring doorbells.

A more effective way to meet people is by personal radiation; that is, by joining and working in various organizations and gaining the friendship and respect of other members who might open accounts. It is important, of course, not to become an obvious "glad-hander" who is usually more avoided than patronized.

Many new sales representatives believe that the difficult task of building a list of clients will take only a few months and that after a brief period a substantial clientele can be relied on to provide a good lifetime income with the commissions they will pay. This, however, is not the case. Attrition among traders, especially after a few recommendations have worked out badly, is the rule and not the exception. Referrals by satisfied clients provide less business than might be expected. Losers rarely make any. Even winners are sometimes reluctant to suggest highly speculative ventures to their friends for fear that they will be held accountable for any losses suffered and ultimately lose their friends with no hope of personal gain. (This fear is probably well founded.)

Sales representatives employed by full-line wire houses are often able to convert some of their stock clients into futures clients. Such conversions typically account for about 70 percent of the traders in futures, but although speculators in the securities markets are an obvious source of clients, they are also a source of a number of problems. Sometimes sales representatives become overenthusiastic about the opportunities in futures trading and induce stock clients to trade futures for whom futures trading is unsuitable, and sometimes they overestimate the skill involved in their own or their firms' short-term success in selecting futures positions and underestimate the risk, after which the clients claim misrepresentation. Even in the case of a speculatively inclined client for whom futures trading is suitable it frequently happens that an unsuccessful venture into futures trading on a relatively small scale ultimately causes the loss of the larger stock account, which might well have proved profitable over a period of years. It is for this reason that many executives of brokerage firms look unfavorably at such conversions. Some will separate security and futures activities completely by having different sales representatives handle the different products or even by maintaining entirely separate futures and stock offices. Some will eliminate futures trading from their firm's portfolio of products altogether, which might, however, cause a stock account to be lost to another firm offering a greater variety of financial merchandise.

MAINTAINING A FUTURES CLIENTELE

The ideal way to maintain a profitable futures clientele would be to provide a continuous stream of highly profitable trade suggestions. If sales representatives can do this, they will not need to be unduly concerned with servicing their clienteles because they will have difficulty losing a customer, even intentionally. Registered commodity representatives who have a trading method that has been validated in real time or who have a high degree of market judgment that permits them to select the positions of others will easily build and retain a substantial clientele. Just as surely the sales representatives who pass on shallow opinions based on superficial observations of a quote board, tape, or naive chart cannot in a real sense succeed. Depending entirely on good trading results to maintain a futures clientele will seldom lead to success. If sales representatives suggest unprofitable trades, they will, of course, lose their clients because the clients will lose their money, their faith, or both. Even if the clients select their own positions, the sales representatives will lose them sooner or later either because they will lose their capital or because they will find a way to justify blaming the sales representatives and their firms for the results, although neither had much to do with them. There are, however, some positive courses of action that sales representatives can follow that will help them maintain their clienteles.

The registered commodity representatives of most wire houses have a full line of merchandise. They should not induce their clients to trade in the parts of their line that they prefer either because they are most profitable to them or because they fit their personal biases. Neither should they attempt to persuade their clients to avoid trading in areas in which they themselves have not been successful. Sales representatives handling investment and speculative vehicles would do well, in the long run, as would sales representatives handling anything else, to adapt their product line to the wishes and needs of their clients rather than to adapt the clients to the items they prefer to sell. They should be careful neither to exaggerate nor to understate the profit potential of their security or futures lines. Sales representatives who speak convincingly of annual expectations of 100 percent or more will undoubtedly open many accounts but will just as surely lose them when it becomes evident that they cannot possibly meet the standards they have set for their own performance. Understating objectives can be just as harmful to clients who have invested a small amount of money in a conservative venture yielding a small return when they might have made a greater gain in a more speculative venture. It is always best for sales representatives to tell the truth about their merchandise, as far as they know it, and not attempt to expound when they do not know the facts. They must stop short of the point at which the clients make their own decisions concerning the amount of risk to take. Sales representatives should make every effort to provide honest guidance, but they should never try to be their brother's keeper.

As far as possible, sales representatives should avoid becoming personally responsible for trades. Some may feel that the role of order taker is below their dignity and prefer to insert themselves into trades suggested by their research departments or by their customers, but this is seldom wise. Those who do will learn sooner or later the truth of the aphorism "When I am right, no one remembers—when I am wrong, no one forgets."

SERVICING A FUTURES CLIENTELE

In the servicing of a clientele one of the least popular but most important tasks is record keeping. If a client asks what her position is or when she established it and at what prices, she is entitled to a prompt and correct answer. Sales representatives who are days behind in their posting or do not do it at all do not deserve the continued patronage of their clients. Failure to maintain accurate records can result not only in the justified loss of clients because of poor service but also in costly errors. One of the most important ledgers is the holding record, in which are entered the name, account number, telephone number, and market positions (including prices and dates) as they are taken and liquidated for each client. Entries should be posted in this record book as confirmations are received or, at worst, at the end of each day. It should be available and open to the client's page while the sales representative is speaking to the client. Relying on memory to fill an order can be a serious matter, and using an erroneous account number can have surprisingly grave results. The client who places the order will not get a confirmation and will suspect that his order was neither promptly nor properly handled. Another of the firm's clients who did not place an order will get a confirmation and will wonder whether trading is being carried on in his account without authorization. The back-office effort required to correct the error may cost the brokerage firm more money than it earned for its commission on the trade.

Much more serious, if a posting record is not maintained, is the possibility of allowing a client to think that she is liquidating a position previously liquidated, with the result that an unwanted position is created. A market order may be entered and an open order forgotten which, when filled later, can cause the same position to be established or liquidated twice. Misunderstandings in directions are easier if written records are not consulted. Sales representatives may find that they have tried to liquidate a short position by selling or a long position by buying. They will therefore have two positions instead of one. It may appear that the market will make the latter prove profitable half the time, but for some reason this seldom seems to work out. (Somehow, when someone drops a piece of toast onto the floor, it seems to have an uncanny way of landing buttered side down.) Losses incurred because of these or similar errors are almost invariably borne by the brokerage firm and, in turn, by the sales representatives themselves, at least in part. In most cases the sales representatives deserve their losses. With the advent of computerized record keeping and electronic communications, some of the problems discussed here have been alleviated by some firms, which send daily accounting to branch offices and often to individual sales representatives. Such records, often called "equity runs," indicate positions in each of a sales representative's accounts, including such information as the credit balance, the price at which each open position was established, the margin in use, and the margin excess or deficiency. Such information can eliminate many problems if it is accurate and if it is utilized by the sales representative.

It is also wise for sales representatives to maintain a cross-file organized by futures in order, if they wish, to determine quickly which of their clients or prospects is interested in a given future. This record is especially important in the servicing of clients who rely on the advice of a brokerage firm. If a client enters a position that the firm later recommends should be liquidated and is not called promptly, he will not react happily to the news that he has suffered a loss or lost his profit because the sales representative forgot that he had a position. When a sales representative posts an entry in a customer's file, it takes only a few extra minutes to post an entry in the cross-file. If the news wires, the financial journals, the government, or the firm itself releases any information that could be of interest to clients holding positions in various futures, it is easy for the sales representative to identify them and convey the information to them by mail or telephone. For the sales representative who is trying to increase the size of his clientele, it is also wise to post in his cross-file the positions of potential clients with whom he is in some communication and keep those clients informed of matters that are pertinent to them. His service may prove to be better than that offered by their present brokers, who may be taking their business for granted. Eventually some or all of this business may be acquired. If a sales representative ranks second on the lists of a large number of people who are determining where to place their business, she will ultimately receive a surprising number of accounts as the first choices fall out of favor. This happens frequently as customers become disenchanted with trade selections, when confirmations of trades are not received promptly or are considered to be unsatisfactory, when information is not passed on promptly or accurately, or when a check is not sent out quickly on request. Because a substantial number of traders have more than one account or have traded with more than one broker, being next in line can prove to be most lucrative.

Because most accounts are opened after several contacts, it is important to maintain a lead file. This may be no more than an alphabetic file of prospects, but it can prove to be invaluable. The best-organized files also have a tickler section organized by date. If a prospect suggests calling back at a later time when he expects to have raised some capital or to have returned from a trip, the sales representative can file his card under a future date to remind himself to call again at the proper time.

To service clients well, as well as to determine their suitability for trading, it is most important to establish what is expected when an account is opened. Some clients will prefer to follow the suggestions offered by the firm or the sales representative. It is necessary to find out what kind of information they will need and when and where they wish to be called. Some of them will ask the sales representative to enter trades for them all the time or when they cannot be reached, but if this is allowed by the firm, the understanding between the client and the broker should be quite clear. The understanding, of course, should be supported by any documentation required to avoid accusations of unauthorized discretion.

Other clients prefer to make their own decisions and do not care to be influenced even by comments about their own choices, much less have trades suggested to them. Presuming that such clients do not lose their money or decide to trade elsewhere for reasons beyond the control of the sales representative, all that the latter need do is provide good service. This involves little more than maintaining accurate records, confirming a client's trades promptly, entering orders properly, and making sure that the telephone is answered. A sales representative who has many clients of this kind would do well to form a partnership of some sort with another registered representative to make sure that his phone is answered at once when he is away from his desk or office or on vacation.

It is in handling self-traders that brokers are really able to excel. This is especially true of young brokers who find no need to explain away their lack of experience as they would have to do with a customer who demanded more detailed direction. All that is necessary is to have a good working knowledge of the procedures of the business and to observe and pass on currently important information and facts rather than offhand opinions, glib guesses, and bluffs. The client who makes her own decisions has the right to expect really outstanding personal service in return for the often significant commissions she pays. Sales representatives who limit themselves as much as possible to giving good service and passing on facts requested by their clients will not do so much business in the short run as their bolder counterparts who are willing to make specific suggestions, but they are quite likely to do more in the long run, build a better reputation, and sleep better at night.

Many sales representatives may be dissatisfied with a role that is little more than order taker, but reflection may convince them that it can be more important than it appears. If a sales representative has no reason to believe that neither her personal trade suggestions nor those of her firm will lead to long-term success, she is left with two functions that she can perform well, both of which are vital. One is the proper servicing of the customer's account. The other, which is even more important, is acting as a customer's alter ego to help jog him along the right road. For example, a customer may tell his sales representative that he believes that every position taken should be protected immediately with a stop order, yet he may omit placing such an order. The sales representative who asks "Where do you want your stop?" and causes one to be entered may be performing a service far more important than that done by the sales representative who calls his clients to tell them that wheat is acting well because it has been up for 2 days and that they should consider taking a long position.

Registered commodity representatives who guide their clients toward logical money management can make a vital contribution to their success. They can avoid reinforcing their clients' errors by acting as if all were well. If they do not know, they should say that they do not know. When clients show loser's characteristics, brokers can take steps to induce them to change their ways before it is too late. "You never go broke taking a profit" warns of taking short profits. "I'm locked in" warns of a person who will not take a loss. "I'll watch it" is a clear indication of a lack of planning, which is the most certain way to lose sooner or later. Sales representatives who learn the correct approach to trading, develop sufficient authority to warrant a hearing, and communicate well enough to deliver their messages effectively can build a rewarding futures clientele and serve and maintain it well.

APPENDIX
Preparation for the National Commodity Futures Examinations

The National Futures Association (NFA) Associated Persons Examination (Series 3) is required of anyone who wishes to become registered as a commodity solicitor with the regulated commodity exchanges in the United States. The test itself consists of multiple-choice and true-false questions. In its initial form, it consisted of 125 questions, and the examinees were given 2 hours to answer. A score of 70 percent was designated as a passing grade. The structure of the test is subject to change.

Examinees are provided with reading material and sample test questions by the brokerage houses that employ them and by the NFA. Although the test is periodically updated, there are 10 areas of knowledge that will prove to be of substantial assistance in passing the test.

1. *Government agencies and commodities exchanges.* The organization and responsibilities of many relevant government agencies and commodity exchanges, including the jurisdiction of key exchange committees, are examined.

2. *Glossary of futures markets terms.* A significant amount of time should be spent studying the general definitions of such terms as "normal," "carrying-charge," "inverted," "overbought," "oversold," and many others which describe price relationships and the behavior of the futures markets.

3. *Type and ownership of accounts.* The examinee should be familiar with the various methods of carrying commodity futures accounts and the legal aspects of the major alternatives.

4. *Speculation, hedging, gambling, and investing.* Some time should be devoted to defining these terms and comparing and contrasting their roles.

5. *Margin and margin calls.* The exam will include questions about setting margins and the responsibilities of the exchange, broker, and customer relating to margin activities.

6. *Technical versus fundamental analysis.* The applicant should be able to compare and contrast the elements of each approach to trade selection.

7. *Types of orders.* Study should include orders of all types—their wording, application, and limitations.

8. *Spreading.* The exam will emphasize the theory of spreading, including the types of spreads and their application.

9. *The soybean complex.* The examinee should understand the relationships in the complex, including the crush, reverse crush, and conversion equivalents between soybeans, soybean meal, and soybean oil contracts.

10. *Contract facts.* For each commodity the applicant should know

    contract size,
    reportable limit,
    position limit,
    commission,
    minimum and maximum allowable price fluctuation,
    whether regulated or unregulated,
    contract months traded,
    delivery procedure, including any special rules for retenders.

SAMPLE QUESTIONS

The following are typical questions asked on the exam. An answer key follows the questions (although there are undoubtedly those who would disagree with the answers suggested).

1. Which of the following is *not* necessary for handling a discretionary account?
    (a) Written approval of client before entry of each order
    (b) Written confirmation after the trade
    (c) Original authorization from the customer
    (d) All of the above
2. The basis is
    (a) The difference between one future price and another future price
    (b) The difference between cash and near future prices
    (c) The future price divided by the cash price
    (d) None of the above
3. The protection of customers' funds by special handling procedures is the responsibility of
    (a) The contract market
    (b) The clearinghouse
    (c) The commission market
    (d) The Commodity Futures Trading Commission
4. Every Monday figures are released on visible supplies, as compiled by the
    (a) CFTC
    (b) Clearinghouse
    (c) Chicago Board of Trade
    (d) Department of Agriculture
5. A soybean processor who buys beans and sells the products in the futures market would be placing a(n)
    (a) Reverse crush
    (b) Processor conversion
    (c) Crush hedge (putting on crush)
    (d) Intermarket spread

6. True or false: Speculation in commodities increases the range of price fluctuations.

7. True or false: Open interest in a given delivery month is the total long and short positions held in that month.

8. The CFTC is interested in all of the following except (more than one is possible)
   (a) Limits on maximum positions
   (b) The prohibition of price manipulation
   (c) Testing of all commodity solicitors
   (d) The designation of a futures market as a contract market
   (e) Protection of customers' funds
   (f) Commodity broker registration
   (g) Specification of commodities covered
   (h) Registration of futures commission merchants
   (i) Registration of floor brokers

9. True or false: Bona fide hedgers must abide by position limits.

Answer Key

1. a
2. b
3. a
4. c
5. c
6. False
7. False
8. c, f
9. False

It should be emphasized that there is no necessary correlation between the passing of the examination and the ability to handle commodity accounts effectively. As in many other fields, the examinee often treats the test as a barrier that must be hurdled, not as an indication of real competence or as a substitute for experience.

16

Compliance:
I'll See You
in Court

*"The best way I know of to win an argument
is to start by being in the right."*
LORD HAILSHAM

INTRODUCTION

Trading in futures involves important sums of money. It also involves people. Inevitably, therefore, disputes occur. Some are honest differences of opinion. Some are not so honest. Some of the more common areas of dispute, their causes, and how they are resolved will be discussed here.

This is not a law book. It is not intended to compete with tomes on commodity and security law. It will not present long lists of case references. The thoughts contained herein, however, are based on experience and practical observation. Perhaps some readers of this book—brokers, customers, and even attorneys— might avoid a problem or help solve one by reading on.

SOURCES OF PROBLEMS AND
THEIR PREVENTION

Soliciting the Account

Representatives of commodity firms are basically sales representatives looking for business. Such representatives may be designated with a high-sounding title or euphemism, but they are sales representatives nevertheless. They are attempting to gain revenues for themselves and their firms. There is nothing wrong with this if it is done properly. There is considerable danger, however, if it is done improperly. Unlike most other sales representatives, those who sell futures are fiduciaries. Clients are asked to place trust and confidence in the sales representatives and their firms and are entitled to receive in return the utmost in good faith and fair dealing.

The Registered Commodity Representative. Those who solicit and accept futures business are supposed to be registered by the CFTC. This involves the granting of a license after approval of an application for registration and confirmation that a test has been passed. If sales representatives are not properly registered, their firms have considerable exposure if clients solicited by such sales representatives later complain of damage. Sometimes clerical personnel go beyond the routine giving of quotes and basic information and get into the areas of soliciting and handling accounts. Firms might be well advised to follow a rule of when in doubt, get employees registered.

It should be pointed out that registration in itself does not mean that sales representatives are honest and reliable or that they know what markets are going to do. Registration only means that their personal records are not too bad or at least that they have been deemed to be rehabilitated from past transgressions and that they have passed any examination required by the CFTC or any commodity exchanges. The government and the exchanges certainly intend registration to indicate that a person is qualified to deal with the public or, at least, that the person is not unqualified. Unfortunately, such a license also tends to indicate to some a high degree of credibility and respectability, which is not always deserved. Most disputes with customers involve sales representatives who are properly registered.

Representations. Potential customers are looking for someone who knows what markets are going to do so that they can make a large amount of money quickly from a small capital base. Although most sales representatives have no idea at all what markets are going to do, some are not above implying that they have excellent sources of valuable information. The combination of a customer and a sales representative whose ignorance of the markets differs only in some small degree can be quite dangerous and provides a potentially serious problem for both. If the sales representative professes to have no forecasting ability or sources, he will have difficulty opening most accounts that require more than order taking. If he indicates that he has inside information, that his research department is almost invariably correct, and that he and most of his accounts consistently make large amounts of money, he may find himself in great difficulty one day when asked to prove these points. He may learn the meaning of such ugly terms as "material misrepresentation" and "reasonable basis." The customer, of course, can be damaged by being lulled into underestimating risks and overestimating the size of potential rewards and the probability of obtaining them; the result is the loss of his capital.

The sales representative who makes a call, conducts a sales meeting ("seminar"), or mails literature really should not have a problem, nor should her potential customer. All the sales representative has to do is tell the truth. All the customer has to do is spend a little time investigating the reputation of the sales representative and her firm, understand their products, and remember that potentially large rewards entail risks equally as great or greater virtually without exception.

Opening the Account

Before a customer can trade futures, he or she must open an account with a brokerage house qualified to deal in futures. Most such brokerage houses are registered with the CFTC as futures commission merchants. Opening an account entails completing various documents and depositing funds. These subjects cannot be discussed exhaustively here, but at least the most common areas that lead to trouble can be identified and some solutions suggested.

Suitability.   Lack of suitability, real or alleged, is high on the list of trouble areas. The CFTC, neither through the act which created it nor through subsequent regulations, specifically requires that a customer be suitable. Those who conclude that suitability for trading futures is therefore not required of a customer, however, are almost certainly wrong. The CFTC has long considered suitability requirements and went so far as to have public hearings and request comments on the subject at least as long ago as 1977. When it failed to adopt a specified regulation, the commission indicated that it had been unable to formulate clear standards and that a specific rule would only serve to limit principles considered to be implicit in the Commodity Futures Trading Commission Act of 1974.

Suitability of customers trading securities has long been established by the "know your customer" rules of most major exchanges, by the Rules of Fair Practice of the National Association of Securities Dealers, and by custom. The latter is no small consideration. Custom, which arises out of well-established industry practices, is considered by many to have all the force of law, and this view is probably well taken. It is also possible that a brokerage firm may have a contractual duty to enforce the rules of the exchanges of which it is a member, and it may be bound further by common-law implications concerning fiduciaries. In that a brokerage firm is generally deemed to have a fiduciary relationship with its clients, a suitability requirement would also be deemed to exist. The degree of responsibility to establish suitability requirements probably varies depending upon whether orders are solicited or unsolicited.

Suitability is determined primarily by asking the customer questions and indicating answers on the new-account form or a customer information sheet, sometimes supplemented by credit reports. Although it is not unusual for the sales representative to complete the form, it is usual for the customer to sign it. It is not uncommon for a form to be completed in a cursory or hasty manner, with the result that disputes later arise as to what was said, who said it, and when it was said. Sometimes customers allege that sales representatives completed blank forms on the basis of pure conjecture after they (the customers) signed them. If sales representatives or their customers would complete the forms carefully and if the customers would sign only after reading what was filled in, a substantial number of problems would be avoided.

Suitability requirements basically fall into two areas. One of these involves financial capacity, and the other centers upon the objectives of the customer. Financial capacity is the easier of the two to deal with because it involvers quantitative factors, which always appeal to administrative and regulative minds. A beginning is total net worth. Many believe that the more assets one has, the more one can afford to risk. Many attempts have been made to break down total net worth into components of varying degrees of importance. The component of particular interest to brokers is liquid net worth, which, as the name implies, is available upon short notice. Houses, trust funds, furnishings, and automobiles are of value to the holders but are of little interest to brokers except under extreme circumstances. Cash and cash equivalents are of greater interest. How much of this liquid net worth is to be deposited in the brokerage account is of the greatest interest of all.

The second broad area of suitability is far more complex. A broker's recommendations should be consistent with the temperament, objectives, and needs of a customer. A customer, however, may say one thing today and another tomorrow depending upon the degree of success of his trading. His objectives and attitude may change as his fortunes improve or deteriorate or as he becomes more experienced, but brokerage firms seldom update the forms completed when an account is opened to indicate such changes. A broker has the obligation to know her customer every day and not just on the day that the account is opened. In the latter case the information written on account documents may become invalid with the passage of time.

It is usual to attempt to determine objectives on the basis of such obvious factors as age, education, dependents, employment, and home ownership, but this is not easy. As people get older, some become more conservative and some less. Education is not synonymous with wisdom or good judgment. Dependents may become more or less self-sufficient over time. Lack of employment may indicate that a client is on the brink of starvation, but it may also indicate that he has acquired sufficient wealth to allow the destruction of his alarm clock. Home ownership may be regarded by some as a financial burden and by others as a source of wealth if real estate values rise. Some people are intrinsically more aggressive financially than others, and they have every right to feel about their money as they choose. What is considered necessary by some people may be considered luxurious by others. In that people are often best judged by what they do rather than by what they say, it might be best for brokers to rely most strongly upon how customers have handled their financial affairs in the past.

Risk Letters.   It is always wise to maintain a paper trail where disputes are possible. Accordingly, it has long been usual for cautious brokers to require new customers to sign some kind of form indicating that they are aware of the financial risks of futures trading and even to request from time to time that customers indicate in writing that they are being treated satisfactorily. These procedures have been supplemented by the CFTC, which has prepared a formal risk disclosure statement covering five common areas of dispute which must be provided for a customer, dated, and signed by the customer before an account is opened. The customer's acknowledgment indicates that he or she has received the document and understands it. The language of the disclosure statement must be exactly as follows:

RISK DISCLOSURE STATEMENT

This statement is furnished to you because rule 1.55 of the Commodity Futures Trading Commission requires it.

The risk of loss in trading commodity futures contracts can be substantial. You should therefore carefully consider whether such trading is suitable for you in light of your financial condition. In considering whether to trade, you should be aware of the following:

(1) You may sustain a total loss of the initial margin funds and any additional funds that you deposit with your broker to establish or maintain a position in the commodity futures market. If the market moves against your position, you may be called upon by your broker to deposit a substantial amount of additional margin funds, on short notice, in order to maintain your position. If you do not provide the required funds within the prescribed time, your position may be liquidated at a loss, and you will be liable for any resulting deficit in your account.

(2) Under certain market conditions, you may find it difficult or impossible to liquidate a position. This can occur, for example, when the market makes a "limit move."

(3) Placing contingent orders, such as "stop-loss" or "stop-limit" order, will not necessarily limit your losses to the intended amounts, since market conditions may make it impossible to execute such orders.

(4) A "spread" position may not be less risky than a simple "long" or "short" position.

(5) The high degree of leverage that is often obtainable in futures trading because of the small margin requirements can work against you as well as for you. The use of leverage can lead to large losses as well as gains.

This brief statement cannot, of course, disclose all the risks and other significant aspects of the commodity markets. You should therefore carefully study futures trading before you trade.

Such letters have sometimes helped avoid disputes but not as often as they should have. Sometimes the broker neglects to get the letter signed, gets it signed after rather than before the account becomes active, or fails to retain it. The customer is supposed to understand the statement, not merely read and sign it. If the customer is rushed into signing the form without having a chance to absorb its meaning, the broker may have a legal exposure. This is especially true if the customer is not given a copy of the form. It is also important to note that the form may not cover all circumstances. Certain markets may entail risks which are peculiar to those markets, and this may not be clear from the risk letter. If there are special risks or other material items of information which warrant disclosure or if it appears that the customer did not really understand the risk statement, a signature alone would almost certainly not protect the broker.

Special Types of Accounts.   There are a large number of accounts which require special documentation. These include business accounts which involve partners' rights to act on behalf of one another, corporate accounts which involve the right of a corporation to trade futures and the question of who can act for it, trust accounts which have special restrictions, accounts of minors, joint accounts, and many others.

In every case, the means of avoiding trouble are virtually the same. Whatever should be disclosed should be disclosed fully and clearly. Papers should be completed accurately; understood and acknowledged by the client, who should be given copies; and approved by a supervisor. This approval should involve more than a routine skimming. Poor supervision is not excused by maintaining that there is too much for the supervisor to do.

Deposit of Funds. An important element of opening an account is the deposit of funds. As the relationship between a broker and a client matures, trust and confidence may well grow with it. Initially a broker would be well advised to have good funds in the account before trading begins, regardless of any financial data provided by the client. Most people are honest and reliable, but not all are. Futures trading may result in large profits or losses rather quickly. If a client suffers a large loss and then refuses to deposit money, the broker may find it difficult or impossible to cover the loss and may have to bear it himself. Even if money is eventually collected, getting it may prove to be a costly and time-consuming process.

The term "good money" is a term of art and is worth a few words of explanation. It means that funds are firmly in hand. Cash, cashier's checks, certified checks, and such negotiable government securities as are acceptable for margin purposes exemplify good money. Personal checks, promises to send such checks, and assurances that checks are in the mail are not good money. Brokers who do not have good money on hand at least for initial transactions in the accounts of new customers are taking risks not justified by their potential revenue from commissions.

The amount of money required to be on hand should be at least enough to meet the requirements of positions established, including enough to cover reasonable short-term adversity. Most brokerage houses require that a flat minimum amount be deposited to open an account. Although this amount may not need to be maintained, it at least indicates the ability of a client to make a deposit if required to do so.

If the funds deposited in the account are borrowed, the client's exposure to risk is increased, and this has suitability implications. If a broker knows her client, as she is expected to, it is not unreasonable that she at least should make an attempt to ascertain the source of funds deposited in an account.

Handling the Account

Although the relations between brokers and their clients have many gradations, there are three basic types. In the the first, the client makes all decisions, and the sales representative acts only as an order taker and record keeper. In this case, the fiduciary duties of the broker are minimal but still exist. They involve primarily but not exclusively the accurate and timely handling of orders and the proper administration of the client's account. At the other extreme, the client follows all or most of the sales representative's suggestions and provides little or no direction of his own. In this event the fiduciary responsibility and hence the exposure of the broker are high. The third possibility is the most common relationship, wherein the sales representative and the client compare ideas and action results from their joint inputs. Most but not all of what follows applies to the second and third types of relations.

Trade Suggestions.   If a sales representative suggests that a customer enter a futures position, the customer has no right to assume that a profit is guaranteed, although some people seem to think that this is the case. A sales representative can only offer his or her best judgment and represent it as such.

It is when sales representatives promise more than they can deliver that the basis for trouble is established. Sometimes a source of information is said to be far better than it really is. This is particularly true of technical devices, often of mysterious nature, which are said to have yielded large gains most of the time. Too often, it is impossible to locate all the people who were supposed to have reaped the benefit from the devices. The solution for this is quite simple. If sales representatives tell the truth, have a reasonable basis for a recommendation, and can document it, they rarely face any problem.

A second problem involving trade suggestions has to do with the sizes of positions recommended. A sales representative may recommend a position so large that it is later considered unsuitable for the client, who did not realize the exposure incurred. The recommendation may have been made in good faith, but that does not eliminate the problem. Almost any sales representative can attest to the maddening tendency of recommended trades to fail immediately after the completion of a major campaign, thereby wiping out his entire clientele, but to succeed when only one contract has been placed and that in the account of his brother-in-law, whom he does not like much anyhow.

Documentation of Orders.   When an order had been placed by a customer, whether it was solicited or not, it should be written down and a record immediately made of the time. The order should then be sent promptly to the proper exchange, and the time that it was sent should be immediately recorded. If the order is filled, canceled, or changed, again, a record of the time should be made immediately. Three time stamps are the usual minimum that any order requires. Although mechanics may vary with the firm's procedure, these time notations should be made promptly and accurately, whether done by the sales representative, a wire operator, or exchange floor personnel.

Failure to transmit orders promptly and accurately provides the opportunity for many types of disputes, some involving mere negligence but others, outright fraud. A delay in transmitting a market order may cause a loss because of a price movement during the delay. Of course, the delay may also cause the order to be filled at a better price, and one would think that this problem would average out, but it does not. It has been said that when one drops a piece of toast, the probability is that it will land buttered side down and that this probability increases directly with the cost of the carpet. So it goes with delayed orders. If a limit order is delayed, matters are even worse because the market may be missed altogether.

Orders should be completed before being sent. They should not be transmitted without account numbers or sent in bulk. Incomplete orders provide the opportunity to assign account numbers after the market has moved enough to establish a significant profit or loss in some cases. Sales representatives are then in a position to assign profits to favored customers, including themselves, and to assign losses to those less fortunate. Changing account numbers after an order is filled provides the opportunity for similar abuses or, at least, their appearance.

The solution for most of these problems is for orders to be completed and time-stamped properly and for supervisors to make certain that brokers and clerical personnel are not permitted to engage in loose or questionable procedures. Changes in orders should be satisfactorily explained and documented. The orders and related documentation should then be preserved for no less than 5 years.

Discretion.   The securities markets generally permit time or price discretion by the broker without a formal power of attorney (trading authority). Some futures exchanges, however, permit no discretion whatever without formal authority. Sometimes a broker, having had a long and good relationship with a client, will make trades without authority. This is done at the broker's peril. If there is no power of attorney, any degree of discretion is unauthorized and constitutes a violation of the exchange rules and industry custom. Given enough monetary incentive, even the friendliest client can become quite unfriendly on short notice. Sales representatives who bend the rules may merely be attempting to do their best to serve their clients, but they are taking a risk far beyond any possible reward.

Most problems in this area may be avoided by a broker if no discretion is taken without a properly executed and current trading authority. Of course, the trading authority itself may lead to other problems, which will be noted below. In addition, an unscrupulous client may accuse a sales representative of using discretion when this was not the case. The latter could be eliminated or sharply reduced if brokers generally chose to record or log all telephone calls in a legal manner, but many, especially major firms, consider this to be somehow unprofessional and believe it would be resented by clients. Such recording might lower revenues somewhat, unless all brokers did it, but legal exposure would certainly be reduced if sales representatives and clients knew that telephone calls could be reconstructed.

Record Keeping.   Clients are supposed to receive accurate confirmations of all trades as well as purchase and sale agreements promptly. In addition, they get periodic reports of the status of their accounts, usually monthly, indicating at least the cash balance, the open positions, and the equity. These and any other communications should be reviewed shortly after being received and the broker notified of any discrepancies.

Sales representatives are usually provided with a daily equity run indicating the status of all accounts handled by them, including open positions and the margin excesses or deficiencies. Some keep individual records organized by client or by individual future so that they can inform clients of any relevant news items. Brokers who are especially bright or battle-scarred sometimes keep accurate telephone logs and copies of letters mailed to clients confirming their understanding of how an account should be handled. In the event of a dispute, such records are of great value, but because brokers tend to be sales rather than bookkeeping types, many tend to be quite lax about maintaining such paper trails, sometimes to their great regret.

Churning. There are so many disputes involving churning, real and alleged, that the subject deserves careful attention. Futures trading is usually short-term in nature. It therefore frequently results in a large number of transactions in a short period. Each transaction results in a commission. Many clients who lose money tend to blame the broker and resent the commissions. It is only one more step to accuse the broker of initiating the trades primarily to generate the commissions. Abuse of a client's account by excessive trading in order to increase the broker's profit is churning. Such conduct can create great financial exposure for a broker, ranging from the return of all commissions to large assessments of damages. The latter might include money lost, money which might have been made (benefit of the bargain), or even punitive assessments well in excess of what was lost. Along with outright gross misrepresentations, churning probably ranks among the most dangerous practices by a broker.

Generally, churning involves three necessary conditions: benefit to the broker, excessive trading, and control by the broker. The first of these is usually obvious. If the sales representative benefits from the commissions, either directly or by achieving a higher salary level, larger bonuses, or more job security, he or she profits from churning.

Excessive trading deserves somewhat more consideration. It is tempting to measure excessiveness quantitatively. Typical measures are commissions paid, the number of transactions, and the turnover of capital. If these numbers are large, they are quite useful for impressing judges, hearing officers, and juries, as well they should be.

There is, however, no law of the Medes or Persians to indicate that "excessive" and "many" are synonymous terms. "Excessive" simply means "too many." If one trade is deemed to be unreasonable because it was made for no good reason, it could undoubtedly support a churning allegation. This is not to say, of course, that most churning cases have been and will probably continue to be based on a large volume of transactions.

It is on the third element of churning, namely control, that most cases in this area tend to center. If a broker has a power of attorney which is exercised regularly, control is probable. This fact alone might be reason enough for a broker not to accept such a power. If a broker does not have a power of attorney and has not exercised discretion without authority, the establishment of control must be determined on a case-by-case basis.

Barring authorized or unauthorized discretion, control must be determined by ascertaining how much influence the sales representative has over the client. This does not require any Svengali-Trilby type of relationship; rather, it requires dominance through force of personality or the client's assumption that he knows so little and the broker so much that there is no point in meddling. Control by the broker may be assumed if the broker has suggested all or almost all transactions and all or most of these were accepted by the client with none or few being rejected unless it is clear that the client has sufficient capacity to disagree but chooses to acquiesce to the broker's suggestions.

The three elements above are all that need to be proved to indicate churning, but trading patterns in the account may be utilized to reinforce the suspicion of this abuse. The more common of such patterns include average losses of larger dollar amounts than average profits; losing trades that are typically held longer than winning trades; more frequent trades and the largest losses occurring late in the account's history; few contacts with the client that are initiated by the sales representative, especially when the client is losing; frequent spreading with small profit potentials or to avoid realizing losses; more trading activity than in accounts not controlled by the same sales representative; and notification of adverse trading results that is delayed or misrepresented by the sales representative. If there are a substantial number of day trades in a churned account, typically most will show profits.

Although determining that an account has been churned is not an exact science because some of the above trading patterns may also occur in accounts controlled by the client, it is surprising to note how many of these elements are present in cases where an account has been determined to have been churned.

Margins.   In the securities area, margins are set by the Federal Reserve Board of Governors, although the requirements may be increased by exchanges, individual brokerage houses, or both. In addition, actions to be taken by the brokerage house in the event of deficiencies are clearly defined. In the futures business, the rules are somewhat more flexible and, in some areas, downright vague.

Minimum margins are set and changed by the exchanges in response to volatility, but there is no consistent formula for establishing them. In the event of substantial impairment, additional margin must be deposited, but it is not always clear how long the client has to deposit funds or what happens if she does not. As a result the stage is set for many kinds of conflicts. If margin is demanded without justification or too quickly, the client may be forced out of a position which will then, of course, immediately move in her favor. If margin should have been collected but was not, the position seemingly will inevitably continue to move against the client, who will now maintain that she should not have been permitted to remain in the market and was therefore further damaged by not being forced out.

Day trading creates an especially interesting problem because exchange clearinghouses compute margins only at the close of the trading day, so under exchange rules at least, the day-trading customer has no obligation to deposit anything except the amount of any losses incurred. Although brokers appreciate the commissions being generated on little or no capital, they are aware that a customer who day-trades might one day move too slowly to exit a market before it closes or, worse, be trapped by an adverse limit move. In order to assure liquidity and good faith on the part of the customer, most brokerage firms have a requirement that the original margin for day trades be deposited in whole or in part, even though the trades are opened and closed out on the same day. The amount of the requirement varies widely from firm to firm, and the strictness of the enforcement of this rule against active accounts varies even more.

Disputes involving margin are almost impossible to prevent under present conditions, but they could be reduced somewhat by careful training of sales representatives, rigid supervision practices, and the enforcement of such rules as there are. A client should certainly have some idea of whether he is going to have to deposit funds, and if he has to, he should know by when and in what form. He should not have a position unreasonably liquidated despite the right given brokerage houses by most account agreements to liquidate when they feel the need to do so. Although he is not assured of being notified of liquidation in advance, he should be certain that once a liquidation is threatened, it is carried out to whatever degree necessary and is done when it is supposed to be done.

Some customers become quite perturbed when exchanges raise margin requirements retroactively or when an undermargined account must be restored not just to its maintenance level but to its full original level. The first of these, however, is not unusual, and the latter is universal.

Dealing with Irreconcilable Differences

Regardless of the effort made by a brokerage house in selecting, training, and supervising its sales representatives, disputes in the futures business will continue. Good practices and precautions can eliminate some problems and reduce the amount of exposure in others, but so long as some people, brokerage house employees and customers alike, make mistakes or are dishonest, disputes will happen.

A summary of what each side should consider doing or not doing in case of a conflict might be helpful.

The Complaint.   A client who thinks he has been wronged usually complains first to his sales representative, who usually, but not always, reports the problem to his supervisor. Sometimes, however, the broker himself is aware that he himself has caused the problem, in which case he might make every effort to avoid reporting the problem to anyone. In such cases, the broker might try to lull the customer by assuring him of better days ahead. This presents considerable danger to the customer, who might be told later that he has given up his rights by ratifying the actions of the broker. Ratification usually means that a client was wronged but waited too long to act after he became aware of a problem and understood that he was wronged; it is said that he gave up his rights by knowingly accepting the situation. Brokers, of course, are quite aware that some clients tend to accept bad situations temporarily to see how matters develop, meanwhile planning to act only if matters get worse. This, of course, is unfair to the broker, who will correctly maintain that the customer was obligated to mitigate damage by complaining promptly upon learning of and understanding any alleged mistreatment.

If the broker does as he should and reports to his supervisor, he should be required to submit a detailed written report of his view of what transpired as quickly as possible. From the firm's standpoint, this has many benefits. The story is complete and timely if the sales representative is forthright. It also protects the firm in the event that the sales representative leaves the firm under unfriendly circumstances, has a memory shorter than that of the client, or becomes physically or mentally incapacitated, possibly by being attacked by the client. It might prove wise for the firm to ask that the sales representative's narrative be addressed to the firm's attorney or to a member of its legal department who is an attorney in good standing. This will assure that the document will be considered a privileged communication.

Many disputes can be settled by or through the firm's local management. In many cases, enough goodwill can be retained to allow retention of the customer's account. If a customer senses that a dispute will require formal legal action, she should beware of continuing to deal with the same firm and especially with the same sales representative because of the danger that she will later be deemed to have ratified the situation and thereby be estopped from pursuing her case.

Legal Action. If a complaint to management does not get results, a customer may well next call in an attorney. Although there is all too often no winner of a dispute past this point aside from the attorney, there are few alternative actions open to a customer. As is usually the case, except when a small claim is involved, expert help is almost certainly needed if the customer is to prevail. If an attorney has now entered the fray, and if the client chose the attorney more wisely than she chose her broker, neither should need this book for help past that point, but it might be useful to close with a brief summary of where matters may go next.

The Formal Demand. The client who engages an attorney will tell him the events that led to his problem with the broker and negotiate an arrangement with the lawyer. This might involve the payment of fees based on time or a payment contingent upon results plus expenses. Specifics depend upon such factors as the quality of the case, the quality of the attorney, and the negotiating power of the parties. If the customer has lost enough money, of course, the contingency arrangement might be the only route open to him. This may still leave a problem having to do with the necessary expenses that are likely to be incurred. An established attorney with faith in his ability might be willing to deal with or even enthusiastic about a contingency arrangement in a major dispute, but he might be less enthusiastic about spending his own money.

Typically the first step taken by the attorney is to send a formal demand letter to the brokerage house threatening action by a given date if satisfaction is not provided. The brokerage house might respond with an offer or not respond at all, but usually it will have its own attorney or in-house counsel answer the letter denying any wrongdoing. It will hope that the client will then drop the matter, run out of money, or get hit by a meteorite. The brokerage house might also be convinced, and perhaps be correct in its conviction, that it really was in the right and that the client has been afflicted by a heavy diet of sour grapes. Usually the client pursues the matter.

The Arenas. Basically, the client, advised by his attorney, will select arbitration, reparations, or a court to make his claim. Sometimes, the account papers that a client signed with the brokerage house limit the client's choices in the matter.

His choice of the arena should be carefully discussed with his attorney. There may be considerable differences in cost, the time required to wait for a hearing, and the amount that may be collected. This decision must not be made lightly.

The laws, rules, or regulations deemed to have been violated may affect the arena chosen for hearing the dispute. There are federal laws resulting from the Commodity Exchange Act of 1922 and the CFTC Act of 1974. There are many federal securities laws which attorneys sometimes attempt to utilize in commodity cases. The rules of the exchanges are said to have the force of law, as is trade custom. Common law may be invoked to establish breach of fiduciary duty or fraud. The various states also have laws which may be applied to commodities cases. And individual brokerage houses may even be taken to task for failing to enforce their own rules. Although there is no private right of action for the latter, probably because this would encourage brokerage houses to have no rules, failure to follow rules might well be considered substandard to trade custom.

The CFTC has a reparations procedure which is relatively inexpensive and has a reputation for fairness to both parties. With the small number of administrative judges, however, there is often a large backlog of cases, so the concept of a rapid hearing of disputes has not worked as well as had been hoped. The limited budget allocated to the CFTC has also reduced the ability of the judges to travel extensively, so clients may be forced to pay considerable travel costs for themselves, attorneys, and witnesses.

Some of these problems may be alleviated by the use of arbitration. Arbitrators may be provided by futures or stock exchanges, the National Association of Securities Dealers, the National Futures Association, the American Arbitration Association, or a court. There are said to be material differences among these in costs and waiting times and perhaps even different degrees of possible bias. Generally, however, arbitration may be arranged quickly at a reasonable cost, and a decision in good faith may be expected relatively soon.

If a court trial is chosen, it must be determined whether a state or federal court will be used. This depends largely upon which rules or laws cover the major allegations, although the geographic location of the court may also be a consideration. Major disputes tend to reach a court, especially if the customer is seeking punitive damages. Such actions tend to be the slowest and most expensive, and they place the most stress upon the parties, but alas, even here, risk and reward, as always, seem to go hand in hand.

NOTES FROM A TRADER

It is rare for either a customer or his or her broker to emerge from a dispute with a profit, and engaging in disputes is not the most rewarding use of one's time anyhow. It would appear best for both parties to avoid trouble in the first place. But how? Herewith some ideas for the customer and the broker to think about.

The Customer

Patronize a reputable brokerage house. Select a registered commodity representative with scruples as well as sophistication. There is no need to hurry into the market. It will reopen on the next trading day. Read all documents carefully before signing them. If anything is unclear, ask questions. Sign nothing in blank. Ask for copies and preserve them. If representations are made, take notes. Date them and preserve them too. Read confirmations and statements. If they are not accurate, complain promptly in writing and keep a copy of your complaint. If you selected your broker wisely, you should not need an attorney, but if you do, get a good one. Let the recent law school graduate practice on someone else. You have trouble enough.

The Broker

Your firm has or should have a compliance manual. It has practices that are recommended probably because of the bitter experiences of someone else. Follow its rules and guidelines. Complete new-account forms fully and carefully, and make sure that they are understood by the client. Give the client copies. If you make representations and have some feeling that the client is hearing only about the rewards and not the risks, write the client a letter summarizing what was said. The word "risk" and its synonyms should be mentioned more often than the word "reward" and its synonyms. Keep a copy. If you hate to spend time keeping a calendar, customer and position records, and a telephone log, keep them anyhow. Do not avoid a customer or the margin department when the markets are mistreating you. If there is trouble, hope that it was not caused by you, but whether it was or not, tell your superiors about it immediately. They know all about the rampant disease called "Buyer's Remorse" and will justifiably have little sympathy for a sales representative who causes problems and much less for one who magnifies them by attempting to conceal them. Full disclosure, honest representations, and a paper trail prevent most problems with clients whose memories might prove to be otherwise unduly flexible.

Further your affiant saith not.

PART 5

Choosing
the Game—
Markets

To profit from using the futures and futures options markets,
speculators must know, in general, how the markets operate, the
regulations surrounding these markets, general methods for
analyzing the markets, and how to monitor their investments.
Speculators must also know something about the specific market in
which they are investing, whether beans, bonds, bellies, or bills. That
is, in the final analysis, the decision-making process, or playing the
game, eventually extends to the individual futures contract in which
a commitment is to be made. Because the factors that affect the
prices of copper and corn, for example, are nearly independent, there
is good reason to employ the term "markets for futures" rather than
"the futures market." Chapters 18 through 22 describe and analyze
the active futures contracts. Basically, each future is discussed
within a common framework, which includes the supply, utilization,
price determinants, seasonal effects, and futures contracts of each
market. Futures contracts are generally grouped by their general
type along with other futures contracts of the same type. The
information given, although not exhaustive, provides the trader or
broker with a good grasp of the significant elements that affect
prices. It is important to note that different techniques may be
illustrated in different chapters for individual commodities; however,

the technique for one commodity is transferable to the others. For example, the seasonal analyses for soybeans and pork bellies may be applied as well to wheat or cattle. Similarly, the regression analyses applied to cocoa, gold, and stock index futures should not be viewed as unique to those commodities.

There is a "Sources of Information" section for each specific futures contract. In addition, Chapter 17, "General Sources of Information," provides a summary of the general sources of information that apply to several or all futures contracts.

The specific groups of futures contracts discussed are:

The soybean complex and grains (Chapter 18)
Meats (Chapter 19)
Natural resources: metals and petroleum (Chapter 20)
Financial futures (Chapter 21)
A potpourri of commodities (Chapter 22)

17

General Sources
of Information

BROKER: *That's a great point. I have a*
perfect story to illustrate your point.
CUSTOMER (after the story): *That's a great*
story, but it doesn't illustrate my point.
Why don't you change your story?
BROKER: *I don't have another story. Why*
don't you change your point?

Many brokers refuse to change their story, no matter what the customer's point is, because they do not have another story. This chapter provides general sources of information about futures and related options contracts so that brokers can develop a story about any of their customers' points.

Only general sources of information which relate to all or many of the various types of futures contracts are provided in this chapter. The following chapters on specific futures contracts provide sources of information that are specific to those types of futures and related options contracts.

PERIODICALS

Daily and weekly newspapers and magazines are valuable and timely sources of information. *The Wall Street Journal,* in addition to providing daily data (current prices, volumes, open interests, daily/high/low/life-of-contract prices, etc.) for all futures and related options markets, provides market commentary and interpretation in its regular column "Futures Markets" and in irregular articles. *Barron's* provides market data and market comment and interpretation on a weekly basis. The regular section on commodities, "Commodities Corner," and the regular section on options, "The Strike Price," are particularly informative. The *Journal of Commerce,* a weekly, also covers the futures markets on a regular basis. It provides data, market analysis, and a discussion of regulatory and exchange issues.

Although many local daily newspapers provide market data and market comment, *The New York Times* "Business Day" is particularly good (this emphasis may reflect only that one of the co-authors works in New York). It provides rather detailed data on the futures contracts, and its regular "Futures/Options" section, as well as frequent special articles, is also informative. Other local newspapers should also be followed, particularly in cities that are in the products' producing areas.

There are two valuable monthly periodicals devoted to the futures and options markets. The first is *Futures* magazine (formerly *Commodities*), which provides articles on the futures and options markets, in addition to regularly tracking the performance of commodity pools and reporting on people and exchanges in the futures and options industry. The second is the newer periodical *Intermarket,* which publishes analytical and descriptive articles on the futures and options markets.

Among the magazines, *Forbes* has a regular feature on futures, "Commodities," which provides specific trading strategies for various futures contracts and periodically provides a track record. *Business Week* covers various products underlying futures contracts on an irregular basis. Other business-oriented magazines, such as *Fortune* and *Dunn's Review,* also cover the futures markets on an irregular basis.

The Commodity Research Bureau (Jersey City, N.J.) provides statistics and charts for most commodities as well as its widely accepted indicator of the commodity markets, the CRB Index.

Commodity Yearbook, an annual publication, is an invaluable reference which contains considerable data and also reviews developments in production, demand, international trade, government policies, and futures trading related to all commodities and financial assets underlying futures contracts over recent history.

An excellent journal devoted to the futures markets, *The Journal of Futures Markets* (John Wiley & Sons, Center for the Study of Futures Markets, Columbia University, New York), publishes both practical and theoretical articles on the futures and options markets. The journal provides a valuable meeting place for academics and practitioners. The Center for the Study of Futures Markets at Columbia University provides special academic research reports on various aspects of the futures and options markets.

An excellent reference book on futures markets is *Handbook of Futures Markets: Commodity, Financial, Stock Index, and Options* by Perry J. Kaufman, editor (John Wiley & Sons, New York, 1984). This book contains articles by different authors on specific futures contracts and on futures market techniques.

General encyclopedias also provide excellent discussions of the nature of supply and production and utilization of various commodities.

GOVERNMENT AND REGULATORY AGENCIES

Many government agencies, such as the U.S. Department of Agriculture, the Board of Governors of the Federal Reserve System, and the Securities and Exchange Commission, provide publications on specific futures markets. (Many of these publications are mentioned in the following five chapters on specific futures contracts.) Most of these publications are available from the U.S. Government Printing Office, Washington, D.C. 20401. This section considers only general publications on the futures markets.

The following lists of U.S. government commodity and crop reports are arranged by commodity and show the approximate dates of release.

U.S. Grains

1. Stocks in all positions, all grains—quarterly, about the 22d of January, April, June, October (soybeans excluded in October)
2. Planting intentions, spring crops—January 22 and April 15
3. Winter wheat production—monthly, May 10 through October 10
4. Rye production—monthly, July 10 through August 10
5. Oats, barley production—monthly, July 10 through September 10
6. Corn and sorghum grain production—monthly, July 10 through November 10
7. Acreage and production, next winter wheat crop—December 22
8. Annual summary for all crops other than small grains, final estimates of acreage, yield, production, price, and value—January 15

U.S. Oilseeds

1. Stocks in all positions, soybeans and flaxseed—22d of January, April, June, September
2. Planting intentions, soybeans and flaxseed—January 21 and April 15
3. Cottonseed output for previous season—May 10
4. Flaxseed production—monthly, August 10 through October 10
5. Soybean acreage planted and for harvest—August 12
6. Soybean and peanut production—monthly, August 10 through November 10
7. Soybean and cottonseed crush, stocks of beans, cottonseed, oils, and meal at mills—monthly, about the 25th
8. Annual summary, all oilseeds, production, yield—January 15

U.S. Cotton

1. Annual summary, acreage, production of previous crop—May 10
2. Farmer intentions to plant—January 21 and April 15
3. New-crop acreage—June 28
4. Production estimates—monthly, August 10 through January 10
5. Ginning reports—biweekly, August through March on the 10th and the 24th
6. Consumption stocks—Census Bureau, monthly, about the 20th
7. Cotton statistics, annual bulletin—June 25

U.S. Livestock

1. Cattle and calves on feed—monthly, with key reports quarterly on January 20, April 16, July 19, and October 19
2. Calf crop, last year—February 2
3. Calf crop, current year—July 26
4. Sows farrowing and hog numbers—March 22, June 22, September 22, and December 22
5. Spring pig crop and fall farrowing—June 22
6. Fall pig crop and spring farrowing—December 22
7. Livestock slaughter—monthly, about the 29th
8. Poultry production and hatch—monthly, about the 20th

Parity and Farm Prices.   Issued for most commodities at the end of each month in one comprehensive report.

Miscellaneous

1. Potatoes: USDA acreage yield, production; winter, spring, fall crops—monthly, about the 10th
2. Citrus—indicated production of citrus fruits. Old crop, January through June; new crop, October through December; October estimate carried forward for November—monthly, about the 10th
3. Lumber and plywood—Bureau of Census report on housing starts—monthly, about the 16th
4. CFTC report of traders' commitments in futures (as of the end of the previous month)—monthly, on the 11th

World Acreage and Production Reports by Country.   Formerly issued about the end of each month in the following sequences, and now issued on an irregular basis:

January: wheat, rye, fats and oils
February: cotton, flaxseed, cocoa
March: soybeans, wheat, rye, corn, barley, oats, coffee
April: olive oil, hog numbers, cattle numbers, sheep numbers
May: cotton, cottonseed, lard, tallow and grease, peanuts
June: corn, sugar, coffee, hides
July: citrus, sunflower seed
August: wool
September: wheat and rye (world), barley, oats, coffees, fats and oils, corn (northern hemisphere)
October: cotton, cottonseed, soybeans, cocoa
November: flaxseed, peanuts, sugar
December: cocoa, coffee, olive oil, rapeseed

The Commodity Futures Trading Commission (CFTC) was formed by Congress in 1974 to regulate the trading of futures contracts, options on futures contracts, and options on physical commodities on all U.S. futures exchanges. Among the

CFTC's responsibilities are monitoring the futures and options markets to detect and prevent price distortions and market manipulations and protecting the rights of customers of these markets.

The CFTC provides several regularly published periodicals and special reports. Among its periodicals are its quarterly CFTC report and its *Commitments of Traders Report* ($36 yearly subscription fee), which provides open interest in futures contracts by several categories, including commercial hedgers and speculators. It also publishes an annual report, which provides data and commentary.

Among the other CFTC publications are:

Large Hedger Study
Interagency Study of Futures and Options
Insider Trading Study
Ten-Year History of the Commission
A Spotter's Guide to Commodity Fraud
Advisory Calendar ($65 yearly subscription fee)
Alternatives to CFTC Reparations: Other Ways to Resolve Futures-Related Disputes
An Analysis of Speculative Trading in Grain Futures, Technical Bulletin 1001, October 1949
Basic Facts about Commodity Futures Trading
Before Trading Commodities—Get the Facts
Commodity Futures Trading Commission
Do's and Don'ts about Dealing in Commodities, Fowler West, commissioner, December 1983
Economic Purposes of Futures Trading
Futures Trading in Financial Instruments, Ronald B. Hobson, October 1978
Glossary of Trading Terms
Questions and Answers about How You Can Resolve a Commodity Market-Related Dispute
Survey of Interest-Rate Futures Markets, Naomi L. Jaffee and Ronald B. Hobson, December 1979

The National Futures Association (NFA) is the industrywide self-regulatory body of the futures industry. The primary purpose of the NFA is to assume, through self-regulation, high standards of professional conduct and financial responsibility on the part of the individuals, firms, and organizations that are its members. The NFA was designated as a registered futures association by the CFTC on September 22, 1981, and began operating on October 1, 1982.

The publications of the NFA reflect its charter. Among these publications are:

An Introduction to the National Futures Association
News Facts Actions, a quarterly publication (February, May, August, and November) which discusses various regulatory issues
Annual Review, published annually
Arbitration: A Way to Resolve Futures Related Disputes
The Need for a Coordinated Campaign against Commodity Fraud
A Compliance Guide: Introducing Brokers

An Application Guide: NFA Membership and CFTC Registration
A Compliance Guide: Commodity Pool Operators and Commodity Trading Advisors
Before You Say Yes—15 Questions to Turn Off an Investment Swindler

These and other NFA publications can be obtained from the National Futures Association, 200 West Madison Street, Suite 1600, Chicago, Illinois 60606.

Finally, the Futures Industry Association (FIA), the futures industry trade association, provides several useful publications. Statistically, the FIA *Monthly Volume Report, Open Interest Report, Monthly Options Report,* and *International Report* provide trading volume and open interest data for all futures and options contracts on a monthly basis. The FIA weekly bulletins provide a collection of general articles on the futures markets. The FIA *Congressional Report* discusses congressional issues related to the futures and options markets. The FIA also publishes a monthly newsletter, its *Report,* which provides data and discusses industry issues. An invaluable publication of the FIA is its *Futures Trading Course & Handbook,* which is published as a study guide to help those studying for the Registered Commodity Brokers (Series 3) examination but is also useful as a general reference.

EXCHANGES

The various futures exchanges also provide publications on specific futures markets, which are mentioned in the appropriate following chapters, as well as general futures market publications. They are available on request. In particular, the Chicago Board of Trade has published an annual bibliography of publications on the futures markets since 1977 and a cumulative bibliography through 1976. The Chicago Board of Trade also publishes on an annual basis statistical annuals on each of its product groups which provide cash and futures market data on these products. The Chicago Mercantile Exchange publishes separate annual yearbooks for the Chicago Mercantile Exchange, the International Monetary Market, and the Index and Options Market.

Other exchanges also provide valuable sources of information, most of them at no charge. The addresses of most U.S. futures exchanges are as follows:

Chicago Board of Trade
141 West Jackson Boulevard
Chicago, IL 60604

Chicago Mercantile Exchange
30 South Wacker Drive
Chicago, IL 60606

Coffee, Sugar & Cocoa Exchange, Inc.
Commodities Exchange Center, Inc.
4 World Trade Center
New York, NY 10048

Commodity Exchange, Inc.
Commodities Exchange Center, Inc.
4 World Trade Center
New York, NY 10048

Kansas City Board of Trade
4800 Main Street, Suite 274
Kansas City, MO 64112

MidAmerica Commodity Exchange
175 West Jackson Boulevard
Chicago, IL 60604

Minneapolis Grain Exchange
150 Grain Exchange Building
Minneapolis, MN 55415

New York Cotton Exchange
Commodities Exchange Center, Inc.
4 World Trade Center
New York, NY 10048

New York Futures Exchange
20 Broad Street
New York, NY 10005

New York Mercantile Exchange
Commodities Exchange Center, Inc.
4 World Trade Center
New York, NY 10048

BROKERAGE HOUSES, INVESTMENT BANKS, AND COMMODITY FIRMS

Most firms that offer retail and/or institutional brokerage services in the futures and options markets provide newsletters or other market comments on a regular or irregular basis. It would be partial to mention some without mentioning all, which would be impossible. So ask your brokers to be put on their mailing lists. Such publications provide fundamental and/or technical commentary on specific futures or on classes of futures.

CHARTBOOKS

Several services provide chartbooks, which have charts of prices (high/low/close) and open interest over time. In addition, technical measures such as relative strength indexes are often also provided. Among these services are:

Commodity Perspective (30 South Wacker Drive, Chicago, IL 60606). The chartbook is provided on a weekly basis. An annual *Encyclopedia of Historical Charts* is also published which provides a brief summary of the products as well as the charts.

Spread Scope (P.O. Box 5841, Mission Hills, CA 91345)

Quotron Futures Charts (P.O. Box 1424, Racine, WI 53401)

Dunn & Hargett Commodity Service (22 North Second Street, P.O. Box 1100, Lafayette, IN 47902)

Commodity Chart Service (75 Montgomery Street, Jersey City, NJ 07302)

Graphix Commodity Charts (30 West Washington Street, Chicago, IL 60602)

Commodity Price Charts (219 Parkade, Cedar Falls, IA 50613)

Cybercast Chart Service (P.O. Box 12940, Houston, TX 77217)

Hadady Professional Chart Service (61 South Lake Avenue, Pasadena, CA 91101)

Commodity Trend Service Futures Charts (Old Port Cove, 1224 Highway One, North Palm Beach, FL 33408)

Chart Craft (1 West Avenue, Larchmont, NY 10538)

HAL Time and Price Charts (P.O. Box 223958, Dallas, TX 75222)

Elliott Report Chart Service (P.O. Box 30223, Dallas, TX 75230)

E&S Financial Market Report (30 South Wacker Drive, Chicago, IL 60606)

There is a subscription fee for such privately published chartbooks.

MARKET LETTERS AND ADVISORY SERVICES

Many services provide, usually in written form and on a regular basis, market interpretations and recommendations. These interpretations and recommendations may be based on either fundamental or technical analyses. And they often cover a wide range of futures contracts.

Among the popular market letters and advisory services are:

The Elliott Wave Theorist, Robert Prechter (P.O. Box 1618, Gainesville, GA 30503)

International Moneyline (25 Broad Street, New York, NY 10004)

The Reaper, R. E. McMaster, Jr. (P.O. Box 39026, Phoenix, AZ 85069)

Track records of such services can easily be maintained. Subscription fees are charged for these services.

NOTES FROM A TRADER—GENERAL SOURCES OF INFORMATION

Many traders trade without a system and correspondingly without information—they trade solely on the basis of instinct. This is a major reason why so many traders are losers. Having a system and supporting information does not guarantee trading success, but it certainly enhances the likelihood of success. Yet even in this case, trading instincts may be indispensable.

There are many different sources of both fundamental and technical information, many of which are mentioned in this chapter. This information can be used in a formal model or in a very informal model. Typically, technical forecasting requires less data or information and a more formal model, while fundamental forecasting requires more data or information and a less formal model, although large formal fundamental models are also used by professional traders.

Data and information can help a trader avoid pitfalls and identify opportunities. Traders should develop their own sources of information and also expect useful information from their brokers.

18

The Soybean Complex and Grains

"Plant in the dust and your pockets will bust."
                    Wheat farmer adage

INTRODUCTION

This chapter discusses the markets and the futures contracts based on the U.S. soybean complex and grains and Canadian oilseeds and grains. The commodities considered are the soybean complex, including soybeans, soybean oil, and soybean meal; domestic grains, including wheat, corn, and oats; and Canadian oilseeds and grains, including flaxseed, rapeseed, rye, and barley.

THE SOYBEAN COMPLEX

The soybean complex is composed of the basic agricultural commodity—soybeans—and two soybean products—soybean meal and soybean oil. Although soybeans are grouped with grains for many purposes, they are actually an oilseed rather than a grain. Soybeans are grown primarily for processing into their two products, soybean meal and soybean oil, which are produced by crushing the soybeans. Although soybeans are the major oilseed in the United States and the world, other important oilseeds are cottonseed, peanuts, sunflower seed, rapeseed, flaxseed, copra, and palm kernel. On a worldwide basis, soybeans have accounted for approximately 16 percent of the oilseed crop, peanuts for 11 percent, sunflower seed for 9 percent, and rapeseed for 8 percent.

Soybeans

The United States is the world's largest producer of soybeans, as shown in Table 18-1, accounting for over 60 percent of the world's total. Brazil has been the second largest producer, followed by China and Argentina. Within the United States, soybeans are the third crop in the amount of acreage devoted to their growth, after corn and wheat, and second, after corn, in the value of their product. Soybean production in the United States is principally in the corn belt, with Illinois and Iowa being the major producers, although the share produced by the south and southwest has increased in recent years. Over 150 varieties of soybeans are grown in the United States. Yields of soybeans vary significantly, not only by variety but also by the soil type and the weather of the growing area.

About 50 percent of the U.S. soybean production is processed in the United States, and the other half is exported as soybeans. Japan and the European Economic Community are the major markets for U.S. soybeans, as shown in Table 18-2. Most of the U.S. exports are from the Gulf ports—the soybeans are transported to these ports via the inland rivers. Major grain terminals in Chicago, Minneapolis, Kansas City, and other cities are intermediate points between the farms and the ports or processing plants for many soybeans.

Almost all the soybeans that are not exported directly are processed into soybean meal and soybean oil. Most of the processing capacity in the United States is in the main soybean production areas—Illinois and Iowa account for significant soybean processing. Most other processing plants are in the midwest and along the Mississippi River. In recent years, the number of processing plants has decreased significantly, and their size has increased significantly.

Soybean processing involves separating the oil and the protein from the soybeans—soybeans contain approximately 20 percent oil and 40 percent protein. Various methods are used for processing. Previously in the United States, mechanical methods were used, involving mainly various types of presses, and these methods are still used in many parts of the world. Currently in the United States a solvent extraction method is predominantly used. In the solvent extraction method, which leaves a much smaller amount (approximately 1 percent) of the oil in residue, soybeans are first hulled, cracked, and flaked and then put in a solvent (typically hexane) which dissolves the oil from the soybeans. From this solution, the solvent is evaporated, and what is left is crude soybean oil. The crude soybean oil is degummed and refined before use. The residue soybean cake is cooked and then ground into soybean meal. A bushel of soybeans (60 pounds) will produce about 10.7 pounds of soybean oil and 47.5 pounds of soybean meal. However, because of differences in prices, meal accounts for only 55 to 60 percent of the combined value of meal and oil.

Soybean Meal

Soybean meal is the principal high-protein meal in the world, accounting for approximately two-thirds of the total, with cottonseed, fish, peanuts, sunflower

TABLE 18-1   WORLD PRODUCTION OF SOYBEANS   (in thousands of metric tons)

Year of harvest*	Argentina	Brazil	Canada	China	Colombia	India	Indonesia	Japan	South Korea	Mexico	Romania	Paraguay	Thailand	United States	U.S.S.R.	World total
1977	2,700	9,541	580	7,300	135		523	111	319	470	191	333	90	47,947	540	72,157
1978	3,700	10,240	516	7,565	137		680	190	293	330	230	549	100	50,898	634	77,266
1979	3,600	15,156	671	7,460	154	350	653	192	257	680	383	575	102	61,722	467	93,705
1980	3,500	15,200	690	7,940	89	442	704	174	216	280	448	600	105	48,772	525	80,910
1981	4,150	12,835	607	9,325	99	467	514	212	257	680	268	600	131	54,435	450	86,020
1982	4,000	14,750	848	9,030	127	491	590	226	233	550	301	520	117	59,610	500	93,260
1983†	6,600	15,200	721	9,765	85	700	625	217	226	600	300	550	110	44,518	560	82,345
1984‡	6,600	15,700	934	9,700						550		750		50,642	500	89,719

*Split year includes northern hemisphere crops harvested in the late months of the first year shown combined with southern hemisphere crops harvested in the early months of the following year.

†Preliminary.

‡Forecast.

SOURCE: USDA, Foreign Agricultural Service.

TABLE 18-2   SALIENT STATISTICS OF SOYBEANS IN THE UNITED STATES

Crop year	Thousands of acres: Planted alone	Acreage harvested	Yield per acre, bushels	Farm price, dollars per bushel	Farm value, millions of dollars	Pounds per bushel crushed: Yield of oil	Yield of meal	U.S. exports of soybeans for crop year (Sept.–Aug.), thousands of metric tons*: Grand total	Belgium-Luxembourg	Denmark	Canada	West Germany	Japan	Netherlands	Taiwan	U.S.S.R.
1972–1973	46,885	45,683	27.8	4.37	5,550	10.59	47.04	479.4	8.2	17.4	22.1	54.7	121.0	84.3	19.6	31.5
1973–1974	56,675	55,667	27.8	5.68	8,790	10.76	47.18	539.1	13.2	12.5	37.9	72.9	98.8	101.1	20.5	.7
1974–1975	53,507	51,341	23.7	6.64	8,079	10.51	47.48	420.7	5.6	5.9	26.9	51.0	96.9	77.7	24.4	0
1975–1976	54,550	53,617	28.9	4.92	7,622	10.94	47.27	555.1	17.7	15.1	28.0	45.6	118.1	130.5	32.8	11.4
1976–1977*	50,226	49,401	26.1	6.81	8,776	11.09	47.81	15,351	411	306	462	1,520	3,219	3,007	697	825
1977–1978	58,760	57,830	30.6	5.88	10,383	10.39	47.34	19,061	475	423	264	1,521	3,636	4,086	854	744
1978–1979	64,708	53,663	29.4	6.66	12,450	11.07	47.63	20,117	420	341	352	1,486	3,865	4,012	1,271	1,178
1979–1980	71,632	70,343	32.1	6.28	14,250	10.74	48.01	28,818	584	342	392	1,318	3,868	6,035	780	813
1980–1981	70,037	67,813	26.5	7.57	13,560	11.08	47.93	19,712	670	156	345	1,791	3,816	3,839	1,063	
1981–1982	67,810	66,163	30.1	6.04	12,071	10.70	47.85	25,285	1,404	167	310	2,135	4,196	5,349	1,059	683
1982–1983	70,884	69,442	31.5	5.65	12,594	10.75	47.61	24,634	1,259	160	324	1,813	4,580	4,648	1,300	199
1983–1984†	63,779	62,525	26.2	7.75	12,679	11.26	47.36	20,148	882	113	248	967	4,394	2,988	1,382	408
1984–1985‡	67,735	66,093	28.2	6.00	11,166			23,000								
1985–1986‡	64,360															

*Data prior to 1976–1977 are in millions of bushels.

†Preliminary.

‡Forecast.

SOURCE: USDA, Crop Reporting Board.

seed, rapeseed, and flaxseed accounting for the remainder. Soybean meal is used mainly in the animal feed industry, primarily as a protein supplement in poultry and livestock feed.

As with soybeans, the United States is the world's major soybean meal producer, accounting for approximately 40 percent of total production. Brazil and the European Economic Community each account for 15 to 20 percent of world production. The United States and Brazil are the major exporters of soybean meal. The European Economic Community is the world's major importer of soybean meal, with Japan also a major importer. Approximately 75 percent of the United States soybean meal production is used domestically for animal feed, and the rest is exported. Tables 18-3 and 18-4 provide data on the U.S. supply, distribution, and export of soybean meal.

Soybean Oil

Soybean oil is the world's major edible oil, accounting for about one-third of the world's total. Soybean oil is used mainly in salad and cooking oil, shortening, and margarine, as shown in Table 18-5, for U.S. use. Other world edible oils, in order of importance, are sunflower, palm, cottonseed, coconut, peanut, rapeseed, and olive. The United States is the world's largest producer of soybean oil, accounting for approximately 40 percent of the world's total. Brazil and Argentina are also major producers, accounting for 20 percent and 16 percent, respectively, of the world's total.

In the United States, about 20 percent of the soybean oil produced is exported— Table 18-6 provides data on the importers of U.S. soybean oil. The United States and Brazil are also among the world's largest exporters. The European Economic Community, along with several developing countries, including India, Pakistan, and North Africa, is the major market for soybean oil.[1]

Table 18-7 summarizes the major uses for soybeans, soybean meal, and soybean oil.

Price Determinants

Soybeans have no major use in their own form; they are used only for processing into their products. In addition, there are no trade-offs in the production of meal and oil; that is, no more of one can be produced if less of the other is produced. Thus, soybean products are truly joint products, and the prices of soybeans, meal, and oil are integrally interrelated. However, because there are differences in the demands for oil and meal, the prices of these two can move somewhat semi-independently.

Soybean meal prices are determined mainly by:

- The number and types of animals in the United States and other countries which consume high-protein feed

---

[1] The European Economic Community imports soybeans, processes them, and then exports oil and meal. Brazil has increasingly tended to process its domestically produced soybeans and export soybean meal and oil.

TABLE 18-3   SUPPLY AND DISTRIBUTION OF SOYBEANS IN THE UNITED STATES   (in millions of bushels)

Crop year beginning Sept. 1	Supply					Distribution					
	Stocks, Sept. 1			Production	Total supply	Crushings	Exports	Seed	Feed	Residual	Total distribution
	Farms	Mills, elevators*	Total								
1972–1973	11.8	60.2	72.0	1270.6	1342.6	721.8	479.4	60.8	1.1	19.8	1282.9
1973–1974	9.4	50.2	59.6	1547.5	1607.1	821.3	539.1	56.1	1.2	18.7	1436.4
1974–1975	64.5	106.3	170.9	1216.3	1387.2	701.3	420.7	57.2	1.0	21.7	1198.9
1975–1976	75.1	109.9	188.2	1548.3	1736.5	865.1	555.1	53.5	1.2	15.7	1490.6
1976–1977	86.2	158.8	244.9	1288.6	1533.5	790.2	564.1	61.0	1.0	13.3	1429.6
1977–1978	32.7	70.2	102.9	1767.3	1870.2	926.7	700.5	68.0	1.0	13.0	1703.6
1978–1979	59.0	102.0	161.0	1868.8	2029.8	1018	739.0	75.0	1.0	23.0	1856.0
1979–1980	61.5	112.6	174.1	2260.7	2437	1123	875.0	—	81	—	2079
1980–1981	128.6	229.9	358.5	1797.5	2156	1020	724.0	—	99	—	1843
1981–1982	153.6	159.4	313.0	1989.1	2302	1030	929.0	—	89	—	2048
1982–1983	117.7	136.7	254.5	2190.3	2444	1108	905	—	86	—	2099
1983–1984†	118.6	226.1	344.6	1635.8	1981	983	740	—	83	—	1806
1984–1985‡	68.3	106.5	175.7	1860.8	2037	1000	810	—	87	—	1897

*Also warehouses.
†Preliminary.
‡Estimates.
SOURCE: USDA, Economic Research Service.

TABLE 18-4   U.S. EXPORTS OF SOYBEAN CAKE AND MEAL BY COUNTRY OF DESTINATION   (in thousands of metric tons)

Year beginning Oct. 1	Belgium-Luxembourg	Japan	Canada	Denmark	France	West Germany	Spain	Ireland	Italy	Netherlands	Philippines	Poland	United Kingdom	Yugoslavia	Grand total
1978–1979	3.8	204.5	416.0	65.6	355.1	717.6	253.5	117.9	691.1	748.1	—	243.0	66.8	57.9	5998
1979–1980	13.3	210.0	355.9	48.5	270.2	1013	58.0	74.1	855.7	1490	41.1	400.0	69.0	152.9	7196
1980–1981	48.9	153.7	331.2	0.1	8.0	710.3	21.6	0.5	684.3	1502	0	312.3	56.9	191.4	6154
1981–1982*	13.7	51.7	339.6	0	62.6	630.9	82.3	15.8	947.3	2201	69.7	0	106.9	84.7	6266
1982–1983*	10.7	0	401.4	3.5	3.7	1073	28.6	21.2	953.5	2066	82.5	57.1	72.7	80.1	6449
1983–1984*	7.4	0.5	427.5	0	0	1154	63.0	4.6	493.0	693.1	293.8	278.5	2.5	8.1	4931

*Preliminary.

SOURCE: U.S. Department of Commerce, Bureau of the Census.

TABLE 18-5 SUPPLY AND DISTRIBUTION OF SOYBEAN OIL IN THE UNITED STATES (in millions of pounds)

| Year beginning Oct. 1 | Production Oct. 1 | Stocks, Oct. 1 | Exports and shipments | Total | Food | | | | | Nonfood | | | | | |
					Short-ening	Mar-garine	Cooking and salad oils	Other edible	Total food	Paint and varnish	Resins and plastics	Fatty acids	Other inedible	Foots and loss	Total non-food
1974–1975	7,375	794	1,090	6,518	1,882	1,486	2,680	22	6,070	82	58	16	31	260	448
1975–1976	9,630	561	1,035	7,096	2,416	1,691	3,274	24	7,405	94	96	23	25	294	501
1976–1977	8,578	1,251	1,607	7,454	2,189	1,568	3,165	25	6,947	85	83	26	36	278	507
1977–1978	10,288	771	2,137	8,273	2,279	1,585	3,325	29	7,621	87	79	42	33	308	549
1978–1979	11,323	729	2,411	8,942	2,480	1,593	3,825								
1979–1980	12,105	776	2,690	8,981	2,680	1,643	4,060								
1980–1981	11,270	1,210	1,631	9,113	2,660	1,651	4,041								
1981–1982	10,979	1,736	2,077	9,536	2,991	1,723	4,368	51	9,133						
1982–1983	12,040	1,103	2,025	9,857	2,944	1,615	4,668	58	9,284						
1983–1984*	10,884	1,261	1,700	9,650	3,212	2,480	4,440	100	10,964						
1984–1985†	11,165	795	1,500	9,750											
1985–1986†		710													

*Preliminary.

†Forecast.

SOURCE: USDA, Economic Research Service.

TABLE 18-6 U.S EXPORTS OF SOYBEAN OIL,* BY COUNTRY OF DESTINATION   (in thousands of metric tons)

Year beginning Oct. 1	Australia	Colombia	Canada	Chile	Ecuador	France	Haiti	Peru	India	Israel	Mexico	Morocco	Pakistan	Panama	Egypt	Grand total
1975–1976	18.1	14.2	31.8	1.0	19.5	—	14.3	14.5	15.8	9.9	3.1	4.9	150.8	13.2	0.5	443
1976–1977	20.1	27.3	26.0	12.0	16.2	—	17.2	57.3	252.2	3.1	15.4	3.0	119.2	12.5	1.4	702
1977–1978	21.0	44.1	27.7	22.0	26.0	5.0	13.8	68.6	247.7	6.3	29.6	5.6	95.8	8.3	6.1	933
1978–1979	16.2	84.1	20.9	22.8	22.4	3.6	17.2	29.4	181.1	9.8	5.1	6.0	163.3	19.0	13.9	1059
1979–1980	16.4	82.6	14.8	13.2	35.3	2.9	22.8	36.2	427.7	9.6	31.4	2.3	147.4	17.9	6.0	1220
1980–1981	16.5	60.3	7.8	22.8	38.6	0	22.4	41.2	61.8	5.2	21.6	5.0	125.7	14.7	3.4	739
1981–1982	22.6	77.4	5.4	1.7	36.2	0	8.8	46.8	68.4	0.3	91.1	9.7	259.9	21.7	6.9	942
1982–1983	5.0	69.5	7.5	—	50.4	—	20.4	70.2	54.9	0.4	16.3	9.0	236.7	16.4	3.5	918
1983–1984†	0.3	24.8	10.0˙	—	41.1	—	12.5	24.9	169.4	0.5	84.4	2.5	200.1	15.7	3.6	823

*Crude and refined oil combined as such.

†Preliminary.

SOURCE: U.S. Department of Commerce, Bureau of the Census.

TABLE 18-7   USES OF SOYBEANS, SOYBEAN OIL, AND SOYBEAN MEAL

	Foods	Feed	Industrial	Seed
Whole soybeans	Baked soybeans Dietetic foods Full-fat soy flour Roasted soybeans Soy butter Soy cereal	Puffed soybeans Roasted soybeans Steamed soybeans		Hybridization planting
Soybean oil	(Refined soybean oil) Cooking oil Margarine Mayonnaise Prepared foods Salad oil Spreads		(Refined soybean oil) Adhesives Disinfectants Inks Plastics	
	(Soybean lecithin) Coatings Emulsifiers Nutrients		(Soybean lecithin) Antifoam agents Antiknock additives Dispensing agents	
			(Sterols)	
			(Fatty acids)	
			(Glycerols)	
Soybean meal	(Basic meal) Baby foods Bakery items Beverages Cereals Confections Dietetic foods Meat analogues Meat products Soups	(Basic meal) Millfeeds Livestock feeds Pet foods Poultry feeds (Soybean millfeeds)	(Basic meal) Fertilizers Fillers (Soy flour, grits) Adhesives Coatings	
	(Isolated proteins)			
	(Soy flour, grits)			

SOURCE: *Commodity Trading Manual* (Chicago Board of Trade, 1982).

- Livestock and poultry prices
- The price and availability of other high-protein feed supplements mentioned above
- The level of soybean and soybean meal stocks
- The overall level of domestic and export demand

Soybean oil prices are determined mainly by:

- The price and availability of soybean oil substitutes such as lard, cottonseed oil, and butter

▪ The level of imports of palm oil and coconut oil
▪ The availability of foreign-produced oils, including palm oil and coconut oil, sunflower oil, rapeseed oil, and peanut oil, which affects the demand for and the level of U.S. exports

The price of soybeans is obviously affected by the demands for soybean meal and oil, which are, in turn, affected by the factors mentioned above. In the opposite direction, the prices of soybean meal and oil are affected by soybean prices. Soybean prices are also affected by the worldwide supply of soybeans, which may be affected by weather, strikes, and the levels of stocks on farms, in terminals, or in processing plants.

Government policies in the United States, Brazil, the European Economic Community, and other countries also play an important role in determining supply, exports, imports, and, thus, prices. Brazilian policies have fostered the domestic production and processing of soybeans. In the United States, in many years soybean price support levels have been set (by a formula based on the average soybean prices of previous years), giving soybean producers the option of borrowing money from the Commodity Credit Corporation (CCC) and using the stored soybeans as collateral, as discussed below.

Finally, the level of international exchange rates affects the prices of soybeans, meal, and oil expressed in dollars and, thus, affects the level of exports. For example, during early 1985 the prices of soybeans and soybean products in terms of foreign currencies were high, and the level of U.S. exports was low due to the strength of the dollar. Soybean prices and the prices of other U.S. agricultural goods which are heavily exported were, as a result, quite low.

Because soybean meal and oil are joint products, their prices are interrelated. But because of their different demands, their prices can move differently. For example, if there were a strong demand for meal for feed, there would be an increase in soybean and soybean meal prices. This soybean meal demand and production, however, could lead to a buildup of oil stocks and a decrease in oil prices. In general, the level of soybean processing activity is determined more by the demand for meal than by the demand for oil because meal is bulky and, thus, expensive to store, and it also does not store well for long periods. Soybean oil, on the other hand, is storable; thus, inventories of oil can moderate temporary supply-demand imbalances. Figure 18-1 presents an overview of the structure for pricing soybeans and soybean products.

In recent years the demand for soybean meal has been growing more quickly than the demand for soybean oil. In addition, the value of meal is greater than that of oil in bean processing. For these reasons, even though soybean meal and oil are joint products of soybeans, the price of meal has generally determined the amount of soybeans crushed and, therefore, the domestic supply of oil as well as the supply of meal. Also for these reasons, oil is often considered a by-product of meal rather than a joint product in soybean processing.

Figures 18-2, 18-3, and 18-4 show the considerable variability of soybean, soybean meal, and soybean oil futures prices. Prior to 1972, soybean prices had been fairly stable at approximately $3 per bushel. During 1972 and 1973, however, soybean prices exceeded $12 due to a series of occurrences, including the purchase

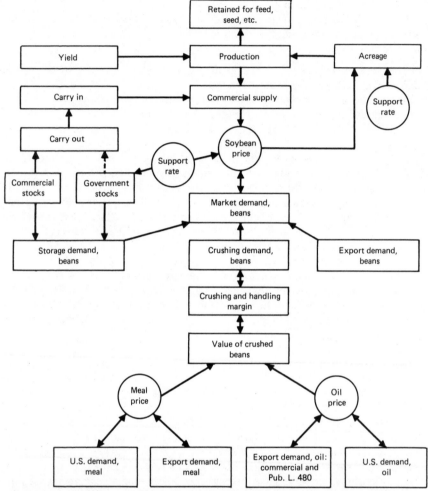

Figure 18-1   Factors influencing prices in the soybean complex. (*Houck et al., Soybeans and Their Products—Markets, Models and Policy.*)

of a large quantity of soybeans by Russia during 1972 due to that country's shortage of sunflower seeds and large livestock production; rain in the United States, which reduced the 1972 crop; a reduced supply of Peruvian fish meal due to the unexplained migration of Peruvian anchovies; a drought in India, which reduced India's supply of peanuts; and other factors. This episode changed the subsequent price behavior of soybeans and their products from being fairly constant to being quite variable over time, as shown in Figures 18-2, 18-3, and 18-4.

Soybean farmers have several ways of marketing or selling their soybeans. The standard way is to harvest the soybeans, deliver them to the local elevator, and then sell them at the prevailing price. There are two alternative ways which have similar results. One is to enter into a cash contract whereby the farmers establish

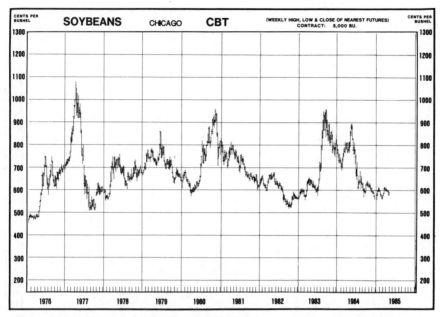

Figure 18-2   Soybeans. [Commodity Year Book 1985, ed. Walter L. Emery (Jersey City, N.J.: Commodity Research Bureau, Inc.).]

the cash price at which they will sell their crops before they harvest them. The other is to sell soybean futures contracts prior to the harvest to establish the sales price. The futures market mechanism provides more flexibility but also more basis risk. The basis risk results from the difference in the grade and location of the farmer's beans relative to those established in the futures contract. Farmers can also delay the pricing of their beans by delivering them to the elevator but delaying the pricing decision—for example, by setting a future price based on a future cash or futures market price.

To soybean processors, soybeans are a purchased input and meal and oil are products sold. Thus, the spread between the price the processors pay for the soybeans and the price at which they sell the meal and oil represents their profit margin, called the "gross processing margin" (GPM). This relationship is the basis for the "crush spread" among soybean, soybean meal, and soybean oil futures contracts, and it is very similar in concept to the crack spread in petroleum futures. Table 18-8 provides an example of a calculation of the GPM. The processor in the example "grosses" 44 cents per bushel. To determine the processor's net profit, other costs must be deducted.

Seasonals in Pricing

Soybeans and soybean products have somewhat different seasonals in their pricing. Soybean prices tend to be at their lowest at harvest time and increase thereafter

Figure 18-3   Soybean meal. [Commodity Year Book 1985, ed. Walter L. Emery (Jersey City, N.J.: Commodity Research Bureau, Inc.).]

to a high in the spring. Soybean oil and meal production and marketing are at their highest after the harvest. Thus, the processing or crushing margin tends to be at its widest shortly after the harvest. But foreign demand also tends to be at its highest at this time and so is an offsetting factor. The production of meal and oil is usually at its lowest in August and September, just before the harvest.

The demand for soybean meal is usually at its highest in the winter, and soybean meal futures prices tend to rise in the late fall or early winter. Cash market meal prices tend to increase from a minimum in early spring to a high in late summer; then they experience a sharp drop in late fall and a subsequent rise until the end of the year. There does not appear to be a seasonal trend in soybean oil futures prices, although cash market oil prices tend to be at their highest in March through April and then decline into summer and rise to the end of the year.

Futures Contracts

The major futures markets for the soybean complex are at the Chicago Board of Trade (CBT), where the soybean futures contract began to be traded during 1936

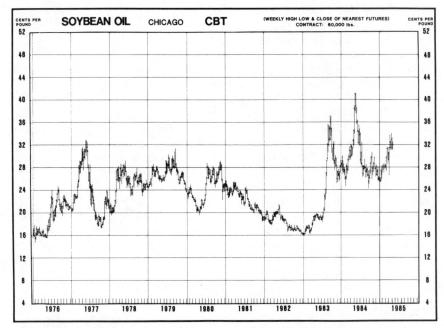

Figure 18-4 Soybean oil. [*Commodity Year Book 1985, ed. Walter L. Emery (Jersey City, N.J.: Commodity Research Bureau, Inc.).]*

and soybean oil and soybean meal futures contracts began to be traded during 1950 and 1951, respectively. The MidAmerica Commodity Exchange (MCE) began trading a soybean futures contract during 1940. The London Commodity Exchange trades futures contracts on soybean meal and oil, and several exchanges in Japan trade soybeans.

The soybean futures contract at the CBT has traditionally been the most active agricultural futures contract in terms of trading volume. The soybean futures contract at the CBT is based on the delivery of 5000 bushels of No. 2 yellow soybeans (substitutions are permitted at specified price differentials) by warehouse receipts from approved warehouses in Chicago, Illinois, and Toledo, Ohio. The

TABLE 18-8 CALCULATION OF GROSS PROCESSING MARGIN

	Price	Yield per bushel of soybeans
Soybeans	$5.70 per bushel	—
Soybean meal	$120.20 per ton	47.9 pounds
Soybean oil	$30.75 per hundred pound	10.6 pounds
Value of meal per bushel: ($120.20/2000) × 47.9 =		$2.88 per bushel
Value of oil per bushel: ($30.75 × 10.6)/100 =		$3.26 per bushel
Total value of meal and oil:		$6.14 per bushel
Cost of soybeans:		− $5.70 per bushel
Gross processing margin:		$0.44 per bushel

delivery months are January, March, May, July, September, and November. Futures prices are quoted in cents per bushel, with 1/4 cent being the minimum price change. The MCE soybean contract is identical in every way except that the size is 1000 bushels.

The sizes of the CBT soybean meal and oil futures contracts are 100 tons and 60,000 pounds (one standard tank car), respectively. Prices are quoted in dollars and cents per ton (with a minimum price change of 10 cents per ton) for the meal contract and in dollars and cents per 100 pounds (with a minimum price change of 1 cent per 100 pounds) for the oil contract. More detailed futures contract specifications are available in Chapter 3.

Soybean processors can use the futures contracts on soybeans, soybean meal, and soybean oil to lock in the GPM. Since processors are at risk due to increases in soybean prices and decreases in soybean meal and oil prices, they can buy soybean futures and sell soybean meal and soybean oil futures to lock in their spread—this is known as the "crush spread" or the "BOM spread" (bean, oil, and meal). The crush spread is put on to protect against a decrease in the GPM. Alternatively, if one thought that the GPM was so low that it would be unprofitable to process beans and that the GPM would, thus, increase, one could put on the reverse crush spread—that is, sell soybean futures and buy meal and oil futures.

Speculative Uses

The futures contracts on the soybean complex have been used extensively for commercial hedging. Soybean farmers have sold soybean futures contracts to protect against price declines before the harvest. Cattle and poultry feeders have bought soybean meal futures and users of soybean oil have bought soybean oil futures to protect against price increases. Soybean processors have also done the crush spread to lock in their GPM.

But the success and activity of the soybean complex futures contracts have not been due to commercial hedgers alone. The soybean complex futures contracts, particularly the soybean futures contract, have also been important speculative vehicles. Speculators can and do buy and sell soybean futures contracts on the basis of the determinants of prices listed above. Since soybeans and their products are actively traded internationally, many foreign as well as domestic factors must be considered in speculating with the soybean complex futures contracts. Soybean futures prices are often very sensitive to exchange rates. The weather in the United States (particularly the amount of rain in July and early August) and in other soybean-producing countries, particularly Brazil, has also always been an important basis for speculation.

Speculators also trade the crush spread and the reverse crush spread on the basis of their forecasts of the GPM. A somewhat related activity of speculators is spreading soybean meal versus soybean oil on the basis of their relative prices.

Several types of spreads are important in soybean speculation. The main soybean spread is the old-crop–new-crop spread. The trading months of bean, meal, and oil futures contracts include January, March, May, July, and September. In addition, there are a November contract for trading bean futures and October and December contracts for trading meal and oil futures. Given the harvesting and processing schedules, September 1 represents the beginning of the new crop year for soybeans. Thus, during January, a long July–short September soybean futures spread would be a spread across years based on speculation on a bountiful new crop. Bullish traders often spread a long nearby contract against a short deferred contract within a crop year instead of just establishing outright long positions. Bearish traders often do the opposite. Speculators also spread soybeans against wheat and corn on the basis of their relative fundamentals or on the basis of their different seasonals. The futures contracts on soybeans and soybean products have long been and remain the premier agricultural speculative vehicles.

Sources of Information—The Soybean Complex

The USDA provides several invaluable sources of information. The USDA's quarterly report on grain stocks in all positions for all grains is particularly useful. The October report, however, is a special soybean report which gives the carry-over of soybeans as of September 1. The USDA also provides the *Preliminary Planting Intention Survey* during January, the *Planting Intentions* report during April, and subsequent crop estimates to provide sequential estimates of the production process. The USDA also publishes the weekly (on Thursday) *Export Sales Report*, which covers export shipments of beans, oil, and meal by destination. The USDA *Fats and Oils Situation* report provides data on and forecasts of the supply and demand for soybeans. The USDA's *Weekly Roundup of World Production and Trade* provides information on foreign supply and demand. Finally, the USDA *Fats and Oils Situation* report provides information on the supply and demand for soybean oil and meal.

The Bureau of the Census publishes monthly reports on the stocks, crushing, exports, and disappearance of soybeans. The National Soybean Processors Association reports on soybean crushing on a weekly basis. The *Oil World*, a trade publication, provides international information on soybeans, oil, and meal. The Chicago Board of Trade, in various publications, also provides information about the cash and futures markets in the soybean complex.

Notes from a Trader

Soybeans are more popular among spreaders than most other markets. In addition to the usual old-crop–new-crop spreads, it is possible to spread oil versus meal or both products versus beans. The September-November spread is appealing to those who expect late crops when the carry-over is small. One should remember that oil and meal prices do not always go in opposite directions and also that one contract of beans does not equal one contract of oil plus one contract of meal—this position emphasizes the oil.

Long oil versus short meal has seldom worked favorably when oil has been in a carrying-charge market. Traders in the reverse crush want carrying charges in beans to indicate large supplies but inversion in at least one of the two products to indicate good demand.

Traders bullish on beans may prefer to go long on nearby contracts versus short on distant contracts rather than establish outright long positions. Bears may wish to sell nearby and buy distant contracts. Traders should be careful about using distant contracts for spreads to reduce margins, for they might find that the open interest is so small that the real risk in the spread is greater than would exist in a net position if adversity developed.

Rain in July and early August is especially critical to new-crop beans; therefore, the market is especially responsive to weather during the late summer. Soybean futures markets have tended to react to government reports more violently than grains, although as the size of the crop in relation to demand continues to expand, this will become less obvious.

As the bean crop year wears on, especially after the December 1 crop estimate, price becomes more and more a function of demand. If there is one "moment of truth" in the bean market, it probably involves the January 1 stocks in all positions.

GRAINS—DOMESTIC

Wheat

Introduction.   Wheat is a universal commodity. It is consumed in virtually every country in the world, grown in most countries in the world, and harvested in every month of the year. Wheat has been universally produced and consumed over the course of history.

Supply.   As shown in Table 18-9, Russia has traditionally been the largest wheat producer in the world, with the United States second. However, in 1984 China increased its production and became the leading wheat producer. Other major producers are India, Canada, and France, with Australia also recently increasing its share of production.

Wheat is actually a grass whose kernels grow in compact heads on the end of the hollow stalks. Wheat produced in the United States can be divided, for the most part, into common and durum. Common wheat is classified according to two primary qualities: by color (red or white) and by hardness (hard or soft). The time of planting, winter or spring, is another category of classification. About half the wheat produced in the United States is winter wheat; that is, it is planted in the fall, lies dormant during the winter (ideally under a snow cover), and is harvested between late May and July, depending on location. Spring wheat is planted as early during the spring as the ground is workable and grows continuously until its harvest in the late summer. Hard wheats, the major portion of U.S. wheat production, are high in protein and contain large quantities of strong, elastic gluten, both of which make them very desirable for bread in the United States.

The three major types of common wheat produced in the United States, as summarized in Table 18-10, are Hard Red winter wheat, Hard Red spring wheat, and Soft Red winter wheat. Hard Red winter wheat is grown in Kansas, Nebraska, Oklahoma, and Texas. These regions have low rainfall and cold winters. Because their winters are too harsh for producing winter wheat, North Dakota and the other north central states produce Hard Red spring wheat, which is the last wheat harvested in the United States, with the harvest occurring during the late summer

TABLE 18-9   WORLD PRODUCTION OF WHEAT (in thousands of metric tons)

Crop year	Argentina	Australia	Canada	China	France	West Germany	India	Italy	Pakistan	Spain	Turkey	United Kingdom	U.S.S.R.	United States	World total*
1978–1979	8,100	18,100	21,100	53,800	21,056	8,118	31,700	9,191	8,400	4,795	13,300	6,615	120,800	48,300	446,800
1979–1980	8,100	16,200	17,200	62,700	19,544	8,061	35,500	8,980	9,900	4,082	13,000	7,169	90,200	58,080	423,700
1980–1981	7,780	10,856	19,158	55,210	23,683	8,156	31,830	9,150	10,857	6,039	13,000	8,472	98,200	64,800	442,700
1981–1982	8,300	16,400	24,803	59,640	22,882	8,314	36,313	8,828	11,473	3,408	13,200	8,710	80,000	75,800	448,500
1982–1983	14,500	8,900	26,700	68,400	25,368	8,632	37,500	8,903	11,300	4,410	13,800	10,315	86,000	75,300	478,600
1983–1984†	12,300	21,900	26,600	81,000	24,828	8,998	42,800	8,514	12,400	4,330	13,300	10,880	78,000	65,900	489,400
1984–1985*	12,700	18,500	21,200	87,700	33,125	10,223	45,100	9,478	10,900	6,044	13,300	14,900	75,000	70,600	516,000

*Estimated.

†Preliminary.

SOURCE: USDA, Foreign Agricultural Service.

TABLE 18-10   WHEAT SUPPLY

Type of wheat	Planting period	Harvesting period	Futures exchange	Producing area	Use
Hard Red winter wheat (high in protein)	Early September–late October	Early June–mid-July	Kansas City Board of Trade	Kansas, Oklahoma, Nebraska, and Texas	Breads
Soft Red winter wheat (low in protein)	Mid-September–late October	Late June–late July	Chicago Board of Trade	Texas and the Great Lakes and Atlantic Coast states	Pastry, crackers, biscuits, cakes
Hard Red spring wheat, other than durum (high in protein)	Mid-April–late May	Late July–early September	Minneapolis Grain Exchange	North Dakota and other north central states	Breads
Durum wheat	Spring	Late summer–early fall	—	North Dakota, South Dakota, and Minnesota	Pasta products

or early fall. Both Hard Red winter and Hard Red spring wheats are used primarily for breads. Soft Red winter wheat is produced in Texas and the Great Lakes and Atlantic Coast states, areas with high rainfall. Soft Red winter wheat is low in protein and is used for making pastry, crackers, biscuits, cakes, and similar products.

Another type of wheat, durum wheat, is grown in North Dakota, South Dakota, and Minnesota and is planted during the spring. Durum wheat is used for making a semolina which is especially suited for the manufacture of macaroni, spaghetti, and other pasta products. A small amount of a third type of wheat, club wheat, is also produced during the winter and spring in some parts of the United States. Tables 18-11 and 18-12 show the U.S. production of winter and spring wheat, respectively, by state. Kansas is the major producer of winter wheat and North Dakota of spring wheat.

Wheat is, thus, harvested in the United States during the summer and early fall, with winter wheat harvested during the early summer and spring wheat harvested during the late summer and early fall. Harvesting begins in the southern portion of the wheat belt during the early summer and moves northward as the summer progresses.

In the supply chain in the United States, wheat is usually sold by the farmers to small country elevators, which in turn sell the wheat to large terminal elevators. The terminal elevators typically sell the wheat to millers (who grind it into flour), to other domestic users of wheat, or to port terminals for export. Storage at terminals is usually lowest at the end of a crop year, around May, and highest soon after the beginning of the new crop year. The level of stocks has an important effect on wheat prices.

Wheat is actively traded internationally. The United States has been the world's largest exporter of wheat, with Canada second. Despite its large production, Russia is the world's largest importer of wheat, followed by China and Japan.

Demand.   The demand for U.S. wheat comes from two sources: exports, which represent approximately 66 percent of production, and domestic use. Exports include both commercial exports and exports via government programs. The largest domestic use is for food consumption. For this purpose, wheat is milled into flour for use in making breads, pastries, pastas, and breakfast foods. Table 18-10 summarizes the major uses of the various types of wheat. The demand for wheat is fairly stable over time. The use of wheat as a livestock feed and the use of wheat for seeds are other minor domestic uses.

Price Determinants.   Although there are many determinants of wheat prices, the major price determinant is worldwide weather conditions, particularly in the world's major producing countries of Russia, China, and the United States. The main reason for the importance of weather is that due to the nature of wheat products as a consumer staple, the demand for wheat products is fairly stable. Thus, supply is the major determinant of price and is usually responsible for imbalances in the demand-supply relationship. Government policies, often weather-induced, also affect wheat prices.

The advent of volatile grain prices occurred during 1974 and 1975 when Russian

TABLE 18-11   PRODUCTION OF WINTER WHEAT IN THE UNITED STATES   (in millions of bushels)

Year	Colo-rado	Idaho	Illinois	Indiana	Kansas	Michi-gan	Missouri	Mon-tana	Nebraska	Ohio	Okla-homa	Ore-gon	Pennsyl-vania	Texas	Wash-ington	Total U.S.
1976	51.6	39.2	72.2	54.0	339.0	33.1	58.1	98.6	94.4	64.0	151.2	56.1	9.0	103.4	132.7	1564.1
1977	56.1	32.4	67.5	55.8	344.9	33.0	68.6	81.2	103.3	72.4	175.5	45.2	8.9	117.5	95.2	1540.4
1978	57.3	41.8	33.4	28.9	300.0	16.4	28.6	83.7	81.6	42.1	145.8	47.3	7.1	54.0	117.0	1222.4
1979	67.6	35.7	53.8	44.4	410.4	31.6	70.4	57.4	86.7	63.4	216.6	48.0	7.3	138.0	94.6	1601.2
1980	107.2	51.9	75.4	53.9	420.0	35.2	89.0	54.8	108.3	67.1	195.0	72.0	9.3	130.0	143.0	1895.4
1981	83.9	55.7	92.5	62.1	305.0	41.5	115.5	89.3	104.4	72.6	172.8	73.2	9.7	183.4	161.3	2103.5
1982	81.5	53.0	67.5	43.3	458.5	23.0	74.8	80.6	101.5	51.6	227.7	59.4	8.2	144.0	125.4	2073.6
1983	117.0	55.6	64.4	49.5	448.2	35.8	70.3	79.1	98.9	58.8	150.5	62.0	7.6	161.0	162.5	1988.3
1984*	110.4	56.7	70.4	48.3	431.2	45.6	84.1	67.0	81.0	48.4	190.8	66.2	8.4	150.0	148.8	2060.6

*Preliminary, December estimate.

SOURCE: USDA, Crop Reporting Board.

TABLE 18-12   PRODUCTION OF ALL SPRING WHEAT IN THE UNITED STATES   (in millions of bushels)

	Durum wheat							Other spring wheat									
Year	Ari-zona	Cali-fornia	Minne-sota	Mon-tana	North Dakota	South Dakota	Total durum	Colo-rado	Idaho	Minne-sota	Mon-tana	North Dakota	Ore-gon	South Dakota	Utah	Wash-ington	Total U.S.
1976	23.9		2.7	8.6	90.5	1.6	134.9	1.6	29.2	123.5	60.2	193.6	4.2	20.5	1.3	11.3	449.7
1977	6.1		2.8	4.8	60.5	3.3	80.0	1.1	18.4	125.6	44.9	167.0	2.4	51.7	0.6	6.1	425.1
1978	6.4		3.8	8.7	102.1	3.8	133.3	2.0	33.6	87.8	53.7	180.1	4.6	44.0	1.4	11.2	419.8
1979	5.3		2.8	6.8	84.5	3.6	106.7	2.6	38.4	85.8	52.3	165.1	9.3	46.0	1.6	23.4	426.2
1980	12.4	7.8	3.4	7.6	73.2	4.1	108.4	3.1	44.2	96.9	57.4	105.5	5.4	37.4	1.4	17.2	370.5
1981	18.3	14.7	5.4	11.0	130.8	5.8	185.9	4.0	34.1	134.0	72.5	197.4	4.2	52.8	1.4	7.0	509.3
1982	7.0	11.6	3.0	9.9	110.8	3.5	145.9	3.5	41.8	120.8	89.9	209.3	4.1	58.8	1.6	13.4	545.5
1983	5.0	6.3	1.2	4.1	54.3	2.1	73.0	5.1	36.1	75.1	53.7	135.0	3.6	36.4	1.4	10.1	358.5
1984*	7.2	9.4	1.6	3.6	78.6	3.1	103.4	4.9	24.7	103.7	34.1	183.6	2.8	61.7	1.8	11.6	431.4

*Preliminary, December estimate.

SOURCE: USDA, Crop Reporting Board.

grain production dropped to approximately 140 million metric tons from over 220 during the previous season. Due to significant Russian imports, wheat prices and the prices of other grains increased significantly. But the U.S. embargo on grain shipments after the Afghanistan imbroglio and a better Russian grain crop sent the prices of wheat and other grains plummeting in 1977. The 1980 drought in the United States increased wheat prices, this time to new highs.

Thus, weather and government policies—government policies at times being a response to the weather—are the primary determinants of wheat prices. Government policies may include stable commercial policies or more irregular, politically induced policies such as embargoes or wars. Some of the stable commercial government policies are discussed below.

Other determinants of wheat prices are:

- Exchange rates (For example, recently the strong U.S. dollar has curtailed U.S. exports of wheat.)
- The level of the carry-over of stocks (in either private or government hands) from one crop year to another
- The availability of domestic commercial storage and freight-car facilities (which affects wheat prices in the short run)
- Changes in production or consumption patterns throughout the world, which tend to be gradual

Figure 18-5 shows the price of the CBT futures contract, including the price increases during 1975 due to Russian imports and during 1980 due to the drought in the United States. Since wheat is a worldwide commodity which is significantly internationally traded, wheat prices are internationally determined.

Seasonals in Pricing.   In general, although different futures contract months and the cash market have somewhat different seasonal price moves, wheat prices tend to decline prior to and during the early part of the harvest into June and then rise from then until the end of the year, as shown in Figure 18-6. Wheat prices then continue to decline during the early harvest because winter wheat is the first crop harvested and the storage space is plentiful. These price changes in the futures markets precede the changes in the cash market by a month or more.

Futures Contracts.   Four wheat futures contracts are traded in the United States. The largest wheat futures contract is at the Chicago Board of Trade, which began trading during May 1923, on the same day on which the CBT corn futures began to be traded. The contract is based on Soft Red winter wheat (No. 2), a variety grown in the Chicago area. Other types of wheat are also deliverable at par, a premium, or a discount to the standard deliverable. Delivery is made at Chicago, or at Toledo at a discount. The contract is for delivery of 5000 bushels. The MidAmerica Commodity Exchange trades a contract based on 1000 bushels of wheat, but otherwise that contract is identical to the CBT contract.

The Minneapolis Grain Exchange trades a futures contract based on Hard Red spring wheat for delivery at Minneapolis–St. Paul or Duluth-Superior. The Kansas City Board of Trade trades a contract based on Hard Red winter wheat for delivery in Kansas City, Missouri-Kansas. Both contracts are for delivery of 5000 bushels.

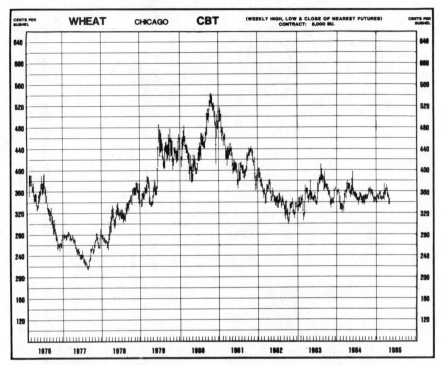

Figure 18-5 Wheat. [*Commodity Year Book 1985, ed. Walter L. Emery* (*Jersey City, N.J.: Commodity Research Bureau, Inc.*).]

All four contracts are traded in the March, May, July, September, and December contract months. Since the harvest begins on July 1, the July futures contract month is the first contract month of the new crop year.

The Winnipeg Commodity Exchange also trades a wheat contract, which is on a 100-tonne broad lot of Canadian wheat (in Canadian dollars), and the London Grain Futures Market trades a contract on 100 long tons (2240 pounds), or approximately 3863 bushels of European wheat (in British pounds).

Pricing of Futures Contracts. In general, wheat futures contracts within the same crop year are traded as carrying-charge markets. That is, the price of a distant contract month exceeds the price of a nearby month by the carrying charges between the contract months. Carrying charges include storage, interest, and insurance. However, because of variations in prices and interest rates, the carrying charges between months are not very stable. While wheat futures contracts are not traded precisely as pure carrying-charge markets such as gold, the users of the wheat futures markets are aware of the current approximate carrying charges, which do affect the pricing of the futures contracts.

When a deferred contract is traded at a premium in excess of carrying charges, the market is bullish on long-term prices (or bearish on current prices). In this case, speculators may buy the nearby contract and sell the deferred contract and

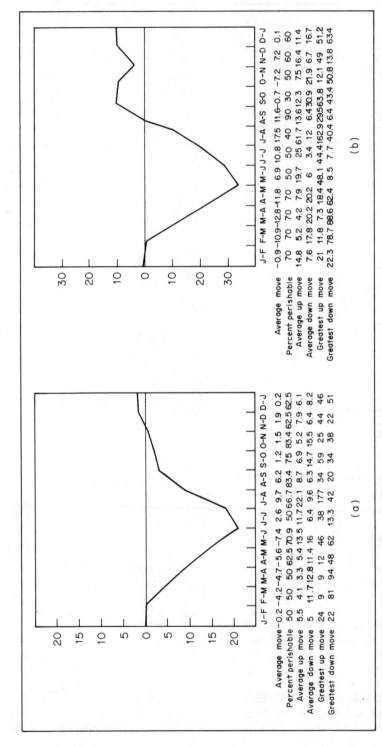

Figure 18-6 Wheat seasonality. (a) Cash Chicago wheat, 24 years; (b) Chicago wheat, nearest futures, 10 years. [*Gruschow and Smith, Profits through Seasonal Trading (New York: John Wiley & Sons, 1980).*]

(a)

	J-F	F-M	M-A	A-M	M-J	J-J	J-A	A-S	S-O	O-N	N-D	D-J
Average move	-0.2	-4.2	-4.7	-5.6	-7.4	2.6	9.7	6.2	1.2	1.5	1.9	0.2
Percent perishable	50	50	62.5	70.9	50	66.7	83.4	75	83.4	62.5	62.5	62.5
Average up move	5.5	4.1	3.3	5.4	13.5	11.7	22.1	8.7	6.9	5.2	7.9	6.1
Average down move	5	11.7	12.8	11.4	16	6.4	9.6	6.3	14.7	15.5	6.4	8.2
Greatest up move	24	9	9	12	46	38	177	34	59	25	44	46
Greatest down move	22	81	94	48	62	13.3	42	20	34	38	22	51

(b)

	J-F	F-M	M-A	A-M	M-J	J-J	J-A	A-S	S-O	O-N	N-D	D-J
Average move	-0.9	-10.9	-12.8	-11.8	6.9	10.8	17.5	11.6	-0.7	-7.2	7.2	0.1
Percent perishable	70	70	70	50	50	40	90	30	50	60	60	
Average up move	14.8	5.2	4.2	7.9	19.7	25	61.7	13.6	12.3	7.5	16.4	11.4
Average down move	7.6	17.8	20.2	20.2	6	3.4	12	6.4	30.9	21.9	6.7	16.7
Greatest up move	21	11.8	7.3	18.4	48.1	44.4	162.9	29	563.8	12.1	49	51.2
Greatest down move	22.3	78.7	88.6	62.4	8.5	7.7	40.4	6.4	43.4	50.8	13.8	634

deliver on the deferred contract. When the deferred contract is traded at a premium that is less than the carrying charges, the market is bearish on long-term prices (or bullish on current prices). In an extreme case, the curve will invert; that is, deferred futures prices will be less than nearby futures prices. This may happen when there is an extreme shortage in the current market.

Speculative Uses.   Wheat has been a popular speculative commodity since its inception due primarily to the familiarity of the U.S. population with the production and use of wheat. Wheat futures are bought and sold by speculators on the basis of the price determinants discussed above. The increase in the level and variability of international trade in recent years, particularly the variability of imports by Russia, has made weather in foreign countries, which may cause foreign-crop shortages, and the political environment in these countries important bases for speculation. Weather—including rainfall, temperature, and even snowfall—in various parts of the United States is also an important basis for the speculator. The yield of the important winter wheat crop can vary greatly from year to year, depending on the amount of snow cover. When snow cover is light, the danger of topsoil blowing away is serious. Changes in government policies by the United States and other exporting and importing countries are also considered by speculators.

Speculators also trade wheat on a seasonal basis. Since wheat has a normal tendency to reach its low price during harvest time and then rise to a high price after December, when supplies become scarcer, speculators typically build up long positions during and after the harvest as the dealers sell futures to hedge. The speculators then gradually liquidate those positions until the spring as the hedgers buy back their short positions. Speculators are the highest bidders during the harvest and offer at the lowest prices during the winter; thus, they exert a contraseasonal force which tends to eliminate, except for carrying charges, any seasonal price fluctuation in the large and efficient market for wheat.

Several types of spreads are used by wheat speculators. A common type of spread, as in other agricultural products, is the old-crop–new-crop spread. Because July is the beginning of the new crop year, a May-July spread is an old-crop–new-crop spread. New-crop months usually are traded at a premium to earlier old-crop months, but the new-crop months may be traded at a discount if there are expectations of a small demand for or a large supply of the new crop. The old-crop–new-crop spread, thus, represents a speculation on the basis of the price of the new crop relative to the price of the old crop.

One of the favorite spread vehicles for speculators has been the spread of long December wheat versus short December corn. This trade, when the position is put on about June 1 and taken off on November 1, has had a profitable average in past years. This tendency is perhaps the result of both wheat and corn prices declining during the respective harvest periods. Because the wheat harvest occurs during the summer months and the corn harvest during the fall, the speculator putting on the spread typically goes long on wheat during its harvest and simultaneously sells corn before its harvest. The theory is that the hedging pressure in wheat will soon be replaced by the bullish effect of hedge lifting, whereas with the later corn crop, the bearish effect of hedging will be later. This version of the wheat-corn spread is based on their different seasonalities.

The wheat-corn spread is also a common spread on the basis of the wheat-corn price ratio, independent of their seasonalities. A rule of thumb is that wheat prices should be 115 percent of corn prices. However, as Figure 18-7 shows, there is considerable variation in this ratio.

Intermarket spreads among the Chicago, Kansas City, and Minneapolis contracts may also prove profitable when there is unusual variation in the supply of and demand for the various types of wheat or when a price adjustment is necessary to overcome changes in the costs of transportation from one market to another.

Some international spreaders also spread between U.S. wheat futures contracts and the Winnipeg or British wheat futures contracts—each of these spreads, however, has risk due to exchange rate changes. A correction must also be made for the different sizes of the contracts.

Notes from a Trader. Fundamentalists sometimes tend to underestimate the difficulty of analyzing the wheat situation. One of the complications is the great number of areas in which wheat is grown. Weather patterns and political developments in all parts of the world and during all seasons have great influence. Countries such as India and Russia may have large surpluses one year and shortages the next. Smaller producers, such as France, Argentina, and Australia, may

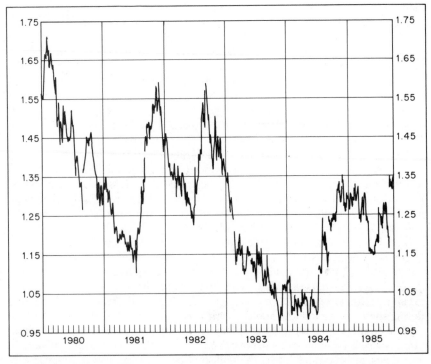

Figure 18-7 Wheat future closing price (nearby)/corn future closing price (nearby).

influence the world market with exports to a degree far beyond what would be expected, given the size of their crops. The use of wheat exports to achieve political ends does not make the analyst's job any easier.

Many traders frequently get trapped by crop scares. Of course, wheat, like all other crops, is sometimes damaged, but more often than not timely rains seem to arrive just about the time that the last speculative long position is established. A common outcome is that a slight damage has occurred in a few scattered areas but the crop is doing beautifully elsewhere. Traders should remember that the type of wheat grown in the United States is adapted to dry weather and can be hurt by too much rain almost as readily as by too little. An old saw among some wheat growers is "Plant in the dust and your pockets will bust."

Spreads, both old-crop–new-crop spreads and spreads between wheat contracts on different exchanges, are popular as discussed above. While the speculative use of wheat futures, like the commodity itself, is a staple, this use will wax and wane as crop shortages and political activities cause significant variations in wheat prices.

Corn

Introduction.   Ancient history shows that corn is one of the oldest agricultural products, dating back as far as 5000 B.C. in Mexico. Although wheat, discussed above, is a grain used primarily for human consumption, corn (and also oats, as discussed below) is used primarily for animal consumption.

Supply.   Corn is a member of the grass family. Its growth requires fertile soil, a temperate climate, and significant moisture during the growing season. Given these growing requirements, as shown in Table 18-13, the United States is the world's largest producer of corn by a significant amount, with China second, followed by Brazil, Russia, Romania, and Yugoslavia. As shown in Table 18-14, most corn in the United States is grown in the corn belt, principally Iowa, Illinois, Indiana, Minnesota, Nebraska, Ohio, and Missouri. Corn is the leading agricultural crop in the United States in terms of acreage planted and value of product. In the United States, corn is planted in the spring, between May 1 and June 15, and harvested between early October and late November. October 1, thus, represents the beginning of the new crop year.

There are several different types of corn, classified by the characteristics of the kernel which affect the use. Dent corn, so named because of a dent at the top of the kernel at maturity, accounts for about 90 percent of all corn grown in the United States and is used primarily as an animal feed. Flint corn is harder than dent corn and is used for the same purpose. Sweet corn has a higher sugar content than other types of corn and is used for human consumption. Popcorn has an extremely hard coat, which is why its kernels explode when heated, producing popcorn. Other types of U.S. corn are of minor significance.

Demand.   As shown in Table 18-15, most of the corn consumption in the United States is for animal feed, mainly for beef cattle, hogs, poultry, dairy cattle, and sheep. Thus, the sizes of the livestock and poultry herds are the main determinants

TABLE 18-13 WORLD PRODUCTION OF CORN OR MAIZE (in millions of metric tons)

Crop year	United States	Argentina	Brazil	Mexico	South Africa	France	China	India	Italy	Bulgaria	Hungary	Yugoslavia	Romania	Indonesia	U.S.S.R.	World total
1979–1980	201.7	6.4	20.2	9.2	10.8	10.4	60.0	5.6	6.2	3.2	7.3	10.1	12.4	3.6	8.4	424.2
1980–1981	168.6	12.9	22.6	10.4	14.6	9.2	62.6	7.0	6.4	2.3	6.5	9.3	10.3	4.0	9.5	406.8
1981–1982	206.2	9.6	22.9	12.5	8.4	9.0	59.2	6.9	7.2	2.4	7.0	9.8	11.9	4.5	8.0	438.9
1982–1983	209.2	9.0	19.5	7.0	4.1	10.4	60.3	6.5	6.8	3.4	7.8	11.1	12.6	3.2	13.5	437.7
1983–1984*	106.0	9.5	21.0	9.3	4.4	10.4	68.2	7.9	6.7	3.3	6.5	10.7	12.0	5.1	16.5	350.0
1984–1985†	194.5	11.0	20.5	9.5	6.5	10.0	72.5	7.2	6.9	3.1	6.5	11.0	11.0	4.0	12.1	445.3

*Preliminary.
†Estimated.

SOURCE: USDA, Foreign Agricultural Service.

TABLE 18-14 PRODUCTION OF CORN (FOR GRAIN) IN THE UNITED STATES, BY STATE (in millions of bushels)

Year	Illinois	Indiana	Iowa	Kansas	Kentucky	Michigan	Minnesota	Missouri	Nebraska	North Carolina	Ohio	Pennsylvania	South Dakota	Wisconsin	Texas
1977	1163	633.4	1092	161.3	132.3	197.2	600.0	201.4	648.5	88.7	380.1	106.7	126.9	291.2	161.7
1978	1240	669.6	1478	153.0	119.9	194.4	643.8	200.1	762.8	121.6	379.1	115.9	177.6	294.0	144.0
1979	1414	675.4	1664	172.0	132.6	237.5	606.0	240.0	822.3	128.4	417.5	121.6	210.9	317.2	132.3
1980	1066	602.9	1463	110.9	103.6	247.0	610.1	109.7	603.5	103.8	440.7	96.0	121.9	348.4	117.0
1981	1454	654.0	1759	148.1	149.0	273.6	744.7	213.4	791.2	140.9	360.0	134.4	180.6	378.0	127.5
1982	1499	790.0	1578	139.1	154.5	293.2	734.5	199.0	748.0	155.4	456.0	126.1	193.7	361.8	119.7
1983	624.1	340.9	743.9	85.6	46.1	165.6	367.1	72.9	470.5	76.8	224.0	72.5	104.4	223.1	104.8
1984*	1247	705.5	1445	108.8	146.0	220.1	689.1	154.4	799.3	145.8	460.2	148.5	186.3	344.5	144.2

*Preliminary, December estimate.
SOURCE: USDA, Crop Reporting Board.

TABLE 18-15   DISTRIBUTION OF CORN IN THE UNITED STATES   (in millions of bushels)

Year beginning Oct. 1	Shipments									Seed	Livestock feed[d]	Exports (including grain equivalents of products)	Total utilization	Domestic disappearance
	Wet corn milling (grind)	Corn-meal[a]	Corn flour, etc.	Hominy grits (food)	Break-fast foods[b]	Starch	Glucose and dextrose	Fuel alco-hol[c]	Total ship-ments					
1975–1976	343	18	15	11	24				482	20	3603	1711	5804	4093
1976–1977	362	17	17	10	25				505	20	3608	1684	5805	4121
1977–1978	398		121						470	20	3744	1948	6282	4334
1978–1979	425		124						601	19.5	4323	2133	7077	4944
1979–1980	455		127						655	20.0	4508	2433	7616	5183
1980–1981	480		160			130	185	75	735	20.2	4133	2355	7223	4868
1981–1982	510		162			125	190	120	811	19.4	4202	1967	6980	5013
1982–1983	540		163			125	190	180	898	14.5	4522	1870	7290	5420
1983–1984[e]	585		161			125	190	210	975	18.9	3726	1866	6566	4700
1984–1985[f]	620		160				190	250	1050	20.0	4001	2075	7126	5051

[a]Regular and degermed.

[b]It is assumed that sizable quantities of corn flour are purchased by breakfast food manufacturers from the dry milling industry.

[c]Fuel, industrial and beverage alcohol.

[d]Feed and waste (residual, mostly feed).

[e]Preliminary.

[f]Forecast.

SOURCE: USDA, Commodity Economics Division.

of the price of corn. In the past, most corn was fed to animals on the farms that produced the corn. Now, however, corn is also sold to country, terminal, and port elevators for distribution elsewhere in the United States or for export. Storage on and off the farm is typically greatest at the beginning of the crop year, October, and declines until the end of the crop year in September.

Corn also has many other uses. The corn kernel, which consists of hard and soft starch, hull, and germ, is the basis of the corn-refinery industry, which uses a wet-milling process to produce starch. The starch is then used in the paper, textile, laundry, and food industries. Starch is also converted into syrup and sugar for use in the candy and food industries. The conversion of starch into sweeteners such as corn syrup, dextrose, and HFCS (high-fructose corn syrup) for use in soft drinks, candy, and bakery products has greatly increased corn's share of the sweetener market in recent years.

The dry-milling industry produces cereals (such as cornflakes), cornmeal, and other such products from corn. Although corn is not used nearly as much for making bread in the United States as wheat, mainly because corn does not contain the gluten that makes wheat flour rise, corn is used to make cornmeal, which is used in cornmeal mush, johnnycake, tortillas, and other bread substitutes. An increase in the use of dry-processed corn for brewing and industrial purposes also occurs when the price of corn decreases to a level at which corn can compete with barley and rice.

Hominy, which is corn from which the hulls have been removed, is consumed widely in the south in the form of hominy grits. Popcorn is a common product of one type of corn. Corn oil, a by-product extracted from the corn germ, is used as a cooking oil and a base for mayonnaise, salad dressing, and margarine. The use of corn to make alcohol and for seed is relatively small.

Finally, as shown in Table 18-16, exports account for approximately 25 percent of U.S. corn production. As shown, Japan is the major importer of U.S. corn, with Mexico, Russia, and the European Economic Community countries next in size.

Price Determinants.   The price of corn, through the supply-demand balance, depends on one important supply factor and one important demand factor. The supply factor is the weather. Since the United States is the world's largest corn producer and exporter, extremely wet fields during the planting time or the lack of rain during the growing season in the United States significantly reduces the crop yield and causes an increase in corn prices.

The major determinant of corn prices on the demand side is the size of livestock and poultry herds. Since livestock and poultry feed represents the largest use of corn, large and growing livestock herds in the United States put upward pressure on corn prices.

Other factors that affect corn prices are:

- The size of livestock and poultry herds in other countries.
- The level of production of other corn producers and exporters.
- The supply and price of competing feed grains.
- The relationship between the corn input prices and the prices of outputs of corn, such as hogs, through the corn-hog ratio. The corn-hog ratio, however, is extremely variable in the short run, as shown in Figure 19-7. However, the size

TABLE 18-16 U.S. EXPORTS* OF CORN (INCLUDING SEED), BY COUNTRY OF DESTINATION (in thousands of metric tons)

Year beginning Oct. 1	U.S.S.R.	Belgium Luxembourg	Canada	Egypt	West Germany	Greece	Israel	Italy	Japan	Mexico	Netherlands	Norway	Spain	United Kingdom	Total, all exports
1978–1979		2,023	364	617	1,435	1,186	258	1,503	8,979		2,193	63	1,747	1,990	53,903
1979–1980	5,342	1,622	597	874	1,521	1,119	562	2,072	11,193	3,834	2,108	36	2,503	1,828	61,801
1980–1981	4,947	2,065	551	1,129	1,264	718	547	1,859	12,586	3,790	1,773	65	2,651	1,395	59,820
1981–1982†	7,646	1,974	342	1,348	1,136	734	403	655	10,588	554	1,428	57	5,686	1,091	49,965
1982–1983†	3,159	2,303	263	1,638	332	221	420	89	13,179	3,987	421	69	2,871	755	47,500
1983–1984†	6,500			1,500					13,600	3,300			2,800		48,260

*Exports of grain only. Does not include corn exported under the food for relief or charity program.

†Preliminary.

SOURCE: USDA, Foreign Agricultural Service.

of hog herds responds more quickly to changes in corn prices than the size of cattle herds.

▪ The relationship between corn prices and the prices of other grains such as wheat, through the wheat-corn ratio. Wheat prices have tended to be about 115 percent of corn prices, but as shown in Figure 18-7, there is considerable variability.

▪ The carry-over of corn stocks (in private or government hands) to the new crop year.

▪ The aggressiveness of government price support policies.

▪ The development of corn substitutes.

▪ Long-term changes in production methods and consumption patterns for corn or products that use corn as an input.

▪ Political factors, including embargoes or wars, involving corn-producing, corn-exporting, or corn-importing countries (for example, the Russian grain embargo during 1980 and 1981).

Figure 18-8 shows the CBT corn futures prices in recent years. The same price increases that occurred in 1980 for corn also occurred for soybeans and wheat for the same basic reasons.

Government Policies.   There are several government programs, some fairly complicated, designed to support farmers and farm prices. These programs involve, in effect, purchasing grains and other agricultural products from farmers, restricting the acreage planted, and/or other actions.

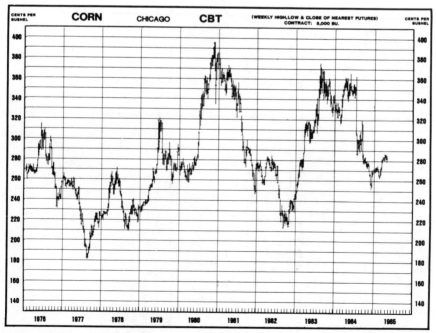

Figure 18-8   Corn. [*Commodity Year Book 1985*, ed. *Walter L. Emery* (*Jersey City, N.J.: Commodity Research Bureau, Inc.*).]

A common program is the government loan program. According to this program, each year the government sets two prices, a loan price and a trigger-level release price. When the price of the agricultural product is below the loan price, the government will lend the farmer an amount equal to this price at a subsidized rate of interest for 9 months, and the farmer will release the crop to the Commodity Credit Corporation (CCC). The purpose of the loan is to permit farmers to repay basic operating costs but sell the crop later if prices increase. This movement of the crop into the loan decreases the free-market supply and causes the crop price to remain at approximately the loan level. At the end of 9 months, the farmer has three choices. He or she can repay the loan plus interest, surrender the crop to the CCC with the interest forgiven, or enter into a reserve loan program.

Under the reserve loan program, in turn, the farmer receives a 3-year loan for a given amount per bushel and agrees to store the grain for 3 years or until the grain price reaches a specified trigger-release level. During this time, the government pays the farmer a storage charge. If the grain price, however, reaches the trigger-release level, the farmer may repay the loan plus interest and withdraw the grain from the loan program. At the end of the 3-year program, the farmer can repay the loan plus interest, surrender the crop to the CCC, or renew the program for 2 more years. At the trigger-release level, farmers typically withdraw their grain from the loan program and sell it, and the government will also sell its holdings—this level, thus, usually establishes a ceiling on the grain price. During 1984, the trigger-level release price for wheat was $4.45 per bushel and the loan rate was $3.30 per bushel. For corn, the two prices were $3.03 and $2.55, respectively. Other government policies affecting grains include an optional acreage reduction program (ARP) and a payment-in-kind (PIK) program.

Seasonals in Pricing.   There is a seasonal pattern to corn prices. Corn prices typically decline during the harvest period, that is, during October and November. Storage space is usually full at these times, particularly because most other crops are harvested earlier, and corn producers are forced to sell corn on the market. Prices usually increase during December, stabilize during the early spring, and then, as storage supplies are depleted, increase until late summer and the new harvest. Speculators tend to exert a countercyclical force on these price variations as with wheat.

Futures Contracts.   Corn futures contracts are traded at the Chicago Board of Trade and the MidAmerica Commodity Exchange. The CBT corn futures contract began to be traded in May 1923, on the same day the CBT wheat futures contract began to be traded. The only difference between the two contracts is in the size of the contracts, with the former contract being for 5000 bushels and the latter for 1000 bushels. Both contracts are traded in the March, May, July, September, and December contract months, with December being the first month of the new crop year. Both contracts are based on No. 2 yellow corn for par delivery in Chicago and for delivery at a discount in four other cities.

Pricing of Futures Contracts.   Corn, much like wheat, is traded as a modified carrying-charge market. If stocks are large, deferred contracts will sell at premiums equal to or in excess of full carrying charges (storage, interest, and insurance).

However, if corn is scarce, deferred contracts will sell at small premiums or even at a discount to the nearby contract. In this case, prices are likely to rise. New-crop months are usually traded at a premium to earlier old-crop months, although the new-crop may be traded at a discount if it is believed that there will be a large supply. These relationships are consistent with a commodity trader's old proverb: "Buy discounts and sell carrying charges."

Speculative Uses.   Corn futures can be bought or sold on the basis of the fundamental determinants of corn prices described above. Speculation in corn based on weather and government policies has been common by those in the agricultural sector.

In addition, the same types of spreads can be done for corn as for wheat. A common type of spread is the old-crop–new-crop spread. Corn is also spread against other grains. As mentioned above, the corn-wheat spread has been a common type of spread on the basis of different seasonals or different fundamental price determinants of corn and wheat. Another type of intermarket spread is the corn-hog spread, based on the relationship between the price of corn, an input, and hog prices, the output.

The CBT corn futures contract has a larger open interest than any other futures contract. Speculators account for a significant portion of this open interest.

Oats

Introduction.   Oats are a cereal grass; they grow in cool, temperate climates and can grow even in poor soils. Their ability to grow in soils poorer than the soils used for growing other grains such as wheat and barley is one reason for their widespread cultivation.

Supply.   Oats are produced in most countries in the world. Russia is the largest producer of oats in the world, as shown in Table 18-17, followed by the United States, West Germany, Canada, and Poland. The production of oats, both worldwide and in the United States, declined through the 1970s. Recent U.S. production has been at its lowest levels since the 1880s. The reason for the decline in the United States is the shift of acreage from oats to other higher-value crops.

Nearly all oats are consumed in the country of production—less than 5 percent of the world's oats production is exported. However, during 1984 the United States imported more than 5 million bushels of oats for the first time since the 1950s.

In the United States, as shown in Table 18-18, the leading oats-producing states are South Dakota, Minnesota, and North Dakota. Most oats produced in the United States are white oats, although red and gray oats are also produced. Oats in the United States are planted in the spring, between early April and late May, and are harvested between mid-July and late August.

Demand.   Oats are used mainly as a livestock feed. Most oats are consumed by livestock on the producing farm. Oats are excellent for feeding horses, breeding animals, young stock, and poultry. A major reason for the decline in the production of oats is the decline in the number of horses and mules employed as work animals.

TABLE 18-17   WORLD PRODUCTION OF OATS   (in thousands of metric tons)

Crop year	Argentina	Australia	Canada	China	Denmark	France	Netherlands	Poland	Spain	Sweden	Turkey	United States	U.S.S.R.	United Kingdom	West Germany	World total
1975–1976	433	1,141	4,466		367	1,948	158	2,920	609	1,345	390	9,551	12,495	795	3,445	47,044
1976–1977	530	1,073	4,831		256	1,402	103	2,695	505	1,251	400	7,930	18,113	764	2,497	48,744
1977–1978	570	991	4,303	1,515	288	1,928	94	2,561	421	1,416	370	10,901	18,407	790	2,714	51,508
1978–1979	676	1,763	3,621	1,500	206	2,203	140	2,492	553	1,550	370	8,730	18,507	706	4,049	51,753
1979–1980	522	1,411	2,978	1,600	163	1,845	109	2,186	456	1,524	370	7,643	15,200	542	3,697	45,165
1980–1981	433	1,128	3,028	1,800	160	1,927	94	2,245	680	1,567	355	6,652	15,544	601	3,249	44,543
1981–1982	339	1,619	3,188	1,700	175	1,774	115	2,731	445	1,816	325	7,391	15,000 ·	620	3,200	45,346
1982–1983*	524	800	3,776	1,800	177	1,726	136	2,621	474	1,658	315	8,602	15,500	590	3,777	48,308
1983–1984†												6,923				

*Preliminary.
†Estimated.
SOURCE: USDA, Foreign Agricultural Service.

TABLE 18-18   PRODUCTION OF OATS IN THE UNITED STATES, BY STATE   (in millions of bushels)

Year	Illinois	Indiana	Iowa	Michigan	Minnesota	Missouri	Nebraska	New York	North Dakota	Ohio	Pennsylvania	South Dakota	Texas	Wisconsin	California
1979	15.6	6.4	63.0	18.9	84.9	2.0	21.2	18.0	37.0	20.3	18.4	94.4	16.8	55.9	4.1
1980	14.0	5.9	62.0	20.1	82.7	2.0	15.6	17.9	13.5	19.4	19.0	66.0	12.6	58.7	4.3
1981	13.5	5.5	59.5	21.1	90.1	4.6	15.8	17.9	44.2	17.0	20.0	70.5	18.9	52.6	3.6
1982	11.8	6.7	54.2	28.4	97.9	3.3	26.7	18.2	55.7	23.5	19.8	123.5	10.7	49.3	3.4
1983	12.6	4.6	38.3	15.6	77.0	2.5	13.6	11.4	63.6	15.4	16.2	79.2	24.0	45.1	2.9
1984*	10.7	5.0	47.4	21.7	78.0	1.6	15.0	10.4	50.0	13.2	16.0	86.8	8.8	53.8	3.5

*Preliminary, December estimate.
SOURCE: USDA, Crop Reporting Board.

As a livestock feed, oats have the highest protein among cereal grains and are also high in carbohydrates.

Small amounts of oats, about 5 percent of production, are used for rolled oats, oatmeal, other cereals, and other human foods and for seeds. As indicated, only a small amount of oats is exported. Table 18-19 provides data on the utilization of oats in the United States.

Price Determinants.   Since oats are used primarily as an animal feed, the number and mix of the livestock and poultry fed are primary determinants of oats prices. In addition, the price of competing feed grains, particularly corn, affects oats prices. A bushel of oats weighs somewhat more than one-half as much as a bushel of corn. On the basis of relative feeding values, a bushel of oats is worth somewhat more than one-half as much as a bushel of corn. Overall, by weight, oats usually sell at 85 to 90 percent of the price of corn. Thus, the corn-oats price ratio is a determinant of oats prices.

Because of the ability of oats to withstand cool weather, the annual oats supply is less subject to bad weather than many other feed grains. However, the carry-over of oats, including the stocks at terminals, affects oats prices. Government programs also affect the price of oats. In 1984, the average loan level for oats was $1.31 per bushel, while the target price was $1.60. The PIK program for corn also resulted in the use of oats as a cover on corn acreage. Figure 18-9 provides the price of the CBT oats futures contract in recent years.

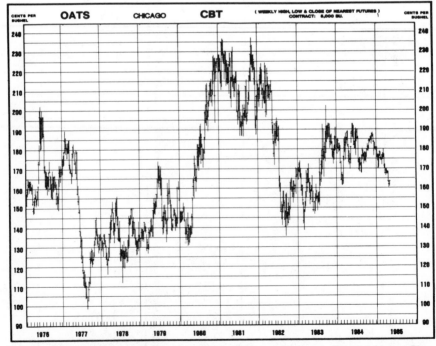

Figure 18-9   Oats. [Commodity Year Book 1985, ed. Walter L. Emery (Jersey City, N.J.: Commodity Research Bureau, Inc.).]

TABLE 18-19   OATS SUPPLY AND UTILIZATION IN THE UNITED STATES

Crop year beginning June 1	Acreage, millions of acres		Yield, bushels per acre	Production	Total supply	Millions of bushels					Farm price, dollars per bushel	National average supply rate, dollars per bushel
	Planted	Harvested				Feed and residual	Other domestic uses	Exports	Total use	Ending stocks		
1980–1981	13.4	8.7	53.0	459	696	432	74	13	520	177	1.79	1.16
1981–1982	13.6	9.4	54.2	510	688	453	76	7	536	152	1.89	1.24
1982–1983*	14.0	10.3	57.8	593	748	441	85	3	529	220	1.48	1.31
1983–1984*	20.3	9.1	52.6	477	727	466	78	2	546	181	1.69	1.36
1984–1985*	12.4	8.1	58.1	472	674	401	80	3	484	190	1.70	1.31
1985–1986*	12.9											

*Preliminary.

SOURCE: USDA, Economic Research Service.

Seasonals in Pricing.   Cash oats prices tend to reach their lows during the July-August harvest and then increase until the end of the year. Oats prices then tend to decline again from January until they reach their harvest period lows.

Futures Contracts.   Futures contracts based on oats are traded on the Chicago Board of Trade, the MidAmerica Commodity Exchange, and the Winnipeg Commodity Exchange. The CBT contract is based on 5000 bushels of oats delivered via warehouse receipt from warehouses in Chicago at par or at Minneapolis or St. Paul at a 7½-cent discount. The trading months are July, September, December, March, and May. Given the timing of the harvest period, July is the first contract month of the new crop. The MCE contract is for 1000 bushels but is identical to the CBT contract in every other way.

The Winnipeg Commodity Exchange contract is based on the delivery of a 100-tonne broad lot, 20-tonne job lot of Canadian oats at Thunder Bay, Ontario. The contract is traded in Canadian dollars.

Speculative Uses.   The speculative uses of oats are similar to those of corn. The corn-oats price ratio is an important basis for intermarket spreading. Because the corn harvest is later than the oats harvest, a buy oats–sell corn spread through the oats harvest period has often been used. The speculative use of the oats market tends to be much less than uses of futures contracts based on the soybean complex, wheat, and corn.

Notes from a Trader—Corn and Oats.   The enormous size of the corn crop and the substantial volume of corn hedging produce a futures market which seems to be somewhat ponderous at times. Moves are usually slow, turns are rounding, and the market can absorb relatively large orders without reacting violently. The corn futures market is a popular market for the relatively new speculator because there is less risk of large sudden adverse moves than in most other markets. Some, however, have called the corn futures market a "sleeping giant" because when it begins to move, it can go further than expected, and occasionally its movements are sharper than what traders are used to experiencing.

When the U.S. corn crop is compared with the corn crops of other countries, its overwhelming size is evident. But that does not mean that the crops of other countries are not without influence. For example, Argentina's importance is out of proportion to the size of its crop because it sells a high percentage of its production into world trade rather than as domestic feed.

Many traders, in attempting to analyze corn, forget that it is basically a feed grain and that many substitutes other than the obvious soybean meal and oats are available. Sorghums of various types are grown in great quantity but are overlooked by many traders because they are not traded heavily on domestic exchanges.

For both corn and oats, weather, particularly at certain times of the year, can be extremely important. In the case of corn, for example, subsoil moisture is usually entirely exhausted by the middle of July, and rain from that time until the middle of August may be critical to avoid severe damage. Too much rain, however, during the same period can prevent storage because of the crop's excess moisture, and the result may be crash marketing and low prices. Conversely, continuing rain can even postpone the harvest until the fields dry, and this postponement is another cause of short-term tightness.

Even worse, the rain may be followed by an early frost, which can severely damage the wet corn and the bank accounts of those who had been selling corn because they regarded the rain as bearish. Late drought may appear bearish, but it may have a beneficial effect if it arrives after the corn crop is made and serves only to dry the corn and the fields. Oats mature earlier than wheat and are not as hardy. They need adequate moisture and may be severely damaged by hot weather near the end of their growing season.

The oats market performs more like a thin market than one would expect from the apparently large crop. One reason is that the small size of a bushel of oats is sometimes forgotten—the crop is not as big as it appears. Furthermore, the oats market is sometimes dominated by a few large trade houses, and so its response to small speculative activity may be greater than had seemed likely.

In spreading oats against corn, most traders regard one contract of corn as equivalent to two contracts of oats, but large traders should keep in mind the thinness of the oats market to avoid suffering a loss greater than expected. Liquidity is seldom a problem in the popular corn-wheat spread, but it may be one for those who choose to spread Chicago oats, particularly a maturing contract of oats, against a more distant contract.

Sources of Information—Wheat, Corn, and Oats. The USDA provides substantial invaluable information on the U.S. grain markets. The USDA *Wheat Situation* report, issued during March, May, August, and November, provides information on supply, demand, disappearance, stocks, prices, government policies, and foreign aspects of the wheat markets. *Winter Wheat Seedling*, issued during late December, supplements these reports. The USDA *Feed Situation* report, published during February, April, May, August, and November, and the weekly USDA *Feed Market News* provide additional information on the grain markets. The USDA weekly, *Grain Market News*, provides more timely information on all aspects of the grain markets, including government activities.

Stocks in All Positions, published quarterly (January, April, July, and October) by the USDA, provides information on stocks and disappearance by location. The weekly *U.S. Export Sales Report*, issued by the USDA Foreign Agricultural Service, and the USDA publications *Foreign Agriculture* and *Weekly Roundup of World Production and Trade* provide data on export sales.

The USDA *Hog and Pigs* report (March, June, September, and December), *Cattle on Feed* report (monthly for seven states), and *Livestock* and *Meat Situation* reports also provide information on the uses of grains.

Among the other relevant USDA publications are:

Planting Intentions—mid-January and mid-April
Prospective Planting report—March 15
Crop Production report—monthly, on the 10th of the month
Annual Summary (of crop production)—third week in December
Eggs, Chickens, and Turkeys report—monthly

The trade publication *Feedstuffs* also provides information on feed demand. *Banking News*, a weekly trade publication, provides substantial information on wheat from planting to utilization.

The *Annual Report* and other publications of the CBT provide significant information on the cash and futures markets for grains. Finally, the CFTC provides information, including its *Commitments of Traders in Commodity Futures*.

CANADIAN MARKETS

The last group of agricultural products discussed in this chapter is traded not on U.S. futures exchanges but on the Winnipeg Commodity Exchange (WCE). The WCE trades via a mechanism that is similar to the technique used by U.S. futures exchanges, not in the London mode. All these contracts are traded, of course, in Canadian dollars. The four agricultural products discussed in this section are flaxseed and rapeseed, both oilseeds like soybeans, and rye and barley, both members of the grass family which are cereal grains like wheat.

Flaxseed

Introduction. Although there are two types of flaxseed, the major type, called linseed, is produced for its seed, which is crushed to produce linseed oil and linseed meal. In this respect, flaxseed is similar to soybeans. The second type of flaxseed is grown for its fiber, which is used to produce linen.

Supply. Flaxseed has been grown since prehistoric times. Argentina is currently the largest producer of flaxseed, as shown in Table 18-20, followed by Canada, India, Russia, and the United States. However, because Argentina and India crush most of their flaxseed domestically and export it as linseed oil and meal, Canada is the world's largest exporter of flaxseed. Japan, Europe (including the United Kingdom), and, to some extent, the United States (depending on the level of domestic flaxseed production) are the major importers of flaxseed. The level of the world production of flaxseed during the last decade has been fairly constant. Canadian flaxseed, the basis for delivery on the WCE futures contract, is grown mainly in the three prairie provinces (Alberta, Saskatchewan, and Manitoba), particularly in the northern areas, although small amounts are grown in eastern Canada.

Flaxseed is grown in temperate climates in drained sandy loam. Canadian flaxseed is generally sown in May and June and harvested in September and October.

Demand. Most flaxseed is crushed to produce linseed oil and linseed meal—approximately 42 percent of flaxseed's weight yields linseed oil. Most linseed oil is used as an industrial oil—as a drying oil in outside paints, varnishes, and printing inks and as an oil for linoleum and other industrial products. Linseed meal, which usually has a protein content of more than 4.2 percent, is a valuable supplement in livestock and poultry feed. Table 18-21 shows the supply and distribution of flaxseed in the United States.

TABLE 18-20 WORLD PRODUCTION OF FLAXSEED (in thousands of metric tons)

Crop year	Argen-tina	Aus-tralia	Czech-oslovakia	Canada	Ethiopia	Egypt	France	Hun-gary	India	Mex-ico	Poland	Ro-mania	Turkey	Uru-guay	United States	U.S.S.R.	World total
1976–1977	750	12		277	50		16		431	8	49	50	7	46	199	337	2347
1977–1978	855	35		653	50		44		527	18	38	50	6	40	409	300	2941
1978–1979	810	28		572	50		43		527	18	38	50	6	40	277	300	2468
1979–1980	600	14		815			31		535	15	52		3	31	305	250	2687
1980–1981	610	7	15	442		27	35	10	423	8	29	44	3	21	196	196	2096
1981–1982	600	7	12	468		18	18	11	483	12	24	38	2	14	185	165	2086
1982–1983*	765	6	15	752		106	31	11	476	1	15	43	2	6	261	150	2648
1983–1984†	703		15	447		68	29	11	440	1	20	40		11	175	234	2250
1984–1985†	500		15	676		68	35	12	480	1	20	42		12	178	215	2290

*Preliminary.

†Estimate.

SOURCE: USDA, Foreign Agricultural Service.

TABLE 18-21 U.S. SUPPLY AND DISTRIBUTION OF FLAXSEED (in thousands of bushels)

Year beginning June 1	Supply							Distribution				
	Stocks, June 1											
	Farm	Term-inal	All other	Total stocks	Imports	Pro-duction	Total supply	Seed	Crushing	Exports	Other*	Total dis-tribution
1975–1976	1,120	——— 1,100 ———		3,031	148	15,553	18,732	1,054	11,791	953	44	13,842
1976–1977	1,830	——— 3,060 ———		4,890	2,168	7,580	14,638	1,043	10,677	196	−239	11,667
1977–1978	1,070	——— 1,934 ———		2,961	859	14,280	18,100	557	11,615	1,001	−388	12,785
1978–1979	2,890	——— 2,606 ———		5,315	1,557	8,614	15,486	724	13,009	91	−924	12,900
1979–1980	977	——— 1,607 ———		2,584	1,916	12,014	16,514	650	12,425	174	−1,753	11,322
1980–1981	2,681	——— 2,337 ———		5,018	2,510	7,728	15,256	547	11,927	76	27	12,447
1981–1982	1,136	——— 1,597 ———		2,733	3,502	7,289	13,524	691	11,231	11	359	11,563
1982–1983	1,175	——— 775 ———		1,950	1,921	10,278	14,149	486	8,722	638	691	10,299
1983–1984†	1,956	——— 1,258 ———		3,212	4,756	6,903	14,871	454	12,733	52	84	13,103
1984–1985‡				1,716	4,707	7,022	13,445	593		45	0	12,093

*Other disappearance represents cleaning loss, waste, and residual.

†Preliminary.

‡Forecasts.

SOURCE: USDA, Statistical Reporting Service.

Futures Contract. A futures contract on flaxseed is traded at the Winnipeg Commodity Exchange for delivery in October, December, March, May, and July. October is the first month of the new crop year. The trading unit is a 100-tonne broad lot, 20-tonne job lot. Delivery is at Thunder Bay, Ontario. The standard weight of flaxseed for delivery is 56 pounds per bushel. Figure 18-10 shows the futures prices of this contract in recent years.

Rapeseed

Introduction. Rapeseed, like flaxseed, is an oilseed which has been used since ancient times—it was used in lamps and as a cooking oil. Rapeseed is in the same family as several U.S. vegetables, including turnips, from which it got its name— *rapum* is the Latin word for "turnip." The commercial production of rapeseed did not accelerate, however, until the development of the steam engine, for which rapeseed oil was used as a lubricant, and until, in more recent times, rapeseed began being used as a food oil.

Supply. As shown in Table 18-22, China is the world's largest producer of rapeseed, followed by India and Canada. France has also become a major producer of rapeseed and exports a significant portion of its crop. Most of Canada's production is in the three prairie provinces; originally it was mainly in the northern areas of these provinces, but there is increasing production in the southern prairies. During

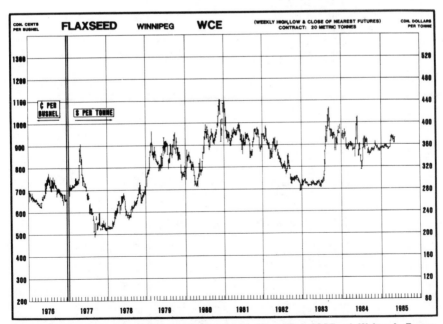

Figure 18-10   Flaxseed and linseed oil. [*Commodity Year Book 1985, ed. Walter L. Emery (Jersey City, N.J.: Commodity Research Bureau, Inc.).*]

TABLE 18-22 WORLD PRODUCTION OF RAPESEED (in thousands of metric tons)

Year*	Canada	China	Czecho-slovakia	Den-mark	France	East Germany	West Germany	India	United Kingdom	Bangla-desh	Pak-istan	Poland	Sweden	Yugo-slavia	World total
1972	2,155	1,000	107.0	51	722.0	234.0	248.7	1,433		106.0	301.0	430.0	327.0		6,624
1973	1,300	1,050	117.0	92	661.0	246.0	242	1,808		98	287.0	512.0	339		7,001
1974	1,207	1,075	85	112	690	200	301	1,692		107	293	523	351		7,022
1975	1,163	1,090	115	115	532	250	194	2,300		110	305	726	327		7,989
1976	1,749			90	561							980	279		
1977	1,973	1,180	162	77	388	308	282	1,650	142	134	236	708	236	40	7,890
1978	3,497	1,868	166	91	568	318	331	1,860	155	137	248	691	289	73	10,721
1979	3,411	2,402	80	150	510	201	321	1,428	198	118	247	233	264	93	10,081
1980	2,484	2,384	214	225	1,103	277	377	2,002	300	122	252	572	285	68	11,107
1981	1,849	4,065	200	290	990	—	363	2,382	325	123	238	496	282	65	12,372
1982†	2,246	5,656	178	350	1,147	280	535	2,472	580	120	246	433	320	79	14,783
1983†	2,632	4,287	315	260	939	320	599	2,566	580	125	242	533	320	137	14,267
1984‡	3,246	4,000						2,700							16,170

*Harvest generally occurs in the first half of the calendar year given in all major producing countries except Canada.

†Preliminary.

‡Estimate.

SOURCE: USDA, Foreign Agricultural Service.

the last decade, the world's production of rapeseed has approximately doubled—rapeseed now represents approximately 12 percent of the world's production of oilseeds. India has become the major exporter of rapeseed, with China and India being other major exporters. Japan and Europe are major importers.

Canadian rapeseed may be seeded in either the fall or the spring, depending on the severity of the winter. Spring planting, the more common type, occurs in May and early June. The harvest occurs from August through October.

Demand.   Rapeseed, like flaxseed, is crushed into oil and meal. In addition, rapeseed, like flaxseed, yields 42 percent of its weight as oil. Rapeseed oil is used for margarine, shortening, and cooking and salad oil, and to some extent it is used as an industrial lubricant. The prospects for the increased edible use of rapeseed oil continue to be good. The U.S. Food and Drug Administration unofficially gave rapeseed oil the status of "generally regarded as safe" for edible use, and this is expected to increase its use. Rapeseed oil has also replaced soybean oil as the main ingredient in margarine and cooking fats in the United Kingdom.

Rapeseed meal, which has a protein content higher than 40 percent, is a valuable supplement in livestock and poultry feed. Japan, the major importer of rapeseed, has greatly increased its use of rapeseed in recent years as an animal feed.

Rapeseed competes in world markets with 12 other vegetable oils, and its price is influenced significantly by these vegetable oils and six other animal or marine sources of oil, ranging down in volume from soybeans, peanuts, and sunflowers through tallow, fish, and whales. The growth in rapeseed production is a reflection of the increased use of rapeseed and its resulting value as a cash crop.

Futures Contract.   The Winnipeg Commodity Exchange trades a futures contract on rapeseed for the delivery months of January, March, June, September, and December. September is the first month of the new crop year. The size of the contract is a 100-tonne broad lot, 20-tonne job lot for delivery in Vancouver, British Columbia, with alternative delivery points in Saskatchewan and Alberta. The standard weight of rapeseed for delivery is 50 pounds per bushel. Figure 18-11 provides the recent prices of this futures contract.

Rye

Introduction.   Rye is also a cereal grass that was grown in prehistoric times. It is currently grown on all continents in the world except Africa.

Supply.   As shown in Table 18-23, Russia is by far the world's largest producer of rye, followed by Poland, East Germany, and West Germany. The United States and Canada are modest producers of rye, although rye production has decreased in recent years in the United States while it has increased in Canada. Canadian rye is produced mainly in the three prairie provinces. And although Canadian rye production is modest, Canada is the major exporter of rye in the world because 60 percent of its production has been exported. Russia and Poland are major importers. The level of world rye production has been very stable during the last 15 years.

TABLE 18-23　WORLD PRODUCTION OF RYE　(in thousands of metric tons)

Crop year	Argen- tina	Aus- tria	Canada	Czecho- slovakia	Den- mark	France	Germany West	Germany East	Hun- gary	Nether- lands	Po- land	Spain	Tur- key	U.S.S.R.	United States	World total
1971–1972	256	448	557	619	150	308	3,188	1,754	182	209	7,827	269	900	10,600	1,252	29,605
1972–1973	500	402	344	633	155	350	2,954	1,947	171	151	8,149	263	755	9,600	741	28,212
1973–1974	613	400	363	688	140	327	2,693	1,699	175	105	8,268	252	690	10,759	660	28,859
1974–1975	306	415	480	671	168	315	2,559	1,949	175	78	7,881	254	560	15,218	483	32,629
1975–1976	273	347	523	530	163	292	2,126	1,563	147	63	6,270	241	750	9,064	457	23,702
1976–1977	330	410	440	561	214	284	2,100	1,455	156	65	6,922	214	740	13,991	381	29,397
1977–1978	170	351	392	540	320	375	2,546	1,500	142	74	6,257	205	690	8,471	462	23,440
1978–1979	210	410	605	625	315	435	2,548	1,895	136	68	7,434	251	620	13,603	665	30,698
1979–1980	202	278	525	486	257	355	2,189	1,830	92	49	5,201	221	620	8,100	569	21,727
1980–1981	155	383	448	575	199	405	2,184	1,917	139	39	6,566	284	525	10,205	419	25,268
1981–1982	149	320	927	544	208	342	1,793	1,797	115	29	6,731	212	520	9,500	478	24,375
1982–1983*	244	348	888	600	226	330	1,703	2,117	120	26	7,812	170	500	14,000	496	30,289
1983–1984†															689	
1984–1985†															823	

*Preliminary.

†Estimate.

SOURCE: USDA, Foreign Agricultural Service.

Figure 18-11   Rapeseed. [*Commodity Year Book 1985, ed. Walter L. Emery (Jersey City, N.J.: Commodity Research Bureau, Inc.).*]

Because rye grows in soil conditions in which other cereal grains would not grow and in extremely cold climates, rye is grown in soil and climate conditions in which other grains, even winter wheat, could not be grown. Most of Canada's rye crop is sown in September and October, lies dormant throughout the winter, and is harvested in late July and August.

The U.S. government supports U.S. rye production. The 1984 national average loan rate was $2.17 per bushel.

Demand.   Rye has several uses. Rye is the only cereal grass other than wheat that can be used to make bread. However, bread made from pure rye flour is extremely dense and dark; as a result, it is known as "black bread." Most rye bread, thus, is made from a combination of rye and wheat flours. Rye bread and rye cereal are staple foods in some countries, particularly the northern European countries and Russia.

Rye is used in the United States and Canada for human food, animal feed, industrial applications, and seed. About 20 percent of the rye consumed is used by the milling and baking industries for making bread. Approximately 38 percent is used for animal feed, although in the United States rye is not regarded as a desirable livestock feed. About 10 percent of the rye production is distilled for the manufacture of whiskey. Table 18-24 provides data on the supply and use of rye in the United States.

Futures Contract.   A rye futures contract is traded on the Winnipeg Commodity Exchange for delivery during October, December, March, May, and July. The October contract is the first contract of the new crop year. The contract size is a 100-tonne broad lot, 20-tonne job lot for delivery in Thunder Bay, Ontario. The standard weight of rye for futures delivery is 56 pounds. Figure 18-12 shows the recent futures prices of this contract.

Barley

Introduction.   Barley is a member of the grass family and a cereal grain. It was cultivated in prehistoric times and was used significantly for bread throughout the history of Europe.

Supply.   As shown in Table 18-25, Russia is the world's largest producer of barley. Other major producers of barley are the United States, Canada, the United King-

Figure 18-12   Rye. [*Commodity Year Book 1985*, ed. *Walter L. Emery* (*Jersey City, N.J.*: *Commodity Research Bureau, Inc.*).]

TABLE 18-24 SALIENT STATISTICS OF RYE IN THE UNITED STATES

Year beginning June 1	Supply, thousands of bushels						Disappearance, thousands of bushels								Acreage, millions of acres		Yield per harvested acre, bushels
	Stocks, June 1						Domestic use										
	Privately owned*	Government†	Total stocks	Production	Imports	Total supply	Food	Alcoholic beverages	Seed	Feed‡	Total	Exports	Total disappearance	Planted	Harvested for grain	
1971–1972			29,331	49,223	241	78,795	5,195	3,005	5,262	16,276	29,738	2,177	31,915	4,842	1,751	28.1
1972–1973			46,880	28,256	154	75,290	5,122	3,038	5,321	16,458	29,939	6,535	36,474	3,458	1,050	26.9
1973–1974			38,816	24,677	1	63,494	6,250	2,547	4,967	8,042	21,806	27,513	49,319	3,380	955	25.8
1974–1975	14,175	—	14,175	17,506	277	31,958	5,459	1,386	4,215	7,811	18,871	6,465	25,336	2,828	784	22.3
1975–1976	6,622	—	6,622	15,924	944	23,524	4,172	2,060	4,217	7,554	18,003	1,117	19,120	2,829	728	21.9
1976–1977	4,404	—	4,404	14,891	248	19,500	3,696	1,930	4,217	5,304	15,147	38	15,100	2,652	719	20.7
1977–1978		—	4,418	16,543	127	21,100	3,648	1,875	4,806	7,000	17,100	24	17,100	2,652	677	24.4
1978–1979	4,137	—	4,137	24,065	145	28,200	3,690	2,369	4,600	8,100	18,800	400	19,200	2,865	926	26.0
1979–1980	8,973	—	8,973	22,389	7	31,369	3,523	2,116	4,034	7,082	16,755	2,422	19,177	2,921	869	25.8
1980–1981	12,000	192	11,970	15,958	10	28,685	3,515	2,050	4,150	6,600	16,400	7,494	23,900	2,488	650	24.6
1981–1982	4,000	145	4,030	18,187	432	23,399	3,458	2,242	4,160	8,200	18,100	1,529	19,600	2,566	685	26.6
1982–1983§			3,012	19,533	3,043	26,955	3,315	2,256	4,240	9,600	19,600	194	19,800	2,533	677	28.9
1983–1984¶			5,822	27,116	1,600	35,100	3,500	2,100	4,800	15,000	25,400	1,000	26,400	2,707	896	30.3
1984–1985¶			8,100	32,392	1,000	41,500	3,500	2,000	4,500	18,000	28,000	1,000	29,000	2,971	981	33.0

*Includes total loans.

†Uncommitted, government only.

‡Residual; approximates total feed use.

§Preliminary.

¶Forecast.

SOURCE: USDA, Economics Service.

TABLE 18-25 WORLD PRODUCTION OF BARLEY (in thousands of metric tons)

Crop years	China	United States	Australia	Canada	Republic of Korea	Denmark	Morocco	France	India	Japan	U.S.S.R.	West Germany	Spain	Turkey	United Kingdom	World total
1978–1979	7,000	9,776	4,006	10,387	1,348	6,301	2,326	11,321	2,311	326	62,077	8,608	8,608	4,750	9,850	182,600
1979–1980	7,500	8,334	3,703	8,460	1,508	6,657	1,886	11,196	2,142	406	47,900	8,184	6,252	5,000	9,609	160,200
1980–1981	7,600	7,859	2,682	11,259	859	6,044	2,210	11,758	1,624	375	43,400	8,826	8,705	5,300	10,326	164,000
1981–1982	7,500	10,436	3,450	13,724	749	6,044	1,039	10,231	2,293	383	37,500	8,687	4,757	5,900	10,230	157,000
1982–1983	6,900	11,233	1,939	13,966	780	6,387	2,334	10,190	2,012	390	41,000	9,460	4,900	6,000	10,884	164,500
1983–1984*	6,900	11,081	4,937	10,296							54,200					169,000
1984–1985†	6,900	12,988	5,475	10,252							40,500					172,700

*Preliminary.
†Estimated.
SOURCE: USDA, Foreign Agricultural Service.

TABLE 18-26 WORLD BARLEY SUPPLY AND DEMAND (in millions of metric tons)

Crop year	Exports						Imports		Production	Utilization				Stocks*		
	Australia	Canada	EC-10	Total non-U.S.	U.S.	Total exports	U.S.S.R.	Total imports	Production	Western Europe	Non-U.S.	U.S.	Total utilization	Non-U.S.	U.S.	Total stocks
1979–1980	2.9	3.0	3.2	10.0	1.2	11.3	2.3	11.3	160.2	51.4	157.6	8.2	165.8	13.8	4.2	18.0
1980–1981	1.5	4.0	4.6	12.4	1.8	14.2	4.0	14.2	164.0	52.0	157.2	7.6	164.8	14.1	3.0	17.1
1981–1982	1.7	5.5	3.5	12.8	2.0	14.8	3.6	14.8	157.0	48.3	149.1	8.1	157.2	13.7	3.2	16.9
1982–1983	0.6	6.1	3.9	12.5	1.0	13.5	2.2	13.5	164.5	49.5	152.6	8.9	161.6	15.1	4.7	19.8
1983–1984	3.7	4.2	3.3	13.6	2.1	15.8	0.5	15.8	169.0	49.0	165.0	9.8	174.8	9.8	4.1	13.9
1984–1985†	4.1	3.0	6.0	16.2	2.2	18.4	3.4	18.4	172.7	50.2	157.0	9.8	166.8	14.3	5.6	19.9

*End of crop year season.
†Preliminary.
SOURCE: USDA, Foreign Agricultural Service.

dom, France, and China. During the last several years, the world's production of barley has been fairly stable, although previously barley production had increased. Australia, Canada, and France are the major exporters of barley. Russia, Japan, Europe, and Poland are major importers. Table 18-26 shows world supply and demand data for barley.

Barley is the most versatile of the cereal grains—it can be grown in all climates, from subarctic to subtropic due to its shorter growing season and its greater tolerance to cold and heat. In Canada, where the barley deliverable on the WCE is grown, seeding occurs during May and the harvest occurs during August. Barley and wheat compete in their demands on acreage in Canada.

The level of production and the price of barley are related to the level of production and the price of other feed grains, such as corn and sorghum. Barley, as a substitute for corn, is usually traded at a price that is approximately 80 percent of the price of corn. The price of barley for malting in beer has been adversely affected, however, by the increased consumption in the United States of light beers, which require much less malt. Malting barley continues to sell at a premium of up to $1 a bushel relative to the price of feed barley. The 1983 government program for barley included a loan rate of $2.16 per bushel and a target price of $2.60 per bushel.

Demand.   Unlike wheat, barley is used chiefly as an animal feed, mainly for hogs and increasingly for cattle. Another significant use of barley, as shown in Table 18-27, is as a malt in beer and other alcoholic beverages. In the United States, one-third of the use of barley is in alcoholic beverages. In Asia and Africa, barley is used as a food, for soup and barley flour. Barley has a minor food use in the United States.

Futures Contract.   A futures contract based on barley is traded on the Winnipeg Commodity Exchange for delivery during October, December, March, May, and July. The October contract is the first contract of the new crop year. The contract size is a 100-tonne broad lot, 20-tonne job lot for delivery in Thunder Bay, Ontario. Figure 18-13 provides a plot of the prices of this futures contract during recent years.

Speculative Uses of Canadian Futures Contracts

The speculative uses of the four contracts traded exclusively on the Winnipeg Commodity Exchange are similar to the speculative uses of the oil and grain futures contracts on the U.S. futures exchanges. These include time spreads, including old-crop–new-crop spreads, and intermarket spreads, including spreads against competing oilseed and grain futures contracts.

Two aspects of these four contracts make them different, however, from the contracts on U.S. futures exchanges. First, the trading volume on these four contracts is typically substantially less than on related contracts on the U.S. markets, and so the markets are much thinner. Thus, price moves can be much greater in response to smaller fundamental reasons. Second, the major producers of com-

TABLE 18-27 SALIENT STATISTICS OF BARLEY IN THE UNITED STATES (in millions of bushels)

Year and periods beginning June 1	Supply				Disappearance								Ending stocks		
	Beginning stocks	Production	Imports	Total supply	Domestic use					Exports	Total disappearance		Government-owned*	Privately owned†	Total stocks
					Food	Alcoholic beverages	Seed	Feed and residual	Total						
1977–1978	126.4	427.8	9.4	563.6	6.0	133.1	16.7	177.5	333.3	57.2	390.5		—	173.1	173.1
1978–1979	173.1	454.8	10.5	638.4	6.0	147.5	13.6	217.6	384.7	25.7	410.4		2.5	225.5	228.0
1979–1980	228.0	383.2	11.8	623.0	7.0	150.9	14.0	204.2	376.1	54.8	430.9		3.2	188.9	192.1
1980–1981	192.1	361.1	10.2	563.4	7.0	155.3	13.2	173.9	349.4	76.7	426.1		3.4	133.9	137.3
1981–1982	137.3	473.5	9.6	620.4	6.9	150.9	16.3	198.4	372.5	100.1	472.6		3.3	144.5	147.8
1982–1983	147.8	515.9	10.7	674.4	7.2	145.5	17.4	240.4	410.5	47.2	457.7		6.0	210.7	216.7
June–Sept.	147.8	515.9	5.1	668.8	2.5	51.3	1.3	92.2	147.3	25.4	172.7		3.9	492.2	496.1
Oct.–Dec.	496.1	—	1.9	498.0	1.8	32.1	2.8	40.7	77.4	6.5	83.9		4.8	409.3	414.1
Jan.–Mar.	414.1	—	2.2	416.3	1.8	35.5	3.9	68.5	109.7	12.7	122.4		5.8	288.1	293.9
Apr.–May	293.9	—	1.5	295.4	1.1	26.6	9.4	39.0	76.1	2.6	78.7		6.0	210.7	216.7
1983–1984‡	216.7	508.3	7.1	732.1	7.0	145.0	19.9	279.5	451.4	91.5	542.9		11.9	177.3	189.2
June–Sept.	216.7	508.3	3.4	728.4	2.5	53.8	1.2	132.0	189.5	23.4	212.9		9.3	506.2	515.5
Oct.–Dec.	515.5	—	1.5	517.0	1.7	29.8	2.4	83.2	117.1	32.9	150.0		11.4	355.6	367.0
Jan.–Mar.	367.0	—	1.2	368.2	1.7	35.2	3.9	33.9	74.7	25.1	99.8		12.0	256.4	268.4
Apr.–May	268.4	—	1.0	269.4	1.1	26.2	12.4	30.4	70.1	10.1	80.2		11.9	177.3	189.2
1984–1985§	189.2	605.7	10.0	804.9	2.5	175.0		274.9	449.9	100.0	549.9		10.0	573.5	255.0
June–Sept.	189.2	605.7	3.6	798.5	2.5	52.7	1.2	128.9	185.3	29.7	215.0		10.0	573.5	583.5

*Uncommitted inventory.

†Includes quantity under loan and farmer-owned reserve.

‡Preliminary.

§Estimate.

SOURCE: USDA, Commodity Economics Division.

modities for delivery on the four Canadian contracts are, in most cases, other countries, so conditions in other countries can have a much greater effect on the prices of these commodities than on soybean, wheat, and corn prices. Rye, in particular, is basically a European crop, and the much smaller Canadian crop is very thin.

Sources of Information—Canadian Markets

An important source of information on the Canadian markets is the Winnipeg Commodity Exchange (678 Grain Exchange Building, Winnipeg, Manitoba, Canada R3B OV7), which trades the commodities. Among other publications, the exchange's *Quarterly Summary* is particularly useful.

The Canadian government also provides useful information. The Canadian Grain Commission, Statistics Branch (280 Grain Exchange Building, Winnipeg, Manitoba, Canada R3B OT6), provides the publication *Statistics*.

The Dominion Bureau of Statistics (Ottawa, Canada) provides *Crop Reports and Estimates*, and the Agriculture, Fisheries and Food Products Branch, Department of Industry and Trade (Ottawa, Canada), provides general information. Finally, the Sanford Evans Service Limited (P.O. Box 6900, Winnipeg, Manitoba, Canada R3C 3B1) provides an *Annual Summary* on these markets.

Figure 18-13   Barley. [*Commodity Year Book 1985*, ed. *Walter L. Emery (Jersey City, N.J.: Commodity Research Bureau, Inc.).]

Notes from a Trader—Canadian Markets

Those who trade flax and rapeseed for the first time after some experience in corn and wheat may have to revise their ideas about price movements and ranges. The great price volatility in these commodities sometimes makes close stops almost meaningless. Spreaders between old and new crops may find one or even both sides of their spreads in unusually thin markets, which can lead to the disorderly execution of market or stop orders. Partial rather than complete fills of limit orders are not uncommon.

Both flax and rapeseed are sometimes, but not always, responsive to European oil prices. In the case of both commodities, oil is usually a more important end product than solids or fibers. Flax tends to be quite responsive to weather conditions in Saskatchewan, Manitoba, and Alberta, particularly to dryness in July. Trends, particularly in flax, are long and strong. Those who like to probe against markets for tops or bottoms may do well to try elsewhere.

Those who trade rye should realize that it is basically a European crop and that the smaller Canadian market is quite thin. This might produce problems where liquidity is important, especially in the case of liquidation under adverse conditions.

There are three important reasons for the volatility of the rye market: (*a*) the crop is small, and a relatively small change in the supply-demand balance will often have significant price consequences; (*b*) there is a smaller amount of hedging pressure and trade buying than with most other grains; and (*c*) because the rye market is relatively thin, rye prices often fluctuate more than the prices of the other grains.

The Meat Futures Contracts

The price of pig,
Is something big;
Because its corn, you'll understand,
Is high-priced, too;
Because it grew
Upon the high-priced farming land.
If you'd know why
That land is high,
Consider this: its price is big
Because it pays
Thereon to raise
The costly corn, the high-priced pig.

H. J. DAVENPORT

This chapter discusses the futures contracts based on livestock and meats. It is divided into beef, which includes the futures contracts on live cattle and feeder cattle, and pork, which includes the futures contracts on hogs and pork bellies.

CATTLE AND FEEDER CATTLE

Introduction

Cattle are raised in several countries throughout the world, as shown in Table 19-1 (which also includes buffalo). India raises significantly more cattle than any

TABLE 19-1 WORLD CATTLE AND BUFFALO NUMBERS (in millions of head)

Year	Argentina	Australia	Brazil	Canada	China	Colombia	France	West Germany	India	Poland	Turkey	Mexico	South Africa	U.S.S.R.	United Kingdom	United States	World total
1981	58.8	25.2	93.0	12.2	95.0	24.4	23.6	15.1	245.6	11.3	16.9	34.0	13.2	115.1	13.1	114.4	943
1982	57.9	24.6	93.0	12.1		24.2	23.5	15.0	246.6	11.5	17.0	34.7	13.4	115.9	13.0	115.4	946
1983	58.0	22.5	93.0	11.6		24.1	23.7	15.1	247.7	11.0	17.1	33.9	13.1	117.2	13.2	115.0	944
1984	58.3	21.8	93.3	11.3		24.0	23.6	15.6	248.7	11.1	17.2	33.9	12.9	119.4	13.1	113.7	947
1985*	58.4	22.5	93.6	11.1		23.8	23.3	15.5	249.7	11.2	17.3	33.9	12.9	121.0	12.6	109.8	948

*Estimate.

SOURCE: USDA, Foreign Agricultural Service.

other country; the United States and Russia, raising approximately equal amounts, are second only to India.

Although there is some international trade in cattle, unlike most grains, most cattle are consumed in the country of production. As shown in Table 19-2, the United States imports modest amounts of beef and exports very little. Table 19-3 shows recent relevant cattle production statistics for the seven major cattle-producing states in the United States.

The production of beef in the United States utilizes more land and creates more market value than the production of any other livestock or grain crop in the country. In most years, the cattle and calves sold for beef produce as much income as wheat, corn, soybeans, and cotton combined. Beef production also accounts for the greatest single use of feed.

Beef, the major ultimate product of the cattle industry, is used almost exclusively for human consumption. Thus, the U.S. consumer is the major source of demand for beef, and the demand is for both home use and restaurant and other institutional use. The major inputs into beef production are calves, land, feed grains (particularly corn), and capital. Consider the supply of and demand for beef separately.

Supply

The production of beef requires the breeding and raising of cattle. Because different names are used for cattle of different sexes at different stages of development, it is useful to summarize this terminology prior to discussing the supply chain. The appropriate terms and their definitions are as follows:

Cow.   A mature female that has had a calf.
Heifer.   A female that has not yet produced a calf (and is under 3 years of age).
Bull calf.   A male calf, not yet castrated.
Steer.   A castrated male.
Bull.   An uncastrated male, capable of reproduction.
Yearling.   A calf that has been fed on pasture for approximately 1 year.

The relationships among these types of cattle are summarized in Figure 19-1. Figure 19-2 shows the timing of various aspects of the cattle cycle. The most important times in the cycle are as follows:

■ There are 14 to 18 months between when a heifer calf is born and when the heifer is bred.

■ The gestation period for a calf is 9 months; that is, it takes 9 months after the heifer is bred before the calf is born.

■ There are approximately 17 to 19 months between when a bull calf is born and when the fed steer is slaughtered.

There are three sectors of the cattle industry. The first is the ranch, also called the cow-calf operation, which produces calves, or feeder cattle. The second is the feedlot, or cattle-feeding, sector, which produces fat cattle, or slaughter cattle, from feeder cattle. The third is the packer, which produces beef from fed cattle. In the United States, the breeding of cattle occurs mainly in the grazing and pasture areas from the Rocky Mountains on the west to the western edge of the

TABLE 19-2 U.S. BEEF SUPPLY AND UTILIZATION

Year	Commercial production	Farm production	Beginning stocks	Imports	Total supply	Exports	Shipments	Military purchases	Ending stocks	Total disappearance	Per capita disappearance, pounds	Retail weight per capita, pounds	Population, millions
					Millions of pounds								
1981:													
I	5,561	61	328	447.80	6,397.80	61.40	10.09	49	342	5,935.30	26.16	19.36	226.90
II	5,435	26	342	418.00	6,221.00	46.96	9.64	58	297	5,809.40	25.55	18.90	227.40
III	5,541	26	297	508.77	6,372.70	47.09	10.38	53	235	6,027.23	26.44	19.56	228.00
IV	5,677	62	235	368.49	6,342.49	60.47	5.70	35	257	5,984.33	26.18	19.37	228.60
Year	22,214	175	328	1,742.99	24,459.99	215.92	35.80	195	257	23,756.27	104.32	77.20	227.70
1982:													
I	5,455	59	257	367.93	6,138.93	55.45	12.54	36	212	5,822.93	25.42	18.81	229.10
II	5,363	25	212	538.37	6,138.37	65.56	14.74	39	190	5,829.07	25.39	18.79	229.60
III	5,730	26	190	655.72	6,601.72	55.83	15.09	35	248	6,247.80	27.14	20.08	230.20
IV	5,818	60	248	377.16	6,503.16	72.90	12.93	25	294	6,098.32	26.42	19.55	230.80
Year	22,366	170	257	1,939.18	24,732.18	249.74	55.30	135	294	23,988.13	104.28	77.17	229.90
1983*:													
I	5,527	64	294	527.89	6,412.89	66.81	10.35	28	299	6,008.73	25.95	19.20	231.50
II	5,556	27	299	516.67	6,398.67	61.96	10.27	34	254	6,038.44	26.02	19.22	232.00
III	6,015	28	254	539.04	6,836.04	71.62	9.14	34	268	6,453.28	27.74	20.53	232.60
IV	5,962	64	268	347.47	6,641.47	71.71	10.47	25	325	6,209.29	26.66	19.73	233.20
Year	23,060	183	294	1,931.07	25,468.07	272.10	40.23	121	325	24,709.74	106.38	78.72	232.30
1984:													
I	5,708	61	325	470.5	6,564.5	90.0	10.8	24	326	6,113.6	26.16	19.36	233.70
II	5,819	26	326	371.0	6,542.0	70.5	13.2	36	303	6,119.3	26.13	19.34	234.20
III	5,949	26	303	513.7	6,791.7	86.6	14.2	27	320	6,343.9	27.03	20.00	234.70
IV	5,933	61	320	467.9	6,781.9	81.6	9.1	25	358	6,308.2	26.74	19.78	236.00
Year	23,409	174	325	1,823.1	25,731.1	328.8	47.3	112	358	25,885.1	106.06	78.48	234.60

*Preliminary.

SOURCE: USDA, Economic Research Service.

TABLE 19-3   U.S. CATTLE STATISTICS FOR SEVEN STATES*

Year	Cattle on feed (January 1)	Cattle placed on feedlots during year	Cattle marketings during year
1981	7863	17,814	17,198
1982	7201	20,261	18,007
1983	8316	19,727	18,680
1984	8006	20,772	18,785

*In thousands of head of cattle; for the seven states of Arizona, California, Colorado, Iowa, Kansas, Nebraska, and Texas.
SOURCE: USDA, Economic Research Service.

corn belt states on the east and, north to south, from Canada to Texas. The cattle are then shipped to feedlots in the feed-grain production areas in the corn belt and sections of Texas and Oklahoma.

Cow-Calf Operation.   The purpose of the cow-calf operation is to produce calves. These calves are produced by using breeding cows, a small number of bulls, and a large amount of forage land. The size of the operation varies considerably, but a typical number of breeding cows is 75, with one bull per 20 cows. Depending on the rainfall and the resulting greenery of the land, it may require from 4 to 200 acres per cow-calf combination.

The cow herd is usually bred in the late summer, and the calves are, given the 9-month gestation period, born the following spring. This cycle provides good weather for the calf's infancy and better forage for the calf's early grazing. Calves remain with their mothers for approximately their first 6 months, with all their nourishment coming from nursing. After 6 to 8 months, the calves are weaned, that is, removed from their mother's milk, and during the last part of the weaning they are fed increasing amounts of grass and grain. Weaned calves usually weigh 350 to 500 pounds.

Although some weaned calves are immediately sent to feedlots, most go through

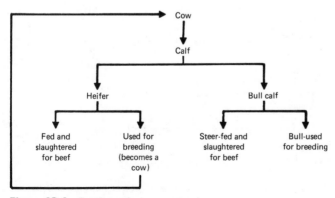

Figure 19-1   Cattle cycle.

an intermediate stage called the "stocker operation," wherein they are fed summer grass, winter wheat, or some other type of roughage. This phase lasts approximately 6 to 10 months, after which time the animals weigh 650 to 800 pounds and are called yearlings—these yearlings are also called feeder cattle (calves that go directly to the feedlot are also often called feeder cattle). At this time, the animals are ready to go to feedlots. It is such yearling feeder cattle that are the basis for the feeder cattle futures contract. The stocker may be part of the cow-calf operation or may be in a different business—in the latter case the stocker may either buy the calves from the cow-calf operation or simply receive a fee for the feeding services.

As discussed below, the cow-calf sector is the driving force of the cattle cycle. Decisions made by the rancher regarding herd size determine the number of calves that will be produced later, the number of cattle ready for slaughter, and the beef supply. The most important decision made in the cow-calf sector is the number of calves that are held back from feeding. In stable times, about 20 percent of all the breeding cows in each breeding cycle must be replaced due to the failure to conceive. Thus, if out of 100 cows, 20 must be replaced, then 20 out of the 80 calves born, or 25 percent, must be used to replace the cow herd. However, if due to rising beef prices cattle herds are being expanded (the accumulation phase of the cattle cycle), more than 25 percent of the calf crop will be withheld and fewer calves will reach feeding; thus, temporarily, even more upward pressure will be put on beef prices. During the liquidation phase of the cattle cycle, when cattle herds are being contracted due to low beef prices, the retention rate for calves with regard to feeding is lower, and more calves will reach feeding; thus, temporarily, more downward pressure is put on beef prices.

Another factor which affects the size of the cow herd is the rate of cow slaughter, independent of the percentage of conception. When reducing the size of the cow herd is desired due to decreasing beef prices, the rate of cow slaughter will increase, further decreasing beef prices. The opposite will occur during times of increasing beef prices. Cow slaughter represents a substantial source of the domestic supply of ground and processed beef. Thus, both the rate of cow slaughter and the rate of calf or heifer retention affect the current and future size of the cattle herd.

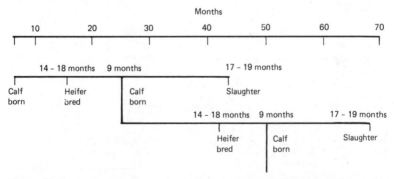

Figure 19-2   Beef production cycle. (*U.S. Department of Agriculture, Economics, Statistics, and Cooperatives Service, February 1979.*)

Since the profit margin of cow-calf operations is often small and these operations are very land-intensive, the appreciation of the grazing land represents an important source of profitability to this sector.

The Feedlot. The feedlot, or cattle-feeding, sector turns feeder cattle into fed cattle ready for slaughter by keeping the cattle in pens and feeding them high-protein feed for rapid weight gain. Both steers and heifers are placed in feedlots, although more steers are placed due to the heifer retention necessary to maintain cow herds. Cows are not usually placed in feedlots prior to slaughter. Table 19-4 shows the weights of feeder steers when they are put into feedlots and the seasonal pattern of shipments. Usually steers are fed until they weigh 1000 to 1200 pounds and heifers until they weigh from 850 to 1000 pounds before slaughter.

In earlier years, feeder cattle were typically fed only on pasture before slaughter. However, the economics of beef production, due to increasing land values and the costs of capital and also consumer preferences for leaner beef, have made feedlots the main location for producing slaughter cattle—feedlots produce heavier and leaner slaughter cattle. The feedlot is, thus, a rather recent sector of the cattle industry.

Feedlots are divided into two types by size. Farmer feedlots are defined as having a capacity of 1000 head or fewer at a time. Feedlots with larger capacities are called commercial feedlots. There are important differences between these two types. Although over 95 percent of all feedlots are farmer feedlots, they account for less than 25 percent of total fed-cattle sales due to their smaller size. In addition, although essentially all cattle on farmer feedlots are owned by the farmer, almost 50 percent of the cattle on a commercial feedlot are owned by someone other than the owner of the feedlot. Separate ownership of the cattle and the feedlot is called custom feeding, which shifts the price risk of fed cattle from the feedlot to the owner of the cattle (that is, the "customer" of the feedlot).

Another difference is that farmer feedlots also produce most of their feed, while commercial feedlots purchase essentially all their feed from feed producers. Partially as a result, farmer feedlots use more roughage and less protein concentrate than commercial feedlots. Thus, the feeding practices and the results of feeding of the two feedlots are very different. The major differences are as follows:

- The farmer feedlot has a lower ratio of pounds of feed per pound of gain.
- The farmer feedlot has a lower ratio of pounds of gain per day than the commercial feedlot.
- Farmer feedlots keep cattle on feed longer than commercial feedlots.

Extremely hot or cold weather decreases the efficiency of feeding by all three measures for both farmer and commercial feedlots.

The feed used by feedlots is a combination of grain, protein supplement, and roughage. The grain component is usually corn, milo, or, at times, wheat when wheat prices are low. The protein supplement is usually soybean, cottonseed, or linseed meal. The roughage is usually alfalfa, silage, prairie hay, or some other local roughage, such as a derivative of sugar beets.

The choice of feed depends on the relative prices of each type. The feeder compares the cost of adding a pound of weight gain with the price of beef on the

TABLE 19-4   FEEDER STEERS SHIPPED (number shipped monthly by weight to eight markets combined: South St. Paul, Kansas City, Omaha, Sioux City, Sioux Falls, Oklahoma City, St. Louis National Stock Yards, and South St. Joseph)

	1001 pounds and up	901–1000 pounds	801–900 pounds	701–800 pounds	501–700 pounds	All weights
1981:						
Jan.	5,876	5,526	7,430	11,618	23,909	54,359
Feb.	4,089	5,440	4,414	8,684	21,861	44,488
Mar.	7,102	4,832	8,512	15,142	31,764	67,352
Apr.	7,691	6,312	13,942	27,602	48,315	103,862
May	4,501	4,375	9,878	19,500	25,254	63,508
June	2,675	6,510	15,814	28,744	27,105	80,848
July	2,186	5,478	13,912	20,481	20,958	63,015
Aug.	5,357	6,468	8,905	17,980	18,396	57,106
Sept.	3,592	5,546	12,938	15,951	21,506	59,533
Oct.	4,419	4,910	11,195	19,473	25,302	65,299
Nov.	4,392	4,208	6,903	8,484	22,354	46,341
Dec.	4,119	4,637	6,579	8,723	16,627	40,685
1982:						
Jan.	2,490	5,649	12,552	11,732	19,833	52,256
Feb.	3,290	6,639	9,610	11,183	27,272	57,994
Mar.	3,034	5,038	12,788	24,021	47,123	92,004
Apr.	2,786	4,490	7,695	21,145	33,745	69,861
May	2,001	3,757	10,297	23,169	24,661	63,885
June	2,031	3,857	10,094	17,629	19,950	53,561
July	1,979	3,126	8,048	11,138	14,729	39,020
Aug.	4,189	5,220	10,670	13,139	18,640	51,858
Sept.	3,858	3,871	8,296	14,796	23,078	53,899
Oct.	4,592	5,477	10,550	13,912	23,569	58,100
Nov.	4,208	5,191	8,436	11,275	23,445	52,513
Dec.	3,716	5,350	7,532	10,761	21,071	48,430
1983:						
Jan.	3,409	6,513	9,185	11,291	23,200	53,598
Feb.	3,749	4,574	5,600	7,003	18,171	39,097
Mar.	5,517	5,923	7,579	15,318	32,592	66,929
Apr.	3,932	6,020	9,834	20,407	29,069	69,262
May	1,496	4,781	13,116	20,913	24,727	65,033
June	4,460	5,703	13,217	26,428	19,714	69,522
July	1,103	4,173	9,375	11,936	8,832	35,419
Aug.	994	5,186	15,721	15,005	15,351	52,257
Sept.	995	4,537	8,627	13,834	14,847	42,840
Oct.	1,472	4,815	10,512	17,746	20,811	55,356
Nov.	1,667	3,028	8,253	10,855	19,966	43,769
Dec.	2,123	4,432	6,755	8,955	14,210	36,475

SOURCE: USDA, Livestock Division, *Livestock, Meat & Wool Market News.*

market. Thus, since corn is always a major component of the feed, the ratio of the price of corn to the price of beef is an important indicator of the profitability of the feedlot. If feed prices decrease or fed-cattle prices increase, the cattle will be kept on feed somewhat longer to a somewhat heavier weight, and vice versa. Obviously, any widening between the price of feeder cattle, the major input to the feedlot, and the price of slaughter cattle due to imbalances in their supplies will also increase the profitability of the feedlot sector.

Because approximately 10 pounds of grain is required to produce 1 pound of beef, transportation costs are lower if feedlots are located near where feed is produced and the cattle are transported to the beef markets than if feedlots are located near the beef markets and the grain is transported to the feedlots. As a result, since most feed is grown in the corn belt and plains states, most feedlots are now located in these states, with the trend toward the corn belt states, where feed is more abundant and cheaper. Table 19-5 shows the inventories of cattle and calves in various categories in recent years.

The Packer. The packer purchases fed cattle, slaughters them, and sells essentially every part of the slaughtered cattle. In recent years, packers have located their slaughterhouses near the feedlots where slaughter cattle are produced, which, as indicated above, have been increasingly located in the corn belt states rather than near the markets for beef. Earlier in the history of beef, packers located their slaughterhouses near the primary market outlets, which were also terminal markets. At that time, most fed cattle were marketed through these terminal markets.

Many other fed cattle were marketed through auctions near the feedlots, which, in earlier times, were near either where the calves were produced or the markets for beef. Recently, however, commercial feedlots have been selling about 90 percent and farmer feedlots over 60 percent of their fed cattle directly to packers. The importance of terminal markets and auctions has, thus, decreased significantly in the marketing chain for fed cattle.

The packer has two major sources of revenue: the sale of beef, either in carcass form or in boxed form, and the sale of hide and offal or drop (hide, trimmed fat, variety meats, bones, blood, glands, etc.). The packer buyer can determine the value of slaughter cattle from the value of beef and its by-products. To do so, the packer buyer must estimate the dressing percentage (the carcass is usually approximately 62 percent of the live weight), the quality grade (prime, choice, good, etc.), and the yield grade (1 to 5, with the higher grades indicating a lower fraction of merchantable retail cuts in the carcass) of the slaughter cattle. For example, a 1000-pound choice yield grade 3 may produce a 650-pound carcass which yields 495 pounds of salable beef. About 50 to 55 percent of the carcass is sold as steaks and roasts, 5 percent as stewing beef, and the remainder as hamburger.

The Pipeline Method. One way to consider the supply of beef and, thus, predict the price of beef is through a pipeline approach in which the various stages of beef production are considered as parts of a pipeline and the inputs to and outputs of the pipeline are analyzed at various stages in the pipeline. U.S. government data on the inputs and outputs are used. Each quarter, the USDA estimates the number of cattle put on feed in the 13 major cattle-feeding states. This figure, with some subjectivity, can be translated into forecasts of fed slaughter cattle, total slaughter cattle, and beef production two quarters later, since, as indicated above, the typical length of feeding is almost two quarters.

Figure 19-3 summarizes this method of forecasting beef production and the potential errors in the forecast. At the first step of the forecast, states other than the 13 major states account for approximately 13 percent of cattle placed on feed, and this fraction varies. At the next level of the forecast, fed steers and heifers

TABLE 19-5 CATTLE AND CALVES ON U.S. FARMS (thousands of head, by class)

	Jan. 1, 1981	July 1, 1981	Jan. 1, 1982	July 1, 1982	Jan. 1, 1983	July 1, 1983	Jan. 1, 1984
Cattle and calves	114,321	124,800	115,604	124,140	115,199	123,540	114,040
Cows and heifers that have calved	49,586	51,004	50,331	49,990	49,154	49,600	48,800
Beef cows	38,726	40,084	39,319	38,970	38,079	38,520	37,660
Milk cows	10,860	10,920	11,012	11,020	11,076	11,080	11,140
Heifers 500 pounds and over	17,766	18,365	18,328	18,550	18,830	18,570	18,598
For beef cow replacement	6,136	6,233	6,615	6,120	6,343	5,800	6,195
For milk cow replacement	4,345	4,628	4,532	4,780	4,533	4,880	4,541
Other heifers	7,285	7,495	7,181	7,650	7,954	7,890	7,862
Steers 500 pounds and over	15,519	16,253	15,501	16,340	16,225	16,840	16,391
Bulls 500 pounds and over	2,547	2,638	2,618	2,610	2,615	2,560	2,550
Heifers, steers, and bulls under 500 pounds	28,904	36,549	28,827	36,650	28,375	35,970	27,701

SOURCE: USDA, Crop Reporting Board.

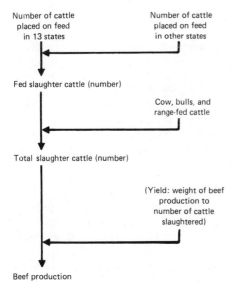

Figure 19-3   Cattle pipeline approach.

account for only about 70 percent of the total, with cows, bulls, and range-fed steers making up the remainder. Finally, the yield of slaughtered cattle averaged about 630 pounds per animal from 1979 to 1983, but this yield also varies. From the number of placements in the 13 states, however, the beef production two quarters later can be estimated with a margin of error. Of course, the USDA also publishes data on fed cattle, slaughter, and beef production with which these earlier forecasts can subsequently be compared.

The Cattle Cycle.   The production of cattle, hence beef, differs from the production of most other farm products because of the existence of a distinct, fairly regular, long-term cyclical variation in the number of cattle produced. This cyclical change in the size of the cattle herd is called the cattle cycle. There have been seven cattle cycles since 1896, averaging about 12 years in length but ranging from 9 to 16 years and comprising, on the average, 7 years of herd expansion and 5 years of herd contraction.

There are several reasons for the cattle cycle. One reason is the life span of the cattle themselves. As indicated above, it is over 2½ years from the time a cow is bred until steak is produced from its offspring. Another reason is the heavy investment required to enter most phases of the cattle business. Changes in the demand for beef and changes in the availability and cost of feed also influence the cattle cycle. For example, a severe drought is almost certain to cause a reduction in herds, whereas abundant feed supplies coupled with low herd numbers encourage an increase. Good grazing conditions encourage producers of feeder cattle to hold back their stock. Feedlot operators will be willing to pay more for the yearlings if feed grains such as corn are abundant enough to ensure reasonably low feed prices. The fundamentalist wishing to analyze the factors affecting the cattle cycle can use some ratio between the price of cattle and that of feed. The cattle price used could be the average farm selling price of choice steers. It might also be necessary to consider both corn- and range-fed cattle by combining a cattle-corn ratio and a cattle-hay ratio, assuming that the price of hay measures pasture conditions for range-fed cattle.

The expansion phase of the typical cattle cycle begins when producers decide to expand their breeding stock in response to rising prices or expectations that prices will rise, and the prices of breeding stock then accordingly begin to rise because the latter are held back to expand the herds. Cows, heifers, and heifer calves are all withheld to be used for herd expansion, and calves, yearlings, and steers are withheld to be fed (finished) to an older age and a heavier weight. When the larger numbers of new calves from the expanded herds mature, slaughter begins to increase because fully finished steers must be marketed regardless of the stage of the cycle. Prices then begin to fall, and marketing becomes still heavier. Prices then begin to break, the liquidation phase of the cycle begins, and prices fall even more, by the greatest amount for breeding stock and the least for high-grade fed cattle. The slaughter of cows and calves is then increased because herd expansion is no longer considered desirable, and this fact depresses cattle prices even more. Finally, herds become so small that prices begin to firm, cattle producers realize that the bottom of the cycle has been reached, and the expansion of the number of cattle is ready to begin again with the rise in steer prices coupled with the increasing scarcity of cow beef as cows are again held back for breeding. As indicated, both the expansion phase and the liquidation phase may last for years, with the buildup typically requiring considerably more time than the liquidation.

One of the early signs of an impending expansion in the number of cattle is the withholding of cows, calves, and heifers from slaughter so that they can be used for rebuilding herds. This creates an interesting problem for packers and consumers. Cow prices fluctuate more than steer prices, and cow meat is used for lower-priced products such as hamburger and sausage meat. Just when consumers are ready to switch to such low-cost substitutes from higher-priced cuts of beef, they find that their prices are increasing proportionately more than the prices of more expensive cuts.

There are consistent relationships between the phase of the cattle cycle and both the slaughter weights of steers and the cost of feeding. These relationships are expressed by the beef-corn price ratio. When cattle feeders become sufficiently optimistic to begin accumulating cattle, the average live weight of steers begins to rise because they are withheld to be finished to heavier weights. The rise in cattle prices usually tends to be more rapid than the accompanying rise in feed costs, and feeding to heavier weights remains profitable, even though the most economical weight gains take place in young animals and the conversion efficiency ratio declines sharply as animals become heavier. Feeders who wait too long find themselves withholding their cattle and seeking higher prices at a time when the cycle is in its liquidation phase, and they may then have difficulty recovering even the cost of production. At this point selling may assume almost panic proportions.

The relationship between the phase of the cattle cycle and beef and cattle price changes should also be noted. While the relationship is somewhat weak, prices tend to begin rising during the latter part of the contraction and continue to rise until cattle prices have risen sufficiently to make cattle breeding, raising, and feeding once again profitable, at which time the contraction ends and the expansion begins. Then, as the expansion continues and reaches a mature stage, the herd becomes overbuilt and prices tend to peak and begin to decrease.

Two measures are suggestive of the phase of the cattle cycle. One is the ratio of breeding cows to people. A ratio of 24 cows per 100 people has been considered an equilibrium level, with a higher ratio interpreted as an indication of oversupply and an impending contraction. The ratios of cattle and calf slaughter to either the total cattle inventory or the previous year's calf crop are also used as indicators of oversupply. If either ratio is below its accepted equilibrium level (0.36 and 0.85, respectively), the interpretation is that the slaughter level is too low, the cattle herd is building too quickly, and prices will soon decrease.

The price relationships of the varying grades of cattle also vary over the cattle cycle. When marketing is light, the price premium for high grades tends to be highest because cattle are coming out of feedlots at lighter weights. When prices begin to decrease in response to increasing supplies, feeders extend the feeding period of more cattle to heavier weights, and the early stage of liquidation may be indicated. This retention of some of the lighter cattle so that they can be fed to heavier weights reduces the relative scarcity of the heavier higher grades of beef, and the premium narrows. When marketing becomes heavy, feeders may have to market their heavy cattle at low prices and lose money.

Cattle on feed may be owned by packers, chain retailers, speculators, farmer feeders, commercial feeders, or ranchers, with farmer and commercial feeders dominating. Many cattle in custom feedlots are fed for absentee owners under contract. The cattle drives so popular in movie westerns have been replaced by less romantic assembly-line tactics. The range cowboy, the small cattle ranch, and the small feedlot have all declined significantly. The stockyards in the big cities have also felt the changing times. Because of the spiraling costs of transportation and feed, as well as the decreasing supply of grassland, the trend has been toward large, mechanized feedlots in order to achieve such benefits of size as volume buying. In warm areas, cattle may be kept in shaded pens provided with sprinkler systems to reduce temperatures and settle the dust. Special diets have been developed for hot regions. Large lots maintain their own feed-mixing mills, and many have developed their own formulas. Many feedlots, especially in the far west, are geared toward producing the popular choice grade of beef. The prime grade, preferred by more expensive restaurants, is becoming increasingly scarce.

Much of the risk in the cattle business is absorbed by the owners of cattle on the cow-calf operations or on feedlots. Once the owners are committed to producing or feeding calves or yearlings, they have little choice but to bring their animals to a marketable weight, regardless of the fluctuations of cattle or feed prices. In addition to the costs of inventory and feed, they must pay for transportation, marketing, taxes, administration, shrinkage, labor, insurance, repairs, veterinary services, and interest. To reduce the risk, some lots sell their cattle some months in advance of their being finished, with provisions for a price adjustment in accordance with the actual condition of the cattle when delivery time arrives. This selling may be by agreement or via the futures markets.

Producers of calves, feeder cattle, or fed cattle face a classic economic capital budgeting decision. Due to the production lag, they must make an investment on the basis of current and expected costs of inputs and expected output prices. The price they receive for their output depends on the price of beef at the time of their sale, which is several months later due to the production lag for both feeder cattle and fed cattle, as indicated above. Important input prices are the prices of corn and feeder cattle for producers of fed cattle and the price of corn for producers of feeder cattle. Weather conditions affect the supply and price of corn and, to a lesser extent, the supply and price of feeder cattle. Thus, for given beef prices, the lower the price of corn or feeder cattle, the more cattle will be placed on feed, since there will be an expected increase in the profitability of producing fed cattle. This future increase in supply will lead to an increase in the supply of beef, which will, in turn, mitigate the degree of price increase. However, there are potentially countervailing factors. For example, lower corn prices will cause the demand for and price of feeder cattle to increase, which will, to some extent, mitigate the degree of price increase for fed cattle. Lower corn prices will also increase the price of feeder cattle relative to the price of fed cattle, thus affecting the relative profitabilities of these two sectors.

A second important aspect of supply is that since there are more ranches than feedlots and more feedlots than packers, the degree of concentration increases up the production chain; thus, producers tend to be price takers rather than price makers. A third aspect of supply is that beef and cattle, unlike most grains, are perishable. When ready for production, they can be stored for only a short period of time. Thus, since supply cannot be stored for sale at a later time, excesses or deficiencies in supply affect prices quickly and significantly.

Demand

Beef is used almost exclusively for human consumption, and there are some differences in the types of beef used for various classes of consumption, as well as differences in the sources of the beef. For example, cows and bulls are used mainly for ground and processed beef, while fed steers are used mainly for select cuts. Different grades of beef are bought by restaurants, by other institutions such as hospitals and dormitories, and for household use.

Beef is also used for dogfood. Other aspects of the demand for beef are considered in the discussion of price determinants below. In addition to the use of beef for human food, extraneous parts of cattle are used for other purposes. For example, skins, fat, bone, blood, hair, and other nonmeat products which are by-products of beef production are used to make leather, soap, animal feed, camera film, and other products.

Price Determinants

As for any other commodity, the price of beef and, thus, the price of fed cattle, feeder cattle, calves, and cows depend mainly on supply and demand. In turn, the two factors that affect supply are production costs and, to reverse the causality, beef prices. The production costs of fed cattle are determined mainly by the price of feed and feeder cattle; feed accounts for approximately 30 percent and feeder cattle approximately 56 percent of total production costs. Decreases in either of these costs, with beef prices constant, would stimulate beef production.

Some indicators of supply, mentioned above, are as follows. The size of the cow herd is an indicator of beef available one year later. As indicated, the number of cattle on feed by weight category and the number placed on feed are shorter-term indicators of beef supply. The beef-corn price ratio, which affects the number of cattle on feed and the length of the feeding period, also affects the beef supply. On a very short-term basis, the number of fed cattle marketed is an important indicator of beef production.

Interest rates also affect the cost of production through their effect on land-financing costs, which influence the production of feeder cattle, and their effect on fed-cattle prices due to the capital intensity and the relatively long feeding time for producing fed cattle. Finally, weather can also affect supply. For example, drought can affect range and pasture conditions and the quality and availability of feeder cattle. Weather conditions also affect the price of feed for feedlots and, directly or indirectly, through the length of the feeding period, the timing of the supply of fed cattle. Good or bad weather, even at the time of marketing, can affect the number of cattle marketed at the time and the short-run price of cattle.

Several factors affect the demand for beef. The first is personal income. While a rise in income usually translates into a smaller increase in the demand for food than for other items, the demand for beef, especially high-quality beef, has usually responded more quickly to a rise in income than the demand for most other foods. An increase in population also causes an increase in the demand for beef, but increases in population occur slowly and predictably enough that population increases do not affect beef prices significantly.

The second factor influencing demand is often called "taste." Taste is, unlike consumer income and other determinants of demand, very subjective and not measurable—it refers to how well consumers like a product and is independent of all other influences on demand, including price. That is, the greater the taste for a product, the more of the product the consumer will purchase, even at the same price. Taste may affect the seasonal demand for some goods; for example, during the Thanksgiving season, the demand for turkey increases and the demand for beef decreases. During the last few years, there has been a secular decrease in the demand for beef in the United States, probably due to greater health consciousness. For example, the per capita consumption of beef peaked in 1976 and has decreased since then, while the per capita demand for chicken and pork has grown.

Finally, the prices and supplies of beef substitutes also affect the demand for beef. Since pork and chicken are also sources of animal protein, their prices and supplies affect beef demand and prices. Because of the substitutability of beef with pork and chicken, when the prices of pork and chicken decrease relative to beef prices, the demand for beef decreases, and vice versa. An example of this occurred during 1973 and 1974, when beef and pork supplies decreased. Consumers attempted to substitute chicken for beef and pork, with the result that while beef and pork prices increased less than they would have without the substitution, chicken prices increased significantly, even though there was no significant decrease in supply.

Over the last several decades there have been continued changes in the relative consumption of beef, pork, and chicken. During 1984, the per capita consumption of beef was 106.1 pounds, while the per capita consumption of pork and chicken was 65.2 and 54.8 pounds, respectively. However, only since about 1950 has beef been the most consumed meat—between 1938 and 1952 the per capita consumption of pork was slightly greater than that of beef. The per capita consumption of pork, however, is currently less than it was during the earlier 1940s. The per capita consumption of chicken, while always in third place, after beef and pork consumption, and currently still significantly less than that of beef, is now only slightly less than that of pork.

Since 1976, however, the per capita consumption of beef has declined from 127.5 pounds to 106.1 pounds, while the per capita demands for pork and chicken have increased from 58.6 to 65.2 pounds and from 43.3 to 54.8 pounds, respectively, as shown in Table 19-6. A major reason for the large absolute decrease and even larger relative decrease in the demand for beef has been related to the "taste" for beef, in turn related to a concern regarding medical research which has indicated that excessive red meat may contribute to heart disease and possibly cancer. Thus, the consumption of chicken rather than beef has been regarded as more consistent with being healthy. There has also recently been some concern about the use of antibiotics in feeding cattle, hogs, and poultry. The consumption of fish, despite rising fish prices, has increased significantly because of the perceived health factors. Other reasons why chicken consumption has increased are that the chicken industry has developed convenience foods with chicken to a greater extent than the meat industry has with meat and has developed more efficient production methods for chicken using a few large "chicken factories." The last major innovation in the beef industry occurred 20 years ago when Iowa Beef Products began shipping boxed beef—that is, beef cut in large pieces—rather than whole beef carcasses. The decrease in beef consumption has had significant negative effects on the profitability and size of all phases of the beef industry, from the cow-calf operations to the packers.

Despite the fact that total expenditures on meat (beef, pork, broilers, and turkeys) have continued to increase, the percentage of total income spent on meat has continually decreased from over 4 percent in 1979 to under 3 percent in early 1985.

As with the demand for most other farm products, the demand side of beef is dominated by a few buyers, whereas there is a large number of suppliers. Public demand is expressed to an important degree by the buyers for large packing houses and grocery chains. All beef produced will be consumed quickly at some price because of the limited storage facilities. Because demand is less volatile than supply in the short run, the current market price depends heavily on the available supplies of beef in relation to those of competitive meats. In the ultimate response to the public's demand for beef, ranchers buy breeding stock, grain farmers buy feeders, packing houses buy fat cattle, and retailers buy sides of beef.

Exports and imports are of relatively little importance in the analysis of cattle prices. Imports of beef are comparatively small because of shipping costs, although the United States does import some beef from countries such as Australia, New Zealand, Argentina, Ireland, Mexico, and Canada. Some live cattle are also imported from Canada and Mexico. The United States is a net exporter of beef products such as tallow, grease, and hides. It also exports a small amount of beef, primarily to Canada.

Figures 19-4 and 19-5 show the prices of the Chicago Mercantile Exchange live cattle and feeder cattle futures contracts.

Seasonal Effects

While the analysis of the cattle cycle is useful for long-term price forecasting, it is of limited value for forecasting prices over a few months or quarters. For this purpose, the analysis of seasonal changes in cattle and beef production and prices is important.

There is no planting or harvest season for cattle, as there is for other crops, but there is a period of high production. A highly generalized, seasonal cycle is as follows. Most calves are born within 45 days of April 1 and weaned within 45 days of October 1. The 350- to 450-pound calf is then usually "rough-wintered" for about 6 months, during which time he gains about 100 pounds. Then he is "summerized" for 6 months and gains about 225 pounds. He then goes to a feedlot, where he eats corn instead of grass and gains weight at the rate of about 2 pounds a day for about 210 days. After a typical young steer has eaten his corn for the 210 days, he is about 26 months old, weighs about 1150 pounds, is a medium choice steer, and is ready to go to a stockyard for slaughter. The rate of slaughter tends to be fairly level throughout the year, but there is a tendency to reach a maximum in October and a minimum in February. Feeding operations make cattle that were taken off grass in the fall available for slaughter in the spring. In the fall, the cattle slaughtered tend to be grass-fed and hence of a lower grade than the better-finished cattle available in greater abundance in the spring and summer. The prices of cattle sold off grass grazing land, including stocker and feeder cattle and cows as well as the lower-grade slaughter steers, are lowest around October. These same classes reach their highest price levels in the spring, when the grazing season begins and the demand is strong for stocker cattle.

TABLE 19-6 CONSUMPTION OF MEATS IN THE UNITED STATES

Year	Beef Total, pounds	Beef Per capita, pounds	Pork Total, pounds	Pork Per capita, pounds	Chicken Total, pounds	Chicken Per capita, pounds
1975	25,397	118.8	11,853	55.4	8,572	40.6
1976	27,593	127.5	12,667	58.6	9,226	43.3
1977	27,048	124.0	13,202	60.5	9,627	44.8
1978	25,998	117.9	13,293	60.3	10,294	47.5
1979	23,522	105.5	15,353	68.8	11,280	51.6
1980	23,320	103.4	16,574	73.5	11,295	50.1
1981	23,756	104.3	15,927	69.9	11,767	51.7
1982	23,998	104.3	14,425	62.7	12,222	53.2
1983	24,710	106.4	15,369	66.2	12,511	53.8
1984	24,885	106.1	15,384	65.2	12,842	54.8

SOURCE: USDA, Economic Research Service.

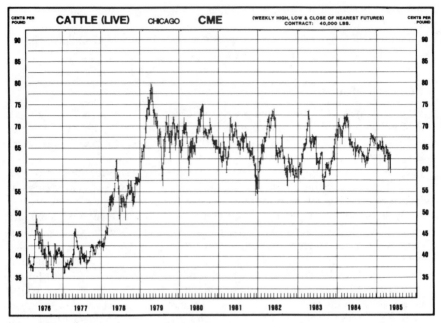

Figure 19-4 Cattle and calves. [*Commodity Year Book 1985, ed. Walter L. Emery (Jersey City, N.J.: Commodity Research Bureau, Inc.).*]

In the corn belt, the prices of fed cattle take a different course than those of grass-fed cattle coming off the range. Cattle go to the feedlots in greatest volume from September to November and remain there from 3 to 12 months, depending on the degree of finish desired and their age when they entered. Prices are relatively lowest for each grade of cattle as it becomes available in greatest supply. Commercial-grade cattle are priced lowest in the fall, when the prices of better grades are near their highs. Good-grade cattle are cheapest in winter, when they are ready for marketing after their relatively short feeding period. The higher choice grade is most plentiful in the spring, and the highest grade, prime, which requires the longest feeding period, is ready for the market in its greatest quantity in summer.

Despite the seasonal breeding and feeding patterns, the production of beef has only a small seasonal, tending to rise slightly from the second to the fourth quarter after declining slightly from the first to the second quarter. Similarly, there is a fairly weak seasonal for the prices of beef, tending to reach a trough in February and a peak in August. The lack of a relationship between price and seasonal production indicates that demand, as well as supply, and also cyclical effects influence beef prices.

Futures Pricing

As discussed in other chapters, some futures contracts, such as those on metals, are priced very precisely on a cash-and-carry basis. Others, such as those on grains, are priced on a cash-and-carry basis within a crop year, but the price relationship changes across crop years. Contracts of either type are priced on a cash-and-carry basis because they can be stored and carried from one contract month to another and, thus, delivered and redelivered in more than one contract month. Cattle, however, as indicated above, are "perishable"; that is, they must be slaughtered within a short period of time after they have reached the stage where they are ready for slaughter, and they cannot be carried from one contract month to another. For this reason, cattle and feeder cattle futures contracts are not traded on a cash-and-carry basis. The futures prices of different months are related only by expected changes in the supply-demand relationship over time. This noncarry type of pricing is often called "expectational."

Futures Contracts

There are three active futures contracts based on the cattle complex. The major contract is the live cattle futures contract at the Chicago Mercantile Exchange (CME). The MidAmerica Commodity Exchange also trades a live cattle futures contract; it is one-half the size of the CME contract but identical in every other respect. The CME also trades a futures contract based on feeder cattle.

The advent of the live cattle futures contract was an important event in the history of the futures industry. The announcement by the CME in 1964 that it

Figure 19-5   Cattle and calves. [*Commodity Year Book 1985, ed. Walter L. Emery* (Jersey City, N.J.: Commodity Research Bureau, Inc.).]

was about to begin trading in live cattle was regarded as revolutionary. Over a period exceeding 100 years, futures trading had been considered necessarily confined to inanimate products which had certain rigid characteristics. Products traded on a futures market, it was believed, had to have grade standards that were more precise and more generally accepted than those for cattle in order to be delivered and successfully accepted against futures contracts. Interchangeability of contract units seemed to require something more homogeneous than live steers, which vary so much in weight and quality. Trading was also confined to products that could be stored over long periods of time, which obviously was not possible for live steers. Even beef is not extensively stored because the limited storage facilities are expensive and consumers do not like frozen beef. Most important, it was thought that a successful futures market must be supported by the trade or those engaged in the production or processing of the product. New markets that had not received the support of the trade had failed to survive. Much of the nation's packing industry not only did not encourage the formation of a futures market for live beef cattle but also actively opposed it. In addition, the board of directors of the American Meat Institute, which represented the majority of U.S. meat packers, voted unanimously in opposition to the establishment of a futures market for live beef cattle. These groups may have had some concern that futures trading might become a vehicle for expanding governmental controls over the livestock and meat industry. The Chicago Mercantile Exchange, however, was not dissuaded, especially after the success of its pork bellies futures market had started in 1961. Trading in live beef cattle began in November 1964. Enough interest was expressed almost from the beginning by speculators, cattle raisers, and even some packers to make the new contract a success from the start. This contract marked an important event in the evolution of futures trading.

The trading unit for the CME live cattle contract is 40,000 pounds of USDA estimated yield grade 1, 2, 3, or 4 of choice-quality live steers averaging between 1050 and 1200 pounds, with no individual steer weighing in excess of 100 pounds above or below the average weight for the delivery unit. In addition, no individual steer weighing less than 950 pounds or more than 1300 pounds is deliverable. There are also several other delivery specifications involving hot yield, weight deviations, health, merchantability, and breeding. Some of these criteria are subjective—USDA graders inspect the cattle and determine their deliverability with respect to these subjective criteria.

The delivery months of the live cattle futures contract are February, April, June, August, October, and December. Par delivery points are Peoria, Illinois; Joliet, Illinois; Omaha, Nebraska; Sioux City, Iowa; and Greeley, Colorado. The minimum price fluctuation is 0.025 cent per pound or $10 per contract.

The par delivery unit of the CME feeder cattle contract is 44,000 pounds of feeder steers averaging between 575 and 700 pounds. No individual animal may weigh in excess of 50 pounds more or less than the average weight of the unit. There are several other delivery specifications, including muscle thickness, health, and merchantability. USDA graders make all decisions regarding deliverability and discounts from par, if any.

The delivery months of the feeder cattle contract are January, March, April, May, August, October, and November. Par delivery points are Omaha, Nebraska;

Oklahoma City, Oklahoma; and Sioux City, Iowa. Delivery can also be made at several other points at varying discounts. The minimum price fluctuation is 0.025 cent per pound or $11 per contract.

Speculative Uses

While the live and feeder cattle futures contracts have been used extensively by hedgers, they have also been popular speculative vehicles. They are bought and sold on the basis of the price determinants discussed above. Speculation prior to important USDA announcements is particularly common.

Intercontract spreads between the live and feeder cattle contracts on the basis of changes in the phase of the cattle cycle or even temporary price discrepancies and between either cattle contract and the corn contract are practiced. Spreads between the live cattle contract and the live hog contract are also common. Finally, because the cattle contracts are not priced on a carry basis, intracontract spreads in both are volatile and attract speculators for this reason.

Sources of Information

There are several important sources of information on the cattle futures contracts, issued by the government, trade associations, and private agencies. Among the important USDA publications (from various USDA divisions) are:

1. *Livestock & Meat Outlook & Situation* (six times a year)—provides historical data summaries and analysis
2. *Cattle* (published in February and July)—shows cattle inventories on January 1 and July 1
3. *Livestock Slaughter* (monthly)—gives meat production and slaughter by weight and number for previous month
4. *Cattle on Feed* (monthly)—provides placements and marketings of cattle and calves on feed
5. *Livestock, Meat & Wool Market News* (weekly)—provides information on livestock receipts and slaughter
6. *Feed Situation* (quarterly)—reviews feed grain industries

Other USDA publications on cattle and beef are also available.

The *Yellow Sheets* provided by the National Provisioner on a daily basis give daily information on the cattle and beef markets. The daily pink *Meat Sheets* published by Meat Sheet, Inc., provide similar information.

The Chicago Mercantile Exchange provides an excellent report on livestock and meat fundamentals and summaries of their contract specifications. The Chicago Mercantile Exchange *Year Book* is also a valuable source of statistics on the cattle and cattle futures markets.

Notes from a Trader

In most years the cattle futures market is a good trading vehicle. Except for unusually surprising reports, the market is one of the less volatile. The length of time required for significant changes in the cattle cycle causes long trends in the futures market. There may be long periods of narrow ranges which might try the patience of more aggressive traders.

The analysis of this market may prove easier than that of some others because of the dominance of the supply side and the relative availability of figures. Some data, however, such as cattle-on-feed figures, may prove inaccurate at times. There is also less reliance on government support programs than in the case of many other commodities.

Intercontract spreads between live cattle and feeder cattle, based on changes in the phase of the cattle cycle, and between live cattle and corn, based on shorter-run profitability considerations, are also practiced. Speculators also transact intercontract spreads between live cattle and hogs on the basis of differences in their production cycles or differences in their demands. Intracontract spreads in the live-cattle market may also prove attractive because there is no normal carrying-charge relationship.

HOGS AND PORK BELLIES

Introduction

In general, the process of raising hogs for the production of pork and pork bellies, from which bacon is made, is similar to that of raising cattle for the production of beef. While hogs are raised in several countries in the world, there is little world trade in pork and pork bellies—most production is consumed in the country of production. As shown in Table 19-7, China is the largest producer of hogs in the world, with Russia and the United States second and third, respectively. Brazil, West Germany, Poland, Mexico, Japan, France, and other European countries are also significant producers.

In the United States, as shown in Table 19-8, hog production is concentrated in the corn belt. Iowa is the major producer, with over 25 percent of the nation's total. Approximately two-thirds of the U.S. total is produced by Illinois, Minnesota, Indiana, Nebraska, and Missouri, in addition to Iowa. Table 19-9 shows the major statistics for hog production in the United States.

Supply

The definition of some terms is necessary, as with cattle, for understanding the production of hogs and pork:

Farrowing. The act of giving birth.
Gilts. Female swine that have not given birth to a litter.
Boars. Male hogs used for breeding.
Stags. Boars castrated after sexual maturity.
Barrows. Male hogs castrated before maturity (equivalent to steers in cattle production)—barrows gain weight more rapidly than boars.

The hog cycle is considerably shorter than the cattle cycle for physiological reasons. The gestation period for hogs is approximately 4 months or somewhat

TABLE 19-7 WORLD HOG NUMBERS IN SPECIFIED COUNTRIES (in millions of head)

Year	Brazil	Canada	Denmark	France	West Germany	Hungary	Italy	Japan	Mexico	Philippines	Poland	Spain	China*	United Kingdom	United States	U.S.S.R.	World
1976	36.0		7.6	11.5	19.8	7.0	8.9	7.5	12.0	6.5	21.6		1976–	7.7	49.3	57.9	1976–
1977	36.8		7.9	11.5	20.6	7.9	9.1	8.1	12.3	5.7	16.8		1980	8.2	54.9	63.1	1980
1978	37.6		8.2	11.5	21.4	7.9	9.4	8.8	12.6	6.9	20.6		average	7.7	56.5	70.5	average
1979	36.0		9.2	11.3	22.6	8.0	8.9	9.5	12.7	7.4	21.1		(296.2)	8.0	60.4	73.5	(670.9)
1980	36.5	10.1	9.5	11.4	22.4	8.4	8.8	10.0	12.8	7.9	21.0	10.5		7.8	67.3	73.9	
1981	35.0	10.2	9.7	11.7	22.6	8.3	8.9	10.1	15.4	7.6	18.7	11.0	305.4	7.8	64.5	73.4	708.7
1982	33.5	10.0	9.8	11.8	22.3	8.3	9.0	10.0	16.2	7.6	19.1	10.7	293.7	7.9	58.7	73.3	692.4
1983	33.5	10.1	9.5	11.7	22.5	9.0	9.1	10.3	16.5	8.0	17.6	11.7	300.8	8.2	54.5	76.7	700.3
1984†	33.0	10.4	9.0	11.2	23.4	9.8	9.2	10.4	15.8	7.8	15.8	12.1	298.5	7.8	56.7	78.5	705.9
1985‡	33.0	10.4	9.1	10.1	22.1	9.8	9.1	10.5	15.0	7.5	16.6	12.1	296.8	7.8	54.0	79.5	700.2

*Mainland.

†Preliminary.

‡Estimate.

SOURCE: USDA, Foreign Agricultural Service.

TABLE 19-8 HOGS AND PIGS ON U.S. FARMS ON DECEMBER 1 (in thousands of head)

Year	Geor-gia	Illi-nois	Indi-ana	Iowa	Kan-sas	Ken-tucky	Minne-sota	Mis-souri	Ne-braska	North Car-olina	Ohio	South Dakota	Ten-nessee	Wis-consin	Total
1979	2360	6950	4850	16,200	2090	1470	4900	4650	4150	2650	2120	2000	1400	1830	67,318
1980	3250	6600	4600	16,100	1900	1220	5100	3980	3900	2460	2150	1860	1140	1680	64,462
1981	1520	6450	4100	16,300	1770	1040	4300	3400	4100	1980	2050	1710	900	1380	58,698
1982	1450	5600	4400	14,400	1670	960	4000	3500	3800	2150	1920	1580	750	1220	54,534
1983	1350	5400	4200	15,000	1650	1000	4400	3600	4000	2350	2200	1730	950	1280	56,694
1984*	1200	5400	4300	14,200	1600	880	4300	3450	3700	2300	1970	1600	1100	1300	54,043

*Preliminary.

SOURCE: USDA, Crop Reporting Board.

TABLE 19-9 SALIENT STATISTICS OF PIGS AND HOGS IN THE UNITED STATES

Year	Pig crop Spring* Sows farrowed‡	Pig crop Spring* Pigs saved‡	Pig crop Fall† Sows farrowed‡	Pig crop Fall† Pigs saved‡	Total pig crop	Value of hogs on farms, Dec. 1 Dollars per head	Value of hogs on farms, Dec. 1 Total, millions of dollars	Hog marketings, thousands of head	Quantity produced (live weight, millions of pounds)	Value of production, millions of dollars	Hogs slaughtered — Commercial Federally inspected	Hogs slaughtered — Commercial Other	Hogs slaughtered — Commercial Total	Hogs slaughtered — Farm	Hogs slaughtered — Total
1976	5,777	42,177	5,850	42,218	84,395	47.00	2,583	75,747	18,160	7,856	70,454	3,330	73,784	1,175	74,959
1977	6,050	42,960	6,009	43,202	86,162	63.20	3,575	80,939	19,021	7,485	74,019	3,285	77,303	1,139	78,442
1978	6,034	42,481	6,398	46,031	88,512	83.20	5,023	81,271	19,466	9,066	74,139	3,176	77,315	1,102	78,417
1979	7,176	50,571	7,322	52,241	102,792	56.00	3,775	92,327	22,595	9,416	85,425	3,674	89,099	1,080	90,179
1980	7,229	52,288	6,855	49,432	101,720	74.70	4,821	100,388	23,352	8,847	91,882	4,192	96,074	1,100	97,174
1981	6,440	47,605	6,268	46,248	93,853	70.10	4,114	95,895	21,783	9,521	87,850	3,697	91,547	897	92,444
1982	5,664	41,575	5,884	43,614	85,189	89.90	4,903	86,653	19,441	10,180	79,328	1,867	82,191	654	81,850
1983	6,301	47,409	6,176	45,746	93,155	58.80	3,331				84,392		87,584		
1984§	5,686	42,322	5,856	44,154	86,476	75.00	4,054						85,156		
1985¶	5,393	40,124													

*December–May.
†June–November.
‡In thousands of head.
§Preliminary.
¶Breeding intentions.
SOURCE: USDA, Statistical Reporting Service.

less (some say 3 months, 3 weeks, and 3 days); that is, farrowing occurs approximately 4 months after breeding. Since it takes approximately 1 month to breed a sow, each sow is bred approximately twice a year.

Litters range from 5 to 15 pigs, with a recent average of slightly less than 9. The pigs are weaned, that is, taken away from their nursing mothers, 6 weeks after birth. Between farrowing and weaning, an average of slightly less than two pigs are lost, more during severe winters, so an average of about seven pigs survive weaning. The litter size reported by the USDA refers to pigs surviving weaning. Although the sows can produce two litters each year for several years, they become heavier the more litters they produce and, as a result, sell at a discount. Sows are, thus, typically slaughtered after producing only one or two litters.

Gilts reach both sexual maturity and slaughter weight at about 6 months of age. So, at 6 months of age, gilts can be either withheld from slaughter and added to the supply of breeding sows or slaughtered. Barrows are also fed to approximately 6 months of age before slaughter. Figure 19-6 summarizes the hog production cycle.

On the basis of the hog production cycle, the hog cycle is considered to be about 4 years, versus about 12 years for the cattle cycle, although hog cycles may range from 3 to 6 years. During the last 50 years, there have been 12 hog cycles averaging 4.1 years and comprising expansions of approximately 2.4 years and contractions of approximately 1.7 years.

During the feeding process, pigs are fed a combination of grain (mainly corn, but also oats or soybeans) and a commercial protein supplement, with additions of vitamins, minerals, and antibiotics. Recently, hogs have been slaughtered when they weigh about 220 pounds. When the price of feed is high relative to hog prices, hogs are usually slaughtered at lighter weights; at lower feed prices relative to hog prices, they are fed to heavier weights.

During recent years, hogs and pork have become much leaner. For example, between 1956 and 1980, pork production increased by 60 percent, while the number of hogs slaughtered increased by only 22 percent. And while the amount of pork produced per hog increased by more than 30 percent (to 170 pounds), only 4 percent of this was due to an increase in the average weight of hogs slaughtered (to 240 pounds). Another indication of the production of leaner hogs

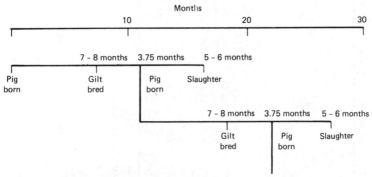

Figure 19-6   Pork production cycle. (*U.S. Department of Agriculture, Economics, Statistics, and Cooperatives Service, February 1979.*)

is that during this period the average lard production per hog declined from approximately 33 pounds to 13 pounds.

Feed costs represent a higher fraction of the total costs of hog production than in the case of cattle production. Whereas for hogs, feed costs represent approximately 38 percent of total costs and replacement animals 46 percent, for cattle, as indicated, the corresponding proportions are 31 percent and 56 percent. On the average, about 4.4 pounds of feed are needed for each pound of slaughter hog. The costs of corn and soybean meal are the dominant feed costs. It is for these reasons that the hog-corn ratio is an important indicator of profitability and future supply in the hog industry. The increased volatility of grain prices discussed in the previous chapter and the relatively long production period for slaughter hogs, thus, provide a difficult planning situation for hog producers.

When hogs are ready for slaughter, they can be sold directly to packers or through terminal markets or auctions. As with cattle, an increasing fraction has been marketed directly to packers—in 1980, over three-fourths of the total sales were to packers.

While there are obvious similarities between cattle and hog production, there are also important differences. One is that while cattle production usually involves two or three separate businesses (the cow-calf operation, the feeder, and, perhaps, the intermediate stocker cattle phase), hogs are typically produced in a single unit, often called a "farrow-to-finish" operation. That is, the pigs usually remain at the same location from farrowing to finish. There are several reasons for the stationary location in hog production. First, hogs cannot convert grass and grazing roughage into protein, and so there is no equivalent of a stocker operation. Second, sows, baby pigs, and hogs all eat essentially the same feed. Finally, young pigs are very sensitive to stress and disease, and as a result, feeder pigs cannot be effectively moved from one location to another. Relocation can slow weight gains and extend the feeding period. For these reasons, about 80 percent of all pigs spend their entire lives in the same farrow-to-finish operation.

Although hog production remains an important part of American agriculture, hog producers, like cattle producers, have become fewer in number and larger in size. For example, in 1981 less than 5 percent of the total hog operations in the United States accounted for over 45 percent of all hogs produced—these operations had in excess of 500 hogs. Consistent with this increased size, hog production has become very capital-intensive, using expensive buildings and equipment. The increased capital, in addition to decreasing costs, enhances the production of hogs during severe winters and hot summers in the corn belt.

In the past, all females were bred at the same times, once in the spring and once in the fall, and so a distinct seasonal in hog production was created. Hog marketings were, thus, very high during the winter and very low during the summer. Now hog production is much more uniform throughout the year. While marketings are still lowest in July, they have increased relatively during this time. Hog marketings have minor peaks in March through April and in October through November.

The Pipeline Approach. As with the supply of beef, the supply of newly produced pork can be forecast by considering the production cycle. The first step in the pipeline approach for pork involves the number of farrowings, that is, the number of pigs born. The USDA, on a quarterly basis (the 22d of March, June, September, and December) in its *Hogs and Pigs* report, provides data on the number of pigs saved (surviving weaning) and the number of sow farrowings for the 10 largest hog-producing states (Georgia, Illinois, Indiana, Iowa, Kansas, Minnesota, Missouri, Nebraska, North Carolina, and Ohio), which produce over 75 percent of the total hogs in the United States. From the number of pigs saved and the number of sow farrowings the total national pig crop can be estimated. Since it takes approximately 6 months to bring a newborn pig to a slaughter weight of 200 to 240 pounds, the total number of hogs slaughtered 6 months later can be estimated. From the hog slaughter, the amount of pork production can also be forecast.

Variations Affecting the Pipeline Approach. Each of the forecasts is based on estimates, and errors can enter at each step. First, the 10 major states do not always produce the same fraction of pigs in the United States. Second, and more important, the relation between pigs produced and hogs slaughtered 6 months later is variable. The period between birth and slaughter can vary due to weather and the price of feed relative to the price of pork—relatively high feed prices will result in earlier slaughters at lighter weights, and vice versa. Another factor that affects this relationship is the number of gilts withheld from slaughter in order to be added to the breeding herd. During the expansion phase of the hog cycle, gilts are withheld from slaughter, and the hog slaughter will be less relative to farrowings. During the contraction phase, sows are culled from the herd and gilts are not withheld from slaughter, and the number of hogs slaughtered increases relative to pig farrowings. The USDA provides weekly data on the female portion of total hog slaughter.

The estimate of the amount of pork produced from hogs slaughtered depends on the amount of pork per hog, or the yield. Recently, hogs have yielded about 172 pounds of pork. Table 19-10 shows the recent quantities produced at the three stages of the pipeline.

Demand

Pork has always played an important role in the U.S. diet, although the per capita consumption of pork has increased by much less than that of beef and chicken since 1940. Pork is consumed in several different forms. At the packing plant, the hog is slaughtered and cut into halves or quarters for shipment to a processor, or cut into smaller pieces called wholesale cuts. According to estimates, a 220-pound hog will yield about 153 pounds of pork, trimmings, and lard with proportions as follows: fresh hams, 18.5 percent; pork bellies, 17.5 percent; loins, 15.0 percent; fat back, clear plate, and fat trimmings, 18.0 percent; picnics, 8.5 percent; and other, 22.5 percent. The six main commercial cuts of pork are hams and loins, the largest; picnics (a hamlike cut from the front leg of the hog); Boston butts; bellies; and spareribs.

These cuts account for over 40 percent of the weight and 90 percent of the value of hogs. Each cut has different characteristics. While loins and butts are sold fresh, most of the other cuts are processed. This represents another major difference between the cattle and hog industries—while most beef is used fresh

TABLE 19-10   PIG CROP, HOG SLAUGHTER, AND PORK PRODUCTION, 1979–1983 (by quarters*)

	I	II	III	IV
	Pig Crop—10 States (in Millions of Head)			
1979	16.289	22.108	19.921	19.042
1980	17.418	21.889	18.001	18.922
1981	15.863	20.741	18.134	17.853
1982	14.059	17.943	16.254	17.548
1983	15.543	21.063	17.675	17.611
	Hog Slaughter, Commercial (in Millions of Head)			
1979	20.040	21.740	22.082	25.237
1980	24.236	25.039	22.157	24.641
1981	23.678	22.594	21.278	24.025
1982	21.714	20.712	18.940	20.825
1983	20.211	21.403	21.292	24.336
	Pork Production, Commercial (in Millions of Head)			
1979	3399	3754	3775	4347
1980	4126	4299	3756	4252
1981	4073	3881	3605	4157
1982	3693	3550	3240	3638
1983	3483	3726	3644	4208

*All quarters are calendar quarters except for pig crop, which begins with a December–February quarter.
SOURCES: Pig crop—USDA, Economic Statistical Service, *Hogs and Pigs;* slaughter and production—USDA, Economic Statistical Service, *Livestock and Meat Situation.*

soon after slaughter, a large portion of pork is processed and becomes storable. For example, hams and picnics can be smoked, canned, or frozen, and pork bellies can be stored for up to 1 year before processing. The storability of pork products means that forecasts of futures supplies must consider not only new production but also stocks, particularly for pork bellies.

The various cuts of pork also have different seasonals in demand. For example, the demand for ham is particularly large before Christmas and Easter, while the demand for pork bellies usually peaks during late summer.

Because there is a futures contract on one particular cut of hogs—pork bellies— we will consider this hog product in more detail. The pork belly is the layer of meat and fat from the underside of a hog. Each hog has two bellies, one on each side, which extend from the front to the rear legs. Each belly weighs between 10 and 20 pounds, depending on the size of the hog. Bellies are divided into five 2-pound weight ranges—10 to 12, 12 to 14, 14 to 16, 16 to 18, and 18 to 20 pounds— with most bellies in the middle ranges. Bellies typically account for about 12 percent of the total weight of hogs and about 17 percent of total pork production. Almost all bellies are cured, smoked, and sliced into bacon by either the firm that slaughters the hog or another firm. There is also a well-developed cash market for pork bellies between packers and processors, which is fostered by the demand for bellies for delivery on the pork belly futures contract.

While the amount of pork frozen and available for subsequent use is small overall—less than 2.5 percent of total pork production is frozen—approximately 7 to 10 percent of the bellies produced are frozen. The seasonal low of frozen stocks is in late summer through early fall, while the high is during the late spring. The period June–September represents the months of greatest movement of bellies out of freezers in response to the peak summer demand for bacon. Tables 19-11 and 19-12 show the recent cold storage holdings of pork and pork bellies, respectively, by month.

Price Determinants

Pork prices are determined by basic supply-demand factors. On the supply side, the phase of the hog cycle has an important effect on prices. Data on the size of the pig crop, hog slaughter, slaughter weights, and the fraction of females in slaughter, as discussed above, can be used in forecasting supplies.

The ratio of the price of corn, the major feed for hogs, to the price of hogs affects the profitability of raising hogs and the future supply. A low ratio of corn price to hog price indicates that feeding is profitable, which will, in the short run, lead to hogs being fed to heavier weights and in the longer run to breeding herds being expanded. These factors tend to contract supply in the very short run but expand supply in the longer run, with the opposite effect on prices.

During recent years, the price of corn has become a smaller fraction of the total costs of producing hogs as other feed supplements and protein meals have been used as feed and as fixed costs, due to buildings and equipment, have increased. Thus, while still useful, the hog-corn price ratio is somewhat less useful as an indicator of the profitability of producing hogs. The hog-corn price ratio is the price of hogs per hundred pounds divided by the price of corn per bushel. Data on the hog-corn ratio, as shown in Table 19-13, are closely watched in this regard. Figure 19-7 shows a plot of the hog-corn ratio in recent years.

On the demand side, pork prices are affected in the long run by the size and age mix of the population and the consumer taste for pork relative to the taste for other products, such as beef and chicken. In the short run, the real income of consumers and the prices of these competing products affect the demand for pork. Prior to about 1950, the per capita consumption of pork was higher than that of either beef or chicken. Since then, however, the per capita consumption of pork has remained approximately constant, while that of beef and chicken has increased considerably. As a result, per capita pork consumption has recently been considerably below the per capita consumption of beef and only slightly above that of chicken. For example, in 1980 the U.S. per capita consumption was approximately 108 pounds for beef, 67 pounds for pork, and 50 pounds for chicken. During the last decade, however, the demand for beef has decreased relative to the demand for pork.

Seasonals

Some aspects of the seasonals in the production of pork and pork bellies are discussed above. While seasonal production patterns have become less pronounced

TABLE 19-11 COLD-STORAGE HOLDINGS OF FROZEN PORK* IN THE UNITED STATES ON FIRST OF MONTH (in millions of pounds)

Year	January	February	March	April	May	June	July	August	September	October	November	December
1980	280.8	285.6	270.4	291.2	345.3	356.5	313.9	263.7	217.3	222.0	269.3	320.7
1981†	348.6	350.8	355.9	360.6	403.5	394.4	346.5	283.4	225.1	206.7	238.3	255.2
1982†	264.4	247.3	246.3	274.1	—	—	264.1	—	—	183.0	—	—
1983†	219.0	224.2	215.8	234.7	272.7	293.0	280.4	253.0	214.1	210.0	240.0	295.2
1984†	300.6	295.1	311.7	350.7	390.4	437.7	405.2	345.0	269.5	256.6	275.6	269.4
1985†	274.1	291.9	283.8									

*Excludes lard.
†Preliminary.
SOURCE: USDA, Crop Reporting Board.

TABLE 19-12 U.S. FROZEN PORK BELLY STORAGE STOCKS (in thousands of pounds, as of first of the month)

Year	January	February	March	April	May	June	July	August	September	October	November	December
1976	44,722	37,386	38,526	51,176	60,144	63,799	49,258	25,773	8,689	5,858	9,708	24,946
1977	42,906	38,338	36,364	52,806	69,539	80,658	62,695	29,901	9,640	5,241	4,230	20,642
1978	23,747	19,013	15,738	39,631	70,976	82,343	75,027	44,787	21,015	7,482	20,013	40,964
1979	54,367	39,432	37,172	57,744	69,689	86,065	78,935	53,373	21,800	11,077	17,739	42,156
1980	70,201	69,635	67,800	85,444	98,163	106,869	96,967	68,616	34,410	21,867	42,186	72,127
1981	97,365	90,181	94,661	104,357	125,469	132,568	117,795	72,998	36,094	16,228	18,060	35,058
1982	54,639	46,167	41,855	66,061	—	—	72,593	—	—	7,558	—	—
1983	31,292	33,592	33,400	44,304	54,510	64,671	63,468	48,409	26,642	15,672	20,047	52,924
1984	78,648	71,568	78,169	95,009	112,205	127,527	115,034	85,630	43,626	22,321	24,048	38,333
1985*	57,361	53,623	51,730									

*Preliminary.
SOURCE: USDA, Crop Reporting Board.

TABLE 19-13 HOG-CORN PRICE RATIO* AT OMAHA

Year	January	February	March	April	May	June	July	August	September	October	November	December	Average
1980	16.5	16.1	15.2	12.3	12.0	13.8	15.3	16.1	15.6	15.2	13.8	13.5	14.6
1981	13.0	13.3	12.4	12.3	12.9	15.2	15.9	18.1	19.8	18.7	17.5	16.8	15.5
1982†	18.4	20.1	19.8	19.8	21.8	22.1	23.3	27.9	28.1	27.2	22.8	23.0	22.9
1983†	23.2	21.7	18.6	15.4	15.2	14.7	14.4	14.6	13.8	12.9	11.9	14.5	15.9
1984†	16.0	15.3	14.5	14.5	14.3	14.8	16.6	16.8	16.0	16.4	18.4	19.6	16.1
1985†	18.8												

*Ratio computed by dividing average price of packer and shipper purchases of barrows and gilts by average price of No. 2 yellow corn, both at Omaha. This ratio represents the number of bushels of corn required to buy 100 pounds of live hogs.

†Preliminary.

SOURCE: USDA, Economic Research Service.

for pork in recent years, these seasonals are still more pronounced than for beef. While farrowings are now more regular throughout the year, they are still at their lowest in midwinter. Hog marketings reach a peak in March through April and a considerably higher peak during the fourth quarter. In addition, the production seasonal is not as strong as the farrowing cycle because even though there is a period of about 6 months from farrow to slaughter, farmers adjust the length of their feeding program to avoid gluts of hogs and pork on the market at any one time.

Even though the seasonals of pork production have been mitigated, hog prices tend to be at their lowest during late spring and the late fourth quarter, when hog marketings are at their greatest, and they tend to reach a peak in August, when marketings are low.

A factor that reduces the effect of the stronger seasonal in farrowings, compared with the equivalent in beef production, is the fact that inventories are more important in pork, particularly pork bellies, than they are in beef. Since pork production is at its lowest in the third quarter, pork belly inventories tend to peak in June, prior to the third quarter peak in demand, and to trough in October, prior to the next production peak. Inventories of other pork products, typically three times as great as pork belly inventories, behave similarly to pork belly inventories.

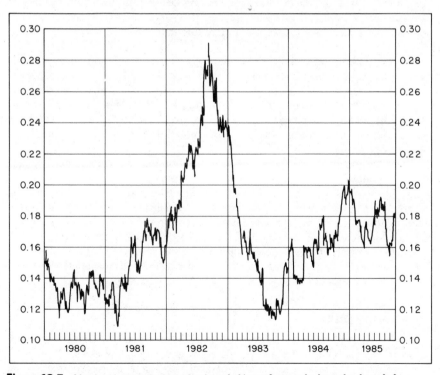

Figure 19-7   Live hog future closing price (nearby)/corn future closing price (nearby).

It is likely that seasonal patterns in production and in prices will continue to become less pronounced.

Futures Contracts

There are futures contracts based on frozen pork bellies and live hogs, both traded on the Chicago Mercantile Exchange. Pork belly futures trading began during September 1961, became active during 1964, and has experienced significant trading volume and open interest since 1965. The pork belly futures contract is based on 38,000 pounds of frozen pork bellies from one federally inspected packing plant that is also approved by the Chicago Mercantile Exchange. Each belly must be USDA-approved, cannot have more than 75 minor defects (a schedule of defects is provided by the exchange), and must be produced from a barrow, gilt, or sow— no bellies from stags and boars are permitted. Bellies in the 12- to 14-pound or 14- to 16-pound range are eligible for par delivery. Bellies that have more than 75 minor defects and that are in the 16- to 18-pound range are deliverable at discounts.

Deliveries are made in Chicago at par, although deliveries can also be made at other exchange-approved delivery points at allowances specified by the exchange. The delivery months are February, March, May, July, and August. Given the minimum level of pork bellies in storage during October, the February to August contracts in the same calendar year represent the same crop year. Prices are quoted in cents per pound, with a minimum price fluctuation of 0.025 cent per pound, or $9.50 per contract.

Futures trading in live hogs began during February 1966, and during recent years the trading volume has exceeded that of pork bellies. Each contract is based on 30,000 pounds of USDA Grade 1, 2, 3, or 4 barrows and gilts. The delivery unit must average between 200 and 230 pounds, with at least 90 hogs in each unit in the 200- to 230-pound range. Hogs in the 190- to 200-pound and 230- to 240-pound ranges are deliverable at a discount, while hogs below 190 pounds or above 240 pounds are not deliverable.

Prices are quoted in cents per pound, with a minimum price fluctuation of 0.025 cent per pound, or $7.50 per contract. The delivery months are February, April, June, July, August, October, and December. Since hogs are not storable, there is no crop year in the live hog futures contract. Par delivery can be made at Peoria, Illinois, although delivery can also be made at approved delivery points in other hog-producing states at 25-cent and 50-cent discounts per hundredweight.

Futures contracts based on feeder pigs have been considered but have not been attempted because, as indicated above, it is inefficient to transport feeder pigs, and most pigs remain on the same farrow-to-finish operation.

Speculative Uses

The live hog and particularly the pork belly futures contracts have been very popular speculative vehicles for speculators who wish to "buy 'em" or "sell 'em" on the basis of the pricing factors discussed above. The pork belly contract is one of the most volatile futures contracts, with many limit-up and limit-down days.

The recent prices of the live hog and pork belly futures contracts are shown in Figures 19-8 and 19-9. This volatility relates primarily to variations in the level of

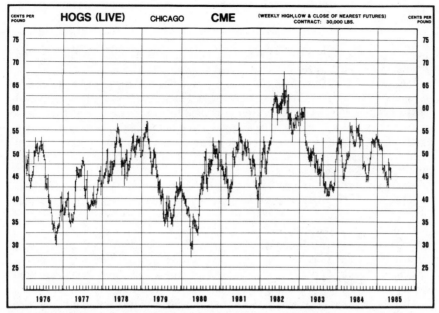

Figure 19-8 Hogs (live). [*Commodity Year Book 1985, ed. Walter L. Emery (Jersey City, N.J.: Commodity Research Bureau, Inc.).*]

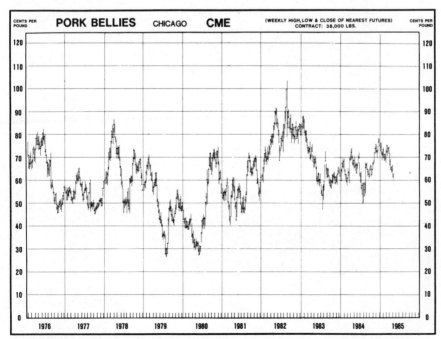

Figure 19-9 Pork bellies. [*Commodity Year Book 1985, ed. Walter L. Emery (Jersey City, N.J.: Commodity Research Bureau, Inc.).*]

hog production, variations in the levels of inventories, changes in the hog-corn price ratio, and, at times, speculative psychology.

Despite being very related, the futures prices of hogs and pork bellies are determined differently. Hogs are not storable, and so the prices of the various months of the live hog futures contract are not related by storage costs, and there is no crop year in hogs. The prices of the various months of the pork belly futures contract are related by carry, and pork bellies have a crop year. Thus, intracommodity spreads in the live hog contract are extremely variable, and considerable profits, or losses, can result.

Since pork bellies can be stored for several months, contracts within the same crop year, from February through August, represent bellies in the same crop year. Thus, "belly spreads" can be done within a crop year or across crop years. An August contract against a February contract of the following year is a popular spread across crop years because bellies received on delivery on the August contract cannot be delivered against the February contract, and the spread is, therefore, extremely volatile. Other spreads across crop years are also very volatile, as they are in grains, while intra-crop-year spreads are less volatile.

The live hog and pork belly futures contracts are also used for intercommodity spreads. A popular intercommodity spread, hogs against bellies, is based on differences in the demands for these products and the frozen storage of bellies. Figure

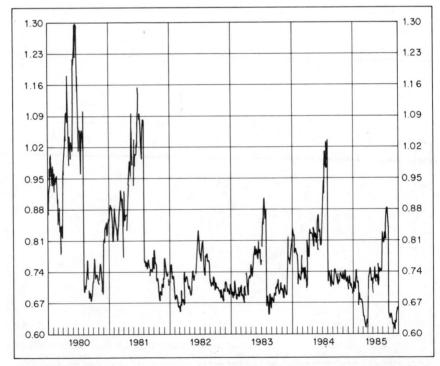

Figure 19-10   Live hog future closing price (nearby)/pork belly future closing price (nearby).

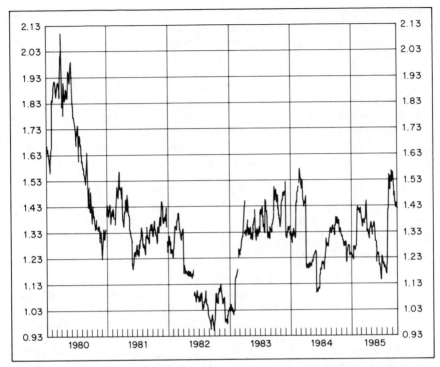

Figure 19-11   Live cattle future closing price (nearby)/live hog future closing price (nearby).

19-10 provides a plot of their price ratio in recent years. As indicated, this spread has also been fairly volatile.

The live hog–live cattle spread is also a common spread. It is based on differences in the seasonal and cyclical production levels of these two meat substitutes. Figure 19-11 shows the recent volatility of this spread. The hog-corn spread, discussed above, is a popular spread involving the hog contract.

Sources of Information

The most important source of information is probably the *Hogs and Pigs* report, published quarterly by the Crop Reporting Board of the Statistical Reporting Service of the USDA on the 22d of March, June, September, and December. This report, based on a survey taken about 3 weeks earlier, covers all 50 states during December and June and the 10 major hog-producing states during March and September. The report provides data by state on the number of sow farrowings, the number of pigs saved per sow, and the total number saved. It also gives producers' intentions for sow farrowings during the next two quarters.

Cold Storage, from the same USDA division, is published each month (on or about the 20th) and provides freezer inventories of bellies, picnics, hams, loins, spareribs, trimmings, and total pork at the end of the preceding month. It also provides data on freezer inventories of beef, poultry, and many other commodities.

The *Livestock Slaughter* report, also published monthly (on or about the 20th) by the USDA, provides data on hog slaughters. *Livestock and Meat Statistics*, an annual published by the USDA, provides more detailed data on a historical basis. The weekly *Livestock, Meat & Wool Market News*, also published by the USDA, provides extensive data on hogs and pork. The *Livestock & Meat Outlook & Situation* is published by the USDA six times a year and provides historical information on the livestock and meat markets. *Feed Situation*, a quarterly published by the USDA, provides data on the feed industries. Two sources of information on daily prices provided by private sources are also closely watched: the *Yellow Sheet* and the pink *Meat Sheet*.

The Chicago Mercantile Exchange *Year Book* contains daily prices, volume, and open interest for each contract, daily cash prices, and useful statistical information related to the supply of and demand for hogs, pork, and pork bellies.

Notes from a Trader

Pork bellies provide a favorite vehicle for day traders because the typical day's price range can easily cover the reduced commission granted for day trades and provide a reasonable profit. Because of the volatility of the market and the popularity of day trading in the market, the last minutes of trading are often particularly volatile, and execution prices are often disappointing.

The belly market lends itself well to spreads such as the February-July or February-August spread. Nearby contracts usually gain enough on the distant in bull markets and lose enough in bear markets to make these spreads attractive, especially considering the lower margin and reduction in risk.

The response of the market opening to the news of the day may be out of proportion to its significance, particularly in the case of the morning hog run, storage movement, or hog prices. Also, the market tends to anticipate important reports, such as those on the pig-crop or cold-storage supply, more accurately than other markets, such as grains.

Because the market is so much better oriented to changes in supply than to changes in demand, it is easier for traders to determine meaningful relationships than in more two-sided markets. If one is stubborn and willing to fight markets, it is advisable to choose markets other than pork bellies or hogs.

20

Natural Resources: Metals and Petroleum

"Luck," continued the gambler reflectively, "is a mighty queer thing. All you know about it is that it's bound to change. And it's finding out when it's going to change that makes you."
BRET HARTE
The Outcasts of Poker Flat

This chapter covers futures contracts based on materials that are extracted from the earth, specifically metals, both precious and industrial metals, and petroleum and petroleum products. The futures contracts based on these commodities have increased in importance and trading volume in recent years.

METALS

This section discusses the precious and industrial metals that are the basis for futures contracts.

Precious Metals

The precious metals on which there are futures contracts are gold, silver, platinum, and palladium.

Gold

Introduction.   Gold has excellent industrial properties, including electrical conductivity, malleability, and durability and indestructibility. While gold is used to some extent in electronic applications, it has two other properties that increase its value and, for this reason, limit its industrial use.

First, gold is lustrous and does not lose its luster. This quality and its malleability, which permits it to be pounded into very thin sheets, make it very desirable for jewelry.

Due to its domestic and international monetary roles and its use for storing (or often hoarding) value and also to its use for jewelry, and for other unexplained reasons, gold has always had value in excess of its value for industrial use. These uses limit the industrial use of gold and make it a precious metal rather than an industrial metal.

While gold has had value for international exchange for centuries, the "modern era" of gold for this purpose began in 1944 with the Bretton Woods Agreement. This agreement set several important international monetary policies. Among them was the provision for the conversion of gold into U.S. dollars, by the U.S. government, at $35 per ounce. Interestingly, this was done more to stabilize the price of the dollar than to stabilize the price of gold.

Gradually, however, the dollar weakened against gold. In 1965 and 1968, the gold reserve requirements for U.S. member bank reserves and U.S. Federal Reserve notes, respectively, were removed. These changes made possible the beginning of a free market for gold, primarily in Zurich. The weakening of the dollar continued when, on August 15, 1971, the Smithsonian Agreement terminated the $35-per-ounce price of gold (and with this the fixed exchange rate between the dollar and other foreign currencies). Gold prices were allowed to float and be determined by the free international market for gold.

Finally, during 1974 the U.S. government announced that U.S. citizens could hold gold legally beginning on December 31, 1974. Prior to this, many U.S. citizens held gold illegally overseas. In response to this change in policy, on December 31, 1974, gold futures contracts began to be traded on several exchanges. This began the period of extreme volatility in gold prices. The pinnacle of gold prices was achieved during January 1980, when the price of gold rose to $850 per ounce. At the beginning of 1985, it was below $300 per ounce.

Supply.   The two major producers of gold, as shown in Table 20-1, are South Africa and the Soviet Union, neither of which has been a political ally of the United States. This situation has created some ambiguity in the U.S. policies of supporting gold prices (or at least establishing a price floor), particularly during the times when these countries increased the supply of gold in order to add to their monetary reserves.

South Africa is the largest gold producer, responsible for more than 50 percent of the world's gold production. A significant amount of this production is sold as gold coins—the Krugerrand—many of which are hoarded. This method of distribution helps support gold prices.

The Soviet Union is the second largest producer of gold. While data on Soviet production are not divulged, it is probably close to 25 percent of the world's total.

TABLE 20-1 WORLD MINE PRODUCTION OF GOLD [in thousands of fine ounces (troy ounces)]

Year	Aus-tralia	Zaire (Congo)	Canada	China	Colom-bia	Ghana	India	Japan	Mexico	Nicara-gua	Papua New Guinea	Philip-pines	Zim-babwe	South Africa	United States	U.S.S.R.*	Total World*
1971	672	172	2243		189	698	119	255	151	121		637	502	31,389	1495	6700	46,495
1972	755	141	2079		188	724	106	243	146	112		607	502	29,245	1450	6900	44,843
1973	554	134	1954		216	723	105	188	133	85		572	800	27,495	1176	7100	43,297
1974	513	131	1698		265	614	101	140	134	83		538	800	24,388	1127	7300	40,124
1975	527	103	1654		309	524	91	144	145	70		503	600	22,938	1052	7500	38,476
1976	503	91	1692		300	532	101	138	163	76		501	387	22,936	1048	7700	39,024
1977	625	80	1734		257	481	97	149	213	66	740	559	402	22,502	1100	7850	38,906
1978	648	76	1735	150	246	402	89	145	202	74	751	587	399	22,649	999	8000	39,057
1979	597	73	1644	200	269	357	85	128	190	61	630	535	388	22,617	964	8160	38,830
1980	548	41	1627	225	510	353	79	102	196	60	452	644	368	21,669	970	8300	39,205
1981	591	64	1673	1700	529	341	80	99	203	62	540	753	371	21,121	1379	8425	41,249
1982†	867	62	2081	1800	482	331	72	104	196	52	564	834	426	21,355	1466	8550	43,057
1983*	1035	60	2274	1900	429	303	69	101	209	47	582		430	21,847	1957	8600	44,533
1984*	1100		2500	2000										22,000	1902	8600	45,000

*Estimated

†Preliminary.

SOURCE: U.S. Bureau of Mines.

Canada and the United States are the third and fourth largest gold producers, respectively. In the United States, gold is produced mainly as a by-product of other mining activities.

Since gold has been held by private individuals, international agencies, and national governments, gold supplies come not only from new production but also from dishoarding by these groups. The United States and the International Monetary Fund (IMF) have been major dishoarders via gold auctions.

The fineness of gold is measured in karats. Twenty-four-karat gold is pure gold, so each karat is one twenty-fourth part of pure gold in an alloy.

Table 20-2 provides additional statistics on the supply of and demand for gold in the United States.

Demand. Over 50 percent of the use of gold satisfies a combination of demand for jewelry and industrial purposes. The largest industrial uses are for electronics, space and defense, and dentistry. The majority of the other uses of gold are for gold coins, much of which is for hoarding, and other forms of hoarding gold.

Price determinants. The price of gold is determined more by its role as an international medium of exchange and store of value than by its industrial use.

Due to the pivotal role of the U.S. dollar in the international financial system, when the dollar is strong against other foreign currencies, it is also usually strong against gold (and the price of gold is low), and vice versa. Thus, the factors discussed in Chapter 21 that tend to make the dollar strong against foreign currencies also tend to make the dollar strong against gold and the dollar price of gold low. Among these factors are high U.S. interest rates, low U.S. inflation, and a U.S. balance of payments surplus. Since the United States is a major importer of crude oil, decreasing oil prices also usually strengthen the dollar against many other foreign currencies and against gold.

Political factors also affect the price of gold, sometimes at the expense of the strength of the dollar. Wars and political unrest in other parts of the world often strengthen gold against the dollar, even though the dollar may become stronger against other foreign currencies.

Changes in the balance between supply and demand also affect the price of gold. Increased sales by the producing countries, such as South Africa and the Soviet Union, or by international agencies or governments, such as the IMF or the United States, tend to decrease the price of gold. The increased industrial demand for gold or a decline in industrial gold stocks also tend to decrease the price of gold.

Finally, the price of gold relative to the price of the other major precious metal, silver, also tends to affect the price of gold. The gold-silver price ratio is a closely watched indicator of both the price of gold and the price of silver. The use of this indicator may seem unusual in view of the ratio's variability, as shown in Figure 20-1. While for a century before 1980, the price of gold was 32 times the price of silver, the ratio declined to 17 during January 1980 and increased to 60 during 1982 before declining again. This ratio is closely watched regardless of the fundamental factors affecting gold and silver prices independently.

Futures contracts. Gold futures trading began on December 31, 1974, on several exchanges, including Comex, the Chicago Board of Trade, the International Monetary Market (of the Chicago Mercantile Exchange), and the MidAmerica

TABLE 20-2 SALIENT U.S. GOLD STATISTICS (in thousands of troy ounces)

Year	Mine production	Value, millions of dollars	Refinery production New (domestic)	Refinery production Secondary[a]	Exports[b]	Imports[b] for consumption	Stocks, Dec. 31 Treasury Dept.[c]	Stocks, Dec. 31 Futures exchange	Stocks, Dec. 31 Earmarked[d]	Consumption Industrial[e]	Consumption Dental	Consumption Industrial	Consumption Jewelry and arts	Consumption Total	Price, dollars per troy ounce[f]
1977	1,100	163.2	956	2,454	8,671	4,454	277.6	1.8	378.7	2.0	728	1,209	2,658	4,863	148.31
1978	999	193.3	962	3,085	5,509	4,690	276.4	2.7	366.2	1.7	706	1,313	2,651	4,738	193.55
1979	964	296.6	795	2,883	16,492	4,630	264.6	2.5	359.3	0.9	646	1,406	2,688	4,785	307.50
1980	970	594.1	773	3,824	6,119	4,542	264.3	5.0	354.5	0.9	341	1,287	1,505	3,215	612.56
1981	1,379	633.9	801	3,085	6,437	4,652	264.1	2.4	350.6	0.6	314	1,210	1,703	3,276	459.64
1982	1,466	551.0	718	3,040	2,970	4,920	264.0	2.3	348.6	0.8	358	1,102	1,954	3,423	375.91
1983[g]	1,957	829.9	885	2,960	3,139	4,593	263.4	2.5	341.4	0.6	360	1,028	1,668	3,060	424.00
1984[h]	1,902	686.0	748	2,942	4,981	7,869	262.8	2.4	337.9	0.8	364	1,070	1,685	3,124	360.66

[a]Old and new scrap.

[b]Excludes coinage.

[c]Includes gold in Exchange Stabilization Fund.

[d]Gold held for foreign and international official accounts at New York Federal Reserve Bank.

[e]Including space and defense.

[f]Engelhard selling quotations.

[g]Preliminary.

[h]Estimate.

SOURCE: U.S. Bureau of Mines.

Figure 20-1   Gold futures (nearby)/silver futures (nearby).

Exchange. The trading volume on these contracts has continued to grow, and the Comex gold futures contract is now the third largest futures contract in terms of trading volume and open interest. Currently three gold futures contracts are traded actively, the major one being at Comex (100 troy ounces), with smaller-size futures contracts at the CBT (1 kilogram) and the MidAmerica Exchange (33.2 troy ounces). Except for their size, these contracts are essentially the same. More detailed specifications of these contracts are provided in Chapter 3.

Speculative uses.   Gold producers, fabricators, traders, and distributors use gold futures contracts to hedge their inventories. In addition, gold spreads can be used to hedge short-term interest rates. For example, a short nearby gold–long deferred gold futures spread locks in a 3-month borrowing cost.

But gold futures contracts are premier speculative vehicles. While there are many other ways to speculate in gold, such as with gold coins and gold bullion, gold futures contracts, due to their high leverage, low transaction costs, and the reputability of the markets, are the most popular vehicles for speculating in gold. Most gold futures contract speculation is standard "buy-'em" and "sell-'em" speculation based on the factors discussed above and other factors.

There are two other important factors in the gold markets in addition to the fundamental factors. They are technical and emotional. Technical factors play an important role in the gold futures markets.

And, as in any other speculative market, emotions play an important role in pricing. It is for this reason that gold prices could go from $35 per ounce in 1971 to $850 in 1980 to below $300 in 1982 and early 1985, with few fundamental changes in the market for industrial gold over this period. Figure 20-2 provides a plot of recent gold futures prices.

Because gold has been an important speculative vehicle for centuries, for both individuals and institutions, gold is likely to remain the world's premier speculative commodity. Gold futures markets have begun in several foreign countries (Tokyo; Hong Kong; London; Sydney, Australia; Singapore; and Winnipeg, Canada), and several other foreign countries are planning gold futures markets.

And options on the gold futures contract which began to be traded at Comex during October 1982 have become very liquid and provide a new dimension for

Figure 20-2   Gold. [*Commodity Year Book 1985*, ed. *Walter L. Emery* (*Jersey City, N.J.: Commodity Research Bureau, Inc.*).]

gold speculation. The risk-reward combinations of gold options for speculators are discussed in Chapter 9.

Silver

Introduction.   While gold is a metal which has desirable industrial properties but whose value is determined by its monetary use, silver is a metal which has the opposite combination. Silver has historically been used for monetary purposes. In the United States, silver, like gold, has been used in coins and has had its price supported by the U.S. government. But its use and value for monetary purposes has recently decreased significantly. In 1965, the Coinage Act eliminated the use of silver in dimes and quarters and reduced the silver content in half-dollars from 90 to 40 percent. On July 14, 1967, the Treasury halted its sales of silver at $1.2929 per fine ounce, begun in 1963, and the price of silver immediately increased to $1.87 per ounce.

To prevent the melting down of old silver coins, which became profitable at $1.38, a ban on melting down coins was issued during 1967. In addition, the Treasury minted more than $8 billion of "clad" dimes and quarters between 1965 and 1967, which was about two-thirds of the supply during the preceding 25 years.

In the middle of 1967, Congress authorized the Secretary of the Treasury to rule that outstanding silver certificates worth about $150 million were either destroyed, lost, or privately held and would not be presented for redemption. After June 24, 1968, any remaining certificates were no longer redeemable in silver. The international demand for silver for monetary purposes has also declined. Silver coinage has also been discontinued in Britain, Canada, and Australia.

Meanwhile, the price of silver has increased due to its technical and industrial properties—high electrical and thermal conductivity, malleability, ductility, sonority, the ability to achieve a high polish, and resistance to corrosion—all of which have made it useful in photography, electronics, communications, computers, and jewelry.

Currently, the value of silver is determined mainly by its industrial uses and to a somewhat lesser extent by its decorative uses, including its use for jewelry; its value is not based on monetary purposes. This change in the way in which silver is valued has increased the price volatility of silver.

Supply.   The supply of silver comes from both primary sources—mine production—and secondary sources—scrap production and dishoarding. Over 70 percent of the mine production of silver comes not from silver mines but as a by-product of the mining of other metals, such as nickel, copper, lead, zinc, and gold.

Most newly mined silver comes from Mexico, Peru, Canada, the United States, and Australia (among the noncommunist countries), as shown in Table 20-3. The U.S.S.R. is also a major producer. Recently, most of the increase in silver production has come from Mexico and Australia.

The secondary supply of silver results from scrap production (the majority of secondary production) and dishoarding. The major secondary sources are the recycling of silverware, jewelry, and other old silver; the melting down of coins; the recovery of silver from camera and x-ray film; and the depletion of government stocks of silver.

TABLE 20-3 WORLD MINE PRODUCTION OF SILVER, BY SELECTED COUNTRIES [in millions of fine ounces (troy ounces)]

Year	Poland	Argentina	Australia	Zaire (Congo)	Bolivia*	Canada	Morocco	West Germany	Honduras	U.S.S.R.†	Japan	Mexico	Peru	United States	Yugoslavia	World Total†
1976	17.8	2.25	25.03	2.47	5.34	41.20	2.05	1.03	3.18	44.0	9.30	42.64	35.58	34.33	4.63	316.4
1977	20.7	2.45	27.53	2.73	5.81	42.24	2.82	1.06	2.82	45.0	9.60	47.03	39.73	38.17	4.68	331.3
1978	21.9	2.16	26.12	4.39	6.29	40.73	3.13	0.80	2.79	46.0	9.66	50.78	37.02	39.39	5.13	345.0
1979	22.6	2.21	26.76	3.89	5.74	36.87	3.28	1.04	2.43	46.0	8.68	52.17	39.25	37.90	5.21	348.1
1980	24.6	2.36	24.65	2.73	6.10	33.34	3.15	1.06	1.77	46.0	8.60	50.05	44.42	32.33	4.79	344.0
1981	30.58	2.52	23.91	2.58	6.39	36.30	2.12	1.13	1.82	46.5	9.01	52.92	46.94	40.68	4.44	361.8
1982‡	21.06	2.68	29.16	1.75	5.47	42.25	2.64	1.28	2.10	46.9	9.84	59.18	53.64	40.25	3.34	383.8
1983†	24.90	2.64	32.15	2.00	5.09	35.56	2.85	1.28	2.50	47.2	9.88	61.44	55.87	43.42	3.99	390.6
1984†						38.0				48.0		62.0	58.0	41.61		400.0

*Exports.

†Estimate.

‡Preliminary.

SOURCE: U.S. Bureau of Mines.

The supply of newly mined silver has been relatively insensitive to the price of silver, since it is mainly a by-product of the production of other metals. On the other hand, the secondary supply of silver has been very sensitive to the price of silver.

Demand. The United States is the largest user of silver in the world, and the U.S.S.R. is second. Table 20-4 shows the level of uses of silver by the noncommunist countries.

The main uses of silver in the United States are industrial, as indicated above and shown in Table 20-5. Approximately one-half of the U.S. use of silver is for photography. Silver is critical for photography because it is the only material which magnifies light (or the photons of light) approximately a billion times. The second largest use of silver is for electrical purposes—silver is used because it conducts electricity and heat very effectively and does not oxidize in air.

Silver is also used for batteries (for which purpose silver is superior to lead) and for dental and medical purposes. In addition, silver is used for jewelry, silverware, mirrors, and medals and coins. The use for official coins has decreased significantly worldwide in recent years.

Price determinants. Silver futures prices are related to spot silver prices on a "carry basis"; that is, the silver futures price equals the spot price of silver plus the costs of financing, storage, and insurance over the period until delivery on the futures contract.

As suggested above, the spot price of silver is determined mainly by industrial use rather than monetary value. The exception to this is that the value of gold, as discussed above, is determined primarily by monetary value and the price of silver is loosely related to the price of gold by the gold-silver ratio as discussed above. Via the gold-silver ratio, silver prices also continue to be indirectly linked to the factors that affect the price of gold, such as the level of interest rates, inflation, the balance of payments, and economic growth.

The value of silver, on an industrial basis, is determined by the balance between supply and demand. Over the last several years, the industrial use has exceeded the newly mined supply, with the supply deficiency coming from secondary sources. The demand for silver for monetary uses has also declined. Overall, however, the demand continues to exceed the newly mined supply.

Supply factors include silver stocks and inventories held by suppliers and users of silver, the level of production in various countries, political factors such as labor strikes in producing countries, and the discovery of new sources of silver. The level of demand for various uses, including photography, medical and dental applications, silverware, and jewelry, represents the demand side. Secondary supply, including the level of hoarding and dishoarding of silver, which in turn depends on the level of prices, also affects prices. The interaction between supply and demand and, at times, "market psychology" determine silver prices.

Futures contracts. As with gold, speculators can speculate in silver with bullion, jewelry, and coins (particularly from Canada, Mexico, and Hungary). But futures contracts are the most popular speculative vehicles for silver.

There are three domestic silver futures contracts. The only significant difference between them is in size. The most heavily traded silver futures contract, at Comex, is based on 5000 ounces; it has recently been the sixth largest futures contract

TABLE 20-4 WORLD° SILVER CONSUMPTION (in millions of troy ounces)

| Year | Industrial uses | | | | | | | | | Coinage | | | | | | | World total |
	Canada	France	West Germany	India	Italy	Japan	United Kingdom	United States	World total	Canada	France	West Germany	Austria	Mexico	United States	World total	
1971	6.0	15.6	59.9	16.0	30.5	46.5	25.0	129.1	351.4	0.2	0.4	19.2	3.2		2.5	28.3	379.7
1972	7.4	16.5	60.0	13.0	32.0	54.3	27.0	151.7	388.9	0.1	0.3	22.6	5.8		2.3	38.4	427.3
1973	8.6	14.3	64.7	13.0	41.5	69.0	31.0	195.9	477.8	1.4	0.1	9.5	6.6		0.9	29.2	507.0
1974	9.6	15.5	59.9	15.0	38.6	46.5	25.0	177.0	409.4	8.9	0.1	8.8	5.6		1.0	27.9	436.9
1975	10.6	21.2	38.9	13.0	28.9	46.4	28.0	157.7	376.8	10.4	5.2	4.3	13.4		2.7	38.8	415.6
1976	9.5	19.0	50.8	18.0	32.1	60.7	28.0	170.5	437.5	8.4	6.7	2.9	6.9		1.3	29.7	467.2
1977	8.8	20.6	59.5	17.6	33.8	63.2	32.2	153.6	433.6	0.3	6.9	2.6	3.0	4.2	0.4	23.4	457.0
1978	9.0	22.2	47.2	20.0	41.8	64.8	29.0	160.2	442.6	0.3	11.1	3.6	4.5	6.3	0.1	36.3	478.9
1979	8.1	21.5	46.1	19.0	31.1	66.4	26.5	157.2	434.2	0.3	7.7	3.7	5.0	5.0	0.1	27.8	462.0
1980	8.7	20.2	29.1	19.0	21.8	61.7	20.5	124.7	354.5	0.2			4.3	6.1	0.1	13.7	368.2
1981	8.5	20.6	28.0	19.0	12.4	59.8	18.5	116.6	336.8	0.2			3.0			9.0	345.8
1982	9.0	18.6	33.6	22.5	9.3	63.2	20.0	118.8	348.7	0.3			4.0		2.5	12.8	361.5
1983	8.5	18.6	31.1	21.8	9.0	71.5	18.0	116.3	349.5	0.4			2.0		11.2	18.6	368.1
1984†	9.0	17.0	32.1	25.7	14.7	76.7	19.0	119.0	371.0	0.3				2.0	3.0	8.3	379.3

*Noncommunist areas only.

†Preliminary.

SOURCE: Handy & Harman.

TABLE 20-5 U.S. CONSUMPTION OF SILVER, BY END USE (in thousands of troy ounces)

Year	Bearings	Brazing alloys and solders	Catalysts	Dental and medical	Electroplated ware	Electrical and electronic products		Jewelry	Mirrors	Photographic materials	Sterling ware	Coins, medallions*	Total net industrial consumption	Coinage	Total consumption
						Batteries	Contacts and conductors								
1976	273	11,198	12,267	1,942	9,534	3,490	32,329	10,995	4,622	55,350	19,815	8,240	170,559	1,315	171,874
1977	523	12,362	8,883	2,232	6,844	5,783	31,316	8,059	2,131	53,679	16,690	4,252	153,613	91	153,704
1978	373	10,987	8,197	2,033	7,274	6,029	30,756	6,766	1,862	64,299	17,908	2,727	160,165	45	160,210
1979	332	10,912	5,637	2,295	8,065	4,583	33,506	5,358	1,850	65,978	13,088	4,676	157,258	168	157,426
1980	649	8,508	3,035	2,212	4,350	5,976	27,796	5,893	672	49,825	9,082	4,693	124,694	72	124,766
1981	297	7,718	3,830	1,709	3,904	3,803	26,411	5,368	581	51,025	4,407	2,622	116,670	179	116,849
1982	228	7,384	2,418	1,688	3,254	4,167	27,730	6,260	970	51,769	6,579	1,832	118,840	1,846	120,686
1983†	170	5,837	2,414	1,532	3,154	2,637	26,298	6,885	970	51,826	7,022	2,979	116,291	2,128	118,419
1984‡	259	5,918	2,447	1,574	3,461	2,671	25,632	5,760	968	55,316	3,639	2,563	114,770	2,665	117,435

*Includes commemorative objects.

†Preliminary.

‡Estimate.

SOURCE: U.S. Bureau of Mines.

in terms of trading volume. Since a standard silver bar is 1000 ounces of 0.999 fine silver, this contract represents 5 bars. Both the Chicago Board of Trade and the MidAmerica Exchange have contracts based on 1000 ounces of silver (1 bar). All are for 0.999 fine silver.

The London Metal Exchange (LME) trades a futures contract based on 10,000 ounces of 0.999 fine silver. The trading of the LME contract is dissimilar to that of the three U.S. futures contracts in that the LME contract is much more like a forward contract, as discussed below.

Beginning on October 4, 1984, Comex also listed an option on its silver futures contract, and it has developed considerable liquidity. It provides the types of opportunities for speculation as discussed in Chapter 9 with regard to other options on futures contracts.

Speculative uses.   Silver producers, traders, fabricators, and other users use the silver futures contracts to hedge their inventories and prospective purchases of silver. These uses are consistent with the predominant industrial use of silver.

The use of the silver futures contracts is also popular with speculators. The major reasons for speculators' interest in silver are that silver, like gold, is a quasi-monetary metal, and it exhibits extreme price volatility. Silver prices rose from approximately $5 per ounce during 1978 to over $50 per ounce in January 1980 during the publicized buying spree by the Hunt family.[1] Silver prices retreated to below $5 during 1982, rose to over $12 during early 1983, and fell back to below $6 during 1985. Figure 20-3 provides a plot of recent silver futures prices.

The factors to consider when speculating in silver futures are:

- The gold-silver price ratio and, indirectly, the factors, mentioned above, that affect gold prices
- The industrial demand for silver for medical, photographic, and other purposes
- The demand for gold for jewelry
- The supply of gold from mines and from dishoarding, particularly by governmental authorities
- The level of silver stockpiles and inventories
- The psychology of silver—most important, as with all other commodities

Platinum

Introduction.   Platinum and palladium are principal metals of the platinum group, which also includes iridium, osmium, rhodium, and ruthenium. These two metals have very similar metallurgical properties, both being inert and resistant to tarnish; as a result, they are often used interchangeably in many applications.

Platinum is white and can be given a beautiful, permanent polish. Under normal conditions, platinum is virtually inert and much tougher than gold, and it cannot be corroded by acids.

Supply.   Platinum production comes mainly from three countries: South Africa, Russia, and Canada. In South Africa, platinum is produced as a primary product—

---

[1] For an interesting description of this episode, read *Beyond Greed,* by Stephen Fay (New York: The Viking Press, 1982).

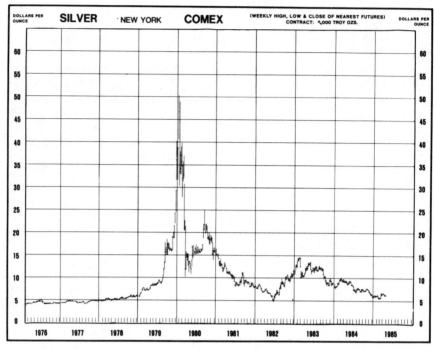

Figure 20-3 Silver. [*Commodity Year Book 1985, ed. Walter L. Emery [Jersey City, N.J.: Commodity Research Bureau, Inc.].]*

South African ores are typically 60 percent platinum and 25 percent palladium. In Russia, platinum is produced mainly as a by-product of the production of palladium and nickel. In Canada, also, platinum is a by-product of nickel production. The United States produces very little platinum, the small amount it does produce being a by-product of gold and copper refining. Table 20-6 provides the supply of all the platinum-group metals by country. Table 20-7 provides data on other aspects of platinum supply, trade, and demand in the United States.

Demand. Although, because of its high value, platinum can be considered a precious metal, it has limited use for coins or for hoarding. In addition, only a small amount is used in jewelry (the use for jewelry is less than 5 percent of total use).

The automobile industry has become the major user of platinum, accounting for approximately 50 percent of total U.S. use. The use of platinum in catalytic converters for emission control (that is, for reducing the emission of unburned hydrocarbons and carbon monoxide) began in the 1975 model year. Platinum is used in the catalytic converters because it can withstand high temperatures and is resistant to attack by acids and other gases.

About 25 percent of U.S. platinum use is by the petroleum and chemical industries, where platinum is used mainly as a catalyst in the production of gasoline, plastic, fertilizers, and explosives. Platinum is also used in the electrical industry (for example, as a catalyst in fuel cells), for medical purposes (including its use

TABLE 20-6 WORLD MINE PRODUCTION OF PLATINUM-GROUP METALS (in troy ounces)

Year	Aus-tralia	Zim-babwe	Fin-land	Canada	Colom-bia*	Ethi-opia	Japan	South Africa	U.S.S.R.	United States	Yugo-slavia	World total†
1979	9,645	—	1,643	197,943	12,933	108	34,637	3,017,000	3,200,000	7,300	5,916	6,487,125
1980	12,603	9,774	900	410,757	14,345	113	41,334	3,100,000	3,250,000	3,348	4,919	6,848,093
1981	14,989	7,500	3,601	382,658	14,801	125	36,269	3,110,000	3,350,000	7,318	3,601	6,930,862
1982	13,900	4,469	8,809	228,425	20,000	125	43,273	2,600,000	3,500,000	8,033	3,480	6,430,514
1983‡	13,900	4,000	9,000	167,019	20,080	125	58,582	2,600,000	3,600,000	6,257	3,300	6,482,183
1984†				200,000				2,800,000	3,600,000	6,000		6,700,000

*Placer platinum.
†Estimate.
‡Preliminary.
SOURCE: U.S. Bureau of Mines.

TABLE 20-7 SALIENT STATISTICS OF PLATINUM AND ALLIED METALS IN THE UNITED STATES. (in troy ounces)

Year	Net import reliance as a percentage of apparent consumption	Production, crude[a]	Refinery New metal	Refinery Secondary metal	Stocks as of Dec. 31[b] Platinum	Stocks as of Dec. 31[b] Palladium	Stocks as of Dec. 31[b] Other	Stocks as of Dec. 31[b] Total	Imports for consumption	Value of imports, millions of dollars	Exports Platinum	Exports Other groups[c]	Exports Other[d]
1979	89	7300	8392	309,022	305,022	323,865	131,812	761,282	3,479,128	840.5	207,832	522,195	189,218
1980	87	3348	2300	330,923	502,185	353,002	118,074	973,261	3,501,782	1177	289,454	302,457	173,053
1981	83	7318	5607	391,637	401,389	398,933	117,856	918,178	2,849,617	800.3	391,194	258,745	213,426
1982	81	8033	7078	344,160	604,632	384,184	117,812	1,106,628	2,493,706	553.9	175,805	262,764	423,576
1983[e]	90	6257	5884	287,149	431,417	412,074	97,520	941,011	3,218,022	752.8	184,599	261,188	782,967
1984[f]	91	6000	6000	370,000	623,358	553,834	147,197	1,324,389	4,474,106	1118.1	220,885	375,802	565,543

[a]From crude platinum placers and by-product platinum-group metals.

[b]In hands of refiners, importers, and dealers.

[c]Palladium, rhodium, iridium, osmium, ruthenium, and osmium metals and alloys.

[d]Ore and concentrates, waste, scrap, and sweepings.

[e]Preliminary.

[f]Estimate.

SOURCE: U.S. Bureau of Mines.

in pacemakers), and in the glass industry. The United States is the world's largest consumer of platinum. Table 20-8 provides data on the uses of platinum and other platinum-group metals in the United States.

Pricing. Platinum futures prices are based on the cost of carry; that is, the futures price equals the cash price plus the cost of carrying the metal until futures delivery day, similar to the pricing of gold and silver futures contracts. Since platinum is primarily an industrial metal, its price is based mainly on the balance between supply and demand. Among the major factors that affect this balance are mine output, secondary production, and automobile sales. The degree of U.S. government stockpiling of platinum, another important price determinant, has varied over time. Under President Reagan, stockpiling of platinum began again due to the use of platinum for defense purposes.

Because platinum is to some extent a precious metal, platinum prices are also thought to be related to gold prices. Typically, platinum prices exceed gold prices due to the relative scarcity of platinum. Due to this perceived relationship, some of the factors that affect gold prices also affect platinum prices. Among these factors are the level of interest rates, the level of economic activity, and the stability of the international political environment. However, the relationship between platinum and gold prices is extremely variable. During early 1980, the price of platinum reached $1000 per ounce and exceeded the price of gold by $300. Since then, however, platinum prices have been somewhat below gold prices at most times.

There are three different markets and prices for platinum. The producer price is the contract price between the world's principal suppliers (mainly South African mining firms) and large U.S. users (mainly automobile companies). The producer prices are set on a forward basis and are maintained at fairly stable levels. The dealer price is set by 20 to 30 metals dealers or traders who get their supplies from Russia, other producers, and secondary supply.

The third type of market and price is the futures market and price. The New York Mercantile Exchange trades a platinum futures contract based on 50 troy ounces of platinum. Both dealer and futures prices are fairly volatile.

Speculative uses. Speculators base their decisions on platinum on either of two factors. First, they can base their assessment of platinum prices on the supply-demand balance, considering platinum as an industrial metal and considering auto sales, mine production, etc. Or they can base their assessment of platinum prices on platinum as a precious metal, considering international political stability, particularly with South Africa and Russia, and interest rates. At different times, each type of assessment may be correct. As shown in Figure 20-4, platinum prices have exhibited considerable volatility.

Palladium. Palladium has many of the same properties as platinum; mainly, it is inert and thus has many of the same industrial uses as platinum. However, palladium is much softer and easier to work than platinum, being more like silver and gold in this regard.

Most palladium is mined in the same three countries that mine platinum: Russia, South Africa, and Canada. There is also a significant secondary supply of palladium from recycling. Russia is the largest producer of palladium, responsible for about

TABLE 20-8 PLATINUM-GROUP METALS SOLD TO CONSUMING INDUSTRIES IN THE UNITED STATES (in thousands of troy ounces)

Year	Automotive Plati-num	Automotive Others*	Chemical Plati-num	Chemical Others*	Electrical Plati-num	Electrical Others*	Dental and medical Plati-num	Dental and medical Others*	Jewelry and decorative Plati-num	Jewelry and decorative Others*	Petroleum Plati-num	Petroleum Others*	All platinum-group metals Plati-num	All platinum-group metals Palla-dium	All platinum-group metals Other* metals	All platinum-group metals Total
1972			225.9	363.5	92.4	443.5	30.5	95.5	20.7	29.3	98.8	31.4	545.3	876.0	140.9	1562.2
1973			239.0	334.1	117.4	551.1	27.9	136.3	22.4	38.9	123.6	20.3	658.5	1012.5	160.9	1833.9
1974	350.0	15.0	350.0	150.0	98.6	452.6	25.5	125.7	23.0	35.3	139.5	26.7	943.7	886.1	151.2	1981.0
1975	273.0	97.0	148.8	166.9	73.6	153.1	17.1	115.9	22.9	29.5	108.0	5.4	698.6	541.5	68.6	1308.7
1976	481.0	194.9	83.6	154.7	89.3	197.5	26.9	140.4	34.7	14.8	59.1	7.7	851.1	657.1	94.9	1603.1
1977	354.3	125.9	84.4	196.6	90.2	254.5	27.1	113.9	25.8	22.1	74.8	13.6	789.8	700.5	102.0	1592.3
1978	597.5	201.8	149.7	186.5	106.4	346.5	44.1	208.0	27.7	25.1	108.4	19.2	1196.3	917.9	145.4	2259.6
1979	803.2	248.3	98.6	264.9	115.8	457.4	27.1	244.9	51.0	21.6	170.0	27.9	1408.9	1132.6	214.5	2756.0
1980	517.1	214.2	119.0	165.6	150.1	376.1	25.8	245.4	27.6	22.6	144.0	26.7	1118.2	912.0	175.7	2205.9
1981	446.7	160.6	78.1	152.4	111.7	388.3	18.7	255.8	16.0	19.6	88.3	22.9	872.6	889.2	158.8	1920.7
1982	477.8	144.8	63.6	200.6	90.0	348.4	22.8	312.1	10.3	12.7	21.6	21.7	780.1	926.3	166.8	1873.3
1983†	508.5	191.8	65.4	99.8	74.7	404.8	16.7	261.7		10.6	38.0	51.1	796.7	921.8	195.4	1914.0
1984‡													1024.0	1080.0	180.9	2284.9

*Palladium, iridium, osmium, rhodium, and ruthenium.
†Preliminary.
‡Estimate.
SOURCE: U.S. Bureau of Mines.

70 percent of total production. South Africa produces about 25 percent and Canada 3 percent of the world's total production.

Palladium is used mainly in electrical applications; due to its excellent electrical properties and low cost, it is used in electrical contacts, temperature thermocouple devices, and resistors. This accounts for approximately one-third of the total U.S. use. The use of palladium for catalytic emission-control devices in automobiles accounts for approximately 20 percent of the U.S. use. Palladium is also used in the chemical industry, for petroleum cracking and hydrogenation, and in the dental and medical fields. And it is used in jewelry, to turn yellow gold white.

Palladium prices are significantly lower than platinum prices, mainly because palladium is a less effective catalyst in industrial applications. For example, when platinum prices exceeded $1000 per ounce in early 1980, palladium prices increased only to slightly higher than $300. More recently, platinum prices have been near $300 and palladium prices near $100. Figure 20-5 shows the recent palladium prices.

As with platinum, there are three different markets and prices for palladium: producer markets and prices, dealer markets and prices, and futures markets and prices. For this metal also, producer prices are relatively stable and dealer and futures prices volatile.

The New York Mercantile Exchange trades a palladium futures contract based on 100 troy ounces of palladium. The delivery mechanism for both the platinum

Figure 20-4   Platinum. [*Commodity Year Book 1985*, ed. *Walter L. Emery* (*Jersey City, N.J.: Commodity Research Bureau, Inc.*).]

Figure 20-5 Palladium. [*Commodity Year Book 1985, ed. Walter L. Emery [Jersey City, N.J.: Commodity Research Bureau, Inc.].]*

and palladium futures contracts is a certificate or a depository receipt from a depository which is in the New York metropolitan area and which is approved by the exchange.

Speculation on palladium is based on many of the same factors that affect speculation on platinum. Since palladium is not a precious metal, as is platinum, its price is not perceived to be set on this basis. For example, palladium is not perceived to have a price relationship with gold. Because Russia and South Africa are the dominant suppliers of palladium, international political considerations are relevant, however. In general, palladium prices are determined mainly by supply-demand balance and the specific sources of demand and supply.

Notes from a Trader—Precious Metals. Gold has been a major speculative vehicle for several years. Fundamentalists consider gold primarily as a financial asset and, in this regard, as an inflation hedge. When inflation is high, interest rates are high, while bond prices are low, and gold prices are high. Thus, interest rates are a major fundamental determinant of gold prices. The politics of gold is important, involving the politics of the producing countries, mainly South Africa and Russia, and of major holding and using countries, most importantly the United States.

The gold market is a very technical market. At times, gold has shown sustained trends—upward, downward, and sideways. At times, also, gold shows considerable short-term variability, and at other times it will have a price movement similar to the surface of a bowling alley. The most uncertain and unstable times are the times of highest gold prices. The gold futures contract is very liquid, particularly during unstable times.

Silver prices tend to follow gold prices at times through the gold-silver ratio, but they march to their own beat at other times. Silver prices can be very volatile for short periods of time and stable for long periods of time. Do not take a vacation at the wrong time with a silver position.

The markets for platinum and palladium are much smaller and less liquid than the gold and silver markets. The deliverable supplies of these metals are also much smaller than those of gold and silver, and so small changes or potential changes in supply can cause significant price changes.

Commercial Metals

The futures contracts on commercial metals are based on copper and aluminum.

Copper

Introduction. Copper, the "red metal," is a long-established commercial metal with many industrial uses and is the basis for one of the oldest futures contracts currently traded. The importance of copper is based on its excellent industrial properties. Copper is an excellent electrical conductor, has a high resistance to corrosion, is malleable and strong, and has a lustrous appearance. For these reasons, copper is used in electrical and plumbing applications, in jewelry, as an alloy, and in several other applications. Copper is produced and utilized in many parts of the world and, as a result, is an internationally actively traded commodity.

Supply. Copper is produced in open pits, and large amounts of earth and ore must be moved to produce the metal. This process requires large amounts of capital and labor; in addition, it has recently encountered government pollution controls. All of these factors have increased the cost of copper production.

Copper is mined mainly in the form of copper sulfide ore, which also typically contains trace amounts of gold, silver, and platinum. Pure copper is produced from copper ore via a three-step process: milling, smelting, and refining. The milling process is essentially crushing and grinding the copper ore and producing copper concentrates by putting the output of these processes through a flotation process. Smelting, by applying intense heat to the copper concentrates, produces blister copper containing approximately 99 percent pure copper. Pure copper is then produced by electrolytically refining the blister to remove the remaining impurities. The output of the refinery stage is copper cathode—approximately 300 pounds of 3½-foot squares of 99.9 percent pure copper—the most common form of copper traded.

Copper production results from newly mined copper and the processing of scrap copper. Newly mined copper comes mainly from four areas in the world—the western slopes of the Andes mountains in Chile and Peru, South Africa (mainly

Zaire and Zambia), the U.S.S.R., and North America, including the United States and Canada. As shown in Table 20-9, these countries account for approximately 65 percent of the world's mine production. U.S. mine production comes mainly from the western states, with Arizona responsible for 65 percent of the U.S. total.

Open-pit mining continues to be the dominant method of copper production. As mines have tended to be depleted, the grade of ore mined has declined over time, but increased productivity due to better technology and recovery methods has tended to offset this effect on the cost of producing copper.

The recycling of copper is feasible due to copper's resistance to corrosion. The secondary, or scrap, production of copper has been an increasing source of copper. Table 20-10 provides other data on the supply, stocks, and trading of copper in the United States.

Demand.   Copper is exclusively an industrial metal; thus, refined copper is consumed mainly by developed countries. Its industrial use is based on its excellent electrical and heat conductivity, corrosion resistance, strength, ductility, and malleability. Copper may also be easily alloyed with nickel and silver.

The United States is the largest consumer of copper, followed by the U.S.S.R. and Japan. These three countries together account for approximately one-half of the world's total consumption. While the United States and the U.S.S.R. are also major producers, Japan must import most of its copper. Other industrial countries, such as the United Kingdom, West Germany, and China, are also major users of copper.

Copper is used in a wide variety of applications. Table 20-11 shows the major classes of consumption in the United States. The largest use of copper is, due to its electrical conductivity, in the electrical industry. In this industry, it is used for wiring and electrical parts in electronic and telecommunications applications, including radios and televisions. Copper is also used in plumbing because of its resistance to corrosion. Due to this corrosion resistance and its ability to conduct heat, it is used in radiators, cooling systems, and solar heating applications. In these uses, copper is used substantially by the housing and automobile industries.

Copper is also used in coins and jewelry because of its strength and shiny appearance. Finally, copper is used in the production of brass and bronze, as well as in many other alloys.

Price determinants.   While much copper is mined by developing countries, most copper is consumed by the industrial, developed countries. Thus, copper exports are an important source of foreign exchange for the developing copper-producing countries. Since no single nation has a monopoly on the source or production of copper, copper is a world commodity.

Because copper is a commercial metal, used particularly by the housing, automotive, and electrical industries, its demand is affected by the general state of the economy and, in particular, by the state of the housing and automotive sectors of the economy. Thus, during recessions or economic slowdowns, the demand for copper declines and its price softens. On the other hand, copper usage typically increases when the economy is strong, and the price of copper, therefore, increases. Copper prices are, thus, fairly volatile over the business cycles.

Increases in the price of copper are, however, limited, particularly when the economy is strong, by competition from substitutes such as steel, plastic, aluminum, and, more recently, fiber optics.

TABLE 20-9 WORLD MINE PRODUCTION OF COPPER (CONTENT OF ORE) (in thousands of metric tons)

Year	Australia	Canada*	Chile	China	Finland	Japan	Mexico	Peru	Zambia	Poland	Zaire	South Africa	Philippines	United States*	U.S.S.R.†	World total†
1979	237.6	636.4	1063	200	41.1	59.1	107.1	390.7	588.3	325.0	430.4	190.6	298.3	1444	855	7691
1980	243.5	716.4	1068	200	36.9	52.6	175.4	366.8	595.8	346.1	539.5	200.7	304.5	1181	900	7739
1981	231.3	691.3	1081	200	38.5	51.5	230.5	342.1	588.0	294.0	555.1	208.7	302.3	1538	940	8191
1982	245.3	612.4	1241	200	34.8	50.7	239.1	369.4	567.8	376.0	519.0	188.7	292.1	1147	970	8072
1983§	256.0	625.0	1257	200	35.0	46.0	250.0	335.6	542.8	380.0	535.0	210.8	273.0	1038	1000	8044
1984‡	250	625	1250	200				370	540	380	525		250	1087	1000	8120

*Recoverable.

†Smelter production.

‡Estimate.

§Preliminary.

SOURCE: U.S. Bureau of Mines.

TABLE 20-10 U.S. SALIENT STATISTICS OF COPPER (in thousands of metric tons)

| | New copper produced | | | | | Second-ary recov-ered[b] | Imports[c] | | Exports | | Stocks, Dec. 31 | | | Apparent con-sumption[f] | |
| | From domestic ores | | | From foreign ores[a] | Total new | | Unmanu-factured | Re-fined | Ore, concen-trate[d] | Re-fined[e] | N.Y. Commodity Exchange | Primary producers (refined) | Blister and materials in solution | Primary copper | Pri-mary and old copper[g] |
Year	Mines	Smelters	Refin-eries												
1975	1282	1247	1167	143	1309	335	294	133	305	156	91	187	283	1191	1526
1976	1457	1326	1291	106	1396	380	485	346	218	102	182	172	291	1656	2036
1977	1364	1265	1280	77	1357	410	396	351	91	47	167	212	314	1622	2032
1978	1358	1270	1327	122	1449	502	532	403	187	92	163	153	263	1819	2321
1979	1447	1313	1413	104	1517	604	282	204	231	74	90	64	275	1735	2432
1980	1181	994	1126	89	1215	613	547	427	107	14	163	49	272	1638	2175
1981	1538	1295	1430	114	1544	598	430	331	151	24	170	151	277	1748	2278
1982[h]	1147	941	1065	162	1227	518	506	258	195	31	248	268	233	1324	1760
1983[h]	1038	888	1004	178	1182	455	644	460	50	81	371	154	174	1688	2020
1984[h]	1087	990	1086	115	1201	450	540	445	69	91	251	122	232		2151

[a]Also from matte, etc., refinery reports.
[b]From old scrap only.
[c]For consumption.
[d]Blister (copper content).
[e]Ingots, bars, etc.
[f]Withdrawals from total supply on domestic account.
[g]Old scrap only.
[h]Preliminary.

SOURCE: U.S. Bureau of Mines.

TABLE 20-11 CONSUMPTION OF REFINED COPPER* IN THE UNITED STATES (in thousands of metric† tons)

Year	By-products						By class of consumer						Total consumption
	Cathodes	Wirebars	Ingot and ingot bars	Cakes and slabs	Billets	Other	Wire mills	Brass mills	Chemical plants	Secondary smelters	Foundries	Miscellaneous	
1975	527.9	722.8	72.5	97.7	75.7	4.1	1061.3	439.0	0.5	4.5	14.0	15.3	1534.5
1976	846.0	768.0	93.5	123.8	84.0	8.6	1346.0	574.9	0.5	3.1	15.4	19.7	1991.9
1977	965.5	861.3	90.2	115.0	103.3	11.2	1511.2	628.6	N.A.	6.6	N.A.	N.A.	2185.0
1978†	1026.1	794.7	111.9	117.1	114.6	24.9	1517.4	619.2	0.4	7.5	12.4	32.3	2189.3
1979	1099.0	701.9	92.1	105.6	129.5	30.4	1499.6	610.2	0.4	6.3	11.9	30.1	2158.4
1980	960.2	583.0	67.6	84.3	117.4	49.7	1308.9	511.6	0.3	5.0	10.9	25.3	1862.1
1981	1198.9	489.2	66.7	121.8	101.9	46.7	1449.6	536.2	0.4	5.4	11.3	22.2	2025.2
1982	1211.0	195.1	45.1	92.4	82.2	32.4	1232.8	393.2	0.4	4.4	7.6	19.7	1658.1
1983‡	1448.1	41.4	53.2	115.3	101.8	7.7	1233.9	500.3	0.6	3.2	11.3	18.3	1767.5
1984§							1416.3	578.1		2.6			2027.0

*Primary and secondary.

†Data prior to 1978 are in thousands of short tons.

‡Preliminary.

§Estimate.

SOURCE: U.S. Bureau of Mines.

On the supply side, labor negotiations and strikes involving the major copper-producing companies in both the developing and developed countries affect copper supplies and, thus, prices. Copper inventories serve as a buffer and, depending on the level of inventories, can affect prices either positively or negatively. In addition, political and social disruptions, particularly in developing countries, affect copper supplies and prices. Disruptions in the international transportation system may also affect copper prices.

There is an important seasonal in copper prices that relates to the use of copper in housing and automobile production. Copper prices tend to be strong in the early spring due to the purchase of copper by the housing and automobile industries for their peak production levels during late spring and summer. Copper prices, thus, usually reach peaks during the February–April period. After the peak demand during late spring, copper demand declines during the summer, and prices soften during the summer and fall. The strength of the production cycles, particularly those related to housing starts, affects the degree of price increase during the early spring.

Copper prices have exhibited considerable volatility, as shown in Figure 20-6.

Futures contracts.   There are two active copper futures contracts. A copper futures contract has been traded at Comex since 1933. And a copper futures contract has been traded at the LME (London Metal Exchange) since 1883. Thus, copper is the basis for one of the oldest commodity futures contracts in existence.

The Comex futures contract is based on 25,000 pounds of copper electrolytic cathodes. Electrolytic wirebars and ingot bars, fire-refined high-conductivity ingot

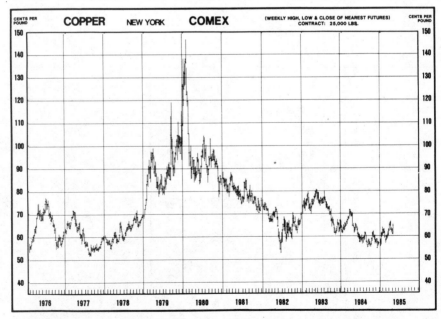

Figure 20-6   Copper. [*Commodity Year Book 1985*, ed. *Walter L. Emery* (*Jersey City, N.J.: Commodity Research Bureau, Inc.*).]

bars, and fire-refined ingot bars are also deliverable at various premiums and discounts. The trading months are the three nearby months and the January, March, May, July, September, and December months up to 23 months in the future.

The LME trades all of its futures contracts quite differently from Comex. The LME does not have a central clearinghouse which stands between all trades, collects initial margin, and marks each position to-the-market. In the LME, rather, each trader, or ring dealer, is a principal, that is, the guarantor of its trades. In addition, margins are not collected, and positions are not marked to-the-market. This system is, thus, based on member financial solvency.

The LME trades two copper futures contracts. The first, which is quite active, is a contract based on high-grade copper wirebars and copper cathodes. The second is based on standard copper cathodes and is less actively traded. Each contract is based on 25 metric tons.

The LME trades on the basis of specific dates, spot and 3 months forward, rather than specific futures months as at Comex and other U.S. futures exchanges. Delivery is via warehouse receipts from warehouses throughout Europe.

In general, the quality of copper cathodes deliverable on the LME contract is slightly higher than the quality of copper cathodes deliverable at Comex, so the LME cathode contract is traded at a slight premium to the Comex contract.

Aluminum

Introduction. Aluminum is the third most abundant element in the earth's crust, after oxygen and silicon. Aluminum also has a combination of physical and chemical properties that makes it one of the earth's most valuable substances. Aluminum is light in weight, is strong (at least in alloyed forms), has high thermal and electrical conductivity, is resistant to corrosion, reflects heat and light, and is malleable and nonmagnetic. Because of these properties and its relatively low cost due to its abundance, aluminum is used in many industrial applications.

Supply. Despite the abundance of aluminum, its wide distribution around the world, and its versatility, the large-scale production and, thus, the significant usage of aluminum did not occur until the late 1800s. A major reason for the delay in the utilization of aluminum was that aluminum, unlike many other metals, is not found free in nature. It is found combined with oxygen in an ore called bauxite. Bauxite is found on all continents except Antarctica, with most of it in Jamaica, Australia, Brazil, and Africa. The United States and Russia have very little bauxite. Most bauxite ore is at the earth's surface, and it can be mined in an open-pit manner.

Recently, Australia has been the biggest producer of bauxite, with approximately 30 percent of the world's total. Guinea (17 percent), Jamaica (14 percent), and Surinam (7 percent) are also major bauxite producers. In 1974, the International Bauxite Association (IBA) was formed to help bauxite-exporting countries increase their control of supply. Almost 90 percent of the western world's bauxite reserves are in IBA members.

In 1886, Hall in the United States and Heroult in France independently discovered the electrolytic process for producing aluminum metal. Two years later,

Bayer in Austria discovered the chemical process for treating bauxite. These two processes are still the basis for producing aluminum.

The production of aluminum from bauxite is a two-step process. In the first step, called refining, basically still using Bayer's process, most of the oxygen is removed from bauxite, and a nonmetallic white powder called alumina is produced by a series of chemical processes. The remainder of the oxygen is then removed from alumina to produce aluminum in the second step, called smelting, via the process developed by Hall and Heroult. In this process, which is very energy-intensive, alumina is dissolved, and the oxygen is separated from the aluminum electrically. Smelter aluminum is 99.50 percent pure. Further refining can produce 99.90 percent pure aluminum.

Pure aluminum is malleable and corrosion-resistant and is an excellent conductor of electricity, but it lacks strength and hardness. For this reason, aluminum is usually alloyed with other metals, typically copper, manganese, magnesium, silicon, and zinc, to improve its properties. Aluminum can also be easily fabricated into many shapes by various metal-working processes, such as rolling, forging, drawing, and extruding.

Until World War II, Alcoa (the Aluminum Company of America) represented 100 percent of the U.S. aluminum capacity, and the United States produced 45 percent of the world's total. But more than 42 countries now produce aluminum. As shown in Table 20-12, the United States is the world's leading producer, with approximately 25 percent, and Russia, Canada, West Germany, and Norway are other major producers. Six large integrated corporations have ownership of 40 percent of the world's aluminum production capacity. They are the Aluminum Company of America (Alcoa), Reynolds Metals Co., and Kaiser Aluminum & Chemical Corp. in the United States, Alcan Aluminum, Ltd. (Alcan) in Canada, Alusuisse International N.V. in Switzerland, and Pechiney Ugine Kuhlmann in France. However, governments, mostly of developing countries, have significant ownership of the world's aluminum production capacity. But the government-owned share declines from stage to stage in the production process. Government-owned capacity is responsible for over one-half of the world's bauxite, one-quarter of its alumina, and less than 20 percent of its aluminum. Political and economic actions taken by these governments, thus, can significantly affect aluminum supplies.

As with other metals, secondary supplies are an important part of the total supply of aluminum. Secondary supplies have been responsible for about one-third of total supplies. "Old scrap" comes mainly from beverage cans and automobiles. "New scrap" is produced by fabricators and is usually recycled immediately. Tables 20-13 and 20-14 provide various data on the supply of aluminum in the United States.

Demand. Because of aluminum's desirable physical and chemical properties, including its light weight and strength, its many applications and total use have been growing significantly. In many applications, it has replaced other materials, such as glass and tin in bottles and cans, copper in the electrical uses, and zinc in the automobile industry.

The largest use of aluminum is in the beverage and food packaging industry, which accounts for approximately one-third of aluminum's total use. Aluminum's use for siding, windows, doors, and screens by the building and construction

TABLE 20-12   WORLD PRODUCTION OF ALUMINUM (in thousands of short tons)

Year	Australia	Austria	Canada	China	France	West Germany	Hungary	Italy	Japan	Norway	Spain	Switzerland	Brazil	United Kingdom	United States	U.S.S.R.	World total
1977	273	101	1073	385	440	818	79	287	1310	686	233	88	184	386	4539	1810	15,189
1978	290	101	1156	400	431	816	79	298	1166	704	234	88	205	382	4804	1840	15,578
1979	297	102	904	400	436	817	79	297	1114	732	286	91	263	396	5023	1930	16,044
1980	335	104	1177	400	476	806	81	299	1203	720	426	95	287	413	5130	1940	16,944
1981	418	104	1230	400	480	804	82	298	849	698	437	91	283	374	4948	1980	16,596
1982*	420	104	1174	410	430	797	82	298	387	702	404	83	330	265	3609	2070	14,802
1983†	475	104	1091	381	398	730	82	216	282	716	394	84	442	275	3353	1996	13,865
1984†	710		1230	380		750				780					4099	2100	15,170

*Preliminary.

†Estimate.

SOURCE: U.S. Bureau of Mines.

489

TABLE 20-13 SALIENT STATISTICS OF ALUMINUM IN THE UNITED STATES (in thousands of short tons)

Year	Net import reliance as a percentage of apparent consumption	Production Primary	Production Secondary	Primary sold[a]	Recovery from scrap Old	Recovery from scrap New	Total apparent consumption	Net shipments[b] by producers Wrought products Plate, sheet, foil	Rolled structural shapes[c]	Extruded shapes[d]	All	Castings Permanent mold	Die	Sand	All	Total all net shipments
1976	9	4251	1155	6145	409	1062	5083	3178	493	1071	4858	189	605	110	923	5780
1977	7	4539	1271	6566	531	1074	5492	3423	467	1198	5210	220	652	113	1004	6214
1978	11	4804	1323	7143	575	1098	6045	3643	583	1311	5673	229	666	126	1044	6717
1979	4	5023	1401	6922	614	1163	5888	3592	618	1263	5615	241	635	143	1040	6655
1980	[e]	5130	1389	6003	680	1058	5065	3346	606	1165	5242	193	443	121	769	6011
1981	[e]	4948	1537	6054	836	1137	5087	3414	520	1110	5169	146	578	119	910	6079
1982	7	3609	1616	5610	862	974	4818	3030	431	1005	4558	120	529	89	803	5361
1983[f]	17	3696	1773	6654	904	1050	5543	3579	475	1149	5301	140	481	112	750	6051
1984[g]	9	4518	1668		915	1054	5875									

[a]To domestic industry.

[b]Consists of total shipments less shipments to other mills for further fabrication.

[c]Also rod, bar, and wire.

[d]Also rod, bar, tube, blooms, and tubing.

[e]Net exports.

[f]Preliminary.

[g]Estimate.

SOURCE: *Commodity Year Book 1985*, Commodity Research Bureau, Jersey City, N.J.

TABLE 20-14 U.S. SUPPLY AND DISTRIBUTION OF ALUMINUM (in thousands of short tons)

Year	Apparent consumption	Production		Imports	Exports	Inventories Dec. 31	
		Primary	From old scrap			Private	Government
1979	5888	5023	614	840	773	2563	2
1980	5065	5130	680	713	1483	2538	2
1981	5087	4948	836	935	867	3303	2
1982	4818	3609	862	968	824	3090	2
1983*	5543	3696	904	1203	855	2497	2
1984†	5875	4518	915	1628	809	2943	2

*Preliminary.
†Estimate.
SOURCE: U.S. Bureau of Mines.

industries accounts for about one-fourth of its total use. The transportation sector, including cars, buses, trucks, and bicycles, accounts for about 12 percent of the U.S. use of aluminum. The electrical sector accounts for approximately 12 percent, using aluminum for power transmission and electrical machinery. Air conditioners, refrigerators, cooking utensils, and other consumer products account for about 7 percent of aluminum's total U.S. use. The use of aluminum in other machinery and equipment, paint, explosives, and defense applications (aluminum is one of the four controlled materials in the U.S. Department of Commerce's Defense Materials System) accounts for most of its remaining use.

Price determinants.   Aluminum prices are determined on the basis of the supply and demand factors discussed above. Overall, the supply of aluminum is more broadly based and more economically, as opposed to politically, determined than copper supply. In addition, aluminum's sources of demand are broader and have smaller seasonal and cyclical influences than copper's. These considerations tend to make aluminum prices more rationally based and less volatile. However, since aluminum and copper are substitutes in many applications, factors that affect one tend also to affect the other to some extent.

To some extent, as in platinum and palladium pricing, there are three types of pricing in the commercial exchange of aluminum. Traditionally, the first type of price, the producer price, has been set by major producers of aluminum as a long-run equilibrium price to assure stable prices for producers and consumers. Producer prices are the last to increase in a strong market and the last to decrease in a weak one. These prices for refined output were initiated by oligopolistic producers who controlled production at all levels.

But as the aluminum market has become more competitive and secondary sources of aluminum have become more important, another level of pricing, merchant pricing, has increased in importance. Metal merchants, or dealers, buy aluminum outside the producer market via secondary smelters, independent refiners, and manufacturer inventories. They then sell to mills and manufacturing firms which cannot obtain it from producers at the time. This market has grown in size and importance since the 1970s. Merchant prices are more volatile than producer prices.

A third type of price, the futures price, has become important since the introduction of aluminum futures contracts in 1978 and 1983. Futures prices, like merchant prices, are fairly volatile.

Since aluminum smelting is very energy-intensive, energy prices have an important effect on aluminum prices. The availability and cost of capital for all stages of aluminum production and technological advances in the production processes also have important effects. Since developing countries are significant at all stages of the aluminum production process, their political and economic policies affect aluminum prices.

Since aluminum is used in both many consumer applications and many industrial applications, its demand is not as volatile over the business cycle as the demand for metals that have few uses or are used solely for industrial applications. Table 20-15 and Figure 20-7 show the recent spot and futures prices for aluminum, respectively.

Futures contracts.   Aluminum futures contracts have been introduced much more recently than the copper futures contracts. The LME aluminum futures

TABLE 20-15 AVERAGE PRICE OF ALUMINUM (VIRGIN 99.5% UNALLOYED INGOT) AT NEW YORK (in cents per pound, carload lots)

Year	Jan.	Feb.	Mar.	Apr.	May	June	July	Aug.	Sept.	Oct.	Nov.	Dec.	Average
1982	76.50	76.50	76.50	76.50	76.50	76.50	76.50	76.50	76.50	76.00	76.00	76.00	76.38
1983	76.00	76.00	76.00	76.00	76.00	76.00	76.00	76.33	78.98	81.00	81.00	81.00	77.53
1984	81.00	81.00	81.00	81.00	81.00	81.00	N.A.	N.A.	N.A.	N.A.	N.A.	N.A.	81.00
1985	N.A.	N.A.											

SOURCE: American Metal Market.

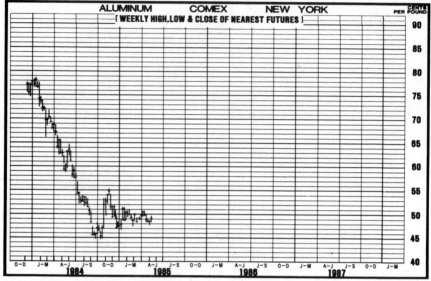

Figure 20-7 Aluminum (April 19, 1985). [*Commodity Year Book 1985, ed. Walter L. Emery (Jersey City, N.J.: Commodity Research Bureau, Inc.).*]

contract began to be traded during 1978, and the Comex contract began on December 8, 1983.[2]

As discussed for copper, the trading methods of these two exchanges are quite different. One important difference is that the LME trades for spot and 3-month-forward delivery as opposed to specific contract months as in all U.S. futures markets. Also, on the LME, the ring dealers are the principals and are responsible for clearing trades; as a result, there are no margins, while on the Comex the clearing organization is behind all trades, and there is the usual U.S. margining procedure. The Comex trading months are the current, or spot, month; the next two calendar months; and any January, March, May, July, September, and December months within 23 months of the current month.

The LME contract is quoted in the British currency (pound sterling) per metric ton, while the Comex contract is quoted in cents per pound. Thus, two corrections must be made for spreads between these two contracts. The first is for the currency difference, which can be hedged with the British pound futures contract. The second is for the denomination or quantity difference—there are 2204.6 pounds in a metric ton. Of course, as indicated above, since the LME trades 3 months forward and Comex in specific months, a correction may also be necessary due to a difference in the time to expiration of the futures contracts.

The LME contract is based on a lower-grade aluminum and thus has a lower price. Specifically, the LME contract is based on the delivery of 99.5 percent pure primary aluminum, while the Comex contract is based on the delivery of 99.7

---

[2] In addition to contracts on copper and aluminum, the LME trades contracts on silver, lead, tin, zinc, and nickel.

percent pure primary aluminum, although 99.5 percent aluminum is deliverable at a discount of 1 cent per pound.

The Comex aluminum contract requires the delivery of 40,000 pounds of aluminum (with a delivery variance of 2 percent) in ingots, sows, or T-bars. Since this size is that of an ocean shipping container, the Comex contract is easier to utilize than the LME contract, which is based on 25 metric tons (55,115.5 pounds). The LME contract has no price limits, while the Comex contract has a price limit of 5 cents per pound (which equals $2000 on the basis of a delivery unit of 40,000 pounds).

The aluminum futures contracts, the newest of the metals futures contracts, have been moderately successful and have provided a valuable alternative to other metals futures contracts for speculators and hedgers.

Speculative uses.   Aluminum futures are used to speculate on the price of aluminum on the basis of the factors discussed above. On the one hand, aluminum prices can be thought to be less volatile than copper prices because the main use of aluminum is for packaging, a consumer staple good, the demand for which is less volatile than the demand for copper on both a seasonal basis and a cyclical basis—the major uses of copper (housing, automobile, and industrial uses) have, as discussed above, significant seasonal and cyclical variations. On the other hand, aluminum is a substitute for copper in many industrial applications, which argues for aluminum and copper prices being closely related and similarly volatile. It is these similarities and differences that make the "ali-copper" spread an interesting basis for speculation. This spread may become as popular as the gold-silver and soybean crush spreads.

Typically, aluminum prices are lower than copper prices. However, aluminum went to a premium over copper in 1983 for the first time since World War II for supply-demand reasons. During the preceding recession the demand for both copper and aluminum decreased. While aluminum producers curtailed production, copper producers, mainly developing country–owned facilities that needed the foreign exchange from copper exports, continued production. During the ensuing recovery, when the demand for both aluminum and copper increased, there were greater inventories of copper, and, thus, the supply of copper increased more quickly, causing aluminum prices to increase more than copper prices. For such reasons, the aluminum-copper spread is, to some extent, an economic-political supply spread.

Another important aspect of this spread relates to energy costs. Aluminum production is much more energy-intensive than copper production, so changes in energy costs, either up or down, affect aluminum prices to a greater degree. Of course, energy prices can also be used as a basis for speculating on aluminum prices alone.

Aluminum futures are priced, as other metal markets are, on a carrying-charge basis; that is, the futures price equals the spot price plus the cost of carrying the metal to the futures delivery day, mainly the financing cost. Pure aluminum time spreads can be used in ways that are similar to the ways spreads are used in other carry markets. Speculators may choose to "buy a time spread" (that is, buy the nearby contract and sell the deferred contract). They may also choose a "bull spread" if they think that supplies will be low, or tight, due to shortages in the spot market or shortages for delivery in the futures market; for example, exchange-certified warehouse receipts will not be adequate for meeting delivery requirements, or demand will be great because economic activity will accelerate.

Aluminum futures, on a naked basis, can also be used as vehicles for speculation based on other supply, demand, and pricing factors discussed in this section.

Notes from a Trader—Commercial Metals. While the precious metals are traded more like financial assets, copper and aluminum are commercial metals and are traded like other commercial commodities such as lumber. And, in fact, copper and lumber are both closely related to the housing cycle, and announcements regarding housing may affect their prices significantly. The demands for both copper and aluminum are susceptible to replacement by existing and new materials. The copper market is much more liquid than the much newer aluminum market.

PETROLEUM AND PETROLEUM PRODUCTS

This section discusses the futures contracts based on petroleum and petroleum products, namely crude oil, heating oil, gasoline, and propane.

Introduction

Prior to the early 1970s, the market for petroleum and petroleum products was a relatively stable market, with stable prices and a stable distribution system. Crude oil was sold via long-term agreements between the major international oil companies, mainly the so-called seven sisters, and the producing countries. Insignificant amounts of crude oil were sold via the spot markets. Crude oil and its products, thus, showed little price volatility. Several political and economic factors changed this environment, thereby increasing price volatility and providing a need for futures contracts on petroleum and petroleum products to hedge the associated price risks.

The formation of OPEC (the Organization of Petroleum Exporting Countries) and the oil embargo during 1973 and 1974 terminated the stable petroleum distribution system, transferring much of the control of crude oil supplies and prices from the major international oil companies to the governments of the oil-producing countries.

The Iranian crisis of 1978 and 1979 continued these trends. Control continued to accrue to the oil-producing countries rather than the international oil companies. An increase in the volume of crude oil sales occurred via the spot market rather than long-term agreements. These changes led to greater price volatility, initially for crude oil and then for refined products; the development of oil-trading companies which traded on the spot markets; an increase in the share of total transactions being conducted on the spot markets; and an increase in the flexibility of independent oil companies. The entire distribution chain, from producer to refiner to wholesaler to retailer of refined products, was affected by these changes. The decontrol of domestic U.S. oil prices during 1981 continued these trends.

These political and economic changes created a need for a method for dealing with the increased volatility in the prices and supplies of petroleum and petroleum products. To understand how the petroleum and petroleum-related futures contracts filled this need, it is necessary to understand the supply system—that is, the production and distribution systems—for petroleum and its products.

Supply

Crude oil, or petroleum, is a natural resource—it is "mined" from the earth. Crude oil is produced in many countries in the world, as shown in Table 20-16. The Soviet Union and the United States are the two largest producers of crude. Great Britain and Mexico are large producers which have significantly increased their production in recent years. But during the last decade, most publicity about crude oil production has centered on several eastern oil-producing countries, including Saudi Arabia, Iran, Iraq, and Kuwait, and the African countries of Libya, Nigeria, and Algeria, which are major exporters of petroleum and which, during the 1970s, increased their supply and the control of this supply.

During the late 1970s and early 1980s, however, the crude production of most of these countries declined, mainly because of decrease in crude imports in developed countries in response to the higher crude prices and energy conservation efforts. For example, in the United States overall petroleum consumption remained unchanged during 1983 due to conservation efforts, including mandatory automobile fuel efficiency standards, incentives for insulating residential and commercial buildings, and tax incentives for industry for conserving energy. The normal market decrease in demand due to higher prices and the conservation efforts led to an oversupply of petroleum (particularly in the OPEC countries), a weakening of the OPEC cartel, and a significant decline in oil prices during the early and mid-1980s. Table 20-17 shows the decrease in imports of petroleum and petroleum products by the United States since 1979.

From the natural resource petroleum, several petroleum products are produced through a process that is called, in general, refining. Currently there are futures contracts on crude oil and several petroleum products. In this sense, the futures contracts on the petroleum complex are similar to those on the so-called soybean complex. Before considering these individual futures contracts, consider, in general, the petroleum production process, called refining, and the nature of the products themselves.

The basic process of refineries is the distillation process. Via the distillation process, a liquid is first heated to vaporize it, and the vapor, or gas, is then cooled to condense it into a liquid. Crude oil contains several components, or hydrocarbon compounds (also called "cuts" or "fractions"), with different boiling points. As crude oil is heated to higher temperatures, the lighter compounds boil first and successively heavier and heavier compounds then boil. The sequential boiling and condensation of these different components separates the various cuts of petroleum. Figure 20-8 shows a typical distillation curve for crude oil, with the lighter compounds boiling at lower temperatures. Crudes from different sources have somewhat different distillation curves, that is, somewhat different fractions of the various components.

TABLE 20-16 WORLD PRODUCTION OF CRUDE PETROLEUM, BY SPECIFIED COUNTRIES (in thousands of barrels per day)

Year	Alger-ia	Cana-da	China	Libya	Iran	Iraq	Ku-wait	Nigeria	Mex-ico	Indo-nesia	United King-dom	U.S.S.R.	Saudi Arabia	United States	Vene-zuela	World total
1978	1161	1313	2082	1983	5242	2563	2131	1897	1209	1635	1082	11,185	8301	8707	2166	60,057
1979	1154	1496	2122	2092	3168	3477	2500	2302	1461	1591	1568	11,460	9532	8552	2356	62,535
1980	1012	1435	2114	1787	1662	2514	1656	2055	1936	1577	1622	11,773	9900	8597	2168	59,538
1981	805	1285	2012	1140	1380	1000	1125	1433	2313	1605	1811	11,909	9815	8572	2102	55,900
1982	710	1372	2045	1150	2214	1012	823	1295	2748	1339	2065	12,080	6483	8649	1895	53,458
1983*	675	1450	2120	1076	2426	1005	1064	1241	2686	1385	2291	12,034	5086	8688	1768	52,981
1984†	642	1407	2208	1072	2187	1203	1117	1382	2758	1468	2492	11,827	4649	8757	1811	53,719

*Preliminary.

†Estimate.

SOURCE: Energy Information Administration.

TABLE 20-17 IMPORTS* OF PETROLEUM AND PRODUCTS INTO THE UNITED STATES (in thousands of barrels (42 gallons per barrel))

| Year | Crude | Total refined | As-phalt | Fuel oil | | Finished gaso-line | Jet fuel | Kero-sene | Liquefied petro-leum gases | Lubri-cants | Petro-chemical feed-stocks | Special naph-thas | Un-finished oils | Wax |
				Dis-tillate	Re-sidual									
1976	1,935,012	705,256	3,905	53,520	517,325	47,774	27,983	3,163	47,436	1,361	1,370	45	11,735	654
1977	2,397,468	767,925	1,483	90,504	492,581	78,434	27,117	6,869	58,927	3,270	4,954	972	11,239	—
1978	2,329,700	722,900	907	63,288	494,640	69,518	31,346	4,031	40,889	2,978	2,994	1,750	9,913	—
1979	2,400,900	685,600	1,448	70,489	420,144	66,006	28,566	3,298	62,576	3,441	3,934	3,480	21,372	0
1980	1,946,200	582,500	1,414	51,900	343,600	51,071	29,521	3,690	56,711	2,667	10,245	3,354	19,659	0
1981	1,654,200	534,200		63,100	292,100									
1982	1,352,400	514,000		34,000	283,100									
1983†	1,317,800	525,900		63,500	255,200									
1984‡	1,370,000	613,000		103,000	246,000									

*Includes shipments to noncontiguous territories.

†Preliminary.

‡Estimate.

SOURCE: U.S. Bureau of Mines.

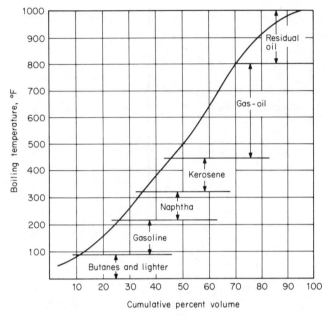

Figure 20-8   Crude-oil distillation curve and its fractions. [*William L. Leffler, Petroleum Refining for the Non-Technical Person* (*Tulsa, Okla.: Pennwell Publ. Co., 1979*), *p. 7.*]

Although there are many processes that are ancillary to the basic distillation process in a refinery (such as cracking, polymerization, and reforming), some of which increase the output of the lighter products, mainly gasoline, and increase the octane of gasoline, the main process in a refinery is distillation. Table 20-18 shows typical recent refinery yields by product. Table 20-19 shows the recent levels of production of refined petroleum products in the United States.

Demand: Petroleum and Petroleum Products

This section discusses the demand for and uses of petroleum and some of its major products which are or may be the basis for futures contracts.

Crude Oil.   Crude oil, as extracted from the earth, varies considerably by location. Crude oil is categorized and evaluated according to three characteristics. The first is sulfur content, which is important because sulfur is a pollutant. Low-sulfur crude oil (called "sweet") contains less than 0.5 percent sulfur by weight; high-sulfur crude ("sour") contains more than 1 percent sulfur by weight; and intermediate-sulfur crude has a sulfur content between 0.5 percent and 1.0 percent. This characteristic of crude oil has become more important in recent years as worldwide pollution control standards have become stricter.

The second characteristic is density. Low-density, or "light," crude oil is desirable because it yields more higher-value light products, such as gasoline, jet fuel, and light-distillate fuel oil. Density is measured in terms of API (American Petroleum

TABLE 20-18 REFINERY YIELDS OF MAJOR PETROLEUM PRODUCTS FROM CRUDE, U.S. TOTALS (percentages)

Item	1982	1981	1980	1979	1978
Gasoline*	46.2	44.5	44.5	43.0	44.1
Jet fuel	8.3	7.9	7.4	6.9	6.6
Ethane (including ethylene)	†	0.1	†	0.1	0.1
Liquefied gases	2.2	2.4	2.4	2.3	2.3
Kerosene	0.9	0.9	1.0	1.3	1.0
Distillate fuel oil	21.5	20.5	19.7	21.5	21.4
Residual fuel oil	8.8	10.4	11.7	11.5	11.3
Petrochemical feedstocks	3.4	4.5	5.1	4.7	4.1
Special naphthas	0.4	0.6	0.7	0.6	0.7
Lubricants	1.2	1.3	1.3	1.3	1.3
Wax	0.1	0.1	0.1	0.1	0.1
Coke	3.4	3.1	2.7	2.6	2.5
Asphalt	2.7	2.7	2.9	3.1	3.2
Road oil	†	†	0.1	†	0.1
Still gas	4.6	4.5	4.0	3.8	3.7
Miscellaneous	0.7	0.7	0.8	0.8	0.9
Shortage	-4.4	-4.0	-4.4	-3.6	-3.4
Total‡	100.0	100.0	100.0	100.0	100.0

*Based on total gasoline minus input of natural gas liquids and other hydrocarbons.

†Less than 0.05 percent.

‡Totals may not sum due to rounding.

SOURCE: U.S. Department of Energy, *Crude Petroleum, Petroleum Products, and Natural Gas Liquids* and *Petroleum Supply Annual*, final summaries.

Year	Asphalt[a]	Aviation gasoline	Fuel oil Distillate	Fuel oil Residual	Gasoline[b]	Petrochemical feedstocks	Special naphthas	Miscellaneous products	Jet fuel	Kerosene	Liquefied gases[c] (for fuel)	Lubricants	Liquefied gases[d] Total	At LPG[e]	At LRG[f]
1978	172.9	13.9	1156	608.6	2631	223.1	36.7	47.0	353.9	56.3	87.5	69.5	561.1	431.5	129.5
1979	168.8	13.7	1151	615.6	2515	252.1	36.6	42.7	369.2	66.8	84.7	71.0	568.0	443.9	124.1
1980	141.2	12.8	974.1	578.4	2394	254.6	36.5	38.5	365.6	50.1	87.0	65.1	561.8	440.9	120.8
1981	123.5	11.5	953.8	482.1	2349				353.2	43.6		60.6	573.4	458.6	114.8
1982	119.4	8.9	951.3	390.4	2322				357.0	42.0		51.6	557.5	459.0	98.5
1983	135.7	9.2	896.5	310.9	2323				373.2	40.0		53.8	599.2	479.6	119.6
1984[g]	140	10	900	320	2400				390	40		55		490	125

[a]5.5 barrels = 1 short ton.
[b]Finished.
[c]Liquefied refinery gases.
[d]Includes ethane and ethylene.
[e]Gas processing plants.
[f]Refineries.
[g]Estimated.
SOURCE: U.S. Bureau of Mines.

Institute) gravity: light crudes have high API gravities (greater than 35°), and heavy crudes have low API gravities (less than 24°). The third characteristic of crude is field of origin, which is important because it summarizes many other characteristics, such as viscosity, pour point, color, flash and fine points, and metals content.

The demand for crude oil comes almost exclusively from refineries. In addition to the continuing long-term agreements and the growing spot markets in the distribution of crude oil, there are a large number of swap transactions whereby refiners or other purchasers of crude oil swap crude of different grades for different delivery points (location swaps) or for delivery at different times (time swaps). Swaps by grade may be necessary because different refineries do not refine efficiently all types of crude; they refine only a limited range of types of crude. In addition, shifts in demand for the various crude products (for example, toward heating oil and away from gasoline) cause refiners to swap for different grades of crude, but again only within the technological restrictions of the refinery. Time swaps permit refiners to vary the time at which they take delivery of crudes so that they can accelerate or decelerate refining.

Heating Oil.   Heating oil is part of a family of petroleum products called distillates (see "gas-oil" in Figure 20-8 and "distillate fuel oil" in Table 20-18). These products, which are refined at approximately 350 to 800°F, represent the middle range of refinery products. Distillates are divided into two groups: No. 1 oil and No. 2 oil. (A third group, No. 4 oil, is sometimes added, but insignificant amounts of this product are produced.) No. 1 oil includes kerosene, which is used for burning in stoves and lamps (jet fuel also has a similar boiling range).

No. 2 oil represents about 85 percent of the distillate group and about 17 percent of a typical barrel of crude oil. No. 2 oil is also known as heating oil, more commonly known as gas oil in Europe. Diesel fuel is very close to heating oil, but while most diesel fuel can be burned as heating oil, the opposite is not true. No. 2 fuel oil is commonly used for domestic and small commercial heating. Its most important characteristics are its burning characteristics and its sulfur content.

Given the use of No. 2 oil, the demand for and, thus, the stock of heating oil are seasonal. Since the demand for heating oil is greatest in the winter, heating oil stocks are greatest in October and November, at the start of the heating season, and reach a minimum during February and March, when the demand for heating oil is coming to an end. June and July are the beginning of the summer-fill period.

As a source of heat, heating oil competes with electricity and natural gas and, to a lesser extent, with coal and liquefied petroleum gas (LPG). During the last decade, heating oil has lost a significant share of the home heating market to electricity. Even within the seasonal demand for heating oil, the demand for and often the price of heating oil increase as the temperature drops. Due to weather differences, the demand for heating oil is also regional.

Gasoline.   As shown in Figure 20-8 and Table 20-18, gasoline accounts for the largest proportion of refinery output. In fact, many of the recent technological advances in refinery processes have been made to increase the quantity and quality of the gasoline output. Gasoline is used almost entirely for transportation, mainly by passenger cars.

In general, there are four grades of gasoline: regular and premium, each either leaded or unleaded. The fraction of unleaded gasoline produced has grown substantially since 1975, when federal controls were initiated. Unleaded gasoline now accounts for over one-half of the total gasoline market, and its use is expected to continue to grow as older automobiles not subject to controls are replaced.

The demand for gasoline is also seasonal, being greatest during the summer driving months. Thus, gasoline stocks peak in April through May and trough in September through October. This seasonal effect is, thus, almost the opposite of the seasonal effect for heating oil. The complementarity in the demands for heating oil and gasoline permits the more efficient use of refineries and storage facilities.

The two most important characteristics of gasoline are vapor pressure and octane. Vapor pressure is the surface pressure it takes to keep the liquid from turning to a vapor or gas, and it must be high enough to permit the car to start, particularly in cold weather, and low enough so that the gas does not vaporize too easily. Octane is a measure of the "engine knock" the gasoline produces—the higher the octane, the less the knock. While lead can be added to raise the octane level and reduce knock, refineries must now use other techniques.

Propane (Liquefied Petroleum Gas—LPG). Propane, or LPG (also called "tank gas"), is a gas under atmospheric conditions, but under higher pressure or at a lower temperature it becomes a liquid.[3] Propane is a minor source of heat; it is used in camp stoves and in outdoor stoves and grills and also, to some extent, for residential and commercial space heating. It is also used as a source of heat in the agricultural sector. For these heating purposes, LPG is very clean and portable. Its major use, however, is as an energy source and feedstock for petrochemical plants. Propane can be converted into ethylene and propylene, which are building blocks for the chemical industry, including the production of plastic.

There are two major sources of propane. First, propane is a normal by-product of the refining process, a by-product whose output has increased significantly in recent years due to technological changes. It is also produced at gas-processing plants along with butane.

Other Refinery Products. The crude oil and refinery products mentioned above are all the basis for current futures contracts. There are, in addition, other refinery products, such as the ones discussed briefly below.

Kerosene and jet fuel. While these two products have similar boiling points, kerosene is used for burning in stoves and lamps and has few quality restrictions, while jet fuel must meet rigid quality restrictions.

Residual fuel oil. The three types of residual fuel oil are referred to as No. 5 and No. 6 heating oils and Bunker C fuel oil. They are typically used to provide steam and heat for large buildings and for industry, including the production of electricity, and to power ships.

---

[3] To be precise, while propane is the major liquefied petroleum gas, there are others, such as butane, butane-propane mixture, and ethane-propane mixture.

Price Determinants

During recent years, the factors that determine the price of petroleum and petroleum products have been widely and publicly discussed. These factors can, as usual, be summarized by supply and demand.

Supply, it has been learned, depends not only on the level of crude available but also on the way in which the crude oil is sold and distributed. The OPEC cartel has both limited the available amount of crude supplied and increased its price. These actions have induced a reduction in demand for many crude products, mainly gasoline; the lower demand is due to normal market responses and also to public policies in the consuming nations. The balance between supply and demand and the related strength or weakness of the OPEC oil cartel have been major determinants of the level of supply and the price of crude oil. These factors are a combination of government policies and market economics.

Factors which disrupt the supply channels, such as wars and blockages, also affect the supply. Weather is an important determinant of demand, particularly for heating oil in cold climates, but also for gasoline in the summer.

The balance of supply and demand in the various links in the production chain is also important. The amount of crude in transit via ships, the amount of products in storage in pipelines or tanks, and how close to capacity refineries are operating and with what mix of products are all important indicators of the supply-demand balance and prospective price changes for specific petroleum products.

Futures Contracts

Futures contracts on the petroleum complex began on November 14, 1978, when the New York Mercantile Exchange introduced a futures contract on heating oil No. 2. From this beginning, petroleum futures have grown in number and trading volume and have become an important part of the futures industry and the petroleum industry. There are now futures contracts on several other petroleum-related products. Several exchanges, however, have listed several petroleum futures contracts since 1978 which have not succeeded. Table 20-20 summarizes the futures contracts based on petroleum and petroleum products that are considered active. Detailed specifications are provided in Chapter 3.

There is a futures contract based on crude oil for delivery in Cushing, Oklahoma. It was listed on March 30, 1983, by the New York Mercantile Exchange (NYME). Despite its recent listing, the crude oil futures contract has been the tenth most active futures contract in terms of trading volume. The crude oil futures contract is based on the delivery of light sweet oil. The following streams are deliverable:

Domestic	*Foreign*
West Texas Intermediate	U.K. Brent Blend
Mid-Continent Sweet	Nigerian Brass Blend
Low Sweet Mix	Nigerian Bonny Light
New Mexican Sweet	Norwegian Ekofisk
North Texas Sweet	Tunisian Zarzaitine/El Borma
Oklahoma Sweet	Algerian Saharan Blend
South Texas Sweet	

TABLE 20-20 PETROLEUM FUTURES CONTRACTS*

Underlying product*	Date listed and exchange	Trading volume (January–September 1984)	Price basis	Unit of trading	Minimum price fluctuations	Contract months
Heating oil No. 2	1978 New York Mercantile Exchange	1,464,420	FOB seller's exshore facility in New York Harbor	1000 barrels (42,000 gallons)	0.01 cent per gallon ($4.20 per contract)	All calendar months, up to 18 months
Gasoline (leaded)	1981 New York Mercantile Exchange	571,317	FOB seller's exshore facility in New York Harbor	1000 barrels (42,000 gallons)	0.01 cent per gallon ($4.20 per contract)	All calendar months, up to 18 months
Crude oil	1983 New York Mercantile Exchange	1,204,600	FOB buyer's designated pipeline storage facility in Cushing, Oklahoma	1000 barrels (42,000 gallons)	$0.01 per barrel ($10 per contract)	All calendar months, up to 18 months
Gasoline (unleaded)	1984 New York Mercantile Exchange		FOB seller's exshore facility in New York Harbor (other options also available)	1000 barrels (42,000 gallons)	0.01 cent per gallon ($4.20 per contract)	All calendar months, up to 15 months
Propane (LPG)	1981 (reintroduced in 1981 after original introduction in 1971) Petroleum Associates (New York Cotton Exchange)	16,238	FOB licensed facilities in Mont Belvieu, Texas, or Conway, Kansas	1000 barrels (42,000 gallons)	0.01 cents per gallon ($4.20 per contract)	All contract months, up to 12 months
Gas oil	International Petroleum Exchange (IPG)—London	N.A.	FOB-approved facilities in Amsterdam, Rotterdam, or Antwerp	100 metric tons (735.7 barrels or 30,895 gallons)	$0.25 per metric ton ($25 per contract)	Nine consecutive calendar months, including the current month

*Detailed specifications are provided in Chapter 3.

Despite the fact that there are several deliverable grades, the crude oil futures contract tracks West Texas Intermediate (WTI) crude. Many of the other grades are not, in practice, delivered in Cushing. In addition to delivery according to the delivery specifications of the futures contracts, many contracts are settled by exchange for physicals (EFP); that is, through mutual agreement between the long and the short, the contract is settled by delivery of a nondeliverable grade at a nondelivery point or on a nondelivery day or at a nondelivery time of day at a mutually acceptable price.

The original NYME heating oil No. 2 contract is for delivery in New York Harbor. The NYME listed a contract on October 5, 1981, on leaded gasoline for New York Harbor delivery, and this contract has become quite active.

The International Petroleum Exchange (IPE) in London trades a gas-oil contract for Netherlands delivery. The gas-oil deliverable grade is similar to but somewhat lower than the heating oil No. 2 on the NYME futures contract. The New York Cotton Exchange, in 1981 (after an original unsuccessful introduction in 1971), listed a contract based on LPG.

The NYME listed a contract on unleaded gasoline on December 3, 1984. This contract has developed liquidity and, as indicated above, is becoming increasingly useful as more automobiles use unleaded gasoline.

The futures price relationships of petroleum futures contracts—that is, the relationships between the prices of the various contract months—are due to a combination of several phenomena. Petroleum and its products are storable, so it may seem that their futures contracts would be priced like the contracts of other storables, such as metals; that is, futures prices would increase the longer it takes to reach the maturity of the futures contracts. Table 20-21 shows the prices of several contract months at a specific time for the NYME crude oil, leaded gasoline, and heating oil No. 2 futures contracts. While storage costs do provide an upward bias for these futures contracts with longer maturity periods, the data in Table 20-21 demonstrate that this is not the only phenomenon and that these futures contracts are not priced like gold.

As indicated above, there is a seasonal aspect to both gasoline and heating oil which provides a seasonal component for their pricing. The summer months are the time of peak demand for gasoline and the winter months for heating oil. This

TABLE 20-21   PETROLEUM PRODUCTS FUTURES PRICE RELATIONSHIPS   (Friday, January 4, 1985)

	Crude oil (NYME), dollars per barrel	Gasoline—leaded regular (NYME), cents per gallon	Heating oil No. 2 (NYME), cents per gallon
February	25.18	63.72	70.24
March	25.19	64.38	69.16
April	25.16	65.10	67.03
May	25.13	65.85	66.05
June	25.10	66.60	65.85
July	24.90	—	66.20
December	25.06	67.10	71.00

provides a seasonal aspect for gasoline and heating oil pricing, as there is for the pricing of grains.

Finally, the strength of the demand for the products affects the price relationships. Since these products can be stored in their means of transportation, the strength of the demand for the products, both current and expected, can cause changes in the price relationships. Typically, when the demand is weak, the prices of deferred futures contracts tend to be lower. The data in Table 20-21 exhibit elements of these different factors which make the pricing of these petroleum-related futures contracts quite complex.

The NYME heating oil and gasoline contracts refer to New York Harbor delivery. The prices, thus, reflect seasonal factors, such as the weather in the northeast United States, which may be different from weather in other parts of the country. Thus, basis relationships for hedges outside the northeast can be affected by such factors.

The petroleum business also tends to be regionalized—each region may have different demand characteristics. But because New York Harbor is linked to the Gulf Coast by pipeline, the basis between these two locations tends to be relatively stable. But basis changes can occur for locations away from these points.

Understanding these price relationships is critical for understanding the basis, which is defined as the futures price minus the cash price in these markets. And understanding the basis is critical to using these contracts for effective hedging. In defining the basis for a hedge, the reference location of the cash price must be specified.

Figures 20-9, 20-10, and 20-11 show the recent futures prices for heating oil, crude oil, and leaded gasoline.

Speculative Uses

Obviously, the petroleum-related futures contracts can be used for hedging by participants in the markets for petroleum and petroleum products. Examples of hedge uses are as follows:

- An oil-trading company, to hedge the forward purchase of crude oil, sells crude oil futures contracts.
- A refiner, to hedge an inventory of gasoline from refinery output, sells gasoline futures contracts.
- A gasoline jobber, to hedge the forward sale of gasoline, buys gasoline futures contracts.

Another type of hedge, which can also be used as a strategy for speculation, is the so-called crack hedge, based on the crack spread. The crack hedge or spread is based on the price relationship between crude oil (a refinery input) and gasoline and heating oil (refinery outputs). The crack hedge or spread, thus, relates to the profit margin of the refinery and is called the gross cracking margin. To hedge or speculate on the basis of a crack spread, refinery ratios must be specified. While the ratio of 3 barrels of crude oil to produce 2 barrels of gasoline and 1 barrel of heating oil is often used, for simplicity assume that 2 barrels of crude produce 1 barrel of gasoline and 1 barrel of heating oil.

Figure 20-9 Heating oil. [*Commodity Year Book 1985, ed. Walter L. Emery* (*Jersey City, N.J.: Commodity Research Bureau, Inc.*).]

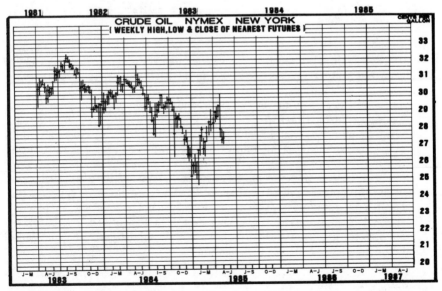

Figure 20-10 Crude oil. [*Commodity Year Book 1985, ed. Walter L. Emery* (*Jersey City, N.J.: Commodity Research Bureau, Inc.*).]

Figure 20-11   Gasoline. [*Commodity Year Book 1985*, ed. *Walter L. Emery [Jersey City, N.J.: Commodity Research Bureau, Inc.].]

Although all three of these futures contracts are in terms of 1000 barrels (42,000 gallons), the crude contract is priced in terms of dollars per barrel and the gasoline and heating oil contracts in terms of cents per gallon. To spread among these contracts, it is necessary to convert all three to common terms. A refiner-hedger or refiner-speculator who expected crude prices to increase relative to gasoline and heating oil prices would "sell the crack," that is, buy two crude oil futures contracts and sell one gasoline futures contract and one heating oil futures contract.

Futures contracts on petroleum and petroleum products have provided speculative opportunities on products which, since the 1970s, have exhibited considerable price volatility and have been continuously in the national and international headlines. The most obvious way to speculate in these contracts is to buy or sell one of these futures contracts on the basis of national and international political and economic factors such as the following:

- OPEC strengthening or fragmenting. (Crude oil prices are most sensitive to the solidarity of OPEC.)
- Announcements of petroleum stockpiles.
- The discovery of new oil sources.

- Unseasonally warm or cold weather.
- Energy conservation efforts succeeding or failing.
- Strong or weak seasonals in demand.

Intercontract spreads can also be done to take advantage of relative price changes—for example, between crude oil and gasoline, crude oil and heating oil, or gasoline and heating oil. The latter may be interesting in view of the different seasonals for these products.

Intracontract spreads—that is, buying one month and selling another month of the same futures contract—are appropriate ways to speculate on the basis of the seasonals in gasoline and heating oil. As indicated, the gasoline season goes from May to September, while the heating oil season goes from October through April. As a result, gasoline futures prices for June and July delivery tend to begin rising in March, and heating oil futures prices for December and January delivery tend to begin rising in September or October. Intracontract spreads based on these seasonals are common. Of course, while these trends are typical, changes in weather patterns or consumption patterns may alter them.

More sophisticated speculators can also engage in arbitrage, which can be regarded as a more sophisticated form of spreading. One form of arbitrage is between New York heating oil and London gas oil. Although the contracts are similar, the NYME specifications are for a somewhat higher grade, and the NYME contract is worth about 2 cents more per gallon than the IPE contract. Although both contracts are quoted in terms of U.S. dollars, adjustment is necessary because the IPE contract is for 100 metric tons, while the NYME contract is for 42,000 gallons. The conversion is that 100 metric tons equals 30,954 U.S. gallons. Another complicated form of arbitrage is the crack spread mentioned above, which is a more sophisticated intercontract spread.

The petroleum futures complex, which began in 1978 and has grown and broadened significantly, has become an important futures group for hedgers and speculators. Its growth, broadening, and importance are likely to continue to increase.

Notes from a Trader

Although the petroleum products futures group is fairly new, this group of futures contracts has become very large and comprises several popular trading vehicles. Crude oil is one of the most actively traded commodities in the world, and the crude oil futures contract reflects this huge cash market. Crude oil futures traders follow international oil politics, particularly those related to OPEC, and watch for possible disruptions in the supply chain due to wars, strikes, or other stoppages. Inventory levels, both in transit and in storage, are also watched as a basis for trading. Weather also affects the prices of petroleum products; in particular, warm or cold weather in the United States or Europe has an effect on heating oil prices.

Basis risk can also add to the risk of speculation in these markets. For example, there may be, at times, a considerable difference in the price changes of, for example, North Sea Brent crude oil and West Texas Intermediate (WTI) crude, on which the pricing of the futures contract is based, and there may be a significant difference between the New York Harbor delivery and the Cushing, Oklahoma, delivery, which is the basis for the futures contract.

A frequent aspect of these markets, particularly the market for crude oil, is their backwardation, that is, the contract price being lower the more distant the contract month, even though these markets are negative carry markets. For this reason, buyers in these markets may want to use the deferred contracts.

Both fundamental and technical methods are used in these markets. The crude oil futures contract has a minimum price movement, or "tic," of $10, or 1 cent per barrel, while the products have a value of $21 per contract, or 5 cents per barrel. The liquidity of these futures markets, particularly for crude oil and heating oil, is considerable.

APPENDIX
Sources of Information

SILVER

Silver Institute, 1001 Connecticut Avenue, NW, Washington, D.C. 20036
Silver Users Association, 1717 K Street, NW, Washington, D.C. 20036

PLATINUM, PALLADIUM, GOLD, AND U.S. SILVER COINS
Government Agencies

U.S. Department of the Interior, Bureau of Mines, Washington, D.C. 20241:
Mineral Industry Surveys—statistics and trade developments; published quarterly
Minerals and Materials—a monthly survey; statistics published monthly
Minerals Yearbook—statistics and long-range developments; published at intervals
   of approximately 5 years

Periodicals

American Metal Market, 7 East 12 Street, New York, NY 10003
Coin Age, Behn-Miller Publications, Incorporated, Sparta, IL
Coin World, Sidney Printing and Publishing Company, Sidney, OH
Metal Bulletin Monthly, 45/46 Lower Marsh, London, England
Metals Week, 1221 Avenue of the Americas, New York, NY 10020
The Platinum Metals Review, Johnson, Matthey and Company, Ltd., London, England

Trade Associations

Gold Institute, Washington, D.C.
International Precious Metals Institute, Brooklyn, NY
Silver Institute, 1001 Connecticut Avenue, NW, Washington, D.C. 20036
Silver Uses Association, 1717 K Street, NW, Washington, D.C. 20036

Other

Metal Statistics, Fairchild Publications, 7 East 12 Street, New York, NY 10003; and
   statistical summary by the publishers of *American Metal Market*
Yearbook of the American Bureau of Metal Statistics, American Bureau of Metal Statistics, New York, NY

ALUMINUM

Annual

Commodity Year Book, Commodity Research Bureau, Inc., 75 Montgomery Street, Jersey City, NJ 07302

Metal Statistics, American Metal Market (Fairchild Publications, Inc.), 7 East 12 Street, New York, NY 10003

Mineral Industry Survey—Aluminum (annual issue and annual preliminary issue), U.S. Bureau of Mines, Washington, D.C. 20241

Yearbook (nonferrous metals), American Bureau of Metal Statistics, 420 Lexington Avenue, New York, NY 10017

Monthly

CRU Metal Monitor (Aluminum), Commodities Research Unit, Ltd., 31 Mount Pleasant, London WC1 XOAD

Mineral Industry Survey—Aluminum, U.S. Bureau of Mines, Washington, D.C. 20241

Weekly

Metal Bulletin, Metal Bulletin, Inc., 708 Third Avenue, New York, NY 10017

Metals Week, McGraw-Hill, Inc., 1221 Avenue of the Americas, New York, NY 10020

Daily

American Metal Market, Fairchild Publications, Inc., 7 East 12 Street, New York, NY 10003

PETROLEUM AND PETROLEUM PRODUCTS

General Energy Publications

American Petroleum Institute. *Standard Definitions for Petroleum Statistics.* Washington, D.C.

American Society for Testing and Materials. *ASTM Specifications for Petroleum Products.* Philadelphia, 1978.

British Petroleum Company, Limited. *Our Industry Petroleum.* London, 1977.

International Petroleum Encyclopedia. Tulsa, Okla.: Penwell Publishing Company.

Wolbert, G. S. *U.S. Oil Pipelines.* Washington, D.C.: American Petroleum Institute, 1979.

Periodicals

Crude Petroleum, Petroleum Products, and Natural Gas Liquids; Energy Data Report; Monthly Energy Review; Monthly Petroleum Statement: Petroleum Market Shares; Sales of LP Gases and Ethane; and *Weekly Petroleum Status Report.* U.S. Department of Energy.

Energy User News. Washington, D.C.: Fairchild Publishing Company.

Fuel Oil Week. Washington, D.C.: Observer Publishing Company.

National Petroleum News. New York, N.Y.: McGraw-Hill.

Oil and Gas Journal. Tulsa, Okla.: Penwell Publishing Company.

Oil Buyer's Guide. Lakewood, N.J.: Petroleum Publications, Incorporated.

Oil Daily. New York, N.Y.: Oil Daily, Incorporated.

The Petroleum Economist. London: Petroleum Press Bureau Limited.

The Petroleum Intelligence Weekly. New York, N.Y.: Petroleum and Energy Intelligence Weekly, Incorporated.

Platt's Oilgram. New York, N.Y.: McGraw-Hill.

Survey of Current Business. U.S. Department of Commerce, Bureau of Economic Analysis.

Associations

American Gas Association, Arlington, VA
American Petroleum Institute, Washington, D.C.
American Petroleum Refiners Association, Washington, D.C.
American Society for Testing and Materials, Philadelphia, PA
Gas Processors Association, Tulsa, OK
Gas Research Institute, Chicago, IL
Independent Petroleum Association of America, Washington, D.C.
Independent Refiners Association of America, Washington, D.C.
National LP-Gas Association, Oak Brook, IL
National Oil Jobbers Council, Incorporated, Washington, D.C.
National Petroleum Council, Washington, D.C.
National Petroleum Refiners Association, Washington, D.C.
Petroleum Industry Research Foundation, Incorporated, New York, NY

Refining

Leffler, W. L. *Petroleum Refining for the Non-Technical Person.* Tulsa, Okla.: Penwell Books, 1979.
National Petroleum Council. *Refinery Flexibility.* Washington, D.C., December 1980.
U.S. Department of Energy. *Trends in Refinery Capacity and Utilization.* September 1978.

Crude

Banks, F. E. *Political Economy of Oil.* Lexington, Mass.: Lexington Books, 1980.
Oil and Gas Journal. *Evaluation of World's Important Crudes.* Tulsa, Okla.: The Petroleum Publishing Company, 1973.
———. *A Guide to World Export Crudes.* Tulsa, Okla.: The Petroleum Publishing Company, 1976.
Wyant, F. R. *The United States, OPEC, and Multi-national Oil.* Lexington, Mass.: Lexington Books, 1977.

Heating Oil

R. Shriver Association. *Middle Distillate Market Profile Report.* U.S. Department of Energy, July 1979.
Schmidt, F. P. *Fuel Oil Manual.* New York: Industrial Press, Incorporated, 1969.

Gasoline

American Petroleum Institute. *Gasoline Marketing.* Washington, D.C., December 1976.
———. *Recent Changes in Retail Gasoline Marketing.* Washington, D.C., January 1981.
Ethyl Corporation. *The Story of Gasoline.* New York, 1964.
Seiferlein, K. E. *Motor Gasoline Supply and Demand 1967–1978.* U.S. Department of Energy, Energy Information Administration, August 1978.

Propane

Butane-Propane News, Incorporated. *An Introduction to LP-Gases.* Arcadin, Calif., 1973.
Leffler, W. L. *The Technology and Economic Behavior of the U.S. Propane Industry.* Tulsa, Okla: The Petroleum Publishing Company, 1973.

21

The Financial
Futures Markets

*"Cardinal rules for the financial futures
markets: bad news for the economy is good
news for the bond and bill markets, bad news
for the dollar relative to foreign currencies,
and either good or bad news for the stock
market."*

There are three categories of financial futures markets. This chapter discusses
them in the chronological order of their listing as futures contracts as follows: (1)
foreign currencies, (2) interest rates, and (3) stock indexes.

THE FOREIGN CURRENCY FUTURES MARKETS

Introduction

Six foreign currency futures markets were listed by the International Monetary
Market (IMM), a division of the Chicago Mercantile Exchange (CME), on May
16, 1972. They were the British pound, the Canadian dollar, the West German
mark, the Japanese yen, the Mexican peso, and the Swiss franc. These contracts
continue to be traded today, with all but the Mexican peso being very active.

The collapse of the Smithsonian Agreement in March 1973, which led to a free
float of all currencies, contributed greatly to the subsequent development of these
markets. These markets have, in turn, contributed to the more volatile international

financial system. Figure 21-1 shows some recent major events and the variability of the dollar.

The listing of the foreign currency futures contracts was greeted with much skepticism. First, these were the first futures contracts listed on financial instruments, and many observers did not believe there could be successful futures trading on financial instruments. Second, there was and still is a well-developed bank forward market for foreign currencies, which many believed made the foreign currency futures markets unnecessary.

But today the foreign currency ("forex") futures markets are prospering and, indeed, are among the largest and fastest-growing futures markets. Obviously, the foreign currency futures markets have filled a need. These markets have succeeded for several reasons.

First, the interbank forward markets are available only in fairly large denominations ($1 million and over), and only corporations which are good credit risks, mainly large corporations, have access to them. To such large users of deferred (futures or forward) foreign currency contracts, however, there are advantages of the interbank forward markets over the futures markets, and such users continue to use the bank forward markets. Some of the advantages of the bank forward markets are shown in Exhibit 21-1. For these reasons, large corporations which have access to the bank foreign currency forward markets continue to use them.

There are, however, some advantages of foreign currency futures markets over the bank forward markets. As indicated, the foreign exchange futures markets are available in smaller denominations and have lower credit standards. Also, once a foreign exchange forward contract has been established, it is difficult and expensive to liquidate this position before making or taking delivery of the foreign currency on the delivery day of the forward contract. With futures contracts, it is as easy and inexpensive to liquidate the position without making or taking delivery

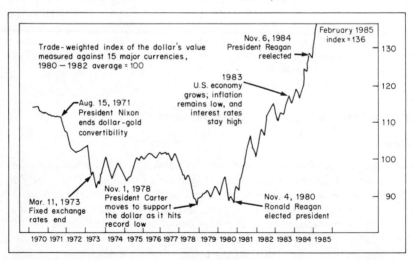

Figure 21-1 Reagan's new dollar strategy. (*The New York Times, Mar. 3, 1985.*)

EXHIBIT 21-1   Advantages of Foreign Currency Forward Markets over Futures Markets

	Forward markets	Futures markets
Forward dates	Available on any day.	Delivery days are one day per contract—contracts mature on a quarterly basis.
Amounts	Available in any amount.	Available in integral multiples of minimum dollar value of futures contract.
Transaction costs	Higher for relatively small amounts but lower for relatively large amounts.	Lower for relatively small amounts, but higher for relatively large amounts.
Related services	Foreign currency forward markets are often provided in conjunction with other bank services, such as consultation and borrowing services.	Foreign currency futures markets are provided independently.

as it was to initially establish the position. Thus, it is much easier to trade or manage a position in the futures markets than in the forward markets.

Many small corporations and companies do not have access to the bank foreign currency forward markets. Neither do retail speculators. And these users, primarily retail speculators, were among the primary early users of the foreign currency futures markets. These markets had found a niche.

But the developers of the IMM and the foreign currency futures contracts formulated a procedure which made it easier for another important class of users to indirectly use the foreign currency futures contracts. This class of users consisted of the same banks that make the foreign currency forward markets. The procedure was class B arbitrage, an IMM policy which made banks confident about making their forward markets available to firms that arbitraged between the foreign currency futures and forward markets. This provided two important advantages for the forex (foreign currency) futures markets. The first advantage was additional trading volume and, thereby, increased liquidity. The second was appropriate pricing. Because of this arbitrage, the prices of the less liquid futures markets more accurately reflected the prices of the more liquid forward markets.

This innovation was crucial in the development of the foreign currency futures markets. Because of its success, class B arbitrage is no longer as common as it once was. The banks are now arbitraging the foreign currency forward markets against the futures markets directly, thereby earning the arbitrage profits themselves rather than letting the class B arbitrageurs earn the profits. And the futures markets have become more liquid, particularly late in the U.S. trading day after the European foreign exchange markets have closed, at which time the futures markets are often more liquid than the bank forward markets. The futures markets frequently lead the forward markets in price changes, even earlier in the day.

Another group of U.S. commercial firms that uses the forex futures markets is agricultural firms that arbitrage between the U.S. agricultural markets and foreign agricultural markets, mainly the European and Canadian markets. These firms, which must hedge their forex exposure as part of their overall arbitrage, often have floor presences on the major exchanges, including the IMM; thus they have better information and lower transaction costs in the forex futures markets than in the forward markets.

Today the forex futures markets are an integral component of the world's forex markets. But the forex futures markets became successful mainly due to speculators' use of these markets. And speculators remain the major users of these markets.

In general, the IMM has active trading in five foreign currencies and less active trading in three others. The denominations of these contracts are expressed in terms of the number of units of the foreign currency. These eight contracts and their denominations are shown in Exhibit 21-2. As indicated above, the dollar value of these contracts is much less than the typical $1 million minimum of the bank forward market.

There is another important practical difference between the forex futures and forward markets for most foreign currencies, namely the way in which prices are quoted. Forex futures prices are quoted in essentially the same way other futures prices are quoted, that is, in dollars or cents per unit of the underlying asset. Thus, for example, for the British pound, the futures price is quoted as $1.20 per British pound, and for the West German mark, the futures price is quoted as $0.40 per DM.

The bank forward markets quote prices for some foreign currencies in a different way. While the bank markets quote prices for the British pound, the Canadian dollar, and the Mexican peso the same way as the futures markets, the bank markets quote the prices of other foreign currencies in terms of the number of units of the foreign currency per U.S. dollar—that is, they use the reciprocal of the way in which prices are quoted in the futures markets. For example, if the price of the DM is quoted as $0.40 per DM in the futures market, it will be quoted

EXHIBIT 21-2 Foreign Currency Futures Contracts

Currency	Denomination, in number of units of foreign currency	Futures price, dollars per unit of foreign currency*	Approximate dollar value*
A. Active contracts:			
British pound	25,000	1.2145	$30,362.50
Canadian dollar	100,000	0.7289	72,890.00
Deutsche mark	125,000	0.3230	40,375.00
Japanese yen	12,500,000	0.003986	49,825.00
Swiss franc	125,000	0.3824	47,800.00
B. Less active contracts:			
Mexican peso	1,000,000	0.00362	3,620.00
Dutch guilder†	125,000	—	—
French franc†	250,000	—	—

*Closing prices of April 1, 1985 (June contract).
†Futures prices not listed.

as 2.50 DM per U.S. dollar (1/0.40 = 2.50) in the bank market. Thus, speculators will have to make a simple calculation to convert bank rates to futures rates for these currencies.

Determinants of Exchange Rates

Foreign exchange rates, at least those commonly recognized in the United States, are price relationships between the U.S. dollar and the foreign currencies. Foreign exchange rates, as quoted in the futures markets, give the number of U.S. dollars and cents that must be paid for one unit of the foreign currency, whether it be a Canadian dollar, a British pound, a DM, or some other currency. Thus, exchange rates give the value of one currency relative to another currency, not the absolute value of either currency.[1]

As a result of this relativity, the effect of any U.S. economic or financial variable on the exchange rate of the dollar with respect to another currency can be determined by comparing the economic or financial variable for the United States with the same variable for the country of the foreign currency.

Some of the major economic, financial, and potential variables that affect exchange rates are discussed below.

Balance of Payments.   The balance of payments was originally a simple concept designed to measure for the United States the dollar outflows from the United States to foreign countries relative to the inflows of foreign currencies from foreign countries. But as the international financial flows have become more complicated, so has the balance of payments concept. Now various balance of payments concepts based on the net inflows and outflows of U.S. dollars according to various types of transactions are discussed. Among them are:

Merchandise (goods)
Services
Direct investments
Security purchases
Bank claims and liabilities
Government assets abroad

Exhibit 21-3 provides an example of the balance of payments accounts.

If more dollars flow out of the United States than foreign currency into the United States, then the balance of payments, according to one or a combination of these types of transactions, is said to be in deficit; if more dollars flow in than out, the balance of payments is said to be in surplus.

In general, a balance of payments surplus usually causes the dollar to become stronger relative to foreign currencies (the dollar value of foreign currencies declines) because there are fewer dollars in foreign countries. A balance of payments

---

[1] If the number of dollars required to buy a unit of foreign currency decreases (that is, if the exchange rate, as quoted in the futures markets, decreases), the dollar is "stronger" and the foreign currency is weaker. In the opposite case, the dollar is "weaker" and the foreign currency is stronger.

EXHIBIT 21-3 Quarterly Series, U.S. International Transactions*

Revised, Seasonally Adjusted (millions of dollars)

Quarters		Trade flows				Current account balance	Direct investment abroad	Direct investment in U.S.	Security purchases abroad	Security purchases in U.S.	Capital flows		U.S. government assets abroad	Foreign official assets in U.S.	Monetary base effect†
		Merchandise exports	Merchandise imports	Service exports	Service imports						Bank claims on foreigners	Bank liabilities to foreigners			
1981	II	60,064	67,373	34,729	24,740	1,117	5,709	5,186	1,566	4,336	15,002	8,063	2,396	-3,075	210
	III	57,812	66,214	35,540	24,851	427	1,124	5,363	726	323	15,310	16,478	1,272	-5,908	-547
	IV	58,416	66,224	35,160	24,239	1,192	745	9,989	2,918	1,649	42,199	21,380	724	8,539	-100
1982	I	55,482	62,546	34,600	25,266	165	-46	3,159	650	2,616	33,343	25,856	1,892	-3,221	-242
	II	55,118	60,921	36,156	26,624	1,927	-1,636	3,630	502	4,641	39,403	26,125	2,832	1,399	119
	III	52,079	64,442	35,079	25,947	-4,976	1,140	3,264	3,410	2,041	21,405	10,884	3,349	2,477	389
	IV	48,519	59,758	32,417	25,086	-6,314	-1,934	4,812	3,541	4,161	16,919	3,057	3,036	2,664	980
1983	I	49,246	58,523	31,865	23,958	-2,943	-793	2,305	1,866	5,927	18,175	10,244	1,917	-252	-342
	II	48,745	63,615	32,610	25,452	-9,560	232	3,327	3,257	5,753	-3,894	1,698	1,235	1,739	-487
	III	50,437	67,938	34,383	26,591	-11,846	3,873	3,322	1,571	2,856	2,871	14,792	675	-2,703	-1,232
	IV	51,829	71,236	34,473	27,801	-17,213	1,568	2,345	983	2,807	8,239	22,325	2,382	6,555	505
1984	I	54,164†	79,805†	36,456†	28,071†	-19,408†	3,191†	1,862†	-244†	3,037†	334†	9,763†	2,646†	-2,859†	159

*The signs in this table do *not* indicate whether a particular transaction is an inflow or an outflow. In this table a negative sign indicates a reduction in the stock of a particular class of assets during a particular time period.

520

†Not seasonally adjusted; quarterly averages of end-of-month data. Beginning with the first quarter of 1979, official U.S. holdings of assets dominated in foreign currencies are revalued monthly at market exchange rates. As of July 1980, the monetary base effect includes the addition of official U.S. holdings of Swiss-franc-denominated assets. Consequently, this series after July 1980 is not directly comparable to that reported for previous periods.

‡Preliminary.

Merchandise exports and imports: the current dollar value of physical goods which are exported from and imported into the United States.

Service exports and imports: receipts and reinvestment of earnings on U.S. investments abroad and payments and reinvestment of earnings on foreign investments in the United States (interest, dividends, and branch earnings), sales and purchases of military equipment, expenditures for U.S. military stations abroad, and payments and receipts associated with foreign travel and transportation.

Current account: the sum of merchandise and service exports less merchandise and service imports and unilateral transfers, which are private transfers representing gifts and similar payments by Americans to foreign residents and government transfers representing payments associated with foreign assistance programs.

Direct investment: private-sector capital transactions which result in the ownership of 10 percent or more of the voting securities or other ownership interests in foreign enterprises by U.S. residents either by themselves or in affiliation with others, including reinvested earnings of incorporated foreign affiliates of U.S. firms; private-sector transactions which result in the ownership of 10 percent or more (before 1974, 25 percent or more) of the voting securities or other ownership interests in U.S. enterprises by foreigners, including reinvested earnings of incorporated U.S. affiliates of foreign firms.

Security purchases: U.S. private-sector net purchases of foreign equity and debt securities with no contractual maturity or a maturity of more than 1 year; foreign-private-sector and international financial institution net purchases of U.S. equity and debt securities with no contractual maturities or maturities of more than 1 year and U.S. Treasury securities.

Bank claims and liabilities: changes in claims on private-sector foreigners (loans, collections outstanding, acceptances, deposits abroad, claims on affiliated foreign banks, foreign government obligations, and foreign commercial and finance paper) and liabilities to private-sector foreigners and international financial institutions (demand, time, and savings deposits, certificates of deposit, liabilities to affiliated foreign banks, and other liabilities) reported by U.S. banks for their own accounts and for the custody accounts of their customers.

U.S. government assets abroad: changes in U.S. official reserve assets (gold, special drawing rights, foreign currency holdings, and reserve position in the International Monetary Fund) and changes in other U.S. government assets abroad.

Foreign official assets in U.S.: foreign official agencies' net purchases of U.S. government securities, obligations issued by U.S. government corporations and agencies, securities issued by state and local governments, and changes in liabilities to foreign official agencies reported by U.S. banks.

deficit usually causes the dollar to become weaker relative to foreign currencies (the dollar value of foreign currencies increases) because there are more dollars in foreign countries. The emphasis in the last two sentences should be on the word "usually" because these economic principles, like most others, are often violated. To judge whether the dollar will become stronger or weaker, however, the balance of trade, which includes the balance for merchandise (goods) and services, is most often used.

Interest Rates. Typically, high interest rates in the United States relative to foreign interest rates make the dollar stronger because the higher rates cause flows of foreign currencies into the United States which are invested in the high-interest securities or are deposited in banks. There is a large pool of funds in the world which goes from short-term investments in one country to such investments in another on the basis of short-term interest rates. This so-called hot money is sensitive even to small interest rate changes.

An important relationship between the exchange rate between two currencies and their two interest rates is called the "interest rate arbitrage theory." For example, assume that the interest rates on 1-year securities in the United States and England are 10 percent and 6 percent, respectively. In this case, the 1-year futures rate on the U.S. dollar should be 4 percent weaker than today's (spot) exchange rate relative to the British pound. When this relationship holds, on a rate-of-return basis, investors and borrowers are indifferent about which of these two currencies they invest in and borrow, respectively. It is this relationship that closely links the forex markets to the Eurodollar market and the interest rate market for other currencies. Arbitrageurs conduct transactions among currencies and debt instruments which cause the interest rate arbitrage relationship to be approximately correct among currencies. This relationship, and the arbitrageurs who conduct transactions on the basis of the relationship, can be overwhelmed, however, by strong sentiments and expectations of other participants, including traders, in the foreign currency markets. Significant premiums and discounts can persist.

Economic Growth. The strength of the U.S. economy has typically had an effect on the strength of the dollar. At different times, this effect has operated in different ways. A stronger U.S. economy has often led to a weaker dollar because a stronger U.S. economy, relative to the strength of the economy of other countries, leads to a greater balance of payments deficit and, hence, to a weaker dollar.

At other times, however, a stronger economy has led to a stronger dollar. The mechanism for this relationship has been monetary policy. Participants in the forex markets assume that a stronger economy will lead to a tighter monetary policy to control inflation, which, in turn, will lead to higher interest rates, more inflows of foreign investment, and, thus, a stronger dollar. A stronger economy also often leads to higher interest rates and a stronger dollar through an increase in the demand for credit.

A stronger U.S. economy may also be perceived as an indication of political stability in the United States, which also often leads to a stronger dollar.

Inflation.   Inflation often affects exchange rates, but at different times in different ways and by different amounts. Inflation typically affects the dollar by making U.S. goods more expensive relative to foreign goods, thus increasing U.S. imports, decreasing exports, causing a balance of payments deficit, and leading to a weaker dollar.

At other times inflation will be assumed to lead to higher interest rates either directly or through its relationship with economic growth, which will lead to an inflow of foreign funds and a stronger dollar. The first effect usually dominates, however, and U.S. inflation leads to a weaker dollar.

Given the level of interest rates, an increase in inflation causes a decrease in the real, inflation-adjusted rate of return. Through this mechanism, an increase in inflation also often weakens the dollar.

Political Conditions.   Political conditions in different countries affect exchange rates. Political unrest or even the election or potential election of a government viewed to be inflationary, antibusiness, or socialistic often leads to a stronger dollar relative to that country's currency. If the other country is a key country, the dollar may strengthen relative to many or all other currencies. World political uncertainties often lead to a stronger dollar. Economic or political events in a country such as a strike or the threat of a strike in a key industry also usually weaken that country's currency relative to the dollar.

Overview of Determinants.   Many other factors also affect exchange rates. In addition, the importance of different factors will be different at different times, depending on the psychology of the markets. For example, at times the U.S. balance of trade will have a major impact on the strength of the dollar, and at other times the level of interest rates will be the dominant influence and the balance of trade will have only a marginal influence. At times, an increase in U.S. inflation will weaken the dollar substantially, and at other times it will not affect the dollar.

Speculative Uses

As indicated, prior to the advent of the foreign currency futures markets, large institutions used the bank forward markets for their forward forex transactions. In particular, they often speculated in the foreign exchange markets via these markets. The foreign currency futures markets added little to their possibilities.

Retail investors, however, had no access to foward foreign exchange markets. Thus, with the advent of the foreign currency futures markets, retail investors could use these markets to speculate in the forex markets, and they have in significant amounts. The liquidity and relatively low transaction costs have made the forex futures markets attractive markets to use for speculation.

In fact, these futures contracts have become very large. For example, the deutsche mark and Swiss franc futures contracts, measured in terms of trading volume, have been the eighth and eleventh largest futures contracts recently. The trading volume of the five active currencies in the aggregate would make them rank as the third largest futures contract. Speculators account for much of this trading volume.

The speculative uses of the forex futures markets are, in concept, relatively simple. Speculators buy forex futures contracts when they believe that the foreign currency will become stronger relative to the dollar (that is, the dollar will become weaker). And they sell forex futures contracts when they believe that the foreign currency will become weaker relative to the dollar (that is, the dollar will become stronger). Speculators have shown a particular interest in "shorting the dollar," that is, buying forex futures contracts.

Retail speculators can also speculate on the basis of moves of one foreign currency against another foreign currency, with the strength of the dollar not involved, by buying a futures contract in the currency they think will be strong and selling a futures contract in the currency they think will be weak—that is, conducting an intercontract spread. For example, to speculate on the basis of the British pound strengthening against the Japanese yen, one would buy the British pound futures and sell the Japanese yen futures. There would, thus, be a profit on this spread if the pound strengthened against the yen, independent of what happened to either vis-à-vis the dollar.

Foreign currency speculators use both technical methods and the fundamental factors for foreign currency speculation. As discussed in Chapter 9, there are also options on foreign currency futures contracts.

The forex markets trade and are monitored worldwide on a 24-hour-a-day basis, and they are among the most widely followed markets, in addition to being among the most exciting markets in which to speculate. They have also exhibited considerable price variability, as shown in Figures 21-2 through 21-6 for the five major foreign currency futures contracts.

Notes from a Trader—Foreign Currency Futures

The rapid growth of the foreign currency futures markets is a reflection of the broad appeal of "trading the dollar" against foreign currencies and the foreign currency futures markets as good trading vehicles.

Currency trading is primarily fundamental, although technical methods are also used. Fundamentalists watch U.S. and foreign interest rates and the factors that affect these interest rates. Balance of trade announcements are also closely watched. Government foreign exchange rate policies and even rumors of changes in these policies may have significant, sudden effects on forex futures prices. Traders also trade foreign currencies against each other by using two futures contracts.

Currency futures prices evidence both long trends and considerable daily volatility. The currency futures markets are very liquid, although they tend to be thinner in the afternoon, particularly on Friday, when the London markets are closed.

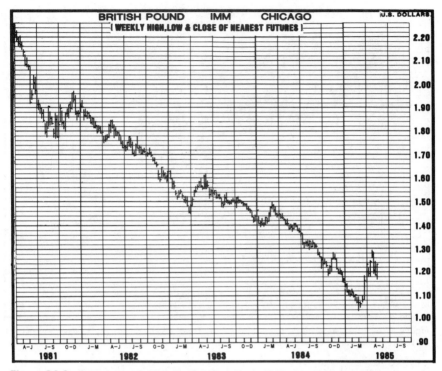

Figure 21-2 British pound. [*Commodity Year Book 1985, ed. Walter L. Emery (Jersey City, N.J.: Commodity Research Bureau, Inc.).*]

Figure 21-3 Canadian dollar. [*Commodity Year Book 1985, ed. Walter L. Emery (Jersey City, N.J.: Commodity Research Bureau, Inc.).*]

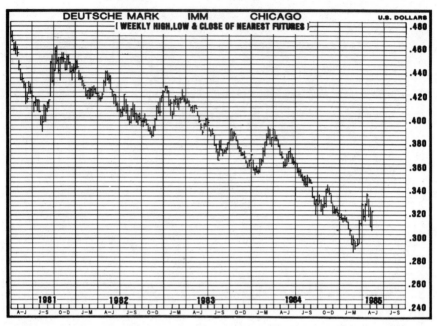

Figure 21-4 Deutsche mark. [*Commodity Year Book 1985, ed. Walter L. Emery* (Jersey City, N.J.: Commodity Research Bureau, Inc.).]

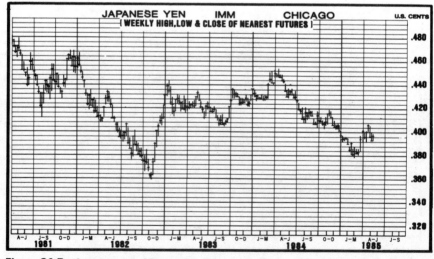

Figure 21-5 Japanese yen. [*Commodity Year Book 1985, ed. Walter L. Emery* (Jersey City, N.J.: Commodity Research Bureau, Inc.).]

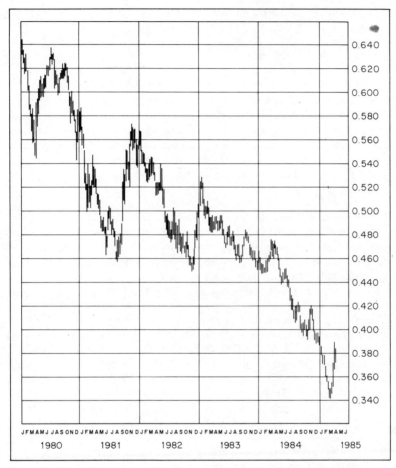

Figure 21-6   Swiss franc weekly range—nearest futures (International Monetary Market; weekly high, low—Friday close; U.S. dollars).

THE INTEREST RATE FUTURES MARKETS

Introduction

As indicated above, the first financial futures contracts, the foreign currency futures contracts, began during May 1972. Even at that time, few conceived that there would also be futures contracts on "interest rates," that is, on fixed-income securities. Given that there were futures contracts on agricultural products, metals, foreign currencies, and other commodities, it seems obvious that there would be futures contracts on fixed-income securities in the world's most sophisticated financial system. But this was not the case.

Yet some thought that there should be such futures contracts. On October 20,

1975, a GNMA-CDR futures contract based on a government-guaranteed mortgage certificate began to be traded on the CBT. Within 3 months, on January 6, 1976, a futures contract on a 90-day Treasury bill began to be traded on the IMM.

Since that time, the interest rate futures markets have grown in trading volume, types of users, types of uses, and number of contracts available, and the interest rate futures contracts currently represent the largest complex of futures contracts.

With respect to the contracts available, many futures contracts have been listed by several different exchanges, but relatively few have succeeded and become actively traded. While there has been much discussion with respect to why some interest rate futures contracts succeeded and others failed, and there remains much uncertainty in this regard, all the successful futures contracts have at least two ingredients—they all have commercial hedge users as well as speculative users.

The best way to structure the interest rate futures contracts is the same way the cash fixed-income securities are structured—by maturity (short term, intermediate term, and long term) and by credit risk (public and private credit risk). The currently available and actively traded interest rate futures contracts are listed in Exhibit 21-4 according to this structure. The existing options on these futures contracts are also indicated.

On public debt instruments, there is a short-term futures contract (on 90-day Treasury bills), as well as two intermediate-term futures contracts (on 10-year Treasury notes and on GNMA-CDRs) and a long-term futures contract (on 20-year Treasury bonds). On private debt instruments, there are only short-term futures contracts on 90-day Eurodollars and 90-day commercial bank certificates of deposit. There are also options on the long-term futures contract (the Treasury bond futures contract), a short-term contract (the Eurodollar futures contract), and an intermediate-term Treasury note futures contract.

Hedge Uses

The interest rate futures markets have been used since their inception for hedging. As the markets have developed, the types of hedgers and the nature of the hedge uses have expanded.

Treasury security dealers began using the Treasury bill and bond futures contracts for hedging their Treasury portfolios soon after the contracts were listed. Savings and loan institutions and mortgage bankers began using the GNMA-CDR and Treasury bond futures contracts to hedge their GNMA portfolios.

The current major hedge users of the interest rate futures markets are as follows. Savings and loan institutions, savings banks, and commercial banks use the Treasury bill, CD, and Eurodollar futures contracts to hedge their future issues of liabilities (and their asset-liability maturity "gap") against rising interest rates. Portfolio managers use the Treasury bond futures and options contracts to hedge their portfolios against rising rates, to increase their flexibility in rapidly increasing or decreasing the amounts they have invested in bonds, or to enhance the yields on their portfolios. They also use the Treasury bond futures options to develop new risk-return combinations for their portfolios. Mortgage bankers and insurance companies have also developed new uses for these markets.

EXHIBIT 21-4 Interest Rate Futures Contracts

Credit	Short term	Intermediate term	Long term
Public	90-day Treasury bill (January 1976; IMM)	GNMA-CDR (October 1975; CBT)	20-year Treasury bond (August 1977; CBT)
		10-year Treasury note (May 1982; CBT)	
Private	90-day bank CD (August 1981; IMM)		
	90-day Eurodollar (December 1981; IMM)		
Option	90-day Eurodollar (March 1985; IMM)	10-year Treasury note (May 1985; CBT)	20-year Treasury bond (October 1982; CBT)

Determinants of Interest Rates

The prices of interest rate futures contracts move inversely to the interest rates on these contracts in the same way that the prices and interest rates of all fixed-income instruments (bonds, notes, or bills) move inversely. Specifically, if interest rates rise, prices decrease, and vice versa. Thus, a long position in the interest rate futures contracts profits from decreasing interest rates (and increasing prices), and vice versa. A short position profits from increasing rates (and declining prices).

A fundamental concept in the interest rate markets is the yield curve. A yield curve shows the relationship between the yield and the maturity of fixed-income securities that are the same in every way except maturity. Yield curves are typically considered for Treasury securities because the Treasury has debt outstanding for virtually all maturities.

Typically, when the general level of interest rates is low, long-term interest rates (30-year maturity) are greater than short-term interest rates (90-day maturity), and the yield curve is "upward-sloping," or "positive," as shown by the bottom curve in Figure 21-7. When the general level of interest rates is high, however, short-term interest rates are usually higher than long-term rates, and, as shown by the top curve in Figure 21-7, the yield curve is "downward-sloping," or "negative."

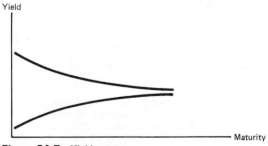

Figure 21-7 Yield curves.

From Figure 21-7 it is clear that short-term rates change by more over the interest rate cycle than long-term rates; that is, short-term rates are more volatile.

However, given equal yield changes, the price of a long-term instrument changes by more than the price of a short-term instrument. For example, if the interest rates of $1 million of 90-day Treasury bills and 30-year Treasury bonds (12 percent coupon) increased from 12.00 percent to 12.50 percent (or by 50 basis points—0.01 percent of interest rate is called 1 basis point), the price of the 90-day bill would decrease by $1250 and the price of the bond would decrease by $38,947.

Because of this price response to yield changes, even though short-term interest rates are more volatile over the interest rate cycle, long-term prices are more volatile.[2] Because of these differences, interest rate forecasters usually distinguish between forecasting short-term and long-term interest rates.

Forecasting interest rates is as common, difficult, and successful (or unsuccessful) as forecasting stock prices. Several different types of indicators are used to forecast interest rates. The first and most widely used type of indicator relates to monetary variables suggestive of the posture of the Board of Governors of the Federal Reserve System (hereinafter the "Fed") in conducting monetary policy. The Fed can, within some limits, cause interest rates to increase by enacting "tighter" monetary policy and cause interest rates to decrease by enacting "looser" monetary policy.

In fact, scrutinizing the Fed's behavior for clues of the Fed's posture toward tightness or ease has led to a new profession: the "Fed watcher." Several variables are considered important indicators of this policy. The first variable is the money supply, most important the MI measure of money supply, which includes checking account balances and some types of savings deposits. Although money supply has long been watched as an indicator of Fed posture, the way in which it is interpreted has changed. The current interpretation is that if MI increases significantly, the Fed will have to tighten monetary policy in the future to lower the growth of MI, and as a result interest rates will increase, and vice versa. The financial community awaits the Fed's announcement of the money supply at 4:30 p.m. (EST) every Thursday afternoon.

Other monetary variables announced (and released) with the money supply by the Fed which are also closely watched include borrowings by commercial banks from the Fed, excess bank reserves, total growth in bank reserves, and commercial loans made by commercial banks.

Many interest rates are watched to detect the Fed's influence on them. The fed funds rate, however, is the interest rate most closely watched in this regard. The fed funds rate is the rate at which commercial banks lend to one another on an overnight basis. A high fed funds rate is usually interpreted to mean that bank reserves are inadequate for the needs of the banking system and that Fed policy

---

[2] This difference in price volatility between long- and short-term instruments is the reason why the denomination of the Treasury bill futures contract is $1 million and the denomination of the Treasury bond futures contract is $100,000. Given this difference in denominations, the prices of both futures contracts tend to vary by approximately the same dollar amounts over the interest rate cycle.

is, therefore, tight. Fed watchers spend their careers watching and analyzing these and many other monetary variables and their effects on interest rates.

The behavior of the U.S. Department of the Treasury (hereinafter the "Treasury") is also analyzed for its impact on interest rates. The most important aspect of Treasury behavior is the budget deficit and actions to finance this deficit. The deficit is financed by the regular auction of Treasury debt instruments with maturities ranging from 91 days (and on an irregular basis shorter maturities) to 30 years. Increases in the deficit and increases in the size of one or more of these auctions typically increase interest rates, particularly the interest rate of the maturity of the issue auctioned. If the auction is very strong, however, interest rates, particularly the interest rate of the maturity auctioned, often decrease.

Because the strength of the economy affects interest rates, economic indicators are watched and analyzed to determine their effect on interest rates. Watching economic variables and assessing their effect on bond, note, or bill prices, however, tends to create a perverse mentality. Typically, a strong economy causes a strong demand for borrowing and, thus, leads to high interest rates. Due to this relationship, typically when the economy is strong, interest rates are high and the prices of debt instruments are low. Conversely, when the economy is weak, interest rates are low and the prices of debt instruments are high. So interest rate analysts describe economic variables indicating a weaker economy, such as lower GNP growth or higher unemployment, as "bullish," and they are, indeed, bullish for bond, note, and bill prices, even though they are bearish for the real economy.

Among the economic variables that are closely watched and analyzed are:

1. GNP growth (on a quarterly basis)
2. Index of industrial production (monthly)
3. Retail sales (monthly)
4. Unemployment rate (monthly)
5. Index of leading indicators (monthly)
6. Price indexes, such as:
   - CPI (consumer price index)—monthly
   - PPI (producer price index)—monthly
   - GNP deflator—quarterly
7. Housing data:
   - Housing starts (monthly)
   - New-home sales (monthly)
8. Consumer demand data:
   - Retail sales (monthly)
   - Automobile sales (three times a month)
9. Business purchases:
   - Durable goods orders (monthly)
   - Construction spending (monthly)

Interest rate forecasters analyze these and many other economic and financial variables in different ways. Some forecasters construct complicated mathematical models ("econometric models"), which incorporate the relationships in the form of mathematical equations, to forecast interest rates. They are called econometric forecasters. Others simply mentally digest all these variables and then opine their forecast. They are called judgmental forecasters. Of course, as in all other markets, some forecast on a technical rather than fundamental basis.

Many interest rate forecasters, whether they are forecasters by profession or avocation, now participate in the interest rate futures markets for speculative purposes due to the leverage, low entry costs, and low transaction costs of these markets. The advent of the interest rate (and stock index) futures markets has substantially expanded the number of speculative users of the futures markets. Many occupations expose their practitioners to interest rates and stock prices but not to agricultural prices. Many investors in these occupations had never participated in the futures markets but are now using the interest rate and stock index futures markets.

Speculative Uses

The interest rate futures markets have grown considerably—recently the Treasury bond futures contract has been the largest futures contract, in trading volume, by a significant margin; the Eurodollar futures contract is the fourth largest. Much of the trading volume in these contracts is due to speculation. Options on Treasury bond futures have also grown considerably—if they were included among the futures contracts, they would be the fourth largest. Speculators use the interest rate futures markets in many ways. The basic principle in their use is that on debt securities, as interest rates increase, prices decrease, and vice versa. The most common way speculators speculate is by buying an interest rate futures contract if they think interest rates of that maturity will decrease and prices will increase, and selling the futures contract if they think interest rates will increase and prices will decrease. It is not surprising that the interest rate futures contracts are used by speculators for pure bull or bear plays. Agricultural, metal, and other futures contracts had been used in these ways for years. In addition, there are many more speculators who have views on interest rates than who have views on soybeans, cattle, or silver prices. Today, all the interest rate futures contracts are used for these bull or bear plays.

Speculators have also used the futures contracts for spreading in several different ways. The first type of spread is the intercontract "yield curve spread." For example, speculators may think that the 30-year/90-day Treasury yield curve is going to become steeper; that is, 30-year yields will increase by more than 90-day yields, and 30-year prices, thus, will decrease by more than 90-day prices. In this case, they will sell the Treasury bond futures contract and buy the 90-day Treasury bill futures contract to profit from this expectation.[3] If speculators think the yield curve will flatten, they will buy the Treasury bond futures contract and sell the 90-day Treasury bill futures contract, properly weighted.

While the 30-year/90-day futures spread is based on changes in the slope of the 30-year/90-day Treasury yield curve, similar futures spreads are based on

---

[3] This spread must be weighted on the basis of the difference in price changes between these two contracts in response to equal yield changes and the contract sizes.

changes in the 10-year/90-day or 30-year/10-year Treasury yield curves by using combinations of the T-note/T-bill and T-bond/T-note futures contracts, respectively, properly weighted.

Quality spreads are also used in the short-term futures markets. Quality spreads are based on the difference in quality between government securities, which have a higher quality and a lower credit risk than private-sector securities, and private securities. In the context of the short-term futures markets, 90-day Treasury bills have a higher quality and a lower credit risk than 90-day CDs and 90-day Eurodollars. Due to the difference in credit risks, CD and Eurodollar yields are higher than T-bill yields, and, thus, CD and Eurodollar futures prices are lower than T-bill futures prices. CD and Eurodollar yields also tend to increase relative to T-bill yields (CD and Eurodollar futures prices tend to decrease relative to T-bill futures prices) when:

- The general level of yields increases and there is a "flight to quality" by investors—that is, a preference for lower-credit-risk, higher-quality Treasury bills and a move away from high-credit-risk, lower-quality private-sector securities.
- There is a banking "scare"; that is, banks are perceived to be vulnerable and have increased credit risk.

Under these circumstances, the appropriate futures quality spread is to buy the 90-day Treasury bill futures contract and sell the CD or Eurodollar futures contract.

On the other hand, if it is perceived that there will be a shift from 90-day Treasury bills to 90-day private-sector instruments because the spread between Treasury bills and private securities is unduly narrow or the general level of yields will decrease, the appropriate strategy is to sell 90-day Treasury bill futures contracts and to buy 90-day CD or Eurodollar futures contracts. There is no similar quality spread involving the long-term or intermediate-term futures contracts due to the absence of futures contracts based on private debt in these maturity ranges.

Another type of spread used by speculators is the intracontract spread, which is the sale of one month of a futures contract and the purchase of another month of the same futures contract. The sale of a June and the purchase of a September Treasury bond futures contract, for example, is an intracontract spread. This type of spread is somewhat subtle and can be used as either a bull or bear strategy or a yield curve play, depending on which contract is bought and which is sold and also on the relationship between the number of contracts bought and the number sold.[4]

There are typically significant margin reductions for intercontract and intracontract spreads, making these trades efficient in terms of funds use. On the basis of funds used, these spreads are often as risky as naked long and short positions.

Speculators use these various futures market strategies. Speculators could use the cash fixed-income markets instead of the futures markets for these purposes. There are several reasons, however, for preferring the futures markets. The first reason is leverage. While institutions with high credit ratings can buy fixed-income

---

[4] See Frank J. Jones, "Turtles, Tails, Spreads and All That," *The Journal of Futures Markets,* 1, No. 4 (1981), 565–596.

securities on a highly leveraged basis, speculators cannot. In the futures markets, however, speculators can achieve high leverage (and not pay interest on borrowings, since they do not have to borrow to achieve leverage). Second, the futures markets have much lower transaction costs than the cash markets, and so the speculator can trade more actively. Also, in relation to transaction costs, the futures markets are much more liquid than the cash markets. Finally, in many strategies it is necessary to have a short position. It is difficult for most institutions and impossible for speculators to short many cash instruments. Thus, speculators use futures rather than cash instruments for these transactions.

The recent histories of Treasury bond, GNMA, Treasury note, Treasury bill, and Eurodollar futures prices are shown in Figures 21-8 through 21-13.

Notes from a Trader—Interest Rate Futures

The interest rate futures markets have become a great attraction for fundamentalists and technicians. Fundamentalists watch long-term trends, mainly with regard to inflation and GNP, and several short-term factors, mainly the periodic economic and financial announcements, including the index of industrial production, GNP, employment and the unemployment rate, the CPI, and the PPI. Fed policy may be the most widely watched indicator of interest rates. The weekly announcements of M1 and bank borrowing from the Fed and the monthly M2

Figure 21-8   Interest rates—T-bonds. [*Commodity Year Book 1985*, ed. *Walter L. Emery* [*Jersey City, N.J.: Commodity Research Bureau, Inc.*].]

Figure 21-9 Interest rates—Ginnie Mae. [Commodity Year Book 1985, ed. Walter L. Emery (Jersey City, N.J.: Commodity Research Bureau, Inc.).]

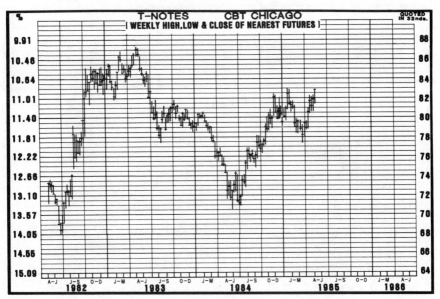

Figure 21-10 Interest rates—T-notes. [Commodity Year Book 1985, ed. Walter L. Emery (Jersey City, N.J.: Commodity Research Bureau, Inc.).]

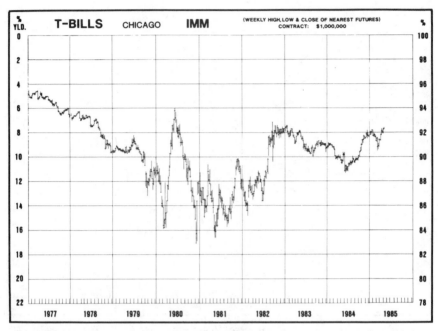

Figure 21-11 Interest rates—T-bills. [*Commodity Year Book 1985*, ed. *Walter L. Emery (Jersey City, N.J.: Commodity Research Bureau, Inc.)*.]

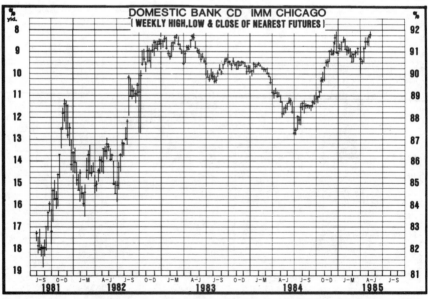

Figure 21-12 Interest rates—domestic bank CD. [*Commodity Year Book 1985*, ed. *Walter L. Emery (Jersey City, N.J.: Commodity Research Bureau, Inc.)*.]

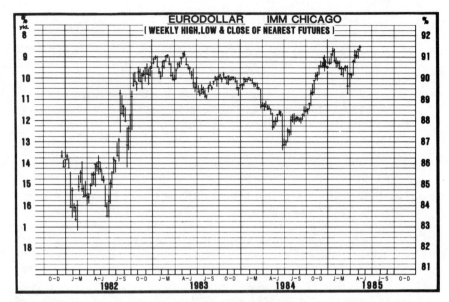

Figure 21-13   Interest rates—Eurodollar. [*Commodity Year Book 1985, ed. Walter L. Emery (Jersey City, N.J.: Commodity Research Bureau, Inc.).*]

and M3 announcements also often have significant effects on interest rates. Finally, different aspects of Treasury policy, particularly the announcement of auctions and the auctions themselves, are closely watched and may affect interest rates significantly. Many of these announcements occur in the afternoon after the futures close or in the morning before the futures opening. Gap openings after unexpected announcements are frequent. Traders become very nervous, and often inactive, before important announcements.

Fundamentalists not only take long and short positions on the basis of these factors but also transact intracontract spreads and intercontract spreads on the basis of perceived changes in the slope of the yield curve. Fundamentalists often "buy the rumor and sell the news" with respect to these factors. Every type of technical method is used by interest rate futures traders. The interest rate futures markets exhibit both considerable short-term volatility and long trends.

The interest rate futures markets, particularly for Treasury bonds and Eurodollars, are extremely liquid, and the bid-ask spreads are very thin. The fact that the interest rate futures group has become the largest futures group attests to the fact that traders enjoy the action in these markets.

THE STOCK INDEX FUTURES MARKETS

Introduction

The stock index futures markets began on February 24, 1982, with the listing of the Value Line Composite Index futures contract by the Kansas City Board of

Trade. Three additional stock index futures contracts are also traded, as indicated in Exhibit 21-5.

Stock index futures contracts were not expected to be traded as early as 1982, if at all. The major reason for this caution was regulatory jurisdiction. The CFTC has regulatory jurisdiction over all futures contracts, and the SEC has jurisdiction over the stock market. There were, nevertheless, several questions with respect to whether the CFTC had exclusive jurisdiction over stock index futures contracts.

During December 1981, however, SEC Chairman John Shad and CFTC Chairman Philip Johnson negotiated their Shad/Johnson Agreement, according to which the CFTC had regulatory jurisdiction over all futures contracts based on broadly based stock indexes which were settled in cash. Soon after, the CFTC approved for trading the first three contracts listed in Exhibit 21-5.[5] Before the approval, however, the Fed, for the first time, became involved in setting margins on futures contracts. The Fed "induced" the exchanges to set margins on these contracts at a level where the dollar value was equal to 10 percent of the initial dollar value of the contracts. This level was higher than the margins that would have been set by traditional methods. As the stock index price levels have increased, however, the dollar level of the margins has remained constant, and the percentage level of margin has, therefore, decreased.

Several stock index futures contracts based on specific industry sectors have also been approved for trading. However, only one has been listed for trading—a futures contract on the NYSE Financial Index by the NYFE—and it has not been successful. The prospects for futures on sector indexes are not bright. Options on narrow stock indexes have also been listed by stock and stock option exchanges, but these also, for the most part, have not attracted a following and become liquid.

The broad stock index futures contracts, however, have grown quickly, have become an integral part of the nation's equity markets, and now have a greater dollar volume of trading than on the New York Stock Exchange, as shown in Figure 21-14.

Fundamentals for Use of Stock Index Futures Contracts

Commercial hedgers have used the stock index futures contracts for a variety of purposes. The hedge and investment uses of stock index futures contracts can be considered in the context of portfolio management strategies used by stock market professionals and concepts developed by academic and applied researchers of the stock market.

In general, there are two types of price risk in the stock market. The first type of risk relates to changes in the price level of the overall stock market—the level

---

[5] Futures contracts for 10 narrow industry stock indexes (10 stocks each) and one midsize (50 stocks) stock index were submitted to the CFTC by the CBT and not approved by the CFTC. And Dow Jones and S&P 500 Index futures contracts that were submitted to the CFTC by the CBT and Comex, respectively, were approved by the CFTC but were prevented from being traded by judicial actions initiated by the developers of the indexes.

EXHIBIT 21-5 Stock Index Futures Contracts

Exchange	Stock index	Date listed	Number of stocks	Calculation of index
Kansas City Board of Trade	Value Line Composite Index	Feb. 24, 1982	1700+	Equal weighting; geometric average
Chicago Mercantile Exchange	Standard & Poor's 500 Stock Index	Apr. 21, 1982	500	Capitalization (market value) weighting; arithmetic average
New York Futures Exchange	New York Stock Exchange Composite Index	May 6, 1982	1500+	Capitalization (market value) weighting; arithmetic average
Chicago Board of Trade	Major Market Index	July 23, 1984	20	Price weighting; arithmetic average

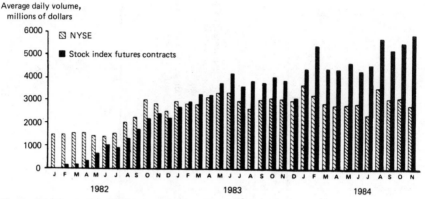

Average daily volume,
millions of dollars

Figure 21-14 **Stock index futures: dollar value of daily trading.**

of the overall market is often measured by a broad index such as the S&P 500 Stock Index or the NYSE Composite Index. The second type of risk relates to changes in the prices of individual stocks relative to the price level of the overall stock market. The first type of price risk is called market risk, or systematic risk, and the second type is called stock-specific risk, or nonsystematic risk. Thus, overall stock market risk can be divided as shown in Exhibit 21-6.

With respect to market risk, the prices of some stocks are equally as volatile as the price level of the overall stock market, while the prices of other stocks are more or less volatile than the price level of the overall stock market. A statistic used in stock market analysis called the "beta coefficient" is used to measure the volatility of the price of a specific stock relative to the price volatility of the overall market (to be precise, the volatility of returns, which include dividends, is used rather than the volatility of prices). Very volatile stocks are often called "high-beta" stocks, and less volatile stocks are called "low-beta" stocks. For example, the price of a volatile stock may increase by 1½ percent when the price level of the overall market increases by 1 percent—such a stock has a beta of 1.5. The price of a low-beta stock, which is less volatile than the overall market, may, for example, increase by 0.5 percent when the price level of the overall market increases by 1 percent—

EXHIBIT 21-6 Stock Market Risk.

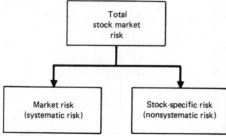

such a stock has a beta of 0.5. Two benchmarks for beta are the overall market, which is usually measured by the S&P 500 Stock Index or the NYSE Composite Index and which has a beta of 1.0, and a risk-free investment, such as a Treasury bill, which has a beta of zero.

Given the average volatility of a stock relative to the volatility of the market, the prices of some stocks track the trend of the market, and are adjusted for this average volatility very closely (are well "correlated" with the market), and the prices of others deviate frequently and substantially (are poorly correlated with the market). The former type tracks the market closely and has little stock-specific risk relative to the market; the latter type tracks the market poorly and has a high degree of stock-specific risk. So in considering the price behavior of individual stocks relative to the market, two characteristics must be studied: the average volatility of the stock relative to the volatility of the market (the beta) and how closely the price of the stock tracks the overall stock market when adjusted for the volatility (the correlation).

In general, portfolio managers can make their portfolios behave more like the overall market in terms of being more highly correlated with the market and having the same volatility as the market by diversifying their portfolios across many stocks. Obviously, if a portfolio had stocks representing every stock in an index, the behavior of the portfolio, in terms of both correlation and volatility, would agree with the behavior of the index. However, a high degree of correlation with the overall index and a similar volatility can be achieved with a stock portfolio in which the number of stocks is much smaller than the number in the index. For example, with respect to volatility, if a stock that increased in price by 1.5 percent and a stock that increased by 0.5 percent when the market increased by 1 percent were combined in equal amounts in a portfolio, the portfolio would move, on the average, by 1 percent when the market moved by 1 percent. Thus, by properly diversifying a portfolio among stocks, a portfolio manager can make the portfolio behave more like the index.

Portfolio managers, large and small, deal with stock-specific risk and market risk in two different ways. First, they reduce or eliminate the risk of having different volatilities than the market and stock-specific risk, as indicated above, by diversifying their portfolios across many stocks. Their portfolios then have only market risk, and the same degree of market risk as the overall market.

Portfolio managers deal with market risk, if at all, in a very different way. In times of expected bull markets—that is, in times of expected stock market price increases—they adjust their portfolios to include more volatile stocks so that the value of the portfolios increases more than the price level of the overall stock market.

On the other hand, in times of expected bear markets—that is, in times of expected stock market price decreases—they adjust their portfolios to include less volatile stocks so that the value of their portfolios decreases less than the price level of the overall stock market. In the limit, during times of expected bear markets, portfolio managers liquidate stocks and make less risky investments, such as in money market instruments. To the extent that they do this, they are, of course, not in the stock market at all.

Basically, then, portfolio managers implement two distinct types of strategies. The first strategy is "stock selection," that is, trying to select stocks to buy that will outperform the market and, to a lesser extent, trying to select specific stocks to short that will underperform the market. The second type of strategy is "market timing," that is, switching to very volatile stocks during times of expected bull markets and to low-volatility stocks or even money market instruments during times of expected bear markets. This market timing strategy is one form of "asset allocation," that is, shifting among equities, money, and bonds. Of course, market timing strategies may interfere with stock selection strategies or reduce the effectiveness of portfolio diversification.

There may, however, be strategic problems in both stock selection and market timing strategies using only the stock market. First, assume that investors wish to make a stock selection decision. They purchase a specific stock on the assumption that the price of that stock will increase because the stock will outperform the market. Assume that they are correct and that the stock does outperform the market. But assume that the overall market declines so that even though the stock outperforms the market, the price of the stock also declines. Thus, they are correct in their assessment of the stock along with the market, but they lose money.

Second, assume that investors wish to make a market timing investment based on the expectation of a rising market. To do so, they buy one or a few stocks. Assume that they are correct and that the stock market does increase. Assume also, however, that the stock or stocks they have purchased underperform the market and that the prices of the stocks decrease, even though the stock market increases. Thus, despite the fact that their assessment is correct and the stock market increases, they lose money.

There may, thus, be problems in implementing both stock selection and market timing strategies in the stock market. However, with stock index futures contracts, the problems in implementing both types of strategies can be reduced or eliminated.

Consider, first, the implementation of the stock selection strategy, that is, investors who wish to purchase a stock that they believe will outperform the market. To implement this strategy they could, under certain circumstances for some stocks, buy the stock and short the futures contract.[6] Then, given that they are correct and the stock does outperform the market, they will earn a net profit even if the market moves down. This occurs because any declines in the overall market generate profits on the short futures position which countervail the effect of the market on the price of the individual stock, leaving a net profit due to the stock outperforming the market. Thus, under these circumstances, investors can implement a stock selection strategy without having to be concerned with market, or systematic, risk. This strategy permits investors to buy superior stocks during the times of expected bear markets.[7]

---

[6] The effectiveness of this strategy depends on the degree of correlation of the price of the specific stock or stocks with the overall market.

[7] The effectiveness of being able to implement this "hedged" stock selection strategy depends on the correlation of the price of the stock with the price of the overall market. The average volatility of the price of the specific stock relative to the overall market can be adjusted for in this type of strategy by varying the dollar value of the futures contract sold relative to the dollar value of the specific stock being hedged in a way that depends on the relative volatility. But if the correlation of the price of the stock with the market is weak, no adjustment can be made, and this type of hedge strategy is, thus, risky.

Second, consider the market timing decision. If investors thought the stock market was going to go up but were uncertain with respect to the price behavior of a specific stock or small group of stocks, they could buy a stock index futures contract, thus sharing in the price movement of the overall stock market without being affected by the price of any individual stock relative to the market.[8] Contrariwise, if investors thought the market was going down, they could sell stock index futures contracts. This is a common use of stock index futures for speculators.

Both individuals and stock market professionals can, thus, use stock index futures contracts to separate market risk from stock-specific risk and implement either a stock selection strategy or a market timing strategy without having unintended effects reduce the effectiveness of the strategy. In these cases, if investors are right in their assessment of an individual stock or the market, they profit.

Stock portfolios are more closely related to the overall market and, thus, have a higher component of systematic risk and a lower component of specific risk than individual stocks. Broad portfolios can, thus, be hedged more effectively than individual stocks—there would, of course, also be less chance of outperforming the market. The amount by which a stock outperforms, or underperforms, the market after an adjustment for volatility (or beta) is called the "alpha" of the stock. At the limit, a large, broad portfolio of stocks could be hedged essentially perfectly with broad stock index futures contracts. The return on such a hedged portfolio, however, would be equal to the short-term interest rate.

Because of the close correlation between the S&P 500 and NYSE Composite stock indexes and broad portfolios of stocks, portfolio managers use the stock index futures contracts based on these indexes to quickly increase and decrease their exposure to the stock market by buying and selling stock index futures contracts, respectively. The low transaction costs and high liquidity of the stock index futures markets make it advantageous to use the stock index futures markets for such asset allocations.

Such hedging and investment techniques have been used by pension fund managers, block traders, stock underwriters, equity dealers, and specialists and other participants in the stock market.

Determinants of Stock Index Futures Prices

There are two aspects to determining the prices of stock index futures contracts: determining the level of the index and determining the futures price given the index. The "basis" between the index and the futures price is defined as the

---

[8] Due to the higher leverage of the futures contracts relative to purchasing stocks, the difference between what is desired to be invested in equities and what must be put up in margin for futures contracts could be put in Treasury bills to earn the risk-free interest rate. For example, if investors desire to invest $80,000 in "the market," they can buy stock index futures contracts which have a total market value of approximately $80,000 but require a margin deposit of approximately only $7000 and put the difference of $73,000 in risk-free Treasury bills.

futures price minus the index. The determinants of the basis are discussed under "Expectations," below. The determinants of the level of the index will be discussed first.

The determinants of stock market levels, as measured by stock indexes, are widely discussed and, at least by wise and honest individuals, not well understood. There are, however, two different approaches to providing the level of the stock market: technical and fundamental. And, in turn, there are two types of technical approaches. The first includes charting and several algorithms such as oscillators and relative strength indicators, which are discussed in Chapter 7. The second technical approach uses stock market indicators such as short interest, specialist short interest, advance/decline ratios, and odd lot buying and selling.

The fundamental approach could not even be summarized well here. One of the authors, however, co-authored an entire book on the stock market.[9] In addition, some of the major, commonly recognized fundamental determinants of the level of the stock market are listed and briefly discussed below.

Corporate Profits. Higher corporate profits, which usually lead to higher dividends, typically lead to higher stock prices (are "bullish").

Interest Rates (Bill and Bond Prices). Higher interest rates cause profits and dividends to be discounted more in determining stock prices, and so higher interest rates typically lead to lower stock prices (are "bearish").[10] Another way to express this relationship is that since high interest rates lead to low bond prices, and stock and bond prices should move together (since they are substitutes in many portfolios), high interest rates should lead to low stock prices. Stock and bond prices often, but not always, move together.

High corporate profits, which cause high stock prices, and high interest rates, which cause low stock prices, often occur together. Which of these two, then, dominates? There is not a general answer to this question. They have each had their days (and months and years). Determining which is dominant at a time is part of the art of predicting stock market levels.

Economic Conditions. A strong economy usually causes high corporate profits and tends to increase stock prices for this reason. But a strong economy also often leads to high interest rates, which tend to cause stock prices to decrease.

Another way of summarizing the level of the overall stock market or the price of an individual stock is through the price-to-earnings ratio. The price of a stock (or the overall market) can be expressed as the price-to-earnings ratio multiplied by the earnings. Often factors which tend to make earnings increase, such as more favorable economic conditions, make the price-to-earnings ratio decrease

---

[9] See Richard J. Teweles and Edward S. Bradley, *The Stock Market,* 4th ed. (New York: John Wiley & Sons, 1982).

[10] A common model of stock prices is the dividend discount model, which says that the stock price is the discounted value of all future dividends. According to this model, an increase in profits and a decrease in interest rates both lead to an increase in stock prices.

because, for example, more favorable economic conditions cause interest rates to increase.

Expectations.   Expectations of almost any economic, financial, political, or social factor also affect the overall stock market. Thus, expectations can be said to determine which dominates, earnings or the price-to-earnings ratio. Often attributing stock price changes to expectations is an admission of almost complete ignorance about the cause of the changes.

Given the likely movements in a stock index underlying a futures contract, the relationship between the futures price and the index—that is, the basis—should be analyzed. There is a formula which gives the conceptual (theoretical) relationship between the index and the futures price, usually called the fair value. This formula says that the fair value of the futures price should equal the current level of the index plus the net cost of carrying the stocks representing the index until the maturity of the futures contract. This net carry cost equals the short-term financing cost, as measured by the Treasury bill of the appropriate maturity, minus the dividend yield of the index. This relationship can be represented by the following equation:

$$PF = I + FC - DY$$

where PF = futures price fair value
   I = stock index
   FC = financing cost
   DY = dividend yield

Thus, if the current level of the index is 100, the annual financing cost is 12 percent, and the dividend yield is 8 percent, the fair value of the futures price with 3 months (one-fourth of a year) to maturity will be $PF = 100 + (\frac{1}{4}) (100)$ $(0.12 - 0.08) = 101$. Similarly, the fair value of the futures price with 6 months to maturity will be approximately 102 and the 9-month fair value of the futures price approximately 103.

The basis between the fair value of the futures price and the index, $PF - I$, thus, will equal the dollar value of the net carry cost from the date in question to the maturity of the futures contract. This basis obviously becomes zero as time passes because the dollar value of the net carry cost declines. At the maturity of the futures contract, the futures price equals the index—this is convergence.

Even though the basis, $PF - I$, should, in concept, equal the net carry cost, $FC - DY$, called the basis "fair value," it often does not. The basis may actually be at a premium or a discount to fair value. Analysts watch this basis continuously. The spread varies significantly both on an intraday basis and on a day-to-day basis, as shown in Figure 21-15.

One reason why this basis is watched is for market information. Some assert that premiums provide a bullish signal and indicate that there will be a subsequent increase in the value of the index. Discounts, accordingly, provide a bearish signal. The basis for this assertion is that due to their greater liquidity, changes in the stock index futures contracts precede changes in the underlying market in either direction.

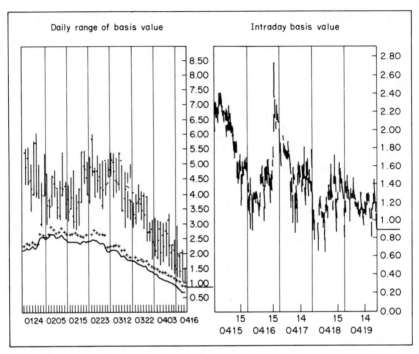

Figure 21-15   S&P 500 Index vs. June S&P 500 Future. Daily fair value estimate (T-bill—financed)—line; daily fair value estimate (CD-financed)— +.

The second reason for watching the basis relates to the rate of return on a portfolio of stocks hedged with stock index futures contracts. Consider a broad portfolio of stocks hedged with one of the broad stock index (S&P 500 or NYSE Composite) futures contracts. Over the holding period of the short futures contract, the futures price will decline relative to the index by the initial spread, which is the short-term financing cost minus the dividend yield $(FC - DY)$. Since the hedge consists of a short futures contract, this futures price decrease will cause a profit of equal amount $(FC - DY)$ over the hedge. But by holding the stock portfolio, the holder also earns the dividend yield. Adding these two returns $[(FC - DY) + DY]$ gives the financing cost, as measured by an approximation of the Treasury bill rate.

Thus, the return to a broad stock portfolio perfectly hedged with stock index futures contracts is the Treasury bill rate. This seems appropriate—a risk-free return (the Treasury bill rate) for a risk-free investment (a hedged stock portfolio). Investors, small or large, who hedge their broad stock portfolios with stock index futures contracts will earn approximately the Treasury bill rate. This is the case, however, only if the futures contract is initially priced at fair value. If the basis is initially at a premium, the hedger is selling futures at a higher price and, thus, earns a profit higher than the Treasury bill rate on the hedge. Rates of return of over 20 percent have been available on this type of transaction. If the basis is initially at a discount, the return will be less than the Treasury bill rate. Any investors planning to hedge a stock portfolio should be aware of whether they are hedging when the market is at a premium or a discount.

Some aggressive traders use the premium and discount phases of the stock index futures market actively. They buy a broad portfolio of stocks, up to 200 stocks, to replicate the index, and they sell futures when the spread is at a premium and sell or short a portfolio of stocks and buy futures when the spread is at a discount. This is called a swaps strategy.

An important aspect of the stock index futures markets is that since many individuals own stock, many of the trading techniques available to commercial and professional traders are also realistic for smaller speculators. This is not true for many other futures markets in which speculators are not involved in the markets for the underlying products.

Speculative Uses

The stock index futures markets have been actively used by both speculators and commercial hedgers. Recently, the S&P 500 futures contract has been the second largest futures contract in terms of trading volume, much of this activity being speculative. Speculators have accepted these markets for several reasons. One is the low (10 percent or less) margin, which may be high relative to other futures margins but is low relative to the stock market margin, which is 50 percent. The second is the lower transaction costs of the futures markets compared with the transaction costs of the stock market. The lower costs allow speculators to trade more actively.

It is also as easy to short futures contracts to implement a bearish stock market view as it is to go long on futures contracts to implement a bullish view, whereas in the stock market, it is more difficult to go short. For these reasons and others,

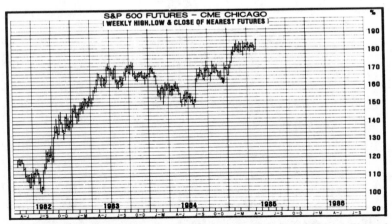

Figure 21-16   S&P 500 futures prices. [*Commodity Year Book 1985*, ed. *Walter L. Emery* (*Jersey City, N.J.: Commodity Research Bureau, Inc.*).]

Figure 21-17   NYSE Composite futures prices. [*Commodity Year Book 1985, ed. Walter L. Emery* (*Jersey City, N.J.: Commodity Research Bureau, Inc.*).]

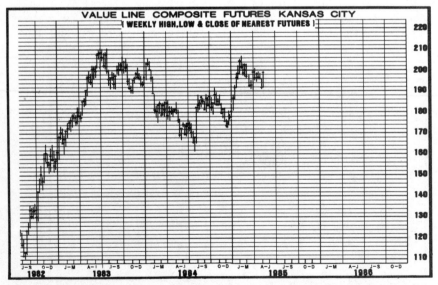

Figure 21-18   Value Line Composite futures prices. [*Commodity Year Book 1985, ed. Walter L. Emery* (*Jersey City, N.J.: Commodity Research Bureau, Inc.*).]

Figure 21-19 Dow Jones Industrial Average/S&P 500.

speculators have also used these markets for long-term position trading. Figures 21-16, 21-17, and 21-18 provide plots of the S&P 500, NYSE Composite, and Value Line Composite Index futures prices—their considerable volatility has also been attractive to speculators.

Independent of attempts to predict the level of different stock market indexes, differences in the changes among the various stock indexes can be used as a basis for speculative strategies. The S&P 500 Stock Index and NYSE Composite Index are broad, capitalization-weighted indexes and can be considered as synonymous with "the market." However, as indicated above, the Value Line is more representative of small stocks. And for long periods of time small stocks, as a group, may have different price movements than the overall market or large stocks. In this regard, there is a much-discussed January effect, according to which small stocks outperform the overall market during January. This differential performance has occurred during most recent years.

The Major Market Index (MMI) is highly correlated with the Dow Jones Industrial Average—30 high-capitalization stocks. These few high-capitalization stocks at times also have different price movements than the overall market and small stocks.

Differentiating the various indexes can be used either for buying or selling outright the various contracts or for spreading between the contracts. Day-to-day and month-to-month differences in the movements of these indexes are significant. For these reasons, the stock index futures markets have been actively used for spreading among markets. Figures 21-19, 21-20, and 21-21 show the ratios of the Dow Jones Industrial Average (as a surrogate of the Major Market Index), the Value Line Composite Index, and the New York Stock Exchange Composite Index to the S&P 500. The first two ratios show considerable variation, while the third ratio shows considerably less variation, since both indexes in the ratio are broad-based indexes.

Thus, due to the possibility of transacting in the overall stock market in one decision, the low transaction costs, low margins, liquidity, and the ease of shorting, stock index futures contracts have been used extensively by speculators for simply buying or selling in the market, spreading among various indexes, implementing various hedging strategies, and many other purposes. They also follow the stock index futures markets as indicators of the stock market itself.

Figure 21-20   Value Line Composite/S&P 500.

Figure 21-21   NYSE Composite/S&P 500.

Notes from a Trader—Stock Index Futures

The availability of stock index futures contracts has made it much easier to trade in the stock market due to their low transaction costs, including both commissions and bid-ask spreads, and the availability of instruments based on "the stock market" by various measures rather than solely on individual stocks. Speculators may trade in the overall stock market via the S&P 500 and NYSE Composite Stock Index futures contracts, and they may trade the "high-cap" component of the stock market via the MMI contract and "small-cap" stocks via the Value Line contract.

The fundamental and technical methods used for analyzing individual stocks and the stock market have been adapted to the stock index futures markets. Some say that the advent of the stock index futures contracts has increased the use of technical methods in the stock market. Some traders use the degree of richness or cheapness of the contracts to make their buy-sell decisions, while others simply buy or sell on the basis of their evaluation of the underlying market, often thereby creating the richness or cheapness.

Most of the trading volume and open interest for these contracts is in the nearby contract month, indicating that most people are simply trading in the stock market with a short-term view, not spreading or investing on a long-term basis. The S&P 500 contract is extremely liquid, with very narrow bid-ask spreads. The other stock index futures contracts are also quite liquid.

APPENDIX
Sources of Information

This section provides general sources of information on all financial futures and specific sources on foreign currencies, interest rates, and stock indexes.

GENERAL SOURCES OF INFORMATION ON FINANCIAL FUTURES

Current market quotes and, in some cases, market commentary and analysis are provided by market vendor services. Among these are Telerate, Bunker Remo, GTE, and Quotron.

Although mentioned in Chapter 17 among the general sources of information, periodicals such as *The Wall Street Journal, Barron's,* and *The New York Times* "Business Day" are particularly important sources of information about the financial futures markets.

An important chart book for the financial futures market is the *Financial Futures Chart Book.*

FOREIGN CURRENCIES

Among the important sources are:

Euromoney, Euromoney Publications, PLC, 14 Finsbury Circus, London EC2, England.

Financial Times (London), 75 Rockefeller Plaza, New York, NY 10020.

World Financial Markets, Morgan Guaranty Trust Company, 23 Wall Street, New York, NY 10004.

Various publications of the Federal Reserve Bank of New York.

International Economic Conditions, Federal Reserve Bank of St. Louis.

Dufey, G., and I. H. Giddy. *The International Money Market.* Englewood Cliffs, N.J.: Prentice-Hall, 1978.

Kubarych, Roger. *Foreign Exchange Markets in the United States.* New York: Federal Reserve Bank of New York, 1978.

Riehl, H. *Foreign Exchange Markets: A Guide to Foreign Currency Operations.* New York: McGraw-Hill, 1979.

International Currency Review, 11 Regency Place, London SW1 2EA, England.

INTEREST RATE FUTURES

The Bank Credit Analyst.

Publications of the Federal Reserve Bank of St. Louis—such as *Monetary Trends, National Economic Trends,* and *U.S. Financial Data.*

Federal Reserve Bulletin, Board of Governors of the Federal Reserve System.

Technical Data on Telerate Systems is a good source of timely market comment and analysis.

STOCK INDEX FUTURES

The Outlook, Standard & Poor's.
New York Stock Exchange—various publications.
Securities and Exchange Commission—various publications.

OTHER SOURCES OF INFORMATION

Journal of Commerce, 99 Wall Street, New York, NY 10005 (daily, Monday–Friday).
The Wall Street Journal, 200 Burnett Road, Chicopee, MA 01201 (daily, Monday–Friday).

22

A Potpourri
of Commodities

*"Cotton is planted in the spring, mortgaged
in the summer, and left in the fields in the
winter."*

This chapter discusses four internationally traded commodities—coffee, sugar,
cocoa, and cotton—and two commodities that are primarily U.S.-produced—
orange juice and lumber—although there is a growing production of these two
commodities from elsewhere within the hemisphere.

COFFEE

Introduction

Coffee was probably first used by the Ethiopians during ancient times. Its use
apparently spread from Ethiopia to various Arabian countries, Egypt, and Turkey
in the early 1600s and into Europe by way of Italy. In the 1600s, coffee was the
main nonalcoholic drink of Europe and the Americas, with the exception of Great
Britain and its possessions, which switched to tea. Coffeehouses were common in
the United States quite early in the country's history, and coffee consumption in
the United States quickly exceeded that of the coffee-producing countries.

As the demand for coffee in the United States and other western countries
continued to grow prior to World War II, the supply continued to come almost

exclusively from South and Central America, mainly Brazil. Since World War II, however, African countries have also become major producers.

Currently, coffee is the most active internationally traded beverage, with substantially greater trading activity than tea and cocoa. Coffee is one of the most active internationally traded commodities overall, considering even grains and other raw materials. A major reason for the active international trade is that coffee production, like that of tea and cocoa, is concentrated in the tropical and subtropical areas of the world, while consumption is in the United States, other parts of North America, and Europe.

Supply

There are two general types of coffee. The first is arabica, which is a very popular, mild coffee produced mainly in Brazil, Colombia, and other Latin American countries. As a result, arabicas are often subdivided into Brazilians, Colombians, and other mild coffees. The second type of coffee is the robusta, grown mainly in Africa, on a hardier plant than arabicas. Because robustas do not have the flavor of arabicas, robustas are used mainly in lower-quality blends and instant coffee.

As shown in Table 22-1, Brazil is the dominant coffee producer in the world. While Brazil now produces approximately 33 percent of the world's total, as recently as the 1930s Brazil produced approximately 60 percent of the world's coffee. Colombia is the world's second largest producer of coffee, producing significantly more than any other country, except Brazil. Brazil and Colombia produce arabicas. Mexico, El Salvador, Guatemala, and other South and Central American countries are also important producers of arabicas. Virtually all robustas are grown in Africa, with the Ivory Coast being the major robusta producer, followed by Uganda. However, approximately one-fourth of Africa's total production is of arabica, mainly in Ethiopia and Kenya. In terms of price and quality, Colombian milds are usually followed, in order, by other milds, unwashed arabicas, and robustas. Table 22-2 shows the world's major exporters of coffee.

In general, arabicas are grown in altitudes over 2000 feet with moderate and uniform temperatures. Robustas are grown at elevations of 500 to 2000 feet and are fairly resistant to disease. In order for coffee to be grown on an important commercial scale, the trees must have intense sunlight, rich soil, and warm rains. Coffee thrives in most tropical and subtropical areas. A botanical oddity is that the best coffees grow in areas in which the coffee plant does not grow wild. It is interesting to note also that coffee does not grow in or around Mocha.

The supply of coffee, like that of any other crop, depends to a considerable degree on natural conditions, although the range of conditions adequate for satisfactory coffee production is wide. The trees require at least 40 inches of rain each year, and the berries require considerable moisture before they mature. Dry weather is preferable during the harvest. Temperatures should be in the high 60s, although somewhat warmer temperatures are tolerable. Frost and wind, however, are mortal enemies of the coffee tree. Although many types of soil are acceptable, the difference in the quality of the coffee produced due to the nature of the soil may be quite material. It is widely believed that coffee grown in locations shaded from the full heat of the sun is superior. Coffee, of course, is also affected by

TABLE 22-1 WORLD GREEN COFFEE (TOTAL) PRODUCTION (in thousands of 60-kilo bags—132.276 pounds per bag)

Crop year	Angola	Brazil	Cameroon	Colombia	Costa Rica	Ethiopia	Guatemala	India	Indonesia	Ivory Coast	Mexico	Salvador	Uganda	Zaire (Congo, K)	World total
1978–1979	613	20,000	1634	12,600	1749	3142	2827	1842	4788	4742	4022	3423	1944	1293	79,074
1979–1980	260	22,000	1658	12,712	1522	3188	2647	2495	4803	3973	3600	3322	2042	1316	81,908
1980–1981	586	21,500	1959	13,500	2140	3264	2702	1977	5365	6090	3862	2940	2133	1526	86,344
1981–1982	392	33,000	1953	14,342	1782	3212	2653	2540	5785	4160	3900	2386	2885	1425	98,062
1982–1983	330	17,750	1929	13,300	2300	3670	2530	2170	4750	4510	4530	3100	3200	1354	83,399
1983–1984*	260	30,000	1058	13,000	2070	3700	2340	1670	5150	1417	4370	2517	3400	1480	90,359
1984–1985*	300	27,000	2117	12,800	2350	3600	2600	2830	5300	4833	4480	3000	3500	1550	93,608

*Preliminary.
SOURCE: USDA, Foreign Agricultural Service.

TABLE 22-2 WORLD GREEN COFFEE (EXPORTABLE)* PRODUCTION (in thousands of 60-kilo bags)

Crop† year	Angola	Brazil	Cameroon	Colombia	Costa Rica	Ethiopia	Guatemala	Indonesia	Ivory Coast	Kenya	Mexico	Salvador	Uganda	Zaire (Congo, K)	World total
1978–1979	568	12,000	1606	10,970	1533	1432	2517	3738	4677	1181	2915	3226	1905	1123	60,028
1979–1980	220	14,000	1626	10,962	1311	1555	2336	3723	3908	1468	2310	3122	2001	1141	62,258
1980–1981	545	13,500	1926	11,675	1932	1664	2381	4137	6026	1648	2362	2740	2090	1346	66,064
1981–1982	350	24,500	1915	12,492	1539	1396	2328	4630	4095	1434	2450	2686	2840	1240	77,170
1982–1983	287	9,750	1904	11,445	2077	2040	2195	3636	4445	1501	2830	2900	3154	1169	62,707
1983–1984‡	216	21,500	1032	11,140	1837	2050	2000	4010	1352	2049	2670	2317	3353	1295	69,094
1984–1985‡	255	18,500	2092	10,935	2115	1935	2260	4100	4763	1000	2780	2300	3452	1350	72,032

*Exportable production represents total harvested production minus estimated domestic consumption.
†Coffee marketing year begins in July in some countries and in others about October.
‡Preliminary.
SOURCE: USDA, Foreign Agricultural Service.

diseases, insects, and fungi. In addition, wars have affected prices considerably because so much of what is grown must be shipped long distances to consuming countries.

Most of the world's coffee comes from a tree known as the Arabica, which apparently originated in Ethiopia but now grows in most coffee-producing regions. The trees produce small white flowers which fall off the trees and are soon replaced by small clusters of cherries that grow along the limbs of the trees for a period of 6 or 7 months. They change in color as they mature from green to deep red. Arabica trees take about 5 years to mature enough to bear fruit, unlike the robusta variety, which requires only 2 or 3 years. Robustas, which have become commercially important only during about the last 75 years, are popular among producers partly because of their rapid growth to maturity and their resistance to disease. They have succeeded, however, in capturing only a relatively small amount of the world's consumption because of the less popular aroma and flavor of the coffee produced from them.

Most coffee trees produce the first full crop in about their fifth year. Each tree produces about 1 pound of marketable coffee each year until it is 25 or 30 years old, although some are productive much longer. The beans ripen at various times in different countries and are harvested, usually by hand, over a period of 4 to 6 weeks. The cherries, which are picked, consist of a sweet pulpy fruit usually covering two flat beans. There are two principal methods of preparing green coffee beans for the market. The first is the so-called wet method. With the wet method, after the outer pulp is mechanically removed from the berries, the berries are washed and put into tanks for fermentation, which affects both the flavor and the color of the coffee. The berries are washed again, then dried to remove the inner skin. It is surprising that no commercial use has yet been discovered for the pulp, despite long efforts to find one. Areas that do not have adequate water and that have long periods of hot, dry weather use the natural method, or dry method, of drying the berries in the sun. While the advantage of this process is that berries can be separated according to their readiness, its effectiveness depends on the constancy of the weather. The wet method, used for most of the higher-priced mild coffees, produces higher prices than the dry, or natural, method.

The producing countries also perform two other functions before shipping the beans. One is classification by size and the other is grading. When these steps have been completed, the coffee is packed in heavy bags for storage or shipment to market. Green coffee can be stored for long periods with little change in quality.

Coffee is then blended, roasted, and packaged for sale to the consumer. The blending and roasting are necessary because green coffees are not homogeneous products. Blending, as indicated, is a highly skilled, secret process for getting the best possible combination of aroma, flavor, appearance, and price. It is done in order to encourage maximum market demand, unify the characteristics of the different components, and allow a favorable dollar return to the seller.

Because there are different harvest periods for coffee in different parts of the world, coffee is harvested continuously throughout the year. Brazilian coffee is harvested from April to August. For this reason, and due to the variability of Brazilian weather, coffee prices are subject to weather shocks during June and

July each year. Colombia harvests coffee from October through March. In Africa, the Ivory Coast harvest is from November through April.

In addition to the usual requirements such as proper soil, labor, adequate financing, and assured markets, coffee presents some special problems. The investment required is large. The trees are subject to a wide variety of highly destructive insects, fungi, and disease. Worst of all, the yield from even the best trees is very unpredictable. The crop from a given tree can vary by 10 times from its minimum to its maximum, and the tree can produce bumper crops for several years in a row and then have sparse yields for the next several years with no apparent pattern. With so much land available for coffee growing in countries that can produce coffee and the ever-growing demand for coffee, the probability of wide variations in supply, both long-term and short-term, is high.

The marketing process for coffee is relatively simple. After the green coffee leaves the producing country, it enters a marketing chain which ends with blenders, roasters, and distributors. Because coffee has essentially a single end use—as a beverage—its distribution pattern is well defined.

The export of green coffee is handled by a small number of firms, which deliver the coffee into jobbers' or roasters' warehouses in a number of ports, among the most important of which are New York, New Orleans, San Francisco, Le Havre, and Antwerp.

Utilization

Coffee is extremely popular in many parts of the world. The United States is the world's largest importer of coffee, with Europe a close second. Table 22-3 shows the origin of U.S. coffee imports. Coffee is used almost exclusively as a beverage; less than 1 percent is used for other purposes, such as flavoring, candies, and desserts. Coffee is not consumed because of its capacity to quench thirst, nor does it have any nutritive value. Rather, the popularity of coffee, like that of tea, which has the same characteristics, is due to its being a stimulant as a result of its caffeine.

Unlike its supply, the demand for coffee varies little over time and responds only to a small degree even to reasonable changes in price or purchasing power, mainly because coffee has only one purpose, has no substitute acceptable to most of its consumers, and is regarded as a necessity by most of them. In addition, a stabilizing effect on price results from the fact that green coffee is storable at a relatively low cost for long periods, which evens out, to some degree, the effects of occasional significant changes in supply. This short-term, highly inelastic demand for coffee, coupled with great changes in supply, has led over many years to attempts to control the supply and marketing of crops, the burning of supplies, and demands for subsidies to growers and exporters by producing countries.

Green coffee beans are used to produce both regular coffee and instant coffee. Both regular and instant coffees are typically blends of several types of coffees. While all coffee blends are different and their composition is regarded as proprietary, a typical regular blend for U.S. consumption is composed of a mixture of Colombian or Central American milds and Brazilians, with the grade of the blend increasing as the portion of the other milds increases and the portion of the

TABLE 22-3   ORIGIN OF COFFEE IMPORTS (FOR CONSUMPTION) INTO THE UNITED STATES   (in thousands of 60-kilo bags)

Year	Angola	Brazil	Colom-bia	Costa Rica	Domin-ican Repub-lic	Ecua-dor	Ethi-opia	Guate-mala	Indon-esia	Ivory Coast	Mexico	Peru	Phil-ippines	Salva-dor	Vene-zuela	Grand total
1971	1590	6536	2642	350	338	404	1130	813			1286			645	246	22,686
1972	1297	6152	2711	294	401	490	965	689	744	977	1070			391	243	20,769
1973	1693	4596	2868	284	507	435	1062	1110	626	1150	1641			1047	174	21,789
1974	2396	2725	3090	268	381	512	505	1096	942	749	1324			1111	246	19,245
1975	1202	3748	3400	192	336	694	533	874	765	966	1662	432		1018	182	20,289
1976	871	3092	2688	179	551	767	703	749	1082	1330	1869	461	44	1045	288	19,788
1977	49	2453	1951	272	585	505	288	832	860	673	1406	654	6	1037	155	14,808
1978	304	2694	2808	334	461	1044	461	942	1177	775	1390	954	62	627	239	18,133
1979	40	1890	3891	516	548	638	549	1123	1294	834	1934	565	96	1123	121	19,396
1980	120	3505	3404	298	343	539	406	1374	1315	438	1337	573	179	1374	35	18,153
1981	21	3243	1727	226	359	701	547	645	1516	602	1393	439	270	779	27	16,555
1982*	63	3372	1710	248	500	773	578	844	1118	998	1377	513	308	919	16	17,416
1983	27	3417	1755	226	430	857	519	887	1079	674	1495	439	276	1214	26	16,449
1984*	5	3866	2170	258	447	961	423	1118	1030	1144	1553	557	296	1052	88	17,734

*Preliminary.

SOURCE: U.S. Department of Commerce.

Brazilians decreases. The goal of blenders is to vary the ingredients of the blend in response to the availability of the various coffees at a low cost but retain the same flavor. This flexibility is necessary because, with the possible exceptions of Brazilian and Colombian beans, no other sources are sufficiently large to be able to guarantee adequate supplies every year.

The use of robustas has increased in recent years for two reasons. First, robustas have been increasingly used in regular coffee despite their lower quality. Second, the use of instant coffee (solubles) has increased, and although instant coffees are also blends, robustas are the main component. The use of instant coffee has increased, particularly internationally, due to its convenience and also because the quality of instant coffee has improved.

Due to the principal use of coffee as a beverage, the short-run demand for coffee is fairly inelastic in response to both price and income changes. However, long-run trends have affected the demand for coffee. Over the last two to three decades, the demand for coffee in the United States has declined, as measured both by the percentage of the population consuming coffee and by per capita consumption. This decline has been due to an aversion to caffeine as a result of increased health consciousness and to an increased use of soft drinks, particularly by the young, who then continue to consume more soft drinks as they become older. However, in other countries (particularly Japan, Eastern Europe, and parts of the former British Empire which have shifted from tea) the demand for both regular and instant coffees has grown sufficiently to offset the decline in the United States.

Price Determinants

The price of coffee depends on both supply and demand. However, because, as indicated above, the demand for coffee is fairly stable, the supply is the major determinant of short-run changes in the price of coffee. And weather is the major determinant of short-run changes in supply. The months of June and July are the freeze-scare months in Brazil and other South American producing countries. This Brazilian frost period is the main uncertainty affecting coffee prices.

One of the most extraordinary price rises in the history of any commodity occurred in early 1954, when the price rose very quickly to more than 95 cents a pound in the spot and futures markets and more than $1.35 at the retail level. Starting on the night of July 5, 1953, huge blasts of frigid air swept over the entire southern regions of South America, and the coffee-growing areas of Brazil were enveloped in freezing weather for 2 days and 3 nights. Because damage to coffee trees from cold is not immediately apparent, the scope of the disaster was not at first readily understood. By September and October, however, it was becoming obvious that what had happened was one of the greatest calamities ever to strike a crop. According to Brazilian coffee officials, more than 904 million coffee trees were destroyed or damaged. The result was a huge speculation in both cash and futures. Panicked consumers stood in line to buy coffee at ever-increasing prices, while those who had coffee to sell withheld it, anticipating even higher prices.

While weather is the most important factor which influences the supply and price of western hemisphere coffees, insects are the major problem with eastern hemisphere production.

Actual or potential dock strikes may also affect coffee prices by initially causing a buildup of inventories and later either a shortage if the strike materializes or a need to liquidate excesses if the strike does not materialize. Wars and potential instability may affect the transport of coffee and its price.

Green coffee can be stored for a long time period under the right conditions. And because coffee is grown in countries with moderate temperatures and humidities, conditions permit storage in most producing countries. Thus, coffee can be stored in producing as well as consuming countries. Stored stocks tend to mitigate the price swings caused by the combination of price-inelastic demand and weather-induced supply changes. The level of inventories of green coffee in producing or consuming countries is an important determinant of coffee prices.

The marketing policies of major coffee-producing countries are also major determinants of coffee prices. In this regard, the role of Brazil, the world's dominant coffee producer, is pivotal. During the 1930s, as indicated, Brazil produced over 60 percent of the world's coffee. During this period, Brazil stored and even destroyed significant portions of its coffee production. While these policies did support high prices for Brazilian coffee in the short run, they also made possible the increased penetration of the coffee market by Colombia and other Central American and African countries.

Another aspect, in addition to size, of Brazil's coffee crop is also important. Unlike the crop in most Latin American countries whose temperature and rainfall are very regular, Brazil's crop is subject to both droughts and frosts. Brazilian weather conditions, thus, often cause significant price increases.

There have been attempts to stabilize coffee prices since the 1930s. Early attempts were made primarily by Brazil. The basis for the current, much broader International Coffee Agreement (ICA) was set during early 1976, which was a difficult time to implement a price stabilization program because the severe Brazilian frost of July 1976 drove the price of type C coffee from 90 cents per pound to $3.40 during April 1977. Since that time, however, the price support program has been fairly effective.

According to the ICA, a total export quota is set. For example, for 1986 this quota was 58 million bags (132 pounds each). From this, an export quota for each country in the International Coffee Organization (ICO) is set. The quota in 1986 was designed to achieve the current price range of $1.20 to $1.40 per pound. Each producing country then categorizes its coffee production into exports permitted according to the quota, domestic consumption, and exports to non-ICO members (primarily Eastern European). The remaining production must be stored at a cost to the producing company or country. As prices decline, tighter quotas are set; as prices rise, the quotas are relaxed. The ICO has recently been effective, since both producer and consumer countries have seen it to their advantage to participate, and most coffee trade occurs between ICO members. Large supplies over a long period, however, could induce consuming countries to withdraw from or not cooperate with the policies of the ICO. As supplies increased during the mid-1980s, noncompliance with standards increased. There are 75 members of the ICO, including the United States and other principal coffee-consuming and -producing countries. Overall, the ICO has been one of the most successful international commodity price-stabilization groups.

Seasonals

Because coffee is grown in so many parts of the world and is harvested throughout the year, there is no clear seasonal in coffee prices. The ease of storing coffee further tends to even out seasonal influences. The coffee year is assumed to begin on July 1, although this date has little significance and there is no effective crop year in coffee.

However, because of Brazil's significance as a producer, its susceptibility to frosts and droughts, and its April-to-August harvesting season, the June–July period is subject to volatile, uncertain price movements. While the possibility of a freeze in Brazil or other South or Central American countries is small, the rewards of being long outweigh the risks, and there is, thus, an aversion to being short on coffee during this period. Even rumored freezes can increase coffee prices significantly.

Futures Contracts

Coffee futures contracts began to be traded in the United States at the New York Coffee Exchange during 1882. Futures trading on sugar was added during

Figure 22-1   Coffee, type C contract. [*Commodity Year Book 1985*, ed. *Walter L. Emery* (*Jersey City, N.J.: Commodity Research Bureau, Inc.*).]

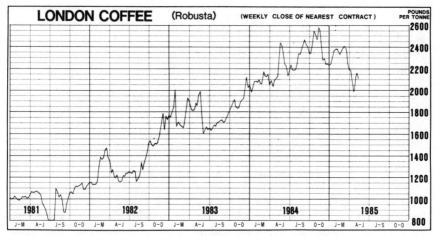

Figure 22-2   London coffee (robusta). [*Commodity Year Book 1985*, ed. *Walter L. Emery* (*Jersey City, N.J.: Commodity Research Bureau, Inc.*).]

1916, and the exchange's name was changed to the New York Coffee and Sugar Exchange. It became the New York Coffee, Sugar and Cocoa (NYCSC) Exchange in 1979, when it merged with the New York Cocoa Exchange.

Two types of coffee futures contracts have been traded recently at the NYCSC Exchange: type C on arabica coffee from 19 countries, excluding Brazil, and type B on Brazilian coffee. Only the type C contract is currently traded at the NYCSC Exchange—the type B contract was formally suspended during 1982, after several years of inactivity. A type U futures contract (on robusta coffee) is traded in the London Coffee Terminal Market. The difference in the locations of these contracts reflects primarily their proximities to the locations of the underlying coffee—New York to South America and London to Africa. Between 1968 and 1970 the NYCSC Exchange also traded a type U (robusta) contract, and during the 1960s it also traded the other coffee contracts.

The NYCSC Exchange type C contract calls for the delivery of 37,500 pounds (approximately 250 bags) of washed arabica coffee from any of 19 countries, not including Brazil; coffee from several countries is deliverable either at par or at discounts ranging from 100 to 800 points (cents per pound), but only Colombian coffee is deliverable at a premium (200 points). Delivery is made at ports in New York and New Orleans. The trading months are March, May, July, September, and December. Prices are quoted in cents per pound, with a minimum price fluctuation of 1/100 cent per pound, or $3.75 per contract.

Figures 22-1 and 22-2 provide recent futures prices for the NYCSC Exchange type C contract and the London robusta coffee contract.

Speculative Uses

Due to the volatility of the prices of coffee futures contracts shown in Figures 22-1 and 22-2, speculators have been active simply buying or selling the contracts on the basis of the price determinants discussed above. A common speculation is based on the weather in Brazil. Even though Brazilian coffee is not deliverable on either contract, Brazil's supply is so large that bad weather in Brazil which reduces the size of the Brazilian crop affects all coffee prices.

Spreading between the NYCSC Exchange and London contracts on the basis of the belief that the arabica-robusta relationship is out of line is common, although the relationship between these two futures depends not only on relative coffee prices but also on the dollar-pound exchange rate. Intracontract spreads in coffee are less interesting than in many other commodities because coffee has no crop year.

The analysis of the prices of coffee futures is simpler than for most other commodities. The sources of supply and areas of demand are well defined. The United States is the prime consumer, amd coffee demand is fairly stable regardless of price. The sources of volatility are on the supply side, but even these sources are easy to identify and include severe growing problems in Brazil or interference with shipping due to wars, long strikes, or other factors. These factors can affect coffee prices significantly because of the enormous influence on U.S. consumers, who have no domestic source of coffee except Hawaii, which produces only relatively small amounts. Because the coffee market is often fairly thin, the risk of long, unexpected changes in supply may cause extended violent price moves.

Sources of Information

The Foreign Agricultural Service of the USDA issues the circular *Coffee* on a quarterly basis (March, June, September, and December). This publication provides estimates of coffee production. The National Coffee Association also issues several statistical reports. The International Coffee Organization of London publishes *General Statistical Documents*. Finally, the New York Coffee, Sugar and Cocoa Exchange provides several sources of useful information.

Notes from a Trader—Coffee

For the fundamentalist, coffee analysis is simpler than the analysis of most other commodities. The sources of coffee and the locations of demand are well defined. The United States is the prime consumer of coffee, and there are few signs of any change in the consumption habits of coffee drinkers in this country. Despite the inroads made by soft drinks, most U.S. adults drink coffee regardless of price and with little consideration of current purchasing power. Warnings of hazards to health to date have affected consumption only in those who consume quite large amounts or those who have health problems such as heart trouble. The International Coffee Agreement, unlike most other such agreements, has a history of being effective.

The greatest potential hazard to a trader is the disruption of the sources of supply, but even these are easy to define. Such disruptions usually involve growing problems in Brazil, such as hot, dry weather during the late summer or early fall, and interference with shipping, such as a war or long strike. The effect of weather on coffee production in Brazil during the late summer and early fall is particularly important. Coffee trees usually flower several times before developing coffee beans. Droughts in Brazil during September and October cause the trees to miss flowerings and prices to rise sharply. However, subsequent rain can then cause significant price decreases. Such factors can have a special influence on coffee prices because of the significant influence of U.S. consumers, who have no domestic source of supply except Hawaii, which produces only relatively small amounts. At times, even rumors about Brazilian weather and supply cause significant price changes. The main change in coffee patterns in the last several years has been that made by instant, or soluble, coffee, which is becoming more popular because of its simplicity of preparation despite its inadequacies in aroma and flavor.

The coffee market tends to be thin, and this condition, combined with the risk of large and unexpected supply changes, may cause extended violent moves. The coffee market is no place for the underfinanced or the timid. Inverted markets are frequent in coffee and, therefore, popular with those who like to buy discount contracts on the theory that the price level is probably understated and they will make money sooner or later.

SUGAR

Introduction

Sugar and other sweeteners have played an important role in U.S. history. Although Columbus brought sugarcane to the New World, the colonies depended primarily on molasses imports as a sweetener. The Sugar Act passed by the British in 1764, which imposed a tax on molasses imports, contributed to the beginning of the American Revolution. Sugarcane production began in the southeastern United States in 1794, and the first sugar beet factory was established in California in 1838.

A century and a half ago, sugar was the king of commerce. To England, its holdings in Antilles represented more wealth than its 13 colonies, and sugar was the most important trade commodity. In France, where Napoleon ruled, frustration over the English blockade of sugarcane imports resulted in the emperor's decree that 70,000 acres of sugar beets be planted to help make France self-sufficient. From such lofty and crucial beginnings, sugar is now only one of several internationally traded commodities and one whose role as a sweetener is being threatened by substitutes.

Supply

Sugar, which is sucrose, is produced from both sugarcane and sugar beets. Though the location of the production, the nature of production, and the processing techniques for these two sources of sugar are different, refined sugar produced from each is indistinguishable.

Sugarcane is a tall, bamboolike tropical grass which requires 1 to 2 years after it is planted before it can be harvested, and then it issues new shoots for approximately 10 years; that is, it is a perennial. It ranges from 8 to 12 feet in height and is about 1 inch in diameter. Sugarcane is grown in the warm, moist climate of the tropical and subtropical zones. Brazil has been the major producer of sugarcane, followed by India and Cuba, as shown in Table 22-4. In the United States, sugarcane is grown in Florida, Louisiana, Texas, and Hawaii, although the growing season varies, being as short as 12 months in Louisiana and as long as 2 years in Hawaii.

Sugar beets are white, tapering roots that are about 1 foot long and weigh about 2 pounds. They are planted in the early spring and harvested before the first winter freeze. Sugar beets are grown in temperate zones. As shown in Table 22-4, Russia is the major producer of beet sugar, with France, Mexico, West Germany, Poland, and the United States being other major producers. In the United States, sugar beets are grown in 16 states, mainly in California and the Red River Valley of Minnesota and North Dakota and South Dakota, all west of the Mississippi River except Ohio and Michigan.

Although almost every country in the world produces sugar, sugar is still actively internationally traded. The major exporters are Cuba, Brazil, Australia, the Philippines, and France. The largest importers are the United States, Japan, Russia, and England. Some of the world's largest sugar producers export rather than consume their production. On the other hand, the United States is one of the world's largest sugar producers but also one of the largest importers, importing approximately half of the entire amount used. Table 22-5 shows the total U.S. supply and utilization, including imports and exports.

The United States grows both sugar beets and sugarcane. Because its climate is mainly temperate, beet planting predominates in the United States, and only in the southernmost states and Hawaii is sugarcane planted in any quantity. Sugarcane does particularly well on the coasts of Louisiana, where there are tropical temperatures and a moist sea breeze. Sugar beets thrive in Colorado, where there are moderate temperatures and a definite annual spring-fall cycle, and in several other states west of the Mississippi.

At any particular time of the year, sugar is being planted or harvested somewhere in the world, but there are, nevertheless, significant seasonal variations. On the other hand, sugar beets are usually harvested in the fall, with planting occurring during the spring. For the latter reason, the world sugar crop year runs from September through the following August.

Centrifugal sugar accounts for more than 85 percent of the world's sugar production and virtually all the sugar traded. Noncentrifugal sugar is produced by an alternate process and is consumed almost exclusively in the country where it is grown.

Harvested sugar beets and sugarcane must be submitted to considerable complicated processing before becoming raw sugar and a product of trade. The main steps are extraction, purification, evaporation, crystallization, and centrifuging. Raw sugar is further refined by means of a long series of processes. The growing, processing, and refining of both beet and cane sugars are very capital-intensive.

During the processing, sugar beets are sliced, pressed, and then processed directly into refined white sugar or into an intermediate product called "thick juice." Thick juice can be stored in tanks at the refinery and then processed into refined white sugar as needed. The processing plants are located in the producing

TABLE 22-4 WORLD PRODUCTION OF SUGAR (CENTRIFUGAL SUGAR—RAW VALUE) (in thousands of metric tons)

Crop year	Australia (cane)	Brazil (cane)	China (mainland)	Cuba (cane)	Hawaii (cane)	India (cane)	Indonesia (cane)	Philippines (cane)	Poland (beet)	West Germany	United States Beet	United States Cane	U.S.S.R. (beet)	Mexico	France	World total, all
1977–1978	3322	8863	2450	7200	934	8201	1125	2397	1819	3076	2820	1497	8825	3029	4268	92,454
1978–1979	2978	7740	2558	7500	962	7071	1372	2347	1763	2997	2984	1436	9300	3058	4000	91,264
1979–1980	2967	6990	2507	6500	928	5170	1331	2325	1582	3095	2612	1488	7800	2763	4257	84,560
1980–1981	3389	8508	3000	7542	951	6542	1338	2373	1134	2988	2857	1547	7196	2518	4262	88,466
1981–1982	3434	8393	3400	8207	821	9727	1742	2503	1873	3688	3011	1603	6413	2842	5576	100,555
1982–1983	3535	9300	4132	7200	915	9508	1731	2521	2141	3591	2483	1712	7392	3078	4833	101,348
1983–1984*	3170	9400	3803	8200	862	7025	1758	2367	2000	2725	2422	1552	8700	3242	3870	95,553
1984–1985†	3550	8890	3769	8200	839	7343	1787	1888	1890	2900	2595	1469	7800	3350	4350	97,546

*Preliminary.

†Estimated.

SOURCE: USDA, Foreign Agricultural Service.

TABLE 22-5 U.S. SUGAR (CANE AND BEET) SUPPLY AND UTILIZATION (in thousands of short tons—raw value)

| | Supply | | | | | | | | Utilization | | | | Domestic disappearance | | |
| | Production | | | Offshore receipts | | | Begin-ning stocks | Total supply | Total use | Ex-ports | Net changes in invisible stocks | Refin-ery loss adjust-ment* | Im-ported blends and mix-tures | Military and civilian | |
Year	Cane	Beet	Total	For-eign	Terri-tories	Total								Total	Per capita
1977	2666	3423	6089	6138	102	6240	3498	15,827	11,336	22	201	14	—	11,099	94.2
1978	2535	3067	5602	4683	52	4735	4491	14,828	11,074	48	29	108	4	10,889	91.4
1979	2727	3066	5793	5027	47	5074	3754	14,621	10,921	73	−12	103	—	10,756	89.3
1980	2684	3052	5736	4495	178	4673	3701	14,110	11,028	689	72	78	—	10,189	83.6
1981	3043	3182	6225	5025	48	5073	3082	14,380	10,919	1191	−94	53	—	9,769	79.4
1982	2776	3160	5936	2964	80	3044	3461	12,441	9,373	137	23	53	7	9,160	73.7
1983†	3094	2588	5682	3186	67	3253	3068	12,003	9,433	300	144	72	105	8,917	71.1
1984‡	2829	3059	5888	3594	24	3618	2570	12,076	8,990	429	20	51	115	8,530	67.4
1985‡							3086								

*Residual.

†Preliminary.

‡Estimate.

SOURCE: USDA, Agricultural Marketing Service.

areas because it is not efficient to transport sugar beets due to their perishability and bulk.

Sugarcane refiners in the United States receive cane from sources throughout the world as well as the domestic markets, and refining is, thus, not seasonal. The imported cane sugar is in the form of raw sugar (96 percent sucrose), which is produced from sugarcane in several tropical countries and shipped to the United States for further processing. Processing and refinery plants are located mainly in Louisiana but also in other Atlantic and Gulf Coast cities close to ports into which sugarcane is imported.

Refined sugar is then sold by the refiners directly to the end users in the food industry, wholesalers, brokers who locate buyers for the sugar, and companies that prepare the sugar for sale as liquid or solid sugar. It may be sold to the U.S. government, according to the price support program.

Utilization

In the United States (the world's largest consumer of sugar) and other major sugar-consuming countries, the major users of sugar as an input for producing other products are bakers, makers of beverages, and confectioners. Table 22-6 shows the major uses of sugar in the United States. The largest use, however, is the direct sale of refined sugar in stores. While the total consumption and per capita consumption of sugar have grown considerably over the last 40 years, these measures of sugar use for the United States have declined in the last decade, as shown in Table 22-5, due to the uses of other sweeteners and the lower use of sweeteners in general.

During recent years, domestically produced beet and cane sugar have been responsible for 35 to 60 percent of the total sweetener consumption in the United States (20 to 30 percent for beet sugar and 15 to 30 percent for cane sugar), imported cane sugar for 30 to 45 percent, and corn sweeteners for 10 to 20 percent, with minor contributions from other sweeteners, such as honey and maple syrup. The per capita consumption of refined sugar in the United States has decreased significantly in recent years, even though the per capita consumption of all sweeteners has increased, due primarily to the increased use of corn sweeteners, particularly high-fructose corn sweetener (HFCS).

Price Determinants

Most internationally traded sugar is priced on a long-term forward basis. A smaller amount of sugar is traded on a current-market basis. Although the same factors affect the prices on both markets, they affect the prices of the former method of sales with a longer lag.

There are several economic and political determinants of sugar prices, on both the demand side and the supply side. On the demand side, per capita income and population are important economic determinants. Although at high levels of income, sugar consumption depends less on the level of per capita income (that is, the income elasticity of demand is low), increases in the level of income and population growth in third world countries have led to an increase in sugar con-

TABLE 22-6 SUGAR, REFINED—DELIVERIES BY TYPE OF PRODUCT OR BUYER IN THE UNITED STATES (in thousands of short tons)

Year	Bakery and cereal products	Bever-ages	Confec-tionery*	Insti-tutions	Dairy products	Proc-essed foods	Other food uses	Retail gro-cers†	Whole-sale grocers‡	Other uses§	Total de-liveries	In con-sumer-size packages	To indus-trial users
1977	1387	2454	951	217	567	745	543	1288	2095	104	10,351	2460	923
1978	1308	2608	912	230	531	689	412	1180	1996	161	10,027	2267	909
1979	1289	2441	911	276	480	681	483	1239	2038	126	9,934	2410	867
1980	1337	2161	932	303	450	535	589	1169	1881	120	9,477	2347	703
1981	1306	1852	983	259	459	484	581	1161	2001	126	9,212	2425	737
1982	1296	1583	940	177	404	450	526	1086	1951	106	8,519	2310	727
1983	1387	1248	1087	195	385	454	431	1168	1713	131	8,199	2314	567
1984¶	1395	900	1106	209	406	430	415	1100	1741	125	7,828	2170	671

*And related products.
†Chain stores, supermarkets.
‡Jobbers, sugar dealers.
§Used largely for pharmaceuticals and some tobacco.
¶Preliminary.
SOURCE: USDA, Statistical Reporting Service.

sumption. While sugar prices also affect the demand for sugar, the effect of prices on sugar demand is fairly small; that is, sugar demand is fairly price-inelastic, at least in the short run. The short-run price inelasticity of demand causes significant sugar price changes in response to changes in sugar supply. The strength of the U.S. dollar also affects the demand for sugar somewhat.

However, in the long run, high sugar prices have caused significant shifts from sugar to other sweeteners, both natural sweeteners, particularly HFCS, and artificial sweeteners, such as aspartame and saccharine. While the market share of HFCS as a sweetener has doubled in the last two decades, thus mitigating sugar price increases, the use of HFCS is limited because it is available only in liquid form. However, HFCS will likely continue to be used increasingly for beverages, bakery products, cereal products, and several other processed items.

Because the demand for sugar is, in the short run, relatively price-inelastic, changes in the supply affect prices significantly. In this regard, the weather and other crop conditions, including acreage planted and yields, in sugar-producing countries affect sugar production and, as a result, sugar prices. Weather is an important determinant of supply, particularly for sugarcane. Since sugarcane accumulates the greatest percentage of its sugar in its final period of growth and must be quickly harvested once it is mature to ensure a maximum yield, an unusual amount of rain at harvest time may reduce cane sugar yields. In addition, both cane and beets are subject to disease from more than 40 insect pests. The leafhopper in Hawaii has caused a decrease in cane yields of as much as 80 percent over three successive crops.

Another economic factor which affects sugar prices is the reportable positions of sugar stocks, which measure the balance between supply and demand. The September 1 stock, at the change of the crop year, is particularly significant. In this regard, the ratio of sugar stocks to sugar consumption is a useful indicator of prospective sugar price changes—sugar prices tend to increase as this ratio decreases. This indicator has tended to vary between 20 and 36 percent.

Overall, a significant portion of the world's sugar is insulated from the free market due to national price support programs, as in the United States and Europe. Due to the price support and subsidy programs in the United States, Europe, and other countries, there is a tendency for world supply to outrun world demand. For example, the European Economic Community, a net exporter prior to 1973, subsidizes its sugar beet producers and was a significant exporter of sugar during 1984. A large share of world trade in sugar is a result of bilateral and multilateral agreements, usually on a forward contractual basis. The open market has, thus, become a residual market. For these reasons, small changes in the supply of or demand for sugar can cause substantial price changes. This excess supply and price variability is supported by the short-run elasticity of supply of sugar due particularly to the multiharvesting of sugarcane during the year. Sugar beets, however, are annual crops, and so the supply can be changed more effectively in the short run due to price changes.

Two political-economic factors which affect U.S. sugar prices are international agreements regarding sugar, mainly the International Sugar Agreement, and U.S. policies regarding sugar.

International Sugar Agreement. The International Sugar Agreement (ISA), first established in 1937 and more recently (at the beginning of 1978) put into effect, is a multinational agreement designed to stabilize the world price of sugar. According to the intended mechanism, participating countries build up reserve stocks and impose export quotas when world sugar prices are low and release stocks and remove quotas when prices are high. The effectiveness of the ISA has been limited, however, due to limited support from and limited participation by sugar-producing countries, particularly the European Economic Community countries. The ISA expired on December 31, 1984. At the Geneva Conference of the International Sugar Organization (ISO) during June and July 1984, attempts to establish a new international agreement with economic provisions to stabilize prices failed due to the weak state of the sugar market and international politics. However, a new administrative agreement was made. While this administrative ISA does not have any authority to restrict exports or maintain price levels, it is a structure for facilitating the collection and exchange of statistics and for continuing negotiations.

Government Programs. Sugar receives the same type of price support as many of the grains. During 1981, the trigger level for loans for sugar was set at 17 cents per pound of raw sugar at the refinery. When sugar prices are below this level, the refiner receives 17 cents per pound, which is paid to the sugarcane or beet grower until the refiner chooses to repay the loan plus interest or default to the Commodity Credit Corporation as discussed in Chapter 18.

There is also a dual program based on duties and market stabilization prices for raw sugar imported into the United States. Given a duty, which was 2.8125 cents per pound during 1982, an adjustable fee is charged such that the sum of the market price of sugar plus the duty, fee, and transportation costs equals the market stabilization price. During 1982, the fee was 2.14180 cents per pound, and the market stabilization price was 19.68 cents per pound.

U.S. import quotas were also introduced during 1982 to complement the price support programs. It is due to these three U.S. government programs to support U.S. sugar prices that U.S. sugar prices are significantly higher than world sugar prices, as reflected in the prices of the two sugar futures contracts discussed below. During 1985, the government lowered its import quotas to increase the degree of protection for both U.S. beet producers and U.S. cane producers. However, CCC stocks continued to increase as sugar producers found it more attractive to sell their sugar to the government.

Over the last decade, world sugar prices have been volatile with long periods of surplus, due to the factors discussed above, and shorter periods of shortages and price increases. Prior to the 1960s, sugar prices were fairly stable due to international sugar agreements. But the dissolution of these agreements since that time has contributed to the volatility.

The short-run inelasticity of demand and the subsidization of sugar production, particularly in the United States and Europe, led to the chronic oversupply of sugar and low prices for extended periods of time. However, when there is a shock on the supply side due to weather or pests, the short-run inelasticity of supply mitigates the supply response to this condition, and prices increase significantly.

Due to the reduced demand and increasing supply, including the considerable supply induced by government policies, world sugar prices declined to less than 3 cents per pound during July 1985, even though the production cost of efficient producers was 9 cents and the cost of other producers was much higher. Many experts forecast that the sugar market will remain in an oversupply condition.

Seasonality

The demand for sugar tends to be highest during the summer, when soft-drink consumption is high and the canning season is approaching, and lowest in the late winter. Refined-sugar production in the United States has little seasonal variation, since sugar can be harvested in tropical regions throughout the year and there is a steady flow of sugarcane into the United States. On the other hand, sugar beets grown in the United States and other countries with temperate climates are planted in the spring and harvested in the fall, and there is maximum production of refined beet sugar between October and February, with November and December typically being the months of maximum production. Due to the harvesting of sugar beets, refinery storage is highest at the beginning of the crop year and lowest at the end of the crop year—the crop year runs from September to August, consistent with the beet harvesting season.

Although the seasonal in the prices of refined sugar is weak, sugar prices tend to reach a minimum during June and a peak during October. These seasonals are atypical of crop seasonals for which price peaks occur at the time of planting and troughs at the time of harvesting.

Futures Contracts

In the United States, there are two sugar futures contracts traded at the New York Coffee, Sugar and Cocoa (NYCSC) Exchange and one traded at the Mid-America Commodity Exchange. Of the two NYCSC Exchange sugar contracts, one is for world sugar (No. 11 sugar)—that is, sugar that is not within the protected U.S. market—and the other is for the protected U.S. market (No. 12 sugar—domestic). The No. 11 sugar (world) contract is based on raw sugar from 26 producing countries, deliverable in the country of origin, while the No. 12 sugar (domestic) contract is based on the same raw commodity, but the sugar is deliverable at four U.S. locations: New York, Philadelphia, Baltimore, and New Orleans. The sugar deliverable on the No. 12 sugar (domestic) contract is either produced in the United States or imported and has had its transportation and import duties paid. The No. 11 sugar (world) contract is based on free sugar that is subject to the import restrictions and fees of the consuming country.

Both NYCSC Exchange contracts are based on 112,000 pounds (50 long tons).[1] The trading months of both contracts are January, March, May, July, and September, but the No. 11 sugar contract is traded, in addition, in October, while the No. 12 sugar contract is traded, in addition, in November.

---

[1] 1 long ton equals 2240 pounds.

The MidAmerica Commodity Exchange also trades a domestic contract. It is based on 40,000 pounds of free-flowing bulk extrafine granulated sugar, deliverable in Chicago. There are also three foreign sugar futures contracts: (1) raw sugar and white sugar (world sugar) at the London Sugar Terminal Market, (2) No. 12 domestic sugar at the Tokyo Sugar Exchange, and (3) white sugar (world sugar) at the International Market of White Sugar of Paris.

Figures 22-3 and 22-4 provide recent price histories of the NYCSC Exchange No. 11 sugar and No. 12 sugar contracts. During October 1982 the NYCSC Exchange began trading an option on its No. 11 sugar (world) futures contract. This options contract provides the same type of speculative and hedging potential on sugar that was discussed in general in Chapter 9.

Speculative Uses

While sugar futures have substantial hedge uses for sugar-producing companies and countries, sugar refiners, and sugar users, sugar futures have also been extensively used by speculators. Speculators buy or sell the futures contracts outright on the basis of the price determinants discussed above. As indicated in Figures 22-3 and 22-4, there have been substantial moves in sugar—these moves tend to be long, whether up or down.

Sugar futures contracts, within a crop year, are usually traded on a cash-and-carry basis. When a deferred month is traded at a premium which exceeds the

Figure 22-3   No. 11 sugar (world). [*Commodity Year Book 1985*, ed. *Walter L. Emery (Jersey City, N.J.: Commodity Research Bureau, Inc.).*]

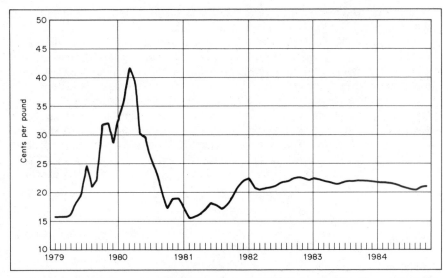

Figure 22-4   No. 12 sugar (domestic), New York, NYCSC Exchange. Monthly average sugar spot prices (domestic), August 1979–May 1985.

cost of carry to a deferred month, the market is bullish on long-term prices, and vice versa. New-crop months, those beginning with the June contract, are usually traded at a premium to prior old-crop months, although new-crop prices may be at a discount if a large supply is expected in the new crop year. Speculators also conduct intracontract spreads within the crop year or across crop years, or they spread world sugar contracts against domestic contracts.

Sources of Information

There are several important government and private sources of information on sugar. These include the following:

1.   The USDA, through its Foreign Agricultural Service and its Agricultural Marketing Service, provides several sources of data, including *Foreign Agriculture, Sugar and Sweetener Situation,* and *Crop Production.*

2.   F. O. Licht's *International Sugar Report* and *World Sugar Statistics* provide data on world sugar markets.

Notes from a Trader—Sugar

World sugar is one of the few commodities for which there can be a spread between U.S. and London markets. The spread for world sugar, however, depends not only on the sugar prices but also on the dollar-pound exchange rate. The world sugar contract in the United States shows more volatility and is, thus, a better trading vehicle than the domestic sugar contract because fluctuations in the latter are tempered by U.S. quotas and other support policies.

The contract for 112,000 pounds results in an unusually high move of $11.20 per point, which represents relatively high leverage during a price move. Sugar markets sometimes erupt suddenly after quiet periods of months or even years and may catch both the trader and his or her margin clerk unawares.

Many traders who rely most heavily on fundamentals tend to overemphasize cane sugar because of the influence of headlines regarding tropical hurricanes and political upheaval, whereas sugar beet crops do not often provide newsworthy events. The sugar from beets, however, is identical with the sugar from cane, and so the importance of beet sugar is often underestimated. In addition, a high percentage of beet sugar is produced in European countries, from many of which accurate crop news is difficult to obtain.

COCOA

Introduction

Cocoa has been used in Central America, where it is grown, for centuries. It has been so dominant as a drink at times that it has also been a medium of exchange. The use of cocoa spread to Europe during the sixteenth century, but cocoa beans were used only to make a drink until the nineteenth century, when two developments diversified their use. In 1828, a Dutch manufacturer discovered that some of the fat of the cocoa bean, called cocoa butter, could be removed and combined with sugar—the manufacturer ground cocoa beans to produce chocolate. Later in the nineteenth century, a Swiss candy maker discovered that adding milk to the chocolate, thus making milk chocolate, improved the taste of the chocolate.

Supply

Cocoa trees, from which cocoa beans are derived and from which all cocoa and chocolate products are made, grow in tropical climates where the rainfall exceeds 50 inches per year. They grow in an area between 20° north and 20° south of the equator. Prior to the twentieth century, cocoa production was dominated by South and Central American countries, but since then West African countries have become the dominant producers. As shown in Table 22-7, the Ivory Coast is the world's largest producer of cocoa beans, followed closely by Brazil. Ghana, Nigeria, and Asia and Oceania are also significant producers.

Due to the differences in the sources of production and the uses of cocoa, over two-thirds of all cocoa production is traded internationally. The United States is the world's largest importer of cocoa, followed by West Germany, the Netherlands, Russia, England, and France, as shown in Table 22-8. As shown in Table 22-9, the Ivory Coast, Ghana, Brazil, and Nigeria all export more than 140,000 tons of cocoa beans.

Cocoa and chocolate are made from the seeds, or cocoa beans, from the cocoa tree. To be precise, the tree on which cocoa beans are grown is the cacao tree,

TABLE 22-7 WORLD PRODUCTION OF COCOA BEANS IN PRINCIPAL PRODUCING COUNTRIES (in thousands of metric tons)

Crop year*	Brazil	Cameroon	Colombia	Dominican Republic	Ecuador	Equatorial Guinea†	Ghana	Ivory Coast	Malaysia	Mexico	Papua New Guinea	Nigeria	Sao Tome and Principe	Trinidad and Tobago	Venezuela	World total
1980–1981	351	120	36	33	85	8	258	412	49	32	27	155	7	3	14	1685
1981–1982	315	120	39	43	88	8	225	456	61	42	29	182	5	3	15	1725
1982–1983	339	106	40	43	55	9	179	360	68	43	28	156	5	3	14	1542
1983–1984†	308	109	41	42	55	9	159	405	90	38	30	125	5	3	14	1529
1984–1985§	375	115	42	44	100	10	176	475	125	40	30	150	6	3	15	1807

*Crop years are for the 12 months—October 1 to September 30.
†Includes Fernando Po and Rio Muni.
‡Preliminary.
§Forecast.
SOURCE: USDA, Foreign Agricultural Service.

TABLE 22-8 IMPORTS OF COCOA BUTTER—SELECTED COUNTRIES (in metric tons)

Year	Argentina	Australia	Austria	Belgium	Canada	Finland	France	West Germany	Italy	Japan	Netherlands	Norway	Sweden	Switzerland	United Kingdom	United States	U.S.S.R.	Yugoslavia
1980	1868	4532	2485	12,388	3717	2057	14,285	22,790	1211	6,264	16,445	1855	4155	9,117	29,597	34,658	—	1054
1981	1923	4410	3461	11,960	4505	2228	14,170	29,358	1667	10,352	11,021	1875	4234	10,208	19,549	43,196	—	1965
1982	1734	5419	3382	12,281	4860	2333	14,008	30,564	1631	10,615	16,225	2083	4451	9,982	25,820	37,325	—	1009
1983*		6067	3535	12,128	5313	2428	16,690	30,581	2151	9,947	20,224	1892	4704	10,224	31,581	47,981	—	
1984†		6600	3900	12,200	5600	2300	17,100	35,000	2000	9,000	25,000	2100	4500	9,950	29,500	53,000	—	

*Preliminary.
†Estimate.
SOURCE: Gill & Duffus Group PLC.

TABLE 22-9   WORLD EXPORTS OF COCOA BEANS BY PRINCIPAL PRODUCING COUNTRIES   (in thousands of metric tons)

Year	Brazil	Costa Rica	Dominican Republic	Ecuador	Equatorial Guinea	Cameroon	Ghana	Malaysia	Ivory Coast	Papua New Guinea	Nigeria	Sao Tome and Principe	Trinidad and Tobago	Venezuela	Togo	Grand total
1980	123.6	2.2	23.4	14.1	6.0	80.5	218.6	30.6	305.3	28.8	133.9	7.0	2.1	7.8	14.5	1046
1981	125.2	2.0	27.3	24.1	7.5	82.4	180.9	42.4	437.2	27.8	109.0	6.0	3.0	8.0	17.2	1146
1982	143.5	1.9	38.2	38.0	7.5	66.4	217.1	57.7	326.3	28.2	136.7	6.0	2.4	9.5	10.1	1138
1983*	152.8	0.7	38.3	07.0	8.0	80.1	177.3	57.2	286.4	26.3	152.3	3.1	2.0	9.5	09.5	1076

*Preliminary.

SOURCE: USDA, Foreign Agricultural Service.

but due to a misspelling many years ago, probably by English importers, it has come to be known as the cocoa tree and its bean as cocoa beans.

Cocoa production requires considerable time. Cocoa trees do not produce usable quantities of beans for the first 5 years after planting. The quantity of beans produced then increases until the trees reach their peak yield at 15 years, and this yield is maintained through the thirtieth year. Yields then decline until the trees are no longer commercially viable, between the fortieth and fiftieth years. Because of this long cycle, the supply of cocoa beans is extremely inelastic in the short run. Temporary high prices do not cause new plantings, and temporary low prices will not temper the production from trees that are currently producing.

Cocoa beans ripen over several months, so the harvest is not a short-term activity. This continuous supply throughout the year also reduces the seasonableness of cocoa production. For most growing areas, the "main-crop" period is from October through March—more than three-fourths of the world's cocoa crop is produced in this period. The smaller-yield "midcrop" period is from May to August. Brazil's midcrop (called the "Temporao"), however, is usually larger than its main crop.

Because cocoa beans cannot be stored long in the tropical climates in which they are produced, they are typically sold to consuming countries for processing. However, the producing countries, particularly Brazil, are also increasingly processing the beans. The marketing and sales policies of various producing countries differ considerably. The Ghanaian, Nigerian, and other West African crops are, almost without exception, purchased from cocoa farmers by government marketing agencies, which then sell them to buyers for export at administratively determined prices. By contrast, Brazilian farm production is sold through free market channels, although the Brazilian government may establish minimum selling prices and export quotas.

There have been some important implications of these marketing differences. During the last decade, there have been significant increases in Brazilian and Malaysian production. These increases were, to a large extent, a response to the price increases of the period 1975–1977 and resulted from the fact that the cocoa producers themselves received these higher prices for their supply. However, the producers in the Ivory Coast and Ghana did not receive these higher prices because the governments maintained the prices paid to producers at earlier levels while charging more for the beans they sold for export. Thus, while the governments of the Ivory Coast and Ghana have increased their revenue, the production in these countries did not increase.

Brazil has also increased its processing capacity. Domestic processing not only increases the value added for the country but also improves the country's ability to store cocoa because chocolate liquor is more storable than cocoa beans. This enables the country to hold back supplies when prices are low and sell them when prices are high and also reduces transportation costs.

The mature cocoa tree is about 25 feet high. It produces small flowers and fruit during all seasons of the year. The ripe fruit, or pod, resembles a long cantaloupe and has 20 to 40 seeds that look like almonds. The pods are cut from the tree with long knives. They are then cut open, and the beans are taken out.

The beans are fermented via heat. If fermented naturally, the beans are put in piles, covered with banana leaves, and allowed to ferment. Fermentation, which takes approximately 2 to 9 days, generates heat, which kills the bean's germ and activates enzymes which give cocoa its unique flavor.

After fermentation, the beans are dried, by either natural or mechanical means, to prevent molding. Natural drying is simply drying the beans in the sun where they were fermented. Once fermented and dried, these beans become the commercially traded cocoa beans and are bagged for shipment. While cocoa beans are storable, they are not stored where they are produced because they deteriorate quickly in tropical weather.

Once sent to processors, cocoa beans are subject to several processing steps. They are first cleaned; then several types of beans are blended, and the blend of beans is roasted. Blends of beans are used to provide the flavor, color, and aroma desired and to utilize the many types of beans that are received and the types of beans available at a particular time. After roasting, the thin shells, or hulls, of the beans are cracked and removed. Cocoa seeds with shells removed are called "nibs"— the nib is the meat of the cocoa seed. Nibs contain about 54 percent cocoa butter, the natural fat of the cocoa bean.

The nibs, which are very dry, are then crushed and ground mechanically to release the cocoa butter. This mixture of cocoa butter and finely ground nibs is called chocolate "liquor." Due to the heat generated by the crushing, the liquor is a liquid which can be molded to form various shapes. All chocolate products are formed from the chocolate liquor—either the liquor is used as is or it is further processed. The chocolate products include baking chocolate, cocoa, milk chocolate, and sweet and semisweet chocolate.

Baking chocolate is simply the commercial form of chocolate liquor and is used in many baked products. The liquor is cooled and solidified into cakes to produce baking chocolate. Most chocolate liquor is subject to further processing, however. The liquor is pressed hydraulically, and varying degrees of the cocoa butter are squeezed out. This extracted cocoa butter has a variety of uses, but its dominant use is in the manufacture of chocolate candy.

After the cocoa butter has been squeezed out, the remaining mass from the liquor is a large, hard cake called the cocoa cake, which can then be ground into its final usable form, cocoa powder, which is a fine, reddish-brown powder. This powder is judged for quality by the amount of fat (cocoa butter) contained in it. This powder is used as a hot drink by adding milk and sugar or is used by confectioners, bakers, and other food processors. Cocoa used as a drink contains a minimum of 22 percent fat; this is the highest grade of cocoa powder.

Milk chocolate, the most popular of all chocolate products, represents the most common use of cocoa butter. Milk chocolate is manufactured by combining chocolate liquor, sugar, and whole milk with extra cocoa butter. These ingredients are mixed, blended, and rolled, and the resulting milk chocolate is sold as bars, solid chocolate, or candy coatings.

Sweet chocolate and semisweet chocolate are made in the same way as milk chocolate, except that milk is not added to the mixture. These chocolates are sold to confectioners for candy production and are used for the home production of candy, cookies, cakes, and other goods.

Utilization

Cocoa can be considered a unique product because its uses are very limited and it has no major substitutes. Its major end products are milk chocolate, sweet and semisweet chocolate, and cocoa powder. These uses make it a "luxury" good, and as a result it is consumed mainly by high-income countries, mainly the United States, West Germany, Russia, and the Netherlands.

The end products are used directly; as parts of other candy products; by confectioners for other uses; for baking cakes, cookies, and other goods; or as a beverage.

Price Determinants

Because, as indicated, cocoa has few uses and no substitutes, its price depends on its own supply and demand characteristics. Both supply and demand affect cocoa prices.

Current, prospective, or even rumored changes in supply have the greatest impact on cocoa prices. This is due to the fact that as a result of the nature of supply and the areas in which cocoa is produced, it is difficult to estimate supply, particularly in Ghana, Nigeria, and other African countries. Weather, pests, other crop diseases, and shipping strikes, either actual or rumored, can also affect supply and prices. A severe harmattan (a dry, dust-laden wind from the Sahara Desert) in the Ivory Coast will reduce the supply of this large producer. The importance of these factors, as well as the likelihood of rumors, is enhanced because a small number of countries, many of them remote, produce most of the total cocoa production.

On the demand side, because cocoa products are mainly luxury goods, prices have a relatively minor effect on cocoa consumption, while income and population growth have significant effects. However, the manufacturers' use of extenders such as cocoa powder during periods of high prices does cause cocoa use to decrease in response to high cocoa prices. With respect to income, cocoa consumption should continue to grow not only in America and Europe but also in South America and Africa. Cocoa consumption, however, has not grown with income in Asia.

Another commodity whose price may affect cocoa consumption is sugar. Since sugar is a major ingredient of chocolate, an increase in sugar prices should cause an increase in chocolate prices and a decrease in chocolate consumption. However, sugar candy is a major competitor for chocolate, so an increase in sugar prices should cause an increase in chocolate consumption for this reason. Overall, the two effects of sugar prices on chocolate consumption tend to nullify each other. A strong dollar, however, tends to decrease the world price of cocoa.

Given the various components of the cocoa bean production chain—cocoa beans, cocoa butter, chocolate liquor, and cocoa powder—it is reasonable to ask which component determines the prices of the others. In an attempt to derive the maximum amount of cocoa butter from the chocolate liquor, an excess of cocoa powder is usually produced—its price, thus, depends on its own demand characteristics, and its price is often very low. The importance of cocoa butter in producing milk chocolate, sweet chocolate, and semisweet chocolate makes it the dominant cocoa bean product, and its price, thus, tends to determine the prices of both chocolate liquor and cocoa beans.

Cocoa prices are also affected by inventories, which reflect the balance between supply and demand. "Afloat" inventories, in the very short run, and, in the longer run, the level of general inventories affect cocoa prices. Whereas inventories were previously accumulated only in consuming countries, producing countries are now also increasingly processing cocoa beans and storing chocolate liquor, and so inventories are internationally more balanced. Cocoa stocks equal to 3 to 9 months of use are held by manufacturers, with 6 months considered normal, so that the manufacturers can weather price increases. These inventories tend to stabilize prices. The maintenance of large inventories also allows chocolate manufacturers to maintain supplies of various types of cocoa beans so that they have the ingredients for the various blends of chocolate they produce.

Another factor that affects cocoa prices is national policies, as mentioned above. National policies have had a major impact on the supply of cocoa in several countries. Internationally, the International Cocoa Agreement (ICCA) was established to stabilize the world price of cocoa between specified upper and lower bounds. If prices fall below the lower bound, the ICCA can accumulate cocoa stocks; if prices rise above the upper bound, the ICCA can release these stocks. Recently, these price levels have been $1.10 and $1.50 per pound. For several reasons, including the absence of the world's largest producer (the Ivory Coast) and largest consumer (the United States) from its membership and the lack of funds to purchase cocoa for the buffer stock, the ICCA has not been effective in maintaining world cocoa prices. An unsuccessful attempt was made to renegotiate the agreement during March 1985.

On the basis of these factors, the major swings in cocoa prices are likely to continue. Figure 22-5 shows the recent price history of the NYCSC Exchange cocoa futures contract.

Seasonals

As indicated, cocoa is harvested throughout much of the year, and, in addition, a significant amount of cocoa is stored. For these reasons, despite the strong seasonal in cocoa consumption, there is only a very weak seasonal in cocoa prices. There is a weak tendency for cocoa prices to reach their lowest levels late in the first quarter and peak during July and August, consistent with the main-crop harvest period of October to March.

Futures Contracts

Cocoa futures contracts are actively traded on the New York Coffee, Sugar and Cocoa (NYCSC) Exchange and the London Terminal Market. There are also small cocoa futures markets in Paris, Amsterdam, and Hamburg.

In the United States, after the New York Cocoa Exchange merged with the New York Coffee and Sugar Exchange in 1979 to form the New York Coffee,

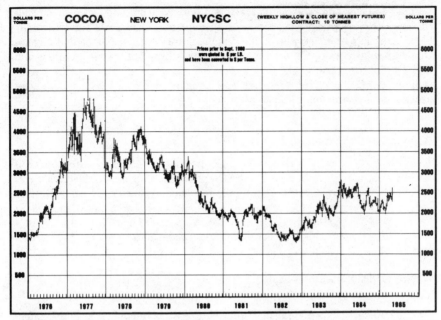

Figure 22-5   Cocoa. [*Commodity Year Book 1985*, ed. *Walter L. Emery* (*Jersey City, N.J.: Commodity Research Bureau, Inc.*).]

Sugar and Cocoa Exchange, it moved with Comex, the New York Cotton Exchange, and the New York Mercantile Exchange to the new trading facilities at the Commodity Exchange Center in the World Trade Center. This joint move provided more traders for the cocoa contract and, thus, more liquidity. During the same year, the size of the contract was changed from 30,000 pounds to 10 metric tons (22,046 pounds), which brought the contract into conformance with the London contract, making it easier to trade against the London contract.

The NYCSC Exchange contract provides for the delivery of Grade A deliverable cocoa (including Ghana, Nigeria, and the Ivory Coast) at a premium of $160 per ton, Grade B deliverable cocoa (including Brazil, Central America, and Venezuela) at a premium of $80 per ton, and Grade C deliverable cocoa (including Sanchez, Haiti, and Malaysia) at par. Delivery can be made at ports in New York, Delaware, and Hampton Roads (Virginia). The delivery months are March, May, July, September, and December, and the minimum price fluctuation is $1 per ton, or $10 per contract.

The cocoa futures contract at the London Cocoa Terminal Market Association has been traded since 1928. It is, of course, traded in British pounds.

Speculative Uses

Cocoa speculators both day-trade on the basis of very short-run price changes and position-trade on the basis of longer-run price changes, and their trading is, in general, based on the fundamental factors discussed above and technical considerations. The supply of cocoa beans is an important element of fundamentally based trading, particularly the supply from countries such as Ghana and Nigeria whose supply data are often difficult to obtain—thus, rumors are frequent and have significant impacts.

Spreading between the New York and London contracts, which includes an exchange rate component, is also practiced.

Sources of Information

The USDA, through its monthly *Foreign Agricultural Circular,* provides crop estimates for foreign countries. The USDA publication *Sugar and Sweetener Reports* provides information on cocoa supply and demand periodically. Gill & Duffus, Ltd., also provides a weekly service on world supply and demand, the quarterly *Cocoa Market Report,* and the annual *Cocoa Statistics.* The Census Bureau provides monthly information on cocoa and cocoa products, U.S. imports, and grind.

Notes from a Trader—Cocoa

Trading cocoa presents special problems for both fundamentalists and technicians. The fundamentalists must rely on supply figures which are notoriously unreliable to make up the price model. The technicians, on the other hand, often face relatively wide bid-ask spreads, commissions and margin requirements that are higher than average, and price movements that represent only $3 per point.

There is no forecasting value in comparing the size of a given midcrop with the size of the following main crop. There is, however, a higher correlation between a late main crop and substandard production. The trend in production and consumption is more important than the respective supply and demand levels. Seasonal studies should also be watched by fundamentalists.

COTTON

Introduction

Cotton is the fibrous overcoat of a seed—the fiber varies in color, length, and weight and in several other ways. Cotton was cultivated in China over 5000 years ago. It was introduced to the west from Persia and India over routes established by Alexander the Great. Weaving techniques were introduced into Spain in the thirteenth century and from there into the Netherlands and, in turn, England in the seventeenth century. The first American mill was established in Rhode Island in 1790. But the invention of the cotton gin, which increased productivity 50 times, by Eli Whitney in 1793 finally made possible the production of enough cotton to supply a commercial textile industry. The cotton gin removes the cotton fibers from the seeds.

Supply

Cotton is grown in over 75 countries throughout the world. Until World War II, the United States was clearly the dominant producer of cotton. But, as shown in Table 22-10, recently China and Russia have joined the United States as the dominant cotton producers. It is interesting to note that the problems Russia has encountered in its grain-producing industries have not affected its cotton industry. China uses a very labor-intensive method of producing cotton, and its crop has been relatively unaffected by bad weather. Turkey and Egypt are other major cotton producers. In the United States, Texas is the leading cotton producer, followed by Mississippi, California, Arizona, and Arkansas.

The four largest consumers of cotton recently have been China, Russia, the United States, and India, as shown in Table 22-11. Japan is the world's largest importer of cotton. France is also a large importer.

Although most of the cotton that is traded internationally is upland cotton, there are many different varieties of this general type of cotton. Upland cotton is differentiated from Sea Island cotton, the type first grown in the southeast, mainly in Georgia and South Carolina. In addition to including most U.S. cotton, upland cotton includes most medium-staple and medium-long-staple cottons in the world, although there are some long-staple and extra-long-staple cottons grown in Egypt, the Sudan, and Peru.

Upland cottons comprise a variety of combinations of grade, staple, and micronaire. Grade is based on three factors: color, foreign matter, and preparation. Color refers to brilliance or spotted character. Foreign matter is the amount of impurity, including dirt, bark, and leaf, in the cotton, which is affected by the types of harvesting and ginning. Preparation refers to the roughness and uniformity of the cotton.

A second characteristic of cotton is the length of its staple: short staple is under $1\frac{3}{16}$ inch; medium and medium-long staple is between $1\frac{3}{16}$ inch and $1\frac{3}{32}$ inches; long staple is from $1\frac{1}{8}$ to $1\frac{5}{16}$ inches; and extra-long staple is over $1\frac{3}{8}$ inches. Upland cottons have medium and medium-long staples.

The third characteristic of cotton, micronaire, also called "mike," is measured by an instrument, whereas the other characteristics are determined by observation. Micronaire determines the maturity of cotton and is measured by airflow through the cotton. This is an important characteristic because overly mature or immature cotton has less value than mature cotton.

The growth of cotton requires about 180 days of no-frost weather. Cotton grows best in hot weather with adequate, uniformly spaced applications of moisture. Variations from these requirements can cause substantial reductions in the size and quality of the crop. As a result, there are four cotton-producing regions in the United States. The first is the southeast (the Carolinas, Georgia, and Alabama), which was the original cotton-growing region in the United States and currently dominates the textile industry. It is not now a major cotton-producing region, however, mainly because it is used for other crops, such as soybeans. The second region is the five-state area of Arkansas, Louisiana, Mississippi (the second largest producer of cotton in the United States), Missouri, and Tennessee. This region grows upland cotton with staples from $1\frac{1}{32}$ to $1\frac{1}{8}$ inches.

TABLE 22-10 WORLD PRODUCTION OF COTTON (in thousands of bales*)

Year beginning Aug. 1	Argentina	Brazil	People's Republic of China	Egypt	India	Iran	Mexico	Pakistan	Israel	Sudan	Colombia	Turkey	United States	U.S.S.R.	World total
1975–1976	645	1800	10,700	1762	5350	640	910	2370	225	500	560	2215	8,500	11,730	54,321
1976–1977	740	2510	10,000	1828	4950	720	1045	2006	247	735	685	2190	10,650	12,050	57,487
1977–1978	1015	2125	9,450	1840	5680	820	1627	2651	295	915	645	2650	14,525	12,700	63,836
1978–1979	800	2530	10,000	2022	6190	610	1570	2183	365	640	373	2200	10,856	11,830	59,482
1979–1980	667	2629	10,158	2221	6274	458	1509	3343	346	523	573	2200	14,629	12,410	64,938
1980–1981	384	2857	12,433	2428	6090	290	1620	3282	359	441	531	2290	11,122	13,165	64,527
1981–1982	696	2939	12,975	2291	6473	338	1440	3438	420	706	406	2244	15,641	12,975	70,579
1982–1983	511	2985	11,950	2117	6320	427	840	3775	399	959	153	2241	11,963	11,950	67,515
1983–1984†	735	2310	12,282	1853	5878	409	1008	2188	427	1006	337	2388	7,771	12,282	67,187
1984–1985‡	750	3858	11,652	1862	6640	425	1200	3750	441	1038	574	2691	13,292	11,652	81,505

*U.S. figures are for running bales (500 pounds); all others are for 478-pound (net weight) bales.

†Preliminary.

‡Estimate.

SOURCE: International Cotton Advisory Committee.

TABLE 22-11 WORLD CONSUMPTION* OF ALL COTTONS IN SPECIFIED COUNTRIES (in thousands of bales—478 pounds net†)

Year beginning Aug. 1	Argentina	Brazil	People's Republic of China	Poland	France	West Germany	India	Italy	Japan	Mexico	Pakistan	United Kingdom	United States	U.S.S.R.	World total
1975–1976	538	2041	10,700	697	931	1022	6100	901	3250	835	2150	494	7300	8750	61,043
1976–1977	538	2091	11,400	697	957	962	5500	923	3150	760	1800	491	6702	8750	60,594
1977–1978	478	2241	12,100	697	846	807	5320	841	3000	740	1900	415	6514	8800	60,825
1978–1979	503	2440	12,700	727	822	777	5626	979	3300	760	1950	447	6352	8888	63,005
1979–1980	468	2589	13,444	782	846	789	5925	1047	3400	757	1972	400	6506	8916	65,320
1980–1981	385	2526	14,938	752	767	792	6314	971	3285	759	2102	220	5891	8971	66,149
1981–1982	359	2619	16,094	697	743	813	5809	994	3423	708	2351	207	5264	8984	65,781
1982–1983	443	2639	16,813	689	765	929	6228	1000	3275	630	2549	207	5503	9039	67,670
1983–1984‡	503	2400	17,200	689	746	970	6453	980	3100	475	2208	234	5926	9100	69,262
1984–1985§	517	2400	17,000	700	738	990	6531	1000	3250	500	2425	234	5400	9150	69,766

*Includes estimates for hand spinning in some countries. Excludes cotton burned or otherwise destroyed.

†Except for the U.S. bales, which are running bales.

‡Preliminary.

§Estimate.

SOURCE: International Cotton Advisory Committee.

The third region is the High Plains of Texas around Lubbock, which is intensively devoted to cotton. This area grows upland cotton with staples averaging approximately 1 inch—for this reason, the cotton sells at a discount to other U.S. cotton. The cotton produced in this region bears the highest risk of any U.S. crop due to droughts during the planting and growing seasons and severe hailstorms and early frosts in the northern areas and at higher altitudes. Oklahoma is another producer of cotton in this region.

The San Joaquin Valley of California developed cotton production during 1920 due to USDA and state policies to develop an alternative supply of Egyptian-type cotton. California is the third largest producer of cotton in the United States. Other western cotton producers are Arizona and New Mexico. Cotton in these states is grown on irrigated land with high per-acre yields. A less important cotton-producing area is the Rio Grande Valley in Texas, which is fairly small but is the earliest-planted region—it is planted in mid-March, 2½ months before planting in the High Plains.

The planting season for cotton in the United States begins as early as mid-March in the Rio Grande Valley of Texas and as late as mid-June in the High Plains of Texas. But the majority of U.S. cotton is planted during April. Similarly, although the harvest occurs as early as late June in the Rio Grande Valley and as late as December in the High Plains, most of the harvesting occurs in October and November. The crop year for cotton is considered to begin on August 1.

Utilization

Approximately one-half of the cotton consumed in the United States is used in the manufacture of clothes. The remainder is used for household and industrial uses. Given these uses, the demand for cotton is fairly stable.

While synthetic materials have not affected the worldwide demand for cotton, they have affected the U.S. demand. Synthetics have made major inroads in the U.S. market, and the 1982 U.S. consumption of cotton was at its lowest since 1911. Since the introduction of rayon in the 1930s and the more recent introduction of polyester, synthetics have grown in use due to their lower cost, their resilience, and the fact that they do not need to be ironed. In addition, there has been an increase in the level of cotton and noncotton textile imports from the Far East and China.

After cotton is harvested, various types of buyers (ginners, brokers, mill buyers, and shippers) begin to accumulate it from the growers and from each other for marketing purposes. Figure 22-6 shows the physical flow of cotton. October–November and February–March are periods of heavy mill consumption.

The different demand factors for both raw cotton and finished products exert their influence on different time schedules, and their total influence is complex and difficult to predict. Much of the raw cotton is acquired by vertically integrated companies that spin the raw cotton into yarn, weave the yarn into cloth, and finish the cloth. Most plants, integrated or not, are located along the Atlantic seaboard.

Some of the end uses for cotton are trousers, bedding, shirts, towels, men's underwear, fabrics, and dresses. Cotton's share of the textile market has decreased to less than 50 percent in recent years due to inroads made by synthetic fibers.

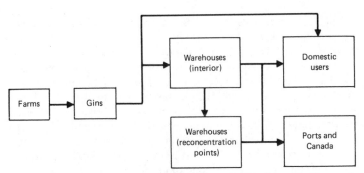

Figure 22-6   Physical flow of U.S. cotton. (*USDA, Economic Research Service*.)

Price Determinants

Cotton prices are determined by demand changes, supply changes, and government policies. Demand changes are important and their impact is significant, but such changes occur slowly. As indicated, the introduction of synthetics has reduced the use of cotton in the United States substantially. On the other hand, the increases in the use of cotton denim have increased cotton use. Imports of foreign cotton and noncotton textiles have also reduced U.S. cotton production.

On the other hand, changes in supply can affect cotton prices significantly and quickly. Planting intentions and acreage allotments give early indications of production levels. But weather developments throughout the planting, growing, and harvesting seasons can sometimes materially affect both the quantity and quality of production. In general, too little rainfall tends to retard germination and plant growth, whereas too much moisture reduces fruiting and causes late maturity. Temperature extremes also reduce the quality and quantity of the crop. For example, rain and cold weather may delay planting, and if there is any great amount of late cotton as a result, early frosts may kill it before it can reach maturity. A wet and cool fall can result in heavy boll rot. Insect pests—boll weevils, bollworms, and thrips—abound, but they can be successfully held down by insecticides if rain does not wash the insecticides off the plants.

The stocks of cotton, as measured by the free-market carry-over, also affect prices. A large carry-over will mitigate price increases, but a small carry-over will make it easy for prices to increase.

Government policies also affect cotton prices—during this century, they have had as great an effect on cotton prices and production as on the prices and production of any other commodity. The government may also have had as great an effect on cotton production as the weather. Government protection of cotton began in 1929, when the Agricultural Marketing Act established a loan rate for cotton at 16 cents per pound. Later, during the 1940s, 1950s, and 1960s, under a program of U.S. price supports, foreign cotton production grew considerably, and the U.S. cotton carry-over also grew considerably, reaching 17 million bales in the mid-1960s, with the Commodity Credit Corporation owning almost three-fourths of the total. Basically, U.S. farmers were growing for government consumption rather than for the U.S. private market or for export.

While the government moved toward a free-market orientation during the 1970s, there is still an extremely complex government support program for cotton which includes parity and loan levels, acreage reduction programs (ARP), and payment-in-kind (PIK) and export programs and which continues to provide signals for farmers that are not consistent with market needs. Because of price support loans for cotton above world prices, farmers continue to produce cotton and turn it over to the government. And U.S. textile manufacturers who cannot afford the high supported U.S. cotton prices and are prevented from importing lower-priced foreign cotton because of import quotas continue to become less competitive internationally.

For example, the 1985 program for upland cotton had a target price of 81 cents per pound, while that for strict low-middling, 1 1/16-inch cotton was 57.3 cents per pound. To become eligible for the target price and loan provision, farmers had to plant no more than 70 percent of their upland cotton base acreage and devote the rest of their acreage to conservation uses. There were other complex parts of this program. There was also a government program for U.S. extra-long-staple (ELS) cotton. There was no payment-in-kind component for the 1985 program. This program was considered attractive for farmers, and government cotton stocks are likely to increase.

Table 22-12 shows recent U.S. data on the supply of and demand for cotton which affect U.S. cotton prices.

Seasonals

Cotton prices follow the expected seasonal cycle, reaching a late-fall low during the harvest period and then a subsequent high between May and July, although this seasonal pattern is not completely reliable.

Futures Contracts

The New York Cotton Exchange (NYCE) was established in September 1870. A cotton futures market was established in New Orleans 5 months later, and subsequently, cotton futures exchanges were organized in Liverpool, Bremen, Alexandria, and Bombay, all places where spot cotton was traded.

In the early 1920s, cotton futures trading volume reached its peak, and even in the late 1940s the dollar volume of cotton futures traded equaled the trade in all other commodities combined and exceeded by several times the dollar volume of stocks traded on the New York Stock Exchange. The government price and production control programs which started during the depression of the 1930s, however, progressively supplanted the influence of the free market. Because of this and other factors, the world role of the United States as a cotton producer has declined, and the activity of cotton futures contracts has correspondingly decreased.

During the 1950s and early 1960s, trading volume for the existing cotton contract was very low, due primarily to the effect of government programs on cotton

TABLE 22-12 SUPPLY AND DISTRIBUTION OF ALL COTTON IN THE UNITED STATES (in thousands of bales—480 pounds net weight)

Crop year beginning Aug. 1	Supply												Distribution		
	Carry-over, Aug. 1						Ginnings								
	Privately owned				CCC-held	Total stocks	Current crop* less ginnings	New crop†	Total‡	Imports	City crop	Total	Mill consumption	Exports	Total
	At mills	In public storage	Elsewhere	Total											
1978–1979	1120	2537	400	4057	1269	5326	10,405	72	10,477	4	0	15,807	6352	6180	12,532
1979–1980	928	1967	250	3145	637	3782	14,190	200	14,390	5	0	18,177	6506	9229	15,735
1980–1981	955	1280	250	2485	542	3027	10,627	44	10,671	28	1	13,897	5891	5926	11,817
1981–1982	883	1035	25	1943	652	2595	15,106	40	15,146	26	0	17,767	5264	6567	11,831
1982–1983	830	1510	300	2640	3759	6399	11,486	2	11,488	3	0	17,907	5513	5207	10,720
1983–1984§	755	1890	150	2795	4766	7561	7,502	165	7,665	9		15,075	5926	6786	12,712
1984–1985¶	795	1171	350	2316	590	2906							5300	6065	11,365

*Less ginnings prior to August 1.
†Ginnings prior to August 1 end of season.
‡Includes in-season ginnings.
§Preliminary.
¶Estimate.

SOURCE: USDA, Economic Research Service.

prices, including the buildup of government (CCC) stocks. However, on March 22, 1967, the New York Cotton Exchange initiated the trading of a new No. 2 cotton futures contract. Both volume and open interest grew substantially during the 1970s following the liquidation of the government stock and the resulting three bull markets. The futures contract is based on 100 bales, or 50,000 pounds of cotton. The price is quoted in cents per pound, and the minimum fluctuation is ¹⁄₁₀₀ cent per pound, or $5 per contract. The contract calls for delivery at ports in New Orleans, Houston, and Galveston and at interior points in Memphis and Greenville. The deliverable product is strict low-middling, 1¹⁄₁₆-inch premium mike: "strict low-middling" refers to the grade, which is low due mainly to machine picking, which gathers impurities; "1¹⁄₁₆-inch" refers to the staple length; and "premium mike" refers to the micronaire. The crop year for U.S. cotton begins on August 1. The delivery months are October, December, March, May, and July.

The new No. 2 cotton futures contract has remained a successful futures contract for speculation and hedging. The open interest is approximately 20,000 contracts, and there is a reasonable trading volume.

Figure 22-7 shows the recent price history of the NYCE No. 2 cotton futures contract.

Figure 22-7   No. 2 cotton. [*Commodity Year Book 1985*, ed. *Walter L. Emery* (*Jersey City, N.J.: Commodity Research Bureau, Inc.*).]

Sources of Information

The USDA is the main source of information on cotton. Particularly useful are its *Cotton and Wool Situation* reports and its weekly *Cotton Market Review*. In addition, the USDA (Economic Research Service) publishes the *Cotton Situation Report* in January, March, May, July, September, and October—this is also a particularly useful report.

The U.S. Census Bureau publishes several reports that provide data on ginnings, cotton consumption, stocks at mills and in storage, cotton goods inventories, and unfilled orders, as well as other statistics. The *Weekly Trade Report* of the New York Cotton Exchange is a useful source of general information on cotton and exchange trading. The International Cotton Advisory Committee and the National Cotton Council also publish useful reports.

Notes from a Trader—Cotton

Long-term changes have in the past affected the trading volume of the cotton futures contract and continue to affect it. Trading went from very active early in the century to moribund during the 1950s and early 1960s to very active again. Currently, long-run changes, mainly the growing use of synthetics and an increase in cotton imports, seem to be again reducing activity. However, the demand for natural fibers seems to be such that the U.S. use of cotton and the ability of U.S. producers to supply the cotton will keep the cotton futures contract active.

There are several types of cotton. In evaluating supply-and-demand conditions, traders should make certain that the conditions they are considering affect the type of cotton that is represented by their contracts. It is disconcerting to consider an increase in the demand for short-staple cotton as favorable to one's long position only to find that the demand for long-staple cotton is declining.

The cotton futures contract does not lend itself well to intercommodity spreads. The cotton spreader is limited to intramarket spreads, either within a crop year or across crop years.

ORANGE JUICE

Introduction

While oranges are grown in several countries throughout the world, the United States has been the world's dominant grower, as shown in Table 22-13. However, very recently Brazil's orange production has grown to equal that of the United States. Spain, Japan, and Italy are also major orange growers. In the United States, Florida is the dominant source of oranges, as shown in Table 22-14; it is responsible for approximately 67 percent of the U.S. crop. California is also a significant grower, responsible for approximately 30 percent, with Arizona and Texas also growing small amounts.

Oranges have been grown in Florida since the 1500s and in California since the 1700s. The Florida orange differs from the California orange due to the variation in the climates of the two states; the Florida orange is juicier, contains less acid, and is paler in color and thinner-skinned.

TABLE 22-13 WORLD PRODUCTION OF ORANGES (INCLUDING TANGERINES) (in thousands of metric tons)

Season	Al-geria	Argen-tina	Brazil	Aus-tralia	Greece	Israel	Italy	Japan	Mexico	Mo-rocco	Spain	Turkey	South Africa	United States	World total
1974–1975	480	1014	4,065	438	539	1016	2098	3952	1110	583	2479	622	499	9,913	30,660
1975–1976	480	958	4,065	389	567	995	1931	4234	905	552	2643	645	564	10,170	30,918
1976–1977	506	990	3,754	391	533	968	2258	3575	1283	784	2489	671	463	10,144	30,567
1977–1978	508	990	4,321	352	455	949	1950	4120	750	1070	1914	785	600	9,268	28,479
1978–1979		925	6,471	451	506	992	1959	3637	1398	827	2526	806	600	8,310	24,050
1979–1980		921	9,282	448	360	943	2104	3945	1810	1024	2597	835	565	10,734	38,502
1980–1981		921	9,872	381	561	812	2057	3229	1720	965	2605	862	569	9,514	36,725
1981–1982*		820	10,853	414	745	1123	2131	3150	1820	988	2468	850	577	6,895	35,446
1982–1983†					691	977	1800	3242	1600	999	2405	860		8,635	
1983–1984†														6,566	

*Preliminary.

†Estimate.

SOURCE: USDA, Foreign Agricultural Service.

TABLE 22-14 U.S. SALIENT STATISTICS OF ORANGES AND ORANGE JUICE

Season	Production, millions of boxes*					Farm price, dollars per box	Farm value, millions of dollars	Frozen concentrated orange juice—Florida, millions of gallons				Florida crop processed chilled products, millions of boxes					Yield per box, gallons
	Arizona	California	Florida	Texas	Total			Carry-in	Pack	Total supply	Total season movement	Frozen concentrates	Juice	Sections and salads	Other processed products	Total processed products	
1976–1977	4.0	45.3	186.8	6.9	243.0	3.34	811.2	29.7	178.7	196.2	180.9	148.7	27.3	.4	8.8	185.2	1.07
1977–1978	2.6	42.6	167.8	6.1	220.1	5.45	1198.7	29.1	185.0	200.8	185.1	132.2	25.3	.4	8.1	166.0	1.23
1978–1979	2.9	37.3	164.0	6.4	210.6	6.15	1296.0	33.5	206.2	221.9	206.1	130.2	22.8	.3	6.5	159.8	1.34
1979–1980	3.5	59.4	206.7	4.0	273.6	4.76	1304.2	37.4	256.4	293.8	239.0	174.9	24.4	.3	7.0	206.6	1.34
1980–1981	2.6	65.3	172.4	4.3	244.6	4.85	1327.7	57.3	249.6	306.9	240.6	145.3	19.6	.2	6.4	171.5	1.21
1981–1982	3.1	41.9	125.8	5.9	176.7	5.30	1295.3	69.0	214.9	283.9	230.5	105.2	16.3	.2	4.5	126.1	1.28
1982–1983	3.8	76.1	139.6	5.7	225.2	6.61	1167.8	53.4	228.4	281.8	239.0	114.6	18.1	.2	2.7	135.5	1.48
1983–1984†	1.8	48.3	116.7	2.5	169.3	6.56	1457.0	42.8	239.9	282.7	228.3	94.0	17.0	.4	3.1	114.4	1.29
1984–1985†	2.7	54.0	104.0	—	160.7			54.4									1.33

*Fruit ripened on trees but destroyed prior to picking is not included.

†Preliminary.

SOURCE: USDA, Economic Research Service; Florida Citrus Processors Association.

The popularity of frozen orange juice, especially since World War II, has caused an increase in the production of oranges and also the development of the orange juice concentrate industry in Florida and its growth to its present capacity of approximately 300 million gallons a year. Frozen concentrated orange juice (FCOJ) was invented by Dr. L. G. MacDowell of the Florida Citrus Commission and two colleagues in 1947, the year the patent was given. Several scientists had previously concentrated orange juice but had found that the orange flavor disappeared with the water. Dr. MacDowell's innovation was to first overconcentrate the juice by reducing it to a thick, syrupy liquid and then add fresh orange juice and other flavorings to restore the natural taste and appearance lost during the evaporation process.

Sugar is the important ingredient in FCOJ. When processors buy fruit for concentrate, they are concerned with "pounds solids," not oranges; that is, they want solids dissolved in the juices. These solids, which remain as concentrate after the water is evaporated, consist primarily of sugar. Oranges get sweeter as the crop year progresses. Valencias provide the best juice because they have the greatest number of pounds of solids per box. Florida produces most of the FCOJ in the United States, and about 75 percent of its orange production is used for FCOJ.

Supply

Florida is the dominant orange grower in the United States and in the world. There are different harvesting periods in Florida for different types of oranges. The most active harvesting period for early and mid-season varieties is the last 2 weeks of January. The harvest period for late oranges is from mid-April to mid-June. The late oranges are primarily Valencia oranges, which are valued for their juice flavor and are the main ingredient in the production of FCOJ. The processing period for the Florida orange crop is from January until June or July. The crop year for Florida oranges, thus, is considered to be from December of one year until November of the next year.

The total U.S. supply of FCOJ is subject to considerable variability because Florida is the dominant producer and its growing region is subject to damaging freezes, which severely reduce supply. In this regard, Florida FCOJ production is similar to Brazilian coffee production. The FCOJ season begins in October with the USDA's crop estimate for the following year. At this time the concern over the winter freeze begins. Although there is no scientific evidence to support the statement that winter freezes should occur near full moons, recent freezes have, in fact, occurred near full moons. For this reason, prices tend to rise prior to the monthly full moons and, if a freeze does not occur, decline thereafter. The December full moon is particularly significant because a freeze at that time not only would lower the current orange yield but also could kill the trees, thus causing supply problems for several years. Thus, the potential increase in the futures price prior to the December full moon and the decrease afterward are particularly significant.

Since the beginning of FCOJ futures contracts, there have been six major freezes—during the winters of 1971–1972, 1976–1977, 1980–1981, 1981–1982, 1983–1984, and 1984–1985. With regard to the four freezes of the 1980s, the loss from prefreeze projections was 23 percent during 1980–1981, 28 percent during 1981–1982, 39 percent during 1983–1984, and 17 percent during 1984–1985 according to the USDA Statistical Reporting Service. Few crops respond as adversely to severe weather as oranges. While mildly adverse weather will cause lower juice yields, a drop in temperature to 25°F damages the tree as well as the fruit, and lower temperatures may destroy the trees (replacement trees require 5 years to produce). Although artificial heat is used to protect the oranges and trees during a freeze, its effectiveness is limited.

Production responded well to the two freezes during the 1970s, although more tree plantings were shifted to southern Florida from north central Florida. But the consecutive freezes of 1980–1981 and 1981–1982 reduced Florida yields, particularly the latter freeze, which also affected southern Florida.

Brazilian orange production has increased significantly in recent years, as indicated above. Central American production has also increased, but to a lesser extent. The reduced Florida production due to four freezes in 5 years has provided a U.S. market for Brazilian production. Florida orange producers are concerned that given their recent freezes and the improved production and processing capacity and ability of Brazil, with the Brazilian government support, Brazil's contribution to worldwide supply and supply to the U.S. market will continue to increase.

Utilization

Most oranges were once shipped fresh and squeezed into juice in the home. Now significant parts of the crop are converted into concentrates which can be frozen and stored. In fact, the dominant use for some types of oranges, such as Florida Valencias, is for juice. Although the orange is used primarily for its juice, there are useful by-products. These include the peel, which can be candied, dried, or made into marmalade, pectin, or orange oil, which is used for flavoring or perfumes. The pulp can also be used for livestock feed. The demand for orange juice in the United States has continued to increase. Recently, however, the use of chilled juice has grown more than the use of frozen orange juice.

After FCOJ leaves the processor's plant, it is sent to institutional distributors, to wholesale grocers, or to supermarket chains.

Price Determinants

While the price of any commodity is affected by both supply and demand, supply has the dominant influence on orange and orange juice prices. And, as indicated, weather has a greater effect on the supply of oranges and orange juice than on the supply of almost any other commodity. Winter freezes, particularly during the freeze-scare period, usually considered to be from late November to mid-February in Florida, affect the supply of oranges and the price of FCOJ significantly. Even threatened or rumored freezes may have short-run effects on FCOJ prices.

In addition to warmth, an orange tree requires considerable moisture, and in some areas irrigation is required. Drought during blooming is especially serious. Trees might also suffer from inadequately drained soil, too much irrigation, and insects. Sudden heat waves can cause young fruit to fall off the trees. Strong winds may also prove dangerous.

In extremely warm areas oranges may ripen during the fall and winter months, but in cooler climates they ripen in the spring or summer a year after blooming. Some ripen early, some in midseason, and some late. In California, they ripen throughout the year.

Current supply is affected by the amount of frozen orange juice concentrate produced (the pack), movement to retail outlets, and stocks on hand. Juice available for concentrates is affected by variables such as the number of trees, the amount of fruit per tree, the size of the oranges, and drop.

On the demand side, the size of the population and the income level affect prices. Because the demand for FCOJ is more elastic with respect to price than the demand for many other commodities, a change in price will affect the level of demand. Table 22-14 provides some data on the U.S. supply of and demand for oranges and orange juice.

Up through the 1970s, the Florida supply of FCOJ was the only supply factor in determining prices. However, with increasing Brazilian production and the four severe freezes during the early 1980s, imports of Brazilian oranges and FCOJ have begun to influence U.S. prices. Large imports during these four freezes mitigated the degree of price increases. Continued and increased imports of Brazilian oranges and FCOJ may not only make inroads in Florida production but also, to some extent, stabilize prices during Florida freezes. Overall, unlike the market for most other commodities, the market for FCOJ has been primarily a domestic U.S. market. However, it appears that the U.S. FCOJ market will become a more international market in the future, with significant imports.

Figure 22-8 shows the significant volatility of FCOJ futures prices recently, including the significant increases during early 1981, 1982, 1984, and 1985 due to the freezes.

Seasonals

FCOJ futures prices tend to reach a peak prior to the harvest, typically during November, and then decline to a trough just after the harvest, usually during June. Even though this seasonal is fairly strong over several seasons, it is unreliable for any particular season—specific supply and demand factors, particularly the former, often prevail.

There is also particular volatility prior to and during the freeze-scare period, which is from late November until mid-February in Florida. Significant price changes often occur after the first official Florida orange crop estimate is given in October.

Futures Contracts

A futures contract on FCOJ began to be traded at the New York Cotton Exchange during 1966. The contract was developed with considerable support from the growers, the processors, and the canners of concentrate, and the contract proved

Figure 22-8 Orange juice. [*Commodity Year Book 1985, ed. Walter L. Emery (Jersey City, N.J.: Commodity Research Bureau, Inc.).*]

immediately successful. The open interest exceeded 5000 contracts within 18 months, and trading volume was heavy.

The contract is based on the delivery of 15,000 pounds of frozen orange juice concentrate from Florida warehouses licensed by the exchange. The minimum price change is 0.05 cent per pound, or $7.50 per contract. The trading months are January, March, May, July, September, and November. As indicated, the crop year for Florida oranges and the marketing year for FCOJ are considered to be from December 1 to November 30. Brazil's growing season is considered to begin on July 1.

Speculative Uses

Speculation in the FCOJ contract is done by both retail speculators and trade speculators in the orange and orange juice industries. Given the importance of weather to supply, much speculation is based on forecasts of weather and actual weather conditions. Cold, excess rain, and excess dryness all cause sharp changes in FCOJ futures prices. Trade speculators include orange growers and the cash market fruit dealers (the "bird dogs"); the latter usually constantly vary their hedges on the basis of changing conditions.

Although there is a crop year in FCOJ and intracontract crop spreads can be done, they are not a common type of speculative trade.

Sources of Information

Given the importance of Florida in the production of oranges, publications from Florida, as well as from the USDA, are very important sources of information on oranges and FCOJ.

The USDA *Fruit Situation* report is issued four times a year (in February, July, September, and November); it summarizes the available supply and consumption figures and provides analysis. The USDA also publishes the annual *Summary of Citrus Fruit Industry* during October; among other things, this publication estimates the orange crop for the following season. The USDA also issues *Monthly Cold Storage Reports* (released during the middle of each month), which indicates the frozen orange juice stocks at the beginning of each month. Finally, the USDA issues the *Crop Production Report* six times a year; this report summarizes the conditions of Florida oranges and citrus crops.

Weekly Statistics, from the Florida Canners Association, provides weekly statistics on carry-over, pack, movement, goods on hand, and utilization for Florida fruits and fruit juices. The Florida Citrus Manual regularly publishes the *Triangle* and also a weekly summary of citrus statistics.

The Florida Crop and Livestock Reporting Service of the Florida Department of Agriculture publishes the annual *Citrus Summary,* which provides data on acreage, production, utilization, prices, and shipments of citrus fruits from all states. The reporting service also provides other statistical information on a more frequent basis. The Florida Citrus Processors Association provides movement data each Thursday.

Finally, *Traders Position,* released by the New York Cotton Exchange each Tuesday, provides the positions of traders during the previous week.

Notes from a Trader—Orange Juice

Trading the frozen orange juice contract is attractive for those who find sudden significant price changes appealing. For those whose pocketbooks or nerve cannot stand sudden adversity of possibly considerable magnitude, other markets may provide better trading vehicles.

With all the factors affecting orange juice prices, one factor dominates: Florida weather. Reports of cold waves, drought, or untimely rainfall can affect prices drastically. The short history of the orange juice futures market, the absence of other similar futures markets, and the relatively recent history of the orange juice concentrate industry do not present the fundamentalist with nearly as much basic information as is available for other commodities.

The trader should beware of judging demand by the size of the concentrate movement immediately after a price increase. Chain stores and other major buyers are normally offered a brief period of price protection during which they can build stocks—which they naturally do whenever a significant price increase is announced.

LUMBER

Introduction

The increasing demand for new houses in the United States since World War II and the resulting general increase in construction have been the major reasons for the phenomenal growth of the softwood industry in the United States. Wood is divided into two categories: hardwood and softwood. There are two ways to distinguish these two types. First, relatively soft woods with an open grain are classified as softwoods, while relatively hard woods with a closed grain are classified as hardwoods. Second, softwoods have exposed seeds, usually in the form of cones (thus, they are called "conifers")—they are also called "evergreens," since they retain their needles throughout the year. On the other hand, hardwoods conceal their seeds in a fruit. They also have leaves and are typically deciduous; that is, they lose their leaves in the fall. Only softwood is considered in this section because it is the type of wood mainly used in construction and on which futures contracts have been based.

The lumber industry is distributed widely throughout the United States—all 50 states engage in lumber production. About 80 percent of all lumber produced is softwood. The western states, mainly Oregon, Washington, and northern California, produce about 65 percent of the softwood, with the southern states, mainly eastern Texas, southeastern Oklahoma, and all states east to the Atlantic Coast and south of the Ohio River, producing about 25 percent. Essentially, all the hardwood is produced in the eastern states.

While lumber imports have increased to over 30 percent of U.S. consumption, virtually all of these imports are from Canada, mainly imports of softwoods such as Douglas fir, western pine, and cedar. Most Canadian softwood is produced in British Columbia. The United States also exports a modest amount of lumber. The United States imports very little Canadian plywood, compared with lumber imports, due to a U.S. duty and different grading systems. Thus, the lumber industry, unlike most of the other commodity industries considered, is predominantly a domestic industry, with the exception of participation by Canada. Africa, Asia (with the possible exception of Japan), and Europe are not important participants in the U.S. lumber industry.

Because the only currently active futures contract is based on lumber (two-by-fours) and there is no futures contract based on plywood, the emphasis in this chapter is on lumber. Plywood, however, is considered in less detail.

Supply

There are several steps in the production of lumber and plywood. The first is the logging, or harvesting, of the timber—that is, cutting down the tree and transporting it to the mill. The logging may be done by small independent concerns, by companies that also include the mill, or by large, integrated lumber companies. But in any case, the logging is, to a large extent, done on land not owned by the logger.

The ownership of commercial forestland is divided between lumber firms, private individuals, local and state governments, and the federal government. In the United

States, over half of the softwood timber is publicly owned. Loggers bid competitively for "stumpage" on both government-owned and privately owned lands. Stumpage costs are important costs in the production of lumber and plywood.

The trees are felled with chain saws or mobile machines, skidded to a collection point, and transported to a mill by water or truck. Due to rugged terrain, it may be difficult to transport the logs. Bad weather, particularly rain (which makes the ground muddy) and fire (caused by dry weather), can make it even more difficult. Independent loggers sell their logs to mills at market prices, and their transportation route depends on the mill to which they have sold the logs, whereas integrated companies (those which include both loggers and mills) have regular transportation routes.

The second part of the lumber industry is the sawmill. At the mill, the logs are either stored in water or stored in open air—if stored in open air, they are sprayed to protect them from insects and to prevent moisture loss. In addition, the logs are debarked—the bark chips are sold for various uses. At this point, the logs are either sawed for lumber production or peeled for plywood production. Logs used for plywood (veneer logs) sell at premiums of approximately 60 percent to logs used for lumber (sawlogs).

The sawlogs are sawed to size depending on the size of the logs; passed through an edger, which evens the edges; and brought to a trimmer, which trims the ends. The lumber is then sorted by grade and size and then, in some cases, seasoned— that is, dried by either kiln or air to remove the moisture. Over half the lumber is kiln-dried, only a small amount is air-dried, and the remainder is sold green. Finally, the lumber is planed to make the surfaces smooth. Then, the lumber is prepared for shipping by being banded (with a steel band), wrapped (with a plastic sheet or a waterproof paper sheet), and loaded onto railroad cars. Wholesalers then play an important part in marketing the lumber, at times selling the lumber in transit from the mills.

Plywood is produced in a very different manner. The logs are cut into 8-foot 4-inch peeler blocks, which are subjected to hot water to make them easy to peel. The blocks are then peeled while being rotated on a lathe—a large stationary knife peels off a ribbon of wood known as veneer. The veneer is then cut into sheets and dried. Several veneer sheets are stacked (with the grains of adjacent sheets perpendicular to one another), glued, and then subjected to heat and pressure. The plywood, which is very strong for its weight, is then graded for smoothness and for knotholes and other defects. Plywood is also typically transported by rail— except in the south, where it is usually transported by truck.

Table 22-15 provides some statistics regarding lumber in the United States, while Table 22-16 provides monthly data on lumber production.

Utilization

The major demand for softwood lumber comes from five broad categories. The uses, with their recent percentage of all U.S. softwood consumption in parentheses, are residential construction (40 percent); nonresidential construction (14 percent); repairs and remodeling (29 percent); and materials handling and other uses (3

TABLE 22-15 SALIENT STATISTICS OF LUMBER IN THE UNITED STATES

| Year | Industrial roundwood* used for | | | | | Imports | Exports | Apparent consumption | Fuelwood consumption* | Apparent production and consumption, all products* | National forest stumpage prices, dollars per 1000 board feet | | | | | |
	Lumber	Pulp products	Plywood and veneer	Other products†	Total†						All eastern hardwoods	Douglas fir	Southern pine	Western hemlock	Ponderosa pine	Maple
1976	5475	3805	1355	380	11,815	2840	1870	12,785	600	13,390	34.90	176.20	87.00	79.70	101.80	36.60
1977	5730	3645	1425	385	11,960	3310	1795	13,475	1030	14,505	37.90	225.90	100.30	89.30	131.40	41.20
1978	5825	3745	1460	400	12,240	3755	1845	14,145	1570	15,720	41.10	250.30	134.50	113.60	164.70	57.40
1979	5680	4110	1370	405	12,510	3655	2135	14,030	2270	16,300	46.80	394.40	155.20	200.80	239.00	33.90
1980	4860	4390	1175	385	11,645	3250	2350	12,550	3115	15,665	52.40	432.20	155.40	212.70	206.10	37.40
1981	4395	4135	1180	355	10,710	3165	2100	11,775	3650	15,425	50.90	350.20	172.00	163.40	195.20	41.50
1982	3890	3955	1070	325	9,965	3010	1995	10,975	3685	14,665	56.40	118.20	127.20	44.50	66.90	34.30
1983†											60.10	161.60	140.60	62.20	104.00	25.00

*Millions of cubic feet.

†Excludes fuelwood. Includes cooperage logs, poles and piling, fence posts, etc.

‡Preliminary.

SOURCE: National Lumber Manufacturers Association, U.S. Department of Commerce, and Forest Service.

TABLE 22-16 LUMBER PRODUCTION* IN THE UNITED STATES (in millions of board feet)

Year	Jan.	Feb.	Mar.	Apr.	May	June	July	Aug.	Sept.	Oct.	Nov.	Dec.	Total
1976	2821	2804	3144	3209	2960	2949	2963	3265	3226	3305	2972	2921	35,760
1977	2822	2930	3388	3260	3253	3160	2975	3290	3368	3268	2839	2944	37,667
1978	2843	2904	3222	3127	3203	3333	2988	3263	3285	3333	3102	2931	37,657
1979	2877	2877	3306	3119	3219	3143	3018	3355	3131	3412	2914	2631	37,061
1980	2798	2855	2879	2257	2307	2486	2479	2783	2818	2903	2480	2329	31,632
1981	2523	2542	2818	2780	2651	2588	2483	2554	2307	2379	1831	1765	29,592
1982	1810	1891	2148	2281	2251	2338	2376	2560	2445	2333	2247	2004	25,795
1983†	2484	2481	2682	2623	2645	2718	2585	2714	2748	2787	2504	2345	31,479
1984†	2740	2678	3104	2983	2828	2968	2685	2933	2776	3154			

*Adjusted with Census reports on lumber production.

†Preliminary.

SOURCE: National Lumber Manufacturers Association.

percent), with the latter including furniture, other manufactured products, railroad rails, and exports.

In residential construction, which represents the largest use of softwood, the lumber is used for framing the structure (that is, forming the skeleton of the structure), and the plywood is used for sheathing (that is, providing the initial cover of the structure). The construction of single-family residential dwellings is critical to the demand for lumber because each single-family dwelling uses twice as much or more lumber and plywood as a multifamily dwelling. Often steel or metal studs are substituted for lumber in multifamily dwellings.

Price Determinants

The determinants of the price of lumber relate mainly to supply and demand factors—government policies have only a minor effect on the lumber industry. On the supply side, consider the costs of production. The major costs of lumber production are raw material costs, transportation costs, and labor costs. Stumpage costs are the major raw material costs. Stumpage costs depend on the willingness of commercial forestland owners, including the government, to lease the land and the price they charge. As indicated, veneer logs are considerably more expensive than sawlogs. There are two phases of transportation and the transportation costs. The first phase is transporting the logs from where they are felled to the mill. Weather may affect the cost of this phase of transportation. Rain or melting snow, particularly during the spring, can cause mud. On the other hand, dry weather, particularly during the summer, can cause fires or threats of fire, which may cause logging to stop.

The second phase is transportation from the mill to the market. Since most lumber and plywood is transported by rail, railroad strikes may prevent delivery of the lumber or plywood to the market—such strikes cause lumber prices to rise, at least in consumption areas away from the mills. Railcar shortages will have an effect similar to that of railroad strikes. Reductions in the level of mill operations due to mill strikes or a shortage of logs also tend to raise lumber prices. Stocks of lumber and plywood in consumption areas or at the sawmills will alleviate these supply problems for a short time, if transportation from the mills to the consumption areas is not interrupted.

On the demand side, while lumber and plywood have many uses, residential construction is the dominant use. Thus, housing starts, published monthly by the U.S. Department of Commerce, are, on a seasonally adjusted annual basis, an important indication of lumber and plywood demand. Housing authorizations and housing competitions are also closely watched indicators of lumber and plywood demand. The housing cycle in the United States is very volatile, and this volatility, in turn, can cause significant volatility in the lumber-producing industry. For example, the capacity utilization of the sawmill industry has recently ranged from a low of 50 percent during 1981 and early 1982 to a high of 94 percent during 1983.

Given the sensitivity of the demand for housing to mortgage interest rates, the level of interest rates and the posture of monetary policy are watched as leading indicators of the demand for lumber and plywood. Lumber prices, on the demand side, may also be affected by substitutes. Steel or aluminum studs have been used to replace lumber in construction. Also, plastics and hybrids have replaced lumber in some decorative rather than structural applications, and plastics have been used for applications such as furniture shutters and millwork. The increased use of such competitive materials is likely to continue.

The U.S. dollar–Canadian dollar exchange rate affects the demand for lumber. A stronger U.S. dollar or a weaker Canadian dollar leads to greater imports from Canada and less U.S. production. Government programs, both direct and indirect, also affect the demand for lumber. Obviously, programs that support housing, such as programs sponsored by GNMA, FHA, and VA, and policies that affect interest rate, such as monetary policy, affect the demand for lumber and plywood indirectly. Timber management programs run by the Forest Service of the U.S. Department of Agriculture affect lumber supply and prices more directly. But government programs have not significantly affected the lumber industry directly by setting price levels as they have done in the grain and cotton industries.

While lumber and plywood have very similar uses and their prices usually move together, this is not always the case. During 1979 and 1980, these two prices diverged considerably.

The recent prices of the lumber futures contract, indicating the considerable volatility, are shown in Figure 22-9.

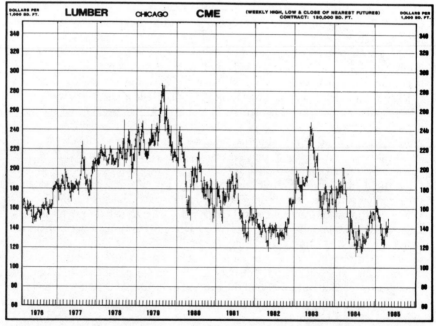

Figure 22-9   Lumber. [*Commodity Year Book 1985*, ed. *Walter L. Emery* [Jersey City, N.J.: *Commodity Research Bureau, Inc.*].]

Seasonals

There are seasonals to both the demand for and the supply of lumber, and a fairly strong and reliable seasonal in prices results from these demand and supply seasonals. The demand for lumber for construction is strongest during the spring and summer. Sawmills accumulate an inventory of logs in the late summer and fall, before the winter interferes with logging. These logs are then prepared for use and stored from the fall until the spring.

Lumber prices reach their lows in the fall, after the construction season, and rise until spring or early summer as construction begins. Prices then tend to decline until the fall.

Futures Contracts

Currently, the only active futures contract based on wood products is the contract on random-length lumber at the Chicago Mercantile Exchange. It was initiated in 1969 and has undergone several changes since then. The futures contract on random-length lumber is based on the delivery of 130,000 board feet of two-by-fours of random lengths—the lengths vary from 8 feet to 20 feet. (The exchange provides a schedule of the acceptable range of percentages for deliveries of each length from 8 feet to 20 feet.) The following species of softwoods are deliverable: alpine fir, Engelmann spruce, hem-fir, lodgepole pine, and spruce-pine-fir. The deliverable grades are "construction and standard" for the "light framing" classification and No. 1 and No. 2 for the "structural light framing" classification, and the lower grades—standard and No. 2—may not be more than one-half of the delivery unit. Delivery can be made via two railroad flatcars from the Canadian provinces of British Columbia and Alberta and the states of Washington, Oregon, California, Montana, Idaho, Nevada, and Wyoming. The delivery months are January, March, May, July, September, and November. The minimum price fluctuation is 10 cents per board foot, or $10 per contract.

Because delivery of the lumber is via railroad cars, lumber delivered on one futures contract cannot be redelivered on a contract of a later month. For this reason, the prices of various contract months are not related on a cash-and-carry basis; that is, they do not differ strictly by the carry cost between the two months. Thus, intracontract spreads have considerable volatility and risk.

The Chicago Board of Trade began a western plywood futures contract in 1969. Although this contract was active for several years, particularly from 1974 to 1977, it has become inactive. It required the delivery of 76,032 square feet of ½-inch plywood from Oregon, Washington, Idaho, Montana, or northern California. Delivery was accomplished by means of a warehouse receipt or shipping certificate, and so the plywood was redeliverable from one contract to another. Plywood futures contracts have also been unsuccessfully introduced by two other exchanges.

Speculative Uses

Speculators trade lumber futures on the basis of the price determinants discussed above. Housing starts are used significantly as a basis of speculation. Strikes, prospective strikes, or even rumored strikes, as well as weather, are also the basis for speculative activity.

As indicated above, because different contract months are not related by carry costs, intracontract spreads are very volatile and are frequently transacted by speculators. With the absence of plywood futures contracts, intercontract spreads are not common for lumber speculators.

Sources of Information

The Forest Service of the U.S. Department of Agriculture and the U.S. Department of Commerce provide several publications which are important for users of the lumber futures contract. Among them are:

> *Production, Prices, Employment and Trade in Pacific Northwest Forest Industries* (quarterly)—USDA, Forest Service
> *Construction Activity* (monthly)—Department of Commerce
> *Housing Starts* (monthly)—Department of Commerce, Bureau of the Census

The Western Wood Products Association (WWPA), a trade association, provides subscribers with several publications which also provide data on and analysis of the lumber industry:

> *Barometer* (weekly)
> *F.O.B. Price Summary Past Sales* (monthly)
> *Western Lumber Facts* (monthly)
> *Statistical Year Book*

The Southern Pine Association and the American Plywood Association, both trade groups, also provide publications on lumber. Three other trade publications that provide valuable information are:

> *Random Lengths* (weekly)
> *Crow's Weekly Letter* (weekly)
> *F. W. Dodge Construction Bulletin* (monthly)

The Chicago Mercantile Exchange provides statistics and other information on lumber and the lumber industry.

Notes from a Trader—Lumber

There are several interesting aspects of the lumber contract. The first is that it is primarily a domestic contract, with Canada being the only non-U.S. supplier on the contract. It is not necessary to analyze the weather and politics of a distant, obscure country in order to trade this contract. Second, this contract is more related to the financial markets, through mortgage interest rates, than the contract for any other commodity. Lumber prices tend to react inversely to interest rate changes. There is also very little intercontract spreading with any other commodity futures contract. And intracontract spreads tend to be very volatile due to the lack of a carry relationship between different contract months.

Bibliography

I. FUTURES TRADING AND COMMODITY EXCHANGES

Anderson, R. W. "The Industrial Organization of Futures Markets," *The Industrial Organization of Futures Markets: Structure and Conduct,* ed. R. W. Anderson. Lexington, Mass.: Lexington Books, 1984.

Arrow, Kenneth. "Future Markets: Some Theoretical Perspectives," *The Journal of Futures Markets,* 1, No. 2 (1981), 107–116.

Arthur, Henry B. "Economic Risk, Uncertainty and the Futures Market," in *Futures Trading Seminar,* vol. 3. Madison, Wis.: Mimir, 1966.

Baer, J. B., and O. G. Saxon. *Commodity Exchanges and Futures Trading: Principles and Operating Methods.* New York: Harper, 1949.

Bailey, Fred, Jr. "What Every Banker Should Know about Commodity Futures Markets," reprint of the following articles from *Banking:* "What a Futures Market Is and How It Works" (October 1967); "Hedging for Country Grain Elevators" (November 1967); "How Farmers Can Use the Futures Markets" (December 1967); "The Cattle Feeder and the Futures Market" (January 1968).

Bakken, H. H. *Theory of Markets and Marketing.* Madison, Wis.: Mimir, 1953.

Barnes, R. M. *Taming the Pits: A Technical Approach to Commodity Trading.* New York: Wiley, 1979.

Besant, Lloyd, et al., eds. *Commodity Trading Manual.* Chicago: Chicago Board of Trade, 1980.

Blau, G. "Some Aspects of the Theory of Futures Trading," *Review of Economic Studies,* 8 (1), No. 31 (1944–1945), 1–3a.

Boyle, J. E. *Speculation and the Chicago Board of Trade.* New York: Macmillan, 1920.

Campbell, D. A. "Trading in Futures under the Commodity Exchange Act," *George Washington Law Review,* 26, No. 2 (January 1958), 215–254.

Chicago Board of Trade. Symposium proceedings, 1948 to date.

Chicago Board of Trade, Futures Trading Seminar, Commodity Marketing Forum for College Teachers of Economics, Chicago, April 28–30, 1965, *Proceedings,* ed. Erwin A. Gaumnitz. Madison, Wis.: Mimir, 1966.

Chicago Board of Trade. *Commodity Trading Manual.* Chicago, 1981.

Commodity Research Bureau. *Understanding the Commodity Futures Markets.* New York, 1977.

Cootner, Paul H. "Common Elements in Futures Markets for Commodities and Bonds," *Proceedings of the American Economic Association,* 51 (May 1961), 173–183.

Corbett, Caroline Louise (Phillips). *Economic Phases of Futures Trading: A Selected List of References.* Washington, D.C.: Commodity Exchange Administration, 1937.

Cox, Charles. "Futures Trading and Market Information," *Journal of Political Economy* (December 1976), 1215–1237.

Dewey, T. H. *A Treatise on Contracts for Future Delivery and Commercial Wagers Including "Options," "Futures," and "Short Sales."* New York: Baker, Voorhis, 1886.

Dow, J. C. R. "A Symposium on the Theory of the Forward Market. II. Addenda to Mr. Kaldor's Note," *Review of Economic Studies*, 7 (1939–1940), 201–202.

———. "A Theoretical Account of Futures Markets," *Review of Economic Studies*, 7 (1939–1940), 185–195.

The Economist (London). Tonbridge, England: The London Metal Exchange, Whitefriars Press, 1958.

Ederington, L. H. "Living with Inflation: A Proposal for New Futures and Options Markets," *Financial Analysts Journal* (January/February 1980), 42–48.

Emery, H. C. "Speculation on the Stock and Produce Exchanges of the United States," in *Studies in History and Economics*, Vol. 7, ed. Faculty of Political Science of Columbia University. New York, 1896.

Geiger, H. Dwight. "The Grain Futures and Cash Markets (and Some of Their Accounting Implications)," *The Arthur Young Journal* (winter 1969).

Gold, Gerald. *Modern Commodity Futures Trading*. New York: Commodity Research Bureau, 1975.

Granger, C. W. J. *Trading in Commodities*, 3d ed. Cambridge, England: Woodhead-Faulkner, 1979.

Gray, Roger W. "Some Current Development in Futures Trading," *Journal of Farm Economics*, 40, No. 2 (May 1958), 344–351.

———. "Search for a Risk Premium," *Journal of Political Economy*, 69, No. 3 (June 1961), 250–260.

———. "The Characteristic Bias of Some Thin Futures Markets," in *Selected Writings on Futures Markets*, Vol. II, ed. A. E. Peck. Chicago Board of Trade, 1977, pp. 83–100.

Grossman, S. J. "The Existence of Futures Markets, Noisy Rational Expectations and Informational Externalities," *Review of Economic Studies*, 44 (3), No. 138 (October 1977), 431–449.

Gunnelson, J. A. "A Study of the Impact of Organizational Changes in Agricultural Commodity Markets," Ph.D. dissertation, Purdue University, 1970.

Harlow, C. V., and R. J. Teweles. "Commodities and Securities Compared," *Financial Analysts Journal* (September–October 1972).

Hawtrey, R. G. "Mr. Kaldor on the Forward Market," *Review of Economic Studies*, 7 (1939–1940), 202–205.

Hearings before the Committee on Agriculture and Forestry, May 1–3, 1957, 85th Cong., 1st Sess., House.

Hearings before a Subcommittee of the Committee on Agriculture and Forestry, Aug. 12, 1957, 85th Cong., 1st Sess., Senate.

Hearings before the Committee on Agriculture and Forestry, Mar. 22–26, 1958, 85th Cong., 2d Sess., Senate.

Hearings on H.R. 904, Apr. 8–10, 1963, 88th Cong., 1st Sess., House.

Hearings before the Subcommittee on Domestic Marketing and Consumer Relations of the Committee on Agriculture on H.R. 11788, Apr. 4–6, 1966, 89th Cong., 2d Sess., House.

Heater, Nancy L. *Commodity Futures Trading, A Bibliography*. University of Illinois College of Agriculture, Department of Agricultural Economics, December 1966.

Hieronymus, T. A. "Should Margins in Futures Trading Be Regulated?" *Commercial and Financial Chronicle*, 173, No. 5004 (Apr. 19, 1951), 1648–1685.

Hoffman, G. W. *Future Trading upon Organized Commodity Markets in the United States*. Philadelphia: University of Pennsylvania Press, 1932.

———. "Past and Present Theory Regarding Futures Trading," *Journal of Farm Economics*, 19 (1937), 300–309.

Hoos, Sidney. "Future Trading in Perishable Agricultural Commodities," *Journal of Marketing*, 6 (1942), 358–365.

Horn, Frederick. *Trading in Commodity Futures*. New York: New York Institute of Finance, 1979.

Houthakker, H. S. "The Scope and Limits of Futures Trading," in Moses Abramovitz et al., *The Allocation of Economic Resources*. Stanford, Calif.: Stanford University Press, 1959.

How to Buy and Sell Commodities, a booklet published by Merrill Lynch, Pierce, Fenner and Smith, New York, January 1969.

"How Well Are the Exchange Markets Functioning?" *Federal Reserve Bank of New York Quarterly Review* (spring 1979), 49–52.

Kaldor, Nickolas. "A Note on the Theory of the Forward Market," *Review of Economic Studies*, 7 (1939–1940), 196–201.

Kamara, A. "Issues in Futures Markets: A Survey," *The Journal of Futures Markets*, 2, No. 3 (1982), 261.

Kaufman, Perry J. *Commodity Trading Systems and Methods*. New York: Wiley, 1978.

———. *Technical Analysis in Commodities*. New York: Wiley, 1980.
———. *Handbook of Futures Markets*. New York: Wiley, 1984.
Larson, Arnold B. "Estimation of Hedging and Speculative Positions in Futures Markets," *Food Research Institute Studies*, 2, No. 3 (1961), 203–212.
Leuthold, Raymond, ed. *Commodity Markets and Futures Prices*. Chicago: Chicago Mercantile Exchange, 1979.
——— and W. G. Tomek. "Developments in the Livestock Futures Literature," *Livestock Futures Research Symposium Proceedings*. Chicago Mercantile Exchange, 1980.
Lindley, A. F. "Essentials of an Effective Futures Market," *Journal of Farm Economics*, 19 (1937), 321–330.
Mehl, J. M. *The Development and Operation of the Commodity Exchange Act*. Washington: Commodity Exchange Authority, 1953.
Mehl, Paul. *A Rapid Method of Calculating Profits Made or Losses Sustained in Privilege Trading on the Chicago Board of Trade*. Washington, D.C.: U. S. Grain Futures Administration, 1931.
———. *Trading in Privileges on the Chicago Board of Trade*, USDA Circular 323, 1934.
Miller, Katherine D. "Futures Trading and Investor Returns: An Investigation of Commodity Market Risk Premiums," thesis, University of Chicago, 1971.
New York Coffee and Sugar Exchange. *History and Operation of the New York Coffee and Sugar Exchange, Inc., 1882–1947*. New York, 1947.
Peck, Anne, ed. *Readings in Futures Markets, 1, 2, 3: Selected Writings of Holbrook Working*. Chicago: Chicago Board of Trade, 1977–1978.
Phillips, J. "The Theory and Practice of Futures Trading," *Review of Marketing and Agricultural Economics* (June 1966).
Powers, Mark J. "Effects of Contract Provisions on the Success of a Futures Contract," *Journal of Farm Economics*, 49, No. 4 (November 1967), 833–843.
———. *Getting Started in Commodity Futures Trading*, 2d ed. Cedar Falls, Iowa: Investor Publications, 1977.
———. "Thin Markets—A Regulatory Perspective," in *Pricing Problems in the Food Industry (with Emphasis on Thin Markets)*, N.C. Project 117, Monograph 7. Madison, Wis., February 1979.
——— and D. J. Vogel. *Inside the Financial Futures Markets*. New York: Wiley, 1982.
Rudnick, R., and L. Carlisle. "Commodities and Financial Futures," *Journal of Taxation Investments* (autumn 1983), 45–55.
Telser, L. G., and H. N. Higinbotham. "Organized Futures Markets: Costs and Benefits," *Journal of Political Economy*, 85 (1977), 969–1000.
Teweles, Richard J., and Charles V. Harlow. "The Commodity Futures Game: Who Wins? Who Loses? Why?" A two-part series in *The Journal of Commodity Trading*, 5, No. 1 (January–February 1970), and 5, No. 2 (March–April 1970).
Teweles, Richard J., Charles V. Harlow, and Herbert L. Stone. *The Commodity Futures Trading Guide*. New York: McGraw-Hill, 1969.
Tomek, William. "Futures Trading and Market Information: Some New Evidence," *Food Research Institute Studies* (1979–1980), 351–359.
U.S. Industrial Commission Report (1900–1901), House Doc. 94, 56th Cong., 2d Sess., House.
Venkataramanan, L. S. *The Theory of Futures Trading*. New York: Asia Publishing, 1965.
Working, Holbrook. "Western Needs for Futures Markets," *Proceedings of the Western Farm Economics Association* (1952), 95–98.
———. "Whose Markets? Evidence on Some Aspects of Futures Trading," *Journal of Marketing*, 19, No. 1 (July 1954), 1–11.
———. "Tests of a Theory Concerning Floor Trading on Commodity Exchanges," *Food Research Institute Studies*, Supplement, 7 (1967), 5–48.

II. HISTORY AND EVOLUTION OF FUTURES TRADING

Anderson, M. A. "Ninety Years Development: Fundamental and Technicalities of Futures Trading Explained," *Cotton Digest*, 21, No. 27 (Mar. 26, 1949), 18–19, 42–43, 46–47.
Boyle, J. E. *Cotton and the New Orleans Cotton Exchange: A Century of Commercial Evolution*. New York: Country Life, 1934.
Carlton, Dennis W. "Futures Markets: Their Purpose, Their History, Their Growth, Their Successes and Failures," *The Journal of Futures Markets*, 4, No. 3 (1984), 237–271.
Cowing, Cedric B. *Populists, Plungers and Progressives: A Social History of Stock and Commodity Speculation, 1860–1936*. Princeton, N.J.: Princeton University Press, 1965.

Dies, E. J. *The Plunger: A Tale of the Wheat Pit*. New York: Covici, 1929; reprinted Salem, N.H.: Ayer Co., 1975.

———. *The Wheat Pit*. Chicago: Argyle, 1925.

Gray, Roger. "The Chicago Wheat Futures Market: Recent Problems in Historical Perspective," *Food Research Institute Studies*. Stanford, Calif: Stanford University Press, 1981, pp. 89–115.

Irwin, H. S. *Evolution of Futures Trading*. Madison, Wis.: Mimir, 1954.

Killough, H. B. "Effects of Governmental Regulation of Commodity Exchanges in the United States," *Harvard Business Review*, 11 (1933), 307–315.

Lermer, G. "The Futures Market and Farm Programs," *Canadian Journal of Agricultural Economics*, 16, No. 2 (June 1968), 27–30.

Miller, Norman C. *The Great Salad Oil Swindle*. New York: Coward-McCann, 1965.

Nimrod, Vance L., and Richard S. Bower. "Commodities and Computers," *Journal of Financial and Quantitative Analysis*, 2, No. 1 (March 1967).

Norris, Frank. *The Pit*. New York: Doubleday, Page, 1903.

Peckron, Harold. "Tax Consequences of Currency Futures after Hoover," *International Tax Journal* (February 1980), 165–177.

Pine, L. G. "London: A Commercial History since the Roman Occupation," supplement to *The Public Ledger*, London (January 1960).

Robinson, H. G. "History and Evolution of Trading in Futures in Potatoes, 1930–1956," Ph.D. dissertation, Ohio State University, 1957.

Sowards, J. K. *Western Civilization to 1660*. New York: St. Martin's, 1965.

Taylor, C. H. *History of the Board of Trade of the City of Chicago*. Chicago: Robert O. Law Co., 1917.

Telser, Lester. "Why Are There Organized Futures Markets?" *The Journal of Law and Economics*, XXIV, No. 1 (1981), 1–22.

Tomek, W. G. "A Note on Historical Wheat Prices and Futures Trading," *Food Research Institute Studies*, 10 (1971).

Williams, J. "The Origin of Futures Markets," *Agricultural History*, 56, (January 1982), 306–316.

Working, Holbrook. "Review of H. S. Irwin, 'Evolution of Futures Trading,'" *Journal of Farm Economics*, 37 (1950), 377–380.

III. ECONOMIC THEORY AND EVIDENCE

Baesel, J., and D. Grant. "Equilibrium in a Futures Market," *Southern Economic Journal*, 49, No. 2 (October 1982), 320–329.

Boulding, Kenneth. *The Skills of the Economist*. Toronto, Canada: Clarke, Irwin, 1958.

Brandow, G. E. *Interrelations among Demand for Farm Products and Implications for Control of Market Supply*, Penn State Agricultural Experiment Station Bulletin 680, 1961.

Carlton, D. "The Disruptive Effect of Inflation on the Organization of Markets," in *Inflation*, ed. R. Hall. Chicago: University of Chicago Press, 1982, pp. 139–152.

Chamberlin, E. H. *The Theory of Monopolistic Competition*. Cambridge, Mass.: Harvard, 1938.

Cornell, B. "Spot Rates, Forward Rates, and Exchange Market Efficiency," *Journal of Financial Economics*, 5, No. 1 (August 1977), 56–66.

Dahl, Reynold. "Futures Markets: The Interaction of Economic Analyses and Regulation: Discussion," *American Journal of Agricultural Economics* (December 1980), 1047–1048.

Fama, Eugene F. "Mandelbrot and the Stable Paretian Hypothesis," *Journal of Business*, 36, No. 4 (October 1963), 420–429.

———. "Efficient Capital Markets: A Review of Theory and Empirical Works," *Journal of Finance*, 25 (1970), 383–423.

Fishman, G. S. *Spectral Methods in Econometrics*. Cambridge, Mass.: Harvard, 1969.

Foote, Richard J. *Analytical Tools for Studying Demand and Price Structure*, USDA Handbook 146, 1958.

Foote, Richard J., and Karl A. Fox. *Analytical Tools for Measuring Demand*, USDA Handbook 64, 1954.

Friedman, M. *Essays in Positive Economics*. Chicago: University of Chicago Press, 1953.

Gardner, Bruce. "Economic Analysis of the Regulation of Agriculture," *American Journal of Agricultural Economics* (November 1979), 732–740.

Gordon, D. F. "A Statistical Contribution to Price Theory: Discussion," *American Economic Review*, Papers and Proceedings, 48 (1958), 201–203.

Gorham, Michael. "The Effects of Inflation on the Rules of Futures Exchanges: A Case Study of the Chicago Mercantile Exchange," *The Journal of Futures Markets* (fall 1981), 337–346.

Goss, Barry, and B. S. Yamey, eds. *The Economics of Futures Trading.* New York: Wiley, 1978.
Granger, C. W. J., and M. Hatanaka. *Spectral Analysis of Economic Time Series.* Princeton, N.J.: Princeton University Press, 1964.
Gray, Roger W., and David J. S. Rutledge. "The Economics of Commodity Futures Markets: A Survey," *Review of Marketing and Agricultural Economics,* 39, No. 4 (1971), 57–108.
Hieronymus, Thomas. *Economics of Futures Trading for Commercial and Personal Profit.* New York: Commodity Research Bureau, 1977.
Houthakker, H. S. *Economic Policy for the Farm Sector.* Washington, D.C.: American Enterprise Institute for Public Policy Research, 1967.
Johnson, D. G. *Forward Prices for Agriculture.* Chicago: University of Chicago Press, 1947.
Jones, Frank J. "The Integration of the Cash and Futures Markets for Treasury Securities," *The Journal of Futures Markets,* 1, No. 1 (1981), 33–57.
————. "The Economics of Futures and Options Contracts Based on Cash Settlement," *The Journal of Futures Markets,* 2, No. 1 (1982), 63–82. (This article was also presented at the annual meeting of the American Finance Association, Dec. 29, 1981, Washington, D.C.)
————. "The Yield Curve: Cash and Futures Markets," Chap. 15 of *The Financial Futures Markets,* eds. Nancy H. Rothstein and James M. Little. New York: McGraw-Hill, 1984, pp. 373–421.
———— and Benjamin Wolkowitz. "The Determinants of Interest Rates on Fixed Income Securities," in *The Handbook of Fixed Income Securities.* Homewood, Ill.: Dow Jones–Irwin, 1983, pp. 91–151.
Kaldor, N. "Speculation and Economic Stability," *Review of Economic Studies,* 7 (1939–40), 1–27.
Keynes, J. M. *A Treatise on Money,* Vol. 2. New York: Harcourt, Brace and World, 1930.
————. *The General Theory of Employment, Interest, and Money.* New York: Harcourt, Brace and World, 1964.
Kogiker, K. C. "A Model of the Raw Materials Markets," *International Economic Review,* No. 8 (February 1967).
Meade, J. E. "Degrees of Competitive Speculation," *Review of Economic Studies,* 17 (1950), 159–167.
Nerlove, Marc. *Distributed Lags and Demand Analysis for Agricultural and Other Commodities,* USDA Handbook 141, 1958.
————. "On the Nerlove Estimate of Supply Elasticity," *Journal of Farm Economics,* 40 (August 1958), 723–728.
———— and William Addison. "Statistical Estimation of Long-Run Elasticities of Supply and Demand," *Journal of Farm Economics,* 40 (November 1958), 861–880.
Panton, Don, and O. Maurice Joy. "Empirical Evidence on International Monetary Market Currency Futures," in *Commodity Markets and Futures Prices,* ed. Raymond Leuthold. Chicago Mercantile Exchange, 1979, pp. 73–86.
Pavaskar, M. G. *Marketing of Cash Crops: Efficiency of Futures Trading.* Bombay, India: Economics and Political Weekly, 1971.
Peck, A. E. "Futures Markets, Supply Response and Price Stability," *Quarterly Journal of Economics,* 90, No. 3 (August 1976), 407–423.
Perrin, R. K. "Analysis and Prediction of Crop Yields for Agricultural Policy Purposes," Ph.D. dissertation, Iowa State University, 1968.
Pindyck, Robert S., and Daniel L. Rubinfeld. *Econometric Models and Economic Forecasts.* New York: McGraw-Hill, 1976.
Scherer, F. M. *Industrial Market Structure and Economic Performance,* 2d ed. Chicago: Rand McNally, 1980.
Scholes, Myron S. "The Economics of Hedging and Spreading in Futures Markets," *The Journal of Futures Markets,* 1, No. 2 (1981), 265–286.
Schultz, H. *The Theory of Measurement of Demand.* Chicago: University of Chicago Press, 1938 (reprinted 1957).
Selvestre, Helios. "Demand Analysis: An Attempt to Develop a Methodology for Detecting the Point in Time Where Structural Changes Took Place," Ph.D. dissertation, Cornell University, 1969.
Taylor, F. M. *Principles of Economics,* 2d ed. Ann Arbor: University of Michigan Press, 1913.
Tesler, L. G. *Economic Theory and the Core.* Chicago: University of Chicago Press, 1978.
Ward, R. W., and F. A. Dasse. "Empirical Contributions to Basis Theory: The Case of Citrus Futures," *American Journal of Agricultural Economics,* 59 (1977), 71–80.
Watson, Donald. *Price Theory and Its Uses.* Boston: Houghton Mifflin, 1963.
Waugh, Fredrick V. *Demand and Price Analysis: Some Examples from Agriculture,* USDA Technical Bulletin 1316, 1964.

Weymar, F. Helmut. "The Supply of Storage Revisited," *American Economic Review*, 56 (December 1966), 1226–1234.

Williams, J. B. "Speculation and the Carryover," *Quarterly Journal of Economics*, 51 (May 1936), 436–455.

Wilmouth, R. K. "Don't Destroy Market's Economic Function," *Commodities* (August 1981), 28.

Working, Holbrook. "Economic Functions of Futures Markets," reprinted in *Selected Writings of Holbrook Working*, comp. Anne Peck. Chicago Board of Trade, 1977.

———. "The Investigation of Economic Expectations," *American Economic Review*, 39, No. 3 (May 1949), 150–166.

———. "Theory of Price Storage," *American Economic Review*, 39, No. 6 (December 1949), 1254–1262.

World, H., and L. Jureen. *Demand Analysis: A Study in Econometrics*. New York: Wiley, 1953.

IV. TRADERS: BEHAVIOR AND RETURNS

Baruch, Bernard. *My Own Story*. New York: Holt, 1957.

Bauer, D. "Prince of the Pit," *The New York Times Magazine* (Apr. 25, 1976), 30–31.

Bernstein, J. *The Investor's Quotient: The Psychology of Successful Investing in Commodities and Stocks*. New York: Wiley, 1980.

Cantril, Hadley. *The Invasion from Mars*. New York: Harper and Row, 1966.

Cootner, P. H. "Returns to Speculators: Telser versus Keynes," *Journal of Political Economy*, 68, No. 4 (August 1960), 396–414, followed by L. G. Telser, "Reply," pp. 404–415, and P. H. Cootner, "Rejoinder," pp. 415–418.

Fee, R. "Tale of Wealthy Cowards and Bankrupt Heroes," *Successful Farming*, 73 (January 1975), 18–19.

Glick, Ira O. "A Social Psychological Study of Futures Trading," Ph.D. dissertation, Department of Sociology, University of Chicago, 1957.

Greenstone, Wayne. "Foreign Commodity Trader: A Regulatory Dilemma," *Administrative Review* (fall 1978), 535–548.

———. "The Wiscope Affair: CFTC Closes in on Foreign Traders," *Commodities* (May 1979).

Harlow, Charles. "Notes from a Trader: When Should a Commodity Position Be Liquidated?" *Commodities*, 5, No. 9 (September 1976), 28.

Harper, C. J. "Belly Trader," *Newsweek* (June 28, 1976), 8.

Harris, Thomas A. *I'm OK*. New York: Harper and Row, 1967.

Hays, D. "Why Pros Like Trends . . . and Trade Contrarily," *Commodities* (February 1977), 30–31.

Houthakker, H. S., and L. G. Telser. "Commodity Futures II: Gains and Losses of Hedgers and Future Speculators," Cowles Commission Discussion Paper, *Economics*, No. 2090 (December 1952).

Hudson, Robert. "Customer Protection in the Commodity Futures Market," *Boston University Law Review* (January 1978), 1–43.

Hultgren, Ralph. "The Market Millionaires," *Commodities*, 4, No. 2 (February 1975), 16–22.

Kroll, Stanley. *The Professional Commodity Trader*. New York: Harper and Row, 1974.

Le Bon, Gustave. *The Crowd*. New York: Viking, 1960.

Lefevre, Edwin. *Reminiscences of a Stock Operator*. New York: American Research Council, 1923.

Longstreet, Roy W. *Viewpoints of a Commodity Trader*. New York: Frederick Fell, 1968.

MacKay, Charles. *Extraordinary Popular Delusions and the Madness of Crowds*. London: Page, 1932.

"The Market Millionaires" (fourth in a series of interviews with commodity traders who have made their fortunes in the futures markets), *Commodities*, 5, No. 1 (January 1976), 16–18.

Market Vane Commodity Letter, Pasadena, Calif.

Matuszewski, T. I. "Trader's Behaviour—An Alternative Explanation," *Review of Economic Studies*, 25 (1958), 126–130.

McMaster, R. E., Jr. *Trader's Notebook 1978*. Phoenix, Ariz.: The Reaper, 1978.

Meger, Richard. "Investor Preferences for Future Straddles," *Journal of Financial and Quantitative Analysis* (March 1977), 105–120.

Mitchell, Mark. "The Regulation of Commodity Trading Advisors," *Emory Law Journal* (fall 1978), 957–1003.

Morris, J. "Over 100 Banks Use Futures," *American Banker* (Apr. 6, 1983), 3, 38.

Neill, Humphrey. *The Art of Contrary Thinking*. Caldwell, Ohio: Caxton, 1960.

Oster, Merrill J. "How the Young Millionaires Trade Commodities. Part 1," *Commodities*, 5, No. 3 (March 1976), 12–16.

———. "How the Young Millionaires Trade Commodities. Part 2," *Commodities*, 5, No. 4 (April 1976), 22–27.

"Publicly Held Brokers: After the Feast, a Mini-Famine," *Financial World*, 145, No. 16 (Aug. 15, 1976), 31.

Reisman, David. *The Lonely Crowd*. New Haven, Conn.: Yale, 1950.

Rockwell, C. S. "Normal Backwardation Forecasting, and the Returns to Speculators," *Food Research Institute Studies*, Supplement, 7 (1967), 107–130.

Schwed, Fred, Jr. *Where Are the Customers' Yachts?* Springfield, Mass.: John Magee, 1955.

Stein, J. L. "Speculative Price: Economic Welfare and the Idiot of Chance," *Review of Economics and Statistics*, 63 (1981), 223–232.

V. INDIVIDUAL COMMODITY STUDIES

Abbott, Susan. "How International Commodity Agreements Affect Futures," *Commodities* (December 1981), 42–43.

ACLI International. "Cocoa—A Special Report," *Commodity Research Bulletin* (New York, April 1980).

Ainsworth, Ralph M. *Profitable Grain Trading*. Greenville, S.C.: Traders Press, 1980.

Akari, Hossein, and John Thomas Cummings. *Agricultural Supply Response, A Survey of the Econometric Evidence*. New York: Praeger, 1976.

Aliber, Robert A. *The International Money Game*, 2d ed. New York: Basic Books, 1976.

Angell, G. "A Technical Approach to Trading Interest Rate Futures Markets," *Commodities*, 6, No. 6 (June 1977), 46–48.

Armore, S. J. *The Demand and Price Structure for Food Fats and Oils*, USDA Technical Bulletin 1068, June 1953.

Aronson, J. R. *The Soybean Crushing Margin, 1953–62: An Economic Analysis of the Futures Market for Soybeans, Soybean Oil and Soybean Meal*. Worcester, Mass.: Clark University, 1964.

Atwood, E. C., Jr. *Theory and Practice in the Coffee Futures Market*. Princeton, N.J.: Princeton University Press, 1959.

Bacon, P., and R. Williams. "Interest Rate Futures: New Tool for the Financial Manager," *Financial Management*, 5, No. 1 (spring 1976), 32–37.

Bakken, H., ed. *Futures Trading in Livestock—Origins and Concepts*. Madison, Wis.: Mimir, 1970.

Ball, Jayne. "The New Potato Futures Market," *Commodities* (August 1979), 40–42.

Ballinger, Roy A. *A History of Sugar Marketing through 1974*, Agricultural Economic Report 328. U. S. Department of Agriculture, Economics, Statistics and Cooperative Service, 1978.

Bierwag, G. O., and G. G. Kaufman. "Coping with the Risk of Interest Rate Fluctuations: A Note," *Journal of Business*, 50, No. 3 (July 1977), 364–370.

Bohnsack. "Financial Futures Markets: Hedging Convergence and Options Up Ahead," *The Money Manager* (June 26, 1978).

Brand, Simon S. "The Decline in the Cotton Futures Market," *Food Research Institute Studies*, 4, No. 3 (1964).

Breimyer, Harold F. *Demand and Prices for Meat*, USDA Technical Bulletin 1253, 1961.

Brown, C. A. "Future Trading in Butter and Eggs," *Journal of Farm Economics*, 15 (1933), 670–675, followed by E. A. Duddy, "Discussion," 675–676.

Brown, William A. *Corn Price Action*. Libertyville, Ill.: Comtab, 1975.

———. *Wheat Price Action*. Libertyville, Ill.: Comtab, 1975.

———. *Soybean Price Action*. Libertyville, Ill.: Comtab, 1976.

Burger, A. E., R. Lang, and R. Rasche. "The Treasury Bill Futures Markets and Market Expectations of Interest Rates," *Federal Reserve Bank of St. Louis Review* (June 1977), 2–9.

Burrows, J. C., W. Hughes, and J. Valette. *An Economic Analysis of the Silver Industry*. Lexington, Mass.: Heath, 1974.

Caves, Richard E. "Organization, Scale, and Performance of Grain Trade," *Food Research Institute Studies*, Vol. 16e. Stanford, Calif.: Stanford University Press, 1977–1978, pp. 107–123.

Chapman, S. J., and Douglas Knoop. "Dealings in Futures on the Cotton Market," *Royal Statistical Journal*, 69 (1906), 321–364.

Chicago Board of Trade. *An Introduction to Financial Futures*. Chicago, 1981.

Chicago Mercantile Exchange. *Opportunities in Interest Rates: Treasury Bill Futures.* Chicago, 1977.

Cocoa Market Report. Gill and Duffus, London quarterly.

Coffee: Production and Marketing Systems, Comptroller General's Report to Congress, No. ID-77-54, Oct. 28, 1977.

Coninx, Raymond G. F. *Foreign Exchange Today.* New York: Wiley, 1978.

Corbin, Frederick T. *World Soybean Conference II* (Proceedings). Boulder, Colo.: Westview Press, 1980.

Cross, C. Richard. "Interest Rate Futures: Portfolio Managers Find a New Tool," *Money Manager* (June 25, 1977).

Danis, Tom. *An Economic Analysis of Egg Prices in 1969,* Chicago Mercantile Exchange Research Report 1, April 1970.

Dominick, B. A., Jr., and F. W. Williams. *Future Trading and the Florida Orange Industry.* Florida Agricultural Experiment Stations, December 1965.

Doyle, Thomas L., Jr. *Live Cattle, Live Hogs and Frozen Pork Bellies.* Los Altos, Calif.: Futures Research Co., 1976.

Drake, A. F., and V. I. West. *Econometric Analysis of the Edible Fats and Oils Economy,* Agricultural Experiment Station Bulletin 695, University of Illinois, Urbana, 1963.

Dugey, Gunter, and Ian H. Giddy. *The International Money Market.* Englewood Cliffs, N.J.: Prentice-Hall, 1978.

Dushek, Charles, and Carol Harding. *Trading in Foreign Currencies, Speculative Practices and Techniques.* Chicago: American TransEuro, 1978.

An Economic Study of the U.S. Potato Industry, Agricultural Economic Report 6, USDA, Economic Research Service, 1962.

Ehrich, Rollo. "The Impact of Government Programs on Wheat Futures Markets: 1953–63," *Food Research Institute Studies,* 6, No. 3 (1966).

Emerson, P. M., and W. G. Tomek. "Did Futures Trading Influence Potato Prices?" *American Journal of Agricultural Economics,* 51, No. 3 (August 1969), 666–672.

Emery, Walter L. "How to Analyze the Soybean Futures Market," *Forecasting Commodity Prices.* New York: Commodity Research Bureau, 1975.

———. "Understanding the Soybean Oil Market," *Forecasting Commodity Prices.* New York: Commodity Research Bureau, 1975.

———. "Understanding the Wheat Futures Market," *Forecasting Commodity Prices.* New York: Commodity Research Bureau, 1975.

Ertek, Tumay. "World Demand for Copper, 1948–1963: An Econometric Study," Ph.D. dissertation, University of Wisconsin, 1967.

Evans, W. S. "Canadian Wheat Stabilization Operations, 1929–35," *Wheat Studies,* 12, No. 7 (March 1926), 249–272.

Foote, R. J., John A. Craven, and Robert R. Williams, Jr. "Pork Bellies: Quarterly 3-Equation Models Designed to Predict Cash Prices," Texas Tech. University, 1971. (Mimeographed.)

———, J. W. Klein, and M. Clough. *The Demand and Price Structure for Corn and Total Feed Concentrates,* USDA Technical Bulletin 1061, October 1952.

Freivalds, John. *Grain Trade.* New York: Stein and Day, 1976.

Gallacher, William. "1973 Bellies—Prices to Clear," *Commodities* (March 1973).

Gann, William D. *Rules for Trading in Soybeans, Corn, Wheat, Oats and Rye.* Pomeroy, Wash.: Lambert-Gann Publishing, 1976.

Gerra, M. J. *The Demand, Supply and Price Structure for Eggs,* USDA Technical Bulletin 1204, 1959.

Gotthelf, Edward B. P. "A Systems Approach to Financial Futures Markets," *Commodities,* 7, No. 8 (August 1978), 28–29.

Gray, Roger W. "Speculation Helps the Onion Grower," *Minnesota Farm Business Notes,* University of Minnesota, Institute of Agriculture (March–April 1959).

———. "Onions Revisited," *Journal of Farm Economics,* 45, No. 2 (May 1963), 273–276.

———. "The Attack upon Potato Futures Trading in the United States," *Food Research Institute Studies,* 4, No. 2 (1964), 97–121.

———. "The Prospects for Wool Price Stability," *Proceedings: International Wool Textile Organization Conference,* Brussels, Belgium (June 1967).

———. *Wool Futures Trading in Australia—Further Prospects,* University of Sydney, Department of Agricultural Economics, Research Bulletin 5, 1967.

————. "The Futures Market of Maine Potatoes: An Appraisal," *Food Research Institute Studies,* 11, No. 3 (1972).

Green, Leslie. "Understanding the Frozen Orange Juice Market," in Harry Jiler, ed., *Commodity Year Book.* New York: Commodity Research Bureau, 1968.

Grubel, Herbert G. *Forward Exchange, Speculation, and the International Flow of Capital.* Ann Arbor, Mich.: University Microfilms, 1977.

Gutman, G. O., and B. R. Duffin. "The London Wool Top Futures Market," *Quarterly Review of Agricultural Economics,* 8, No. 4 (Bureau of Agricultural Economics, Canberra, October 1955), 185–192.

Harlow, Arthur. *Factors Affecting the Price and Supply of Hogs,* USDA Technical Bulletin 1247, 1964.

Hee, Olman. "The Effect of Price on Acreage and Yield of Potatoes," *Agricultural Economics Research,* 10 (1958), 131–141.

Hein, Dale. "An Economic Analysis of the U.S. Poultry Sector," *American Journal of Agricultural Economics,* 58, No. 2 (May 1976).

Helmuth, J. "A Report on the Systematic Downward Bias in Live Cattle Futures Prices," *The Journal of Futures Markets,* 1, No. 3, 347–358.

Hieronymus, T. A. "The Economics of Risk in the Marketing of Soybeans and Soybean Products," Ph.D. dissertation, University of Illinois, Urbana, 1949.

————. *Effects of Future Trading on Grain Prices,* Illinois Farm Economics No. 190–191, 1951, pp. 1150–1155.

————. *Futures Trading and Speculation in Soybeans,* University of Illinois Agricultural Extension Service, AE-2777, 1951.

————. "Futures Trading and Speculation in Soybeans by Country Elevators," *Grain and Feed Review,* 40, No. 7 (March 1951), 20, 22, 56, 57.

————. *Appropriate Speculative Limits for Soybean Oil and Lard.* Chicago Board of Trade, 1953.

————. *Farm Speculation in Soybeans,* University of Illinois Department of Agricultural Economics, AERR 9, Urbana, 1965.

Higgins, Richard, and Randall Holcombe. "The Effect of Futures Trading on Price Variability in the Market for Onions," *Atlantic Economic Journal* (July 1980), 44–52.

Hobson, R. *Futures Trading in Financial Instruments.* Commodity Futures Trading Commission, October 1978.

Hoffman, G. "The Effect of Futures Prices on the Short-Run Supply of Fed Cattle and Hogs," in *Livestock Futures Research Symposium,* Chicago Mercantile Exchange, 1979.

Honhon, Georges L. J. "An Econometric Analysis of the Corn Market in an Open Economy," Ph.D. dissertation, University of Illinois, 1970.

Hooker, R. H. "The Suspension of the Berlin Produce and Exchange and Its Effects upon Corn Prices," *Royal Statistical Society Journal,* 64 (1901), 574–604.

Houck, James P. *Demand and Price Analysis of the U.S. Soybean Market,* Agricultural Experiment Station Bulletin 244, Minnesota, 1963.

————. "A Statistical Model of the Demand for Soybeans," *Journal of Farm Economics,* 46 (May 1964), 366–374.

———— and J. S. Mann. *Domestic and Foreign Demand for U.S. Soybeans and Soybean Products,* Agricultural Experiment Station Technical Bulletin 256, University of Minnesota, Minneapolis, 1968.

————, M. E. Ryan, and A. Subotnik. *Soybeans and Their Products: Markets, Models and Policy.* Minneapolis: University of Minnesota Press, 1972.

Inkeles, David M. "How to Analyze the World Sugar Futures Market," *Forecasting Commodity Prices.* New York: Commodity Research Bureau, 1975.

————. "Understanding the Oats Futures Market," *Forecasting Commodity Prices.* New York: Commodity Research Bureau, 1975.

International Coffee Agreement, International Coffee Organization, London, 1976.

International Monetary Market. *Treasury Bill Futures.* Chicago, 1977.

International Monetary Market. *T-Bill Futures: Opportunities in Interest Rates.* Chicago.

Irland, Lloyd C., James P. Olmedo, Jr., and Robert O. McMahon, eds. *Futures Trading: Its Uses in Forest Industry.* New Haven: Yale School of Forestry, 1977.

Jaffe, N., and R. Hobson. *Survey of Interest Rate Futures Markets.* Commodity Futures Trading Commission, December 1979.

Jastram, R. W. *Silver: The Restless Metal.* New York: Wiley, 1981.

Johnson, A. C., Jr. "Whose Markets? The Case for Maine Potato Futures," *Food Research Institute Studies*, 11, No. 3 (1972).

Jones, Frank J. "The Uses and Users of the Stock Index Futures Markets," *Stock Index Futures*, eds. Frank J. Fabozzi and Gregory M. Kipnis. Homewood, Ill.: Dow Jones–Irwin, 1984, pp. 145–166.

Kahl, Kandice H., and William G. Tomek. "Effectiveness of Hedging in Potato Futures," *The Journal of Futures Markets*, 2, No. 1 (1982), 9–18.

Kelly, John. "A Look at Cattle: From Bum Steer to Bull Market?" *Commodities*, 5, No. 9 (September 1976), 22–25.

Kofi, T. A. "Feasibility Analysis of International Commodity Agreements on Cocoa," Ph.D. dissertation, University of California, Berkeley, 1970.

Kohls, R. L. "A Technique for Anticipating Change in the Volume of Eggs Shortage," *Journal of Farm Economics*, 32, No. 4 (November 1950), 663–666.

Kolb, Robert W., and Gerald D. Gay. "The Performance of Live Cattle Futures as Predictors of Subsequent Spot Prices," *The Journal of Futures Markets*, 3, No. 1 (1983), 55–63.

Koudele, J. W. "An Economic Analysis of Trading in Egg Futures, 1934–1954," Ph.D. dissertation, Michigan State University, 1956.

Kubarych, Roger F. *Foreign Exchange Markets in the United States*. New York: Federal Reserve Bank, 1978.

Labys, Walter C. *Dynamic Commodity Models: Specification, Estimation, and Simulation*. Lexington, Mass.: Heath, 1973.

——, M. Ishag Nadiri, and Jose Nunex Del Arco. *Commodity Markets and Latin American Development*. Cambridge, Mass.: Ballinger, 1980.

Langemeier, L., and R. G. Thompson. "Study of Demand, Supply, and Price Relationships on the Beef Sector, Post World War II Period," *Journal of Farm Economics*, 49 (February 1967), 169–183.

"Las Vegas in Chicago: Speculating on Interest Rates Futures," *Forbes* (July 1, 1979), 31–33.

Leuthold, R. M. "Commercial Use and Speculative Measures of the Livestock Commodity Futures Markets," *The Journal of Futures Markets*, 3, No. 2 (1983), 113–135.

—— and Parry Dixon, eds. *Livestock Futures Research Symposium, Proceedings*. Chicago Mercantile Exchange, 1980.

—— and P. A. Hartmann. "A Semi-Strong Farm Evaluation of the Efficiency of the Hog Futures Market," *American Journal of Agricultural Economics*, 61, No. 3 (1979), 482–489.

——, A. J. A. MacCormick, A. Schmitz, and D. G. Watts. "Forecasting Daily Hog Prices and Quantities: A Study of Alternative Forecasting Techniques," *Journal of the American Statistical Association*, 65 (March 1970).

—— and W. G. Tomek. "Developments in the Livestock Futures Literature," in *Livestock Futures Research Symposium*. Chicago Mercantile Exchange, 1979.

Loosigian, Allan M. *Interest Rate Futures*. New York: Dow Jones Books, 1980.

——. *Foreign Exchange Futures*. Homewood, Ill.: Dow Jones–Irwin, 1981.

Lowell, Fred R. *The Wheat Market*. Kansas City, Mo.: Keltner Statistical Service, 1968.

Lutgen, L., and M. Turner. "Successful Futures Trading; Predicting Basis Is the Key," *Hog Farm Management*, 12, No. 11 (November 1975), 48–49.

McCoy, J., et al. "Pricing Feeder Pigs," *Hog Farm Management*, 13, No. 3 (March 1976), 82.

Meinken, K. W. *The Demand and Price Structure for Wheat*, USDA Technical Bulletin 1136, November 1955.

Miller, Stephen Ernest. *Live Hog Futures Prices as Expected Prices in the Empirical Modeling of the Pork Sector*. Chicago Mercantile Exchange, 1977.

——. "Forward Pricing Feeder Pigs," *The Journal of Futures Markets*, 2, No. 4 (1982), 333–340.

Miracle, Diane S. "The Egg Futures Market: 1940–1966," *Food Research Institute Studies*, 11, No. 3 (1972).

"More Competition Needed in Hog Marketing," *Hog Farm Management*, 12, No. 3 (March 1975), 38.

"More Hogs but . . ." *Commodities*, 5, No. 3 (March 1976), 22–26.

Myers, L. H. "Economic Analysis of the Monthly Structure of the Hog Pork Sector of the U.S.," Ph.D. dissertation, Purdue University, 1968.

Olmedo, James, P., Jr., "Understanding the Lumber and Plywood Futures Markets," *Forecasting Commodity Prices*. New York: Commodity Research Bureau, 1975.

Oster, Merrill J. *Multiply Your Money Trading Soybeans.* Cedar Falls, Iowa: Investor Publications, 1981.

Paul, Allen B., Kandice H. Kahl, and William G. Tomek. *Performance of Futures Markets: The Case of Potatoes,* USDA Technical Bulletin 1636, 1981.

Peck, A. E. "Measures and Price Effects of Changes in Speculation on the Wheat, Corn, and Soybean Futures Markets," *Research on Speculation Seminar Report.* Chicago Board of Trade, 1981, 138–149.

Peery, J. S. "Theory and Practice in the Forward Market for Shell Eggs," Ph.D. dissertation, Northwestern University, 1964.

Powers, Mark J. "An Economic Analysis of the Futures Market for Pork Bellies," thesis, University of Wisconsin, 1966.

——— and D. Vogel. *Inside the Financial Futures Markets.* New York: Wiley, 1981.

Puglisi, D. "Is the Futures Market for Treasury Bills Efficient?" *The Journal of Portfolio Management,* 4, No. 2 (winter 1978), 64–67.

Purcell, Wayne D. *Agricultural Marketing: Systems, Coordination, Cash and Futures Prices.* Reston, Va.: Reston, 1979.

Reiman, Ray. "The Hog Farmer Who Came in From the Mud," *Commodities,* 4, No. 5 (May 1975), 26–32.

———. "Cattle, Cattle, Everywhere . . ." *Commodities,* 4, No. 6 (June 1975), 28–33.

———. "Are Hogs Finally Climbing Back on Their Cycle?" *Commodities,* 4, No. 11 (November 1975), 18–24.

Rendleman, R., and C. Carabini, "The Efficiency of the Treasury Bill Futures Market," *Journal of Finance,* 34, No. 4 (September 1979), 895–914.

Rhodes, V. James. *The Agricultural Marketing System.* Columbus, Ohio: Grid, 1978.

Riehl, Heinz, and Rita M. Rodriguez. *Foreign Exchange Markets.* New York: McGraw-Hill, 1977.

Rogers, George B. *Costs and Returns for Poultry and Eggs 1955–1975.* U.S. Department of Agriculture, Economic Research Service, Poultry and Egg Situation 290, June 1976.

Rourke, B. E. "Causes and Predictability of Annual Changes in Supplies and Prices of Coffee," Ph.D. dissertation, Stanford University, 1969.

Roy, Sujit. "Econometric Models for Predicting Short Run Egg Prices," Pennsylvania State University, University Park, Pa., 1971. (Mimeographed.)

Sandor, R. "The Interest Rate Futures Markets: An Introduction," *Commodities,* 5, No. 9 (September 1976), 14–17.

Schwager, Jack. "Hogs: A Period of Transition . . . Finally?" *Commodities,* 5, No. 8 (August 1976), 20–27.

Schwartz, E. W. *How to Use Interest Rate Futures Contracts.* Homewood, Ill.: Dow Jones–Irwin, 1979.

Skadberg, J. M., and G. A. Futrell. "An Economic Appraisal of Futures Trading in Livestock," *Journal of Farm Economics,* 48, No. 5 (December 1966), 1485–1489.

Smith, Courtney. *Commodity Spreads: Techniques and Methods for Spreading Financial Futures Grains, Meats and Other Commodities.* New York: Wiley, 1982.

Smith, J. G. *Organized Produce Markets.* London: Longmans, 1922.

Snape, R. H. "Protection and Stabilization in the World Sugar Industry," Ph.D. dissertation, University of London, 1962.

Sohn, H. K. "A Spatial Equilibrium Model of the Beef Industry in the United States," Ph.D. dissertation, University of Hawaii, 1970.

Stewart, Blair. *An Analysis of Speculative Trading in Grain Futures,* USDA Technical Bulletin 1001, October 1949.

Stone, M. J. C. "The Trade View of the Market," in *The Future of Sugar,* International Sweetener and Alcohol Conference, 1980.

Stuning, William C. "Understanding the Coffee Market," *Forecasting Commodity Prices.* New York: Commodity Research Bureau, 1975.

Taylor, A. E. "Speculation, Short Selling, and the Price of Wheat," *Food Research Institute Wheat Studies* (1931), 231–266.

Telser, L. G. "The Supply of Stocks: Cotton and Wheat," Ph.D. dissertation, University of Chicago, 1956.

———. "Futures Trading and the Storage of Cotton and Wheat," *Journal of Political Economy,* 66, No. 3 (June 1958), 233–255.

———. "The Supply of Speculative Services in Wheat, Corn and Soybeans," *Food Research Institute Studies,* Supplement, 7 (1967), 131–176.

Tewes, T. "Sugar: A Short-Term Forecasting Model for the World Market with a Forecast of the World Market Price for Sugar in 1972–1973," *The Business Economist*, 4 (summer 1972), 89–97.

Trustman, Alan. "The Silver Scam: How the Hunts Were Outfoxed," *Atlantic*, 246 (September 1980), 70–81.

Uribe Compuzano, Andres. *Brown Gold*. New York: Random House, 1954.

U.S. Congress, Senate Committee on Agriculture, Nutrition, and Forestry. *Report on the CFTC on Recent Developments in the Silver Futures Market*, May 1980.

USDA, Agricultural Marketing Service. *Possibilities for Futures Trading in Florida Citrus Fruit and Products*, Marketing Research Report 156, February 1959.

USDA, Commodity Exchange Authority. *Speculation in Onion Futures*, March 1957.

USDA, Commodity Exchange Authority. *Trading in Frozen Pork Bellies*, October 1967.

USDA, Consumer and Marketing Service. *Fats and Oils Situations*, quarterly.

USDA, Economic Research Service. *An Economic Study of the U.S. Potato Industry*, Agricultural Economic Report 6, 1962.

USDA, Economic Research Service. *Demand and Price Analysis for Potatoes*, USDA Technical Bulletin 1380, July 1967.

USDA, Economic Research Service. *Margins, Speculation and Prices in Grains Futures Markets*, December 1967.

USDA, Economic Research Service. *Agriculture—The Third Century*, July 1976.

USDA, Foreign Agricultural Service. *U.S. Coffee Consumption, 1946–1976*, FAS M-275, February 1977.

USDA, Foreign Agricultural Service. *Coffee Production and Trade in Latin America*, FAS M-288, May 1979.

U.S. Federal Trade Commission. *Economic Report of the Investigation of Coffee Prices*.

U.S. Federal Trade Commission. *Report on the Grain Trade*, 7 vols., 1920–1926.

U.S. General Accounting Office. *Beef Marketing: Issues and Concerns*, 1978.

Vaile, R. S. "Speculation and the Price of Grain," *Journal of Marketing*, 12 (1947), 497–498.

Vandenborre, Roger J. "Demand Analysis on the Markets for Soybean Oil and Soybean Meal," *Journal of Farm Economics*, 28 (November 1946), 920–934.

Waldock, Jack. "What Is behind Those Wild Belly Spreads," *Commodities*, 5, No. 1 (January 1976), 24–26.

Walsh, Joseph M. *Coffee, Its History Classification and Description*. Philadelphia: Henry T. Coates and Co., 1894.

Ward, Ronald. "Market Liquidity in the FCOJ Futures Market," *American Journal of Agricultural Economics*, 56, No. 1 (February 1974), 150–154.

Weiss, J. S. "A Spectral Analysis of World Cocoa Prices," *American Journal of Agricultural Economics*, 52 (February 1970), 122–126.

Weisser, M. *The Sydney Wool Futures Market*, Bureau of Agricultural Economics, Wool Economic Research Report 4, Canberra, June 1963.

Wesson, William T. *The Economic Importance of Futures Trading in Potatoes*, USDA Marketing Research Report 241, June 1958.

Weymar, F. Helmut. *The Dynamics of the World Cocoa Market*. Cambridge, Mass.: M.I.T., 1968.

"What's Ahead for Your Cattle Customer?" *AgricFinance*, 18, No. 3 (May/June 1976), 35–40.

Wickizer, L. V. D. *Coffee, Tea, and Cocoa*. Stanford, Calif.: Stanford University Press, 1951.

Witherall, W. H. *Dynamics of the International Wool Market: An Econometric Analysis*, Econometric Research Program Memorandum 91. Princeton, N.J.: Princeton University Press, September 1967.

Working, Holbrook. "Financial Results of Speculative Holding of Wheat," *Food Research Institute Wheat Studies*, 7, No. 81 (July 1931).

——. "Futures Trading and Hedging As Applied to the Wine Industry," *Food Research Institute Studies* (1953).

——. "Economic Functions of Futures Markets," in H. Bakken, ed., *Futures Trading in Livestock—Origins and Concepts*. Madison, Wis.: Mimir, 1970.

Yamey, B. S. "Cotton Futures Trading in Liverpool," *Three Banks Review*, No. 41 (March 1959), 21–38.

VI. REGULATION OF FUTURES TRADING

Anderson, Ronald W. "The Regulation of Futures Contract Innovations in the United States," *The Journal of Futures Markets*, 4, No. 3 (1984), 297–332.

Bagley, William. "Introduction: A New Body of Law in an Era of Industry Growth," *Emory Law Journal* (fall 1978), 849–851.

Blanco, Joseph. "The Mechanics of Futures Trading: Speculation and Manipulation," *Hofstra Law Review* (fall 1977), 27–40.

Bor, Robert. "Some Issues Arising in Consideration of the Futures Trading Act of 1978," *Record of the Association of the Bar of the City of New York* (April 1979), 278–289.

The Bureau of National Affairs. *Securities Regulation and Law Report,* No. 558 (Washington, D.C., June 18, 1980), pp. 2, F-1 to F-12.

Cagan, Phillip. "Financial Futures Markets: Is More Regulation Needed?" *The Journal of Futures Markets,* 1, No. 2 (1981), 169–189.

"CFTC: Kicked While It's Down," *Economist* (Mar. 24, 1979), 141–142.

"CFTC vs. Exchanges: The Cash Price Battle," *Commodities* (October 1977), 56–59.

Chief, William, and Jerry Markham. "The Nation's 'Commodity Cops'—Efforts by the Commodity Futures Trading Commission to Enforce the Commodities Exchange Act," *Business Lawyer* (November 1978), 19–61.

Commodity Futures Trading Commission Regulatory Authority Review: Hearing, Feb. 12 and May 21, 1980, House Committee on Agriculture, 1981.

Commodity Futures Trading Commission Act; Hearings, 93d Cong., 2d Sess., on S. 2485, S. 2578, S. 2837, and H.R. 13113, Senate Committee on Agriculture and Forestry, 1974.

The Commodity Futures Trading Commission Act of 1974, 93d Cong., 2d Sess., H.R. 13113, Pub. L. 93-463, Senate Committee on Agriculture and Forestry, 1974.

Dinur, Daniel. "Tax Consequences in Settlement of Currency Futures Unclear Despite Recent Decision," *Journal of Taxation* (November 1979), 282–287.

Edwards, Franklin R. "The Regulation of Futures and Forward Trading by Depository Institutions: A Legal and Economic Analysis," *The Journal of Futures Markets,* 1, No. 2 (1981), 201–218.

———. "The Clearing Association in Futures Markets: Guarantor and Regulator," *The Journal of Futures Markets,* 3, No. 4 (1983), 369–392.

———. "Futures Markets in Transition: The Uneasy Balance between Government and Self-Regulation," *The Journal of Futures Markets,* 3, No. 2 (1983), 191–205.

———. "The Regulation of Futures Markets: A Conceptual Framework," *The Journal of Futures Markets,* 1 (1984), Supplement, 417–439.

Edwards, Linda N., and Franklin R. Edwards. "A Legal and Economic Analysis of Manipulation in Futures Markets," *The Journal of Futures Markets,* 4, No. 3 (1984), 333–366.

Emery, H. C. "Legislation against Futures," *Political Science Quarterly,* 10 (1886), 62–68.

"Everyone Encounters Commodities Regulation Sooner or Later" (from *Proceedings ABA National Institute,* December 1979), *Business Lawyer,* 35 (March 1980), 691–912.

Filler, Ronald H. "Bring Us Forth from the Land of Duplicative Regulation," *The Journal of Futures Markets,* 1 (1981), Supplement, 449–452.

Fischel, D., and S. Grossman. "Customer Protection in Futures and Securities Markets," *The Journal of Futures Markets,* 4, No. 3 (1984), 271–293.

Futures Trading Act of 1978, Senate Committee on Agriculture, Nutrition and Forestry, 1979.

Goldfein, Lawrence, and Lester Hochberg. "Analysis of IRS's Ruling that Straddle Transactions Lack Requisite Profit Motive," *Journal of Taxation* (September 1977), 142–147.

Greenburg, Stephen. "On Being Regulated: Remarks by a Futures Commission Merchant," *Hofstra Law Review* (fall 1977), 143–147.

Greenstone, Wayne. "Foreign Commodity Trader: A Regulatory Dilemma," *Administrative Law Review* (fall 1978), 535–548.

Johnson, Philip. "The Changing Face of Commodity Regulation," *Practical Lawyer* (December 1974), 27–42.

———. "Futures Image, the Regulators and Other Concerns," *Commodities* (August 1979), 8–10 ff.

Jordan, Leslie, and Richard J. Teweles. "The Expert Witness in Commodities Futures Litigation," *Trial Magazine* (July 1982).

Kane, Edward J. "Regulatory Structure in Futures Markets: Jurisdictional Competition between the SEC, the CFTC, and Other Agencies," *The Journal of Futures Markets,* 4, No. 3 (1984), 367–384.

Killough, H. B. "Effects of Governmental Regulation of Commodity Exchanges in the United States," *Harvard Business Review,* 11 (1933), 307–315.

Lee, Lawrence. "Commodity Futures as Tax Shelters," *Practical Lawyer* (Apr. 15, 1977), 11–22.

Levin, Simon, and Charles Zucker. "Trading in Commodities Can Result in Tax Savings as Well as Investment Advantages," *Taxation for Accountants* (August 1979), 94–102.

Levinson, Arnold. "Abuses in Commodity Markets: The Need for Change in the Regulatory Structure," *Georgetown Law Journal* (February 1975), 751–773.

Lower, Robert. "Regulation of Commodity Options," *Duke Law Journal* (December 1978), 1095–1145.

McCabe, George, and Robert McLeod. "Regulation and Bank Trading in the Futures Market," *Issues in Bank Regulation* (summer 1979), 6–14.

McCall, James. "Taxation: Commodity Straddles as an Income Sheltering Device," *Oklahoma Law Review* (winter 1978), 233–246.

Moylan, James J. "Self-Regulation in the Commodity Futures Industry," *The Journal of Futures Markets*, 1 (1981), Supplement, 501–504.

Paul, Allen. *Treatment of Hedging in Commodity Market Regulation*, U.S. Department of Agriculture Technical Bulletin 1538, 1976.

Peck, A. E. "Increase Speculative Limits?" *Commodities*, 10 (February 1981), 20.

———. "The Role of Economic Analysis in Futures Market Regulation," *American Journal of Agricultural Economics*, 62 (December 1980), 1037–1043.

Peck, Ron. "Tax Consequences of Currency Futures after Hoover," *International Tax Journal* (February 1980), 165–177.

Peltzman, Sam. "Toward a More General Theory of Regulation," *Journal of Law and Economics* (August 1976), 211–240.

Rainbolt, John, II. "Regulating the Grain Gambler and His Successors," *Hofstra Law Review* (fall 1977), 1–25.

Rosen, Jeffrey S. "The Impact of the Futures Trading Act of 1982 upon Commodity Regulation," *The Journal of Futures Markets*, 3, No. 3 (1983), 235–258.

Russo, Thomas, and Edwin Lyon. "The Exclusive Jurisdiction of the Commodity Futures Trading Commission," *Hofstra Law Review* (fall 1977), 57–91.

Saitlin, Sheldon. "Exclusive CFTC Jurisdiction of Commodity Trading Vehicles May Depend upon Form over Substances or, Everyone into the Pool," *Business Lawyer* (November 1977), 241–298.

———. "Additional Developments on the Question of CFTC Exclusive Jurisdiction over Commodity Vehicles," *Business Lawyer* (July 1978), 2195–2198.

Saloner, G. "Self-Regulating Commodity Futures Exchanges," in *The Industrial Organization of Futures Markets: Structure and Conduct,* ed. R. W. Anderson. Lexington, Mass.: Lexington Books, 1984.

Schneider, Howard. "The CFTC: Initial Action and Future Priorities," *Administrative Law Review* (fall 1975), 369–376.

———. "Commodities Law and Predispute Arbitration Clauses," *Hofstra Law Review* (fall 1977), 129–142.

——— and Fred Santo. "Commodity Futures Trading Commission: A Review of the 1978 Legislation," *Business Lawyer* (July 1979), 1755–1770.

Schroeder, Edmund, and Susan Pollack. "Commodities Regulation," *The Review of Securities Regulation* (Apr. 9, 1975), 935–950.

Selig, Stephen, and Wayne Schmittberger. "Tax Aspects of Commodity Futures Trading," *Hofstra Law Review* (fall 1977), 93–114.

Shapiro, Donald. "Commodities, Forwards, Puts and Calls—Things Equal to the Same Things Are Sometimes Not Equal to Each Other," *Tax Lawyer* (spring 1981), 581–604.

Srodes, James. "CFTC Disaster . . . How Long Can Commodity Trading Endure Its Regulators Bungling?" *Financial World* (June 1, 1979), 24–27.

Stassen, John H. "Facts Are Stubborn Things: Section 3 Should Be Revised," *The Journal of Futures Markets*, 1 (1981), Supplement, 457–459.

Stone, James M. "Principles of the Regulation of Futures Markets," *The Journal of Futures Markets*, 1, No. 2 (1981), 117–121.

"Symposium on Commodity Futures Regulation," *Hofstra Law Review* (fall 1977), 1–201.

Teweles, Richard J. "Excessive Trading and the Expert Consultant," *Commodities Law Letter*, IV, Nos. 2 and 3 (April and May 1984).

U.S. Comptroller General. *Report to the Congress: Improvements Needed in Regulation of Commodities Futures Trading.* U.S. Commodity Futures Trading Commission, 1975.

Valdez, Abelando. "Modernizing the Regulation of the Commodity Futures Markets," *Harvard Journal of Legislation* (December 1975), 35–75.

White, Frederick L. "Jurisdiction over Commodity Futures Contracts: Vertical versus Horizontal Regulation," *The Journal of Futures Markets*, 1 (1981), Supplement, 441–443.

————. "Taxation of Commodity Futures Transactions by State or Local Government," *The Journal of Futures Markets,* 1 (1981), Supplement, 491–493.

Working, Holbrook. "Futures Markets under Renewed Attack," *Food Research Institute Studies,* 4, No. 1 (1963), 13–24.

————. "Spoiling the Broth; Congress Acted Unwisely When It Banned Trading in Onion Futures," *Barron's,* 43, No. 5 (Feb. 4, 1963), 11, 22.

Wunder, David. "Commodities Regulation: State and Federal Jurisdiction," *Administrative Law Review* (fall 1975), 377–379.

VII. PRICE BEHAVIOR

Alexander, Sidney. "Price Movements in Speculative Markets: Trends or Random Walks," No. 2, as reprinted in Paul Cootner, ed., *The Random Character of Stock Market Prices.* Cambridge, Mass.: M.I.T., 1964, pp. 338–372.

Allingham, M. G. "Futures Price Oscillations," *Economica* (May 1976), 169–172.

Armstrong, Charles E. "Testing Cycles for Statistical Significance," *Journal of Cycle Research* (October 1961).

Arnold, David B. "An Econometric Study on the Weekly Behavior of the Cash Basis for Corn at Chicago," thesis, University of Illinois, 1969.

Bachelier, Louis. "Theory of Speculation," reprinted in Paul Cootner, ed., *The Random Character of Stock Market Prices.* Cambridge, Mass.: M.I.T., 1964.

Bance, Nigel. "Will the Next Commodity Boom Be like the Last?" *Euromoney* (February 1976), 61.

Barnes, R. M. *Commodity Profits through Trend Trading: Price Models and Strategies.* New York: Wiley, 1982.

Baumol, W. J. "Speculation, Profitability and Stability," *Review of Economics and Statistics,* 39 (August 1957), 263–271.

Bear, R. M. "Martingale Movements in Commodity Futures," Ph.D. dissertation, University of Iowa, 1970.

Beckman, M. J. "On the Determination of Prices in Futures Markets," reprinted in M. J. Brennan, ed., *Patterns of Market Behavior.* Providence, R.I.: Brown University Press, 1965.

Bernstein, J. *The Handbook of Commodity Cycles: A Window on Time.* New York: Wiley, 1982.

Blank, Steve. "Are Commodity Futures Prices 'Accurate'?" *Commodities* (September 1977), 24–26.

Booth, G. Geoffrey, and Fred R. Kaen. "Gold and Silver Spot Prices and Market Information Efficiency," *The Financial Review* (spring 1979), 21–26.

Brinegar, C. S. "A Statistical Analysis of Speculative Price Behavior," Ph.D. dissertation, Stanford University, 1954.

————. "A Statistical Analysis of Speculative Price Behavior," *Food Research Institute Studies,* Supplement, 9 (1970).

Clough, Malcolm. "Relation between Corn and Wheat Futures," *Journal of Farm Economics,* 21 (1939), 500–502.

"Commodity Prices—Scotching the Big-Bank Theory," *Citibank Monthly Economic Letter* (July 1976), 11–15.

Cootner, Paul H. "Stock Prices: Random vs. Systematic Changes," *Industrial Management Review,* 3, No. 2 (spring 1962).

————, ed. *The Random Character of Stock Market Prices.* Cambridge, Mass.: M.I.T., 1964.

Cowles, Alfred, and H. E. Jones. "Some A Posteriori Probabilities in Stock Market Action," *Econometrica,* 5 (1937), 280–294.

"Crop Reports and Prices," *Commodities,* 5, No. 9 (September 1976), 26–27.

Derecho, Stefan D. "Not So Much a Commodity Price Boom, More a Ripple or Two," *Euromoney* (October 1976), 40–43.

"Distributors Eyeing Commodity Markets for New Cost-Price Data," *Industrial Distribution,* 66, No. 5 (May 1976), 40.

Dow, J. C. R. "The Inaccuracy of Expectations: A Statistical Study of the Liverpool Cotton Futures Market 1921/22–1937/38," *Economica,* new series, 8 (1941), 162–175.

Ehrich, R. L. "Cash-Futures Price Relationships for Live Beef Cattle," *American Journal of Agricultural Economics,* 51, No. 1 (February 1969), 26–40.

Fama, Eugene. "The Behavior of Stock Market Price," *Journal of Business* (January 1965).

————, L. Fisher, M. C. Jensen, and R. Roll. "The Adjustment of Stock Prices to New Information," *International Economic Review*, 10 (February 1969), 1–21.

Feduniak, Robert B. "Riding the Next Commodity Wave," *Financial World*, 145, No. 19 (Oct. 1, 1976), 9–12.

Fielitz, B. D. "Stationarity of Random Data: Some Implications for the Distribution of Stock Price Changes," *Journal of Financial and Quantitative Analysis*, 6 (June 1971), 1025–1034.

Fischer, R. *Stocks or Options? Programs for Profits.* New York: Wiley, 1980.

Frey, Norman E., and John W. Labuszewski. "Newspaper Articles and Their Impact on Commodity Price Formation—Case Study: Copper," *The Journal of Futures Markets*, 1, No. 1 (1981), 89–91.

Godfrey, M. D., C. W. J. Granger, and O. Morgenstern. "The Random Walk Hypothesis of Stock Market Behavior," *Kyklos*, 17 (1964), 1–30.

Graham, R. W. "Cash-Future Price Relationships in Corn," M.S. thesis, University of Illinois, Urbana, 1954.

Granger, C. W. J. "Some Aspects of the Random Walk Model of Stock Prices," *International Economic Review*, 9 (1968), 283–287.

————. "What the Random Walk Does Not Say," *Financial Analysts Journal* (May–June 1970), 91–93.

Gray, Roger W. "The Characteristic Bias in Some Thin Futures Markets," *Food Research Institute Studies*, 1, No. 3 (November 1960).

————. "The Relationship among Three Futures Markets," *Food Research Institute Studies*, 2, No. 1 (February 1961).

————. "The Seasonal Pattern of Wheat Futures under the Loan Program," *Food Research Institute Studies*, 3, No. 1 (February 1962).

————. "Fundamental Price Behavior Characteristics in Commodity Futures," *Futures Trading Seminar*, 3 (1966).

————. "Price Effects of a Lack of Speculation," *Food Research Institute Studies*, Supplement, 7 (1977), 177–194.

———— and S. T. Nielsen. "Rediscovery of Some Fundamental Price Behavior Characteristics," paper presented at meeting of Econometric Society, Cleveland, Ohio, September 1963.

Grushcow, J., and C. Smith. *Profits through Seasonal Trading.* New York: Wiley, 1980.

Gusler, G. "Price Discovery II. How Egg Futures Affect Prices," *Egg Producer*, 91, No. 3 (March 1960), 8–9.

Heifner, R. G. "Temporal Relationships among Futures Prices: Comment," *American Journal of Agricultural Economics* (May 1971).

Hendel, J. "Price Making in Organized Commodity Markets," *Marketing Research Commission Report 5*, Western Agricultual Economics Research Council (1963), 71–98.

Hoffman, G. W. *Future Trading and the Cash Grain Markets*, USDA Circular 201, 1932.

————. *Grain Prices and the Futures Markets*, USDA Technical Bulletin 747, January 1941.

Hoose, Sidney, and Holbrook Working. "Price Relations of Liverpool Wheat Futures with Special Reference to the December–March Spread," *Food Research Institute Wheat Studies*, 17 (1940), 101–143.

Houthakker, H. S. *Commodity Futures IV: An Empirical Test of the Theory of Normal Backwardation*, Cowles Commission Discussion Paper, Economics No. 2124, June 1955.

————. *Restatement of the Theory of Normal Backwardation*, Foundation Discussion Paper, Economics No. 44, December 1957.

————. "Systematic and Random Elements in Short-Term Price Movements," *American Economic Review*, 51 (1961).

Irwin, H. S. "Seasonal Cycles in Aggregates of Wheat-Futures Contracts," *Journal of Political Economy*, 43 (1935), 34–49.

————. *Seasonal Tendencies in Wheat Futures Prices.* Washington, D.C.: Grain Futures Administration, 1938.

Jensen, Michael. "Comment," *Financial Analysts Journal* (November–December 1967), 77–85.

———— and George A. Benington. "Random Walks and Technical Theories: Some Additional Evidence," *Journal of Finance*, 25 (1970), 469–481.

Jobman, Darrell. "A Look at Price Ratios," *Commodities*, 5, No. 4 (April 1976), 28–29.

Jones, David L. "The Misbehavior of Commodity Futures Prices," *Commodities*, 4, No. 8 (August 1975), 20.

Kassouf, S. T. "Stock Price Random Walks: Some Supporting Evidence," *Review of Economic Statistics* (May 1968).

Kemp, M. C. "Speculation, Profitability, and Price Stability," *Review of Economics and Statistics,* 45, No. 2 (May 1962), 185–189.

Kendall, M. G. "The Analysis of Economic Times Series—Part I: Prices," *Journal of the Royal Statistical Society,* Series A (General), 116, No. 1 (1953), 11–25.

Keynes, J. M. "Some Aspects of Commodity Markets," *Manchester Guardian Commercial,* European Reconstruction Series, Section 13 (Mar. 29, 1923), 784–786.

Labys, Walter C. "Commodity Price Fluctuations: A Short Term Explanation for Selected Commodities on the American Market," Ph.D. dissertation, University of Nottingham, 1968.

Larson, A. B. "Evidence on the Temporal Dispersion of Price Effects of New Market Information," Ph.D. dissertation, Stanford University, 1960.

————. "Measurement of a Random Process in Futures Prices," *Food Research Institute Studies,* 1, No. 3 (1960).

————. "The Quiddity of the Cobweb Theorem," *Food Research Institute Studies,* 7 No. 2 (1967).

Levy, R. A. "Random Walks: Reality or Myth?" *Financial Analysts Journal* (November–December 1967), 69–77.

Malkiel, B. G., and J. G. Cragg. "Expectation and the Structure of Share Prices," *American Economic Review,* 60 (1970), 601–617.

Mandelbrot, Benoit. "The Variation of Certain Speculative Prices," *Journal of Business,* 36, No. 4 (1963), 394–419.

Manderscheid, L. V. "Influence of Price Support Program on Seasonal Corn Prices," Ph.D. dissertation, Stanford University, 1961.

Mann, Jitendar. "Intraday Commodity Price Movements," *Agricultural Economics Research* (April 1980), 44–47.

Margins, Speculation and Prices in Grains Futures Markets. USDA, Economic Research Service, December 1967.

Marine, C. L. "Effects of Futures Trading on Price Variation," M.S. thesis, University of Illinois, Urbana, 1959.

McCain, Wesley G. "Price Effects of Margin Changes in Commodity Future Markets," Ph.D. dissertation, Stanford University, 1969.

Mehl, Paul. "Trading in Futures and Price Fluctuations," *Journal of Farm Economics,* 16 (1934), 481–495.

————. "Relationship between Daily Price Range and Net Price Change, Opening to Close of the Dominant Corn Future and the Daily Volume of Trading in Corn Futures on the Chicago Board of Trade," U.S. Grain Futures Administration, Washington, D.C., 1938.

————. "Trading in Wheat and Corn Futures in Relation to Price Movements," *Journal of Farm Economics,* 22 (1940), 601–612.

Moore, Arnold. "A Statistical Analysis of Common Stock Prices," Ph.D. dissertation, Graduate School of Business, University of Chicago, 1962.

Muth, John F. "Rational Expectations and the Theory of Price Movements," *Econometrica,* 29 (July 1961), 315–335.

Osborne, M. F. M. "Brownian Motion in the Stock Market," *Operations Research,* 7, No. 2 (March–April 1959), 145–173.

————. "Some Quantitative Tests for Stock Price Generating Models and Trading Folklore," *Journal of the American Statistical Association* (June 1967), 321–340.

"The Outlook for Commodity Prices," *The Bank Credit Analyst,* 28 (1, pt. 3, July 1976), 30–42.

Parzen, E. *Time Series Analysis Papers.* San Francisco: Holden Day, 1968.

Peck, A. E. "Future Markets, Supply Response and Price Stability," *The Quarterly Journal of Economics,* 90, No. 3 (August 1976).

————. "The Question of Bias in Futures Prices," in *Selected Writings on Futures Markets,* Vol. 2, ed. A. E. Peck. Chicago Board of Trade, 1977, pp. 1–4.

Peston, M. H., and B. S. Yamey. "Inter-temporal Price Relationships with Forward Markets: A Method of Analysis," *Economica,* new series, 27 (1960), 355–367.

Pinches, George E., and William R. Kinney, Jr. "The Measurement of the Volatility of Common Stock Prices," *Journal of Finance,* 26 (1971), 119–125.

Praetz, P. D. "The Distribution of Share Price Changes," *Journal of Business,* 45 (January 1972), 49–55.

"Price Conference Report," *Farm Futures,* 4, No. 8 (August 1976), 34–41.

Roberts, Harry. "Stock Market 'Patterns' and Financial Analysis: Methodological Suggestions," *Journal of Finance* (March 1959), 4–5.

Rocca, L. H. "Time Series Analysis of Commodity Futures Prices," Ph.D. dissertation, University of California, Berkeley, 1969.

Rutledge, D. "A Note on the Variability of Futures Prices," in *Selected Writings on Futures Markets,* ed. A. E. Peck. Chicago Board of Trade, 1977.

———. "Trading Volume and Price Variability: New Evidence on the Price Effects of Speculation," International Futures Trading Seminar 1978, Chicago Board of Trade, 161–174.

Samuelson, Paul A. "Intertemporal Price Equilibrium: A Prologue to the Theory of Speculation," *Welwirtschaftliches Archiv,* 79 (December 1957), 181–221.

———. "Proof that Properly Anticipated Prices Fluctuate Randomly," *Industrial Management Review,* 6, No. 2 (spring 1965), 41–49.

———. "A Random Theory of Futures Prices," *Industrial Management Review,* 6 (June 1965).

Sargent, T. J. "Commodity Price Expectations and the Interest Rate," *Quarterly Journal of Economics,* 83 (February 1969), 126–140.

Shelton, J. P. "The Value Line Contest: A Test of the Predictability of Stock Market Changes," *Journal of Business* (July 1967).

Snape, R. H. "Price Relationships on the Sydney Wool Futures Market," *Economica,* new series, 35, No. 138 (May 1968), 169–178.

Sobel, Eugene. "Approximate Best Linear Prediction of a Certain Class of Stationary and Non-Stationary Noise Distorted Signals," *Journal of the American Statistical Association,* 66, No. 334 (June 1971), 363–370.

Spence, A. "The Third World and Commodity Prices: What Next?" *Banker,* 126, No. 608 (October 1976), 1123–1126.

Stein, J. L. "The Simultaneous Determination of Spot and Futures Prices," *American Economic Review,* 51, No. 5 (December 1961), 1012–1025.

Stevenson, Richard, and Robert M. Bear. "Commodity Futures: Trends or Random Walks?" *Journal of Finance,* 25, No. 1 (March 1970), 65–81.

Taussig, F. W. "Is Market Price Determinate?" *Quarterly Journal of Economics,* 35 (May 1921), 394–411.

Telser, Lester G. "Price Relations between May and New Crop Wheat Futures at Chicago since 1885," *Wheat Studies,* 10 (February 1934), 183–228.

———. "A Theory of Speculation Relating Profitability and Stability," *Review of Economics and Statistics,* 41 (1959), 295–301.

Teweles, Richard J., and Charles V. Harlow. "An Inquiry into Non-Random Elements of the Commodity Futures Markets," *Journal of Commodity Trading,* 4 (July–August 1969).

Tomek, W. G., and Roger W. Gray. "Temporal Relationships among Prices on Commodity Futures Markets: Their Allocative and Stabilizing Roles," *American Journal of Agricultural Economics,* 52, No. 3 (August 1970), 372–380.

Turnowsky, Stephen J. "Stochastic Stability of Short-Run Market Equilibrium," *Quarterly Journal of Economics,* 82 (November 1968), 666–681.

12 Years of Achievement under Public Law 480, USDA, Economic Research Service, 1967.

Vaile, Roland. "Cash and Futures Price of Corn," *Journal of Marketing,* 9 (July 1944).

———. "Inverse Carrying Charges in Futures Markets," *Journal of Farm Economics,* 30, No. 3 (August 1948), 574–575.

Vance, Lawrence. "Grain Market Forces in the Light of Inverse Carrying Charges," *Journal of Farm Economics,* 28 (November 1946), 1036–1040.

Watson, Donald S., and Mary A. Holman. *Price Theory and Its Uses,* 4th ed. Boston, Mass.: Houghton Mifflin, 1976.

Weiss, Moshe. "Quantitative Analysis of Egg Price Quotations," Ph.D. dissertation, Cornell University, 1969.

White, G. R. "Some Statistical Aspects of Future Trading on a Commodity Exchange," *Royal Statistical Society Journal,* new series, 99 (1936), 297–329.

Working, Holbrook. "The Post Harvest Depression of Wheat Prices," *Food Research Institute Wheat Studies,* 5 (November 1929).

———. "Price Relations between July and September Wheat Futures at Chicago since 1885," *Food Research Institute Wheat Studies,* 9 (1933), 187–238.

———. "Price Relations between May and New-Crop Wheat Futures at Chicago since 1885," *Food Research Institute Wheat Studies,* 10 (1934), 183–228.

———. "A Random-Difference Series for Use in the Analysis of Time Series," *Journal of the American Statistical Association,* 29, No. 185 (March 1934), 11–24.

———. "Theory of the Inverse Carrying Charge in Futures Markets," *Journal of Farm Economics,* 30, No. 1 (February 1948), 1–28.

———. "Memorandum on Measurement of Cycles in Speculative Prices," *Food Research Institute Studies* (1949).

———. "Professor Vaile and the Theory of Inverse Carrying Charges," *Journal of Farm Economics,* 31, No. 1 (February 1949), 168–172.

———. "A Note on Mr. Meade's Theory of Competitive Speculation," *Review of Economic Studies,* 18 (1951), 188–189.

———. "Price Effects of Scalping and Day Trading," *Proceedings of the Seventh Annual Symposium: Commodity Markets and the Public Interest* (Chicago Board of Trade, 1954).

———. "New Ideas and Methods for Price Research," *Journal of Farm Economics,* 38, No. 5 (December 1956), 1427–1436.

———. "Note on the Correlation of First Differences of Averages in a Random Chain," *Econometrica,* 28 (1960), 916–918.

———. "Price Effect on Futures Trading," *Food Research Institute Studies,* 1, No. 1 (February 1960), 3–31.

———. "Frontiers in Uncertainty Theory: The Evidence of Futures Markets: New Concepts Concerning Futures Markets and Prices," *American Economic Review Papers and Proceedings,* 51, No. 2 (May 1961), 160–163.

———. "New Concepts Concerning Futures Markets and Prices," *American Economic Review,* 52, No. 3 (June 1962), 431–459.

Yamey, Basil S. "Speculation and Price Stability: A Note," and Robert Z. Aliber, "Speculation and Price Stability: A Reply," *Journal of Political Economy,* 74 (April 1966), 206–208.

VIII. PRICE FORECASTING

Ainsworth, R. M. *Profitable Grain Trading.* Mason City, Ill.: Ainsworth Financial Service, 1933.

Appel, Gerald, and Martin E. Zweig. *New Directions in Technical Analysis.* Great Neck, N.Y.: Signalert, 1976.

Ashby, Andrew W. "On Forecasting Commodity Prices by the Balance Sheet Approach," *Journal of Farm Economics,* 46 (August 1964), 633–643.

Ashby, R. B. "Cotton Futures as Forecasters of Cotton Spot Prices," *Journal of the American Statistical Association,* 24, No. 168 (December 1929), 412–419.

Barnes, Robert. *Taming the Pits: A Technical Approach to Commodity Trading.* New York: Wiley, 1979.

———. *1981 Technical Commodity Yearbook.* Florence, Ky.: Van Nostrand Reinhold, 1981.

Bates, J., and C. W. J. Granger. "Combining Forecasts," *Operations Research Quarterly,* 20 (1969), 451–467.

Belveal, L. D. *Commodity Speculation.* Wilmette, Ill.: Commodities Press, 1967.

———. *Commodity Speculation: With Profits in Mind.* Wilmette, Ill.: Commodities Press, 1968.

Benner, Samuel. *Benner's Prophecies of Ups and Downs in Prices,* privately printed. Cincinnati, Ohio, 1875.

Bernstein, L. A. "How Commodity Price Charts Disclose Supply-Demand Shifts," *Commodity Year Book.* New York: Commodity Research Bureau, 1958, pp. 33–42.

Bolton, Hamilton. *The Elliot Wave Principle—A Critical Appraisal.* Montreal: Tremblay and Co., 1980.

Bostian, David. *Intra-Day Intensity Index,* privately printed. Fort Benjamin Harrison, Ind., 1967.

Brooks, William, Henry Wiebe, James Hier, and C. E. Francis. "Testing a Model for Predicting Commodity Futures Prices," *American Economist* (spring 1980), 24–31.

Brown, Robert. *Smoothing, Forecasting and Prediction of Discrete Times Series.* Englewood Cliffs, N.J.: Prentice-Hall, Inc., 1963.

Busby, William T. "A Model for Speculation in Pork Belly Futures," Ph.D. dissertation, University of Southern California, May 1971.

Christian, Roy E. *New Methods for Long Term Stock Market Forecasting.* Aptos, Calif.: Physicians Market Letter, 1966.

Cohen, A. *The Chartcraft Method of Point and Figure Trading.* Larchmont, N.Y.: Chartcraft, 1960.

Collins, Charles. "The Elliott Wave Principle—1966 Supplement," *The Bank Credit Analyst,* Quebec, Canada.

———. "Market Ebb Tide," *Barron's* (March 1970).

Conroy, Robert M., and Richard J. Rendleman, Jr. "Pricing Commodities When Both Price and Output Are Uncertain," *The Journal of Futures Markets,* 3, No. 4 (1983), 439–450.

Cornelius, James, John Ikerd, and A. Nelson. "A Preliminary Evaluation of Price Forecasting Performance by Agricultural Economists," *American Journal of Agricultural Economics* (November 1981), 712–714.

Cornell, B. "The Consumption Based Asset Pricing Model: A Note on Potential Tests and Applications," *Journal of Financial Economics,* 9 (1981), 103–108.

———. "The Relationship between Volume and Price Variability in Futures Markets," *The Journal of Futures Markets,* 1, No. 3 (1981), 303–316.

Cowles, Alfred W. "Can Stock Market Forecasters Forecast?" *Econometrica,* 1 (1933).

Cox, H. *A Common Sense Approach to Commodity Futures Trading.* New York: Reynolds, 1968.

Cox, J., J. Ingersoll, and S. Ross. "The Relation between Forward Prices and Futures Prices," *Journal of Financial Economics,* 9, No. 4 (December 1981), 321–346.

Dahl, Curtiss. *Consistent Profits in the Commodity Futures Market.* Cincinnati, Ohio: Tri-state Offset Co., 1960.

Devillers, Victor. *The Point and Figure Method of Anticipating Stock Price Movements.* New York: Tender Press, 1972.

Dewey, Edward R. *Cycles, The Science of Prediction.* New York: Holt, 1949.

———. "The 5½ Year Cycle in Corn Prices," *Cycles Magazine* (February 1955).

———. "Samuel Turner Benner," *Cycles Magazine* (March 1955).

———. "Kick in the Pants Cycles," *Cycles Magazine* (August 1961).

——— and O. G. Mandino. *Cycles: Mysterious Forces That Trigger Events.* New York: Hawthorne, 1971.

Dines, James. *How the Average Investor Can Use Technical Analysis for Stock Profits.* New York: Dines Chart Corp., 1972.

Donchian, R. D. "High Finance in Copper," *Financial Analysts Journal,* 16, No. 6 (November–December 1960), 133–142.

———. "Trend Following Methods in Commodity Price Analysis," *Guide to Commodity Price Forecasting.* New York: Commodity Research Bureau, 1965, pp. 48–60.

Drew, Garfield. "A Clarification of the Odd-Lot Theory," *Financial Analysts Journal* (September–October 1967).

Dunnigan, William. *New Blueprints for Gains in Stocks and Grains,* privately published. San Francisco, Calif., 1956.

Edwards, Robert D., and John Magee. *Technical Analysis of Stock Trends.* Springfield, Mass.: John Magee, 1961.

The Egg-Spread Method. Pasadena, Calif.: Market Research Associates, 1966.

Elliott, R. N. "The Wave Principle," *Financial World* (1939).

———. *Nature's Law—The Secret of the Universe,* privately published. New York, 1946.

Fama, Eugene F. "Forward Rates as Predictors of Future Spot Rates," *Journal of Financial Economics,* No. 3 (1976), 361–377.

Farrell, M. J. "Profitable Speculation," *Economica,* new series, 33, No. 130 (May 1966), 183–193.

"The Fibonacci Numbers," *Time* (April 1969).

Floss, Carl W. *Market Rhythm.* Detroit: Investors Publishing, 1955.

Gann, William D. *Forecasting Rules for Gain—Geometric Angles.* Pomeroy, Wash.: Lambert-Gann Publishing, 1976.

——— and J. L. Gann. *How to Make Profits Trading in Commodities: A Study of the Commodity Market, with Charts and Rules for Successful Trading and Investing.* New York: W. D. Gann and Sons, 1941; rev. ed. 1951.

Gardner, Robert L. *How to Make Money in the Commodity Market.* Englewood Cliffs, N.J.: Prentice-Hall, Inc., 1961.

Gartley, H. M. *Profits in the Stock Market.* New York: H. M. Gartley, 1935.

Gotthelf, Edward B. *The Commodex System.* New York: Commodity Futures Forecast.

Granger, C. W. J. *Forecasting in Business and Economics.* New York: Academic, 1980.

——— and O. Morgenstern. *Predictability of Stock Market Prices.* Lexington, Mass.: Heath, 1970.

Granville, Joseph. *Granville's New Key to Stock Market Profits.* Englewood Cliffs, N.J.: Prentice-Hall, Inc., 1963.

Graver, F., and R. Litzenberger. "The Pricing of Commodity Futures Contracts, Nominal Bonds, and Other Risky Assets under Commodity Price Uncertainty," *Journal of Finance,* 31 (March 1979).

Hamilton, Milo. "Computer Guesstimates 1977–78 Farm Prices," *Soybean Digest,* 37, No. 2 (December 1976), 16–18.

Hamilton, William Peter. *The Stock Market Barometer.* New York: Harper, 1922.

Hardy, Colburn. *The Investor's Guide to Technical Analysis.* New York: McGraw-Hill, 1978.

Harlow, Charles V. *An Analysis of the Predictive Value of Stock Market "Breadth" Measurements.* Larchmont, N.Y.: Investor's Intelligence, 1968.

Hart, John K. *Commodity Trend Service.* Columbus, Ga.

Heiby, Walter. *Stock Market Profits through Dynamic Synthesis.* Chicago, Ill.: Institute of Dynamic Synthesis, 1965.

Hieronymus, T. A. "Forecasting Soybean and Soybean Product Prices," in H. Jiler, ed., *Guide to Commodity Price Forecasting.* New York: Commodity Research Bureau, 1965.

————. *Economics of Futures Trading for Commercial and Personal Profit.* New York: Commodity Research Bureau, 1971.

Hill, John R. *Stock and Commodity Market Trend Trading by Advanced Technical Analysis.* Hendersonville, N.C.: Commodity Research Institute, 1977.

————. *Technical and Mathematical Analysis of the Commodity and Stock Markets.* Chicago, Ill.: Commodity Research Institute.

Hingorani, G. G. "Forecasting Economic Time Series Generated by Random Processes," *Proceedings of the Business and Economic Statistics Section of the Annual Meeting of the American Statistical Association* (1966).

Houthakker, H. S. "Can Speculators Forecast Prices?" *Review of Economics and Statistics,* 39, No. 2 (May 1959), 143–151.

Irwin, H. S. "Technical Conditions Are Important Factors in Short-Time Movements of Wheat Prices," *Journal of Farm Economics,* 18 (1936), 736–742.

Jarrett, F. G. "Short Term Forecasting of Australian Wool Prices," *Australian Economic Papers,* 4 (June–December 1965), 93–102.

Jevons, William Stanley. *The Periodicity of Commercial Crises and Physical Explanation.* University of Manchester, 1875.

————. *The Solar Period and the Price of Corn.* University of Manchester, 1875.

Jiler, Harry, ed. *Forecasting Commodity Prices: How the Experts Analyze the Market.* New York: Commodity Research Bureau, 1975.

Jiler, William. *How Charts Can Help You in the Stock Market.* New York: Commodity Research Publishing Corporation, 1961.

————, ed. *Guide to Commodity Price Forecasting.* New York: Commodity Research Bureau, 1965.

Just, Richard, and Gordon Rausser. "Commodity Price Forecasting with Large Scale Econometric Models and the Futures Market," *American Journal of Agricultural Economics* (May 1981), 197–208.

Kaish, Stanley. "Odd Lot Profit and Loss Performance," *Financial Analysts Journal* (September–October 1969).

Kaufman, Perry, ed. *Technical Analysts in Commodities.* New York: Wiley, 1980.

Keltner, Chester. *How to Make Money in Commodities.* Kansas City, Mo.: Keltner Statistical Service, 1960.

Kewley, Thomas J., and R. A. Stevenson. "The Odd Lot Theory—A Reply," *Financial Analysts Journal* (January–February 1969).

Labys, W. C., and C. W. J. Granger. *Speculation, Hedging and Commodity Price Forecasts.* Lexington, Mass.: Heath, 1970.

Larson, Arnold B. "Price Prediction on the Egg Futures Market," *Proceedings of a Symposium on Price Effects of Speculation in Organized Commodity Markets,* Food Research Studies, 7 (1967), 49–64.

Leslie, Conrad. *Guide for Successful Speculation.* Chicago: Darnell Press, 1970.

Levich, Richard. "An Assessment of Forecasting Accuracy and Market Efficiency in the International Money Market: 1967–1975," *Commodity Markets and Futures Prices,* ed. Raymond Leuthold. Chicago Mercantile Exchange, 1979, pp. 87–124.

Levine, Irving. *Successful Commodity Speculation.* Newark, N.J.: Levro Press, 1965.

Levy, Robert A. *The Relative Strength Concept of Common Stock Price Forecasting.* Larchmont, N.Y.: Investor's Intelligence, 1967.

Lindsay, George. "A Timing Method for Traders," *The Encyclopedia of Stock Market Techniques.* Larchmont, N.Y.: Investor's Intelligence, 1965.

Lowell, Fred R. *Profits in Soybeans.* Kansas City, Mo.: Keltner Statistical Service, 1966.

Mandelbrot, B. "Forecasts of Future Prices, Unbiased Markets and Martingale Models," *Journal of Business,* 39, Part 2 (January 1966), 242–255.

Markstein, David L. *How to Chart Your Way to Stock Market Profits.* West Nyack, N.Y.: Parker Publishing, 1966.

Marquardt, R. "An Evaluation of the Relative Price-Forecasting Accuracy of Selected Futures Markets," *Commodity Markets and Futures Prices,* ed. R. M. Leuthold. Chicago Mercantile Exchange, 1979, pp. 125–142.

———— and Anthony F. McGann. "Forecasting Commodity Prices," *Commodity Journal,* 10, No. 2 (September/October 1975), 29–33.

Martel, R. F. *Charting Supply and Demand for Stock Analysis.* Reading, Pa.: Martel, 1961.

Martin, Larry, and Philip Garcia. "The Price-Forecasting Performance of Futures Marktes for Live Cattle and Hogs: A Disaggregated Analysis," *American Journal of Agricultural Economics* (May 1981), 209–215.

Mishkin, F. S. "Are Market Forecasts Rational?" *American Economic Review,* 71 (June 1981), 295–306.

Murphy, P. J. "Outlook: Here's How You Can Use Shifts in the Stock and Commodities Market to Aid Forecasting," *Purchasing,* 79 (Aug. 19, 1975), 78.

Neill, Humphrey. *Tape Reading and Market Tactics.* Burlington, Vt.: Fraser, 1960.

O'Connor, William. *Stocks, Wheat and Pharaohs.* New York: Werner Books, 1961.

Oliviera, R. A., et al. "Time Series Forecasting Models of Lumber: Cash, Futures and Basis Prices," *Forest Science* (June 1977), 268–280.

Rausser, G. C., and R. E. Just. "Agricultural Commodity Price Forecasting Accuracy: Futures Markets versus Commercial Econometric Models," *International Futures Trading Seminar,* Vol. 6. Chicago Board of Trade, pp. 116–165.

Relative Volume Index. Louisville, Ky.: Trend Way Advisory Service.

Rhea, Robert. *The Dow Theory.* Binghamton, N.Y.: Vail-Ballou, 1932.

Rockwell, C. W. "Profits, Normal Backwardation, and Forecasting in Commodity Futures," Ph.D. dissertation, University of California, Berkeley, 1964.

Runner, Tim Jon. "Pit-falls of Computer Simulations," *Commodity Journal,* 6, No. 4 (July–August 1971).

Schabacker, Richard W. *Technical Analysis and Stock Market Profits.* New York: B. C. Forbes Publishing Company, 1934.

————. *Stock Market Profits.* Burlington, Vt.: Fraser, 1967.

Scheinman, William X. *Why Most Investors Are Mostly Wrong Most of the Time.* New York: Lancer, 1970.

Schulz, John. *The Intelligent Chartist.* New York: WRSM Financial Service, 1962.

Seligman, Daniel. "The Mystique of Point and Figure," *Fortune* (March 1962).

Shellans, S. "Building Technical Trading Models," *Commodities* (December 1980), 46–48.

Shishko, Irwin. "Forecasting Sugar Prices," in H. Jiler, ed., *Guide to Commodity Price Forecasting.* New York: Commodity Research Bureau, 1965.

————. "How to Forecast Cocoa Prices," in H. Jiler, ed., *Guide to Commodity Price Forecasting.* New York: Commodity Research Bureau, 1965.

————. "Techniques of Forecasting Commodity Prices," *Commodity Year Book.* New York: Commodity Research Bureau, 1965, pp. 30–36.

Stoken, D. "Forecasting Pork Belly Futures," *Commodity Year Book.* New York: Commodity Research Bureau, 1966.

Taylor, Robert Joel. "The Major Price Trend Directional Indicator," *Commodities Magazine* (April 1982).

Tomek, William G., and Scott F. Querin. "Random Processes in Prices and Technical Analysis," *The Journal of Futures Markets,* 4, No. 1 (1984), 15–23.

Tomkins, Edwin H. *Systematic Stock Trading.* Riverside, Ill.: The Moore Guide, 1969.

Unacek, Edward, Jr. "An Econometric Analysis and Forecasting Model for Pork Bellies," Ph.D. dissertation, Texas A. and M., 1967.

Van Horne, James, and G. Parker. "Technical Trading Rules: A Comment," *Financial Analysts Journal* (July–August 1968), 128–132.

Walters, James, and Larry Williams. "Measuring Market Momentum," *Commodities Magazine* (October 1972).

Weymar, F. H. "Cocoa, the Effects of Inventories on Price Forecasting," *Commodity Year Book.* New York: Commodity Research Bureau, 1969.

Wheelan, Alexander. *Study Helps in Point and Figure Technique.* New York: Morgan, Rogers and Roberts, 1962.

————. "Point and Figure Procedure in Commodity Market Analysis," *Guide to Commodity Price Forecasting.* New York: Commodity Research Bureau, 1965.

Williams, Larry. *Accumulation—Distribution Studies.* Carmel, Calif.: Williams Reports.

Working, Holbrook. "Quotations on Commodity Futures as Price Forecasts," *Econometrica,* 10 (1942), 39–52.

————. "A Theory of Anticipatory Prices," *American Economic Review,* 48, No. 2 (May 1958), 188–199.

Wyckoff, Richard. *Studies in Tape Reading.* New York: Traders Press, 1972.

IX. MONEY MANAGEMENT AND RISK CONTROL

Baratz, M. S. *Commodity Money Management Yearbook.* New York: Wiley, 1982.

Barger, Harold. "Speculation and the Risk-Preference," *Journal of Political Economy,* 46 (1938), 396–408.

Barnes, Robert M. "A Statistical Method for Setting Stops in Stock Trading," *Operations Research,* 18 (July 1970), 665–688.

Bear, R. M. "Risk and Return Patterns on Overnight Holdings of Livestock Futures," in R. M. Leuthold, ed., *Commodity Markets and Futures Prices.* Chicago Mercantile Exchange, 1970, pp. 13–23.

Bierman, H. "Diversification: Is There Safety in Numbers?" *The Journal of Portfolio Management,* 5, No. 1 (fall 1978), 29–32.

Blume, Marshall E. "On the Assessment of Risk," *Journal of Finance,* 26 (1971), 1–10.

Bodie, Z., and V. Rosansky. "Risk and Return in Futures Markets," *Financial Analysts Journal* (May/June 1980).

Breeden, Douglas. "Consumption Risk in Futures Markets," *The Journal of Finance* (May 1980), 503–520.

Briloff, A. J. "Income Tax Aspects of Commodity Futures Transactions," in H. Jiler, ed., *Guide to Commodity Price Forecasting.* New York: Commodity Research Bureau, 1965.

Cootner, P. H. "Returns to Speculators: Telser versus Keynes," in A. E. Peck, ed., *Readings in Futures Markets: 2: Selected Writings in Futures Markets.* Chicago Board of Trade, 1977.

Dalrymple, Brent B. "Risk Analysis Applied to Commodity Speculation," Ph.D. dissertation, Louisiana State University, 1970.

Diener, William. "Managed Portfolio Approach to Commodity Trading," *Commodities* (November 1979), 38–39.

Elton, Edwin J., and Martin J. Gruber. *Modern Portfolio Theory and Investment Analysis.* New York: Wiley, 1981.

Ensor, Richard, and Boris Antl. *The Management of Foreign Exchange Risk.* London: Euromoney, 1978.

Epstein, R. A. *The Theory of Gambling and Statistical Logic.* New York: Academic, 1969.

Feller, W. *An Introduction to Probability Theory and Its Applications,* Vol. 2, New York: Wiley, 1966.

Gehm, Fred. "Avoiding Avoidable Risk through Portfolio Theory," *Commodities* (July 1980), 46–50.

———. *Commodity Market Money Management.* New York: Wiley, 1982.

———. "Techniques for Making Decisions under Uncertainty," *The Journal of Futures Markets,* 4, No. 1 (1984), 65–73.

Goldberg, Samuel. *Probability: An Introduction.* Englewood Cliffs, N.J.: Prentice-Hall, Inc., 1960.

Goldfein, Lawrence, and Lester Houchberg. "Use of Commodity Straddles Can Effect Impressive Tax Savings," *The Journal of Taxation,* 29, No. 6 (December 1968).

Gray, Roger. "Risk Management in Commodities and Financial Markets," *American Journal of Agricultural Economics* (May 1976), 280–285.

Hadley, G. *Introduction to Business Statistics.* San Francisco, Calif.: Holden-Day, 1968.

Hardy, C. O. *Risk and Risk Bearing.* Chicago: University of Chicago Press, 1923.

Helmuth, J. W. "Futures Trading under Conditions of Uncertainty," Ph.D. dissertation, University of Missouri, Columbia, 1970.

Hieronymus, T. A. *Principles of Inventory and Risk Management,* University of Illinois Agricultural Extension Service AE 2831, 1951.

Irwin, H. S. "The Nature of Risk Assumption in the Trading of Organized Exchanges," *American Economic Review,* 27 (1937), 267–278.

Jackson, Barbara Bond. "Manage Risk in Industrial Pricing," *Harvard Business Review* (July/August 1980), 121–133.

Kaufman, Perry. "Safety-Adjusted Performance Evaluation," *The Journal of Futures Markets* (spring 1981), 17–31.

Knight, Frank H. *Risk, Uncertainty and Profit.* Boston: Houghton Mifflin, 1921; reprinted 1957.

Koppenhaver, Gary. "Risk Aversion and Futures Market Behavior," Ph.D. dissertation, University of Iowa, 1980.

Lee, C. F., and R. M. Leuthold. *Impact of Investment on the Determination of Risk and Return in the Commodity Futures Market.* Chicago Mercantile Exchange, 1980.

Levy, Haim. "The CAPM and Beta in an Imperfect Market," *The Journal of Portfolio Management* (winter 1980), 5–11.

Markowitz, H. M. *Portfolio Selections: Efficient Diversification of Investments.* New York: Wiley, 1959.

Moriarty, E., S. Phillips, and P. Tosini. "A Comparison of Options and Futures in the Management of Portfolio Risk," *Financial Analysis Journal* (January–February 1981), 61–67.

Powers, Mark. "The Almost Riskless Arbitrage," *Commodities* (December 1973), 32–33.

Raynauld, Jacques, and Jacques Tessier. "Risk Premiums in Futures Markets: An Empirical Investigation," *The Journal of Futures Markets*, 4, No. 2 (1984), 189–211.

Rinfret, P. A. "Investment Managers Are Worth Their Keep," *Financial Analysts Journal* (March–April 1968).

Sandor, Richard L., and James E. Rhodes. "The Development of a Trading Strategy," *Commodities Magazine* (July 1982), 22–28.

Schwartz, Marvin. "Scientific Money Management," *Commodity Journal*, 6, No. 3 (May–June 1971).

Shackle, G. L. S. "An Analysis of Speculative Choice," *Economica*, new series, 12 (1945), 10–21.

Sowders, A. G., Jr. "The Commodity Markets and Taxes," *Arthur Young Journal* (July 1960).

Standard Federal Tax Reporter, Code Volume. New York: Commerce Clearing House, 1969.

Teweles, R. J. "Excessive Trading and Expert Consultants," *Commodities Law Letter,* Part I (April 1984), 1–3; Part II (May 1984), 6–7.

Thorpe, Edward O. *Beat the Dealer.* New York: Random House, 1962.

Von Neumann, John, and Oskar Morgenstern. *The Theory of Games and Economic Behavior.* Princeton, N.J.: Princeton University Press, 1947.

Wilson, Allen N. *The Casino Gambler's Guide.* New York: Harper and Row, 1970.

Zweig, M. E. "An Analysis of Risk and Return on Put and Call Option Strategies," Ph.D. dissertation, Michigan State University, 1969.

X. HEDGING

Agri-Finance and William Uhrig. "Lender's Guide to Hedging," *Agri-Finance* (July/August 1976), 21–51.

Anderson, R. W., and J. P. Danthine. "Hedging and Joint Production: Theory and Illustrations," *Journal of Finance,* 35 (May 1980), 489–497.

────── and ──────. "Cross Hedging," *Journal of Political Economy,* 89 (1981), 1182–1196.

────── and ──────. "Hedger Diversity in Futures Markets," *Economic Journal,* 93 (1983), 370–389.

Arthur, Henry B. "Inventory Profits in the Business Cycle," *American Economic Review,* 28, No. 1 (March 1938).

──────. "The Nature of Commodity Futures as an Economic and Business Instrument," *Food Research Institute Studies,* 9, No. 3 (1972).

Bailey, Fred. "Understanding the Mechanics of Making and Taking Delivery," *Commodities* (September 1980), 66–67.

Batlin, Carl Alan. "Interest Rate Risk, Prepayment Risk, and the Futures Market Hedging Strategies of Financial Intermediaries," *The Journal of Futures Markets,* 3, No. 2 (1983), 177–184.

──────. "Production under Price Uncertainty with Imperfect Time Hedging Opportunities in Futures Markets," *Southern Economic Journal* (January 1983).

Benninga, Simon, Rafael Eldor, and Itzhak Zilcha. "Optimal Hedging in the Futures Market under Price Uncertainty," *Economics Letters,* 13 (1983), 141–145.

──────, ──────, and ──────. "The Optimal Hedge Ratio in Unbiased Futures Markets," *The Journal of Futures Markets,* 4, No. 2 (1984), 155–159.

Bobst, Barry, and Joseph Davis. "Effects of Within- and Among- Contract Basis Variation on the Production Hedging of Feeder Cattle," *Mid South Journal of Economics,* 4, No. 1 (1980), 59–64.

Brennan, M. J. "The Supply of Storage," *American Economic Review,* 48, No. 1 (March 1958), 50–72.

──────. "A Model of Seasonal Inventories," *Econometrica,* 17 (April 1959), 228–244.

Cootner, P. H. "Speculation and Hedging," *Food Research Institute Studies,* Supplement, 7 (1967), 65–106.

Costello, John. "Tax Consequences of Speculation and Hedging in Foreign Currency Futures," *Tax Lawyer* (winter 1975), 221–249.

Dale, Charles. "The Hedging Effectiveness of Currency Futures Markets," *The Journal of Futures Markets,* 1, No. 1 (spring 1981), 77–88.

Dew, J. K. "David and Goliath: A Skirmish in the Hedge Rows," *American Banker,* 14 (September 1982), 4–7.

Dorosz, Wanda. "Hedging against Foreign Exchange Risk: An Overview," *Canadian Tax Journal* (November/December 1978), 667–683.

Ederington, Louis. "The Hedging Performance of the New Futures Markets," *The Journal of Finance* (March 1979), 157–170.

English, E. D. "The Use of Commodity Exchanges by Millers," *Proceedings of Fifth Annual Symposium,* Chicago Board of Trade (Sept. 11–12, 1952).

Farmer Use of Futures Markets, Illinois Agricultural Experiment Station AE 3760, 1962.

Franckle, C. T. "The Hedging Performance of the New Futures Market: Comment," *Journal of Finance,* 35, No. 5 (December 1980), 1272–1279.

Goss, Barry. "Aspects of Hedging Theory," *Australian Journal of Agricultural Economics* (December 1980), 210–223.

Graf, T. F. "Hedging—How Effective Is It?" *Journal of Farm Economics,* 35, No. 3 (August 1953), 398–413.

Grammatikos, Theoharry, and Anthony Saunders. "Stability and the Hedging Performance of Foreign Currency Futures," *The Journal of Futures Markets,* 3, No. 3 (1983), 295–305.

Gray, R. W. "The Importance of Hedging in Futures Trading; and the Effectiveness of Futures Trading for Hedging," *Futures Trading Seminar,* Vol. 1, Madison, Wis.: Mimir, 1960.

Gruen, F. H. "The Pros and Cons of Futures Trading for Woolgrowers," *Review of Marketing and Agricultural Economics,* 28, No. 3 (September 1960), 1–12.

Guttentag, Jack M. "A Note on Hedging and Solvency: The Case of a Phoenix," *The Journal of Futures Markets,* 3, No. 2 (1983), 137–141.

Hall, Kristen. "How Hedgers Use Brokerage Firms," *Commodities* (April 1981), 76.

Hardy, C. O., and L. S. Lyon. "The Theory of Hedging," *Journal of Political Economy,* 31, No. 2 (April 1923), 276–287.

Hayenga, Marvin L., and Dennis D. DiPietre. "Hedging Wholesale Meat Prices: Analysis of Basis Risk," *The Journal of Futures Markets,* 2, No. 2 (1982), 131–140.

———, ———, J. Marvin Skadberg, and Ted C. Schroeder. "Profitable Hedging Opportunities and Risk Premiums for Producers in Live Cattle and Live Hog Futures Markets," *The Journal of Futures Markets,* 4, No. 2 (1984), 141–154.

The Hedger's Handbook: A Businessman's Guide to the Commodity Futures Markets. New York: Merrill Lynch, Pierce, Fenner and Smith, 1970.

Hieronymus, T. A. *Making Use of Basis Changes to Earn Income,* University of Illinois Department of Agricultural Economics AE 3537, Urbana, 1959.

———. "Four Ways to Make a Profit on Futures," *Better Farming Methods,* 35, No. 1 (January 1963), 22–25.

———. *Uses of Grain Futures Markets in the Farm Business,* University of Illinois Agricultural Experiment Station Bulletin 696, 1963.

———. *Hedging for Country Elevators,* Agricultural Economics Research Report 91, University of Illinois, March 1968.

———. "How You Can Use the Futures Markets," *Successful Farming,* 60, No. 4 (April 1972), 51, 70–71.

———, F. S. Scott, and W. J. Wills. "Hedging Cattle Feeding Operations," *Illinois Farm Economics,* No. 200 (January 1952), 1272–1276.

Hill, Joanne, and Thomas Schneeweis. "A Note on the Hedging Effectiveness of Foreign Currency Futures," *The Journal of Futures Markets,* 1, No. 4 (winter 1981), 659–664.

Hobson, Karl. *Wheat Prices in 1964—How to Forecast Them, How to Insure Them.* Washington State University, Agricultural Extension Service E.M., 2332, 1963.

Hoffman, G. W. "Hedging by Dealing in Grain Futures," Ph.D. dissertation, University of Pennsylvania, Philadelphia, 1925.

Holthausen, D. "Hedging and the Competitive Firm under Price Uncertainty," *American Economic Review,* 69, No. 5 (December 1979), 989–995.

Howell, L. D. *Analysis of Hedging and Other Operations in Grain Futures,* USDA Technical Bulletin 971, August 1948.

———. *Influence of Certificated Stocks on Spot-Futures Price Relationships for Cotton,* USDA Technical Bulletin 1119, 1955.

———. *Analysis of Hedging and Other Operations in Wool and Wool Top Futures,* USDA Technical Bulletin 1260, January 1962.

——— and L. J. Watson. *Relation of Spot Cotton Prices to Futures Contracts and Protection Afforded by Trading in Futures,* USDA Technical Bulletin 602, January 1938.

Irwin, H. S. *Speculation versus Hedging in Country Elevator Operation.* Washington, D.C.: Commodity Exchange Administration, 1938.

Jackson, Barbara Bond. "Manage Risk in Industrial Pricing," *Harvard Business Review* (July/August 1980), 121–133.

Jaffray, Benjamin. "Hedging in the Corporate Financial Structure," *Industry Research Seminar Proceedings,* Chicago Board of Trade (1980), 4–12, Discussion, 13–19.

Johnson, Leland L. "Hedging, Speculation and Futures Trading in the Coffee Market since World War II," Ph.D. dissertation, Yale University, 1957.

———. "Price Instability, Hedging, and Trade Volume in the Coffee Market," *Journal of Political Economy,* 45 (1957), 306–321.

———. "The Theory of Hedging and Speculation in Commodity Futures," *Review of Economic Studies,* 27 (3), No. 74 (June 1960), 139–151.

Kahl, Kandice, and William Romek. "Effectiveness of Hedging in Potato Futures," *The Journal of Futures Markets* (spring 1982), 9–18.

Kenyon, David, and Neil Shapiro. "Profit Margin Hedging in the Broiler Industry," *Industry Research Seminar Proceedings,* Chicago Board of Trade (1980), 58–70, Discussion, 71–83.

Leuthold, Raymond, and Scott Mokler, "Feeding-Margin Hedging in the Cattle Industry," *International Futures Trading Seminar Proceedings* (1978), 56–68, Discussion, 69–77.

Longson, Ian Geoffrey. *Forecasting the Ontario Hog Basis and the Evaluation of Hedging Strategies for Ontario Hedgers.* Chicago Mercantile Exchange, 1977.

McEnally, R. W., and M. L. Rice. "Hedging Possibilities in the Flotation of Debt Securities," *Financial Management,* 8 (1979), 12–18.

McKinnon, R. I. "Future Markets Buffer Stocks and Income Stability for Primary Producers," *Journal of Political Economy,* 75, No. 6 (December 1967), 844–861.

Nettles, Donald M. *Hedging, the Use of Commodity Markets.* Washington, D.C.: Farm Credit Administration, 1975.

Oster, Merrill. "20 Rules for Successful Commodity Hedging," *Commodities* (October 1976), 20–23.

———. *Commodity Futures for Profit . . . A Farmer's Guide to Hedging.* Cedar Falls, Iowa: Investor Publications, 1979.

Pardue, Benjamin. "International Taxation—Hedging," *Vanderbilt Journal of Transnational Law* (fall 1980), 825–834.

Parrott, Robert. "A Professional's View of Hedging," *Business Horizons* (June 1977), 12–22.

Paul, Allen B. "The Pricing of Binspace—A Contribution to the Theory of Storage," *American Journal of Agricultural Economics,* 52, No. 1 (February 1970), 1.

———. *Treatment of Hedging in Commodity Market Regulation,* U.S. Department of Agriculture Technical Bulletin 1538, 1976.

Peck, Anne. "Reflections of Hedging on Futures Market Activity," *Food Research Institute Studies* (1979–1980), 327–349.

———. "Estimation of Hedging and Speculative Positions on Futures Markets Revisited," *Food Research Institute Studies,* 18 (1982), 181–195.

Rolfo, J. "Optimal Hedging under Price and Quantity Uncertainty: The Case of a Cocoa Producer," *Journal of Political Economy,* 88, No. 1 (February 1980), 100–116.

——— and Howard Sosin. "Alternative Strategies for Hedging and Spreading," Center for the Study of Futures Markets working paper 22, Columbia University, April 1981.

Rutledge, David J. S. "The Relationship between Prices and Hedging Patterns in the United States Soybean Complex," Ph.D. dissertation, Stanford University, 1970.

———. "Hedgers' Demand for Futures Contracts: A Theoretical Framework with Applications to the United States Soybean Complex," *Food Research Institute Studies,* 10, No. 3 (1972).

———. "Estimation of Hedging and Speculative Positions in Futures Markets: An Alternative Approach," *Food Research Institute Studies* (1977–1978), 205–211.

Schrock, Nicholas W. "A Portfolio Analysis of Straddle Operations in the Futures Markets," thesis, University of Oregon, 1967.

Schultz, Theodore W. "Spot and Futures Prices as Production Guides," *American Economic Review,* 39 (May 1949).

Schureman, Thomas R. *Hedging Strategies for Cattle Feeders.* Chicago Mercantile Exchange, 1978.

"Should You Hedge Hogs?" *Commodities,* 5, No. 10 (October 1976), 30–31.

Snape, R. H., and B. S. Yamey. "Test of the Effectiveness of Hedging," *Journal of Political Economy,* 73, No. 5 (October 1965), 540–544.

Soss, Eugene. "Strategy for Hedging Cattle," *Big Farmer*, 47, No. 5 (May/June 1975).
Stevens, W. H. S. "The Relation of the Cash-Future Spread to Hedging Transactions," *Journal of Business*, 2, No. 1 (January 1929), 28–49.
Stoll, Hans. "Commodity Futures and Spot Price Determination and Hedging in Capital Market Equilibrium," *The Journal of Financial and Quantitative Analysis* (November 1979), 873–894.
Telser, L. G. "Safety First and Hedging," *Review of Economic Studies*, 23 (1), No. 60 (1955–1956), 1–16.
Tosini, Paula A., and Eugene J. Moriarty. "Potential Hedging Use of a Futures Contract Based on a Composite Stock Index," *The Journal of Futures Markets*, 2, No. 1 (1982), 83–103.
Urnousky, S. J. "Futures Markets, Private Storage, and Price Stabilization," *Journal of Public Economics* (1979), 301–327.
Wardrep, B. N., and J. F. Buck. "The Efficacy of Hedging with Financial Futures: A Historical Perspective," *The Journal of Futures Markets*, 2 No. 3 (1982), 243–254.
Weiner, Neil S. "The Hedging Rationale for a Stock Index Futures Contract," *The Journal of Futures Markets*, 1, No. 1 (1981), 59–76.
Wiese, Virgil. "Introduction to Hedging," in A. E. Peck, ed., *Readings in Futures Markets, 3: Views from the Trade.* Chicago Board of Trade, 1978, pp. 3–11.
Willingham, C. "Hedging with Commodity Futures Contracts. When Will Ordinary Treatment Result?" *Journal of Taxation* (January 1981), 48–50.
Witte, Willard. "Trade Hedging and the Dynamic Stability of the Foreign Exchange Market," *Quarterly Journal of Economics* (February 1980), 15–30.
Working, Holbrook. "Futures Trading and Hedging," *American Economic Review*, 43, No. 3 (June 1953), 314–343.
———. "Hedging Reconsidered," *Journal of Farm Economics*, 35, No. 4 (November 1953), 544–561.
———. "Price Support and the Effectiveness of Hedging," *Journal of Farm Economics*, 35 (1953), 811–818.
———. "Speculation on Hedging Markets," *Food Research Institute Studies*, 1, No. 1 (1960).
Yamey, B. S. "An Investigation of Hedging on an Organized Produce Exchange," *The Manchester School of Economics and Social Studies*, 19 (September 1951), 305–319.
———. "Addendum" to "An Investigation of Hedging on an Organized Produce Exchange," in P. T. Bauer and B. S. Yamey, *Markets, Market Control and Marketing Reform.* London: Weidenfeld and Nicolson, 1969.

XI. PRICES AND RELATED STATISTICAL DATA

Annual Coffee Statistics. New York: Pan American Coffee Bureau.
Broomhall's Corn Trade Yearbook, 1914 to date.
Chicago Board of Trade Annual Report, 1858 to date.
Chicago Board of Trade Statistical Annual.
Chicago Board of Trade Year Book. Chicago Board of Trade, 141 West Jackson Boulevard, Chicago, Ill.
Chicago Mercantile Exchange Year Book. Chicago Mercantile Exchange, 444 West Jackson Boulevard, Chicago, Ill., 1923 to date.
Cocoa Statistics. London: Gill and Duffus. Published annually.
Commodity Perspective, Encyclopedia of Historical Charts. Chicago: Investor Publications, 1976.
Commodity Year Book. New York: Commodity Research Bureau, 1939 to date.
Commodity Year Book (annual). New York: Commodity Research Bureau, 1929 to date.
Danthine, Jean-Pierre. "Information, Futures Prices and Stabilizing Speculation," *Journal of Economic Theory*, 17 (February 1978), 79–98.
Dobson, Edward G. *Commodities: A Chart Anthology.* Greenville, S.C.: Dobson, 1976.
F. O. Licht's World Sugar Statistics. Ratzeburg, Germany, 1980–1981.
Garbade, K., J. Pomrenze, and W. Silber. "On the Information Content of Prices," *American Economic Review*, 69 (March 1979), 50–59.
Hoffman, G. W., and J. W. T. Duvel. *Grain Prices and the Futures Market: A 15 Year Survey*, USDA Technical Bulletin 747, January 1941.
Kansas City Board of Trade Annual Statistical Report, 1921 to date.
Mann, Jitendar S., and Richard G. Heifner. *The Distribution of Shortrun Commodity Price Movements*, USDA, Economic Research Service, Technical Bulletin 1536, March 1976.

Manthy, R. S. *Natural Resource Commodities—A Century of Statistics.* Baltimore: Johns Hopkins Press for Resources for the Future, 1978.

Minneapolis Grain Exchange. *Annual Report* (formerly Minneapolis Chamber of Commerce, *Annual Report*), 1882 to date.

Naik, A. S. *Effects of Futures Trading on Prices.* Bombay, India: K. R. Samat for Somaiya Publications Pty., Ltd., 1970.

New York Mercantile Exchange Year Book.

The 1978 6-Year Soybean and Oilseed Statistical Summary. Chicago Board of Trade, 1979.

Powers, M. J. "Does Futures Trading Reduce Price Fluctuations in the Cash Markets?" *American Economic Review,* 60, No. 3 (June 1970), 460–464.

Rutledge, D. J. S. "A Note on the Variability of Futures Prices," *Review of Economics and Statistics,* 58, No. 1 (February 1976).

Simonoff, Jeffrey S. "Application of Statistical Methodology to the Evaluation of Timing Devices in Commodities Trading," *The Journal of Futures Markets,* 1, No. 4 (1981), 649–656.

Thomsen, F. L., and R. J. Foote. *Agricultural Prices.* New York: McGraw-Hill, 1952.

USDA, Commodity Exchange Authority. *Commodity Futures Statistics,* annual from 1947.

USDA, Commodity Exchange Authority. *Grain Futures Statistics 1921–1951,* Statistical Bulletin 131, 1952.

USDA, Consumer and Marketing Service. *Cotton Price Statistics.* Published annually.

USDA, Consumer and Marketing Service. *Grain and Feed Statistics.* Published annually.

USDA, Economic Research Service. *Statistics on Cotton and Related Data, 1925–62,* Statistical Bulletin 329, 1963.

Usher, A. P. "The Influence of Speculative Marketing upon Prices," *American Economic Review,* 6 (1916), 49–60.

Working, Holbrook. "Prices of Cash Wheat and Futures at Chicago since 1883," *Food Research Institute Wheat Studies,* 10 (November 1934), 103–117.

―――― and Sidney Hoos. "Wheat Futures Prices and Trading at Liverpool since 1886," *Food Research Institute Wheat Studies,* 15 (November 1938).

XII. SPREADS AND OPTIONS

Angell, George. *Computer-Proven Commodity Spreads.* Windsor, N.Y.: Brightwaters, 1981.

―――― and R. Earl Hadady. *Spread Trading for the Risk-Conscious Speculator.* Pasadena, Calif.: Hadady, 1979.

Ansbacher, Max G. *The New Options Market.* New York: Walker, 1979.

Asay, Michael. "A Note on the Design of Commodity Option Contracts," *The Journal of Futures Markets* (spring 1982), 2–8; "Comment," by Robert McDonald and Daniel Siegel (spring 1983), 43–46; "Reply" (fall 1983), 335–338.

Babbel, David F. "The Rise and Decline of Currency Options," *Euromoney* (September 1980), 141–149.

Beardsley, George. "Proficient 'Spreaders' Prove Profit Is There," *Chicago Tribune* (Aug. 14, 1972), Sec. 3, p. 9.

Bernstein, J. *How to Profit From Seasonal Commodity Spreads: A Complete Guide.* New York: Wiley, 1982.

Bilderman, C. "New Trading Vehicle: Commodity Options Are Growing in Popularity," *Barron's,* 53, No. 11 (Jan. 8, 1973).

Black, Fischer. "Fact and Fantasy in the Use of Options," *Financial Analysts Journal* (July/August 1975), 36–41.

――――. "The Pricing of Commodity Contracts," *Journal of Financial Economics* (January/March 1976), 167–179.

―――― and Myron Scholes. "The Pricing of Options and Corporate Liabilities," *Journal of Political Economics* (May/June 1973).

―――― and ――――. "The Valuation of Option Contracts and a Test of Market Efficiency," *The Journal of Finance,* 27, No. 2 (May 1972), 399–417.

Bokron, N. *How to Use Put and Call Options.* Springfield, Mass.: John Magee, 1975.

Bonen, Thomas. "Latest Wrinkle: Options on Futures," *Banker's Monthly* (Oct. 5, 1982), 8–10 ff.

Borton, Mark, and Harlan Abrahams. "Options on Commodity Futures Contract as Securities in California," *Business Lawyer* (April 1974), 867–878.

Bowe, J. J. "Reviewing the Concepts," *Commodities* (July 1982), 44–47.

Breeden, Douglas. "Futures Markets and Commodity Options," Center for the Study of Futures Markets Working Paper 20, Columbia University, September 1980.

Burns, Joseph A. *Treatise on Markets: Spot, Futures and Options.* Washington, D.C.: American Enterprise Institute for Public Policy Research, 1979.

Byars, Richard, and Shelby Bennet. "Corporate Tax Planning with Commodity Spreads," *Journal of Corporate Taxation* (winter 1981), 375–379.

Camerer, Colin. "The Pricing and Social Value of Commodity Options," *Financial Analysts Journal* (January/February 1982), 62–66.

"Can Commodity Agreements Work?" *Economist,* 244 (Aug. 19, 1972), 60–61.

Carasik, Karen. "Exchange Traded Clearinghouse (Offset) Options," *The Journal of Futures Markets,* Supplement to Vol. 1 (1981), 539–541.

Castelino, Mark G., and Ashok Vora. "Spread Volatility in Commodity Futures: The Length Effect," *The Journal of Futures Markets,* 4, No. 1 (1984), 39–46.

Catlett, Lowell, and Michael Boehlje. "Options as an Alternative to Hedging," *Commodity Journal* (September/October 1980), 1 ff.

—— and ——. "Commodity Options, Hedging and Risk Premiums," *North Central Journal of Agricultural Economics* (July 1982), 95–101.

Chiras, D., and S. Manaster. "The Information Content of Option Prices and a Test of Market Efficiency," *Journal of Financial Economics,* 6 (June/September 1978).

"Commodity Options: London Is Concerned, Too," *Commodities,* 5, No. 11 (November 1976), 18–21.

Commodity Options: On Their Contribution to the Economy. Princeton, N.J.: Mathematica, Inc., 1973.

"Commodity Panel Moving to Permit Trading in Options," *Wall Street Journal,* 188, No. 52 (Sept. 14, 1976), 40.

"Copper as a Currency Hedge," *International Currency Review,* 8, No. 2 (1976), 36–38.

Cracraft, Perry J. *London Options on Commodities: A Primer for American Speculators.* Chicago: Contemporary Books, 1977.

Crum, Bruce. "Remedies: Commodity Options: Implied Civil Remedies for Fraud," *Oklahoma Law Review* (winter 1978), 217–233.

Culver, James. "It's Time to Reconsider Options on Farm Commodities," *Commodities* (January 1982), 18–24.

Dalio, Ray. "A Spread with a Warranty: $25 or 1,075 Pounds, Whichever Comes First," *Commodities,* 4, No. 10 (October 1975), 12–14.

——. "The Hidden Profits in Commodity Arbitrage," *Commodities,* 5, No. 2 (February 1976), 16–18.

Dunning, Dan. "Valuing London Commodity Options," *Commodities* (June 1977), 44–45.

Eckhardt, Walter, Jr. "The American Put: Computational Issues and Value Comparisons," *Financial Management* (autumn 1982), 42–52.

Esserman, Wayne. *Odds on Grain Spreading.* Delphi, Ind.: EWW Publishing, 1979.

"Fast, Sure Game of Grain Arbitrage," *Business Week* (May 31, 1976), 58.

Figlewski, Stephen, and M. Desmond Fitzgerald. "The Price Behavior of London Commodity Options," *Review of Research in Futures Markets,* 1, No. 1 (1982), 90–104; "Discussion," 105–106.

Fishman, Gerald. "Dealer Options," *The Journal of Futures Markets,* Supplement to Vol. 1 (1981), 535–538.

Gammill, James, Jr., and James Stone. "Options, Futures, and Business Risk," *The Journal of Futures Markets* (summer 1982), 141–149.

Gardner, Bruce. "Commodity Options for Agriculture," *American Journal of Agricultural Economics* (December 1977), 986–992.

Giddy, Ian H. "Foreign Exchange Options," *The Journal of Futures Markets,* 3 No. 2 (1983), 143–166.

"Giving Gold Buyers a Call Option," *Business Week* (Feb. 23, 1976), 71–72.

Goodman, Laurie. "How to Trade in Currency Options," *Euromoney* (January 1983), 73–74.

Guither, Harold. "Commodity Exchanges, Agrarian Political Power, and the Anti-option Battle: Comment," *Agricultural History* (January 1974), 126–129.

Hartzog, Jerry. "Options: A New Tool for Managing Risk," *Savings and Loan News* (November 1982), 56–60.

Heifner, R. G. "The Gains from Basing Grain Storage Decisions on Cash-Future Spreads," *Journal of Farm Economics,* 48, No. 5 (December 1966), 1490–1495.

Jacobs, Sol. "Before You Trade Spreads, Beware . . . ," *Commodities,* 3, No. 12 (December 1974), 32–34.

Jobman, Darrell. "Evaluating Commodity Options Firms—Some Views on Trading Approaches," *Commodities,* 5, No. 12 (December 1976), 21–22.

Jones, Frank J. "Spreads: Tails, Turtles and All That," *The Journal of Futures Markets,* 1, No. 4 (1981), 565–596.

Kallard, Thomas. *Make Money in Commodity Spreads.* New York: Optosonic Press, 1974.

Kelne, Nicholas. "Commodity Option Exemptions," *The Journal of Futures Markets,* Supplement to Vol. 1 (1981), 543–545.

Kettler, Paul C. "Big Spreads," *Journal of Finance, Silver Market Letter,* 2, No. 26 (Oct. 5, 1972), 6.

Klemkosky, Robert C., and Terry S. Maness. "The Impact of Options on the Underlying Securities," *Journal of Portfolio Management* (winter 1980), 12–18.

Knezevich, Richard. "Federal Legislation for Commodity Option Trading: A Proposal," *Southern California Law Review* (August 1974), 1418–1452.

Laborde, P. "A Note on Net and Double Gains, or Losses, in Spreading Operations," *The Journal of Futures Markets,* 2, No. 4 (1982), 409–414.

Latane, H., and R. Rendleman. "Standard Deviations of Stock Price Ratios Implied in Option Prices," *Journal of Finance,* 31 (May 1976).

"Leveraging the Leverage (Commodity Options)," *Forbes,* 117, No. 7 (Apr. 1, 1976), 64–66.

Liptor, D. A. "The Special Study of the Options Market: Its Findings and Recommendations," *Securities Regulation Law Journal,* 7, No. 4 (1980), 299–345.

Liuzza, Vincent. "Handling Cash Flow for Futures Spread," *Broiler Industry,* 36, No. 9 (September 1973), 43.

Lofton, Todd. "The No-Risk Spreads (Or, How I Stopped Worrying and Learned to Love the Markets)," *Commodities,* 5, No. 2 (February 1976), 31.

Long, Joseph. "The Naked Commodity Option Contract as a Security," *William and Mary Law Review* (winter 1973), 211–263.

———. "Commodity Options—Revisited," *Drake Law Review* (fall 1975), 75–132.

Long, William, and Thomas Rzepski. "The Exchange Traded GNMA Option," *Mortgage Banker* (September 1980), 34–38.

Manternach, Dan. "Using Butterflies to Spread Soybeans," *Commodities* (November 1980), 50.

McDonald, Robert, and Daniel Siegel. "A Note on the Design of Commodity Options Contracts: A Comment," *The Journal of Futures Markets,* 3, No. 1 (1983), 43–46.

McMillian, L. *Options as a Strategic Investment.* New York: Institute of Finance, 1980.

Mehl, P. *Trading Privileges on the Chicago Board of Trade,* USDA Circular 323, 1934.

Melamed, Leo. "The Futures Market: Liquidity and the Technique of Spreading," *The Journal of Futures Markets,* 1, No. 3 (1981), 405–411.

Mery, Geraldine. "Federal Regulation of Commodity Option Trading—Is the Customer Protected?" *St. Mary's Law Journal* (1977), 53–71.

Meyer, James, and Young Kim. "An Autoregressive Forecast of the World Sugar Future Option Market," *Journal of Financial and Quantitative Analysis* (December 1975), 821–835; "Comment," by O. D. Anderson (December 1977), 879–881; "Comment," by Stephen Taylor and Brian Kingsman (December 1977), 883–890.

Meyer, Richard L. *Profitability of Spread Positions in Pork Bellies over a Ten-Year Period,* 1977.

Murray, Roger F. "A New Role for Options," *Journal of Financial and Quantitative Analysis* (November 1979), 895–899.

Murray, T. J. "Furor over the Commodity Options," *Dun's Review,* 101 (March 1973), 69–72.

Nahum, Biger, and John Hull. "The Valuation of Currency Options," *Financial Management* (spring 1983), 24–28.

Noddings, T. *How the Experts Beat the Market.* Homewood, Ill.: Dow Jones–Irwin, 1976.

"Options Timetable Delayed until December," *Commodities,* 5, No. 12 (December 1976), 23.

Pincus, Joseph A. "Commodity Option Trading," *Commodity Journal,* 8, No. 4 (July/August 1973), 17.

Powers, Mark. "Fact and Fiction about Spreads," *Commodities* (July 1973), 41–47.

Riess, Michael, "Trading London Commodity Options," *Commodities,* 1, No. 4 (June 1972), 10–15.

———. "Trading London Commodity Options, Part II: Tax Aspects," *Commodities,* 1, No. 5 (July 1972), 12–14.

———. "Arbitrage as a Trading Medium," *Commodities,* 2, No. 3 (March 1973), 24–27.

———. "London Commodity Markets," *Commodities*, 3, No. 2 (February 1974), 17–22.

———. "Trading London Commodity Options (R)," *Commodities*, 5, No. 8 (August 1976), 14–19.

"The Risks in London Commodity Options," *Business Week* (Apr. 12, 1986), 86–87.

Rogers, George B. *Price Spreads, Costs, and Productivity in Poultry and Egg Marketing 1955–1974*, U.S. Department of Agriculture, Economic Research Service, Agricultural Economic Report 326, February 1976.

Rubinstein, M. "An Economic Evaluation of Organized Options Markets," *Journal of Comparative Corporate Law and Securities Regulation*, 2 (1979), 49–64.

Sarsoun, Lawrence C. "There's Gold in Them Thar Spreads," *Commodities*, 4, No. 10 (October 1975), 30–34.

Schwager, John. "Understanding Spreading," *Commodities* (October 1974), 10–16.

Shakin B. "Commodities Options: They're Available from London through Some New York Brokers," *Barron's* (Jan. 27, 1975), 11.

Sinquefield, Jean Cairns. "Understanding Options on Futures," *Mortgage Banking* (July 1982), 34–35 ff.

Smith, Clifford W. "Option Pricing: A Review," *Journal of Financial Economics*, 3 (January/March 1976), 3–51.

Smith, Courtney. *Commodity Spread Analysis*. New York: Wiley, 1982.

Sullivan, Joseph. "GNMA Options on the CBOE," *Mortgage Banker* (October 1981), 53 ff.

Thygerson, Kenneth. "Hedging Forward Mortgage Loan Commitments: The Option of Futures and a Future for Options," *American Real Estate and Urban Economics Association Journal* (winter 1978), 357–369.

Tiger, Phillip E. "The Limited Risk Spread," *Commodities*, 3, No. 7 (July 1974), 15–22.

———. "A Pig Spread with a Pedigree," *Commodities*, 4, No. 12 (December 1975), 14–17.

Vesely, Eric. "Introduction: Commodity Options," *Commodity Journal* (July/August 1982), 17–23.

Welch, William. *Strategies for Put and Call Option Trading*. Cambridge, Mass.: Winthrop Publishers, 1982.

Wolf, Avner. "Fundamentals of Commodity Options on Futures," *The Journal of Futures Markets*, 2, No. 4 (1982), 391–408.

Zieg, Kermit, and William Nix. *The Commodity Options Market: Dynamic Trading Strategies for Speculation and Commercial Hedging*. Homewood, Ill.: Dow Jones–Irwin, 1978.

——— and Susannah Zieg. *Commodity Options*. Columbia, Md.: Investor Publications, 1974.

——— and Susannah Zieg. "London Commodity Options—Trading Techniques," *Commodities* (October 1974), 27–31.

——— and Susannah Zieg. "Commodity Double Options," *Commodity Journal* (January/February 1975), 26–31.

Index

About the Authors

RICHARD J. TEWELES, Ph.D., is professor of finance, real estate, and law at California State University at Long Beach. He has also served as a registered representative and executive in the brokerage business, and he has acted as a consultant to over 100 brokerage firms, law firms, exchanges, and regulatory agencies (including the IRS and the Justice Department). He is frequently called upon by TV and radio stations to discuss the various aspects of futures trading and has authored a great many publications on the subject.

FRANK J. JONES, Ph.D., is director of Barclays de Zoete Wedd Government Securities Inc. He was previously managing director of the Financial Futures Department at Kidder, Peabody & Co., Incorporated. He has also served as senior vice president of the New York Stock Exchange for the Options & Index Products Division, as executive vice president and COO of the New York Futures Exchange, and as a vice president and chief economist at the Chicago Mercantile Exchange. He has written several books and articles on the financial futures and options markets, and he is a frequent speaker on topics related to financial futures and options, the financial markets, and futures exchanges.

The Futures Game